# Internet of Things Built Up By

# Digital Inventory

## Guoping Jie

**Internet of Things Built Up By Digital Inventory**

**First Edition**

ISBN-10: 099582035X

ISBN-13: 978-0-9958203-5-7 (Guoping Jie)

www.mathaccounting.com

# ABSTRACT

What kind of the data is the most data in the era of big data? All social members, which include the governments, the organizations, the companies, and the individuals, are interested in the data of the cash, so the most data is the data of the cash. Then, where is the most reliable and the most correct data of cash? Because the data of the cash in all banks is recorded by using of all smart cards automatically, the customers' data of the cash in these banks is the most trustworthy. The data of the cash in the banks can be regarded as a standard or a ruler of measuring other data of the cash. From this idea, I wrote the two books of the "Digital Currency Embedded in Identities of All Society Members I and II". Based on these two books, I have developed and extended a concept of the Digital Inventory. The inventory account is a concomitant of the cash account or the account receivable (account payable) account. There are only two kinds of forms of the three accounts which appear in a transaction sub-equation. First, there must be the cash account with the inventory account in the transaction sub-equation. Of course, this sub-equation may include the account receivable (account payable) account. When the cash is embedded in a social member identity, the inventory is also embedded in a social member identity automatically. Another is that there is not the cash account and is only account receivable (account payable) account with the inventory account in a transaction sub-equation. The lowest subaccount of the account receivable (account payable) account is the telephone number and there is a relationship of one to one between the telephone number and the social member identity. Therefore, when a transaction sub-equation only include the account receivable (account payable) account and the inventory account, the inventory is also embedded in a social member identity automatically. By tracking the embedded identity, the parts of this inventory and its product code will be detected. All inventories embedded in all social members' identities and information of their parts and their product codes will be consisted of the Digital Inventory. The combination of internet and the digital inventory is the Internet of Things. Only digital inventory is a new concept and is also core technology, so the digital inventory will be introduced in detail in this book. The Internet of Things will realize the intelligent recognition, tracking, monitoring and management of all inventories. In this situation, counterfeit and shoddy products will be impossible to occur.

Keywords: digital currency, digital inventory, and internet of things

# Acknowledgements

I wish to take this opportunity to sincerely thank OSAP system (Canada) which gave me a chance to study.

# Contents

## APPENDIXES

# Chapter 1

# Internet of Things Summary

## 1.1 Internet of Things Definition

What kind of the data is the most data in the era of big data? All social members, which include the governments, the organizations, the companies, and the individuals, are interested in the data of the cash, so the most data is the data of the cash. Then, where is the most reliable and the most correct data of cash? Because the data of the cash in all banks is recorded by using of all smart cards automatically, the customers' data of the cash in these banks is the most trustworthy. The data of the cash in the banks can be regarded as a standard or a ruler of measuring other data of the cash. From this idea, I wrote the two books of the "Digital Currency Embedded in Identities of All Society Members I and II". Based on these two books and the great accounting cycle including the interior transactions, I have developed and extended a concept of the Digital Inventory. The inventory account is a concomitant of the cash account or the account receivable (account payable) account in the same transaction. There are three classes of transaction sub-equations for combination the three accounts.

First, there are the cash account with the inventory account in a transaction sub-equation. The transaction sub-equation is:

Cash (1): xxx + Inventory (1): -xxx = Sales (4): xxx + Cost of goods sold (5): -xxx

When the cash is embedded in a social member identity, the inventory is also embedded in this social member identity automatically.

Second, there are these three accounts (the cash account, the inventory account, and the account receivable (or account payable)) in a transaction sub-equation. The transaction sub-equations are:

Cash (1): xxx + Inventory (1): -xxx + Account receivable (1): xxx = Sales (4): xxx + Cost of goods sold (5): -xxx

Or    Cash (1): -xxx + Inventory (1): xxx = Account payable (2): xxx

When the cash is embedded in a social member identity, the inventory is also embedded in this social member identity automatically.

Last one is that there is not the cash account and is only account receivable (account payable) account with the inventory account in a transaction sub-equation. The transaction sub-equations are:

Inventory (1): -xxx + Account receivable (1): xxx = Sales (4): xxx + Cost of goods sold (5): -xxx

Or    Inventory (1): xxx = Account payable (2): xxx

The lowest subaccount of the account receivable (account payable) account is the customer (supplier) telephone number, and there is a relationship of one to one between the telephone number and the social member identity in the two tables of the customers' information and the suppliers' information. In simplification, I only change the column name of the Country to the Identity in this book. Of course, the MathAccouting software should also be changed accordingly. Therefore, when a transaction sub-equation only include the account receivable (account payable) account and the inventory account, the inventory is also embedded in this social member identity automatically.

Please pay attention. There is an exception of the Interior transaction. When a company (an organization) has produced some products which are the sources of all inventories. When a company (an organization) uses the purchased inventories as the some equipment or some parts to produce itself products or as the consumables to consume (do not consider the detail process of the Sales department and the Purchase department for simplification), these transactions are the interior transactions in a company (an organization) and the identity embedded in these inventories does not change. For distinguishing the above transactions, I give the recorder's identity as the inventory's identity. The interior transaction sub-equations respectively are:

Inventory (1): xxx + Working-in-process inventory (1): xxx = 0

Or    Inventory (1): -xxx + Different equipment (1): xxx = 0

Or    Inventory (1): -xxx = Cost of goods manufactured (5): -xxx

Or    Inventory (1): -xxx = Administrative expenses (5): -xxx

These accounts of the Cash, the Account payable, account receivable, the Working-in-process inventory, the Cost of goods manufactured, and the XXX expenses are defined as the judging accounts. When correcting a transaction which includes a judging account, the transaction sub-equation must include a judging account even if its amount is zero.

By tracking the embedded identity, the parts of this inventory and their product codes will be detected. All inventories embedded in all social members' identities and information of their parts will be consisted of digital inventory. The combination of internet and the digital inventory is the Internet of Things. The Internet of Things will realize the intelligent recognition, tracking, monitoring and management of all inventories. In this situation, counterfeit and shoddy products will be impossible to occur. Only digital inventory is a new concept and is also core technology in the internet of things, so the digital inventory will be introduced in detail in this book.

For recording the detail information of all circulating inventory (data), I design a table, seeing the Figure 1.1-1 on the next page. The table will record inventory (purchased inventory and sold inventory) by all social members (all organizations and all individuals) through the MathAccounting software. The detail information of a social member (an organization or an individual) in this table is recorded by other different organizations, so the data is fair, reliable, and correct.

In other words, an organization can build itself inventory flows statement by using of itself data while the Administrators of Industry and Commence can build this organization's inventory flows statement by using of other organizations' data recorded in a table. Of course, this table is in a public database dcj200 of the Administrators of Industry and Commence.

| ID | Amount | Symbol | Multi-subaccount Names | Transaction Date | Recorder | Unit |
|---|---|---|---|---|---|---|
|  |  |  |  |  |  |  |
|  |  |  |  |  |  |  |

Figure 1.1-1   Inventory purchased and inventory sold by all social members table

In addition, every organization has four tables to record detail information of inventory purchased and inventory sold by other organizations or by individuals because the inventory purchased and inventory sold are in different function departments. The Figure 1.1-2 shows two sample tables which records inventory purchased and inventory sold by all organizations respectively. The Figure 1.1-3 shows another two sample tables which records inventory purchased and inventory sold by all individuals respectively.

| Business No. (Suppliers) | Amount | Symbol | Transaction Date | Unit |
|---|---|---|---|---|
|  |  |  |  |  |
|  |  |  |  |  |

| Business No. (Customers) | Amount | Symbol | Transaction Date | Unit |
|---|---|---|---|---|
|  |  |  |  |  |
|  |  |  |  |  |

Figure 1.1-2   Inventory Purchased and Sold by all Organizations Table

| ID (Suppliers) | Amount | Symbol | Transaction Date | Unit |
|---|---|---|---|---|
|  |  |  |  |  |
|  |  |  |  |  |

| ID (Customers) | Amount | Symbol | Transaction Date | Unit |
|---|---|---|---|---|
|  |  |  |  |  |
|  |  |  |  |  |

Figure 1.1-3  Inventory Purchased and Sold by all Individuals Table

Inventory can be divided into two classes of inventory purchased and inventory sold and can be distinguished by the symbols of the "+" and "-". For every social member, the sum of inventory purchased and inventory sold is his or her balance of inventory he or she holds. The individuals may not sell the inventories to other social members, but they may return some inventories to their suppliers.

Due to adding new contents, the MatAccounting software will also be made some changes. Then, all transactions must be entered again. Therefore, I must write these transactions in this book again.

The following Figure 1.1-4 shows the meanings of the inventory's symbols in the transactions of including the account receivable or the account payable and the interior transactions.

| Inventory | Symbols | Meanings | Examples |
|---|---|---|---|
| Including Cash or only Account receivable | -c | Sold to customers to consume | Cash or Account receivable |
| Including Cash or only Account payable | -t | Purchased from suppliers | Cash or Account payable |
| In the interior transaction | -p | Produced products (Sources) | Working-in-process inventory |
| In the interior transaction | -e | Equipment | Car, Computer, Airplane, Buildings |
| In the interior transaction | -f | Transfer into other product | Cost of goods manufactured |
| In the interior transaction | -s | Consumption | Office supply expenses |

Figure 1.1-4  Meanings of Symbols Table

## 1.2 Technical Support and Security of Digital Inventory

The most advantage of the MathAccounting software is that it can embed an identity ID into every dollar in the process of money circulation regardless of the cash receipts and the cash payments. Therefore, the MathAccounting software is the strong technical support and security of the digital currency. All members of the society in the world will touch money and the digital currency is the electric extend of the traditional money, so all identity IDs of society members can be embedded in the money. The inventory account is a concomitant of the cash account or the account receivable (account payable) account in the same transaction. When the MathAccounting software records the data of the cash account automatically, the software also records the relevant information of the inventory account.

In addition, for the multi-subaccount name of the inventory account, every company (organization) can build the different one-level and two-level subaccounts and only need to ensure that the three-level subaccounts are sole. Therefore, the digital inventory is feasible and reliable.

Just as said before, the digital currency is the electric extend of the traditional money, so the digital currency may be divided to the simple digital currency (ideal condition) and the mixed digital currency. In this book, digital inventory is based on the simple digital currency (ideal condition) model.

# Chapter 2

# Simple (Pure) Digital Currency Model

Digital currency and digital inventory are a pair of twins. Simple digital currency model means that there is not any paper money in the process of money circulation. Obviously, it is an ideal society and the MathAccounting software will be a perfect solution of the digital currency. Therefore, digital inventory is also based on the simple (pure) digital currency model.

When all members (except of individuals) of the society use the MathAccounting software to record their business transactions, the Tax Bureau will know the received cash and the paid cash of every member (including individuals). Meanwhile, the Administrators of Industry and Commence will also know where all inventories are.

From the conceptual framework of pyramid pattern (seeing the Figure 1), all society member is divided to four ranks of social members. Below, I will discuss the detail process of money circulation in the four ranks of social members respectively by using of a sample of a small society.

## 2.1 Sample of a Small Society Model

If there is a small society with the 10 organizations and the 30 persons, its conceptual framework of all society members is showed in the Figure 2.1-1 on the next page.

The Figure 2.1-2 on the next page shows some basic information of the 10 organizations on December 31, 2015. Because the 10 organizations will convert to the MathAccounting software on December 31, 2015, the detail information of the dynamic accounting equation for every organization will be introduced later by building 10 reference tables for the 10 organizations respectively. In addition, some multi-subaccounts of the Cash account have not any three-level subaccount, so I do not enter any twin transaction (Cash (1): xxx = Deposits payable (2): xxx) of the Cash transaction during the conversion.

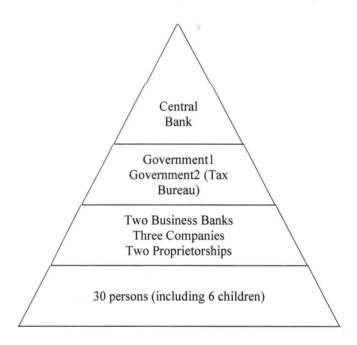

Figure 2.1-1   Pyramid Pattern of Small Society

| Order | Business No. | Name | Phone number | Tax rate | Business Bank1 | Business Bank2 | Balance | Primary Account |
|-------|-------------|------|-------------|----------|----------------|----------------|---------|-----------------|
| 1 | 88-654300 | Cash Management Center | 123456700 | 0 | 1058058.20 | 0 | 1058058.20 | Business Bank1 |
| 2 | 88-654301 | Central Bank | 123456789 | 0 | 0 | 4090.65 | 4090.65 | Business Bank2 |
| 3 | 88-654302 | Government1 | 123456788 | 0 | 1289.11 | 610.08 | 1899.19 | Business Bank1 |
| 4 | 88-654303 | Tax Bureau | 123456787 | 0 | 1003.72 | 1117.96 | 2121.68 | Business Bank1 |
| 5 | 88-654304 | Business Bank1 | 123456786 | 0.3 | - | 0 | 0 | Business Bank1 |
| 6 | 88-654305 | Business Bank2 | 123456785 | 0.3 | 0 | - | 0 | Business Bank2 |
| 7 | 88-654306 | Company1 | 123456784 | 0.3 | 67873.98 | 0 | 67873.98 | Business Bank1 |
| 8 | 88-654307 | Company2 | 123456783 | 0.3 | 0 | 47393.19 | 47393.19 | Business Bank2 |
| 9 | 88-654308 | Company3 | 123456782 | 0.3 | 3906.47 | 6753.89 | 10660.36 | Business Bank2 |

| 10 | 88-654309 | Proprietorship1 | 123456781 | 0.2 | 18783.78 | 0 | 18783.78 | Business Bank1 |
| 11 | 88-654310 | Proprietorship2 | 123456780 | 0.2 | 0 | 8768.69 | 8768.69 | Business Bank2 |
| **12** | **Total** | - | - | - | **1150915.26** | **68734.46** | **1219649.72** | - |

Figure 2.1-2   Organizations Information Table

The following Figure 2.1-3 shows the detail information of the 30 persons (including five children) on December 31, 2015.

| Order | SIN | Name | Employer Name | Business Bank1 | Business Bank2 | Balance | Primary Account |
|---|---|---|---|---|---|---|---|
| 1 | 909876501 | A1 | Central Bank | 15900.10 | 12000.15 | 27900.25 | Business Bank1 |
| 2 | 909876502 | A2 | Central Bank | 12200.11 | 16500.55 | 28700.66 | Business Bank1 |
| 3 | 909876503 | A3 | Government1 | 11800.23 | 16260.10 | 28060.33 | Business Bank1 |
| 4 | 909876504 | A4 | Government1 | 17230.03 | 11400.61 | 28630.64 | Business Bank1 |
| 5 | 909876505 | A5 | Tax Bureau | 15960.96 | 11970.23 | 27931.19 | Business Bank1 |
| 6 | 909876506 | A6 | Tax Bureau | 17200.52 | 11100.54 | 28301.06 | Business Bank1 |
| 7 | 909876507 | A7 | Business Bank1 | 28500.03 | 0 | 28500.03 | Business Bank1 |
| 8 | 909876508 | A8 | Business Bank1 | 15620.65 | 11000.11 | 26620.76 | Business Bank1 |
| 9 | 909876509 | A9 | Business Bank1 | 27700.11 | 0 | 27700.11 | Business Bank1 |
| 10 | 909876510 | A10 | Business Bank2 | 0 | 28600.21 | 28600.21 | Business Bank2 |
| 11 | 909876511 | A11 | Business Bank2 | 11710.41 | 14520.56 | 26230.97 | Business Bank2 |
| 12 | 909876512 | A12 | Business Bank2 | 15720.23 | 11680.34 | 27400.57 | Business Bank2 |
| 13 | 909876513 | A13 | Company1 | 16510.35 | 11810.18 | 28320.53 | Business Bank1 |
| 14 | 909876514 | A14 | Company1 | 17980.41 | 12200.45 | 30180.86 | Business Bank1 |
| 15 | 909876515 | A15 | Company1 | 26250.27 | 0 | 26250.27 | Business Bank1 |
| 16 | 909876516 | A16 | Company2 | 18790.58 | 11300.74 | 30091.32 | Business Bank1 |
| 17 | 909876517 | A17 | Company2 | 0 | 26150.88 | 26150.88 | Business Bank2 |
| 18 | 909876518 | A18 | Company2 | 18260.63 | 10510.99 | 28771.62 | Business Bank1 |
| 19 | 909876519 | A19 | Company3 | 11230.11 | 16910.92 | 28141.03 | Business Bank2 |
| 20 | 909876520 | A20 | Company3 | 11082.23 | 15900.51 | 26982.74 | Business Bank2 |
| 21 | 909876521 | A21 | Company3 | 0 | 26210.18 | 26210.18 | Business Bank2 |
| 22 | 909876522 | A22 | Proprietorship1 | 16510.03 | 11720.14 | 28230.17 | Business Bank2 |
| 23 | 909876523 | A23 | Proprietorship1 | 11960.84 | 15150.21 | 27111.05 | Business Bank2 |
| 24 | 909876524 | A24 | Proprietorship2 | 28100.25 | 0 | 28100.25 | Business Bank1 |
| 25 | 909876525 | A25 | Proprietorship2 | 11230.32 | 16150.25 | 27380.57 | Business Bank1 |
| 26 | 909876526 | A1A8 | Child of A1 and A8 | 0 | 0 | 0 | A1: Business Bank2 |
| 27 | 909876527 | A1A8 | Child of A1 and A8 | 0 | 0 | 0 | A8: - |

| 28 | 909876528 | A12A20 | Child of A12 and A20 | 0 | 0 | 0 | A12: Business Bank1 |
|----|-----------|--------|----------------------|---|---|---|---------------------|
| 29 | 909876529 | A13A25 | Child of A13 and A25 | 0 | 0 | 0 | A13: - |
| 30 | 909876530 | A16A23 | Child of A16 and A23 | 0 | 0 | 0 | A16: - |
| **31** | **Total** | | | **377449.40** | **319048.85** | **696498.25** | **-** |

Figure 2.1-3    Individuals Information Table

The following Figure 2.1-4 shows the cash detail information of the Business Bank1 and the Business Bank2.

| Order | Name | Balance | Self-Cash | Total Deposits | Companies Deposits | Individuals Deposits |
|-------|------|---------|-----------|----------------|--------------------|--------------------|
| 1 | Business Bank1 | 1609115.51 | 80750.85 | 1528364.66 | 1150915.26 | 377449.40 |
| 2 | Business Bank2 | 390884.49 | 3101.18 | 387783.31 | 68734.46 | 319048.85 |
| **3** | **Total** | **2000000.00** | **83852.03** | **1916147.97** | **1219649.72** | **696498.25** |

Figure 2.1-4    Two Business Banks Information Table

The balance of the "Cash" in the Business Bank1 and the balance of the "Cash" in the Business Bank2 are $1,609,115.51 and $390,884.49 respectively. Their sum is $2,000,000 which is also the issued money by the Central Bank.

For simplification, there is not the accounts of the "Net payroll payable", the "Salary tax payable", the "Utility expenses", and the "Office rent expenses". In addition, I do not need to know the detail information of every individual's receipt and payment before December 31, 2015. I only need to know the balances of the 25 individuals on December 31, 2015. These balances are the deposits in the Business Bank1 and the Business Bank2. Therefore, if the multi-subaccount names of the "Cash" account has not any three-level subaccount in a transaction, the amounts of the "Cash" are related to the individuals.

## 2.2 Top Rank of Social Members

The Central Bank is at the top of pyramid pattern from the Figure 2.1-1 on the page 14. It have two financial statements. One is for an abstract Cash Management Center. It only issues money and manages money and manages the planned national budgets because it does not have any equipment and only have interest expenses. Therefore, the abstract Cash Management Center is also given a business number and telephone number which are 88-654300 and 123456700 respectively. Another is for the Central Bank itself. Its function is as same as a government.

The Central Bank issues money and is the source of all money in the society. Meanwhile, it also recycles the money from the other ranks in the society by issuing bonds or bills. It pays the money to governments at all levels according to the national budgets or national tax revenues (hypothesis). Of course, it also pays the money to itself.

## 2.2.1 Sample of the Cash Management Center

### 2.2.1.1 Conversion of the Cash Management Center

The Cash Management Center (the Central Bank) issued money $2,000,000 a few years ago. Now, the Cash Management Center will convert to the MathAccounting software on January 1, 2016. The Figure 2.2-1 and the Figure 2.2-2 show the converting reference table and the multi-subaccount names table.

| Order | Class | Account Name (Subtotal Name) | Balance | Row |
|---|---|---|---|---|
| 1 | 1 | (Current assets) | - | 103 |
| 2 | 1 | Cash | 1058058.20 | 104 |
| 3 | 1 | Planned national budgets | 0 | 106 |
| 4 | 1 | Account receivable | 0 | 108 |
| 5 | 2 | (Current liabilities) | | 203 |
| 6 | 2 | Account payable | 0 | 204 |
| 7 | 2 | Business bank reserves payable | 0 | 204 |
| 8 | 2 | Tax receipts payable | 272062.66 | 206 |
| 9 | 2 | Accrued interest payable | 0 | 208 |
| 10 | 2 | (Long term liabilities) | - | 251 |
| 11 | 2 | Bonds payable | 60000.00 | 252 |
| 12 | 3 | (Owners' capital) | - | 303 |
| 13 | 3 | National capital | 725995.54 | 304 |
| 14 | 3 | Retained earnings | 0 | 306 |
| 15 | 4 | (Revenues) | - | 403 |

| 16 | 4 | Sales | 0 | 404 |
|---|---|---|---|---|
| **17** | **5** | **(Cost)** | - | **431** |
| 18 | 5 | Cost of goods sold | 0 | 432 |
| **19** | **5** | **(Operating and administrative expenses)** | - | **453** |
| 20 | 5 | Interest expenses | 0 | 454 |
| 21 | 5 | Bank fee expenses | 0 | 456 |
| **20** | **4** | **(Other income)** | - | **475** |
| 21 | 4 | Investment incomes | - | 476 |

Figure 2.2-1   Cash Management Center Converting Reference Table

| Order | Class | Multi-subaccount Name | Parent Name | Lowest Subaccount Balance |
|---|---|---|---|---|
| 1 | 1 | Cash receipts from issued money < Financial activities | Cash | 2000000.00 |
| 2 | 1 | 88-654302-i-reserve < Cash receipts from business bank reserves < Financial activities | Cash | 0 |
| 3 | 1 | 88-654303-i-reserve < Cash receipts from business bank reserves < Financial activities | Cash | 0 |
| 4 | 1 | Cash receipts from public markets < Operating activities | Cash | 726395.54 |
| 5 | 1 | 909876501-i-bond01 < Cash receipts from issued bonds < Financial activities | Cash | 5000.00 |
| 6 | 1 | 909876502-i-bond01 < Cash receipts from issued bonds < Financial activities | Cash | 5000.00 |
| 7 | 1 | 909876503-i-bond01 < Cash receipts from issued bonds < Financial activities | Cash | 5000.00 |
| 8 | 1 | 909876507-i-bond01 < Cash receipts from issued bonds < Financial activities | Cash | 5000.00 |
| 9 | 1 | 909876509-i-bond01 < Cash receipts from issued bonds < Financial activities | Cash | 5000.00 |
| 10 | 1 | 909876510-i-bond01 < Cash receipts from issued bonds < Financial activities | Cash | 5000.00 |
| 11 | 1 | 909876511-i-bond01 < Cash receipts from issued bonds < Financial activities | Cash | 5000.00 |
| 12 | 1 | 909876512-i-bond01 < Cash receipts from issued bonds < Financial activities | Cash | 5000.00 |
| 13 | 1 | 909876515-i-bond01 < Cash receipts from issued bonds < Financial activities | Cash | 5000.00 |
| 14 | 1 | 909876516-i-bond01 < Cash receipts from issued bonds < Financial activities | Cash | 5000.00 |
| 15 | 1 | 909876521-i-bond01 < Cash receipts from issued bonds < Financial activities | Cash | 5000.00 |
| 16 | 1 | 909876522-i-bond01 < Cash receipts from issued bonds < Financial activities | Cash | 5000.00 |
| 17 | 1 | 88-654303-c-tax < Cash receipts from public markets-tax < Financial activities | Cash | 34112.53 |
| 18 | 1 | 88-654303-c-tax < Cash receipts from public markets-tax < Financial activities | Cash | 31671.27 |
| 19 | 1 | 88-654303-c-tax < Cash receipts from public markets-tax < Financial activities | Cash | 52674.38 |
| 20 | 1 | 88-654303-c-tax < Cash receipts from public markets-tax < Financial activities | Cash | 71318.63 |
| 21 | 1 | 88-654303-c-tax < Cash receipts from public markets-tax < Financial activities | Cash | 51453.71 |

| | | | | |
|---|---|---|---|---|
| 22 | 1 | 88-654303-c-tax < Cash receipts from public markets-tax < Financial activities | Cash | 20752.91 |
| 23 | 1 | 88-654303-c-tax < Cash receipts from public markets-tax < Financial activities | Cash | 10079.23 |
| 24 | 1 | Cash payments to public markets < Operating activities | Cash | -2000000.00 |
| 25 | 1 | Cash payments for operating expenses < Operating activities | Cash | -400.00 |
| 26 | 1 | Planned national budgets-central bank | Planned national budgets | 0 |
| 27 | 1 | Planned national budgets-government1 | Planned national budgets | 0 |
| 28 | 1 | Planned national budgets-tax bureau | Planned national budgets | 0 |
| 29 | 2 | Business bank reserves-bank1 | Business bank reserves payable | 0 |
| 30 | 2 | Business bank reserves-bank2 | Business bank reserves payable | 0 |
| 31 | 2 | n | Tax receipts payable | 272062.66 |
| 32 | 2 | Bond01-interest payable < Bonds-interest payable | Accrued interest payable | 0 |
| 33 | 2 | Business bank1 reserves-interest payable < Business bank reserves-interest payable | Accrued interest payable | 0 |
| 34 | 2 | Business bank2 reserves-interest payable < Business bank reserves-interest payable | Accrued interest payable | 0 |
| 35 | 2 | Bond01-909876501 < Bond01 | Bonds payable | 5000.00 |
| 36 | 2 | Bond01-909876502 < Bond01 | Bonds payable | 5000.00 |
| 37 | 2 | Bond01-909876503 < Bond01 | Bonds payable | 5000.00 |
| 38 | 2 | Bond01-909876507 < Bond01 | Bonds payable | 5000.00 |
| 39 | 2 | Bond01-88-654309 < Bond01 | Bonds payable | 5000.00 |
| 40 | 2 | Bond01-88-654310 < Bond01 | Bonds payable | 5000.00 |
| 41 | 2 | Bond01-909876511 < Bond01 | Bonds payable | 5000.00 |
| 42 | 2 | Bond01-909876512 < Bond01 | Bonds payable | 5000.00 |
| 43 | 2 | Bond01-909876515 < Bond01 | Bonds payable | 5000.00 |
| 44 | 2 | Bond01-909876516 < Bond01 | Bonds payable | 5000.00 |
| 45 | 2 | Bond01-909876521 < Bond01 | Bonds payable | 5000.00 |
| 46 | 2 | Bond01-909876522 < Bond01 | Bonds payable | 5000.00 |
| 47 | 3 | Nation | National capital | 725995.54 |
| 48 | 5 | Bond01- interest expenses < Bonds-interest expenses | Interest expenses | 0 |
| 49 | 5 | Business bank1 reserves-interest expenses < Business bank reserves-interest expenses | Interest expenses | 0 |
| 50 | 5 | Business bank2 reserves-interest expenses < Business bank reserves-interest expenses | Interest expenses | 0 |
| 51 | 5 | Business bank1 | Bank fee expenses | 0 |

Figure 2.2-2   Cash Management Center Converting Multi-Subaccount Names Table

The Cash Management Center issued one bond, so the "Bonds payable" has one one-level subaccount of the "Bond01-payable" ($60,000, beginning on November 1, 2015, two years, and annual interest rate 4%), seeing the Figure 2.2-3 on this page and the next page, which shows the detail information of the issued bond. Its balance is $60,000. Accordingly, the "Bonds payable" has also many two-level subaccounts and its balance is $60,000 too.

| Order | Bond | Amount | Term | Purchaser Name | Identity |
|---|---|---|---|---|---|
| 1 | Bond01 | 5000 | November 1, 2015, two years, 4% annually | A1 | 909876501 |
| 2 | Bond01 | 5000 | November 1, 2015, two years, 4% annually, pay at end of each year | A2 | 909876502 |
| 3 | Bond01 | 5000 | November 1, 2015, two years, 4% annually, pay at end of each year | A3 | 909876503 |
| 4 | Bond01 | 5000 | November 1, 2015, two years, 4% annually, pay at end of each year | A7 | 909876507 |
| 5 | Bond01 | 5000 | November 1, 2015, two years, 4% annually, pay at end of each year | A9 | 909876509 |
| 6 | Bond01 | 5000 | November 1, 2015, two years, 4% annually, pay at end of each year | A10 | 909876510 |
| 7 | Bond01 | 5000 | November 1, 2015, two years, 4% annually, pay at end of each year | A11 | 909876511 |
| 8 | Bond01 | 5000 | November 1, 2015, two years, 4% annually, pay at end of each year | A12 | 909876512 |
| 9 | Bond01 | 5000 | November 1, 2015, two years, 4% annually, pay at end of each year | A15 | 909876515 |
| 10 | Bond01 | 5000 | November 1, 2015, two years, 4% annually, pay at end of each year | A16 | 909876516 |
| 11 | Bond01 | 5000 | November 1, 2015, two years, 4% annually, pay at end of each year | A21 | 909876521 |
| 12 | Bond01 | 5000 | November 1, 2015, two years, 4% annually, pay at end of each year | A22 | 909876522 |
| 13 | Total | 60000 | | | |

Figure 2.2-3   Cash Management Center Issued Bond Information Table

From the Figure 2.2-1 and the Figure 2.2-2, the dynamic accounting equation on January 1, 2016 must be divided to the "N" transaction sub-equations because of the restriction of the MathAccounting software. Every sub-equation has maximum twelve items. For simplification of not changing the MathAccounting software here, I first enter two initialization sub-equations. All converting transaction sub-equations can be designed and written as the followings.

- The two transaction sub-equations are respectively two initialization sub-equations.

  Account receivable (1): 0 = Account payable (2): 0

  0 = Sales (4): 0 – Cost of goods sold (5): 0

- The transaction sub-equation includes the "Cash" account with the Order 5 to the Order 10 and the "Bonds payable" account with the Order 35 to the Order 40. The third transaction sub-equation is:

  Cash (1): 5000 + Cash (1): 5000 + Cash (1): 5000 + Cash (1): 5000 + Cash (1): 5000 + Cash (1): 5000 = Bonds payable (2): 5000 + Bonds payable (2): 5000 + Bonds payable (2): 5000 + Bonds payable (2): 5000 + Bonds payable (2): 5000 + Bonds payable (2): 5000

- The transaction sub-equation includes the "Cash" account with the Order 11 to the Order 16 and the "Bonds payable" account with the Order 41 to the Order 46. The fourth transaction sub-equation is:

  Cash (1): 5000 + Cash (1): 5000 + Cash (1): 5000 + Cash (1): 5000 + Cash (1): 5000 + Cash (1): 5000 = Bonds payable (2): 5000 + Bonds payable (2): 5000 + Bonds payable (2): 5000 + Bonds payable (2): 5000 + Bonds payable (2): 5000 + Bonds payable (2): 5000

- The transaction sub-equation includes the "Cash" account with the Order 1, the Order 4, the Order 24, and the Order 25, and the "National capital" account with the Order 47. The fifth transaction sub-equation is:

  Cash (1): 2000000 + Cash (1): 726395.54 + Cash (1): -2000000 + Cash (1): -400 = National capital (3): 725995.54

- The transaction sub-equation includes the "Cash" account with the Order 17 to the Order 23 and the "Tax receipts payable" account with the Order 31. The sixth transaction sub-equation is:

  Cash (1): 34112.53 + Cash (1): 31671.27 + Cash (1): 52674.38 + Cash (1): 71318.63 + Cash (1): 51453.71 + Cash (1): 20752.91 + Cash (1): 10079.23 = Tax receipts payable (2): 272062.66

After completing this transaction, the dynamic accounting equation of the Cash Management Center on December 31, 2015 has entered into the database dcj2021.

## 2.2.1.2 Brief Summary of the Cash Management Center

Obviously, there is not any information of the Inventory account in these transaction sub-equations.

## 2.2.2 Sample of the Central Bank

## 2.2.2.1 Conversion of the Central Bank

The Central Bank (Cash Management Center) issued money $2,000,000 a few years ago. Now, the Central Bank will convert to the MathAccounting software on January 1, 2016. The Figure 2.2-4 and the Figure 2.2-5 show the converting reference table and the multi-subaccount names table.

| Order | Class | Account Name (**Subtotal Name**) | Balance | Row |
|-------|-------|----------------------------------|---------|-----|
| **1** | **1** | **(Current assets)** | - | **103** |
| 2 | 1 | Cash | 4090.65 | 104 |
| 3 | 1 | Supplies | 171.53 | 106 |
| **4** | **1** | **(Long term investments)** | - | **141** |
| 5 | 1 | Bonds | 0 | 143 |
| **6** | **1** | **(Equipment)** | - | **171** |
| 7 | 1 | Vehicle | 85000.00 | 172 |
| 8 | 1 | Accumulated amortization: vehicle | -42500.00 | 173 |
| 9 | 1 | Computer | 5900.00 | 174 |
| 10 | 1 | Accumulated amortization: computer | -4916.66 | 175 |
| **11** | **2** | **(Current liabilities)** | | **203** |
| 12 | 2 | Account payable | 1600.00 | 204 |
| **13** | **3** | **(Owners' capital)** | - | **303** |
| 14 | 3 | Budgets capital | 46145.52 | 304 |
| 15 | 3 | Retained earnings | 0 | 306 |
| **16** | **4** | **(Revenues)** | - | **403** |
| 17 | 4 | Sales (received budgets) | 0 | 404 |
| **18** | **5** | **(Cost)** | - | **431** |
| 19 | 5 | Cost of goods sold | 0 | 432 |
| **20** | **5** | **(Operating and administrative expenses)** | - | **453** |

| 21 | 5 | Travelling expenses | 0 | 454 |
|---|---|---|---|---|
| 22 | 5 | Other expenses | 0 | 456 |
| 23 | 5 | Office supplies expenses | 0 | 458 |
| 24 | 5 | Salary expenses | 0 | 460 |
| 25 | 5 | Amortization expenses | 0 | 462 |
| 26 | 5 | Interest expenses | 0 | 464 |
| **27** | **4** | **(Other income)** | - | **475** |
| 28 | 4 | Investment incomes | 0 | 476 |
| 29 | 4 | Deposits interest incomes | 0 | 478 |

Figure 2.2-4   Central Bank Converting Reference Table

| Order | Class | Multi-subaccount Name | Parent Name | Lowest Subaccount Balance |
|---|---|---|---|---|
| 1 | 1 | 88-654301-c-budgets < Cash receipts from central bank budgets < Financial activities | Cash | 685000.00 |
| 2 | 1 | 88-654304-c-interest of investment bond-xx1 < Cash receipts from investments < Investing activities | Cash | 0 |
| 3 | 1 | 88-654305-c-interest of investment bond-xx2 < Cash receipts from investments < Investing activities | Cash | 0 |
| 4 | 1 | 88-654306-t-truck2 < Cash payments for machinery < Operating activities | Cash | -45000.00 |
| 5 | 1 | 88-654306-t-car1 < Cash payments for machinery < Operating activities | Cash | -40000.00 |
| 6 | 1 | 88-654306-t-computer server1 < Cash payments for machinery < Operating activities | Cash | -2800.00 |
| 7 | 1 | 88-654306-t-computer1 < Cash payments for machinery < Operating activities | Cash | -1600.00 |
| 8 | 1 | 88-654306-t-computer2 < Cash payments for machinery < Operating activities | Cash | -1500.00 |
| 9 | 1 | Cash payments for operating expenses < Operating activities | Cash | -197854.41 |
| 10 | 1 | Cash payments for operating expenses < Operating activities | Cash | -196722.75 |
| 11 | 1 | Cash payments for operating expenses < Operating activities | Cash | -195432.19 |
| 12 | 1 | 88-654304-n-investment bondxx1 < Cash payments for investments < Investing activities | Cash | 0 |
| 13 | 1 | 88-654305-n-investment bondxx2 < Cash payments for investments < Investing activities | Cash | 0 |
| 14 | 1 | n | Supplies | 171.53 |
| 15 | 1 | Bondxx1 | Bonds | 0 |
| 16 | 1 | Bondxx2 | Bonds | 0 |
| 17 | 1 | Truck11 < Truck1 < Truck | Vehicle | 45000.00 |
| 18 | 1 | Car11 < Car1 < Car | Vehicle | 40000.00 |
| 19 | 1 | Truck11-accumulated amortization < Truck1-accumulated amortization < Truck-accumulated amortization | Accumulated amortization: Vehicle | -22500.00 |
| 20 | 1 | Car11-accumulated amortization < Car1-accumulated amortization < Car-accumulated amortization | Accumulated amortization: Vehicle | -20000.00 |
| 21 | 1 | Computer server11 < Computer server1 < Computer server | Computer | 2800.00 |

| 22 | 1 | Computer11 < Computer1 | Computer | 1600.00 |
|---|---|---|---|---|
| 23 | 1 | Computer21 < Computer2 | Computer | 1500.00 |
| 24 | 1 | Computer server11-accumulated amortization < Computer server1-accumulated amortization < Computer server-accumulated amortization | Accumulated amortization: Computer | -2333.33 |
| 25 | 1 | Computer11-accumulated amortization < Computer1-accumulated amortization | Accumulated amortization: Computer | -1333.33 |
| 26 | 1 | Computer21-accumulated amortization < Computer2-accumulated amortization | Accumulated amortization: Computer | -1250.00 |
| 27 | 2 | 123456784 | Account payable | 1400.00 |
| 28 | 2 | 123456783 | Account payable | 0 |
| 29 | 2 | 123456782 | Account payable | 200.00 |
| 30 | 2 | 123456781 | Account payable | 0 |
| 31 | 3 | Central Bank | Budgets capital | 46145.52 |
| 32 | 4 | n | Sales (received budgets) | 0 |
| 33 | 5 | n | Supplies expenses | 0 |
| 34 | 5 | 909876501-travelling < Office department-travelling | Travelling expenses | 0 |
| 35 | 5 | 909876501-other < Office department-other | Other expenses | 0 |
| 36 | 5 | 909876502-travelling < Operation department-travelling | Travelling expenses | 0 |
| 37 | 5 | 909876502-other < Operation department-other | Other expenses | 0 |
| 38 | 5 | 909876501-salary < Office department-salary | Salary expenses | 0 |
| 39 | 5 | 909876502-salary < Operation department-salary | Salary expenses | 0 |
| 40 | 5 | Truck11-amortization < Truck1-amortization < Vehicle-truck-amortization | Amortization expenses | 0 |
| 41 | 5 | Car11-amortization < Car1-amortization < Vehicle-Car-amortization | Amortization expenses | 0 |
| 42 | 5 | Computer server11-amortization < Computer server1-amortization < Computer-computer server-amortization | Amortization expenses | 0 |
| 43 | 5 | Computer11-amortization < Computer1-amortization < Computer-amortization | Amortization expenses | 0 |
| 44 | 5 | Computer21-amortization < Computer2-amortization < Computer-amortization | Amortization expenses | 0 |
| 45 | 4 | Accrued interest income-bond-xx1 < Bonds | Investment incomes | 0 |
| 46 | 4 | Accrued interest income-bond-xx2 < Bonds | Investment incomes | 0 |
| 47 | 4 | n | Deposits interest income | 0 |

Figure 2.2-5   Central Bank Converting Multi-Subaccount Names Table

From the above Figure 2.2-4 and the Figure 2.2-5, the dynamic accounting equation on December 31, 2015 must be divided to the "N" transaction sub-equations because of the restriction of the MathAccounting software. Every sub-equation has maximum twelve items. All converting transaction sub-equations can be designed and written as following.

- I first build a transaction sub-equation for the "Account payable" account. The transaction sub-equation includes the "Account payable" account with the Order 27 and the Order 29, the part of the "Cash" account with the Order 1, and initializations of the "Account receivable" account, the "Sales" account, and the "Cost of goods sold" account. The first transaction sub-equation is:

Cash (1): 1600 + Account receivable (1): 0 = Account payable (2): 1400 + Account payable (2): 200 + Sales (4): 0 + Cost of goods sold (5): 0

After entering this transaction, the new balance of the "Cash" account with the Order 1 is $683,400 (= $685,000 - $1,600).

- The transaction sub-equation includes the "Cash" account with the Order 4 to the Order 8, the "Vehicle" account with the Order 17 and the Order 18, and the "Computer" account with the Order 21 to the Order 23. The second transaction sub-equation is:

Cash (1): -45000 + Cash (1): -40000 + Cash (1): -2800 + Cash (1): -1600 + Cash (1): -1500 + Vehicle (1): 45000 + Vehicle (1): 40000 + Computer (1): 2800 + Computer (1): 1600 + Computer (1): 1500 = 0

- The transaction sub-equation includes the part of the "Cash" account with the Order 1, the "Cash" account with the Order 9 to the Order 11, the "Supplies" account with the Order 14, and the "Budgets capital" account with the Order 31. The third transaction sub-equation is:

Cash (1): 635983.34 + Cash (1): -197854.41 + Cash (1): -196722.75 + Cash (1): -195432.19 + Supplies (1): 171.53 = Budgets capital (3): 46145.52

After entering this transaction, the new balance of the "Cash" account with the Order 1 is $47,416.66 (= $683,400 - $-635,983.34).

- The transaction sub-equation includes the rest ($47,416.66) of the "Cash" account with the Order 1, the "Accumulated amortization: Vehicle" account with the Order

19 and the Order 20, and the "Accumulated amortization: Computer" account with the Order 24 to the Order 26. The fourth transaction sub-equation is:

Cash (1): 47416.66 + Accumulated amortization: Vehicle (1): -22500 + Accumulated amortization: Vehicle (1): -20000 + Accumulated amortization: Computer (1): -2333.33 + Accumulated amortization: Computer (1): -1333.33 + Accumulated amortization: Computer (1): -1250 = 0

After completing this transaction, the dynamic accounting equation of the Central Bank on December 31, 2015 has entered into the database dcj2022.

Obviously, there is not any information of the Inventory account in these transaction sub-equations.

### 2.2.2.2 Brief Summary of the Central Bank

Obviously, there is not any information of the Inventory account in these transaction sub-equations.

# 2.3 Second Rank of Social Members

The second rank of the social members is the governments at all levels and includes the Tax Bureau government. Every government pays all expenses of its employees and other expenses (including the office supplies and equipment).

## 2.3.1 Sample of the Government1

### 2.3.1.1 Conversion of the Government1

The Government1 will convert to the MathAccounting software on January 1, 2016. The Figure 2.3-1 and the Figure 2.3-2 show the converting reference table and the multi-subaccount names table.

| Order | Class | Account Name (**Subtotal Name**) | Balance | Row |
|-------|-------|----------------------------------|---------|-----|
| 1 | 1 | **(Current assets)** | - | **103** |
| 2 | 1 | Cash | 1899.19 | 104 |

| | | | | |
|---|---|---|---|---|
| 3 | 1 | Supplies | 122.86 | 106 |
| **4** | **1** | **(Long term investments)** | - | **141** |
| 5 | 1 | Bonds | 15000.00 | 143 |
| **6** | **1** | **(Equipment)** | - | **171** |
| 7 | 1 | Vehicle | 80000.00 | 172 |
| 8 | 1 | Accumulated amortization: vehicle | -36000.00 | 173 |
| 9 | 1 | Computer | 5900.00 | 174 |
| 10 | 1 | Accumulated amortization: computer | -1229.16 | 175 |
| **11** | **2** | **(Current liabilities)** | | **203** |
| 12 | 2 | Account payable | 500.00 | 204 |
| **13** | **3** | **(Owners' capital)** | - | **303** |
| 14 | 3 | Budgets capital | 65192.89 | 304 |
| 15 | 3 | Retained earnings | 0 | 306 |
| **16** | **4** | **(Revenues)** | - | **403** |
| 17 | 4 | Sales (received budgets) | 0 | 404 |
| **18** | **5** | **(Cost)** | - | **431** |
| 19 | 5 | Cost of goods sold | 0 | 432 |
| **20** | **5** | **(Operating and administrative expenses)** | - | **453** |
| 21 | 5 | Travelling expenses | 0 | 454 |
| 22 | 5 | Other expenses | 0 | 456 |
| 23 | 5 | Office supplies expenses | 0 | 458 |
| 24 | 5 | Salary expenses | 0 | 460 |
| 25 | 5 | Amortization expenses | 0 | 462 |
| 26 | 5 | Interest expenses | 0 | 464 |
| **27** | **4** | **(Other income)** | - | **475** |
| 28 | 4 | Investment incomes | 0 | 476 |
| 29 | 4 | Deposits interest incomes | 0 | 478 |

Figure 2.3-1   Government1 Converting Reference Table

| Order | Class | Multi-subaccount Name | Parent Name | Lowest Subaccount Balance |
|---|---|---|---|---|
| 1 | 1 | 88-654301-c-budgets < Cash receipts from central bank budgets < Financial activities | Cash | 677000.00 |
| 2 | 1 | 88-654304-c-interest of investment bond11 < Cash receipts from investments < Investing activities | Cash | 460.00 |
| 3 | 1 | 88-654305-c-interest of investment bond21 < Cash receipts from investments < Investing activities | Cash | 615.00 |
| 4 | 1 | 88-654306-t-truck2 < Cash payments for machinery < Operating activities | Cash | -40000.00 |
| 5 | 1 | 88-654306-t-car1 < Cash payments for machinery < Operating activities | Cash | -40000.00 |
| 6 | 1 | 88-654306-t-computer server1 < Cash payments for machinery < Operating activities | Cash | -2800.00 |

| | | | | |
|---|---|---|---|---|
| 7 | 1 | 88-654306-t-computer1 < Cash payments for machinery < Operating activities | Cash | -1600.00 |
| 8 | 1 | 88-654306-t-computer2 < Cash payments for machinery < Operating activities | Cash | -1500.00 |
| 9 | 1 | Cash payments for operating expenses < Operating activities | Cash | -194872.37 |
| 10 | 1 | Cash payments for operating expenses < Operating activities | Cash | -190271.95 |
| 11 | 1 | Cash payments for operating expenses < Operating activities | Cash | -190131.49 |
| 12 | 1 | 88-654304-n-investment bond11 < Cash payments for investments < Investing activities | Cash | -6000.00 |
| 13 | 1 | 88-654305-n-investment bond21 < Cash payments for investments < Investing activities | Cash | -9000.00 |
| 14 | 1 | n | Supplies | 122.86 |
| 15 | 1 | Bond11 | Bonds | 6000.00 |
| 16 | 1 | Bond21 | Bonds | 9000.00 |
| 17 | 1 | Truck21 < Truck2 < Truck | Vehicle | 40000.00 |
| 18 | 1 | Car11 < Car1 < Car | Vehicle | 40000.00 |
| 19 | 1 | Truck21-accumulated amortization < Truck2-accumulated amortization < Truck-accumulated amortization | Accumulated amortization: Vehicle | -19333.33 |
| 20 | 1 | Car11-accumulated amortization < Car1-accumulated amortization < Car-accumulated amortization | Accumulated amortization: Vehicle | -16666.67 |
| 21 | 1 | Computer server11 < Computer server1 < Computer server | Computer | 2800.00 |
| 22 | 1 | Computer11 < Computer1 | Computer | 1600.00 |
| 23 | 1 | Computer21 < Computer2 | Computer | 1500.00 |
| 24 | 1 | Computer server11-accumulated amortization < Computer server1-accumulated amortization < Computer server-accumulated amortization | Accumulated amortization: Computer | -583.33 |
| 25 | 1 | Computer11-accumulated amortization < Computer1-accumulated amortization | Accumulated amortization: Computer | -333.33 |
| 26 | 1 | Computer21-accumulated amortization < Computer2-accumulated amortization | Accumulated amortization: Computer | -312.50 |
| 27 | 2 | 123456784 | Account payable | 0 |
| 28 | 2 | 123456783 | Account payable | 500.00 |
| 29 | 2 | 123456782 | Account payable | 0 |
| 30 | 2 | 123456781 | Account payable | 0 |
| 31 | 3 | Government1 | Budgets capital | 65192.89 |
| 32 | 4 | n | Sales (received budgets) | 0 |
| 33 | 5 | n | Supplies expenses | 0 |
| 34 | 5 | 909876503-travelling < Office department-travelling | Travelling expenses | 0 |
| 35 | 5 | 909876503-other < Office department-other | Other expenses | 0 |
| 36 | 5 | 909876504-travelling < Operation department-travelling | Travelling expenses | 0 |
| 37 | 5 | 909876504-other < Operation department-other | Other expenses | 0 |
| 38 | 5 | 909876503-salary < Office department-salary | Salary expenses | 0 |
| 39 | 5 | 909876504-salary < Operation department-salary | Salary expenses | 0 |
| 40 | 5 | Truck21-amortization < Truck2-amortization < Vehicle-truck-amortization | Amortization expenses | 0 |
| 41 | 5 | Car11-amortization < Car1-amortization < Vehicle-Car-amortization | Amortization expenses | 0 |

| 42 | 5 | Computer server11-amortization < Computer server1-amortization < Computer-computer server-amortization | Amortization expenses | 0 |
|----|---|------|-----------------------|---|
| 43 | 5 | Computer11-amortization < Computer1-amortization < Computer-amortization | Amortization expenses | 0 |
| 44 | 5 | Computer21-amortization < Computer2-amortization < Computer-amortization | Amortization expenses | 0 |
| 45 | 4 | Accrued interest income-bond11 < Bonds | Investment incomes | 0 |
| 46 | 4 | Accrued interest income-bond21 < Bonds | Investment incomes | 0 |
| 47 | 4 | n | Deposits interest income | 0 |

Figure 2.3-2   Government1 Converting Multi-Subaccount Names Table

From the Figure 2.3-1 and the Figure 2.3-2, the dynamic accounting equation on December 31, 2015 must be divided to the "N" transaction sub-equations because of the restriction of the MathAccounting software. Every sub-equation has maximum twelve items. All converting transaction sub-equations can be designed and written as following.

- I first build a transaction sub-equation for the "Account payable" account. The transaction sub-equation includes the "Account payable" account with the Order 27 and the Order 28, the part of the "Cash" account with the Order 1, and initializations of the "Account receivable" account, the "Sales" account, and the "Cost of goods sold" account. The first transaction sub-equation is:

  Cash (1): 500 + Account receivable (1): 0 = Account payable (2): 500 + Sales (received budgets) (4): 0 + Cost of goods sold (5): 0

  After entering this transaction, the new balance of the "Cash" account with the Order 1 is $676,500 (= $677,000 - $500).

- The transaction sub-equation includes the "Cash" account with the Order 4 to the Order 8, the "Vehicle" account with the Order 17 and the Order 18, and the "Computer" account with the Order 21 to the Order 23. The second transaction sub-equation is:

  Cash (1): -40000 + Cash (1): -40000 + Cash (1): -2800 + Cash (1): -1600 + Cash (1): -1500 + Vehicle (1): 40000 + Vehicle (1): 40000+ Computer (1): 2800 +

Computer (1): 1600 + Computer (1): 1500 = 0

- The transaction sub-equation includes the "Cash" account with the Order 12 and the Order 13, and the "Bonds" account with the Order 15 and the Order 16. The third transaction sub-equation is:

  Cash (1): -6000 + Cash (1): -9000 + Bonds (1): 6000 + Bonds (1): 9000 = 0

- The transaction sub-equation includes the part of the "Cash" account with the Order 1, the "Cash" account with the Order 2 and the Order 3, the "Cash" account with the Order 9 to the Order 11, the "Supplies" account with the Order 14, and the "Budgets capital" account with the Order 31. The fourth transaction sub-equation is:

  Cash (1): 639270.84 + Cash (1): 460 + Cash (1): 615 + Cash (1): -194872.37 + Cash (1): -190271.95 + Cash (1): -190131.49 + Supplies (1): 122.86 = Budgets capital (3): 65192.89

  After entering this transaction, the new balance of the "Cash" account with the Order 1 is $37,229.16 (= $676,500 - $639,270.84).

- The transaction sub-equation includes the rest ($37,229.16) of the "Cash" account with the Order 1, the "Accumulated amortization: Vehicle" account with the Order 19 and the Order 20, and the "Accumulated amortization: Computer" account with the Order 24 to the Order 26. The fifth transaction sub-equation is:

  Cash (1): 37229.16 + Accumulated amortization: Vehicle (1): -19333.33 + Accumulated amortization: Vehicle (1): -16666.67 + Accumulated amortization: Computer (1): -583.33 + Accumulated amortization: Computer (1): -333.33 + Accumulated amortization: Computer (1): -312.5 = 0

After completing this transaction, the dynamic accounting equation of the Government1 on December 31, 2015 has entered into the database dcj203.

## 2.3.1.2 Brief Summary of the Government1

Obviously, there is not any information of the Inventory account in these transaction sub-equations.

## 2.3.2 Sample of the Tax Bureau

### 2.3.2.1 Conversion of the Tax Bureau

The Tax Bureau will convert to the MathAccounting software on January 1, 2016. The Figure 2.3-3 and the Figure 2.3-4 show the converting reference table and the multi-subaccount names table.

| Order | Class | Account Name (**Subtotal Name**) | Balance | Row |
|---|---|---|---|---|
| **1** | **1** | **(Current assets)** | - | **103** |
| 2 | 1 | Cash | 2121.68 | 104 |
| 3 | 1 | Supplies | 166.78 | 105 |
| **4** | **1** | **(Long term investments)** | - | **141** |
| 5 | 1 | Bonds | 13000.00 | 143 |
| **6** | **1** | **(Equipment)** | - | **171** |
| 7 | 1 | Vehicle | 118000.00 | 172 |
| 8 | 1 | Accumulated amortization: vehicle | -43666.67 | 173 |
| 9 | 1 | Computer | 5900 | 174 |
| 10 | 1 | Accumulated amortization: computer | -3687.50 | 175 |
| **11** | **2** | **(Current liabilities)** | | **203** |
| 12 | 2 | Account payable | 1200.00 | 204 |
| 13 | 2 | Tax receipts payable | 0 | 206 |
| **14** | **3** | **(Owners' capital)** | - | **303** |
| 15 | 3 | Budgets capital | 90634.29 | 304 |
| 16 | 3 | Retained earnings | 0 | 306 |
| **17** | **4** | **(Revenues)** | - | **403** |
| 18 | 4 | Sales (received budgets) | 0 | 404 |
| **19** | **5** | **(Cost)** | - | **431** |
| 20 | 5 | Cost of goods sold | 0 | 432 |
| **21** | **5** | **(Operating and administrative expenses)** | - | **453** |
| 22 | 5 | Travelling expenses | 0 | 454 |
| 23 | 5 | Other expenses | 0 | 456 |
| 24 | 5 | Office supplies expenses | 0 | 458 |
| 25 | 5 | Salary expenses | 0 | 460 |
| 26 | 5 | Amortization expenses | 0 | 462 |

| | | | | | |
|---|---|---|---|---|---|
| 27 | 5 | Interest expenses | | 0 | 464 |
| **28** | **4** | **(Other income)** | | **-** | **475** |
| 29 | 4 | Investment incomes | | 0 | 476 |
| 30 | 4 | Deposits interest incomes | | 0 | 478 |

Figure 2.3-3   Tax Bureau Converting Reference Table

| Order | Class | Multi-subaccount Name | Parent Name | Lowest Subaccount Balance |
|---|---|---|---|---|
| 1 | 1 | 88-654301-c-budgets < Cash receipts from central bank < Financial activities | Cash | 718000.00 |
| 2 | 1 | 88-654304-c-tax < Cash receipts from taxation < Financial activities | Cash | 34112.53 |
| 3 | 1 | 88-654305-c-tax < Cash receipts from taxation < Financial activities | Cash | 31671.27 |
| 4 | 1 | 88-654306-c-tax < Cash receipts from taxation < Financial activities | Cash | 52674.38 |
| 5 | 1 | 88-654307-c-tax < Cash receipts from taxation < Financial activities | Cash | 71318.63 |
| 6 | 1 | 88-654308-c-tax < Cash receipts from taxation < Financial activities | Cash | 51453.71 |
| 7 | 1 | 88-654309-c-tax < Cash receipts from taxation < Financial activities | Cash | 20752.91 |
| 8 | 1 | 88-654310-c-tax < Cash receipts from taxation < Financial activities | Cash | 10079.23 |
| 9 | 1 | 88-654304-c-interest of investment bond11 < Cash receipts from investments < Investing activities | Cash | 383.33 |
| 10 | 1 | 88-654305-c-interest of investment bond21 < Cash receipts from investments < Investing activities | Cash | 546.67 |
| 11 | 1 | 88-654306-t-truck2 < Cash payments for machinery < Operating activities | Cash | -40000.00 |
| 12 | 1 | 88-654306-t-car1 < Cash payments for machinery < Operating activities | Cash | -40000.00 |
| 13 | 1 | 88-654306-t-car3 < Cash payments for machinery < Operating activities | Cash | -38000.00 |
| 14 | 1 | 88-654306-t-computer server1 < Cash payments for machinery < Operating activities | Cash | -2800.00 |
| 15 | 1 | 88-654306-t-computer1 < Cash payments for machinery < Operating activities | Cash | -1600.00 |
| 16 | 1 | 88-654306-t-computer2 < Cash payments for machinery < Operating activities | Cash | -1500.00 |
| 17 | 1 | Cash payments for operating expenses < Operating activities | Cash | -195412.62 |
| 18 | 1 | Cash payments for operating expenses < Operating activities | Cash | -193578.19 |
| 19 | 1 | Cash payments for operating expenses < Operating activities | Cash | -190917.51 |
| 20 | 1 | 88-654304-n-investment bond11 < Cash payments for investments < Investing activities | Cash | -5000.00 |
| 21 | 1 | 88-654305-n-investment bond21 < Cash payments for investments < Investing activities | Cash | -8000.00 |
| 22 | 1 | 88-654301-n-tax < Cash payments to central bank < Financial activities | Cash | -272062.66 |
| 23 | 1 | n | Supplies | 166.78 |
| 24 | 1 | Bond11 | Bonds | 5000.00 |
| 25 | 1 | Bond21 | Bonds | 8000.00 |

| | | | | |
|---|---|---|---|---|
| 26 | 1 | Truck21 < Truck2 < Truck | Vehicle | 40000.00 |
| 27 | 1 | Car11 < Car1 < Car | Vehicle | 40000.00 |
| 28 | 1 | Car31 < Car3 < Car | Vehicle | 38000.00 |
| 29 | 1 | Truck21-accumulated amortization < Truck2-accumulated amortization < Truck-accumulated amortization | Accumulated amortization: Vehicle | -18666.67 |
| 30 | 1 | Car11-accumulated amortization < Car1-accumulated amortization < Car-accumulated amortization | Accumulated amortization: Vehicle | -18666.67 |
| 31 | 1 | Car31-accumulated amortization < Car3-accumulated amortization < Car-accumulated amortization | Accumulated amortization: Vehicle | -6333.33 |
| 32 | 1 | Computer server11 < Computer server1 < Computer server | Computer | 2800.00 |
| 33 | 1 | Computer11 < Computer1 | Computer | 1600.00 |
| 34 | 1 | Computer21 < Computer2 | Computer | 1500.00 |
| 35 | 1 | Computer server11-accumulated amortization < Computer server1-accumulated amortization < Computer server-accumulated amortization | Accumulated amortization: Computer | -1750.00 |
| 36 | 1 | Computer11-accumulated amortization < Computer1-accumulated amortization | Accumulated amortization: Computer | -1000.00 |
| 37 | 1 | Computer21-accumulated amortization < Computer2-accumulated amortization | Accumulated amortization: Computer | -937.50 |
| 38 | 2 | 123456784 | Account payable | 500.00 |
| 39 | 2 | 123456783 | Account payable | 400.00 |
| 40 | 2 | 123456782 | Account payable | 300.00 |
| 41 | 2 | 123456781 | Account payable | 0 |
| 42 | 3 | Tax Bureau | Budgets capital | 90634.29 |
| 43 | 4 | n | Sales (received budgets) | 0 |
| 44 | 5 | n | Supplies expenses | 0 |
| 45 | 5 | 909876505-travelling < Office department-travelling | Travelling expenses | 0 |
| 46 | 5 | 909876505-other < Office department-other | Other expenses | 0 |
| 47 | 5 | 909876506-travelling < Operation department-travelling | Travelling expenses | 0 |
| 48 | 5 | 909876506-other < Operation department-other | Other expenses | 0 |
| 49 | 5 | 909876505-salary < Office department-salary | Salary expenses | 0 |
| 50 | 5 | 909876506-salary < Operation department-salary | Salary expenses | 0 |
| 51 | 5 | Truck21-amortization < Truck2-amortization < Vehicle-truck-amortization | Amortization expenses | 0 |
| 52 | 5 | Car11-amortization < Car1-amortization < Vehicle-Car-amortization | Amortization expenses | 0 |
| 53 | 5 | Car31-amortization < Car3-amortization < Vehicle-Car-amortization | Amortization expenses | 0 |
| 54 | 5 | Computer server11-amortization < Computer server1-amortization < Computer-computer server-amortization | Amortization expenses | 0 |
| 55 | 5 | Computer11-amortization < Computer1-amortization < Computer-computer-amortization | Amortization expenses | 0 |
| 56 | 5 | Computer21-amortization < Computer2-amortization < Computer-computer-amortization | Amortization expenses | 0 |
| 57 | 4 | Accrued interest income-bond11 < Bonds | Investment incomes | 0 |
| 58 | 4 | Accrued interest income-bond21 < Bonds | Investment incomes | 0 |
| 59 | 4 | n | Deposits interest income | 0 |

Figure 2.3-4   Tax Bureau Converting Multi-Subaccount Names Table

From the Figure 2.3-3 and the Figure 2.3-4, the dynamic accounting equation on December 31, 2015 must be divided to the "N" transaction sub-equations because of the restriction of the MathAccounting software. Every sub-equation has maximum twelve items. All converting transaction sub-equations can be designed and written as the followings.

- I first build a transaction sub-equation for the "Account payable" account. The transaction sub-equation includes the "Account payable" account with the Order 38 to the Order 40, and the part of the "Cash" account with the Order 1, and initializations of the "Account receivable" account, the "Sales" account, and the "Cost of goods sold" account. The first transaction sub-equation is:

  Cash (1): 1200 + Account receivable (1): 0 = Account payable (2): 500 + Account payable (2): 400 + Account payable (2): 300 + Sales (received budgets) (4): 0 + Cost of goods sold (5): 0

  After entering this transaction, the new balance of the "Cash" account with the Order 1 is $716,800 (= $718,000 - $1,200).

- The transaction sub-equation includes the "Cash" account with the Order 2 to the Order 8 and the "Cash" account with the 22. The second transaction sub-equation is:

  Cash (1): 34112.53 + Cash (1): 31671.27 + Cash (1): 52674.38 + Cash (1): 71318.63 + Cash (1): 51453.71 + Cash (1): 20752.91+ Cash (1): 10079.23 + Cash (1): -272062.66 = 0

- The transaction sub-equation includes the "Cash" account with the Order 11 to the Order 16, the "Vehicle" account with the Order 26 and the Order 28, and the "Computer" account with the Order 32 to the Order 34. The third transaction sub-equation is:

  Cash (1): -40000 + Cash (1): -40000 + Cash (1): -38000 + Cash (1): -2800 + Cash

(1): -1600 + Cash (1): -1500 + Vehicle (1): 40000 + Vehicle (1): 40000 + Vehicle (1): 38000 + Computer (1): 2800 + Computer (1): 1600 + Computer (1): 1500 = 0

- The transaction sub-equation includes the "Cash" account with the Order 20 and the Order 21, and the "Bonds" account with the Order 24 and the Order 25. The fourth transaction sub-equation is:

  Cash (1): -5000 + Cash (1): -8000 + Bonds (1): 5000 + Bonds (1): 8000 = 0

- The transaction sub-equation includes the part of the "Cash" account with the Order 1, the "Cash" account with the Order 9 and the Order 10, the "Cash" account with the Order 17 to the Order 19, the "Supplies" account with the Order 23, and the "Budgets capital" account with the Order 42. The fifth transaction sub-equation is:

  Cash (1): 669445.83 + Cash (1): 383.33 + Cash (1): 546.67 + Cash (1): -195412.62 + Cash (1): -193578.19 + Cash (1): -190917.51 + Supplies (1): 166.78 = Budgets capital (3): 90634.29

  After entering this transaction, the new balance of the "Cash" account with the Order 1 is $47,354.17 (= $716,800 - $669,445.83).

- The transaction sub-equation includes the rest ($47,354.17) of the "Cash" account with the Order 1, the "Accumulated amortization: Vehicle" account with the Order 29 and the Order 31, and the "Accumulated amortization: Computer" account with the Order 35 to the Order 37. The sixth transaction sub-equation is:

  Cash (1): 47354.17 + Accumulated amortization: Vehicle (1): -18666.67 + Accumulated amortization: Vehicle (1): -18666.67 + Accumulated amortization: Vehicle (1): -6333.33 + Accumulated amortization: Computer (1): -1750 + Accumulated amortization: Computer (1): -1000 + Accumulated amortization: Computer (1): -937.5= 0

After completing this transaction, the dynamic accounting equation of the Tax Bureau on December 31, 2015 has entered into the database dcj204.

### 2.3.2.2 Brief Summary of the Tax Bureau

Obviously, there is not any information of the Inventory account in these transaction sub-equations.

# 2.4 Third Rank of Social Members

The third rank of the social members is all organizations or all companies. There are seven companies or organizations in the third rank of the social members.

## 2.4.1 Sample of the Business Bank1

The Business Bank1 has total share capital $1,000,000 and two shareholders of the individual A7 and the individual A9. Their percentages are 60% and 40% respectively.

### 2.4.1.1 Conversion of the Business Bank1

The Business Bank1 will convert to the MathAccounting software on January 1, 2016. The Figure 2.4-1 and the Figure 2.4-2 show the converting reference table and the multi-subaccount names table respectively.

| Order | Class | Account Name (**Subtotal Name**) | Balance | Row |
|-------|-------|----------------------------------|---------|-----|
| **1** | **1** | **(Current assets)** | - | **103** |
| 2 | 1 | Cash | 1609115.51 | 104 |
| 3 | 1 | Supplies | 102.31 | 106 |
| 4 | 1 | Business bank reserves receivable | 0 | 108 |
| 5 | 1 | Accrued interest receivable | 0 | 110 |
| 6 | 1 | Notes receivable | 1010000.00 | 112 |
| **7** | **1** | **(Long term investments)** | - | **141** |
| 8 | 1 | Bonds | 11000.00 | 143 |
| **9** | **1** | **(Equipment)** | - | **171** |
| 10 | 1 | Vehicle | 85000.00 | 172 |
| 11 | 1 | Accumulated amortization: Vehicle | -32916.67 | 173 |
| 12 | 1 | Computer | 5600.00 | 174 |

| | | | | |
|---|---|---|---|---|
| 13 | 1 | Accumulated amortization: Computer | -3966.67 | 175 |
| **14** | **2** | **(Current liabilities)** | - | **203** |
| 15 | 2 | Business bank reserves payable | 0 | 204 |
| 16 | 2 | Account payable | 0 | 206 |
| | 2 | Accrued interest payable | 0 | 208 |
| 17 | 2 | Deposits payable | 1528364.66 | 210 |
| 18 | 2 | Tax payable | 0 | 210 |
| **19** | **2** | **(Long term liabilities)** | - | **251** |
| 20 | 2 | Bonds payable | 150000.00 | 252 |
| **21** | **3** | **(Owners' capital)** | - | **303** |
| 22 | 3 | Share capital | 1000000.00 | 304 |
| 23 | 3 | Retained earnings (Conversion) | 5569.82 | 306 |
| **24** | **4** | **(Revenues)** | - | **403** |
| 25 | 4 | Sales (notes interest) | 0 | 404 |
| **26** | **5** | **(Cost)** | - | **431** |
| 27 | 5 | Cost of notes interest | 0 | 432 |
| **28** | **5** | **(Operating and administrative expenses)** | - | **453** |
| 29 | 5 | Travelling expenses | 0 | 454 |
| 30 | 5 | Other expenses | 0 | 456 |
| 31 | 5 | Office supplies expenses | 0 | 458 |
| 32 | 5 | Salary expenses | 0 | 460 |
| 33 | 5 | Bond interest expenses | 0 | 462 |
| 34 | 5 | Amortization expenses | 0 | 464 |
| 35 | 5 | Interest expenses | 0 | 466 |
| **36** | **4** | **(Other income)** | - | **475** |
| 37 | 4 | Investment incomes | 0 | 476 |
| 39 | 4 | Deposits fee incomes | 0 | 478 |
| **39** | **5** | **(Tax)** | - | **600** |
| 40 | 5 | Tax expenses | 0 | 602 |

Figure 2.4-1   Business Bank1 Converting Reference Table

| Order | Class | Multi-subaccount Name | Parent Name | Lowest Subaccount Balance |
|---|---|---|---|---|
| 1 | 1 | 909876507-i-owners < Cash receipts from owners < Financial activities | Cash | 600000.00 |
| 2 | 1 | 909876509-i-owners < Cash receipts from owners < Financial activities | Cash | 400000.00 |
| 3 | 1 | 909876501-d-deposits < Cash receipts from customers deposits < Operating activities | Cash | 15900.10 |
| 4 | 1 | 909876502-d-deposits < Cash receipts from customers deposits < Operating activities | Cash | 12200.11 |
| 5 | 1 | 909876503-d-deposits < Cash receipts from customers deposits < Operating activities | Cash | 11800.23 |

| 6 | 1 | 909876504-d-deposits < Cash receipts from customers deposits < Operating activities | Cash | 17230.03 |
|---|---|---|---|---|
| 7 | 1 | 909876505-d-deposits < Cash receipts from customers deposits < Operating activities | Cash | 15960.96 |
| 8 | 1 | 909876506-d-deposits < Cash receipts from customers deposits < Operating activities | Cash | 17200.52 |
| 9 | 1 | 909876507-d-deposits < Cash receipts from customers deposits < Operating activities | Cash | 28500.03 |
| 10 | 1 | 909876508-d-deposits < Cash receipts from customers deposits < Operating activities | Cash | 15620.65 |
| 11 | 1 | 909876509-d-deposits < Cash receipts from customers deposits < Operating activities | Cash | 27700.11 |
| 12 | 1 | 909876510-d-deposits < Cash receipts from customers deposits < Operating activities | Cash | 0 |
| 13 | 1 | 909876511-d-deposits < Cash receipts from customers deposits < Operating activities | Cash | 11710.41 |
| 14 | 1 | 909876512-d-deposits < Cash receipts from customers deposits < Operating activities | Cash | 15720.23 |
| 15 | 1 | 909876513-d-deposits < Cash receipts from customers deposits < Operating activities | Cash | 16510.35 |
| 16 | 1 | 909876514-d-deposits < Cash receipts from customers deposits < Operating activities | Cash | 17980.41 |
| 17 | 1 | 909876515-d-deposits < Cash receipts from customers deposits < Operating activities | Cash | 26250.27 |
| 18 | 1 | 909876516-d-deposits < Cash receipts from customers deposits < Operating activities | Cash | 18790.58 |
| 19 | 1 | 909876517-d-deposits < Cash receipts from customers deposits < Operating activities | Cash | 0 |
| 20 | 1 | 909876518-d-deposits < Cash receipts from customers deposits < Operating activities | Cash | 18260.63 |
| 21 | 1 | 909876519-d-deposits < Cash receipts from customers deposits < Operating activities | Cash | 11230.11 |
| 22 | 1 | 909876520-d-deposits < Cash receipts from customers deposits < Operating activities | Cash | 11082.23 |
| 23 | 1 | 909876521-d-deposits < Cash receipts from customers deposits < Operating activities | Cash | 0 |
| 24 | 1 | 909876522-d-deposits < Cash receipts from customers deposits < Operating activities | Cash | 16510.03 |
| 25 | 1 | 909876523-d-deposits < Cash receipts from customers deposits < Operating activities | Cash | 11960.84 |
| 26 | 1 | 909876524-d-deposits < Cash receipts from customers deposits < Operating activities | Cash | 28100.25 |
| 27 | 1 | 909876525-d-deposits < Cash receipts from customers deposits < Operating activities | Cash | 11230.32 |
| 28 | 1 | 88-654300-d-deposits < Cash receipts from customers deposits < Operating activities | Cash | 1058058.20 |
| 29 | 1 | 88-654302-d-deposits < Cash receipts from customers deposits < Operating activities | Cash | 1289.11 |
| 30 | 1 | 88-654303-d-deposits < Cash receipts from customers deposits < Operating activities | Cash | 1003.72 |
| 31 | 1 | 88-654304-d-deposits < Cash receipts from customers deposits < Operating activities | Cash | 0 |
| 32 | 1 | 88-654305-d-deposits < Cash receipts from customers deposits < Operating activities | Cash | 0 |
| 33 | 1 | 88-654306-d-deposits < Cash receipts from customers deposits < Operating activities | Cash | 67873.98 |
| 34 | 1 | 88-654307-d-deposits < Cash receipts from customers deposits < Operating activities | Cash | 0 |
| 35 | 1 | 88-654308-d-deposits < Cash receipts from customers deposits < Operating activities | Cash | 3906.47 |
| 36 | 1 | 88-654309-d-deposits < Cash receipts from customers deposits < Operating activities | Cash | 18783.78 |
| 37 | 1 | 88-654310-d-deposits < Cash receipts from customers deposits < Operating activities | Cash | 0 |

| 38 | 1 | 88-654302-i-bond11 < Cash receipts from issued bonds < Financial activities | Cash | 6000.00 |
|---|---|---|---|---|
| 39 | 1 | 88-654303-i-bond11 < Cash receipts from issued bonds < Financial activities | Cash | 5000.00 |
| 40 | 1 | 88-654305-i-bond11 < Cash receipts from issued bonds < Financial activities | Cash | 7000.00 |
| 41 | 1 | 88-654306-i-bond11 < Cash receipts from issued bonds < Financial activities | Cash | 10000.00 |
| 42 | 1 | 88-654308-i-bond11 < Cash receipts from issued bonds < Financial activities | Cash | 8000.00 |
| 43 | 1 | 88-654309-i-bond11 < Cash receipts from issued bonds < Financial activities | Cash | 5000.00 |
| 44 | 1 | 909876507-i-bond11 < Cash receipts from issued bonds < Financial activities | Cash | 9000.00 |
| 45 | 1 | 909876509-i-bond11 < Cash receipts from issued bonds < Financial activities | Cash | 6000.00 |
| 46 | 1 | 909876513-i-bond11 < Cash receipts from issued bonds < Financial activities | Cash | 3000.00 |
| 47 | 1 | 909876514-i-bond11 < Cash receipts from issued bonds < Financial activities | Cash | 1000.00 |
| 48 | 1 | 88-654305-i-bond12 < Cash receipts from issued bonds < Financial activities | Cash | 3000.00 |
| 49 | 1 | 88-654307-i-bond12 < Cash receipts from issued bonds < Financial activities | Cash | 8000.00 |
| 50 | 1 | 88-654309-i-bond12 < Cash receipts from issued bonds < Financial activities | Cash | 3000.00 |
| 51 | 1 | 88-654310-i-bond12 < Cash receipts from issued bonds < Financial activities | Cash | 6000.00 |
| 52 | 1 | 909876501-i-bond12 < Cash receipts from issued bonds < Financial activities | Cash | 5000.00 |
| 53 | 1 | 909876502-i-bond12 < Cash receipts from issued bonds < Financial activities | Cash | 2000.00 |
| 54 | 1 | 909876504-i-bond12 < Cash receipts from issued bonds < Financial activities | Cash | 7000.00 |
| 55 | 1 | 909876521-i-bond12 < Cash receipts from issued bonds < Financial activities | Cash | 6000.00 |
| 56 | 1 | 88-654305-i-bond13 < Cash receipts from issued bonds < Financial activities | Cash | 6000.00 |
| 57 | 1 | 88-654306-i-bond13 < Cash receipts from issued bonds < Financial activities | Cash | 3000.00 |
| 58 | 1 | 88-654309-i-bond13 < Cash receipts from issued bonds < Financial activities | Cash | 2000.00 |
| 59 | 1 | 909876503-i-bond13 < Cash receipts from issued bonds < Financial activities | Cash | 6000.00 |
| 60 | 1 | 909876505-i-bond13 < Cash receipts from issued bonds < Financial activities | Cash | 4000.00 |
| 61 | 1 | 909876506-i-bond13 < Cash receipts from issued bonds < Financial activities | Cash | 7000.00 |
| 62 | 1 | 909876515-i-bond13 < Cash receipts from issued bonds < Financial activities | Cash | 4000.00 |
| 63 | 1 | 909876517-i-bond13 < Cash receipts from issued bonds < Financial activities | Cash | 5000.00 |
| 64 | 1 | 909876518-i-bond13 < Cash receipts from issued bonds < Financial activities | Cash | 3000.00 |
| 65 | 1 | 909876519-i-bond13 < Cash receipts from issued bonds < Financial activities | Cash | 6000.00 |
| 66 | 1 | 909876521-i-bond13 < Cash receipts from issued bonds < Financial activities | Cash | 4000.00 |
| 67 | 1 | 88-654306-c-accrued interest < Cash receipts from note accrued interest (customers) < Operating activities | Cash | 65625.00 |
| 68 | 1 | 88-654307-c-accrued interest < Cash receipts from note accrued interest (customers) < Operating activities | Cash | 23100.00 |
| 69 | 1 | 88-654308-c-accrued interest < Cash receipts from note accrued interest (customers) < Operating activities | Cash | 30000.00 |

| 70 | 1 | 88-654307-c-accrued interest < Cash receipts from note accrued interest (customers) < Operating activities | Cash | 36416.67 |
|---|---|---|---|---|
| 71 | 1 | 88-654306-c-accrued interest < Cash receipts from note accrued interest (customers) < Operating activities | Cash | 4037.50 |
| 72 | 1 | 88-654305-c-interest of investment bond21 < Cash receipts from investments < Investing activities | Cash | 410.00 |
| 73 | 1 | 88-654305-c-interest of investment bond22 < Cash receipts from investments < Investing activities | Cash | 201.67 |
| 74 | 1 | 88-654306-t-truck1 < Cash payments for machinery < Operating activities | Cash | -45000.00 |
| 75 | 1 | 88-654306-t-car1 < Cash payments for machinery < Operating activities | Cash | -40000.00 |
| 76 | 1 | 88-654306-t-computer server2 < Cash payments for machinery < Operating activities | Cash | -2700.00 |
| 77 | 1 | 88-654306-t-computer2 < Cash payments for machinery < Operating activities | Cash | -1500.00 |
| 78 | 1 | 88-654306-t-computer3 < Cash payments for machinery < Operating activities | Cash | -1400.00 |
| 79 | 1 | Cash payments for operating expenses < Operating activities | Cash | -28061.55 |
| 80 | 1 | Cash payments for operating expenses < Operating activities | Cash | -27953.14 |
| 81 | 1 | Cash payments for operating expenses < Operating activities | Cash | -27312.77 |
| 82 | 1 | 88-654303-n-tax < Cash payments for operating expenses < Operating activities | Cash | -34112.53 |
| 83 | 1 | 88-654306-n-notes1 < Cash payments to notes lenders < Operating activities | Cash | -250000.00 |
| 84 | 1 | 88-654307-n-notes2 < Cash payments to notes lenders < Operating activities | Cash | -140000.00 |
| 85 | 1 | 88-654308-n-notes3 < Cash payments to notes lenders < Operating activities | Cash | -200000.00 |
| 86 | 1 | 88-654307-n-notes4 < Cash payments to notes lenders < Operating activities | Cash | -250000.00 |
| 87 | 1 | 88-654306-n-notes5 < Cash payments to notes lenders < Operating activities | Cash | -170000.00 |
| 88 | 1 | 88-654305-n-investment bond21 < Cash payments for investments < Investing activities | Cash | -6000.00 |
| 89 | 1 | 88-654305-n-investment bond22 < Cash payments for investments < Investing activities | Cash | -5000.00 |
| 90 | 1 | n | Supplies | 102.31 |
| 91 | 1 | Note11-88-654306 | Notes receivable | 250000.00 |
| 92 | 1 | Note12-88-654307 | Notes receivable | 140000.00 |
| 93 | 1 | Note13-88-654308 | Notes receivable | 200000.00 |
| 94 | 1 | Note14-88-654307 | Notes receivable | 250000.00 |
| 95 | 1 | Note15-88-654306 | Notes receivable | 170000.00 |
| 96 | 1 | Bond21 | Bonds | 6000.00 |
| 97 | 1 | Bond22 | Bonds | 5000.00 |
| 98 | 1 | Truck11 < Truck1 < Truck | Vehicle | 45000.00 |
| 99 | 1 | Car11 < Car1 < Car | Vehicle | 40000.00 |
| 100 | 1 | Truck11-accumulated amortization < Truck1-accumulated amortization < Truck-accumulated amortization | Accumulated amortization: Vehicle | -20250.00 |
| 101 | 1 | Car11-accumulated amortization < Car1-accumulated amortization < Car-accumulated amortization | Accumulated amortization: Vehicle | -12666.67 |
| 102 | 1 | Computer server21 < Computer server2 < Computer server | Computer | 2700.00 |

| 103 | 1 | Computer21 < Computer2 | Computer | 1500.00 |
|---|---|---|---|---|
| 104 | 1 | Computer31 < Computer3 | Computer | 1400.00 |
| 105 | 1 | Computer server21-accumulated amortization < Computer server2-accumulated amortization < Computer server-accumulated amortization | Accumulated amortization: Computer | -1912.5 |
| 106 | 1 | Computer21-accumulated amortization < Computer2-accumulated amortization | Accumulated amortization: Computer | -1062.5 |
| 107 | 1 | Computer31-accumulated amortization < Computer3-accumulated amortization | Accumulated amortization: Computer | -991.67 |
| 108 | 2 | Deposits-909876501 | Deposits payable | 15900.10 |
| 109 | 2 | Deposits-909876502 | Deposits payable | 12200.11 |
| 110 | 2 | Deposits-909876503 | Deposits payable | 11800.23 |
| 111 | 2 | Deposits-909876504 | Deposits payable | 17230.03 |
| 112 | 2 | Deposits-909876505 | Deposits payable | 15960.96 |
| 113 | 2 | Deposits-909876506 | Deposits payable | 17200.52 |
| 114 | 2 | Deposits-909876507 | Deposits payable | 28500.03 |
| 115 | 2 | Deposits-909876508 | Deposits payable | 15620.65 |
| 116 | 2 | Deposits-909876509 | Deposits payable | 27700.11 |
| 117 | 2 | Deposits-909876510 | Deposits payable | 0 |
| 118 | 2 | Deposits-909876511 | Deposits payable | 11710.41 |
| 119 | 2 | Deposits-909876512 | Deposits payable | 15720.23 |
| 120 | 2 | Deposits-909876513 | Deposits payable | 16510.35 |
| 121 | 2 | Deposits-909876514 | Deposits payable | 17980.41 |
| 122 | 2 | Deposits-909876515 | Deposits payable | 26250.27 |
| 123 | 2 | Deposits-909876516 | Deposits payable | 18790.58 |
| 124 | 2 | Deposits-909876517 | Deposits payable | 0 |
| 125 | 2 | Deposits-909876518 | Deposits payable | 18260.63 |
| 126 | 2 | Deposits-909876519 | Deposits payable | 11230.11 |
| 127 | 2 | Deposits-909876520 | Deposits payable | 11082.23 |
| 128 | 2 | Deposits-909876521 | Deposits payable | 0 |
| 129 | 2 | Deposits-909876522 | Deposits payable | 16510.03 |
| 130 | 2 | Deposits-909876523 | Deposits payable | 11960.84 |
| 131 | 2 | Deposits-909876524 | Deposits payable | 28100.25 |
| 132 | 2 | Deposits-909876525 | Deposits payable | 11230.32 |
| 133 | 2 | Deposits-88-654300 | Deposits payable | 1058058.2 |
| 134 | 2 | Deposits-88-654302 | Deposits payable | 1289.11 |
| 135 | 2 | Deposits-88-654303 | Deposits payable | 1003.72 |
| 136 | 2 | Deposits-88-654304 | Deposits payable | 0 |
| 137 | 2 | Deposits-88-654305 | Deposits payable | 0 |
| 138 | 2 | Deposits-88-654306 | Deposits payable | 67873.98 |
| 139 | 2 | Deposits-88-654307 | Deposits payable | 0 |
| 140 | 2 | Deposits-88-654308 | Deposits payable | 3906.47 |
| 141 | 2 | Deposits-88-654309 | Deposits payable | 18783.78 |

| 142 | 2 | Deposits-88-654310 | Deposits payable | 0 |
|---|---|---|---|---|
| 143 | 2 | Bond11-88-654302 < Bond11 | Bonds payable | 6000.00 |
| 144 | 2 | Bond11-88-654303 < Bond11 | Bonds payable | 5000.00 |
| 145 | 2 | Bond11-88-654305 < Bond11 | Bonds payable | 7000.00 |
| 146 | 2 | Bond11-88-654306 < Bond11 | Bonds payable | 10000.00 |
| 147 | 2 | Bond11-88-654308 < Bond11 | Bonds payable | 8000.00 |
| 148 | 2 | Bond11-88-654309 < Bond11 | Bonds payable | 5000.00 |
| 149 | 2 | Bond11-909876507 < Bond11 | Bonds payable | 9000.00 |
| 150 | 2 | Bond11-909876509 < Bond11 | Bonds payable | 6000.00 |
| 151 | 2 | Bond11-909876513 < Bond11 | Bonds payable | 3000.00 |
| 152 | 2 | Bond11-909876514 < Bond11 | Bonds payable | 1000.00 |
| 153 | 2 | Bond12-88-654305 < Bond12 | Bonds payable | 3000.00 |
| 154 | 2 | Bond12-88-654307 < Bond12 | Bonds payable | 8000.00 |
| 155 | 2 | Bond12-88-654309 < Bond12 | Bonds payable | 3000.00 |
| 156 | 2 | Bond12-88-654310 < Bond12 | Bonds payable | 6000.00 |
| 157 | 2 | Bond12-909876501 < Bond12 | Bonds payable | 5000.00 |
| 158 | 2 | Bond12-909876502 < Bond12 | Bonds payable | 2000.00 |
| 159 | 2 | Bond12-909876504 < Bond12 | Bonds payable | 7000.00 |
| 160 | 2 | Bond12-909876521 < Bond12 | Bonds payable | 6000.00 |
| 161 | 2 | Bond13-88-654305 < Bond13 | Bonds payable | 6000.00 |
| 162 | 2 | Bond13-88-654306 < Bond13 | Bonds payable | 3000.00 |
| 163 | 2 | Bond13-88-654309 < Bond13 | Bonds payable | 2000.00 |
| 164 | 2 | Bond13-909876503 < Bond13 | Bonds payable | 6000.00 |
| 165 | 2 | Bond13-909876505 < Bond13 | Bonds payable | 4000.00 |
| 166 | 2 | Bond13-909876506 < Bond13 | Bonds payable | 7000.00 |
| 167 | 2 | Bond13-909876515 < Bond13 | Bonds payable | 4000.00 |
| 168 | 2 | Bond13-909876517 < Bond13 | Bonds payable | 5000.00 |
| 169 | 2 | Bond13-909876518 < Bond13 | Bonds payable | 3000.00 |
| 170 | 2 | Bond13-909876519 < Bond13 | Bonds payable | 6000.00 |
| 171 | 2 | Bond13-909876521 < Bond13 | Bonds payable | 4000.00 |
| 172 | 3 | Capital-909876507 | Share capital | 600000.00 |
| 173 | 3 | Capital-909876509 | Share capital | 400000.00 |
| 174 | 3 | n | Retained earnings (Conversion) | 5569.82 |
| 175 | 4 | Note11-interest income | Sales (notes interest) | 0 |
| 176 | 4 | Note12-interest income | Sales (notes interest) | 0 |
| 177 | 4 | Note13-interest income | Sales (notes interest) | 0 |
| 178 | 4 | Note14-interest income | Sales (notes interest) | 0 |
| 179 | 4 | Note15-interest income | Sales (notes interest) | 0 |
| 180 | 5 | Deposit interest expenses | Cost of notes interest | 0 |
| 181 | 5 | 909876509-travelling < Sales department-travelling | Travelling expenses | 0 |

| 182 | 5 | 909876508-other < Purchase department-other | Other expenses | 0 |
|---|---|---|---|---|
| 183 | 5 | 909876507-salary < Office department-salary | Salary expenses | 0 |
| 184 | 5 | Bond11-interest expenses | Bond interest expenses | 0 |
| 185 | 5 | Bond12-interest expenses | Bond interest expenses | 0 |
| 186 | 5 | Bond13-interest expenses | Bond interest expenses | 0 |
| 187 | 5 | Truck11-amortization < Truck1-amortization < Vehicle-truck-amortization | Amortization expenses | 0 |
| 188 | 5 | Car11-amortization < Car1-amortization < Vehicle-car-amortization | Amortization expenses | 0 |
| 189 | 5 | Computer server21-amortization < Computer server2-amortization < Computer-amortization | Amortization expenses | 0 |
| 190 | 5 | Computer21-amortization < Computer2-amortization < Computer-amortization | Amortization expenses | 0 |
| 191 | 5 | Computer31-amortization < Computer3-amortization < Computer-amortization | Amortization expenses | 0 |
| 192 | 4 | Accrued interest income-bond21 <Bonds | Investment incomes | 0 |
| 193 | 4 | Accrued interest income-bond22 <Bonds | Investment incomes | 0 |
| 194 | 4 | n | Deposits fee incomes | 0 |

Figure 2.4-2   Business Bank1 Converting Multi-Subaccount Names Table

Before entering the dynamic accounting equation on December 31, 2015 into the database dcj205, I first enter two initialization sub-equations.

Account receivable (1): 0 = Account payable (2): 0

0 = Sales (notes interest) (4): 0 – Cost of notes interest (5):0

From the Figure 2.4-1 and the Figure 2.4-2, the dynamic accounting equation on December 31, 2015 must be divided to the "N" transaction sub-equations because of the limitation of the MathAccounting software. Every sub-equation has maximum twelve items. The all converting transaction sub-equations can be designed and written as the followings.

- The transaction sub-equation includes the "Cash" account with the Order 3 to the Order 8 and the "Deposits payable" account with the Order 108 to the Order 113. The first transaction sub-equation is:

Cash (1): 15900.1 + Cash (1): 12200.11 + Cash (1): 11800.23 + Cash (1): 17230.03 + Cash (1): 15960.96 + Cash (1): 17200.52 = Deposits payable (2):

15900.1 + Deposits payable (2): 12200.11 + Deposits payable (2): 11800.23 + Deposits payable (2): 17230.03 + Deposits payable (2): 15960.96 + Deposits payable (2): 17200.52

- The transaction sub-equation includes the "Cash" account with the Order 9 to the Order 15 and the "Deposits payable" account with the Order 114 to the Order 120. Because the balances of the "Cash" with the Order 12 and the Order 117 are zero, the second transaction sub-equation is:

Cash (1): 28500.03 + Cash (1): 15620.65 + Cash (1): 27700.11+ Cash (1): 11710.41 + Cash (1): 15720.23 + Cash (1): 16510.35 = Deposits payable (2): 28500.03 + Deposits payable (2): 15620.65 + Deposits payable (2): 27700.11+ Deposits payable (2): 11710.41 + Deposits payable (2): 15720.23 + Deposits payable (2): 16510.35

- The transaction sub-equation includes the "Cash" account with the Order 16 to the Order 22 and the "Deposits payable" account with the Order 121 to the Order 127. Because the balances of the "Cash" with the Order 19 and the Order 124 are zero, the third transaction sub-equation is:

Cash (1): 17980.41 + Cash (1): 26250.27 + Cash (1): 18790.58 + Cash (1): 18260.63 + Cash (1): 11230.11 + Cash (1): 11082.23 = Deposits payable (2): 17980.41+ Deposits payable (2): 26250.27 + Deposits payable (2): 18790.58 + Deposits payable (2): 18260.63 + Deposits payable (2): 11230.11 + Deposits payable (2): 11082.23

- The transaction sub-equation includes the "Cash" account with the Order 23 to the Order 29 and the "Deposits payable" account with the Order 128 to the Order 134. Because the balances of the "Cash" with the Order 23 and the Order 128 are zero, the fourth transaction sub-equation is:

Cash (1): 16510.03 + Cash (1): 11960.84 + Cash (1): 28100.25 + Cash (1): 11230.32 + Cash (1): 1058058.2 + Cash (1): 1289.11 = Deposits payable (2): 16510.03 + Deposits payable (2): 11960.84 + Deposits payable (2): 28100.25 + Deposits payable (2): 11230.32 + Deposits payable (2): 1058058.2 + Deposits payable (2): 1289.11

- The transaction sub-equation includes the "Cash" account with the Order 2, 30, 33, 35, and 36 , the "Share capital" account with the Order 173, and the "Deposits payable" account with the Order 135, 138, 140, and 141. The fifth transaction sub-equation is:

Cash (1): 400000 + Cash (1): 1003.72 + Cash (1): 67873.98 + Cash (1): 3906.47 + Cash (1): 18783.78 = Share capital (3): 400000 + Deposits payable (2): 1003.72 + Deposits payable (2): 67873.98 + Deposits payable (2): 3906.47+ Deposits payable (2): 18783.78

- The transaction sub-equation includes the "Cash" account with the Order 38 to the Order 43 and the "Bonds payable" account with the Order 143 to the Order 148. The sixth transaction sub-equation is:

Cash (1): 6000 + Cash (1): 5000 + Cash (1): 7000 + Cash (1): 10000 + Cash (1): 8000 + Cash (1): 5000 = Bonds payable (2): 6000 + Bonds payable (2): 5000 + Bonds payable (2): 7000 + Bonds payable (2): 10000 + Bonds payable (2): 8000 + Bonds payable (2): 5000

- The transaction sub-equation includes the "Cash" account with the Order 44 to the Order 49 and the "Bonds payable" account with the Order 149 to the Order 154. The seventh transaction sub-equation is:

Cash (1): 9000 + Cash (1): 6000 + Cash (1): 3000 + Cash (1): 1000 + Cash (1): 3000 + Cash (1): 8000 = Bonds payable (2): 9000 + Bonds payable (2): 6000 + Bonds payable (2): 3000 + Bonds payable (2): 1000 + Bonds payable (2): 3000 +

Bonds payable (2): 8000

- The transaction sub-equation includes the "Cash" account with the Order 50 to the Order 55 and the "Bonds payable" account with the Order 155 to the Order 160. The eighth transaction sub-equation is:

  Cash (1): 3000 + Cash (1): 6000 + Cash (1): 5000 + Cash (1): 2000 + Cash (1): 7000 + Cash (1): 6000 = Bonds payable (2): 3000 + Bonds payable (2): 6000 + Bonds payable (2): 5000 + Bonds payable (2): 2000 + Bonds payable (2): 7000 + Bonds payable (2): 6000

- The transaction sub-equation includes the "Cash" account with the Order 56 to the Order 61 and the "Bonds payable" account with the Order 161 to the Order 166. The ninth transaction sub-equation is:

  Cash (1): 6000 + Cash (1): 3000 + Cash (1): 2000 + Cash (1): 6000 + Cash (1): 4000 + Cash (1): 7000 = Bonds payable (2): 6000 + Bonds payable (2): 3000 + Bonds payable (2): 2000 + Bonds payable (2): 6000 + Bonds payable (2): 4000 + Bonds payable (2): 7000

- The transaction sub-equation includes the "Cash" account with the Order 62 to the Order 66 and the "Bonds payable" account with the Order 167 to the Order 171. The tenth transaction sub-equation is:

  Cash (1): 4000 + Cash (1): 5000 + Cash (1): 3000 + Cash (1): 6000 + Cash (1): 4000 = Bonds payable (2): 6000 + Bonds payable (2): 3000 + Bonds payable (2): 2000 + Bonds payable (2): 6000 + Bonds payable (2): 4000

- The transaction sub-equation includes the "Cash" account with the Order 67 to the Order 75 and the part of the "Share capital" account with the Order 172. The eleventh transaction sub-equation is:

Cash (1): 65625 + Cash (1): 23100 + Cash (1): 30000 + Cash (1): 36416.67 + Cash (1): 4037.5 + Cash (1): 410 + Cash (1): 201.67 + Cash (1): -45000 + Cash (1): -40000 = Share capital (3): 74790.84

After entering this transaction, the new balance of the "Share capital" account with the Order 172 is $525,209.16 (= $600,000 - $74,790.84).

- The transaction sub-equation includes the "Cash" account with the Order 79 to the Order 82 and the Order 88 to the Order 89, the "Bonds" with the Order 96 to the Order 97, and the part of the "Cash" account with the Order 1. The twelfth transaction sub-equation is:

Cash (1): -28061.55 + Cash (1): -27953.14 + Cash (1): -27312.77 + Cash (1): -34112.53 + Cash (1): -6000 + Cash (1): -5000 + Bonds (1): 6000 + Bonds (1): 5000 + Cash (1): 117439.99 = 0

After entering this transaction, the new balance of the "Cash" account with the Order 1 is $482,560.01 (= $600,000 - $117,439.99).

- The transaction sub-equation includes the "Cash" account with the Order 83 to the Order 87, the "Supplies" account with the Order 90, the "Notes receivable" account with the Order 91 to the Order 95, and the part of the "Share capital" account with the Order 172. The thirteenth transaction sub-equation is:

Cash (1): -250000 + Cash (1): -140000 + Cash (1): -200000 + Cash (1): -250000 + Cash (1): -170000 + Supplies (1): 102.31 + Notes receivable (1): 250000 + Notes receivable (1): 140000 + Notes receivable (1): 200000 + Notes receivable (1): 250000 + Notes receivable (1): 170000 = Share capital (3): 102.31

After entering this transaction, the new balance of the "Share capital" account with the Order 172 is $525,106.85 (= $525,209.16 - $102.31)

- The transaction sub-equation includes the "Vehicle" account with the Order 98 and 99, the "Accumulated amortization: Vehicle" account with the Order 100 and 101, the "Computer" account with the Order 102 to the Order 104, the "Accumulated amortization: Computer" account with the Order 105 and the Order 107, and the part of the "Share capital" account with the Order 172. The fourteenth transaction sub-equation is:

Vehicle (1): 45000 + Vehicle (1): 40000 + Accumulated amortization: Vehicle (1): -20250 + Accumulated amortization: Vehicle (1): -12666.67 + Computer (1): 2700 + Computer (1): 1500 + Computer (1): 1400 + Accumulated amortization: Computer (1): -1912.5 + Accumulated amortization: Computer (1): -1062.5 + Accumulated amortization: Computer (1): -991.67 = Share capital (3): 53716.66

After entering this transaction, the new balance of the "Share capital" account with the Order 172 is $471,390.19 (= $525,106.85 - $53,716.66)

- The transaction sub-equation includes the "Cash" account with the Order 76 to the Order 78, the rest ($482,560.01) of the "Cash" account with the Order 1, the rest ($471,390.13) of the "Share capital" account with the Order 172, and the "Retained earnings (Conversion)" account with the balance $5,569.82. The fifteenth transaction sub-equation is:

Cash (1): -2700 + Cash (1): -1500 + Cash (1): -1400 + Cash (1): 482560.01 = Share capital (3): 471390.19 + Retained earnings (Conversion) (3): 5569.82

After completing this transaction, the dynamic accounting equation of the Business Bank1 on December 31, 2015 has entered into the database dcj205.

### 2.4.1.2 Brief Summary of the Business Bank1

Obviously, there is not any information of the Inventory account in these transaction sub-equations.

## 2.4.2 Sample of the Business Bank2

The Business Bank2 has total share capital $900,000 and three shareholders of the individual

A11, the individual A17, and the Business Bank1. The percentages of their share capital are 40%, 25%, and 35% respectively.

## 2.4.2.1 Conversion of the Business Bank2

The Business Bank2 will convert to the MathAccounting software on January 1, 2016. The Figure 2.4-3 and the Figure 2.4-4 show the converting reference table and the multi-subaccount names table respectively.

| Order | Class | Account Name (Subtotal Name) | Balance | Row |
|---|---|---|---|---|
| **1** | **1** | **(Current assets)** | - | **103** |
| 2 | 1 | Cash | 390884.49 | 104 |
| 3 | 1 | Supplies | 84.16 | 106 |
| 4 | 1 | Business bank reserves receivable | 0 | 108 |
| 5 | 1 | Accrued interest receivable | 0 | 110 |
| 6 | 1 | Notes receivable | 960000.00 | 112 |
| **7** | **1** | **(Long term investments)** | - | **141** |
| 8 | 1 | Bonds | 29000.00 | 143 |
| **9** | **1** | **(Equipment)** | - | **171** |
| 10 | 1 | Vehicle | 78000.00 | 172 |
| 11 | 1 | Accumulated amortization: Vehicle | -28066.67 | 173 |
| 12 | 1 | Computer | 5900.00 | 174 |
| 13 | 1 | Accumulated amortization: Computer | -3687.5 | 175 |
| **14** | **2** | **(Current liabilities)** | - | **203** |
| 15 | 2 | Business bank reserves payable | 0 | 204 |
| 16 | 2 | Deposits payable | 387783.31 | 206 |
| 17 | 2 | Accrued interest payable | 0 | 208 |
| 18 | 2 | Account payable | 0 | 210 |
| 19 | 2 | Tax payable | 0 | 212 |
| **20** | **2** | **(Long term liabilities)** | - | **251** |
| 21 | 2 | Bonds payable | 140000.00 | 252 |
| **22** | **3** | **(Owners' capital)** | - | **303** |
| 23 | 3 | Share capital | 900000.00 | 304 |
| 24 | 3 | Retained earnings (Conversion) | 4331.17 | 306 |
| **25** | **4** | **(Revenues)** | - | **403** |
| 26 | 4 | Sales (notes interest) | 0 | 404 |
| **27** | **5** | **(Cost)** | - | **431** |
| 28 | 5 | Cost of notes interest | 0 | 432 |
| **29** | **5** | **(Operating and administrative expenses)** | - | **453** |

| | | | | | |
|---|---|---|---|---|---|
| 30 | 5 | Travelling expenses | | 0 | 454 |
| 31 | 5 | Other expenses | | 0 | 456 |
| 32 | 5 | Office supplies expenses | | 0 | 458 |
| 33 | 5 | Salary expenses | | 0 | 460 |
| 34 | 5 | Bond interest expenses | | 0 | 462 |
| 35 | 5 | Amortization expenses | | 0 | 464 |
| 36 | 5 | Interest expenses | | 0 | 466 |
| **37** | **4** | **(Other income)** | | - | **475** |
| 38 | 4 | Investment incomes | | 0 | 476 |
| **39** | **5** | **(Tax)** | | - | **600** |
| 40 | 5 | Tax expenses | | 0 | 602 |

Figure 2.4-3    Business Bank2 Converting Reference Table

| Order | Class | Multi-subaccount Name | Parent Name | Lowest Subaccount Balance |
|---|---|---|---|---|
| 1 | 1 | 909876511-i-owners < Cash receipts from owners < Financial activities | Cash | 360000.00 |
| 2 | 1 | 909876517-i-owners < Cash receipts from owners < Financial activities | Cash | 225000.00 |
| 3 | 1 | 88-654304-i-owners < Cash receipts from owners < Financial activities | Cash | 315000.00 |
| 4 | 1 | 909876501-d-deposits < Cash receipts from customers deposits < Operating activities | Cash | 12000.15 |
| 5 | 1 | 909876502-d-deposits < Cash receipts from customers deposits < Operating activities | Cash | 16500.55 |
| 6 | 1 | 909876503-d-deposits < Cash receipts from customers deposits < Operating activities | Cash | 16260.10 |
| 7 | 1 | 909876504-d-deposits < Cash receipts from customers deposits < Operating activities | Cash | 11400.61 |
| 8 | 1 | 909876505-d-deposits < Cash receipts from customers deposits < Operating activities | Cash | 11970.23 |
| 9 | 1 | 909876506-d-deposits < Cash receipts from customers deposits < Operating activities | Cash | 11100.54 |
| 10 | 1 | 909876507-d-deposits < Cash receipts from customers deposits < Operating activities | Cash | 0 |
| 11 | 1 | 909876508-d-deposits < Cash receipts from customers deposits < Operating activities | Cash | 11000.11 |
| 12 | 1 | 909876509-d-deposits < Cash receipts from customers deposits < Operating activities | Cash | 0 |
| 13 | 1 | 909876510-d-deposits < Cash receipts from customers deposits < Operating activities | Cash | 28600.21 |
| 14 | 1 | 909876511-d-deposits < Cash receipts from customers deposits < Operating activities | Cash | 14520.56 |
| 15 | 1 | 909876512-d-deposits < Cash receipts from customers deposits < Operating activities | Cash | 11680.34 |
| 16 | 1 | 909876513-d-deposits < Cash receipts from customers deposits < Operating activities | Cash | 11810.18 |
| 17 | 1 | 909876514-d-deposits < Cash receipts from customers deposits < Operating activities | Cash | 12200.45 |
| 18 | 1 | 909876515-d-deposits < Cash receipts from customers deposits < Operating activities | Cash | 0 |
| 19 | 1 | 909876516-d-deposits < Cash receipts from customers deposits < Operating activities | Cash | 11300.74 |
| 20 | 1 | 909876517-d-deposits < Cash receipts from customers deposits < Operating activities | Cash | 26150.88 |

| 21 | 1 | 909876518-d-deposits < Cash receipts from customers deposits < Operating activities | Cash | 10510.99 |
|---|---|---|---|---|
| 22 | 1 | 909876519-d-deposits < Cash receipts from customers deposits < Operating activities | Cash | 16910.92 |
| 23 | 1 | 909876520-d-deposits < Cash receipts from customers deposits < Operating activities | Cash | 15900.51 |
| 24 | 1 | 909876521-d-deposits < Cash receipts from customers deposits < Operating activities | Cash | 26210.18 |
| 25 | 1 | 909876522-d-deposits < Cash receipts from customers deposits < Operating activities | Cash | 11720.14 |
| 26 | 1 | 909876523-d-deposits < Cash receipts from customers deposits < Operating activities | Cash | 15150.21 |
| 27 | 1 | 909876524-d-deposits < Cash receipts from customers deposits < Operating activities | Cash | 0 |
| 28 | 1 | 909876525-d-deposits < Cash receipts from customers deposits < Operating activities | Cash | 16150.25 |
| 29 | 1 | 88-654301-d-deposits < Cash receipts from customers deposits < Operating activities | Cash | 4090.65 |
| 30 | 1 | 88-654302-d-deposits < Cash receipts from customers deposits < Operating activities | Cash | 610.08 |
| 31 | 1 | 88-654303-d-deposits < Cash receipts from customers deposits < Operating activities | Cash | 1117.96 |
| 32 | 1 | 88-654304-d-deposits < Cash receipts from customers deposits < Operating activities | Cash | 0 |
| 33 | 1 | 88-654305-d-deposits < Cash receipts from customers deposits < Operating activities | Cash | 0 |
| 34 | 1 | 88-654306-d-deposits < Cash receipts from customers deposits < Operating activities | Cash | 0 |
| 35 | 1 | 88-654307-d-deposits < Cash receipts from customers deposits < Operating activities | Cash | 47393.19 |
| 36 | 1 | 88-654308-d-deposits < Cash receipts from customers deposits < Operating activities | Cash | 6753.89 |
| 37 | 1 | 88-654309-d-deposits < Cash receipts from customers deposits < Operating activities | Cash | 0 |
| 38 | 1 | 88-654310-d-deposits < Cash receipts from customers deposits < Operating activities | Cash | 8768.69 |
| 39 | 1 | 88-654302-i-bond21 < Cash receipts from issued bonds < Financial activities | Cash | 9000.00 |
| 40 | 1 | 88-654303-i-bond21 < Cash receipts from issued bonds < Financial activities | Cash | 8000.00 |
| 41 | 1 | 88-654304-i-bond21 < Cash receipts from issued bonds < Financial activities | Cash | 6000.00 |
| 42 | 1 | 88-654306-i-bond21 < Cash receipts from issued bonds < Financial activities | Cash | 9000.00 |
| 43 | 1 | 88-654308-i-bond21 < Cash receipts from issued bonds < Financial activities | Cash | 12000.00 |
| 44 | 1 | 88-654310-i-bond21 < Cash receipts from issued bonds < Financial activities | Cash | 7000.00 |
| 45 | 1 | 909876507-i-bond21 < Cash receipts from issued bonds < Financial activities | Cash | 4000.00 |
| 46 | 1 | 909876509-i-bond21 < Cash receipts from issued bonds < Financial activities | Cash | 6000.00 |
| 47 | 1 | 909876513-i-bond21 < Cash receipts from issued bonds < Financial activities | Cash | 3000.00 |
| 48 | 1 | 909876514-i-bond21 < Cash receipts from issued bonds < Financial activities | Cash | 5000.00 |
| 49 | 1 | 909876518-i-bond21 < Cash receipts from issued bonds < Financial activities | Cash | 3000.00 |
| 50 | 1 | 909876520-i-bond21 < Cash receipts from issued bonds < Financial activities | Cash | 8000.00 |
| 51 | 1 | 88-654304-i-bond22 < Cash receipts from issued bonds < Financial activities | Cash | 5000.00 |
| 52 | 1 | 88-654307-i-bond22 < Cash receipts from issued bonds < Financial activities | Cash | 6000.00 |

| 53 | 1 | 88-654309-i-bond22 < Cash receipts from issued bonds < Financial activities | Cash | 8000.00 |
|----|---|---|---|---|
| 54 | 1 | 88-654310-i-bond22 < Cash receipts from issued bonds < Financial activities | Cash | 4000.00 |
| 55 | 1 | 909876503-i-bond22 < Cash receipts from issued bonds < Financial activities | Cash | 6000.00 |
| 56 | 1 | 909876504-i-bond22 < Cash receipts from issued bonds < Financial activities | Cash | 7000.00 |
| 57 | 1 | 909876506-i-bond22 < Cash receipts from issued bonds < Financial activities | Cash | 6000.00 |
| 58 | 1 | 909876511-i-bond22 < Cash receipts from issued bonds < Financial activities | Cash | 8000.00 |
| 59 | 1 | 909876519-i-bond22 < Cash receipts from issued bonds < Financial activities | Cash | 3000.00 |
| 60 | 1 | 909876521-i-bond22 < Cash receipts from issued bonds < Financial activities | Cash | 7000.00 |
| 61 | 1 | 88-654306-c-accrued interest < Cash receipts from note accrued interest (customers) < Operating activities | Cash | 56100.00 |
| 62 | 1 | 88-654307-c-accrued interest < Cash receipts from note accrued interest (customers) < Operating activities | Cash | 36000.00 |
| 63 | 1 | 88-654308-c-accrued interest < Cash receipts from note accrued interest (customers) < Operating activities | Cash | 25650.00 |
| 64 | 1 | 88-654307-c-accrued interest < Cash receipts from note accrued interest (customers) < Operating activities | Cash | 27300.00 |
| 65 | 1 | 88-654306-c-accrued interest < Cash receipts from note accrued interest (customers) < Operating activities | Cash | 3760.00 |
| 66 | 1 | 88-654304-c-interest of investment bond11 < Cash receipts from investments < Investing activities | Cash | 536.67 |
| 67 | 1 | 88-654304-c-interest of investment bond12 < Cash receipts from investments < Investing activities | Cash | 189.00 |
| 68 | 1 | 88-654304-c-interest of investment bond13 < Cash receipts from investments < Investing activities | Cash | 90.00 |
| 69 | 1 | 88-654306-c-interest of investment bond31 < Cash receipts from investments < Investing activities | Cash | 268.33 |
| 70 | 1 | 88-654307-c-interest of investment bond41 < Cash receipts from investments < Investing activities | Cash | 313.33 |
| 71 | 1 | 88-654306-t-truck2 < Cash payments for machinery < Operating activities | Cash | -40000.00 |
| 72 | 1 | 88-654306-t-car3 < Cash payments for machinery < Operating activities | Cash | -38000.00 |
| 73 | 1 | 88-654306-t-computer server1 < Cash payments for machinery < Operating activities | Cash | -2800.00 |
| 74 | 1 | 88-654306-t-computer1 < Cash payments for machinery < Operating activities | Cash | -1600.00 |
| 75 | 1 | 88-654306-t-computer2 < Cash payments for machinery < Operating activities | Cash | -1500.00 |
| 76 | 1 | Cash payments for operating expenses < Operating activities | Cash | -27634.61 |
| 77 | 1 | Cash payments for operating expenses < Operating activities | Cash | -26587.92 |
| 78 | 1 | Cash payments for operating expenses < Operating activities | Cash | -28312.35 |
| 79 | 1 | 88-654303-n-tax < Cash payments for operating expenses < Operating activities | Cash | -31671.27 |
| 80 | 1 | 88-654306-n-notes1 < Cash payments to notes lenders < Operating activities | Cash | -220000.00 |
| 81 | 1 | 88-654307-n-notes2 < Cash payments to notes lenders < Operating activities | Cash | -240000.00 |

| | | | | |
|---|---|---|---|---|
| 82 | 1 | 88-654308-n-notes3 < Cash payments to notes lenders < Operating activities | Cash | -180000.00 |
| 83 | 1 | 88-654308-n-notes4 < Cash payments to notes lenders < Operating activities | Cash | -200000.00 |
| 84 | 1 | 88-654309-n-notes5 < Cash payments to notes lenders < Operating activities | Cash | -120000.00 |
| 85 | 1 | 88-654304-n-investment bond11 < Cash payments for investments < Investing activities | Cash | -7000.00 |
| 86 | 1 | 88-654304-n-investment bond12 < Cash payments for investments < Investing activities | Cash | -3000.00 |
| 87 | 1 | 88-654304-n-investment bond13 < Cash payments for investments < Investing activities | Cash | -6000.00 |
| 88 | 1 | 88-654306-n-investment bond31 < Cash payments for investments < Investing activities | Cash | -5000.00 |
| 89 | 1 | 88-654307-n-investment bond41 < Cash payments for investments < Investing activities | Cash | -8000.00 |
| 90 | 1 | n | Supplies | 84.16 |
| 91 | 1 | Note11-88-654306 | Notes receivable | 220000.00 |
| 92 | 1 | Note12-88-654307 | Notes receivable | 240000.00 |
| 93 | 1 | Note13-88-654308 | Notes receivable | 180000.00 |
| 94 | 1 | Note14-88-654308 | Notes receivable | 200000.00 |
| 95 | 1 | Note15-88-654309 | Notes receivable | 120000.00 |
| 96 | 1 | Bond11 | Bonds | 7000.00 |
| 97 | 1 | Bond12 | Bonds | 3000.00 |
| 98 | 1 | Bond13 | Bonds | 6000.00 |
| 99 | 1 | Bond31 | Bonds | 5000.00 |
| 100 | 1 | Bond41 | Bonds | 8000.00 |
| 101 | 1 | Truck21 < Truck2 < Truck | Vehicle | 40000.00 |
| 102 | 1 | Car31 < Car3 < Car | Vehicle | 38000.00 |
| 103 | 1 | Truck21-accumulated amortization < Truck2-accumulated amortization < Truck-accumulated amortization | Accumulated amortization: Vehicle | -16666.67 |
| 104 | 1 | Car31-accumulated amortization < Car3-accumulated amortization < Car-accumulated amortization | Accumulated amortization: Vehicle | -11400.00 |
| 105 | 1 | Computer server11 < Computer server1 < Computer server | Computer | 2800.00 |
| 106 | 1 | Computer11 < Computer1 | Computer | 1600.00 |
| 107 | 1 | Computer21 < Computer2 | Computer | 1500.00 |
| 108 | 1 | Computer server11-accumulated amortization < Computer server1-accumulated amortization < Computer server-accumulated amortization | Accumulated amortization: Computer | -1750.00 |
| 109 | 1 | Computer11-accumulated amortization < Computer1-accumulated amortization | Accumulated amortization: Computer | -1000.00 |
| 110 | 1 | Computer21-accumulated amortization < Computer2-accumulated amortization | Accumulated amortization: Computer | -937.50 |
| 111 | 2 | Deposits-909876501 | Deposits payable | 12000.15 |
| 112 | 2 | Deposits-909876502 | Deposits payable | 16500.55 |
| 113 | 2 | Deposits-909876503 | Deposits payable | 16260.10 |
| 114 | 2 | Deposits-909876504 | Deposits payable | 11400.61 |
| 115 | 2 | Deposits-909876505 | Deposits payable | 11970.23 |
| 116 | 2 | Deposits-909876506 | Deposits payable | 11100.54 |

| 117 | 2 | Deposits-909876507 | Deposits payable | 0 |
|---|---|---|---|---|
| 118 | 2 | Deposits-909876508 | Deposits payable | 11000.11 |
| 119 | 2 | Deposits-909876509 | Deposits payable | 0 |
| 120 | 2 | Deposits-909876510 | Deposits payable | 28600.21 |
| 121 | 2 | Deposits-909876511 | Deposits payable | 14520.56 |
| 122 | 2 | Deposits-909876512 | Deposits payable | 11680.34 |
| 123 | 2 | Deposits-909876513 | Deposits payable | 11810.18 |
| 124 | 2 | Deposits-909876514 | Deposits payable | 12200.45 |
| 125 | 2 | Deposits-909876515 | Deposits payable | 0 |
| 126 | 2 | Deposits-909876516 | Deposits payable | 11300.74 |
| 127 | 2 | Deposits-909876517 | Deposits payable | 26150.88 |
| 128 | 2 | Deposits-909876518 | Deposits payable | 10510.99 |
| 129 | 2 | Deposits-909876519 | Deposits payable | 16910.92 |
| 130 | 2 | Deposits-909876520 | Deposits payable | 15900.51 |
| 131 | 2 | Deposits-909876521 | Deposits payable | 26210.18 |
| 132 | 2 | Deposits-909876522 | Deposits payable | 11720.14 |
| 133 | 2 | Deposits-909876523 | Deposits payable | 15150.21 |
| 134 | 2 | Deposits-909876524 | Deposits payable | 0 |
| 135 | 2 | Deposits-909876525 | Deposits payable | 16150.25 |
| 136 | 2 | Deposits-88-654301 | Deposits payable | 4090.65 |
| 137 | 2 | Deposits-88-654302 | Deposits payable | 610.08 |
| 138 | 2 | Deposits-88-654303 | Deposits payable | 1117.96 |
| 139 | 2 | Deposits-88-654304 | Deposits payable | 0 |
| 140 | 2 | Deposits-88-654305 | Deposits payable | 0 |
| 141 | 2 | Deposits-88-654306 | Deposits payable | 0 |
| 142 | 2 | Deposits-88-654307 | Deposits payable | 47393.19 |
| 143 | 2 | Deposits-88-654308 | Deposits payable | 6753.89 |
| 144 | 2 | Deposits-88-654309 | Deposits payable | 0 |
| 145 | 2 | Deposits-88-654310 | Deposits payable | 8768.69 |
| 146 | 2 | Bond 21-88-654302 < Bond21 | Bonds payable | 9000.00 |
| 147 | 2 | Bond21-88-654303 < Bond21 | Bonds payable | 8000.00 |
| 148 | 2 | Bond21-88-654304 < Bond21 | Bonds payable | 6000.00 |
| 149 | 2 | Bond21-88-654306 < Bond21 | Bonds payable | 9000.00 |
| 150 | 2 | Bond21-88-654308 < Bond21 | Bonds payable | 12000.00 |
| 151 | 2 | Bond21-88-654310 < Bond21 | Bonds payable | 7000.00 |
| 152 | 2 | Bond21-909876507 < Bond21 | Bonds payable | 4000.00 |
| 153 | 2 | Bond21-909876509 < Bond21 | Bonds payable | 6000.00 |
| 154 | 2 | Bond21-909876513 < Bond21 | Bonds payable | 3000.00 |
| 155 | 2 | Bond21-909876514 < Bond21 | Bonds payable | 5000.00 |
| 156 | 2 | Bond21-909876518 < Bond21 | Bonds payable | 3000.00 |

| 157 | 2 | Bond21-909876520 < Bond21 | Bonds payable | 8000.00 |
|---|---|---|---|---|
| 158 | 2 | Band22-88-654304 < Band22 | Bonds payable | 5000.00 |
| 159 | 2 | Bond22-88-654307 < Bond22 | Bonds payable | 6000.00 |
| 160 | 2 | Bond22-88-654309 < Bond22 | Bonds payable | 8000.00 |
| 161 | 2 | Bond22-88-654310 < Bond22 | Bonds payable | 4000.00 |
| 162 | 2 | Bond22-909876503 < Bond22 | Bonds payable | 6000.00 |
| 163 | 2 | Bond22-909876504 < Bond22 | Bonds payable | 7000.00 |
| 164 | 2 | Bond22-909876506 < Bond22 | Bonds payable | 6000.00 |
| 165 | 2 | Bond22-909876511 < Bond22 | Bonds payable | 8000.00 |
| 166 | 2 | Bond22-909876519 < Bond22 | Bonds payable | 3000.00 |
| 167 | 2 | Bond22-909876521 < Bond22 | Bonds payable | 7000.00 |
| 168 | 3 | Capital-909876511 | Share capital | 360000.00 |
| 169 | 3 | Capital-909876517 | Share capital | 225000.00 |
| 170 | 3 | Capital-88-654304 | Share capital | 315000.00 |
| 171 | 3 | n | Retained earnings (Conversion) | 4331.17 |
| 172 | 4 | Note21-interest incomes | Sales (notes interest) | 0 |
| 173 | 4 | Note22-interest incomes | Sales (notes interest) | 0 |
| 174 | 4 | Note23-interest incomes | Sales (notes interest) | 0 |
| 175 | 4 | Note24-interest incomes | Sales (notes interest) | 0 |
| 176 | 4 | Note25-interest incomes | Sales (notes interest) | 0 |
| 177 | 5 | Deposit interest expenses | Cost of notes interest | 0 |
| 178 | 5 | 909876512-travelling < Sales department-travelling | Travelling expenses | 0 |
| 179 | 5 | 909876511-other < Purchase department-other | Other expenses | 0 |
| 180 | 5 | 909876510-salary < Office department-salary | Salary expenses | 0 |
| 181 | 5 | Bond21-interest expenses | Bond interest expenses | 0 |
| 182 | 5 | Bond22-interest expenses | Bond interest expenses | 0 |
| 183 | 5 | Bond23-interest expenses | Bond interest expenses | 0 |
| 184 | 5 | Truck21-amortization < Truck2-amortization < Vehicle-truck-amortization | Amortization expenses | 0 |
| 185 | 5 | Car31-amortization < Car3-amortization < Vehicle-car-amortization | Amortization expenses | 0 |
| 186 | 5 | Computer server11-amortization < Computer server2-amortization < Computer-amortization | Amortization expenses | 0 |
| 187 | 5 | Computer11-amortization < Computer1-amortization < Computer-amortization | Amortization expenses | 0 |
| 188 | 5 | Computer21-amortization < Computer2-amortization < Computer-amortization | Amortization expenses | 0 |
| 189 | 4 | Accrued interest income-bond11 < Bonds | Investment incomes | 0 |
| 190 | 4 | Accrued interest income-bond12 < Bonds | Investment incomes | 0 |
| 191 | 4 | Accrued interest income-bond13 < Bonds | Investment incomes | 0 |
| 192 | 4 | Accrued interest income-bond31 < Bonds | Investment incomes | 0 |
| 193 | 4 | Accrued interest income-bond41 < Bonds | Investment incomes | 0 |

Figure 2.4-4　Business Bank2 Converting Multi-Subaccount Names Table

When entering the dynamic accounting equation into the database dcj205 on December 31, 2015, I first enter three initialization sub-equations.

Cash (1): 0 = Share capital (3): 0

Account receivable (1): 0 = Account payable (2): 0

0 = Sales (notes interest) (4): 0 – Cost of notes interest (5):0

From the Figure 2.4-3 and the Figure 2.4-4, the dynamic accounting equation on December 31, 2015 must be divided to the "N" transaction sub-equations because of the limitation of the MathAccounting software. Every sub-equation has maximum twelve items. All converting transaction sub-equations can be designed and written as following.

- The transaction sub-equation includes the "Cash" account with the Order 4 to the Order 10 and the "Deposits payable" account with the Order 111 to the Order 117. Because the balances of the "Cash" with the Order 10 and the Order 117 are zero, the first transaction sub-equation is:

  Cash (1): 12000.15 + Cash (1): 16500.55 + Cash (1): 16260.1 + Cash (1): 11400.61 + Cash (1): 11970.23 + Cash (1): 11100.54 = Deposits payable (2): 12000.15 + Deposits payable (2): 16500.55 + Deposits payable (2): 16260.1 + Deposits payable (2): 11400.61 + Deposits payable (2): 11970.23 + Deposits payable (2): 11100.54

- The transaction sub-equation includes the "Cash" account with the Order 11 to the Order 17 and the "Deposits payable" account with the Order 118 to the Order 124. Because the balances of the "Cash" with the Order 12 and the Order 119 are zero, the second transaction sub-equation is:

  Cash (1): 11000.11 + Cash (1): 28600.21 + Cash (1): 14520.56 + Cash (1): 11680.34 + Cash (1): 11810.18 + Cash (1): 12200.45 = Deposits payable (2): 11000.11 + Deposits payable (2): 28600.21 + Deposits payable (2): 14520.56 +

Deposits payable (2): 11680.34 + Deposits payable (2): 11810.18 + Deposits payable (2): 12200.45

- The transaction sub-equation includes the "Cash" account with the Order 18 to the Order 24 and the "Deposits payable" account with the Order 125 to the Order 131. Because the balances of the "Cash" with the Order 18 and the Order 125 are zero, the third transaction sub-equation is:

  Cash (1): 11300.74 + Cash (1): 26150.88 + Cash (1): 10510.99 + Cash (1): 16910.92 + Cash (1): 15900.51 + Cash (1): 26210.18 = Deposits payable (2): 11300.74 + Deposits payable (2): 26150.88 + Deposits payable (2): 10510.99 + Deposits payable (2): 16910.92 + Deposits payable (2): 15900.51+ Deposits payable (2): 26210.18

- The transaction sub-equation includes the "Cash" account with the Order 25 to the Order 31 and the "Deposits payable" account with the Order 132 to the Order 138. Because the balances of the "Cash" with the Order 27 and the Order 134 are zero, the fourth transaction sub-equation is:

  Cash (1): 11720.14 + Cash (1): 15150.21 + Cash (1): 16150.25 + Cash (1): 4090.65 + Cash (1): 610.08 + Cash (1): 1117.96 = Deposits payable (2): 11720.14 + Deposits payable (2): 15150.21 + Deposits payable (2): 16150.25 + Deposits payable (2): 4090.65 + Deposits payable (2): 610.08 + Deposits payable (2): 1117.96

- The transaction sub-equation includes the "Cash" account with the Order 32 to the Order 38 and the "Deposits payable" account with the Order 139 to the Order 145. Because the balances of the "Cash" with the Order 32 to the Order 34, the Order 37, the Order 139 to the Order 141, and the Order 144 are zero, the fifth transaction sub-equation is:

Cash (1): 47393.19 + Cash (1): 6753.89 + Cash (1): 8768.69 = Deposits payable (2): 47393.19 + Deposits payable (2): 6753.89 + Deposits payable (2): 8768.69

- The transaction sub-equation includes the "Cash" account with the Order 39 to the Order 44 and the "Bonds payable" account with the Order 146 to the Order 151. The sixth transaction sub-equation is:

Cash (1): 9000 + Cash (1): 8000 + Cash (1): 6000 + Cash (1): 9000 + Cash (1): 12000 + Cash (1): 7000 = Bonds payable (2): 9000 + Bonds payable (2): 8000 + Bonds payable (2): 6000 + Bonds payable (2): 9000 + Bonds payable (2): 12000 + Bonds payable (2): 7000

- The transaction sub-equation includes the "Cash" account with the Order 45 to the Order 50 and the "Bonds payable" account with the Order 152 to the Order 157. The seventh transaction sub-equation is:

Cash (1): 4000 + Cash (1): 6000 + Cash (1): 3000 + Cash (1): 5000 + Cash (1): 3000 + Cash (1): 8000 = Bonds payable (2): 4000 + Bonds payable (2): 6000 + Bonds payable (2): 3000 + Bonds payable (2): 5000 + Bonds payable (2): 3000 + Bonds payable (2): 8000

- The transaction sub-equation includes the "Cash" account with the Order 51 to the Order 56 and the "Bonds payable" account with the Order 158 to the Order 163. The eighth transaction sub-equation is:

Cash (1): 5000 + Cash (1): 6000 + Cash (1): 8000 + Cash (1): 4000 + Cash (1): 6000 + Cash (1): 7000 = Bonds payable (2): 5000 + Bonds payable (2): 6000 + Bonds payable (2): 8000 + Bonds payable (2): 4000 + Bonds payable (2): 6000+ Bonds payable (2): 7000

- The transaction sub-equation includes the "Cash" account with the Order 57 to the

Order 60 and the "Bonds payable" account with the Order 164 to the Order 167. The ninth transaction sub-equation is:

Cash (1): 6000 + Cash (1): 8000 + Cash (1): 3000 + Cash (1): 7000 = Bonds payable (2): 6000 + Bonds payable (2): 8000 + Bonds payable (2): 3000 + Bonds payable (2): 7000

- The transaction sub-equation includes the "Cash" account with the Order 61 to the Order 70 and the part of the "Share capital" account with the Order 168. The tenth transaction sub-equation is:

Cash (1): 56100 + Cash (1): 36000 + Cash (1): 25650 + Cash (1): 27300 + Cash (1): 3760 + Cash (1): 536.67 + Cash (1): 189 + Cash (1): 90 + Cash (1): 268.33 + Cash (1): 313.33 = Share capital (3): 150207.33

After entering this transaction, the new balance of the "Share capital" account with the Order 168 is $209,792.67 (= $360,000 - $150,207.33).

- The transaction sub-equation includes the "Cash" account with the Order 71, the Order 72, the Order 76 to the Order 79, the Order 85 to the Order 89, and the part of the "Cash" account with the Order 1. The eleventh transaction sub-equation is:

Cash (1): -40000 + Cash (1): -38000 + Cash (1): -27634.61 + Cash (1): -26587.92 + Cash (1): -28312.35 + Cash (1): -31671.27 + Cash (1): -7000 + Cash (1): -3000 + Cash (1): -6000 + Cash (1): -5000 + Cash (1): -8000 + Cash (1): 221206.15 = 0

After entering this transaction, the new balance of the "Cash" account with the Order 1 is $138,793.85 (= $360,000 - $221,206.15).

- The transaction sub-equation includes the "Cash" account with the Order 80 to the Order 84, the "Supplies" account with the Order 90, the "Notes receivable" account with the Order 91 to the Order 95, and the part of the "Share capital" account with the Order 168. The twelfth transaction sub-equation is:

Cash (1): -220000 + Cash (1): -240000 + Cash (1): -180000 + Cash (1): -200000 + Cash (1): -120000 + Supplies (1): 84.16 + Notes receivable (1): 250000 + Notes receivable (1): 240000 + Notes receivable (1): 180000 + Notes receivable (1): 200000 + Notes receivable (1): 120000 = Share capital (3): 84.16

After entering this transaction, the balance of the "Share capital" account with the Order 168 is \$209,708.51 (= \$209,792.67 - \$84.16)

- The transaction sub-equation includes the "Cash" account with the Order 2 and the Order 3, "Bonds" account with the Order 96 to the Order 100, the "Share capital" account with the Order 169 and the Order 170, the and the part of the "Share capital" account with the Order 168. The thirteenth transaction sub-equation is:

Cash (1): 225000 + Cash (1): 315000 + Bonds (1): 7000 + Bonds (1): 3000 + Bonds (1): 6000 + Bonds (1): 5000 + Bonds (1): 8000 = Share capital (3): 225000 + Share capital (3): 315000 + Share capital (3): 29000

After entering this transaction, the balance of the "Share capital" account with the Order 168 is \$180,708.51 (= \$209,708.51 - \$29,000)

- The transaction sub-equation includes the "Vehicle" account with the Order 101 and the Order 102, the "Accumulated amortization: vehicle" account with the Order 103 and the Order 104, the "Computer" account with the Order 105 to the Order 107, the "Accumulated amortization: Computer" account with the Order 108 and the Order 110, and the part of the "Share capital" account with the Order 168. The fourteenth transaction sub-equation is:

Vehicle (1): 40000 + Vehicle (1): 38000 + Accumulated amortization: Vehicle (1): -16666.67 + Accumulated amortization: Vehicle (1): -11400 + Computer (1): 2800 + Computer (1): 1600 + Computer (1): 1500 + Accumulated amortization: Computer (1): -1750 + Accumulated amortization: Computer (1): -1000 + Accumulated amortization: Computer (1): -937.5 = Share capital (3): 52145.83

After entering this transaction, the balance of the "Share capital" account with the Order 168 is $128,562.68 (= $180,708.51 - $52,145.83)

- The transaction sub-equation includes the "Cash" account with the Order 73 to the Order 75, the rest ($138,793.85) of the "Cash" account with the Order 1, the rest ($128,562.68) of the "Share capital" account with the Order 168, and the "Retained earnings (Conversion)" account with the balance $24,331.17. The fifteenth transaction sub-equation is:

Cash (1): -2800 + Cash (1): -1600 + Cash (1): -1500 + Cash (1): 138793.85 = Share capital (3): 128562.68 + Retained earnings (Conversion) (3): 4331.17

After completing this transaction, the dynamic accounting equation of the Business Bank2 on December 31, 2015 has entered into the database dcj206.

### 2.4.2.2 Brief Summary of the Business Bank2

Obviously, there is not any information of the Inventory account in these transaction sub-equations.

## 2.4.3 Sample of the Company1

The Company1 has total share capital $200,000 and three shareholders of the individual A12, the individual A15, and the individual A18. Their percentages of the share capital are 40%, 35%, and 25% respectively. The Company1 produces the vehicles and the computers. The Figure 2.4-5 shows its products and sale prices.

| Order | Product (the Lowest-level Subaccount) Names | Multi-subaccount Names | Costs | Sale Prices |
|---|---|---|---|---|
| 1 | Truck1 | Truck1 < Truck < Vehicle | 33700.00 | 45000.00 |
| 2 | Truck2 | Truck2 < Truck < Vehicle | 30000.00 | 40000.00 |
| 3 | Car1 | Car1 < Car < Vehicle | 28000.00 | 40000.00 |
| 4 | Car2 | Car2 < Car < Vehicle | 27000.00 | 39000.00 |
| 5 | Car3 | Car3 < Car < Vehicle | 26000.00 | 38000.00 |
| 6 | Computer server1 | Computer server1 < Computer server < Computer | 1600.00 | 2800.00 |

| 7 | Computer server2 | Computer server2 < Computer server < Computer | 1500.00 | 2700.00 |
|---|---|---|---|---|
| 8 | Computer1 | Computer1 < Computer | 1000.00 | 1600.00 |
| 9 | Computer2 | Computer2 < Computer | 920.00 | 1500.00 |
| 10 | Computer3 | Computer3 < Computer | 830.00 | 1400.00 |
| 11 | Computer4 | Computer4 < Computer | 770.00 | 1300.00 |
| 12 | Truck1- Service package1 | Truck1- Service package1 < Truck-service < Vehicle-service | - | 550.00 |
| 13 | Truck2- Service package2 | Truck2- Service package2 < Truck-service < Vehicle-service | - | 500.00 |
| 14 | Car1- Service package3 | Car1- Service package3 < Car-service < Vehicle-service | - | 490.00 |
| 15 | Car2- Service package4 | Car2- Service package4 < Car-service < Vehicle-service | - | 450.00 |
| 16 | Car3- Service package5 | Car3- Service package5 < Car-service < Vehicle-service | - | 410.00 |
| 17 | Computer server1- Service package6 | Computer server1- Service package6 < Computer server-service < Computer-service | - | 60.00 |
| 18 | Computer server2- Service package7 | Computer server2- Service package7 < Computer server-service < Computer-service | - | 55.00 |
| 19 | Computer1- Service package8 | Computer1- Service package8 < Computer-service | - | 50.00 |
| 20 | Computer2- Service package9 | Computer2- Service package9 < Computer-service | - | 45.00 |
| 21 | Computer3- Service package10 | Computer3- Service package10 < Computer-service | - | 40.00 |

Figure 2.4-5  Company1 Products and Sale Prices Table

For a manufacturing company, the balances of the working-in- process inventory and the cost of goods manufactured must be calculated during a fiscal year.

## 2.4.3.1 Conversion of the Company1

The Company1 will convert to the MathAccounting software on January 1, 2016. The Figure 2.4-6 and the Figure 2.4-7 show the converting reference table and the multi-subaccount names table respectively.

| Order | Class | Account Name (**Subtotal Name**) | Balance | Row |
|---|---|---|---|---|
| **1** | **1** | **(Current assets)** | - | **103** |
| 2 | 1 | Cash | 67873.98 | 104 |
| 3 | 1 | Supplies | 93.79 | 106 |
| 4 | 1 | Account receivable | 6400.00 | 108 |
| 5 | 1 | Inventory | 357130.00 | 110 |
| 6 | 1 | Working-in-process inventory | 367796.65 | 112 |
| **7** | **1** | **(Long term investments)** | - | **141** |
| 8 | 1 | Bonds | 22000.00 | 142 |

| | | | | |
|---|---|---|---|---|
| 9 | 1 | Share | 36000.00 | 144 |
| **10** | **1** | **(Equipment)** | - | **171** |
| 11 | 1 | Vehicle | 121000.00 | 172 |
| 12 | 1 | Accumulated amortization: Vehicle | -48833.33 | 173 |
| 13 | 1 | Computer | 5400.00 | 174 |
| 14 | 1 | Accumulated amortization: Computer | -4275.00 | 175 |
| **15** | **2** | **(Current liabilities)** | - | **203** |
| 16 | 2 | Account payable | 27040.00 | 204 |
| 17 | 2 | Accrued interest payable | 0 | 206 |
| 18 | 2 | Tax payable | 0 | 208 |
| **19** | **2** | **(Long term liabilities)** | - | **251** |
| 20 | 2 | Bonds payable | 50000.00 | 252 |
| 21 | 2 | Note payable | 640000.00 | 254 |
| **22** | **3** | **(Owners' capital)** | - | **303** |
| 23 | 3 | Share capital | 200000.00 | 304 |
| 24 | 3 | Retained earnings (Conversion) | 13546.09 | 306 |
| **25** | **4** | **(Revenues)** | - | **403** |
| 26 | 4 | Sales | | 404 |
| **27** | **5** | **(Cost)** | - | **431** |
| 28 | 5 | Cost of goods sold | | 432 |
| **29** | **5** | **(Operating and administrative expenses)** | - | **453** |
| 30 | 5 | Travelling expenses | 0 | 454 |
| 31 | 5 | Other expenses | 0 | 455 |
| 32 | 5 | Salary expenses | 0 | 456 |
| 33 | 5 | Cost of goods manufactured | 0 | 457 |
| 34 | 5 | Bond interest expenses | 0 | 458 |
| 35 | 5 | Note interest expenses | 0 | 460 |
| 36 | 5 | Amortization expenses | 0 | 462 |
| **37** | **4** | **(Other income)** | - | **475** |
| 38 | 4 | Investment income | | 476 |
| 39 | 4 | Deposits interest income | 0 | 478 |
| 40 | 4 | Service package income | 0 | 480 |
| **41** | **5** | **(Tax)** | - | **600** |
| 42 | 5 | Tax expenses | 0 | 602 |

Figure 2.4-6   Company1 Converting Reference Table

| Order | Class | Multi-subaccount Name | Parent Name | Lowest Subaccount Balance |
|---|---|---|---|---|
| 1 | 1 | 909876512-i-owners < Cash receipts from owners < Financial activities | Cash | 80000.00 |

| 2 | 1 | 909876515-i-owners < Cash receipts from owners < Financial activities | Cash | 70000.00 |
|---|---|---|---|---|
| 3 | 1 | 909876518-i-owners < Cash receipts from owners < Financial activities | Cash | 50000.00 |
| 4 | 1 | 88-654304-i-note11 < Cash receipts from banks < Financial activities | Cash | 250000.00 |
| 5 | 1 | 88-654304-i-note15 < Cash receipts from banks < Financial activities | Cash | 170000.00 |
| 6 | 1 | 88-654305-i-note21 < Cash receipts from banks < Financial activities | Cash | 220000.00 |
| 7 | 1 | Cash receipts from customers < Operating activities | Cash | 0 |
| 8 | 1 | 88-654305-i-bond31 < Cash receipts from issued bonds < Financial activities | Cash | 5000.00 |
| 9 | 1 | 909876501-i-bond31 < Cash receipts from issued bonds < Financial activities | Cash | 3000.00 |
| 10 | 1 | 909876502-i-bond31 < Cash receipts from issued bonds < Financial activities | Cash | 6000.00 |
| 11 | 1 | 909876508-i-bond31 < Cash receipts from issued bonds < Financial activities | Cash | 5000.00 |
| 12 | 1 | 909876511-i-bond31 < Cash receipts from issued bonds < Financial activities | Cash | 7000.00 |
| 13 | 1 | 909876514-i-bond31 < Cash receipts from issued bonds < Financial activities | Cash | 2000.00 |
| 14 | 1 | 909876516-i-bond31 < Cash receipts from issued bonds < Financial activities | Cash | 4000.00 |
| 15 | 1 | 909876518-i-bond31 < Cash receipts from issued bonds < Financial activities | Cash | 2000.00 |
| 16 | 1 | 909876521-i-bond31 < Cash receipts from issued bonds < Financial activities | Cash | 3000.00 |
| 17 | 1 | 909876522-i-bond31 < Cash receipts from issued bonds < Financial activities | Cash | 5000.00 |
| 18 | 1 | 909876524-i-bond31 < Cash receipts from issued bonds < Financial activities | Cash | 3000.00 |
| 19 | 1 | 909876525-i-bond31 < Cash receipts from issued bonds < Financial activities | Cash | 5000.00 |
| 20 | 1 | 88-654304-c-interest of investment bond11 < Cash receipts from investments < Investing activities | Cash | 766.67 |
| 21 | 1 | 88-654304-c-interest of investment bond13 < Cash receipts from investments < Investing activities | Cash | 45.00 |
| 22 | 1 | 88-654305-c-interest of investment bond21 < Cash receipts from investments < Investing activities | Cash | 615.00 |
| 23 | 1 | 88-654306-t-truck1 < Cash payments for machinery < Operating activities | Cash | -45000.00 |
| 24 | 1 | 88-654306-t-truck2 < Cash payments for machinery < Operating activities | Cash | -40000.00 |
| 25 | 1 | 88-654306-t-car3 < Cash payments for machinery < Operating activities | Cash | -36000.00 |
| 26 | 1 | 88-654306-t-computer server2 < Cash payments for machinery < Operating activities | Cash | -2700.00 |
| 27 | 1 | 88-654306-t-computer3 < Cash payments for machinery < Operating activities | Cash | -1400.00 |
| 28 | 1 | 88-654306-t-computer4 < Cash payments for machinery < Operating activities | Cash | -1300.00 |
| 29 | 1 | Cash payments for operating expenses < Operating activities | Cash | -185721.33 |
| 30 | 1 | Cash payments for operating expenses < Operating activities | Cash | -184369.41 |
| 31 | 1 | Cash payments for operating expenses < Operating activities | Cash | -186387.57 |
| 32 | 1 | 88-654303-n-tax < Cash payments for operating expenses < Operating activities | Cash | -52674.38 |
| 33 | 1 | 88-654308-t-operating < Cash payments to suppliers<Operating activities | Cash | -1000.00 |

| 34 | 1 | 88-654309-t-operating < Cash payments to suppliers<Operating activities | Cash | -17000.00 |
|---|---|---|---|---|
| 35 | 1 | 88-654310-t-operating < Cash payments to suppliers<Operating activities | Cash | -12000.00 |
| 36 | 1 | 88-654304-n-investment bond11 < Cash payments for investments < Investing activities | Cash | -10000.00 |
| 37 | 1 | 88-654304-n-investment bond13 < Cash payments for investments < Investing activities | Cash | -3000.00 |
| 38 | 1 | 88-654305-n-investment bond21 < Cash payments for investments < Investing activities | Cash | -9000.00 |
| 39 | 1 | 88-654307-n-company2 share capital < Cash payments for investments < Investing activities | Cash | -36000.00 |
| 40 | 1 | n | Supplies | 93.79 |
| 41 | 1 | 123456789 | Account receivable | 1400.00 |
| 42 | 1 | 123456787 | Account receivable | 500.00 |
| 43 | 1 | 123456783 | Account receivable | 600.00 |
| 44 | 1 | 123456782 | Account receivable | 900.00 |
| 45 | 1 | 123456781 | Account receivable | 1000.00 |
| 46 | 1 | 123456780 | Account receivable | 2000.00 |
| 47 | 1 | Inven111 < Inven11 < Inven1 | Inventory | $10*74 = 740.00$ |
| 48 | 1 | Inven112 < Inven11 < Inven1 | Inventory | $40*95 = 3800.00$ |
| 49 | 1 | Inven121 < Inven12 < Inven1 | Inventory | $0.8*275 = 220.00$ |
| 50 | 1 | Inven122 < Inven12 < Inven1 | Inventory | $50*32 = 1600.00$ |
| 51 | 1 | Inven21 < Inven2 | Inventory | $30*90 = 2700.00$ |
| 52 | 1 | Inven221 < Inven22 < Inven2 | Inventory | $30*30 = 900.00$ |
| 53 | 1 | Inven222 < Inven22 < Inven2 | Inventory | $50*60 = 3000.00$ |
| 54 | 1 | PPUK parts < ASD parts < Inven2 | Inventory | $40*50 = 2000.00$ |
| 55 | 1 | PPGH parts < ASD parts < Inven2 | Inventory | $2*500 = 1000.00$ |
| 56 | 1 | Inven31 < Inven3 | Inventory | $10*40 = 400.00$ |
| 57 | 1 | Inven32 < Inven3 | Inventory | $50*22 = 1100.00$ |
| 58 | 1 | Inven331 < Inven33 < Inven3 | Inventory | $20*25 = 500.00$ |
| 59 | 1 | Inven332 < Inven33 < Inven3 | Inventory | $45*40 = 1800.00$ |
| 60 | 1 | HGFCVB parts < QASXC parts < Inven3 | Inventory | $10*10 = 100.00$ |
| 61 | 1 | PPGHUP parts < ASDUP parts < Inven3 | Inventory | $20*30 = 600.00$ |
| 62 | 1 | Inven411 < Inven41 < Inven4 | Inventory | $5*102 = 510.00$ |
| 63 | 1 | Inven412 < Inven41 < Inven4 | Inventory | $18.5*20 = 370.00$ |
| 64 | 1 | TTTCU parts < TTT parts < Inven4 | Inventory | $20*115 = 2300.00$ |
| 65 | 1 | RRRHJK parts < Inven4 | Inventory | $20*70 = 1400.00$ |
| 66 | 1 | Truck1 part1 < Truck1 parts < Vehicle parts | Inventory | $8700.00*1 = 8700.00$ |
| 67 | 1 | Truck1 part2 < Truck1 parts < Vehicle parts | Inventory | $7600.00*1 = 7600.00$ |
| 68 | 1 | Truck1 part3 < Truck1 parts < Vehicle parts | Inventory | $5800.00*1 = 5800.00$ |
| 69 | 1 | Truck2 part1 < Truck2 parts < Vehicle parts | Inventory | $8500.00*1 = 8500.00$ |
| 70 | 1 | Truck2 part2 < Truck2 parts < Vehicle parts | Inventory | $7200.00*1 = 7200.00$ |
| 71 | 1 | Truck2 part3 < Truck2 parts < Vehicle parts | Inventory | $5400.00*1 = 5400.00$ |
| 72 | 1 | Car1 part1 < Car1 parts < Vehicle parts | Inventory | $8300.00*1 = 8300.00$ |
| 73 | 1 | Car1 part2 < Car1 parts < Vehicle parts | Inventory | $7200.00*1 = 7200.00$ |
| 74 | 1 | Car1 part3 < Car1 parts < Vehicle parts | Inventory | $5100.00*1 = 5100.00$ |

| 75 | 1 | Car2 part1 < Car2 parts < Vehicle parts | Inventory | 7900.00*1 = 7900.00 |
|---|---|---|---|---|
| 76 | 1 | Car2 part2 < Car2 parts < Vehicle parts | Inventory | 6800.00*1 = 6800.00 |
| 77 | 1 | Car2 part3 < Car2 parts < Vehicle parts | Inventory | 4900.00*1 = 4900.00 |
| 78 | 1 | Car3 part1 < Car3 parts < Vehicle parts | Inventory | 7500.00*1 = 7500.00 |
| 79 | 1 | Car3 part2 < Car3 parts < Vehicle parts | Inventory | 6400.00*1 = 6400.00 |
| 80 | 1 | Car3 part3 < Car3 parts < Vehicle parts | Inventory | 4700.00*1 = 4700.00 |
| 81 | 1 | Computer server1 part1 < Computer server parts < Computer parts | Inventory | 600.00*1 = 600.00 |
| 82 | 1 | Computer server1 part2 < Computer server parts < Computer parts | Inventory | 400.00*1 = 400.00 |
| 83 | 1 | Computer server2 part1 < Computer server parts < Computer parts | Inventory | 540.00*1 = 540.00 |
| 84 | 1 | Computer server2 part2 < Computer server parts < Computer parts | Inventory | 380.00*1 = 380.00 |
| 85 | 1 | Computer1 part1 < Computer parts | Inventory | 360.00*1 = 360.00 |
| 86 | 1 | Computer1 part2 < Computer parts | Inventory | 310.00*1 = 310.00 |
| 87 | 1 | Computer2 part1 < Computer parts | Inventory | 320.00*1 = 320.00 |
| 88 | 1 | Computer2 part2 < Computer parts | Inventory | 290.00*1 = 290.00 |
| 89 | 1 | Computer3 part1 < Computer parts | Inventory | 280.00*1 = 280.00 |
| 90 | 1 | Computer3 part2 < Computer parts | Inventory | 260.00*1 = 260.00 |
| 91 | 1 | Computer4 part1 < Computer parts | Inventory | 250.00*1 =250.00 |
| 92 | 1 | Computer4 part2 < Computer parts | Inventory | 240.00*1 = 240.00 |
| 93 | 1 | Truck1-inventory < Truck-inventory < Vehicle-inventory | Inventory | 33700.00*1 = 33700.00 |
| 94 | 1 | Truck2-inventory < Truck-inventory < Vehicle-inventory | Inventory | 30000.00*1 = 30000.00 |
| 95 | 1 | Car1-inventory < Car-inventory < Vehicle-inventory | Inventory | 28000.00*1 = 28000.00 |
| 96 | 1 | Car2-inventory < Car-inventory < Vehicle-inventory | Inventory | 27000.00*2 = 54000.00 |
| 97 | 1 | Car3-inventory < Car-inventory < Vehicle-inventory | Inventory | 26000.00*2 = 52000.00 |
| 98 | 1 | Computer server1-inventory < Computer server-inventory < Computer-inventory | Inventory | 1600.00*3 = 4800.00 |
| 99 | 1 | Computer server2-inventory < Computer server-inventory < Computer-inventory | Inventory | 1500.00*2 = 3000.00 |
| 100 | 1 | Computer1-inventory < Computer-inventory | Inventory | 1000.00*4 = 4000.00 |
| 101 | 1 | Computer2-inventory < Computer-inventory | Inventory | 920.00*4 = 3680.00 |
| 102 | 1 | Computer3-inventory < Computer-inventory | Inventory | 830.00*6 = 4980.00 |
| 103 | 1 | Computer4-inventory < Computer-inventory | Inventory | 770.00*10 = 7700.00 |
| 104 | 1 | Working-truck1 < Working-truck < Working-vehicle | Working-in-process inventory | 29572.91*2 = 59145.82 |
| 105 | 1 | Working-truck2 < Working-truck < Working-vehicle | Working-in-process inventory | 27863.74*3 = 83591.22 |
| 106 | 1 | Working-car1 < Working-car < Working-vehicle | Working-in-process inventory | 26987.33*2 = 53974.66 |
| 107 | 1 | Working-car2 < Working-car < Working-vehicle | Working-in-process inventory | 24549.81*2 = 49099.62 |
| 108 | 1 | Working-car3 < Working-car < Working-vehicle | Working-in-process inventory | 24412.17*3 = 73236.51 |
| 109 | 1 | Working-computer server1 < Working-computer server < Working-computer | Working-in-process inventory | 1556.45*4 = 6225.80 |
| 110 | 1 | Working-computer server2 < Working-computer server < Working-computer | Working-in-process inventory | 1476.29*4 = 5905.16 |

| | | | | |
|---|---|---|---|---:|
| 111 | 1 | Working-computer1 < Working-computer | Working-in-process inventory | 945.12*10 = 9451.20 |
| 112 | 1 | Working-computer2 < Working-computer | Working-in-process inventory | 817.12*10 = 8171.20 |
| 113 | 1 | Working-computer3 < Working-computer | Working-in-process inventory | 732.28*12 = 8787.36 |
| 114 | 1 | Working-computer4 < Working-computer | Working-in-process inventory | 680.54*15 = 10208.1 |
| 115 | 1 | Bond11 | Bonds | 10000.00 |
| 116 | 1 | Bond13 | Bonds | 3000.00 |
| 117 | 1 | Bond21 | Bonds | 9000.00 |
| 118 | 1 | Company2 share capital | Share | 36000.00 |
| 119 | 1 | Truck11 < Truck1 < Truck | Vehicle | 45000.00 |
| 120 | 1 | Truck21 < Truck2 < Truck | Vehicle | 40000.00 |
| 121 | 1 | Car31 < Car3 < Car | Vehicle | 36000.00 |
| 122 | 1 | Truck11-accumulated amortization < Truck1-accumulated amortization < Truck-accumulated amortization | Accumulated amortization: Vehicle | -19500.00 |
| 123 | 1 | Truck21-accumulated amortization < Truck2-accumulated amortization < Truck-accumulated amortization | Accumulated amortization: Vehicle | -17333.33 |
| 124 | 1 | Car31-accumulated amortization < Car3-accumulated amortization < Car-accumulated amortization | Accumulated amortization: Vehicle | -12000.00 |
| 125 | 1 | Computer server21 < Computer server2 < Computer server | Computer | 2700.00 |
| 126 | 1 | Computer31 < Computer3 | Computer | 1400.00 |
| 127 | 1 | Computer41 < Computer4 | Computer | 1300.00 |
| 128 | 1 | Computer server21-accumulated amortization < Computer server2-accumulated amortization < Computer server-accumulated amortization | Accumulated amortization: Computer | -2137.50 |
| 129 | 1 | Computer31-accumulated amortization < Computer3-accumulated amortization | Accumulated amortization: Computer | -1108.33 |
| 130 | 1 | Computer41-accumulated amortization < Computer4-accumulated amortization | Accumulated amortization: Computer | -1029.17 |
| 131 | 2 | 123456083 | Account payable | 13400.00 |
| 132 | 2 | 123456082 | Account payable | 10600.00 |
| 133 | 2 | 123456081 | Account payable | 2040.00 |
| 134 | 2 | 123456080 | Account payable | 1000.00 |
| 135 | 2 | Band31-interest payable < Bonds-interest payable | Accrued interest payable | 0 |
| 136 | 2 | Note11-interest payable < Notes-interest payable | Accrued interest payable | 0 |
| 137 | 2 | Note15-interest payable < Notes-interest payable | Accrued interest payable | 0 |
| 138 | 2 | Note21-interest payable < Notes-interest payable | Accrued interest payable | 0 |
| 139 | 2 | Bond31-88-654305 < Bond31 | Bonds payable | 5000.00 |
| 140 | 2 | Bond31-909876501 < Bond31 | Bonds payable | 3000.00 |
| 141 | 2 | Bond31-909876502 < Bond31 | Bonds payable | 6000.00 |
| 142 | 2 | Bond31-909876508 < Bond31 | Bonds payable | 5000.00 |
| 143 | 2 | Bond31-88-654311 < Bond31 | Bonds payable | 7000.00 |

| 144 | 2 | Bond31-88-654314 < Bond31 | Bonds payable | 2000.00 |
|---|---|---|---|---|
| 145 | 2 | Bond31-909876516 < Bond31 | Bonds payable | 4000.00 |
| 146 | 2 | Bond31-909876518 < Bond31 | Bonds payable | 2000.00 |
| 147 | 2 | Bond31-909876521 < Bond31 | Bonds payable | 3000.00 |
| 148 | 2 | Bond31-909876522 < Bond31 | Bonds payable | 5000.00 |
| 149 | 2 | Bond31-909876524 < Bond31 | Bonds payable | 3000.00 |
| 150 | 2 | Bond31-909876525 < Bond31 | Bonds payable | 5000.00 |
| 151 | 2 | Note11-88-654304 | Notes payable | 250000.00 |
| 152 | 2 | Note15-88-654304 | Notes payable | 170000.00 |
| 153 | 2 | Note21-88-654305 | Notes payable | 220000.00 |
| 154 | 3 | Capital-909876512 | Share capital | 80000.00 |
| 155 | 3 | Capital-909876515 | Share capital | 70000.00 |
| 156 | 3 | Capital-909876518 | Share capital | 50000.00 |
| 157 | 3 | n | Retained earnings (Conversion) | 13546.09 |
| 158 | 4 | Sales-909876513 | Sales | 0 |
| 159 | 5 | 909876513-travelling < Sales department-travelling | Travelling expenses | 0 |
| 160 | 5 | 909876514-travelling < Office department-travelling | Travelling expenses | 0 |
| 161 | 5 | 909876515-travelling < Product department-travelling | Travelling expenses | 0 |
| 162 | 5 | 909876513-other < Sales department-other | Other expenses | 0 |
| 163 | 5 | 909876514-other < Office department-other | Other expenses | 0 |
| 164 | 5 | 909876515-other < Product department-other | Other expenses | 0 |
| 165 | 5 | 909876514-salary < Office department-salary | Salary expenses | 0 |
| 166 | 5 | Supplies expenses | Cost of goods manufactured | 0 |
| 167 | 5 | 909876513-salary < Sales department-salary < Salary expenses | Cost of goods manufactured | 0 |
| 168 | 5 | 909876515-salary < Product department-salary < Salary expenses | Cost of goods manufactured | 0 |
| 169 | 5 | General parts expenses | Cost of goods manufactured | 0 |
| 170 | 5 | Bond31-interest | Bond interest expenses | 0 |
| 171 | 5 | Note11-interest | Note interest expenses | 0 |
| 172 | 5 | Note15-interest | Note interest expenses | 0 |
| 173 | 5 | Note21-interest | Note interest expenses | 0 |
| 174 | 5 | Truck11-amortization < Truck1-amortization < Vehicle-truck-amortization | Amortization expenses | 0 |
| 175 | 5 | Truck21-amortization < Truck2-amortization < Vehicle-truck-amortization | Amortization expenses | 0 |
| 176 | 5 | Car31-amortization < Car3-amortization < Vehicle-car-amortization | Amortization expenses | 0 |
| 177 | 5 | Computer server21-amortization < Computer server2-amortization < Computer-amortization | Amortization expenses | 0 |
| 178 | 5 | Computer31-amortization < Computer3-amortization < Computer-amortization | Amortization expenses | 0 |
| 179 | 5 | Computer41-amortization < Computer4-amortization < Computer-amortization | Amortization expenses | 0 |
| 180 | 4 | Accrued interest income-bond11 < Bonds | Investment incomes | 0 |

| 181 | 4 | Accrued interest income-bond13 < Bonds | Investment incomes | 0 |
|---|---|---|---|---|
| 182 | 4 | Accrued interest income-bond21 < Bonds | Investment incomes | 0 |
| 183 | 4 | n | Deposits interest income | 0 |

Figure 2.4-7  Company1 Converting Multi-Subaccount Names Table

From the Figure 2.4-7, the inventory has two class of the products. The first class of the products with the Order 93 to the Order 103 are themselves produced products which will be sold to other customers. The second class of the products are the purchased products, which will be consumed or transferred into themselves produced products directly, from their suppliers. During conversion, only the first products are added their product codes to the lowest multi-subaccounts. In this book, the product code is simply consisted of the abbreviation of the company name, the produced date, the abbreviation of the product name (or other useful information), and the product order, and is behind the product name. The Figure 2.4-8 shows the changes of the first class of the products' multi-subaccounts. They are the Inventory with the Other 93 to the Other 103, seeing the Figure 2.4-7.

| Order | Class | Multi-subaccount Name | Parent Name | Lowest Subaccount Balance |
|---|---|---|---|---|
| 1 | 1 | Truck1-C1-20150917-T1-011 < Truck-inventory < Vehicle-inventory | Inventory | 33700.00*1 = 33700.00 |
| 2 | 1 | Truck2-C1-20150917-T2-011 < Truck-inventory < Vehicle-inventory | Inventory | 30000.00*1 = 30000.00 |
| 3 | 1 | Car1-C1-20150921-C1-023 < Car-inventory < Vehicle-inventory | Inventory | 28000.00*1 = 28000.00 |
| 4 | 1 | Car2-C1-20150925-C2-027 < Car-inventory < Vehicle-inventory | Inventory | 27000.00*1 = 27000.00 |
| 5 | 1 | Car2-C1-20150925-C2-028 < Car-inventory < Vehicle-inventory | Inventory | 27000.00*1 = 27000.00 |
| 6 | 1 | Car3-C1-20150925-C3-028 < Car-inventory < Vehicle-inventory | Inventory | 26000.00*1 = 26000.00 |
| 7 | 1 | Car3-C1-20150925-C3-029 < Car-inventory < Vehicle-inventory | Inventory | 26000.00*1 = 26000.00 |
| 8 | 1 | Computer server1-C1-20150107-COMS1-039 < Computer server inventory < Computer-inventory | Inventory | 1600.00*1 = 1600.00 |
| 9 | 1 | Computer server1-C1-20150107-COMS1-040 < Computer server inventory < Computer-inventory | Inventory | 1600.00*1 = 1600.00 |
| 10 | 1 | Computer server1-C1-20150108-COMS1-041 < Computer server inventory < Computer-inventory | Inventory | 1600.00*1 = 1600.00 |
| 11 | 1 | Computer server2-C1-20150108-COMS2-045 < Computer server-inventory < Computer-inventory | Inventory | 1500.00*1 = 1500.00 |
| 12 | 1 | Computer server2-C1-20150108-COMS2-046 < Computer server-inventory < Computer-inventory | Inventory | 1500.00*1 = 1500.00 |
| 13 | 1 | Computer1-C1-20150108-COM1-055 < Computer-inventory | Inventory | 1000.00*1 = 1000.00 |

| 14 | 1 | Computer1-C1-20150108-COM1-056 < Computer-inventory | Inventory | $1000.00*1 = 1000.00$ |
|---|---|---|---|---|
| 15 | 1 | Computer1-C1-20150108-COM1-057 < Computer-inventory | Inventory | $1000.00*1 = 1000.00$ |
| 16 | 1 | Computer1-C1-20150108-COM1-058 < Computer-inventory | Inventory | $1000.00*1 = 1000.00$ |
| 17 | 1 | Computer2-C1-20150108-COM2-065 < Computer inventory | Inventory | $920.00*1 = 920.00$ |
| 18 | 1 | Computer2-C1-20150108-COM2-066 < Computer inventory | Inventory | $920.00*1 = 920.00$ |
| 19 | 1 | Computer2-C1-20150108-COM2-067 < Computer inventory | Inventory | $920.00*1 = 920.00$ |
| 20 | 1 | Computer2-C1-20150108-COM2-068 < Computer inventory | Inventory | $920.00*1 = 920.00$ |
| 21 | 1 | Computer3-C1-20150111-COM3-077 < Computer-inventory | Inventory | $830.00*1 = 830.00$ |
| 22 | 1 | Computer3-C1-20150111-COM3-078 < Computer-inventory | Inventory | $830.00*1 = 830.00$ |
| 23 | 1 | Computer3-C1-20150111-COM3-079 < Computer-inventory | Inventory | $830.00*1 = 830.00$ |
| 24 | 1 | Computer3-C1-20150111-COM3-080 < Computer-inventory | Inventory | $830.00*1 = 830.00$ |
| 25 | 1 | Computer3-C1-20150111-COM3-081 < Computer-inventory | Inventory | $830.00*1 = 830.00$ |
| 26 | 1 | Computer3-C1-20150111-COM3-082 < Computer-inventory | Inventory | $830.00*1 = 830.00$ |
| 27 | 1 | Computer4-C1-20150111-COM4-093 < Computer-inventory | Inventory | $770.00*10=7700.00$ |
| 28 | 1 | Computer4-C1-20150111-COM4-094 < Computer-inventory | Inventory | $770.00*10=7700.00$ |
| 29 | 1 | Computer4-C1-20150111-COM4-095 < Computer-inventory | Inventory | $770.00*10=7700.00$ |
| 30 | 1 | Computer4-C1-20150111-COM4-096 < Computer-inventory | Inventory | $770.00*10=7700.00$ |
| 31 | 1 | Computer4-C1-20150111-COM4-097 < Computer-inventory | Inventory | $770.00*10=7700.00$ |
| 32 | 1 | Computer4-C1-20150111-COM4-098 < Computer-inventory | Inventory | $770.00*10=7700.00$ |
| 33 | 1 | Computer4-C1-20150111-COM4-099 < Computer-inventory | Inventory | $770.00*10=7700.00$ |
| 34 | 1 | Computer4-C1-20150111-COM4-100 < Computer-inventory | Inventory | $770.00*10=7700.00$ |
| 35 | 1 | Computer4-C1-20150111-COM4-101 < Computer-inventory | Inventory | $770.00*10=7700.00$ |
| 36 | 1 | Computer4-C1-20150111-COM4-102 < Computer-inventory | Inventory | $770.00*10=7700.00$ |

Figure 2.4-8   Changes of Multi-Subaccount Names Table

Before entering the dynamic accounting equation on December 31, 2015 into the database dcj207, I first enter two initialization sub-equations.

Account payable (2): 0 = Share capital (3): 0

0 = Sales (4): 0 – Cost of goods sold (5):0

All converting transaction sub-equations can be designed and written as the followings.

- I build a transaction sub-equation for the "Account receivable" and the "Account payable" accounts. The transaction sub-equation includes the part of the "Cash" account with the Order 1, the "Account receivable" account with the Order 41 to the Order 46, and the "Account payable" account with the Order 131 to the Order 134. The first transaction sub-equation is:

  Cash (1): 20640 + Account receivable (1): 1400 + Account receivable (1): 500 + Account receivable (1): 600 + Account receivable (1): 900 + Account receivable (1): 1000 + Account receivable (1): 2000 = Account payable (2): 13400 + Account payable (2): 10600 + Account payable (2): 2040 + Account payable (2): 1000

  After entering this transaction, the new balance of the "Cash" account with the Order 1 is $59,360 (= $80,000 - $20,640).

- The transaction sub-equation includes the rest ($59,360) of the "Cash" account with the Order 1, the "Cash" account with the Order 2 to the Order 6, the part of the "Share capital" account with the Order 154, the "Share capital" account with the Order 155 and the Order 156, and the "Notes payable" account with the Order 151 to the Order 153. The second transaction sub-equation is:

  Cash (1): 59360 + Cash (1): 70000 + Cash (1): 50000 + Cash (1): 250000 + Cash (1): 170000 + Cash (1): 220000 = Share capital (3): 59360 + Share capital (3): 70000 + Share capital (3): 50000 + Notes payable (2): 250000 + Notes payable (2): 170000 + Notes payable (2): 220000

  After entering this transaction, the new balance of the "Share capital" account with the Order 154 is $20,640 (= $80,000 - $59,360).

- The transaction sub-equation includes the "Cash" account with the Order 7 to the Order 13 and the "Bonds payable" account with the Order 139 to the Order 144. Because the balance of the "Cash" with the Order 7 is zero, the third transaction sub-equation is:

Cash (1): 5000 + Cash (1): 3000 + Cash (1): 6000 + Cash (1): 5000 + Cash (1): 7000 + Cash (1): 2000 = Bonds payable (2): 5000 + Bonds payable (2): 3000 + Bonds payable (2): 6000 + Bonds payable (2): 5000 + Bonds payable (2): 7000 + Bonds payable (2): 2000

- The transaction sub-equation includes the "Cash" account with the Order 14 to the Order 19 and the "Bonds payable" account with the Order 145 to the Order 150. The fourth transaction sub-equation is:

Cash (1): 4000 + Cash (1): 2000 + Cash (1): 3000 + Cash (1): 5000 + Cash (1): 3000 + Cash (1): 5000 = Bonds payable (2): 4000 + Bonds payable (2): 2000 + Bonds payable (2): 3000 + Bonds payable (2): 5000 + Bonds payable (2): 3000 + Bonds payable (2): 5000

- The transaction sub-equation includes the "Cash" account with the Order 20 to the Order 22, the part of the "Cash" account with the Order 29, and the "Inventory" account with the Order 47 to the Order 54. The fifth transaction sub-equation is:

Cash (1): 766.67 + Cash (1): 45 + Cash (1): 615 + Cash (1): -16386.67 + Inventory (1): 740 + Inventory (1): 3800 + Inventory (1): 220 + Inventory (1): 1600 + Inventory (1): 2700 + Inventory (1): 900 + Inventory (1): 3000 + Inventory (1): 2000 = 0

After entering this transaction, the new balance of the "Cash" account with the Order 29 is -$169,334.66 (= -$185,721.33 + $16,386.67).

- The transaction sub-equation includes the "Cash" account with the Order 23 to the Order 28, the "Vehicle" account with the Order 119 to the Order 121, and the "Computer" account with the Order 125 to the Order 127. The sixth transaction sub-equation is:

Cash (1): -45000 + Cash (1): -40000 + Cash (1): -36000 + Cash (1): -2700 + Cash (1): -1400 + Cash (1): -1300 + Vehicle (1): 45000 + Vehicle (1): 40000 + Vehicle (1): 36000 + Computer (1): 2700 + Computer (1): 1400 + Computer (1): 1300 = 0

- The transaction sub-equation includes the part of the "Cash" account with the Order 29 and the "Inventory" account with the Order 55 to the Order 65. The seventh transaction sub-equation is:

Cash (1): -10080 + Inventory (1): 1000 + Inventory (1): 400 + Inventory (1): 1100 + Inventory (1): 500 + Inventory (1): 1800 + Inventory (1): 100 + Inventory (1): 60000 + Inventory (1): 510+ Inventory (1): 370 + Inventory (1): 2300 + Inventory (1): 1400 = 0

After entering this transaction, the new balance of the "Cash" account with the Order 29 is -$159,254.66 (= -$169,334.66 + $10,080).

- The transaction sub-equation includes the part of the "Cash" account with the Order 29, the "Cash" account with the Order 33 to the Order 35, and the "Inventory" account with the Order 66 to the Order 73. The eighth transaction sub-equation is:

Cash (1): -28700 + Cash (1): -1000 + Cash (1): -17000 + Cash (1): -12000 + Inventory (1): 8700 + Inventory (1): 7600 + Inventory (1): 5800 + Inventory (1): 8500 + Inventory (1): 7200 + Inventory (1): 5400 + Inventory (1): 8300 + Inventory (1): 7200 = 0

After entering this transaction, the new balance of the "Cash" account with the Order 29 is -$130,554.66 (= -$159,254.66 + $28,700).

- The transaction sub-equation includes the part of the "Cash" account with the Order 29, the "Cash" account with the Order 36 to the Order 38, and the "Inventory" account with the Order 74 to the Order 80. The ninth transaction sub-equation is:

Cash (1): -21300 + Cash (1): -10000 + Cash (1): -3000 + Cash (1): -9000 + Inventory (1): 5100 + Inventory (1): 7900 + Inventory (1): 6800 + Inventory (1): 4900 + Inventory (1): 7500 + Inventory (1): 6400 + Inventory (1): 4700 = 0

After entering this transaction, the new balance of the "Cash" account with the Order 29 is -$109,254.66 (= -$130,554.66 + $21,300).

- The transaction sub-equation includes the part of the "Cash" account with the Order 29 and the "Inventory" account with the Order 81 to the Order 91. The tenth transaction sub-equation is:

Cash (1): -3990 + Inventory (1): 600 + Inventory (1): 400 + Inventory (1): 540 + Inventory (1): 380 + Inventory (1): 360 + Inventory (1): 310 + Inventory (1): 320 + Inventory (1): 290+ Inventory (1): 280 + Inventory (1): 260 + Inventory (1): 250=0

After entering this transaction, the new balance of the "Cash" account with the Order 29 is -$105,264.66 (= -$109,254.66 + $3,990).

- The following transactions sub-equation include the rest of the "Cash" account with the Order 29, the part of the "Cash" account with the Order 30, the "Cash" account with the Order 32 and the Order 39, the "Supplies" account with the Order 40, and the "Inventory" account with the Order 92 to the Order 98. The eleventh transaction sub-equation is:

Cash (1): -105264.66 + Cash (1): -8,894.75 + Cash (1): -52674.38 + Cash (1): -36000 + Supplies (1): 93.79 + Inventory (1): 240 + Inventory (1): 33700 + Inventory (1): 30000 + Inventory (1): 28000 + Inventory (1): 54000 + Inventory (1): 52000 + Inventory (1): 4800 = 0

After dividing this transaction sub-equation, I get the following transactions sub-equations respectively:

Cash (1): -48464.66 + Cash (1): -8,894.75 + Cash (1): -52674.38 + Cash (1): -36000 + Supplies (1): 93.79 + Inventory (1): 240 + Inventory (1): 33700 + Inventory (1): 30000 + Inventory (1): 28000 + Inventory (1): 27000 + Inventory (1): 27000 = 0

Cash (1): -56800 + Inventory (1): 26000 + Inventory (1): 26000 + Inventory (1): 1600 + Inventory (1): 1600 + Inventory (1): 1600 = 0

After entering the two transactions, the new balance of the "Cash" account with the Order 30 is -$175,474.66 (= -$184369.41+ $8,894.75).

- The following transactions sub-equation include the part of the "Cash" account with the Order 30, the "Cash" account with the Order 31, the "Inventory" account with the Order 99 to the Order 103, and the "Working-in-process inventory" account with the Order 104 to the Order 108. The eleventh transaction sub-equation is:

Cash (1): -156020.26 + Cash (1): -186387.57 + Inventory (1): 3000 + Inventory (1): 4000 + Inventory (1): 3680 + Inventory (1): 4980 + Inventory (1): 7700 + Working-in-process inventory (1): 59145.82 + Working-in-process inventory (1): 83591.22 + Working-in-process inventory (1): 53974.66 + Working-in-process inventory (1): 49099.62 + Working-in-process inventory (1): 73236.51 = 0

After dividing this transaction sub-equation, I get the following transactions sub-equations respectively:

Cash (1): -135660.26 + Cash (1): -186387.57 + Inventory (1): 1500 + Inventory (1): 1500 + Working-in-process inventory (1): 59145.82 + Working-in-process inventory (1): 83591.22+ Working-in-process inventory (1): 53974.66 + Working-in-process inventory (1):49099.62 +Working-in-process inventory (1):73236.51= 0

Cash (1): -7680 + Inventory (1): 1000 + Inventory (1): 1000 + Inventory (1): 1000 + Inventory (1): 1000 + Inventory (1): 920 + Inventory (1): 920 + Inventory (1):

920 + Inventory (1): 920 = 0

Cash (1): -4980 + Inventory (1): 830 + Inventory (1): 830 + Inventory (1): 830 + Inventory (1): 830 + Inventory (1): 830 + Inventory (1): 830 = 0

Cash (1): -7700 + Inventory (1): 770 + Inventory (1): 770 + Inventory (1): 770 + Inventory (1): 770 + Inventory (1): 770 + Inventory (1): 770 + Inventory (1): 770 + Inventory (1): 770 + Inventory (1): 770 + Inventory (1): 770 = 0

After entering the four transactions, the new balance of the "Cash" account with the Order 30 is -$19,454.4 (= -$175,474.66 + $135,660.26 + $7,680 + $4,980 + $7,700).

- The transaction sub-equation includes the part of the "Cash" account with the Order 30 (increase), the "Working-in-process inventory" account with the Order 109 to the Order 114, and the "Accumulated amortization: Vehicle" account with the Order 122 to the Order 124. The transaction sub-equation is:

Cash (1): 84.51 + Working-in-process inventory (1): 6225.8 + Working-in-process inventory (1): 5905.16 + Working-in-process inventory (1): 9451.2 + Working-in-process inventory (1): 8171.2 + Working-in-process inventory (1): 8787.36 + Working-in-process inventory (1): 10208.1 + Accumulated amortization: Vehicle (1): -19500 + Accumulated amortization: Vehicle (1): -17333.33 + Accumulated amortization: Vehicle (1): -12000 = 0

After entering this transaction, the new balance of the "Cash" account with the Order 30 is -$19,538.91 (= -$19,454.4 - $84.51).

- The transaction sub-equation includes rest (-$19,538.91) of the "Cash" account with the Order 30, the "Bonds" account with the Order 115 to the Order 117, the "Share" account with the Order 118, the "Accumulated amortization: Computer" account with the Order 128 and the Order 130, the rest ($20,640) of the "Share capital" account with the Order 154, and the "Retained earnings (Conversion)" account with the balance $13546.09. The transaction sub-equation is:

Cash (1): -19538.91 + Bonds (1): 10000 + Bonds (1): 3000 + Bonds (1): 9000 + Share (1): 36000 + Accumulated amortization: Computer (1): -2137.5 + Accumulated amortization: Computer (1): -1108.33 + Accumulated amortization: Computer (1): -1029.17 = Share capital (3): 20640 + Retained earnings (Conversion) (3): 13546.09

After completing this transaction, the dynamic accounting equation of the Company1 on December 31, 2015 has entered into the database dcj207.

### 2.4.3.2 Brief Summary of the Company1

The Figure 2.4-9 on the next page shows the partial information of inventory purchased or inventory sold by other social members in the public database dcj200. The balance of the Inventory is -$357,130 after completing conversion on December 31, 2015. The negative balance means that amounts sold by other social members are greater than amounts purchased by other social members. The contents of the column IDM and the column Symbol are meaningless because there is any logic relationship between the entered transaction sub-equations' accounts. Moreover, some multi-subaccounts of the Cash have not any three-level subaccount.

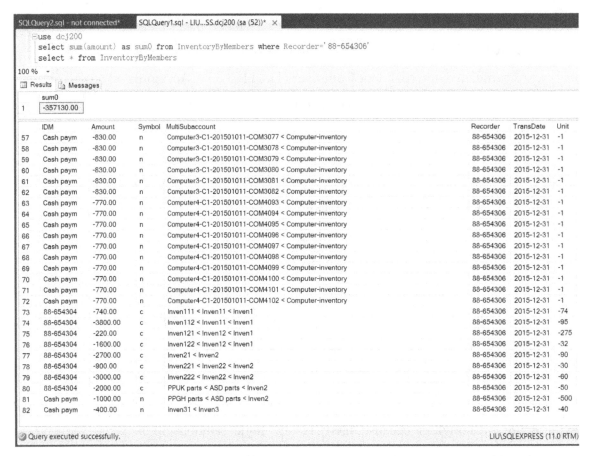

Figure 2.4-9   Company1 Inventory Purchased or Sold by Other Members

## 2.4.4 Sample of the Company2

The Company2 has total share capital $180,000 and three shareholders of the individual A13, the individual A14, and the Company1. Their percentages of the share capital are 50%, 30%, and 20% respectively. The Company2 produces the parts of vehicles and the computers. The Figure 2.4-10 shows its product names, costs, and sale prices.

| Order | Product (the Lowest-level Subaccount) Names | Multi-subaccount Names | Costs | Sale Prices |
|-------|---------------------------------------------|------------------------|-------|-------------|
| 1 | Truck1 part1 | Truck1 part1 < Truck1 parts < Vehicle parts | 5600.00 | 8700.00 |
| 2 | Truck1 part2 | Truck1 part2 < Truck1 parts < Vehicle parts | 4950.00 | 7600.00 |
| 3 | Truck1 part3 | Truck1 part3 < Truck1 parts < Vehicle parts | 3750.00 | 5800.00 |
| 4 | Truck2 part1 | Truck2 part1 < Truck2 parts < Vehicle parts | 5500.00 | 8500.00 |

| | | | | |
|---|---|---|---|---|
| 5 | Truck2 part2 | Truck2 part2 < Truck2 parts < Vehicle parts | 4660.00 | 7200.00 |
| 6 | Truck2 part3 | Truck2 part3 < Truck2 parts < Vehicle parts | 3500.00 | 5400.00 |
| 7 | Car1 part1 | Car1 part1 < Car1 parts < Vehicle parts | 5380.00 | 8300.00 |
| 8 | Car1 part2 | Car1 part2 < Car1 parts < Vehicle parts | 4650.00 | 7200.00 |
| 9 | Car1 part3 | Car1 part3 < Car1 parts < Vehicle parts | 3300.00 | 5100.00 |
| 10 | Car2 part1 | Car2 part1 < Car2 parts < Vehicle parts | 5100.00 | 7900.00 |
| 11 | Car2 part2 | Car2 part2 < Car2 parts < Vehicle parts | 4400.00 | 6800.00 |
| 12 | Car2 part3 | Car2 part3 < Car2 parts < Vehicle parts | 3170.00 | 4900.00 |
| 13 | Car3 part1 | Car3 part1 < Car3 parts < Vehicle parts | 4850.00 | 7500.00 |
| 14 | Car3 part2 | Car3 part2 < Car3 parts < Vehicle parts | 4150.00 | 6400.00 |
| 15 | Car3 part3 | Car3 part3 < Car3 parts < Vehicle parts | 3050.00 | 4700.00 |
| 16 | Computer server1 part1 | Computer server1 part1 < Computer server parts < Computer parts | 390.00 | 600.00 |
| 17 | Computer server1 part2 | Computer server1 part2 < Computer server parts < Computer parts | 260.00 | 400.00 |
| 18 | Computer server2 part1 | Computer server2 part1 < Computer server parts < Computer parts | 350.00 | 540.00 |
| 19 | Computer server2 part2 | Computer server2 part2 < Computer server parts < Computer parts | 250.00 | 380.00 |
| 20 | Computer1 part1 | Computer1 part1 < Computer parts | 235.00 | 360.00 |
| 21 | Computer1 part2 | Computer1 part2 < Computer parts | 202.00 | 310.00 |
| 22 | Computer2 part1 | Computer2 part1 < Computer parts | 208.00 | 320.00 |
| 23 | Computer2 part2 | Computer2 part2 < Computer parts | 189.00 | 290.00 |
| 24 | Computer3 part1 | Computer3 part1 < Computer parts | 182.00 | 280.00 |
| 25 | Computer3 part2 | Computer3 part2 < Computer parts | 169.00 | 260.00 |
| 26 | Computer4 part1 | Computer4 part1 < Computer parts | 162.00 | 250.00 |
| 27 | Computer4 part2 | Computer4 part2 < Computer parts | 156.00 | 240.00 |

Figure 2.4-10   Company2 Products and Sale Prices Table

For a manufacturing company, the Company2 is similar to the Company1. When the Company2 uses the MathAccounting software, the "Working-in-process inventory" is treated as a parent account of the class 1 and the "Cost of goods manufactured" is treated as the parent accounts of the class 5. For simplification, the "Cost of goods manufactured" account has only three one-level subaccounts of the "Supplies expenses", the "Salary expenses" for employees of A16 and A18, and the "Other general parts" in this book.

## 2.4.4.1 Conversion of the Company2

The Company2 will convert to the MathAccounting software on January 1, 2016. The Figure

2.4-11 and the Figure 2.4-12 show the converting reference table and the multi-subaccount names table respectively.

| Order | Class | Account Name (**Subtotal Name**) | Balance | Row |
|---|---|---|---|---|
| **1** | **1** | **(Current assets)** | - | **103** |
| 2 | 1 | Cash | 47393.19 | 104 |
| 3 | 1 | Supplies | 192.45 | 106 |
| 4 | 1 | Account receivable | 15150.00 | 108 |
| 5 | 1 | Inventory | 406970.00 | 110 |
| 6 | 1 | Working-in-process inventory | 309085.02 | 112 |
| **7** | **1** | **(Long term investments)** | - | **141** |
| 8 | 1 | Bonds | 14000.00 | 142 |
| **9** | **1** | **(Equipment)** | - | **171** |
| 10 | 1 | Vehicle | 125000.00 | 172 |
| 11 | 1 | Accumulated amortization: Vehicle | -44083.33 | 173 |
| 12 | 1 | Computer | 5900.00 | 174 |
| 13 | 1 | Accumulated amortization: Computer | -4179.16 | 175 |
| **14** | **2** | **(Current liabilities)** | - | **203** |
| 15 | 2 | Account payable | 7400.00 | 204 |
| 16 | 2 | Accrued interest payable | 0 | 206 |
| 17 | 2 | Tax payable | 0 | 208 |
| **18** | **2** | **(Long term liabilities)** | - | **251** |
| 19 | 2 | Bonds payable | 40000.00 | 252 |
| 20 | 2 | Note payable | 630000.00 | 254 |
| **21** | **3** | **(Owners' capital)** | - | **303** |
| 22 | 3 | Share capital | 180000.00 | 304 |
| 23 | 3 | Retained earnings (Conversion) | 18028.17 | 306 |
| **24** | **4** | **(Revenues)** | - | **403** |
| 25 | 4 | Sales | | 404 |
| **26** | **5** | **(Cost)** | - | **431** |
| 27 | 5 | Cost of goods sold | | 432 |
| **28** | **5** | **(Operating and administrative expenses)** | - | **453** |
| 29 | 5 | Travelling expenses | 0 | 454 |
| 30 | 5 | Other expenses | 0 | 455 |
| 31 | 5 | Salary expenses | 0 | 456 |
| 32 | 5 | Cost of goods manufactured | 0 | 457 |
| 33 | 5 | Bond interest expenses | 0 | 458 |
| 34 | 5 | Note interest expenses | 0 | 460 |
| 35 | 5 | Amortization expenses | 0 | 462 |
| **36** | **4** | **(Other income)** | - | **475** |

| Order | Class | Multi-subaccount Name | Parent Name | Lowest Subaccount Balance |
|---|---|---|---|---|
| 37 | 4 | Investment incomes | | 476 |
| 38 | 4 | Deposits interest incomes | 0 | 478 |
| **39** | **5** | **(Tax)** | **-** | **600** |
| 40 | 5 | Tax expenses | 0 | 602 |

Figure 2.4-11   Company2 Converting Reference Table

| Order | Class | Multi-subaccount Name | Parent Name | Lowest Subaccount Balance |
|---|---|---|---|---|
| 1 | 1 | 909876513-i-owners < Cash receipts from owners < Financial activities | Cash | 90000.00 |
| 2 | 1 | 909876514-i-owners < Cash receipts from owners < Financial activities | Cash | 54000.00 |
| 3 | 1 | 88-654306-i-owners < Cash receipts from owners < Financial activities | Cash | 36000.00 |
| 4 | 1 | 88-654304-i-note12 < Cash receipts from banks < Financial activities | Cash | 140000.00 |
| 5 | 1 | 88-654304-i-note14 < Cash receipts from banks < Financial activities | Cash | 250000.00 |
| 6 | 1 | 88-654305-i-note22 < Cash receipts from banks < Financial activities | Cash | 240000.00 |
| 7 | 1 | Cash receipts from customers < Operating activities | Cash | 0 |
| 8 | 1 | 88-654305-i-bond41 < Cash receipts from issued bonds < Financial activities | Cash | 8000.00 |
| 9 | 1 | 909876504-i-bond41 < Cash receipts from issued bonds < Financial activities | Cash | 4000.00 |
| 10 | 1 | 909876505-i-bond41 < Cash receipts from issued bonds < Financial activities | Cash | 2000.00 |
| 11 | 1 | 909876506-i-bond41 < Cash receipts from issued bonds < Financial activities | Cash | 1000.00 |
| 12 | 1 | 909876510-i-bond41 < Cash receipts from issued bonds < Financial activities | Cash | 3000.00 |
| 13 | 1 | 909876513-i-bond41 < Cash receipts from issued bonds < Financial activities | Cash | 5000.00 |
| 14 | 1 | 909876515-i-bond41 < Cash receipts from issued bonds < Financial activities | Cash | 2000.00 |
| 15 | 1 | 909876519-i-bond41 < Cash receipts from issued bonds < Financial activities | Cash | 3000.00 |
| 16 | 1 | 909876520-i-bond41 < Cash receipts from issued bonds < Financial activities | Cash | 2000.00 |
| 17 | 1 | 909876523-i-bond41 < Cash receipts from issued bonds < Financial activities | Cash | 3000.00 |
| 18 | 1 | 909876524-i-bond41 < Cash receipts from issued bonds < Financial activities | Cash | 5000.00 |
| 19 | 1 | 909876525-i-bond41 < Cash receipts from issued bonds < Financial activities | Cash | 2000.00 |
| 20 | 1 | 88-654304-c-interest of investment bond12 < Cash receipts from investments < Investing activities | Cash | 504.00 |
| 21 | 1 | 88-654305-c-interest of investment bond22 < Cash receipts from investments < Investing activities | Cash | 242.00 |
| 22 | 1 | 88-654306-t-truck1 < Cash payments for machinery < Operating activities | Cash | -45000.00 |
| 23 | 1 | 88-654306-t-truck2 < Cash payments for machinery < Operating activities | Cash | -40000.00 |
| 24 | 1 | 88-654306-t-car1 < Cash payments for machinery < Operating activities | Cash | -40000.00 |
| 25 | 1 | 88-654306-t-computer server1 < Cash payments for machinery < Operating activities | Cash | -2800.00 |

| 26 | 1 | 88-654306-t-computer1 < Cash payments for machinery < Operating activities | Cash | -1600.00 |
|---|---|---|---|---|
| 27 | 1 | 88-654306-t-computer2 < Cash payments for machinery < Operating activities | Cash | -1500.00 |
| 28 | 1 | Cash payments for operating expenses < Operating activities | Cash | -191371.25 |
| 29 | 1 | Cash payments for operating expenses < Operating activities | Cash | -190789.41 |
| 30 | 1 | Cash payments for operating expenses < Operating activities | Cash | -189973.52 |
| 31 | 1 | 88-654303-n-tax < Cash payments for operating expenses < Operating activities | Cash | -71318.63 |
| 32 | 1 | 88-654308-t-operating < Cash payments to suppliers<Operating activities | Cash | -15000.00 |
| 33 | 1 | 88-654304-n-investment bond12 < Cash payments for investments < Investing activities | Cash | -8000.00 |
| 34 | 1 | 88-654305-n-investment bond22 < Cash payments for investments < Investing activities | Cash | -6000.00 |
| 35 | 1 | n | Supplies | 192.45 |
| 36 | 1 | 123456788 | Account receivable | 500.00 |
| 37 | 1 | 123456787 | Account receivable | 400.00 |
| 38 | 1 | 123456784 | Account receivable | 13400.00 |
| 39 | 1 | 123456782 | Account receivable | 600.00 |
| 40 | 1 | 123456781 | Account receivable | 250.00 |
| 41 | 1 | 123456780 | Account receivable | 0 |
| 42 | 1 | Inven111 < Inven11 < Inven1 | Inventory | $10*100 = 1000.00$ |
| 43 | 1 | Inven112 < Inven11 < Inven1 | Inventory | $40*80 = 3200.00$ |
| 44 | 1 | Inven121 < Inven12 < Inven1 | Inventory | $0.8*200 = 160.00$ |
| 45 | 1 | Inven122 < Inven12 < Inven1 | Inventory | $50*60 = 3000.00$ |
| 46 | 1 | Inven21 < Inven2 | Inventory | $30*50 = 1500.00$ |
| 47 | 1 | Inven221 < Inven22 < Inven2 | Inventory | $30*100 = 3000.00$ |
| 48 | 1 | Inven222 < Inven22 < Inven2 | Inventory | $50*40 = 2000.00$ |
| 49 | 1 | PPUK parts < ASD parts < Inven2 | Inventory | $40*60 = 2400.00$ |
| 50 | 1 | PPGH parts < ASD parts < Inven2 | Inventory | $2*200 = 400.00$ |
| 51 | 1 | Inven51 < Inven5 | Inventory | $10*150 = 1500.00$ |
| 52 | 1 | Inven52 < Inven5 | Inventory | $50*50 = 2500.00$ |
| 53 | 1 | Inven531 < Inven53 < Inven5 | Inventory | $25*100 = 2500.00$ |
| 54 | 1 | Inven532 < Inven53 < Inven5 | Inventory | $35*100 = 3500.00$ |
| 55 | 1 | Inven541 < Inven54 < Inven5 | Inventory | $12*100 = 1200.00$ |
| 56 | 1 | Inven542 < Inven54 < Inven5 | Inventory | $15*80 = 1200.00$ |
| 57 | 1 | Inven611 < Inven61 < Inven6 | Inventory | $6.5*100 = 650.00$ |
| 58 | 1 | Inven612 < Inven61 < Inven6 | Inventory | $12.5*100 = 1250.00$ |
| 59 | 1 | Inven621 < Inven62 < Inven6 | Inventory | $18*100 = 1800.00$ |
| 60 | 1 | Inven63 < Inven6 | Inventory | $16*100 = 1600.00$ |
| 61 | 1 | Truck1 part1 < Truck1 parts < Vehicle parts | Inventory | $5600.00*5 = 28000.00$ |
| 62 | 1 | Truck1 part2 < Truck1 parts < Vehicle parts | Inventory | $4950.00*5 = 24750.00$ |
| 63 | 1 | Truck1 part3 < Truck1 parts < Vehicle parts | Inventory | $3750.00*5 = 18750.00$ |
| 64 | 1 | Truck2 part1 < Truck2 parts < Vehicle parts | Inventory | $5500.00*5 = 27500.00$ |
| 65 | 1 | Truck2 part2 < Truck2 parts < Vehicle parts | Inventory | $4660.00*5 = 23300.00$ |

| 66 | 1 | Truck2 part3 < Truck2 parts < Vehicle parts | Inventory | 3500.00*5 = 17500.00 |
|---|---|---|---|---|
| 67 | 1 | Car1 part1 < Car1 parts < Vehicle parts | Inventory | 5380.00*5 = 26900.00 |
| 68 | 1 | Car1 part2 < Car1 parts < Vehicle parts | Inventory | 4650.00*5 = 23250.00 |
| 69 | 1 | Car1 part3 < Car1 parts < Vehicle parts | Inventory | 3300.00*5 = 16500.00 |
| 70 | 1 | Car2 part1 < Car2 parts < Vehicle parts | Inventory | 5100.00*5 = 25500.00 |
| 71 | 1 | Car2 part2 < Car2 parts < Vehicle parts | Inventory | 4400.00*5 = 22000.00 |
| 72 | 1 | Car2 part3 < Car2 parts < Vehicle parts | Inventory | 3170.00*5 = 15850.00 |
| 73 | 1 | Car3 part1 < Car3 parts < Vehicle parts | Inventory | 4850.00*5 = 24250.00 |
| 74 | 1 | Car3 part2 < Car3 parts < Vehicle parts | Inventory | 4150.00*5 = 20750.00 |
| 75 | 1 | Car3 part3 < Car3 parts < Vehicle parts | Inventory | 3050.00*5 = 15250.00 |
| 76 | 1 | Computer server1 part1 < Computer server parts < Computer parts | Inventory | 390.00*10 = 3900.00 |
| 77 | 1 | Computer server1 part2 < Computer server parts < Computer parts | Inventory | 260.00*10 = 2600.00 |
| 78 | 1 | Computer server2 part1 < Computer server parts < Computer parts | Inventory | 350.00*10 = 3500.00 |
| 79 | 1 | Computer server2 part2 < Computer server parts < Computer parts | Inventory | 250.00*10 = 2500.00 |
| 80 | 1 | Computer1 part1 < Computer parts | Inventory | 235.00*20 = 4700.00 |
| 81 | 1 | Computer1 part2 < Computer parts | Inventory | 202.00*20 = 4040.00 |
| 82 | 1 | Computer2 part1 < Computer parts | Inventory | 208.00*20 = 4160.00 |
| 83 | 1 | Computer2 part2 < Computer parts | Inventory | 189.00*20 = 3780.00 |
| 84 | 1 | Computer3 part1 < Computer parts | Inventory | 182.00*20 = 3640.00 |
| 85 | 1 | Computer3 part2 < Computer parts | Inventory | 169.00*20 = 3380.00 |
| 86 | 1 | Computer4 part1 < Computer parts | Inventory | 162.00*20 = 3240.00 |
| 87 | 1 | Computer4 part2 < Computer parts | Inventory | 156.00*20 = 3120.00 |
| 88 | 1 | Working-truck1 part1 < Working-truck1 parts < Working-vehicle parts | Working-in-process inventory | 4709.33*5 = 23546.65 |
| 89 | 1 | Working-truck1 part2 < Working-truck1 parts < Working-vehicle parts | Working-in-process inventory | 4236.78*5 = 21183.90 |
| 90 | 1 | Working-truck1 part3 < Working-truck1 parts < Working-vehicle parts | Working-in-process inventory | 3012.51*5 = 15062.55 |
| 91 | 1 | Working-truck2 part1 < Working-truck2 parts < Working-vehicle parts | Working-in-process inventory | 4684.25*5 = 23421.25 |
| 92 | 1 | Working-truck2 part2 < Working-truck2 parts < Working-vehicle parts | Working-in-process inventory | 2967.59*5 = 14837.95 |
| 93 | 1 | Working-truck2 part3 < Working-truck2 parts < Working-vehicle parts | Working-in-process inventory | 2787.26*5 = 13936.30 |
| 94 | 1 | Working-car1 part1 < Working-car1 parts < Working-vehicle parts | Working-in-process inventory | 4594.23*5 = 22971.15 |
| 95 | 1 | Working-car1 part2 < Working-car1 parts < Working-vehicle parts | Working-in-process inventory | 3758.87*5 = 18794.35 |
| 96 | 1 | Working-car1 part3 < Working-car1 parts < Working-vehicle parts | Working-in-process inventory | 2564.77*5 = 12823.85 |
| 97 | 1 | Working-car2 part1 < Working-car2 parts < Working-vehicle parts | Working-in-process inventory | 4482.66*5 = 22413.30 |
| 98 | 1 | Working-car2 part2 < Working-car2 parts < Working-vehicle parts | Working-in-process inventory | 3577.41*5 = 17887.05 |
| 99 | 1 | Working-car2 part3 < Working-car2 parts < Working-vehicle parts | Working-in-process inventory | 2469.88*5 = 12349.40 |
| 100 | 1 | Working-car3 part1 < Working-car3 parts < Working-vehicle parts | Working-in-process inventory | 4177.56*6 = 25065.36 |
| 101 | 1 | Working-car3 part2 < Working-car3 parts < Working-vehicle parts | Working-in-process inventory | 3327.45*6 = 19964.70 |

| | | | | |
|---|---|---|---|---|
| 102 | 1 | Working-car3 part3 < Working-car3 parts < Working-vehicle parts | Working-in-process inventory | 2285.21*6 = 13711.26 |
| 103 | 1 | Working-computer server1 part1 < Working-computer server1 < Working-computer parts | Working-in-process inventory | 329.00*6 = 1974.00 |
| 104 | 1 | Working-computer server1 part2 < Working-computer server1 < Working-computer parts | Working-in-process inventory | 186.00*6 = 1116.00 |
| 105 | 1 | Working-computer server2 part1 < Working-computer server2 < Working-computer parts | Working-in-process inventory | 285.00*6 = 1710.00 |
| 106 | 1 | Working-computer server2 part2 < Working-computer server2 < Working-computer parts | Working-in-process inventory | 175.00*6 = 1050.00 |
| 107 | 1 | Working-computer1 part1< Working-computer parts | Working-in-process inventory | 208.50*20 = 4170.00 |
| 108 | 1 | Working-computer1 part2< Working-computer parts | Working-in-process inventory | 182.20*20 = 3644.00 |
| 109 | 1 | Working-computer2 part1< Working-computer parts | Working-in-process inventory | 178.80*20 = 3576.00 |
| 110 | 1 | Working-computer2 part2< Working-computer parts | Working-in-process inventory | 157.90*20 = 3158.00 |
| 111 | 1 | Working-computer3 part1< Working-computer parts | Working-in-process inventory | 150.20*20 = 3004.00 |
| 112 | 1 | Working-computer3 part2< Working-computer parts | Working-in-process inventory | 135.90*20 = 2718.00 |
| 113 | 1 | Working-computer4 part1< Working-computer parts | Working-in-process inventory | 128.20*20 = 2564.00 |
| 114 | 1 | Working-computer4 part2< Working-computer parts | Working-in-process inventory | 121.60*20 = 2432.00 |
| 115 | 1 | Bond12 | Bonds | 8000.00 |
| 116 | 1 | Bond22 | Bonds | 6000.00 |
| 117 | 1 | Truck11 < Truck1 < Truck | Vehicle | 45000.00 |
| 118 | 1 | Truck21 < Truck2 < Truck | Vehicle | 40000.00 |
| 119 | 1 | Car11 < Car1 < Car | Vehicle | 40000.00 |
| 120 | 1 | Truck11-accumulated amortization < Truck1-accumulated amortization < Truck-accumulated amortization | Accumulated amortization: Vehicle | -18750.00 |
| 121 | 1 | Truck21-accumulated amortization < Truck2-accumulated amortization < Truck-accumulated amortization | Accumulated amortization: Vehicle | -13333.33 |
| 122 | 1 | Car11-accumulated amortization < Car1-accumulated amortization < Car-accumulated amortization | Accumulated amortization: Vehicle | -12000.00 |
| 123 | 1 | Computer server11 < Computer server1 < Computer server | Computer | 2800.00 |
| 124 | 1 | Computer11 < Computer1 | Computer | 1600.00 |
| 125 | 1 | Computer21 < Computer2 | Computer | 1500.00 |
| 126 | 1 | Computer server11-accumulated amortization < Computer server1-accumulated amortization < Computer server-accumulated amortization | Accumulated amortization: Computer | -1983.33 |
| 127 | 1 | Computer11-accumulated amortization < Computer1-accumulated amortization | Accumulated amortization: Computer | -1133.33 |
| 128 | 1 | Computer21-accumulated amortization < Computer2-accumulated amortization | Accumulated amortization: Computer | -1062.50 |
| 129 | 2 | 123456084 | Account payable | 600.00 |
| 130 | 2 | 123456082 | Account payable | 6000.00 |
| 131 | 2 | 123456081 | Account payable | 500.00 |
| 132 | 2 | 123456080 | Account payable | 300.00 |
| 133 | 2 | Band41-interest payable < Bonds-interest payable | Accrued interest payable | 0 |
| 134 | 2 | Note12-interest payable < Notes-interest payable | Accrued interest payable | 0 |

| 135 | 2 | Note14-interest payable < Notes-interest payable | Accrued interest payable | 0 |
|---|---|---|---|---|
| 136 | 2 | Note22-interest payable < Notes-interest payable | Accrued interest payable | 0 |
| 137 | 2 | Bond41-88-654305 < Bond41 | Bonds payable | 8000.00 |
| 138 | 2 | Bond41-909876504 < Bond41 | Bonds payable | 4000.00 |
| 139 | 2 | Bond41-909876505 < Bond41 | Bonds payable | 2000.00 |
| 140 | 2 | Bond41-909876506 < Bond41 | Bonds payable | 1000.00 |
| 141 | 2 | Bond41-909876510 < Bond41 | Bonds payable | 3000.00 |
| 142 | 2 | Bond41-909876513 < Bond41 | Bonds payable | 5000.00 |
| 143 | 2 | Bond41-909876515 < Bond41 | Bonds payable | 2000.00 |
| 144 | 2 | Bond41-909876519 < Bond41 | Bonds payable | 3000.00 |
| 145 | 2 | Bond41-909876520 < Bond41 | Bonds payable | 2000.00 |
| 146 | 2 | Bond41-909876523 < Bond41 | Bonds payable | 3000.00 |
| 147 | 2 | Bond41-909876524 < Bond41 | Bonds payable | 5000.00 |
| 148 | 2 | Bond41-909876525 < Bond41 | Bonds payable | 2000.00 |
| 149 | 2 | Note12-88-654304 | Notes payable | 140000.00 |
| 150 | 2 | Note14-88-654304 | Notes payable | 250000.00 |
| 151 | 2 | Note22-88-654305 | Notes payable | 240000.00 |
| 152 | 3 | Capital-909876513 | Share capital | 90000.00 |
| 153 | 3 | Capital-909876514 | Share capital | 54000.00 |
| 154 | 3 | Capital-88-654306 | Share capital | 36000.00 |
| 155 | 3 | n | Retained earnings (Conversion) | 18028.17 |
| 156 | 4 | Sales-909876516 | Sales | 0 |
| 157 | 5 | 909876516-travelling < Sales department-travelling | Travelling expenses | 0 |
| 158 | 5 | 909876517-travelling < Office department-travelling | Travelling expenses | 0 |
| 159 | 5 | 909876518-travelling < Product department-travelling | Travelling expenses | 0 |
| 160 | 5 | 909876516-other < Sales department-other | Other expenses | 0 |
| 161 | 5 | 909876517-other < Office department-other | Other expenses | 0 |
| 162 | 5 | 909876518-other < Product department-other | Other expenses | 0 |
| 163 | 5 | 909876517-salary < Office department-salary | Salary expenses | 0 |
| 164 | 5 | Supplies expenses | Cost of goods manufactured | 0 |
| 165 | 5 | 909876516-salary < Sales department-salary < Salary expenses | Cost of goods manufactured | 0 |
| 166 | 5 | 909876518-salary < Product department-salary < Salary expenses | Cost of goods manufactured | 0 |
| 167 | 5 | General parts expenses | Cost of goods manufactured | 0 |
| 168 | 5 | Bond41-interest | Bond interest expenses | 0 |
| 169 | 5 | Note12-interest | Note interest expenses | 0 |
| 170 | 5 | Note14-interest | Note interest expenses | 0 |
| 171 | 5 | Note22-interest | Note interest expenses | 0 |
| 172 | 5 | Truck11-amortization < Truck1-amortization < Vehicle-truck-amortization | Amortization expenses | 0 |

| 173 | 5 | Truck21-amortization < Truck2-amortization < Vehicle-truck-amortization | Amortization expenses | 0 |
|---|---|---|---|---|
| 174 | 5 | Car11-amortization < Car1-amortization < Vehicle-car-amortization | Amortization expenses | 0 |
| 175 | 5 | Computer server11-amortization < Computer server1-amortization < Computer-amortization | Amortization expenses | 0 |
| 176 | 5 | Computer11-amortization < Computer1-amortization < Computer-amortization | Amortization expenses | 0 |
| 177 | 5 | Computer21-amortization < Computer2-amortization < Computer-amortization | Amortization expenses | 0 |
| 178 | 4 | Accrued interest income-bond12 < Bonds | Investment incomes | 0 |
| 179 | 4 | Accrued interest income-bond22 < Bonds | Investment incomes | 0 |
| 180 | 4 | n | Deposits interest income | 0 |

Figure 2.4-12   Company2 Converting Multi-Subaccount Names Table

Just as said before, only the first products are added their product codes to the lowest multi-subaccounts. For simplification, the product batch will be used in the computer parts. In this book, the product batch is simply consisted of the abbreviation of the company name, the produced date, the abbreviation of the product name (or other useful information), and the total product quantity. This product batch is behind the product name. The Figure 2.4-13 shows the changes of the first class of the products' multi-subaccounts. They are the Inventory with the Other 61 to the Other 87, seeing the Figure 2.4-12.

| Order | Class | Multi-subaccount Name | Parent Name | Lowest Subaccount Balance |
|---|---|---|---|---|
| 1 | 1 | Truck1 part1-C2-20150721-T1P1-034 < Truck1 parts < Vehicle parts | Inventory | 5600.00*1 = 5600.00 |
| 2 | 1 | Truck1 part1-C2-20150721-T1P1-035 < Truck1 parts < Vehicle parts | Inventory | 5600.00*1 = 5600.00 |
| 3 | 1 | Truck1 part1-C2-20150721-T1P1-036 < Truck1 parts < Vehicle parts | Inventory | 5600.00*1 = 5600.00 |
| 4 | 1 | Truck1 part1-C2-20150721-T1P1-037 < Truck1 parts < Vehicle parts | Inventory | 5600.00*1 = 5600.00 |
| 5 | 1 | Truck1 part1-C2-20150721-T1P1-038 < Truck1 parts < Vehicle parts | Inventory | 5600.00*1 = 5600.00 |
| 6 | 1 | Truck1 part2-C2-20150721-T1P2-042 < Truck1 parts < Vehicle parts | Inventory | 4950.00*1 = 4950.00 |
| 7 | 1 | Truck1 part2-C2-20150721-T1P2-043 < Truck1 parts < Vehicle parts | Inventory | 4950.00*1 = 4950.00 |
| 8 | 1 | Truck1 part2-C2-20150721-T1P2-044 < Truck1 parts < Vehicle parts | Inventory | 4950.00*1 = 4950.00 |
| 9 | 1 | Truck1 part2-C2-20150721-T1P2-045 < Truck1 parts < Vehicle parts | Inventory | 4950.00*1 = 4950.00 |
| 10 | 1 | Truck1 part2-C2-20150721-T1P2-046 < Truck1 parts < Vehicle parts | Inventory | 4950.00*1 = 4950.00 |
| 11 | 1 | Truck1 part3-C2-20150721-T1P3-045 < Truck1 parts < Vehicle parts | Inventory | 3750.00*1 = 3750.00 |
| 12 | 1 | Truck1 part3-C2-20150721-T1P3-046 < Truck1 parts < Vehicle parts | Inventory | 3750.00*1 = 3750.00 |

| 13 | 1 | Truck1 part3-C2-20150721-T1P3-047 < Truck1 parts < Vehicle parts | Inventory | 3750.00*1 = 3750.00 |
|----|---|---|---|---|
| 14 | 1 | Truck1 part3-C2-20150721-T1P3-048 < Truck1 parts < Vehicle parts | Inventory | 3750.00*1 = 3750.00 |
| 15 | 1 | Truck1 part3-C2-20150721-T1P3-049 < Truck1 parts < Vehicle parts | Inventory | 3750.00*1 = 3750.00 |
| 16 | 1 | Truck2 part1-C2-20150728-T2P1-053 < Truck2 parts < Vehicle parts | Inventory | 5500.00*1 = 5500.00 |
| 17 | 1 | Truck2 part1-C2-20150728-T2P1-054 < Truck2 parts < Vehicle parts | Inventory | 5500.00*1 = 5500.00 |
| 18 | 1 | Truck2 part1-C2-20150728-T2P1-055 < Truck2 parts < Vehicle parts | Inventory | 5500.00*1 = 5500.00 |
| 19 | 1 | Truck2 part1-C2-20150728-T2P1-056 < Truck2 parts < Vehicle parts | Inventory | 5500.00*1 = 5500.00 |
| 20 | 1 | Truck2 part1-C2-20150728-T2P1-057 < Truck2 parts < Vehicle parts | Inventory | 5500.00*1 = 5500.00 |
| 21 | 1 | Truck2 part2-C2-20150728-T2P2-053 < Truck2 parts < Vehicle parts | Inventory | 4660.00*1 = 4660.00 |
| 22 | 1 | Truck2 part2-C2-20150728-T2P2-054 < Truck2 parts < Vehicle parts | Inventory | 4660.00*1 = 4660.00 |
| 23 | 1 | Truck2 part2-C2-20150728-T2P2-055 < Truck2 parts < Vehicle parts | Inventory | 4660.00*1 = 4660.00 |
| 24 | 1 | Truck2 part2-C2-20150728-T2P2-056 < Truck2 parts < Vehicle parts | Inventory | 4660.00*1 = 4660.00 |
| 25 | 1 | Truck2 part2-C2-20150728-T2P2-057 < Truck2 parts < Vehicle parts | Inventory | 4660.00*1 = 4660.00 |
| 26 | 1 | Truck2 part3-C2-20150728-T2P3-053 < Truck2 parts < Vehicle parts | Inventory | 3500.00*1 = 3750.00 |
| 27 | 1 | Truck2 part3-C2-20150728-T2P3-054 < Truck2 parts < Vehicle parts | Inventory | 3500.00*1 = 3750.00 |
| 28 | 1 | Truck2 part3-C2-20150728-T2P3-055 < Truck2 parts < Vehicle parts | Inventory | 3500.00*1 = 3750.00 |
| 29 | 1 | Truck2 part3-C2-20150728-T2P3-056 < Truck2 parts < Vehicle parts | Inventory | 3500.00*1 = 3750.00 |
| 30 | 1 | Truck2 part3-C2-20150728-T2P3-057 < Truck2 parts < Vehicle parts | Inventory | 3500.00*1 = 3750.00 |
| 31 | 1 | Car1 part1-C2-20150816-C1P1-061 < Car1 parts < Vehicle parts | Inventory | 5380.00*1 = 5380.00 |
| 32 | 1 | Car1 part1-C2-20150816-C1P1-062 < Car1 parts < Vehicle parts | Inventory | 5380.00*1 = 5380.00 |
| 33 | 1 | Car1 part1-C2-20150816-C1P1-063 < Car1 parts < Vehicle parts | Inventory | 5380.00*1 = 5380.00 |
| 34 | 1 | Car1 part1-C2-20150816-C1P1-064 < Car1 parts < Vehicle parts | Inventory | 5380.00*1 = 5380.00 |
| 35 | 1 | Car1 part1-C2-20150816-C1P1-065 < Car1 parts < Vehicle parts | Inventory | 5380.00*1 = 5380.00 |
| 36 | 1 | Car1 part2-C2-20150816-C1P2-068 < Car1 parts < Vehicle parts | Inventory | 4650.00*1 = 4650.00 |
| 37 | 1 | Car1 part2-C2-20150816-C1P2-069 < Car1 parts < Vehicle parts | Inventory | 4650.00*1 = 4650.00 |
| 38 | 1 | Car1 part2-C2-20150816-C1P2-070 < Car1 parts < Vehicle parts | Inventory | 4650.00*1 = 4650.00 |
| 39 | 1 | Car1 part2-C2-20150816-C1P2-071 < Car1 parts < Vehicle parts | Inventory | 4650.00*1 = 4650.00 |
| 40 | 1 | Car1 part2-C2-20150816-C1P2-072 < Car1 parts < Vehicle parts | Inventory | 4650.00*1 = 4650.00 |
| 41 | 1 | Car1 part3-C2-20150816-C1P3-070 < Car1 parts < Vehicle parts | Inventory | 3300.00*1 = 3300.00 |
| 42 | 1 | Car1 part3-C2-20150816-C1P3-071 < Car1 parts < Vehicle parts | Inventory | 3300.00*1 = 3300.00 |
| 43 | 1 | Car1 part3-C2-20150816-C1P3-072 < Car1 parts < Vehicle parts | Inventory | 3300.00*1 = 3300.00 |
| 44 | 1 | Car1 part3-C2-20150816-C1P3-073 < Car1 parts < Vehicle parts | Inventory | 3300.00*1 = 3300.00 |

| | | | | |
|---|---|---|---|---|
| 45 | 1 | Car1 part3-C2-20150816-C1P3-074 < Car1 parts < Vehicle parts | Inventory | 3300.00*1 = 3300.00 |
| 46 | 1 | Car2 part1-C2-20150902-C2P1-077 < Car2 parts < Vehicle parts | Inventory | 5100.00*1= 5100.00 |
| 47 | 1 | Car2 part1-C2-20150902-C2P1-078 < Car2 parts < Vehicle parts | Inventory | 5100.00*1= 5100.00 |
| 48 | 1 | Car2 part1-C2-20150902-C2P1-079 < Car2 parts < Vehicle parts | Inventory | 5100.00*1= 5100.00 |
| 49 | 1 | Car2 part1-C2-20150902-C2P1-080 < Car2 parts < Vehicle parts | Inventory | 5100.00*1= 5100.00 |
| 50 | 1 | Car2 part1-C2-20150902-C2P1-081 < Car2 parts < Vehicle parts | Inventory | 5100.00*1= 5100.00 |
| 51 | 1 | Car2 part2-C2-20150902-C2P2-081 < Car2 parts < Vehicle parts | Inventory | 4400.00*1 = 4400.00 |
| 52 | 1 | Car2 part2-C2-20150902-C2P2-082 < Car2 parts < Vehicle parts | Inventory | 4400.00*1 = 4400.00 |
| 53 | 1 | Car2 part2-C2-20150902-C2P2-083 < Car2 parts < Vehicle parts | Inventory | 4400.00*1 = 4400.00 |
| 54 | 1 | Car2 part2-C2-20150902-C2P2-084 < Car2 parts < Vehicle parts | Inventory | 4400.00*1 = 4400.00 |
| 55 | 1 | Car2 part2-C2-20150902-C2P2-085 < Car2 parts < Vehicle parts | Inventory | 4400.00*1 = 4400.00 |
| 56 | 1 | Car2 part3-C2-20150902-C2P3-083 < Car2 parts < Vehicle parts | Inventory | 3170.00*1 = 3170.00 |
| 57 | 1 | Car2 part3-C2-20150902-C2P3-084 < Car2 parts < Vehicle parts | Inventory | 3170.00*1 = 3170.00 |
| 58 | 1 | Car2 part3-C2-20150902-C2P3-085 < Car2 parts < Vehicle parts | Inventory | 3170.00*1 = 3170.00 |
| 59 | 1 | Car2 part3-C2-20150902-C2P3-086 < Car2 parts < Vehicle parts | Inventory | 3170.00*1 = 3170.00 |
| 60 | 1 | Car2 part3-C2-20150902-C2P3-087 < Car2 parts < Vehicle parts | Inventory | 3170.00*1 = 3170.00 |
| 61 | 1 | Car3 part1-C2-20150902-C3P1-084 < Car3 parts < Vehicle parts | Inventory | 4850.00*1 = 4850.00 |
| 62 | 1 | Car3 part1-C2-20150902-C3P1-085 < Car3 parts < Vehicle parts | Inventory | 4850.00*1 = 4850.00 |
| 63 | 1 | Car3 part1-C2-20150902-C3P1-086 < Car3 parts < Vehicle parts | Inventory | 4850.00*1 = 4850.00 |
| 64 | 1 | Car3 part1-C2-20150902-C3P1-087 < Car3 parts < Vehicle parts | Inventory | 4850.00*1 = 4850.00 |
| 65 | 1 | Car3 part1-C2-20150902-C3P1-088 < Car3 parts < Vehicle parts | Inventory | 4850.00*1 = 4850.00 |
| 66 | 1 | Car3 part2-C2-20150902-C3P2-087 < Car3 parts < Vehicle parts | Inventory | 4150.00*1 = 4150.00 |
| 67 | 1 | Car3 part2-C2-20150902-C3P2-088 < Car3 parts < Vehicle parts | Inventory | 4150.00*1 = 4150.00 |
| 68 | 1 | Car3 part2-C2-20150902-C3P2-089 < Car3 parts < Vehicle parts | Inventory | 4150.00*1 = 4150.00 |
| 69 | 1 | Car3 part2-C2-20150902-C3P2-090 < Car3 parts < Vehicle parts | Inventory | 4150.00*1 = 4150.00 |
| 70 | 1 | Car3 part2-C2-20150902-C3P2-091 < Car3 parts < Vehicle parts | Inventory | 4150.00*1 = 4150.00 |
| 71 | 1 | Car3 part3-C2-20150902-C3P3-094 < Car3 parts < Vehicle parts | Inventory | 3050.00*1 = 3050.00 |
| 72 | 1 | Car3 part3-C2-20150902-C3P3-095 < Car3 parts < Vehicle parts | Inventory | 3050.00*1 = 3050.00 |
| 73 | 1 | Car3 part3-C2-20150902-C3P3-096 < Car3 parts < Vehicle parts | Inventory | 3050.00*1 = 3050.00 |
| 74 | 1 | Car3 part3-C2-20150902-C3P3-097 < Car3 parts < Vehicle parts | Inventory | 3050.00*1 = 3050.00 |
| 75 | 1 | Car3 part3-C2-20150902-C3P3-098 < Car3 parts < Vehicle parts | Inventory | 3050.00*1 = 3050.00 |
| 76 | 1 | Computer server1 part1-C2-20150709-COMS1P1-10T < Computer server parts < Computer parts | Inventory | 390.00*10 = 3900.00 |

| 77 | 1 | Computer server1 part2-C2-20150709-COMS1P2-10T < Computer server parts < Computer parts | Inventory | 260.00*10 = 2600.00 |
|---|---|---|---|---|
| 78 | 1 | Computer server2 part1-C2-20150709-COMS2P1-10T < Computer server parts < Computer parts | Inventory | 350.00*10 = 3500.00 |
| 79 | 1 | Computer server2 part2-C2-20150709-COMS2P2-10T < Computer server parts < Computer parts | Inventory | 250.00*10 = 2500.00 |
| 80 | 1 | Computer1 part1-C2-20150715-COM1P1-20T < Computer parts | Inventory | 235.00*20 = 4700.00 |
| 81 | 1 | Computer1 part2-C2-20150715-COM1P2-20T < Computer parts | Inventory | 202.00*20 = 4040.00 |
| 82 | 1 | Computer2 part1-C2-20150715-COM2P1-20T < Computer parts | Inventory | 208.00*20 = 4160.00 |
| 83 | 1 | Computer2 part2-C2-20150715-COM2P2-20T < Computer parts | Inventory | 189.00*20 = 3780.00 |
| 84 | 1 | Computer3 part1-C2-20150715-COM3P1-20T < Computer parts | Inventory | 182.00*20 = 3640.00 |
| 85 | 1 | Computer3 part2-C2-20150715-COM3P2-20T < Computer parts | Inventory | 169.00*20 = 3380.00 |
| 86 | 1 | Computer4 part1-C2-20150715-COM4P1-20T < Computer parts | Inventory | 162.00*20 = 3240.00 |
| 87 | 1 | Computer4 part2-C2-20150715-COM4P2-20T < Computer parts | Inventory | 156.00*20 = 3120.00 |

Figure 2.4-13   Changes of Multi-Subaccount Names Table

Before entering the dynamic accounting equation on January 1, 2016 into the database dcj208, I first enter two initialization sub-equations.

Account payable (2): 0 = Share capital (3): 0

0 = Sales (4): 0 – Cost of goods sold (5):0

All converting transaction sub-equations can be designed and written as the followings.

- I build a transaction sub-equation for the "Account receivable" and the "Account payable" accounts. The transaction sub-equation includes the "Account receivable" account with the Order 36 to the Order 41, the "Account payable" account with the Order 129 to the Order 132, and the part of the "Share capital" account with the Order 152. Because the balances of the "Account receivable" with the Order 41 is zero, the first transaction sub-equation is:

Account receivable (1): 500 + Account receivable (1): 400 + Account receivable (1): 13400 + Account receivable (1): 600 + Account receivable (1): 250 = Account payable (2): 600 + Account payable (2): 6000 + Account payable (2): 500 +

Account payable (2): 300 + Share capital (3): 7750

After entering this transaction, the new balance of the "Share capital" account with the Order 152 is $82,250 (= $90,000 - $7,750).

- The transaction sub-equation includes the part of the "Cash" account with the Order 1, the "Cash" account with the Order 2 to the Order 6, the rest ($82,250) of the "Share capital" account with the Order 152, the "Share capital" account with the Order 153 and the Order 154, and the "Notes payable" account with the Order 149 to the Order 151. The second transaction sub-equation is:

Cash (1): 82250 + Cash (1): 54000 + Cash (1): 36000 + Cash (1): 140000 + Cash (1): 250000 + Cash (1): 240000 = Share capital (3): 82250 + Share capital (3): 54000 + Share capital (3): 36000 + Notes payable (2): 140000 + Notes payable (2): 250000 + Notes payable (2): 240000

After entering this transaction, the new balance of the "Cash" account with the Order 1 is $7,750 (= $90,000 - $82,250).

- The transaction sub-equation includes the "Cash" account with the Order 7 to the Order 13 and the "Bonds payable" account with the Order 137 to the Order 142. Because the balance of the "Cash" with the Order 7 is zero, the third transaction sub-equation is:

Cash (1): 8000 + Cash (1): 4000 + Cash (1): 2000 + Cash (1): 1000 + Cash (1): 3000 + Cash (1): 5000 = Bonds payable (2): 8000 + Bonds payable (2): 4000 + Bonds payable (2): 2000 + Bonds payable (2): 1000 + Bonds payable (2): 3000 + Bonds payable (2): 5000

- The transaction sub-equation includes the "Cash" account with the Order 14 to the Order 19 and the "Bonds payable" account with the Order 143 to the Order 148. The fourth transaction sub-equation is:

Cash (1): 2000 + Cash (1): 3000 + Cash (1): 2000 + Cash (1): 3000 + Cash (1): 5000 + Cash (1): 2000 = Bonds payable (2): 2000 + Bonds payable (2): 3000 + Bonds payable (2): 2000 + Bonds payable (2): 3000 + Bonds payable (2): 5000 + Bonds payable (2): 2000

- The transaction sub-equation includes the rest ($7,750) of the "Cash" account with the Order 1, the "Cash" account with the Order 20 and the Order 21, the part of the "Cash" account with the Order 28, and the "Inventory" account with the Order 42 to the Order 49. The fifth transaction sub-equation is:

Cash (1): 7750 + Cash (1): 504 + Cash (1): 242 + Cash (1): -24756 + Inventory (1): 1000 + Inventory (1): 3200 + Inventory (1): 160 + Inventory (1): 3000 + Inventory (1): 1500 + Inventory (1): 3000 + Inventory (1): 2000 + Inventory (1): 2400 = 0

After entering this transaction, the new balance of the "Cash" account with the Order 28 is -$166,615.25 (= -$191,371.25 + $24,756).

- The transaction sub-equation includes the "Cash" account with the Order 22 to the Order 27, the "Vehicle" account with the Order 117 to the Order 119, and the "Computer" account with the Order 123 to the Order 125. The sixth transaction sub-equation is:

Cash (1): -45000 + Cash (1): -40000 + Cash (1): -40000 + Cash (1): -2800 + Cash (1): -1600 + Cash (1): -1500 + Vehicle (1): 45000 + Vehicle (1): 40000 + Vehicle (1): 40000 + Computer (1): 2800 + Computer (1): 1600 + Computer (1): 1500 = 0

- The transaction sub-equation includes the part of the "Cash" account with the Order 28 and the "Inventory" account with the Order 50 to the Order 60. The seventh transaction sub-equation is:

Cash (1): -18100 + Inventory (1): 400 + Inventory (1): 1500 + Inventory (1): 2500

+ Inventory (1): 2500 + Inventory (1): 3500 + Inventory (1): 1200 + Inventory (1): 1200 + Inventory (1): 650+ Inventory (1): 1250 + Inventory (1): 1800 + Inventory (1): 1600 = 0

After entering this transaction, the new balance of the "Cash" account with the Order 28 is -$148,515.25 (= -$166,615.25 + $18,100).

- The transaction sub-equation includes the part of the "Cash" account with the Order 29, the "Cash" account with the Order 32 to the Order 34, and the "Inventory" account with the Order 61 to the Order 68. The eighth transaction sub-equation is:

Cash (1): -160,950 + Cash (1): -15000 + Cash (1): -8000 + Cash (1): -6000 + Inventory (1): 28000 + Inventory (1): 24750 + Inventory (1): 18750 + Inventory (1): 27500 + Inventory (1): 23300 + Inventory (1): 17500 + Inventory (1): 26900 + Inventory (1): 23250 = 0

After dividing this transaction sub-equation, I get the following transactions sub-equation respectively:

Cash (1): 1000 + Cash (1): -15000 + Cash (1): -8000 + Cash (1): -6000 + Inventory (1): 5600 + Inventory (1): 5600 + Inventory (1): 5600 + Inventory (1): 5600 + Inventory (1): 5600 = 0

Cash (1): -43500 + Inventory (1): 4950 + Inventory (1): 4950 + Inventory (1): 4950 + Inventory (1): 4950 + Inventory (1): 4950 + Inventory (1): 3750 + Inventory (1): 3750 + Inventory (1): 3750 + Inventory (1): 3750 + Inventory (1): 3750 = 0

Cash (1): -50800 + Inventory (1): 5500 + Inventory (1): 5500 + Inventory (1): 5500 + Inventory (1): 5500 + Inventory (1): 5500 + Inventory (1): 4660 + Inventory (1): 4660 + Inventory (1): 4660 + Inventory (1): 4660 + Inventory (1): 4660 = 0

Cash (1): -44400 + Inventory (1): 3500 + Inventory (1): 3500 + Inventory (1): 3500 + Inventory (1): 3500 + Inventory (1): 3500 + Inventory (1): 5380 + Inventory (1): 5380 + Inventory (1): 5380 + Inventory (1): 5380 + Inventory (1): 5380 = 0

Cash (1): -23250 + Inventory (1): 4650 + Inventory (1): 4650 + Inventory (1): 4650 + Inventory (1): 4650 + Inventory (1): 4650 = 0

After entering these transaction, the new balance of the "Cash" account with the Order 29 is -$29,839.41 (= -$190,789.41 - $1,000 + $43,500 + $50,800 + $44,400 + $23,250).

- The transaction sub-equation includes the part of the "Cash" account with the Order 28, the rest (-$29,839.41) of the "Cash" account with the Order 29, and the "Inventory" account with the Order 69 to the Order 75. The ninth transaction sub-equation is:

Cash (1): -110260.59 + Cash (1): -29839.41 + Inventory (1): 16500 + Inventory (1): 25500 + Inventory (1): 22000 + Inventory (1): 15850 + Inventory (1): 24250 + Inventory (1): 20750 + Inventory (1): 15250 = 0

After dividing this transaction sub-equation, I get the following transactions sub-equation respectively:

Cash (1): -12160.59 + Cash (1): -29839.41 + Inventory (1): 3300 + Inventory (1): 3300 + Inventory (1): 3300 + Inventory (1): 3300 + Inventory (1): 3300 + Inventory (1): 5100 + Inventory (1): 5100 + Inventory (1): 5100 + Inventory (1): 5100 + Inventory (1): 5100 = 0

Cash (1): -37850 + Inventory (1): 4400 + Inventory (1): 4400 + Inventory (1): 4400 + Inventory (1): 4400 + Inventory (1): 4400 + Inventory (1): 3170 + Inventory (1): 3170 + Inventory (1): 3170 + Inventory (1): 3170 + Inventory (1):

3170 = 0

Cash (1): -45000 + Inventory (1): 4850 + Inventory (1): 4850 + Inventory (1): 4850 + Inventory (1): 4850 + Inventory (1): 4850 + Inventory (1): 4150 + Inventory (1): 4150 + Inventory (1): 4150 + Inventory (1): 4150 = 0

Cash (1): -15250 + Inventory (1): 3050 + Inventory (1): 3050 + Inventory (1): 3050 + Inventory (1): 3050 + Inventory (1): 3050 + Inventory (1): 3050 = 0

After entering this transaction, the new balance of the "Cash" account with the Order 28 is -$38,254.66 (= -$148,515.25 + $12,160.59 + $37,850 + $45,000 + $15,250).

- The transaction sub-equation includes the part of the "Cash" account with the Order 28 and the "Inventory" account with the Order 76 to the Order 85. The tenth transaction sub-equation is:

Cash (1): -36200 + Inventory (1): 3900 + Inventory (1): 2600 + Inventory (1): 3500 + Inventory (1): 2500 + Inventory (1): 4700 + Inventory (1): 4040 + Inventory (1): 4160 + Inventory (1): 3780 + Inventory (1): 3640 + Inventory (1): 3380 = 0

After entering this transaction, the new balance of the "Cash" account with the Order 28 is -$2,054.66 (= -$38,254.66 + $36,200).

- The transaction sub-equation includes the rest (-$2,054.66) of the "Cash" account with the Order 28, the part of the "Cash" account with the Order 30, the "Inventory" account with the Order 86 and the Order 87, and the "Working-in-process inventory" account with the Order 88 to the Order 95. The eleventh transaction sub-equation is:

Cash (1): -2054.66 + Cash (1): -158059.44 + Inventory (1): 3240 + Inventory (1): 3120 + Working-in-process inventory (1): 23546.65 + Working-in-process inventory (1): 21183.90 + Working-in-process inventory (1): 15062.55 + Working-in-process inventory (1): 23421.25 + Working-in-process inventory (1): 14837.95 + Working-in-process inventory (1): 13936.30 + Working-in-process inventory (1): 22971.15 + Working-in-process inventory (1): 18794.35 = 0

After entering this transaction, the new balance of the "Cash" account with the Order 30 is -$31,914.08 (= -$189,973.52 + $158,059.44).

- The transaction sub-equation includes the rest (-$31,914.08) of the "Cash" account with the Order 30, the "Cash" account with the Order 31, the "Supplies" account with the Order 35, the "Working-in-process inventory" account with the Order 96 to the Order 102, the "Accumulated amortization: Vehicle" account with the Order 120, and the part of the "Accumulated amortization: Vehicle" account with the Order 121. The twelfth transaction sub-equation is:

Cash (1): -31914.08 + Cash (1): -71318.63 + Supplies (1): 192.45 + Working-in-process inventory (1): 12823.85 + Working-in-process inventory (1): 22413.30 + Working-in-process inventory (1): 17887.05 + Working-in-process inventory (1): 12349.40 + Working-in-process inventory (1): 25065.36 + Working-in-process inventory (1): 19964.70 + Working-in-process inventory (1): 13711.26 + Accumulated amortization: Vehicle (1): -18750 + Accumulated amortization: Vehicle (1): -2424.66 = 0

After entering this transaction, the new balance of the "Accumulated amortization: Vehicle" account with the Order 121 is -$10,908.67 (= -$13,333.33 + $2,424.66).

- The transaction sub-equation includes the rest (-$10,908.67) of the "Accumulated amortization: Vehicle" account with the Order 121, the "Accumulated amortization: Vehicle" account with the Order 122, the "Working-in-process inventory" account with the Order 103 to the Order 110, the part of the "Bonds" account with the Order 115. The thirteenth transaction sub-equation is:

Accumulated amortization: Vehicle (1): -10908.67 + Accumulated amortization: Vehicle (1): -12000 + Working-in-process inventory (1): 1974 + Working-in-process inventory (1): 1116 + Working-in-process inventory (1): 1710 + Working-in-process inventory (1): 1050 + Working-in-process inventory (1): 4170 + Working-in-process inventory (1): 3644 + Working-in-process inventory (1): 3576 + Working-in-process inventory (1): 3158 + Bonds (1): 2510.67 = 0

After entering this transaction, the new balance of the "Bonds" account with the Order 115 is $5,489.33 (= $8,000 - $2,510.67).

- The transaction sub-equation includes the "Working-in-process inventory" account with the Order 111, the part of the "Bonds" account with the Order 115, and the "Accumulated amortization: Computer" account with the Order 126 and the Order 128. The fourteenth transaction sub-equation is:

Working-in-process inventory (1): $3004 + Bonds (1): 1175.16 + Accumulated amortization: Computer (1): -1983.33 + Accumulated amortization: Computer (1): -1133.33 + Accumulated amortization: Computer (1): -1062.50 = 0

After entering this transaction, the new balance of the "Bonds" account with the Order 115 is $4,314.17 (= $5,489.33 - $1,175.16).

- The transaction sub-equation includes the rest ($4,314.17) of the "Bonds" account with the Order 115, the "Bonds" account with the Order 116, the "Working-in-process inventory" account with the Order 112 to 114, and the "Retained earnings" account with the balance $18028.17. The fifteenth transaction sub-equation is:

Bonds (1): 4314.17 + Bonds (1): 6000 + Working-in-process inventory (1): 2718 + Working-in-process inventory (1): 2564 + Working-in-process inventory (1): 2432 = Retained earnings (Conversion) (3): 18,028.17

After completing this transaction, the dynamic accounting equation of the Company2 on December 31, 2015 has entered into the database dcj208.

## 2.4.4.2 Brief Summary of the Company2

The Figure 2.4-14 on the next page shows the partial information of inventory purchased or inventory sold by other social members in the public database dcj200.

```
SQLQuery1.sql - LIU...SS.dcj200 (sa (55))*  ×
   use dcj200
   select sum(amount) as sum0 from InventoryByMembers where Recorder='88-654307'
   and TransDate between '2015-01-01' and '2015-12-31'
   select * from InventoryByMembers where Recorder='88-654307' and TransDate between '2015-01-01' and '2015-12-31'
100 %  ▾
```

Results  Messages

| | sum0 |
|---|---|
| 1 | -406970.00 |

| | IDM | Amount | Symbol | MultiSubaccount | Recorder | TransDate | Unit |
|---|---|---|---|---|---|---|---|
| 83 | Cash paym | -4660.00 | n | Truck2 part2-C2-20150728-T2P2-054 < Truck2 parts < Vehicle parts | 88-654307 | 2015-12-31 | -1 |
| 84 | Cash paym | -4660.00 | n | Truck2 part2-C2-20150728-T2P2-055 < Truck2 parts < Vehicle parts | 88-654307 | 2015-12-31 | -1 |
| 85 | Cash paym | -4660.00 | n | Truck2 part2-C2-20150728-T2P2-056 < Truck2 parts < Vehicle parts | 88-654307 | 2015-12-31 | -1 |
| 86 | Cash paym | -4660.00 | n | Truck2 part2-C2-20150728-T2P2-057 < Truck2 parts < Vehicle parts | 88-654307 | 2015-12-31 | -1 |
| 87 | Cash paym | -3500.00 | n | Truck2 part3-C2-20150728-T2P3-053 < Truck2 parts < Vehicle parts | 88-654307 | 2015-12-31 | -1 |
| 88 | Cash paym | -3500.00 | n | Truck2 part3-C2-20150728-T2P3-054 < Truck2 parts < Vehicle parts | 88-654307 | 2015-12-31 | -1 |
| 89 | Cash paym | -3500.00 | n | Truck2 part3-C2-20150728-T2P3-055 < Truck2 parts < Vehicle parts | 88-654307 | 2015-12-31 | -1 |
| 90 | Cash paym | -3500.00 | n | Truck2 part3-C2-20150728-T2P3-055 < Truck2 parts < Vehicle parts | 88-654307 | 2015-12-31 | -1 |
| 91 | Cash paym | -3500.00 | n | Truck2 part3-C2-20150728-T2P3-057 < Truck2 parts < Vehicle parts | 88-654307 | 2015-12-31 | -1 |
| 92 | Cash paym | -5380.00 | n | Car1 part1-C2-20150816-C1P1-061 < Car1 parts < Vehicle parts | 88-654307 | 2015-12-31 | -1 |
| 93 | Cash paym | -5380.00 | n | Car1 part1-C2-20150816-C1P1-062 < Car1 parts < Vehicle parts | 88-654307 | 2015-12-31 | -1 |
| 94 | Cash paym | -5380.00 | n | Car1 part1-C2-20150816-C1P1-063 < Car1 parts < Vehicle parts | 88-654307 | 2015-12-31 | -1 |
| 95 | Cash paym | -5380.00 | n | Car1 part1-C2-20150816-C1P1-064 < Car1 parts < Vehicle parts | 88-654307 | 2015-12-31 | -1 |
| 96 | Cash paym | -5380.00 | n | Car1 part1-C2-20150816-C1P1-065 < Car1 parts < Vehicle parts | 88-654307 | 2015-12-31 | -1 |
| 97 | 88-654307 | 3500.00 | e | Truck2 part3-C2-20150728-T2P3-055 < Truck2 parts < Vehicle parts | 88-654307 | 2015-12-31 | 1 |
| 98 | 88-654307 | -3500.00 | e | Truck2 part3-C2-20150728-T2P3-056 < Truck2 parts < Vehicle parts | 88-654307 | 2015-12-31 | -1 |
| 99 | Cash paym | -4650.00 | n | Car1 part2-C2-20150816-C1P2-068 < Car1 parts < Vehicle parts | 88-654307 | 2015-12-31 | -1 |
| 100 | Cash paym | -4650.00 | n | Car1 part2-C2-20150816-C1P2-069 < Car1 parts < Vehicle parts | 88-654307 | 2015-12-31 | -1 |
| 101 | Cash paym | -4650.00 | n | Car1 part2-C2-20150816-C1P2-070 < Car1 parts < Vehicle parts | 88-654307 | 2015-12-31 | -1 |
| 102 | Cash paym | -4650.00 | n | Car1 part2-C2-20150816-C1P2-071 < Car1 parts < Vehicle parts | 88-654307 | 2015-12-31 | -1 |
| 103 | Cash paym | -4650.00 | n | Car1 part2-C2-20150816-C1P2-072 < Car1 parts < Vehicle parts | 88-654307 | 2015-12-31 | -1 |
| 104 | Cash paym | -3300.00 | n | Car1 part3-C2-20150816-C1P3-070 < Car1 parts < Vehicle parts | 88-654307 | 2015-12-31 | -1 |
| 105 | Cash paym | -3300.00 | n | Car1 part3-C2-20150816-C1P3-071 < Car1 parts < Vehicle parts | 88-654307 | 2015-12-31 | -1 |
| 106 | Cash paym | -3300.00 | n | Car1 part3-C2-20150816-C1P3-072 < Car1 parts < Vehicle parts | 88-654307 | 2015-12-31 | -1 |
| 107 | Cash paym | -3300.00 | n | Car1 part3-C2-20150816-C1P3-073 < Car1 parts < Vehicle parts | 88-654307 | 2015-12-31 | -1 |
| 108 | Cash paym | -3300.00 | n | Car1 part3-C2-20150816-C1P3-074 < Car1 parts < Vehicle parts | 88-654307 | 2015-12-31 | -1 |

Query executed successfully.                                                    LIU\SQLEX

Figure 2.4-14   Company2 Inventory Purchased or Sold by Other Members

## 2.4.5 Sample of the Company3

The Company3 has total share capital $220,000 and three shareholders of the individual A7, A17, and A19. Their percentages of the share capital are 30%, 30%, and 40% respectively. The Figure 2.4-15 shows its product names, costs, and sale prices.

| Order | Product (the Lowest-level Subaccount) Names | Multi-subaccount Names | Costs | Sale Prices |
|---|---|---|---|---|
| 1 | Inven111 | Inven111 < Inven11 < Inven1 | 6.00 | 10.00 |

| 2 | Inven112 | Inven112 < Inven11 < Inven1 | 25.00 | 40.00 |
|---|---|---|---|---|
| 3 | Inven121 | Inven121 < Inven12 < Inven1 | 0.40 | 0.80 |
| 4 | Inven122 | Inven122 < Inven12 < Inven1 | 30.00 | 50.00 |
| 5 | Inven21 | Inven21 < Inven2 | 20.00 | 30.00 |
| 6 | Inven221 | Inven221 < Inven22 < Inven2 | 20.00 | 30.00 |
| 7 | Inven222 | Inven222 < Inven22 < Inven2 | 27.00 | 50.00 |
| 8 | PPUK parts | PPUK parts < ASD parts < Inven2 | 22.40 | 40.00 |
| 9 | PPGH parts | PPGH parts < ASD parts < Inven2 | 1.00 | 2.00 |
| 10 | Inven51 | Inven51 < Inven5 | 6.00 | 10.00 |
| 11 | Inven52 | Inven52 < Inven5 | 30.00 | 50.00 |
| 12 | Inven531 | Inven531 < Inven53 < Inven5 | 15.00 | 25.00 |
| 13 | Inven532 | Inven532 < Inven53 < Inven5 | 21.00 | 35.00 |
| 14 | Inven541 | Inven541 < Inven54 < Inven5 | 7.20 | 12.00 |
| 15 | Inven542 | Inven542 < Inven54 < Inven5 | 7.50 | 15.00 |
| 16 | Inven611 | Inven611 < Inven61 < Inven6 | 4.00 | 6.50 |
| 17 | Inven612 | Inven612 < Inven61 < Inven6 | 7.50 | 12.50 |
| 18 | Inven621 | Inven621 < Inven62 < Inven6 | 10.00 | 18.00 |
| 19 | Inven63 | Inven63 < Inven6 | 8.00 | 16.00 |
| 20 | Inven711 | Inven711 < Inven71 < Inven7 | 21.60 | 36.00 |
| 21 | Inven712 | Inven712 < Inven71 < Inven7 | 18.60 | 31.00 |
| 22 | Inven721 | Inven721 < Inven72 < Inven7 | 12.50 | 22.00 |
| 23 | Inven722 | Inven722 < Inven72 < Inven7 | 12.00 | 20.00 |
| 24 | Inven731 | Inven731 < Inven73 < Inven7 | 10.80 | 18.00 |
| 25 | Inven732 | Inven732 < Inven73 < Inven7 | 9.60 | 16.00 |
| 26 | Inven811 | Inven811 < Inven81 < Inven8 | 15.00 | 25.00 |
| 27 | Inven812 | Inven812 < Inven81 < Inven8 | 14.40 | 24.00 |
| 28 | Inven813 | Inven813 < Inven81 < Inven8 | 13.80 | 23.00 |
| 29 | Inven82 | Inven82 < Inven8 | 12.00 | 20.00 |
| 30 | Inven831 | Inven831 < Inven83 < Inven8 | 10.80 | 18.00 |
| 31 | Inven832 | Inven832 < Inven83 < Inven8 | 9.60 | 16.00 |

Figure 2.4-15   Company3 Products and Sale Prices Table

## 2.4.5.1 Conversion of the Company3

The Company3 will convert to the MathAccounting software on January 1, 2016. The Figure 2.4-16 and the Figure 2.4-17 show the converting reference table and the multi-subaccount names table respectively.

| Order | Class | Account Name (**Subtotal Name**) | Balance | Row |
|---|---|---|---|---|
| **1** | **1** | **(Current assets)** | - | **103** |

| 2 | 1 | Cash | 10660.36 | 104 |
|---|---|---|---|---|
| 3 | 1 | Supplies | 209.88 | 106 |
| 4 | 1 | Account receivable | 17450.00 | 108 |
| 5 | 1 | Inventory | 343370.00 | 110 |
| 6 | 1 | Working-in-process inventory | 365110.00 | 112 |
| **7** | **1** | **(Long term investments)** | - | **141** |
| 8 | 1 | Bonds | 20000.00 | 142 |
| **9** | **1** | **(Equipment)** | - | **171** |
| 10 | 1 | Vehicle | 246000.00 | 172 |
| 11 | 1 | Accumulated amortization: Vehicle | -103466.67 | 173 |
| 12 | 1 | Computer | 5400.00 | 174 |
| 13 | 1 | Accumulated amortization: Computer | -4275.00 | 175 |
| **14** | **2** | **(Current liabilities)** | - | **203** |
| 15 | 2 | Account payable | 3900.00 | 204 |
| 16 | 2 | Accrued interest payable | 0 | 206 |
| 17 | 2 | Tax payable | 0 | 208 |
| **18** | **2** | **(Long term liabilities)** | - | **251** |
| 19 | 2 | Bonds payable | 80000.00 | 252 |
| 20 | 2 | Note payable | 580000.00 | 254 |
| **21** | **3** | **(Owners' capital)** | - | **303** |
| 22 | 3 | Share capital | 220000.00 | 304 |
| 23 | 3 | Retained earnings (Conversion) | 16558.57 | 306 |
| **24** | **4** | **(Revenues)** | - | **403** |
| 25 | 4 | Sales | | 404 |
| **26** | **5** | **(Cost)** | - | **431** |
| 27 | 5 | Cost of goods sold | | 432 |
| **28** | **5** | **(Operating and administrative expenses)** | - | **453** |
| 29 | 5 | Travelling expenses | 0 | 454 |
| 30 | 5 | Other expenses | 0 | 455 |
| 31 | 5 | Salary expenses | 0 | 456 |
| 32 | 5 | Cost of goods sold | 0 | 457 |
| 33 | 5 | Bond interest expenses | 0 | 458 |
| 34 | 5 | Note interest expenses | 0 | 460 |
| 35 | 5 | Amortization expenses | 0 | 462 |
| **36** | **4** | **(Other income)** | - | **475** |
| 37 | 4 | Investment incomes | | 476 |
| 38 | 4 | Deposits interest incomes | 0 | 478 |
| **39** | **5** | **(Tax)** | - | **600** |
| 40 | 5 | Tax expenses | 0 | 602 |

Figure 2.4-16   Company3 Converting Reference Table

| Order | Class | Multi-subaccount Name | Parent Name | Lowest Subaccount Balance |
|---|---|---|---|---|
| 1 | 1 | 909876507-i-owners < Cash receipts from owners < Financial activities | Cash | 66000.00 |
| 2 | 1 | 909876517-i-owners < Cash receipts from owners < Financial activities | Cash | 66000.00 |
| 3 | 1 | 909876519-i-owners < Cash receipts from owners < Financial activities | Cash | 88000.00 |
| 4 | 1 | 88-654304-i-note13 < Cash receipts from banks < Financial activities | Cash | 200000.00 |
| 5 | 1 | 88-654305-i-note23 < Cash receipts from banks < Financial activities | Cash | 180000.00 |
| 6 | 1 | 88-654305-i-note24 < Cash receipts from banks < Financial activities | Cash | 200000.00 |
| 7 | 1 | 88-654306-c-operating < Cash receipts from customers < Operating activities | Cash | 1000.00 |
| 8 | 1 | 88-654307-c-operating < Cash receipts from customers < Operating activities | Cash | 15000.00 |
| 9 | 1 | 909876501-i-bond51 < Cash receipts from issued bonds < Financial activities | Cash | 6000.00 |
| 10 | 1 | 909876502-i-bond51 < Cash receipts from issued bonds < Financial activities | Cash | 4000.00 |
| 11 | 1 | 909876503-i-bond51 < Cash receipts from issued bonds < Financial activities | Cash | 7000.00 |
| 12 | 1 | 909876507-i-bond51 < Cash receipts from issued bonds < Financial activities | Cash | 6000.00 |
| 13 | 1 | 909876508-i-bond51 < Cash receipts from issued bonds < Financial activities | Cash | 7000.00 |
| 14 | 1 | 909876509-i-bond51 < Cash receipts from issued bonds < Financial activities | Cash | 5000.00 |
| 15 | 1 | 909876511-i-bond51 < Cash receipts from issued bonds < Financial activities | Cash | 4000.00 |
| 16 | 1 | 909876512-i-bond51 < Cash receipts from issued bonds < Financial activities | Cash | 8000.00 |
| 17 | 1 | 909876514-i-bond51 < Cash receipts from issued bonds < Financial activities | Cash | 5000.00 |
| 18 | 1 | 909876516-i-bond51 < Cash receipts from issued bonds < Financial activities | Cash | 7000.00 |
| 19 | 1 | 909876517-i-bond51 < Cash receipts from issued bonds < Financial activities | Cash | 5000.00 |
| 20 | 1 | 909876518-i-bond51 < Cash receipts from issued bonds < Financial activities | Cash | 6000.00 |
| 21 | 1 | 909876521-i-bond51 < Cash receipts from issued bonds < Financial activities | Cash | 4000.00 |
| 22 | 1 | 909876522-i-bond51 < Cash receipts from issued bonds < Financial activities | Cash | 6000.00 |
| 23 | 1 | 88-654304-c-interest of investment bond11 < Cash receipts from investments < Investing activities | Cash | 613.33 |
| 24 | 1 | 88-654305-c-interest of investment bond21 < Cash receipts from investments < Investing activities | Cash | 820.00 |
| 25 | 1 | 88-654306-t-truck1 < Cash payments for machinery < Operating activities | Cash | -90000.00 |
| 26 | 1 | 88-654306-t-truck2 < Cash payments for machinery < Operating activities | Cash | -80000.00 |
| 27 | 1 | 88-654306-t-car2 < Cash payments for machinery < Operating activities | Cash | -76000.00 |
| 28 | 1 | 88-654306-t-computer server2 < Cash payments for machinery < Operating activities | Cash | -2700.00 |
| 29 | 1 | 88-654306-t-computer3 < Cash payments for machinery < Operating activities | Cash | -1400.00 |
| 30 | 1 | 88-654306-t-computer4 < Cash payments for machinery < Operating activities | Cash | -1300.00 |
| 31 | 1 | Cash payments for operating expenses < Operating activities | Cash | -190377.25 |

| 32 | 1 | Cash payments for operating expenses < Operating activities | Cash | -189189.46 |
|---|---|---|---|---|
| 33 | 1 | Cash payments for operating expenses < Operating activities | Cash | -184352.55 |
| 34 | 1 | 88-654303-n-tax < Cash payments for operating expenses < Operating activities | Cash | -51453.71 |
| 35 | 1 | Cash payments to suppliers<Operating activities | Cash | 0 |
| 36 | 1 | 88-654304-n-investment bond11 < Cash payments for investments < Investing activities | Cash | -8000.00 |
| 37 | 1 | 88-654305-n-investment bond21 < Cash payments for investments < Investing activities | Cash | -12000.00 |
| 38 | 1 | n | Supplies | 209.88 |
| 39 | 1 | 123456789 | Account receivable | 200.00 |
| 40 | 1 | 123456787 | Account receivable | 300.00 |
| 41 | 1 | 123456784 | Account receivable | 10600.00 |
| 42 | 1 | 123456783 | Account receivable | 6000.00 |
| 43 | 1 | 123456781 | Account receivable | 150.00 |
| 44 | 1 | 123456780 | Account receivable | 200.00 |
| 45 | 1 | Inven111-C3-20150922-In111-1000T < Inven11 < Inven1 | Inventory | $6*1000 = 6000.00$ |
| 46 | 1 | Inven112-C3-20150922-In112-800T < Inven11 < Inven1 | Inventory | $25*800 = 20000.00$ |
| 47 | 1 | Inven121-C3-20150922-In121-20000T < Inven12 < Inven1 | Inventory | $0.40*20000 = 8000.00$ |
| 48 | 1 | Inven122-C3-20150922-In122-1000T < Inven12 < Inven1 | Inventory | $30*1000 = 30000.00$ |
| 49 | 1 | Inven21-C3-20150922-In21-1250T < Inven2 | Inventory | $20*1250= 25000.00$ |
| 50 | 1 | Inven221-C3-20150922-In221-750T < Inven22 < Inven2 | Inventory | $20*750 = 15000.00$ |
| 51 | 1 | Inven222-C3-20150922-In222-400T < Inven22 < Inven2 | Inventory | $27*400 = 10800.00$ |
| 52 | 1 | PPUK parts-C3-20150922-PU-500T < ASD parts < Inven2 | Inventory | $22.4*500 =  11200.00$ |
| 53 | 1 | PPGH parts-C3-20150922-PG-1600T < ASD parts < Inven2 | Inventory | $1.00*1600 = 1600.00$ |
| 54 | 1 | Inven51-C3-20150922-In51-1000T < Inven5 | Inventory | $6*1000 = 6000.00$ |
| 55 | 1 | Inven52-C3-20150922-In52-500T < Inven5 | Inventory | $30*500 = 15000.00$ |
| 56 | 1 | Inven531-C3-20150922-In531-1000T < Inven53 < Inven5 | Inventory | $15*1000 = 15000.00$ |
| 57 | 1 | Inven532-C3-20150922-In532-1000T < Inven53 < Inven5 | Inventory | $21*1000 = 21000.00$ |
| 58 | 1 | Inven541-C3-20150922-In541-1000T < Inven54 < Inven5 | Inventory | $7.2*1000 = 7200.00$ |
| 59 | 1 | Inven542-C3-20150922-In542-1000T < Inven54 < Inven5 | Inventory | $7.5*1000 = 7500.00$ |
| 60 | 1 | Inven611-C3-20151003-In611-1300T < Inven61 < Inven6 | Inventory | $4*1300 = 5200.00$ |
| 61 | 1 | Inven612-C3-20151003-In612-1100T < Inven61 < Inven6 | Inventory | $7.5*1000 = 7500.00$ |
| 62 | 1 | Inven621-C3-20151003-In621-900T < Inven62 < Inven6 | Inventory | $10*900 = 9000.00$ |
| 63 | 1 | Inven63-C3-20151003-In63-1000T < Inven6 | Inventory | $8*1000 = 8000.00$ |
| 64 | 1 | Inven711-C3-20151003-In711-500T < Inven71 < Inven7 | Inventory | $21.60*500 = 10800.00$ |
| 65 | 1 | Inven712-C3-20151003-In712-100T < Inven71 < Inven7 | Inventory | $18.60*100 = 1860.00$ |
| 66 | 1 | Inven721-C3-20151003-In721-744T < Inven72 < Inven7 | Inventory | $12.50*744 = 9300.00$ |

| 67 | 1 | Inven722-C3-20151003-In722-600T < Inven72 < Inven7 | Inventory | 12.00*600 = 7200.00 |
|---|---|---|---|---|
| 68 | 1 | Inven731-C3-20151003-In731-600T < Inven73 < Inven7 | Inventory | 10.80*600 = 6480.00 |
| 69 | 1 | Inven732-C3-20151003-In732-1000T < Inven73 < Inven7 | Inventory | 9.60*1000 = 9600.00 |
| 70 | 1 | Inven811-C3-20151003-In811-600T < Inven81 < Inven8 | Inventory | 15.00*600 = 9000.00 |
| 71 | 1 | Inven812-C3-20151003-In812-600T < Inven81 < Inven8 | Inventory | 14.40*600 = 8640.00 |
| 72 | 1 | Inven813-C3-20151003-In813-600T < Inven81 < Inven8 | Inventory | 13.80*600 = 8280.00 |
| 73 | 1 | Inven82-C3-20151003-In82-600T < Inven8 | Inventory | 12.00*600 = 7200.00 |
| 74 | 1 | Inven831-C3-20151003-In831-600T < Inven83 < Inven8 | Inventory | 10.80*600 = 6480.00 |
| 75 | 1 | Inven832-C3-20151003-In832-800T < Inven83 < Inven8 | Inventory | 9.60*800 = 7680.00 |
| 76 | 1 | Inven31 < Inven3 | Inventory | 10*100 = 1000.00 |
| 77 | 1 | Inven32 < Inven3 | Inventory | 50*100 = 5000.00 |
| 78 | 1 | Inven331 < Inven33 < Inven3 | Inventory | 20*100 = 2000.00 |
| 79 | 1 | Inven332 < Inven33 < Inven3 | Inventory | 45*100 = 4500.00 |
| 80 | 1 | HGFCVB parts < QASXC parts < Inven3 | Inventory | 10*100 = 1000.00 |
| 81 | 1 | PPGHUP parts < ASDUP parts < Inven3 | Inventory | 20*100 = 2000.00 |
| 82 | 1 | Inven411 < Inven41 < Inven4 | Inventory | 5*100 = 500.00 |
| 83 | 1 | Inven412 < Inven41 < Inven4 | Inventory | 18.5*100 = 1850.00 |
| 84 | 1 | TTTCU parts < TTT parts < Inven4 | Inventory | 20*100 = 2000.00 |
| 85 | 1 | RRRHJK parts < Inven4 | Inventory | 20*100 = 2000.00 |
| 86 | 1 | Working-Inven111 < Working-Inven11 < Working-Inven1 | Working-in-process inventory | 4.78*1000 = 4780.00 |
| 87 | 1 | Working-Inven112 < Working-Inven11 < Working-Inven1 | Working-in-process inventory | 20.12*1000 = 20120.00 |
| 88 | 1 | Working-Inven121 < Working-Inven12 < Working-Inven1 | Working-in-process inventory | 0.20*10000 = 2000.00 |
| 89 | 1 | Working-Inven122 < Working-Inven12 < Working-Inven1 | Working-in-process inventory | 25.78*1000 = 25780.00 |
| 90 | 1 | Working-Inven21 < Working-Inven2 | Working-in-process inventory | 14.36*1000 = 14360.00 |
| 91 | 1 | Working-Inven221 < Working-Inven22 < Working-Inven2 | Working-in-process inventory | 14.77*1000 = 14770.00 |
| 92 | 1 | Working-Inven222 < Working-Inven22 < Working-Inven2 | Working-in-process inventory | 25.33*1000 = 25330.00 |
| 93 | 1 | Working-PPUK parts < Working-ASD parts < Working-Inven2 | Working-in-process inventory | 19.84*1000 = 19840.00 |
| 94 | 1 | Working-PPGH parts < Working-ASD parts < Working-Inven2 | Working-in-process inventory | 0.85*6000 = 5100.00 |
| 95 | 1 | Working-Inven51 < Working-Inven5 | Working-in-process inventory | 5.25*5000 = 26250.00 |
| 96 | 1 | Working-Inven52 < Working-Inven5 | Working-in-process inventory | 24.47*1000 = 24470.00 |
| 97 | 1 | Working-Inven531 < Working-Inven53 < Working-Inven5 | Working-in-process inventory | 12.83*1000 = 12830.00 |
| 98 | 1 | Working-Inven532 < Working-Inven53 < Working-Inven5 | Working-in-process inventory | 17.37*1000 = 17370.00 |
| 99 | 1 | Working-Inven541 < Working-Inven54 < Working-Inven5 | Working-in-process inventory | 6.22*1000 = 6220.00 |
| 100 | 1 | Working-Inven542 < Working-Inven54 < Working-Inven5 | Working-in-process inventory | 7.11*1000 = 7110.00 |

| 101 | 1 | Working-Inven611 < Working-Inven61 < Working-Inven6 | Working-in-process inventory | 3.39*5000 = 16950.00 |
|---|---|---|---|---|
| 102 | 1 | Working-Inven612 < Working-Inven61 < Working-Inven6 | Working-in-process inventory | 6.49*1000 = 6490.00 |
| 103 | 1 | Working-Inven621 < Working-Inven62 < Working-Inven6 | Working-in-process inventory | 8.87*1000 = 8870.00 |
| 104 | 1 | Working-Inven63 < Working-Inven6 | Working-in-process inventory | 7.95*1000 = 7950.00 |
| 105 | 1 | Working-Inven711 < Working-Inven71 < Working-Inven7 | Working-in-process inventory | 10.60*1000 = 10600.00 |
| 106 | 1 | Working-Inven712 < Working-Inven71 < Working-Inven7 | Working-in-process inventory | 9.43*1000 = 9430.00 |
| 107 | 1 | Working-Inven721 < Working-Inven72 < Working-Inven7 | Working-in-process inventory | 6.81*1000 = 6810.00 |
| 108 | 1 | Working-Inven722 < Working-Inven72 < Working-Inven7 | Working-in-process inventory | 6.13*1000 = 6130.00 |
| 109 | 1 | Working-Inven731 < Working-Inven73 < Working-Inven7 | Working-in-process inventory | 5.38*1000 = 5380.00 |
| 110 | 1 | Working-Inven732 < Working-Inven73 < Working-Inven7 | Working-in-process inventory | 5.04*1000 = 5040.00 |
| 111 | 1 | Working-Inven811 < Working-Inven81 < Working-Inven8 | Working-in-process inventory | 7.29*1000 = 7290.00 |
| 112 | 1 | Working-Inven812 < Working-Inven81 < Working-Inven8 | Working-in-process inventory | 7.17*1000 = 7170.00 |
| 113 | 1 | Working-Inven813 < Working-Inven81 < Working-Inven8 | Working-in-process inventory | 6.94*1000 = 6940.00 |
| 114 | 1 | Working-Inven82 < Working-Inven8 | Working-in-process inventory | 5.68*1000 = 5680.00 |
| 115 | 1 | Working-Inve831 < Working-Inven83 < Working-Inven8 | Working-in-process inventory | 4.76*3000 = 14280.00 |
| 116 | 1 | Working-Inven832 < Working-Inven83 < Working-Inven8 | Working-in-process inventory | 4.59*3000 = 13770.00 |
| 117 | 1 | Bond11 | Bonds | 8000.00 |
| 118 | 1 | Bond21 | Bonds | 12000.00 |
| 119 | 1 | Truck11 < Truck1 < Truck | Vehicle | 45000.00 |
| 120 | 1 | Truck12 < Truck1 < Truck | Vehicle | 45000.00 |
| 121 | 1 | Truck21 < Truck2 < Truck | Vehicle | 40000.00 |
| 122 | 1 | Truck22 < Truck2 < Truck | Vehicle | 40000.00 |
| 123 | 1 | Car31 < Car3 < Car | Vehicle | 38000.00 |
| 124 | 1 | Car32 < Car3 < Car | Vehicle | 38000.00 |
| 125 | 1 | Truck11-accumulated amortization < Truck1-accumulated amortization < Truck-accumulated amortization | Accumulated amortization: Vehicle | -21000.00 |
| 126 | 1 | Truck12-accumulated amortization < Truck1-accumulated amortization < Truck-accumulated amortization | Accumulated amortization: Vehicle | -21000.00 |
| 127 | 1 | Truck21-accumulated amortization < Truck2-accumulated amortization < Truck-accumulated amortization | Accumulated amortization: Vehicle | -18000.00 |
| 128 | 1 | Truck22-accumulated amortization < Truck2-accumulated amortization < Truck-accumulated amortization | Accumulated amortization: Vehicle | -14666.67 |
| 129 | 1 | Car31-accumulated amortization < Car3-accumulated amortization < Car-accumulated amortization | Accumulated amortization: Vehicle | -16800.00 |
| 130 | 1 | Car32-accumulated amortization < Car3-accumulated amortization < Car-accumulated amortization | Accumulated amortization: Vehicle | -12000.00 |
| 131 | 1 | Computer server21 < Computer server2 < Computer server | Computer | 2700.00 |
| 132 | 1 | Computer31 < Computer3 | Computer | 1400.00 |

| 133 | 1 | Computer41 < Computer4 | Computer | 1300.00 |
|---|---|---|---|---|
| 134 | 1 | Computer server21-accumulated amortization < Computer server2-accumulated amortization < Computer server-accumulated amortization | Accumulated amortization: Computer | -2137.50 |
| 135 | 1 | Computer31-accumulated amortization < Computer3-accumulated amortization | Accumulated amortization: Computer | -1108.33 |
| 136 | 1 | Computer41-accumulated amortization < Computer4-accumulated amortization | Accumulated amortization: Computer | -1029.17 |
| 137 | 2 | 123456084 | Account payable | 900.00 |
| 138 | 2 | 123456083 | Account payable | 600.00 |
| 139 | 2 | 123456081 | Account payable | 1600.00 |
| 140 | 2 | 123456080 | Account payable | 800.00 |
| 141 | 2 | Bond51-interest payable < Bonds-interest payable | Accrued interest payable | 0 |
| 142 | 2 | Note13-interest payable < Notes-interest payable | Accrued interest payable | 0 |
| 143 | 2 | Note23-interest payable < Notes-interest payable | Accrued interest payable | 0 |
| 144 | 2 | Note24-interest payable < Notes-interest payable | Accrued interest payable | 0 |
| 145 | 2 | Bond51-909876501 < Bond51 | Bonds payable | 6000.00 |
| 146 | 2 | Bond51-909876502 < Bond51 | Bonds payable | 4000.00 |
| 147 | 2 | Bond51-909876503 < Bond51 | Bonds payable | 7000.00 |
| 148 | 2 | Bond51-909876507 < Bond51 | Bonds payable | 6000.00 |
| 149 | 2 | Bond51-909876508 < Bond51 | Bonds payable | 7000.00 |
| 150 | 2 | Bond51-909876509 < Bond51 | Bonds payable | 5000.00 |
| 151 | 2 | Bond51-909876511 < Bond51 | Bonds payable | 4000.00 |
| 152 | 2 | Bond51-909876512 < Bond51 | Bonds payable | 8000.00 |
| 153 | 2 | Bond51-909876514 < Bond51 | Bonds payable | 5000.00 |
| 154 | 2 | Bond51-909876516 < Bond51 | Bonds payable | 7000.00 |
| 155 | 2 | Bond51-909876517 < Bond51 | Bonds payable | 5000.00 |
| 156 | 2 | Bond51-909876518 < Bond51 | Bonds payable | 6000.00 |
| 157 | 2 | Bond51-909876521 < Bond51 | Bonds payable | 4000.00 |
| 158 | 2 | Bond51-909876522 < Bond51 | Bonds payable | 6000.00 |
| 159 | 2 | Note13-88-654304 | Notes payable | 200000.00 |
| 160 | 2 | Note23-88-654305 | Notes payable | 180000.00 |
| 161 | 2 | Note24-88-654305 | Notes payable | 200000.00 |
| 162 | 3 | Capital-909876507 | Share capital | 66000.00 |
| 163 | 3 | Capital-909876517 | Share capital | 66000.00 |
| 164 | 3 | Capital-909876519 | Share capital | 88000.00 |
| 165 | 3 | n | Retained earnings (Conversion) | 16558.57 |
| 166 | 4 | Sales-909876519 | Sales | 0 |
| 167 | 5 | 909876519-travelling < Sales department-travelling | Travelling expenses | 0 |
| 168 | 5 | 909876520-travelling < Office department-travelling | Travelling expenses | 0 |

| 169 | 5 | 909876521-travelling < Product department-travelling | Travelling expenses | 0 |
|-----|---|------|------|---|
| 170 | 5 | 909876519-other < Sales department-other | Other expenses | 0 |
| 171 | 5 | 909876520-other < Office department-other | Other expenses | 0 |
| 172 | 5 | 909876521-other < Product department-other | Other expenses | 0 |
| 173 | 5 | 909876520-salary < Office department-salary | Salary expenses | 0 |
| 174 | 5 | Supplies expenses | Cost of goods manufactured | 0 |
| 175 | 5 | 909876519-salary < Sales department-salary < Salary expenses | Cost of goods manufactured | 0 |
| 176 | 5 | 909876521-salary < Product department-salary < Salary expenses | Cost of goods manufactured | 0 |
| 177 | 5 | General parts expenses | Cost of goods manufactured | 0 |
| 178 | 5 | Bond51-interest | Bond interest expenses | 0 |
| 179 | 5 | Note13-interest | Note interest expenses | 0 |
| 180 | 5 | Note23-interest | Note interest expenses | 0 |
| 181 | 5 | Note24-interest | Note interest expenses | 0 |
| 182 | 5 | Truck1-1-amortization < Truck1-amortization < Vehicle-truck-amortization | Amortization expenses | 0 |
| 183 | 5 | Truck1-2-amortization < Truck1-amortization < Vehicle-truck-amortization | Amortization expenses | 0 |
| 184 | 5 | Truck2-1-amortization < Truck2-amortization < Vehicle-truck-amortization | Amortization expenses | 0 |
| 185 | 5 | Truck2-2-amortization < Truck2-amortization < Vehicle-truck-amortization | Amortization expenses | 0 |
| 186 | 5 | Car31-amortization < Car3-amortization < Vehicle-car-amortization | Amortization expenses | 0 |
| 187 | 5 | Car32-amortization < Car3-amortization < Vehicle-car-amortization | Amortization expenses | 0 |
| 188 | 5 | Computer server21-amortization < Computer server2-amortization < Computer-amortization | Amortization expenses | 0 |
| 189 | 5 | Computer31-amortization < Computer3-amortization < Computer-amortization | Amortization expenses | 0 |
| 190 | 5 | Computer41-amortization < Computer4-amortization < Computer-amortization | Amortization expenses | 0 |
| 191 | 4 | Accrued interest income-bond11 < Bonds | Investment incomes | 0 |
| 192 | 4 | Accrued interest income-bond21 < Bonds | Investment incomes | 0 |
| 193 | 4 | n | Deposits interest income | 0 |

Figure 2.4-17   Company3 Converting Multi-Subaccount Names Table

Just as said before, only the first products are added their product codes or their product batch to the lowest multi-subaccounts. For simplification, the product batch is used in all products of the Company3. These changes have been done in the Figure 2.4-17. They are the Inventory with the Other 45 to the Other 75.

Before entering the dynamic accounting equation on December 31, 2015 into the database dcj209, I first enter three initialization sub-equations.

Account payable (2): 0 = Share capital (3): 0

0 = Sales (4): 0 – Cost of goods sold (5):0

Cash (1): 0 = Retained earnings (Conversion) (3): 0

All converting transaction sub-equations can be designed and written as the followings.

- I build a transaction sub-equation for the "Account receivable" and the "Account payable" accounts. The transaction sub-equation includes the "Account receivable" account with the Order 39 to the Order 44, the "Account payable" account with the Order 137 to the Order 140, and the part of the "Cash" account with the Order 31, The first transaction sub-equation is:

  Account receivable (1): 200 + Account receivable (1): 300 + Account receivable (1): 10600 + Account receivable (1): 600 + Account receivable (1): 150 + Account receivable (1): 200 + Cash (1): -13550 = Account payable (2): 900 + Account payable (2): 600 + Account payable (2): 1600 + Account payable (2): 800

  After entering this transaction, the new balance of the "Cash" account with the Order 31 is -$176,827.25 (= -$190377.25 + $13,550).

- The transaction sub-equation includes the "Cash" account with the Order 1 to the Order 6, the "Share capital" account with the Order 162 to the Order 164, and the "Notes payable" account with the Order 159 to the Order 161. The second transaction sub-equation is:

  Cash (1): 66000 + Cash (1): 66000 + Cash (1): 88000 + Cash (1): 200000 + Cash (1): 180000 + Cash (1): 200000 = Share capital (3): 66000 + Share capital (3): 66000 + Share capital (3): 88000 + Notes payable (2): 200000 + Notes payable (2): 180000 + Notes payable (2): 200000

- The transaction sub-equation includes the "Cash" account with the Order 9 to the Order 14 and the "Bonds payable" account with the Order 145 to the Order 150. The third transaction sub-equation is:

Cash (1): 6000 + Cash (1): 4000 + Cash (1): 7000 + Cash (1): 6000 + Cash (1): 7000 + Cash (1): 5000 = Bonds payable (2): 6000 + Bonds payable (2): 4000 + Bonds payable (2): 7000 + Bonds payable (2): 6000 + Bonds payable (2): 7000 + Bonds payable (2): 5000

- The transaction sub-equation includes the "Cash" account with the Order 15 to the Order 20 and the "Bonds payable" account with the Order 151 to the Order 156. The fourth transaction sub-equation is:

Cash (1): 4000 + Cash (1): 8000 + Cash (1): 5000 + Cash (1): 7000 + Cash (1): 5000 + Cash (1): 6000 = Bonds payable (2): 4000 + Bonds payable (2): 8000 + Bonds payable (2): 5000 + Bonds payable (2): 7000 + Bonds payable (2): 5000 + Bonds payable (2): 6000

- The transaction sub-equation includes the part of the "Cash" account with the Order 31, the "Cash" account with the Order 21 to the Order 24, the "Inventory" account with the Order 45 to the Order 48, and the "Bonds payable" account with the Order 157 and the Order 158. The fifth transaction sub-equation is:

Cash (1): -65433.33 + Cash (1): 4000 + Cash (1): 6000 + Cash (1): 613.33 + Cash (1): 820 + Inventory (1): 6000 + Inventory (1): 20000 + Inventory (1): 8000 + Inventory (1): 30000 = Bonds payable (2): 4000 + Bonds payable (2): 6000

After entering this transaction, the new balance of the "Cash" account with the Order 31 is -$111,393.92 (= -$176,827.25 + $65,433.33).

- The transaction sub-equation includes the "Cash" account with the Order 25 to the Order 27 and the "Vehicle" account with the Order 119 to the Order 124. The sixth transaction sub-equation is:

Cash (1): -90000 + Cash (1): -80000 + Cash (1): -76000 + Vehicle (1): 45000 +

Vehicle (1): 45000 + Vehicle (1): 40000 + Vehicle (1): 40000 + Vehicle (1): 38000 + Vehicle (1): 38000 = 0

- The transaction sub-equation includes the part of the "Cash" account with the Order 31, the "Cash" account with the Order 28 to the Order 30, the "Computer" account with the Order 131 to the Order 133, and the "Inventory" account with the Order 49 to the Order 53. The seventh transaction sub-equation is:

Cash (1): -63600 + Cash (1): -2700 + Cash (1): -1400 + Cash (1): -1300 + Computer (1): 2700 + Computer (1): 1400 + Computer (1): 1300 + Inventory (1): 25000 + Inventory (1): 15000 + Inventory (1): 10800 + Inventory (1): 11200 + Inventory (1): 1600 = 0

After entering this transaction, the new balance of the "Cash" account with the Order 31 is -$47,793.92 (= -$111,393.92 + $63,600).

- The transaction sub-equation includes the part of the "Cash" account with the Order 32 and the "Inventory" account with the Order 54 to the Order 64. The eighth transaction sub-equation is:

Cash (1): -112200 + Inventory (1): 6000 + Inventory (1): 15000 + Inventory (1): 15000 + Inventory (1): 21000 + Inventory (1): 7200 + Inventory (1): 7500 + Inventory (1): 5200 + Inventory (1): 7500+ Inventory (1): 9000 + Inventory (1): 8000 + Inventory (1): 10800 = 0

After entering this transaction, the new balance of the "Cash" account with the Order 32 is -$76,989.46 (= -$189,189.46 + $112,200).

- The transaction sub-equation includes the part of the "Cash" account with the Order 31, the "Cash" account with the Order 35 to the Order 37, and the "Inventory" account with the Order 65 to the Order 72. Because the balances of the "Cash" with the Order 35 is zero, the ninth transaction sub-equation is:

Cash (1): -40360 + Cash (1): -8000 + Cash (1): -12000 + Inventory (1): 1860 + Inventory (1): 9300 + Inventory (1): 7200 + Inventory (1): 6480 + Inventory (1): 9600 + Inventory (1): 9000 + Inventory (1): 8640 + Inventory (1): 8280 = 0

After entering this transaction, the new balance of the "Cash" account with the Order 31 is -$7,433.92 (= -$47,793.92 + $40,360).

- The transaction sub-equation includes the rest (-$7,433.92) of the "Cash" account with the Order 31, the part of the "Cash" account with the Order 32, and the "Inventory" account with the Order 73 to the Order 82. The tenth transaction sub-equation is:

Cash (1): -7433.92 + Cash (1): -29926.08 + Inventory (1): 7200 + Inventory (1): 6480 + Inventory (1): 7680 + Inventory (1): 1000 + Inventory (1): 5000 + Inventory (1): 2000 + Inventory (1): 4500 + Inventory (1): 1000 + Inventory (1): 2000 + Inventory (1): 500 = 0

After entering this transaction, the new balance of the "Cash" account with the Order 32 is -$47,063.38 (= -$76,989.46 + $29,926.08).

- The transaction sub-equation includes the rest (-$47,063.38) of the "Cash" account with the Order 32, the part of the "Cash" account with the Order 33, the "Inventory" account with the Order 83 to the Order 85, and the "Working-in-process inventory" account with the Order 86 to the Order 92. The eleventh transaction sub-equation is:

Cash (1): -47063.38 + Cash (1): -65926.62 + Inventory (1): 1850 + Inventory (1): 2000 + Inventory (1): 2000 + Working-in-process inventory (1): 4780 + Working-in-process inventory (1): 20120 + Working-in-process inventory (1): 2000 + Working-in-process inventory (1): 25780 + Working-in-process inventory (1): 14360 + Working-in-process inventory (1): 14770 + Working-in-process inventory (1): 25330 = 0

After entering this transaction, the new balance of the "Cash" account with the

Order 33 is -$118,425.93 (= -$184,352.55 + $65,926.62).

- The transaction sub-equation includes the rest (-$118,425.93) of the "Cash" account with the Order 33, the part of the "Cash" account with the Order 34, and the "Working-in-process inventory" account with the Order 93 to the Order 102. The twelfth transaction sub-equation is:

Cash (1): -118425.93 + Cash (1): -24204.07 + Working-in-process inventory (1): 19840 + Working-in-process inventory (1): 5100 + Working-in-process inventory (1): 26250 + Working-in-process inventory (1): 24470 + Working-in-process inventory (1): 12830 + Working-in-process inventory (1): 17370 + Working-in-process inventory (1): 6220 + Working-in-process inventory (1): 7110 + Working-in-process inventory (1): 16950 + Working-in-process inventory (1): 6490 = 0

After entering this transaction, the new balance of the "Cash" account with the Order 34 is -$27,249.64 (= -$51,453.71+ $24,204.07).

- The transaction sub-equation includes the part of the "Cash" account with the Order 34, the "Supplies" account with the Order 35, the "Working-in-process inventory" account with the Order 103 to the Order 108, the "Accumulated amortization: Vehicle" account with the Order 125 and the Order 126. The thirteenth transaction sub-equation is:

Cash (1): -7999.88 + Supplies (1): 209.88 + Working-in-process inventory (1): 8870 + Working-in-process inventory (1): 7950 + Working-in-process inventory (1): 10600 + Working-in-process inventory (1): 9430 + Working-in-process inventory (1): 6810 + Working-in-process inventory (1): 6130 + Accumulated amortization: Vehicle (1): -21000 + Accumulated amortization: Vehicle (1): -21000 = 0

After entering this transaction, the new balance of the "Cash" account with the Order 34 is -$19,249.76 (= -$27,249.64 + $7,999.88).

- The transaction sub-equation includes the part of the "Cash" account with the Order 34, the "Working-in-process inventory" account with the Order 109 to the Order 113, and the "Accumulated amortization: Vehicle" account with the Order 127. The fourteenth transaction sub-equation is:

Cash (1): -13820 + Working-in-process inventory (1): 5380 + Working-in-process inventory (1): 5040 + Working-in-process inventory (1): 7290 + Working-in-process inventory (1): 7170 + Working-in-process inventory (1): 6940 + Accumulated amortization: Vehicle (1): -18000 = 0

After entering this transaction, the new balance of the "Cash" account with the Order 34 is -$5,429.76 (= -$19,249.76 + $13820).

- The transaction sub-equation includes the part of the "Cash" account with the Order 34, the "Cash" account with the Order 8, the "Working-in-process inventory" account with the Order 114 to the Order 116, and the "Accumulated amortization: Vehicle" account with the Order 128 to 130. The fifteenth transaction sub-equation is:

Cash (1): -5263.33 + Cash (1): 15000 + Working-in-process inventory (1): 5680 + Working-in-process inventory (1): 14280 + Working-in-process inventory (1): 13770 + Accumulated amortization: Vehicle (1): -14666.67 + Accumulated amortization: Vehicle (1): -16800 + Accumulated amortization: Vehicle (1): -12000 = 0

After entering this transaction, the new balance of the "Cash" account with the Order 34 is -$166.43 (= -$5,429.76 + $5,263.33).The transaction sub-equation includes the rest (-$166.43) of the "Cash" account with the Order 34, the "Cash" account with the Order 7, the "Accumulated amortization: Computer" account with the Order 134 to the Order 136, the "Bonds" account with the Order 117 and the Order 118, and the "Retained earnings (Conversion)" account with the balance $16,558.57. The sixteenth transaction sub-equation is:

Cash (1): -166.43 + Cash (1): 1000 + Accumulated amortization: Computer (1): -2137.5 + Accumulated amortization: Computer (1): -1108.33 + Accumulated amortization: Computer (1): -1029.17 + Bonds (1): 8000 + Bonds (1): 12000 = Retained earnings (Conversion) (3): 16558.57

After completing this transaction, the dynamic accounting equation of the Company3 on December 31, 2015 has entered into the database dcj209.

### 2.4.5.2 Brief Summary of the Company3

The Figure 2.4-18 on the next page shows the partial information of inventory purchased or inventory sold by other social members in the public database dcj200.

SQLQuery1.sql - LIU...SS.dcj200 (sa (55))*

```
use dcj200
select sum(amount) as sum0 from InventoryByMembers where Recorder='88-654308'
and TransDate between '2015-01-01' and '2015-12-31'
select * from InventoryByMembers where Recorder='88-654308' and TransDate between '2015-01-01' and '2015-12-31'
```

100 %

Results | Messages

| | sum0 |
|---|---|
| 1 | -343370.00 |

| | IDM | Amount | Symbol | MultiSubaccount | Recorder | TransDate | Unit |
|---|---|---|---|---|---|---|---|
| 16 | Cash paym | -5200.00 | n | Inven611-C3-20151003-In611-1300T < Inven61 < Inven6 | 88-654308 | 2015-12-31 | -1300 |
| 17 | Cash paym | -7500.00 | n | Inven612-C3-20151003-In612-1100T < Inven61 < Inven6 | 88-654308 | 2015-12-31 | -1000 |
| 18 | Cash paym | -9000.00 | n | Inven621-C3-20151003-In621-900T < Inven62 < Inven6 | 88-654308 | 2015-12-31 | -900 |
| 19 | Cash paym | -8000.00 | n | Inven63-C3-20151003-In63-1000T < Inven6 | 88-654308 | 2015-12-31 | -1000 |
| 20 | Cash paym | -10800.00 | n | Inven711-C3-20151003-In711-500T < Inven71 < Inven7 | 88-654308 | 2015-12-31 | -500 |
| 21 | Cash paym | -1860.00 | n | Inven712-C3-20151003-In712-100T < Inven71 < Inven7 | 88-654308 | 2015-12-31 | -100 |
| 22 | Cash paym | -9300.00 | n | Inven721-C3-20151003-In721-744T < Inven72 < Inven7 | 88-654308 | 2015-12-31 | -744 |
| 23 | Cash paym | -7200.00 | n | Inven722-C3-20151003-In722-600T < Inven72 < Inven7 | 88-654308 | 2015-12-31 | -600 |
| 24 | Cash paym | -6480.00 | n | Inven731-C3-20151003-In731-600T < Inven73 < Inven7 | 88-654308 | 2015-12-31 | -600 |
| 25 | Cash paym | -9600.00 | n | Inven732-C3-20151003-In732-1000T < Inven73 < Inven7 | 88-654308 | 2015-12-31 | -1000 |
| 26 | Cash paym | -9000.00 | n | Inven811-C3-20151003-In811-600T < Inven81 < Inven8 | 88-654308 | 2015-12-31 | -600 |
| 27 | Cash paym | -8640.00 | n | Inven812-C3-20151003-In812-600T < Inven81 < Inven8 | 88-654308 | 2015-12-31 | -600 |
| 28 | Cash paym | -8280.00 | n | Inven813-C3-20151003-In813-600T < Inven81 < Inven8 | 88-654308 | 2015-12-31 | -600 |
| 29 | Cash paym | -7200.00 | n | Inven82-C3-20151003-In82-600T < Inven8 | 88-654308 | 2015-12-31 | -600 |
| 30 | Cash paym | -6480.00 | n | Inven831-C3-20151003-In831-600T < Inven83 < Inven8 | 88-654308 | 2015-12-31 | -600 |
| 31 | Cash paym | -7680.00 | n | Inven832-C3-20151003-In832-800T < Inven83 < Inven8 | 88-654308 | 2015-12-31 | -800 |
| 32 | Cash paym | -1000.00 | n | Inven31 < Inven3 | 88-654308 | 2015-12-31 | -100 |
| 33 | Cash paym | -5000.00 | n | Inven32 < Inven3 | 88-654308 | 2015-12-31 | -100 |
| 34 | Cash paym | -2000.00 | n | Inven331 < Inven33 < Inven3 | 88-654308 | 2015-12-31 | -100 |
| 35 | Cash paym | -4500.00 | n | Inven332 < Inven33 < Inven3 | 88-654308 | 2015-12-31 | -100 |
| 36 | Cash paym | -1000.00 | n | HGFCVB parts < QASXC parts < Inven3 | 88-654308 | 2015-12-31 | -100 |
| 37 | Cash paym | -2000.00 | n | PPGHUP parts < ASDUP parts < Inven3 | 88-654308 | 2015-12-31 | -100 |
| 38 | Cash paym | -500.00 | n | Inven411 < Inven41 < Inven4 | 88-654308 | 2015-12-31 | -100 |
| 39 | Cash paym | -1850.00 | n | Inven412 < Inven41 < Inven4 | 88-654308 | 2015-12-31 | -100 |
| 40 | Cash paym | -2000.00 | n | TTTCU parts < TTT parts < Inven4 | 88-654308 | 2015-12-31 | -100 |
| 41 | Cash paym | -2000.00 | n | RRRHJK parts < Inven4 | 88-654308 | 2015-12-31 | -100 |

Query executed successfully. LIU\SQLE

Figure 2.4-18 Company3 Inventory Purchased or Sold by Other Members

## 2.4.6 Sample of the Proprietorship1

The Proprietorship1 is owned by the individual A23 completely and has total share capital $160,000. The Proprietorship1 produces the general parts and the foods. The Figure 2.4-19 shows its product names, costs, and sale prices.

| Order | Product (the Lowest-level Subaccount) Names | Multi-subaccount Names | Costs | Sale Prices |
|---|---|---|---|---|
| 1 | Inven31 | Inven31 < Inven3 | 6.00 | 10.00 |
| 2 | Inven32 | Inven32 < Inven3 | 30.00 | 50.00 |
| 3 | Inven331 | Inven331 < Inven33 < Inven3 | 10.00 | 20.00 |
| 4 | Inven332 | Inven332 < Inven33 < Inven3 | 27.00 | 45.00 |
| 5 | HGFCVB parts | HGFCVB parts < QASXC parts < Inven3 | 6.00 | 10.00 |
| 6 | PPGHUP parts | PPGHUP parts < ASDUP parts < Inven3 | 12.00 | 20.00 |
| 7 | Food111 | Food111 < Food11 < Food1 | 5.00 | 10.00 |
| 8 | Food112 | Food112 < Food11 < Food1 | 5.50 | 11.00 |
| 9 | Food113 | Food113 < Food11 < Food1 | 6.00 | 12.00 |
| 10 | Food121 | Food121 < Food12 < Food1 | 6.50 | 13.00 |
| 11 | Food122 | Food122 < Food12 < Food1 | 7.00 | 14.00 |
| 12 | Food123 | Food123 < Food12 < Food1 | 7.50 | 15.00 |
| 13 | Food211 | Food211 < Food21 < Food2 | 4.00 | 8.00 |
| 14 | Food212 | Food212 < Food21 < Food2 | 4.50 | 9.00 |
| 15 | Food213 | Food213 < Food21 < Food2 | 5.00 | 10.00 |
| 16 | Food214 | Food214 < Food21 < Food2 | 5.50 | 11.00 |
| 17 | Food221 | Food221 < Food22 < Food2 | 6.00 | 12.00 |
| 18 | Food222 | Food222 < Food22 < Food2 | 6.50 | 13.00 |
| 19 | Food23 | Food23 < Food2 | 7.50 | 16.00 |
| 20 | Food311 | Food311 < Food31 < Food3 | 8.50 | 20.00 |
| 21 | Food312 | Food312 < Food31 < Food3 | 11.00 | 24.00 |
| 22 | Food321 | Food321 < Food32 < Food3 | 12.00 | 27.00 |
| 23 | Food322 | Food322 < Food32 < Food3 | 13.00 | 30.00 |

Figure 2.4-19   Proprietorship1 Products and Sale Prices Table

For a producing foods company of the Proprietorship1, the costs of its food products are most the labor and inventory costs. When the Proprietorship1 uses the MathAccounting software, the "Working-in-process inventory" is treated as a parent account of the class 1 and the "Cost of goods sold" is treated as the parent accounts of the class 5. For simplification, the "Cost of goods sold" account has the three one-level subaccounts of the "Supplies expenses", the "Salary expenses" for the A22, and the general parts in this book.

### 2.4.6.1 Conversion of the Proprietorship1

The Proprietorship1 will convert to the MathAccounting software on January 1, 2016. The Figure 2.4-20 and the Figure 2.4-21 show the converting reference table and the multi-subaccount names table respectively.

| Order | Class | Account Name (Subtotal Name) | Balance | Row |
|---|---|---|---|---|
| **1** | **1** | **(Current assets)** | - | **103** |
| 2 | 1 | Cash | 18783.78 | 104 |
| 3 | 1 | Supplies | 155.45 | 106 |
| 4 | 1 | Account receivable | 4540.00 | 108 |
| 5 | 1 | Inventory | 218350.00 | 110 |
| 6 | 1 | Working-in-process inventory | 60420.00 | 112 |
| **7** | **1** | **(Long term investments)** | - | **141** |
| 8 | 1 | Bonds | 18000.00 | 142 |
| **9** | **1** | **(Equipment)** | - | **171** |
| 10 | 1 | Vehicle | 40000.00 | 172 |
| 11 | 1 | Accumulated amortization: Vehicle | -18000.00 | 173 |
| 12 | 1 | Computer | 5400.00 | 174 |
| 13 | 1 | Accumulated amortization: Computer | -3375.00 | 175 |
| **14** | **2** | **(Current liabilities)** | - | **203** |
| 15 | 2 | Account payable | 1700.00 | 204 |
| 16 | 2 | Accrued interest payable | 0 | 206 |
| 17 | 2 | Tax payable | 0 | 208 |
| **18** | **2** | **(Long term liabilities)** | - | **251** |
| 19 | 2 | Bonds payable | 50000.00 | 252 |
| 20 | 2 | Notes payable | 120000.00 | 254 |
| **21** | **3** | **(Owners' capital)** | - | **303** |
| 22 | 3 | Share capital | 160000.00 | 304 |
| 23 | 3 | Retained earnings (Conversion) | 12574.23 | 306 |
| **24** | **4** | **(Revenues)** | - | **403** |
| 25 | 4 | Sales | | 404 |
| **26** | **5** | **(Cost)** | - | **431** |
| 27 | 5 | Cost of goods sold | | 432 |
| **28** | **5** | **(Operating and administrative expenses)** | - | **453** |
| 29 | 5 | Travelling expenses | 0 | 454 |
| 30 | 5 | Other expenses | 0 | 455 |

| | | | | | |
|---|---|---|---|---|---|
| 31 | 5 | Salary expenses | | 0 | 456 |
| 32 | 5 | Cost of goods sold | | 0 | 457 |
| 33 | 5 | Bond interest expenses | | 0 | 458 |
| 34 | 5 | Note interest expenses | | 0 | 460 |
| 35 | 5 | Amortization expenses | | 0 | 462 |
| **36** | **4** | **(Other income)** | | - | **475** |
| 37 | 4 | Investment incomes | | | 476 |
| 38 | 4 | Deposits interest incomes | | 0 | 478 |
| **39** | **5** | **(Tax)** | | - | **600** |
| 40 | 5 | Tax expenses | | 0 | 602 |

Figure 2.4-20   Proprietorship1 Converting Reference Table

| Order | Class | Multi-subaccount Name | Parent Name | Lowest Subaccount Balance |
|---|---|---|---|---|
| 1 | 1 | 909876522-i-owners < Cash receipts from owners < Financial activities | Cash | 160000.00 |
| 2 | 1 | 88-654305-i-note25 < Cash receipts from banks < Financial activities | Cash | 120000.00 |
| 3 | 1 | 88-654306-c-operating < Cash receipts from customers < Operating activities | Cash | 17000.00 |
| 4 | 1 | 88-654304-c-interest of investment bond11 < Cash receipts from investments < Investing activities | Cash | 383.33 |
| 5 | 1 | 88-654304-c-interest of investment bond12 < Cash receipts from investments < Investing activities | Cash | 189.00 |
| 6 | 1 | 88-654304-c-interest of investment bond13 < Cash receipts from investments < Investing activities | Cash | 30.00 |
| 7 | 1 | 88-654305-c-interest of investment bond22 < Cash receipts from investments < Investing activities | Cash | 322.67 |
| 8 | 1 | 909876504-i-bond61 < Cash receipts from issued bonds < Financial activities | Cash | 3000.00 |
| 9 | 1 | 909876505-i-bond61 < Cash receipts from issued bonds < Financial activities | Cash | 4000.00 |
| 10 | 1 | 909876506-i-bond61 < Cash receipts from issued bonds < Financial activities | Cash | 5000.00 |
| 11 | 1 | 909876508-i-bond61 < Cash receipts from issued bonds < Financial activities | Cash | 2000.00 |
| 12 | 1 | 909876510-i-bond61 < Cash receipts from issued bonds < Financial activities | Cash | 3000.00 |
| 13 | 1 | 909876513-i-bond61 < Cash receipts from issued bonds < Financial activities | Cash | 5000.00 |
| 14 | 1 | 909876515-i-bond61 < Cash receipts from issued bonds < Financial activities | Cash | 4000.00 |
| 15 | 1 | 909876516-i-bond61 < Cash receipts from issued bonds < Financial activities | Cash | 2000.00 |
| 16 | 1 | 909876517-i-bond61 < Cash receipts from issued bonds < Financial activities | Cash | 5000.00 |
| 17 | 1 | 909876518-i-bond61 < Cash receipts from issued bonds < Financial activities | Cash | 3000.00 |
| 18 | 1 | 909876519-i-bond61 < Cash receipts from issued bonds < Financial activities | Cash | 5000.00 |
| 19 | 1 | 909876520-i-bond61 < Cash receipts from issued bonds < Financial activities | Cash | 3000.00 |
| 20 | 1 | 909876521-i-bond61 < Cash receipts from issued bonds < Financial activities | Cash | 4000.00 |

| 21 | 1 | 909876522-i-bond61 < Cash receipts from issued bonds < Financial activities | Cash | 2000.00 |
|---|---|---|---|---|
| 22 | 1 | 88-654306-t-truck2 < Cash payments for machinery < Operating activities | Cash | -40000.00 |
| 23 | 1 | 88-654306-t-computer server2 < Cash payments for machinery < Operating activities | Cash | -2700.00 |
| 24 | 1 | 88-654306-t-computer3 < Cash payments for machinery < Operating activities | Cash | -1400.00 |
| 25 | 1 | 88-654306-t-computer4 < Cash payments for machinery < Operating activities | Cash | -1300.00 |
| 26 | 1 | Cash payments for operating expenses < Operating activities | Cash | -124356.77 |
| 27 | 1 | Cash payments for operating expenses < Operating activities | Cash | -120631.54 |
| 28 | 1 | 88-654303-n-tax < Cash payments for operating expenses < Operating activities | Cash | -20752.91 |
| 29 | 1 | Cash payments to suppliers<Operating activities | Cash | 0 |
| 30 | 1 | 88-654304-n-investment bond11 < Cash payments for investments < Investing activities | Cash | -5000.00 |
| 31 | 1 | 88-654304-n-investment bond12 < Cash payments for investments < Investing activities | Cash | -3000.00 |
| 32 | 1 | 88-654304-n-investment bond13 < Cash payments for investments < Investing activities | Cash | -2000.00 |
| 33 | 1 | 88-654305-n-investment bond22 < Cash payments for investments < Investing activities | Cash | -8000.00 |
| 34 | 1 | n | Supplies | 155.45 |
| 35 | 1 | 123456784 | Account receivable | 2040.00 |
| 36 | 1 | 123456783 | Account receivable | 500.00 |
| 37 | 1 | 123456782 | Account receivable | 1600.00 |
| 38 | 1 | 123456780 | Account receivable | 400.00 |
| 39 | 1 | Inven31-P1-20151125-In31-1000T < Inven3 | Inventory | $6.00*1000 = 6000.00$ |
| 40 | 1 | Inven32-P1-20151125-In32-1000T < Inven3 | Inventory | $30.00*1000 = 30000.00$ |
| 41 | 1 | Inven331-P1-20151125-In331-1000T < Inven33 < Inven3 | Inventory | $10.00*1000 = 10000.00$ |
| 42 | 1 | Inven332-P1-20151125-In332-1000T < Inven33 < Inven3 | Inventory | $27.00*1000 = 27000.00$ |
| 43 | 1 | HGFCVB parts-P1-20151125-HGP-1000T < QASXC parts < Inven3 | Inventory | $6.00*1000 = 6000.00$ |
| 44 | 1 | PPGHUP parts-P1-20151125-PPP-1000T < ASDUP parts < Inven3 | Inventory | $12.00*1000 = 12000.00$ |
| 45 | 1 | Food111-P1-20151203-F111-1000T < Food11 < Food1 | Inventory | $5.00*1000 = 5000.00$ |
| 46 | 1 | Food112-P1-20151203-F112-1000T < Food11 < Food1 | Inventory | $5.50*1000 = 5500.00$ |
| 47 | 1 | Food113-P1-20151203-F113-1000T < Food11 < Food1 | Inventory | $6.00*1000 = 6000.00$ |
| 48 | 1 | Food121-P1-20151203-F121-1000T < Food12 < Food1 | Inventory | $6.50*1000 = 6500.00$ |
| 49 | 1 | Food122-P1-20151203-F122-1000T < Food12 < Food1 | Inventory | $7.00*1000 = 7000.00$ |
| 50 | 1 | Food123-P1-20151203-F123-1000T < Food12 < Food1 | Inventory | $7.50*1000 = 7500.00$ |
| 51 | 1 | Food211-P1-20151203-F211-1000T < Food21 < Food2 | Inventory | $4.00*1000 = 4000.00$ |
| 52 | 1 | Food212-P1-20151203-F212-1000T < Food21 < Food2 | Inventory | $4.50*1000 = 4500.00$ |
| 53 | 1 | Food213-P1-20151203-F213-1000T < Food21 < Food2 | Inventory | $5.00*1000 = 5000.00$ |
| 54 | 1 | Food214-P1-20151203-F214-1000T < Food21 < Food2 | Inventory | $5.50*1000 = 5500.00$ |

| 55 | 1 | Food221-P1-20151203-F221-1000T < Food22 < Food2 | Inventory | 6.00*1000 = 6000.00 |
|---|---|---|---|---|
| 56 | 1 | Food222-P1-20151203-F222-1000T < Food22 < Food2 | Inventory | 6.50*1000 = 6500.00 |
| 57 | 1 | Food23-P1-20151203-F23-1000T < Food2 | Inventory | 7.50*1000 = 7500.00 |
| 58 | 1 | Food311-P1-20151203-F311-1000T < Food31 < Food3 | Inventory | 8.50*1000 = 8500.00 |
| 59 | 1 | Food312-P1-20151203-F312-1000T < Food31 < Food3 | Inventory | 11.00*1000 = 11000.00 |
| 60 | 1 | Food321-P1-20151203-F321-1000T < Food32 < Food3 | Inventory | 12.00*1000 = 12000.00 |
| 61 | 1 | Food322-P1-20151203-F322-1000T < Food32 < Food3 | Inventory | 13.00*1000 = 13000.00 |
| 62 | 1 | Inven411 < Inven41 < Inven4 | Inventory | 5*100 = 500.00 |
| 63 | 1 | Inven412 < Inven41 < Inven4 | Inventory | 18.5*100 = 1850.00 |
| 64 | 1 | TTTCU parts < TTT parts < Inven4 | Inventory | 20*100 = 2000.00 |
| 65 | 1 | RRRHJK parts < Inven4 | Inventory | 20*100 = 2000.00 |
| 66 | 1 | Working-Inven31 < Working-Inven3 | Working-in-process inventory | 3.00*600 = 1800.00 |
| 67 | 1 | Working-Inven32 < Working-Inven3 | Working-in-process inventory | 14.00*600 = 8400.00 |
| 68 | 1 | Working-Inven331 < Working-Inven33 < Working-Inven3 | Working-in-process inventory | 5.00*600 = 3000.00 |
| 69 | 1 | Working-Inven332 < Working-Inven33 < Working-Inven3 | Working-in-process inventory | 13.00*600 = 7800.00 |
| 70 | 1 | Working-HGFCVB parts < Working-QASXC parts < Working-Inven3 | Working-in-process inventory | 3.00*600 = 1800.00 |
| 71 | 1 | Working-PPGHUP parts < Working-ASDUP parts < Working-Inven3 | Working-in-process inventory | 6.00*600 = 3600.00 |
| 72 | 1 | Working-Food111 < Working-Food11 < Working-Food1 | Working-in-process inventory | 2.40*600 = 1440.00 |
| 73 | 1 | Working-Food112 < Working-Food11 < Working-Food1 | Working-in-process inventory | 2.50*600 = 1500.00 |
| 74 | 1 | Working-Food113 < Working-Food11 < Working-Food1 | Working-in-process inventory | 3.00*600 = 1800.00 |
| 75 | 1 | Working-Food121 < Working-Food12 < Working-Food1 | Working-in-process inventory | 2.90*600 = 1740.00 |
| 76 | 1 | Working-Food122 < Working-Food12 < Working-Food1 | Working-in-process inventory | 3.00*600 = 1800.00 |
| 77 | 1 | Working-Food123 < Working-Food12 < Working-Food1 | Working-in-process inventory | 3.50*600 = 2100.00 |
| 78 | 1 | Working-Food211 < Working-Food21 < Working-Food2 | Working-in-process inventory | 2.00*600 = 1200.00 |
| 79 | 1 | Working-Food212 < Working-Food21 < Working-Food2 | Working-in-process inventory | 2.00*600 = 1200.00 |
| 80 | 1 | Working-Food213 < Working-Food21 < Working-Food2 | Working-in-process inventory | 2.20*600 = 1320.00 |
| 81 | 1 | Working-Food214 < Working-Food21 < Working-Food2 | Working-in-process inventory | 2.50*600 = 1500.00 |
| 82 | 1 | Working-Food221 < Working-Food22 < Working-Food2 | Working-in-process inventory | 3.00*600 = 1800.00 |
| 83 | 1 | Working-Food221 < Working-Food22 < Working-Food2 | Working-in-process inventory | 3.10*600 = 1860.00 |
| 84 | 1 | Working-Food23 < Working-Food2 | Working-in-process inventory | 3.50*600 = 2100.00 |
| 85 | 1 | Working-Food311 < Working-Food31 < Working-Food3 | Working-in-process inventory | 4.10*600 = 2460.00 |
| 86 | 1 | Working-Food312 < Working-Food31 < Working-Food3 | Working-in-process inventory | 5.00*600 = 3000.00 |
| 87 | 1 | Working-Food321 < Working-Food32 < Working-Food3 | Working-in-process inventory | 6.00*600 = 3600.00 |

| 88 | 1 | Working-Food322 < Working-Food32 < Working-Food3 | Working-in-process inventory | 6.00*600 = 3600.00 |
|---|---|---|---|---|
| 89 | 1 | Bond11 | Bonds | 5000.00 |
| 90 | 1 | Bond12 | Bonds | 3000.00 |
| 91 | 1 | Bond13 | Bonds | 2000.00 |
| 92 | 1 | Bond22 | Bonds | 8000.00 |
| 93 | 1 | Truck21 < Truck2 < Truck | Vehicle | 40000.00 |
| 94 | 1 | Truck21-accumulated amortization < Truck2-accumulated amortization < Truck-accumulated amortization | Accumulated amortization: Vehicle | -18000.00 |
| 95 | 1 | Computer server21 < Computer server2 < Computer server | Computer | 2700.00 |
| 96 | 1 | Computer31 < Computer3 | Computer | 1400.00 |
| 97 | 1 | Computer41 < Computer4 | Computer | 1300.00 |
| 98 | 1 | Computer server21-accumulated amortization < Computer server2-accumulated amortization < Computer server-accumulated amortization | Accumulated amortization: Computer | -1687.50 |
| 99 | 1 | Computer31-accumulated amortization < Computer3-accumulated amortization | Accumulated amortization: Computer | -875.00 |
| 100 | 1 | Computer41-accumulated amortization < Computer4-accumulated amortization | Accumulated amortization: Computer | -812.50 |
| 101 | 2 | 123456084 | Account payable | 1000.00 |
| 102 | 2 | 123456083 | Account payable | 250.00 |
| 103 | 2 | 123456082 | Account payable | 150.00 |
| 104 | 2 | 123456080 | Account payable | 300.00 |
| 105 | 2 | Bond61-interest payable < Bonds-interest payable | Accrued interest payable | 0 |
| 106 | 2 | Note25-interest payable < Notes-interest payable | Accrued interest payable | 0 |
| 107 | 2 | Bond61-909876504 < Bond61 | Bonds payable | 3000.00 |
| 108 | 2 | Bond61-909876505 < Bond61 | Bonds payable | 4000.00 |
| 109 | 2 | Bond61-909876506 < Bond61 | Bonds payable | 5000.00 |
| 110 | 2 | Bond61-909876508 < Bond61 | Bonds payable | 2000.00 |
| 111 | 2 | Bond61-88-654310 < Bond61 | Bonds payable | 3000.00 |
| 112 | 2 | Bond61-88-654313 < Bond61 | Bonds payable | 5000.00 |
| 113 | 2 | Bond61-909876515 < Bond61 | Bonds payable | 4000.00 |
| 114 | 2 | Bond61-909876516 < Bond61 | Bonds payable | 2000.00 |
| 115 | 2 | Bond61-909876517 < Bond61 | Bonds payable | 5000.00 |
| 116 | 2 | Bond61-909876518 < Bond61 | Bonds payable | 3000.00 |
| 117 | 2 | Bond61-909876519 < Bond61 | Bonds payable | 5000.00 |
| 118 | 2 | Bond61-909876520 < Bond61 | Bonds payable | 3000.00 |
| 119 | 2 | Bond61-909876521 < Bond61 | Bonds payable | 4000.00 |
| 120 | 2 | Bond61-909876522 < Bond61 | Bonds payable | 2000.00 |
| 121 | 2 | Note25-88-654305 | Notes payable | 120000.00 |
| 122 | 3 | Capital-909876522 | Share capital | 160000.00 |
| 123 | 3 | n | Retained earnings (Conversion) | 12574.23 |
| 124 | 4 | Sales-909876522 | Sales | 0 |

| 125 | 5 | 909876522-travelling < Sales department-travelling | Travelling expenses | 0 |
|---|---|---|---|---|
| 126 | 5 | 909876523-travelling < Product department-travelling | Travelling expenses | 0 |
| 127 | 5 | 909876522-other < Sales department-other | Other expenses | 0 |
| 128 | 5 | 909876523-other < Product department-other | Other expenses | 0 |
| 129 | 5 | 909876522-salary < Sales department-salary | Salary expenses | 0 |
| 130 | 5 | Supplies expenses | Cost of goods mined | 0 |
| 131 | 5 | 909876523-salary < Product department-salary < Salary expenses | Cost of goods mined | 0 |
| 132 | 5 | General parts expenses | Cost of goods mined | 0 |
| 133 | 5 | Bond61-interest | Bond interest expenses | 0 |
| 134 | 5 | Note25-interest | Note interest expenses | 0 |
| 135 | 5 | Truck21-amortization < Truck2-amortization < Vehicle-truck-amortization | Amortization expenses | 0 |
| 136 | 5 | Computer server21-amortization < Computer server2-amortization < Computer-amortization | Amortization expenses | 0 |
| 137 | 5 | Computer31-amortization < Computer3-amortization < Computer-amortization | Amortization expenses | 0 |
| 138 | 5 | Computer41-amortization < Computer4-amortization < Computer-amortization | Amortization expenses | 0 |
| 139 | 4 | Accrued interest income-bond11 < Bonds | Investment incomes | 0 |
| 140 | 4 | Accrued interest income-bond12 < Bonds | Investment incomes | 0 |
| 141 | 4 | Accrued interest income-bond13 < Bonds | Investment incomes | 0 |
| 142 | 4 | Accrued interest income-bond22 < Bonds | Investment incomes | 0 |
| 143 | 4 | n | Deposits interest income | 0 |

Figure 2.4-21   Proprietorship1 Converting Multi-Subaccount Names Table

Just as said before, only the first products are added their product codes or their product batch to the lowest multi-subaccounts. For simplification, the product batch is used in all products of the Proprietorship1. These changes have been done in the Figure 2.4-21. They are the Inventory with the Other 39 to the Other 61.

Before entering the dynamic accounting equation on January 1, 2016 into the database dcj210, I first enter two initialization sub-equations.

Cash (1): 0 = Share capital (3): 0

0 = Sales (4): 0 - Cost of goods sold (5):0

All converting transaction sub-equations can be designed and written as the followings.

- I build a transaction sub-equation for the "Account receivable" and the "Account payable" accounts. The transaction sub-equation includes the "Account receivable" account with the Order 35 to the Order 38, the "Account payable" account with the Order 101 to the Order 104, and the part of the "Share capital" account with the Order 122, The first transaction sub-equation is:

Account receivable (1): 2040 + Account receivable (1): 500 + Account receivable (1): 1600 + Account receivable (1): 400 = Account payable (2): 1000 + Account payable (2): 250 + Account payable (2): 150 + Account (2): 300 + Share capital (3): 2840

After entering this transaction, the new balance of the "Share capital" account with the Order 122 is $157,160 (= $160,000 - $2,840).

- The transaction sub-equation includes the "Cash" account with the Order 1 to the Order 7, the part of the "Cash" account with the Order 26, the rest ($157,160) the "Share capital" account with the Order 122, and the "Notes payable" account with the Order 121. The second transaction sub-equation is:

Cash (1): 160000 + Cash (1): 120000 + Cash (1): 17000 + Cash (1): 383.33 + Cash (1): 189 + Cash (1): 30 + Cash (1): 322.67 + Cash (1): -20765 = Share capital (3): 157160 + Notes payable (2): 120000

After entering this transaction, the new balance of the "Cash" account with the Order 26 is -$103,591.77 (= -$124,356.77 + $20,765).

- The transaction sub-equation includes the "Cash" account with the Order 8 to the Order 13 and the "Bonds payable" account with the Order 107 to the Order 112. The third transaction sub-equation is:

Cash (1): 3000 + Cash (1): 4000 + Cash (1): 5000 + Cash (1): 2000 + Cash (1): 3000 + Cash (1): 5000 = Bonds payable (2): 3000 + Bonds payable (2): 4000 + Bonds payable (2): 5000 + Bonds payable (2): 2000 + Bonds payable (2): 3000 + Bonds payable (2): 5000

- The transaction sub-equation includes the "Cash" account with the Order 14 to the Order 19 and the "Bonds payable" account with the Order 113 to the Order 118. The fourth transaction sub-equation is:

  Cash (1): 4000 + Cash (1): 2000 + Cash (1): 5000 + Cash (1): 3000 + Cash (1): 5000 + Cash (1): 3000 = Bonds payable (2): 4000 + Bonds payable (2): 2000 + Bonds payable (2): 5000 + Bonds payable (2): 3000 + Bonds payable (2): 5000 + Bonds payable (2): 3000

- The transaction sub-equation includes the "Cash" account with the Order 20 to the Order 25, the "Vehicle" account with the Order 93, the "Computer" account with the Order 95 to the Order 97, and the "Bonds payable" account with the Order 119 and the Order 120. The fifth transaction sub-equation is:

  Cash (1): 4000 + Cash (1): 2000 + Cash (1): -40000 + Cash (1): -2700 + Cash (1): -1400 + Cash (1): -1300 + Vehicle (1): 40000 + Computer (1): 2700 + Computer (1): 1400 + Computer (1): 1300 = Bonds payable (2): 4000 + Bonds payable (2): 2000

- The transaction sub-equation includes the "Cash" account with the Order 30 to the Order 33 and the "Bonds" account with the Order 89 to the Order 92. The sixth transaction sub-equation is:

  Cash (1): -5000 + Cash (1): -3000 + Cash (1): -2000 + Cash (1): -8000 + Bonds (1): 5000 + Bonds (1): 3000 + Bonds (1): 2000 + Bonds (1): 8000 = 0

- The transaction sub-equation includes the part of the "Cash" account with the Order 26, the "Supplies" account with the Order 34, and the "Inventory" account with the Order 39 to the Order 46. The seventh transaction sub-equation is:

  Cash (1): -101655.45 + Supplies (1): 155.45 + Inventory (1): 6000 + Inventory (1):

30000 + Inventory (1): 10000 + Inventory (1): 27000 + Inventory (1): 6000 + Inventory (1): 12000 + Inventory (1): 5000+ Inventory (1): 5500 = 0

After entering this transaction, the new balance of the "Cash" account with the Order 26 is -$1,936.32 (= -$103,591.77 + $101,655.45).

- The transaction sub-equation includes the rest (-$1,936.32) of the "Cash" account with the Order 26, the part of the "Cash" account with the Order 27, and the "Inventory" account with the Order 47 to the Order 56. The eighth transaction sub-equation is:

Cash (1): -1936.32 + Cash (1): -56563.68 + Inventory (1): 6000 + Inventory (1): 6500 + Inventory (1): 7000 + Inventory (1): 7500 + Inventory (1): 4000 + Inventory (1): 4500 + Inventory (1): 5000 + Inventory (1): 5500 + Inventory (1): 6000 + Inventory (1): 6500 = 0

After entering this transaction, the new balance of the "Cash" account with the Order 27 is -$64,067.86 (= -$120,631.54 + $56,563.68).

- The transaction sub-equation includes the part of the "Cash" account with the Order 27 and the "Inventory" account with the Order 57 to the Order 65. The ninth transaction sub-equation is:

Cash (1): -58350 + Inventory (1): 7500 + Inventory (1): 8500 + Inventory (1): 11000 + Inventory (1): 12000 + Inventory (1): 13000 + Inventory (1): 500 + Inventory (1): 1850 + Inventory (1): 2000 + Inventory (1): 2000 = 0

After entering this transaction, the new balance of the "Cash" account with the Order 27 is -$5,717.86 (= -$64,067.86 + $58,350).

- The transaction sub-equation includes the rest (-$5,717.86) of the "Cash" account with the Order 27, the "Cash" account with the Order 28, the part of the "Accumulated amortization: Vehicle" account with the Order 94, and the "Working-in-process inventory" account with the Order 66 to the Order 74. The tenth transaction sub-equation is:

Cash (1): -5717.86 + Cash (1): -20752.91 + Accumulated amortization: Vehicle (1): -4669.23 + Working-in-process inventory (1): 1800 + Working-in-process inventory (1): 8400 + Working-in-process inventory (1): 3000 + Working-in-process inventory (1): 7800 + Working-in-process inventory (1): 3600 + Working-in-process inventory (1): 1440 + Working-in-process inventory (1): 1500 + Working-in-process inventory (1): 1800 = 0

After entering this transaction, the new balance of the "Accumulated amortization: Vehicle" account with the Order 94 is -$13,330.77 (= -$18,000 + $4,669.23).

- The transaction sub-equation includes the part of the "Accumulated amortization: Vehicle" account with the Order 94 and the "Working-in-process inventory" account with the Order 75 to the Order 82. The eleventh transaction sub-equation is:

Accumulated amortization: Vehicle (1): -12660 + Working-in-process inventory (1): 1740 + Working-in-process inventory (1): 1800 + Working-in-process inventory (1): 2100 + Working-in-process inventory (1): 1200 + Working-in-process inventory (1): 1200 + Working-in-process inventory (1): 1320 + Working-in-process inventory (1): 1500 + Working-in-process inventory (1): 1800 = 0

After entering this transaction, the new balance of the "Accumulated amortization: Vehicle" account with the Order 94 is -$670.77 (= -$13,330.77 + $12,660).

- The transaction sub-equation includes the rest (-$670.77) of the "Accumulated amortization: Vehicle" account with the Order 94, the "Accumulated amortization: Computer" account with the Order 98 to 100, the "Working-in-process inventory" account with the Order 83 to 88, and the "Retained earnings (Conversion)" account with the balance $12,574.23. The twelfth transaction sub-equation is:

Accumulated amortization: Vehicle (1): -670.77 + Accumulated amortization: Computer (1): -1687.5 + Accumulated amortization: Computer (1): -875 +

Accumulated amortization: Computer (1): -812.5 + Working-in-process inventory (1): 1860 + Working-in-process inventory (1): 2100 + Working-in-process inventory (1): 2460 + Working-in-process inventory (1): 3000 + Working-in-process inventory (1): 3600 + Working-in-process inventory (1): 3600 = Retained earnings (Conversion) (3): 12574.23

The dynamic accounting equation of the Proprietorship1 on December 31, 2015 has entered into the database dcj210.

### 2.4.6.2 Brief Summary of the Proprietorship1

The Figure 2.4-22 shows the partial information of inventory purchased or inventory sold by other social members in the public database dcj200.

SQLQuery1.sql - LIU...SS.dcj200 (sa (55))*

```
use dcj200
select sum(amount) as sum0 from InventoryByMembers where Recorder='88-654309'
and TransDate between '2015-01-01' and '2015-12-31'
select * from InventoryByMembers where Recorder='88-654309' and TransDate between '2015-01-01' and '2015-12-31'
```

100 %

Results | Messages

| | sum0 |
|---|---|
| 1 | -218350.00 |

| | IDM | Amount | Symbol | MultiSubaccount | Recorder | TransDate | Unit |
|---|---|---|---|---|---|---|---|
| 1 | Cash paym | -6000.00 | n | Inven31-P1-20151125-In31-1000T < Inven3 | 88-654309 | 2015-12-31 | -1000 |
| 2 | Cash paym | -30000.00 | n | Inven32-P1-20151125-In32-1000T < Inven3 | 88-654309 | 2015-12-31 | -1000 |
| 3 | Cash paym | -10000.00 | n | Inven331-P1-20151125-In331-1000T < Inven33 < Inven3 | 88-654309 | 2015-12-31 | -1000 |
| 4 | Cash paym | -27000.00 | n | Inven332-P1-20151125-In332-1000T < Inven33 < Inven3 | 88-654309 | 2015-12-31 | -1000 |
| 5 | Cash paym | -6000.00 | n | HGFCVB parts-P1-20151125-HGP-1000T < QASXC parts < Inven3 | 88-654309 | 2015-12-31 | -1000 |
| 6 | Cash paym | -12000.00 | n | PPGHUP parts-P1-20151125-PPP-1000T < ASDUP parts < Inven3 | 88-654309 | 2015-12-31 | -1000 |
| 7 | Cash paym | -5000.00 | n | Food111-P1-20151203-F111-1000T < Food11 < Food1 | 88-654309 | 2015-12-31 | -1000 |
| 8 | Cash paym | -5500.00 | n | Food112-P1-20151203-F112-1000T < Food11 < Food1 | 88-654309 | 2015-12-31 | -1000 |
| 9 | Cash paym | -6000.00 | n | Food113-P1-20151203-F113-1000T < Food11 < Food1 | 88-654309 | 2015-12-31 | -1000 |
| 10 | Cash paym | -6500.00 | n | Food121-P1-20151203-F121-1000T < Food12 < Food1 | 88-654309 | 2015-12-31 | -1000 |
| 11 | Cash paym | -7000.00 | n | Food122-P1-20151203-F122-1000T < Food12 < Food1 | 88-654309 | 2015-12-31 | -1000 |
| 12 | Cash paym | -7500.00 | n | Food123-P1-20151203-F123-1000T < Food12 < Food1 | 88-654309 | 2015-12-31 | -1000 |
| 13 | Cash paym | -4000.00 | n | Food211-P1-20151203-F211-1000T < Food21 < Food2 | 88-654309 | 2015-12-31 | -1000 |
| 14 | Cash paym | -4500.00 | n | Food212-P1-20151203-F212-1000T < Food21 < Food2 | 88-654309 | 2015-12-31 | -1000 |
| 15 | Cash paym | -5000.00 | n | Food213-P1-20151203-F213-1000T < Food21 < Food2 | 88-654309 | 2015-12-31 | -1000 |
| 16 | Cash paym | -5500.00 | n | Food214-P1-20151203-F214-1000T < Food21 < Food2 | 88-654309 | 2015-12-31 | -1000 |
| 17 | Cash paym | -6000.00 | n | Food221-P1-20151203-F221-1000T < Food22 < Food2 | 88-654309 | 2015-12-31 | -1000 |
| 18 | Cash paym | -6500.00 | n | Food222-P1-20151203-F222-1000T < Food22 < Food2 | 88-654309 | 2015-12-31 | -1000 |
| 19 | Cash paym | -7500.00 | n | Food23-P1-20151203-F23-1000T < Food2 | 88-654309 | 2015-12-31 | -1000 |
| 20 | Cash paym | -8500.00 | n | Food311-P1-20151203-F311-1000T < Food31 < Food3 | 88-654309 | 2015-12-31 | -1000 |
| 21 | Cash paym | -11000.00 | n | Food312-P1-20151203-F312-1000T < Food31 < Food3 | 88-654309 | 2015-12-31 | -1000 |
| 22 | Cash paym | -12000.00 | n | Food321-P1-20151203-F321-1000T < Food32 < Food3 | 88-654309 | 2015-12-31 | -1000 |
| 23 | Cash paym | -13000.00 | n | Food322-P1-20151203-F322-1000T < Food32 < Food3 | 88-654309 | 2015-12-31 | -1000 |
| 24 | Cash paym | -500.00 | n | Inven411 < Inven41 < Inven4 | 88-654309 | 2015-12-31 | -100 |
| 25 | Cash paym | -1850.00 | n | Inven412 < Inven41 < Inven4 | 88-654309 | 2015-12-31 | -100 |
| 26 | Cash paym | -2000.00 | n | TTTCU parts < TTT parts < Inven4 | 88-654309 | 2015-12-31 | -100 |
| 27 | Cash paym | -2000.00 | n | RRRHJK parts < Inven4 | 88-654309 | 2015-12-31 | -100 |

Query executed successfully. LIU\SQLE

Figure 2.4-22 Proprietorship1 Inventory Purchased or Sold by Other Members

## 2.4.7 Sample of the Proprietorship2

The Proprietorship2 is owned by the individual A24 completely and has total share capital $150,000. The Proprietorship1 produces the general parts and the foods. The Figure 2.4-23 shows its product names, costs, and sale prices.

| Order | Product (the Lowest-level Subaccount) Names | Multi-subaccount Names | Costs | Sale Prices |
|---|---|---|---|---|
| 1 | Inven411 | Inven411 < Inven41 < Inven4 | 3.00 | 5.00 |
| 2 | Inven412 | Inven412 < Inven41 < Inven4 | 11.10 | 18.50 |
| 3 | TTTCU parts | TTTCU parts < TTT parts < Inven4 | 12.00 | 20.00 |
| 4 | RRRHJK parts | RRRHJK parts < Inven4 | 12.00 | 20.00 |
| 5 | Food411 | Food411 < Food41 < Food4 | 5.00 | 10.00 |
| 6 | Food412 | Food412 < Food41 < Food4 | 5.50 | 11.00 |
| 7 | Food421 | Food421 < Food42 < Food4 | 6.00 | 12.00 |
| 8 | Food422 | Food422 < Food42 < Food4 | 6.50 | 13.00 |
| 9 | Food43 | Food43 < Food4 | 7.00 | 14.00 |
| 10 | Food44 | Food44 < Food4 | 7.50 | 15.00 |
| 11 | Food511 | Food511 < Food51 < Food5 | 4.00 | 8.00 |
| 12 | Food512 | Food512 < Food51 < Food5 | 4.50 | 9.00 |
| 13 | Food513 | Food513 < Food51 < Food5 | 5.00 | 10.00 |
| 14 | Food514 | Food514 < Food51 < Food5 | 5.50 | 11.00 |
| 15 | Food521 | Food521 < Food52 < Food5 | 6.00 | 12.00 |
| 16 | Food522 | Food522 < Food52 < Food5 | 6.50 | 13.00 |
| 17 | Food53 | Food53 < Food5 | 8.00 | 16.00 |
| 18 | Food611 | Food611 < Food61 < Food6 | 10.00 | 20.00 |
| 19 | Food612 | Food612 < Food61 < Food6 | 12.00 | 24.00 |
| 20 | Food613 | Food613 < Food61 < Food6 | 13.00 | 26.00 |
| 21 | Food614 | Food614 < Food61 < Food6 | 15.00 | 30.00 |
| 22 | Food621 | Food621 < Food62 < Food6 | 13.00 | 26.00 |
| 23 | Food622 | Food622 < Food62 < Food6 | 14.00 | 28.00 |
| 24 | Supplies1 | Supplies1 | 7.00 | 14.00 |
| 25 | Supplies2 | Supplies2 | 8.00 | 16.00 |

Figure 2.4-23   Proprietorship2 Products and Sale Prices Table

For a producing foods company, the costs of its food products are most the labor and inventory costs. When the Proprietorship2 uses the MathAccounting software, the "Working-in-process inventory" is treated as a parent account of the class 1 and the "Cost of goods sold" is treated as the parent accounts of the class 5. For simplification, the "Cost of goods sold" account has only three one-level subaccounts of the "Supplies expenses", the "Salary expenses" for employee A25, and the other general parts in this book.

### 2.4.7.1 Conversion of the Proprietorship2

The Proprietorship2 will convert to the MathAccounting software on January 1, 2016. The Figure 2.4-24 and the Figure 2.4-25 show the converting reference table and the multi-subaccount names table respectively.

| Order | Class | Account Name (**Subtotal Name**) | Balance | Row |
|---|---|---|---|---|
| **1** | **1** | **(Current assets)** | - | **103** |
| 2 | 1 | Cash | 8768.69 | 104 |
| 3 | 1 | Supplies | 167.85 | 106 |
| 4 | 1 | Account receivable | 2400.00 | 108 |
| 5 | 1 | Inventory | 149000.00 | 110 |
| 6 | 1 | Working-in-process inventory | 72350.00 | 112 |
| **7** | **1** | **(Long term investments)** | - | **141** |
| 8 | 1 | Bonds | 17000.00 | 142 |
| **9** | **1** | **(Equipment)** | - | **171** |
| 10 | 1 | Vehicle | 40000.00 | 172 |
| 11 | 1 | Accumulated amortization: Vehicle | -13333.33 | 173 |
| 12 | 1 | Computer | 5400.00 | 174 |
| 13 | 1 | Accumulated amortization: Computer | -2925.00 | 175 |
| **14** | **2** | **(Current liabilities)** | - | **203** |
| 15 | 2 | Account payable | 2600.00 | 204 |
| 16 | 2 | Accrued interest payable | 0 | 206 |
| 17 | 2 | Tax payable | 0 | 208 |
| **18** | **2** | **(Long term liabilities)** | - | **251** |
| 19 | 2 | Bonds payable | 120000.00 | 252 |
| 20 | 2 | Notes payable | 0 | 254 |
| **21** | **3** | **(Owners' capital)** | - | **303** |
| 22 | 3 | Share capital | 150000.00 | 304 |
| 23 | 3 | Retained earnings (conversion) | 6228.21 | 306 |
| **24** | **4** | **(Revenues)** | - | **403** |
| 25 | 4 | Sales | | 404 |
| **26** | **5** | **(Cost)** | - | **431** |
| 27 | 5 | Cost of goods sold | | 432 |
| **28** | **5** | **(Operating and administrative expenses)** | - | **453** |
| 29 | 5 | Travelling expenses | 0 | 454 |
| 30 | 5 | Other expenses | 0 | 455 |

| | | | | | |
|---|---|---|---|---|---|
| 31 | 5 | Salary expenses | | 0 | 456 |
| 32 | 5 | Cost of goods sold | | 0 | 457 |
| 33 | 5 | Bond interest expenses | | 0 | 458 |
| 34 | 5 | Note interest expenses | | 0 | 460 |
| 35 | 5 | Amortization expenses | | 0 | 462 |
| **36** | **4** | **(Other income)** | | - | **475** |
| 37 | 4 | Investment incomes | | | 476 |
| 38 | 4 | Deposits interest incomes | | 0 | 478 |
| **39** | **5** | **(Tax)** | | - | **600** |
| 40 | 5 | Tax expenses | | 0 | 602 |

Figure 2.4-24   Proprietorship2 Converting Reference Table

| Order | Class | Multi-subaccount Name | Parent Name | Lowest Subaccount Balance |
|---|---|---|---|---|
| 1 | 1 | 909876524-i-owners < Cash receipts from owners < Financial activities | Cash | 150000.00 |
| 2 | 1 | 88-654305-i-note25 < Cash receipts from banks < Financial activities | Cash | 0 |
| 3 | 1 | 88-654306-c-operating < Cash receipts from customers < Operating activities | Cash | 12000.00 |
| 4 | 1 | 88-654304-c-interest of investment bond12 < Cash receipts from investments < Investing activities | Cash | 378.00 |
| 5 | 1 | 88-654305-c-interest of investment bond21 < Cash receipts from investments < Investing activities | Cash | 478.33 |
| 6 | 1 | 88-654305-c-interest of investment bond22 < Cash receipts from investments < Investing activities | Cash | 161.33 |
| 7 | 1 | 909876501-i-bond71 < Cash receipts from issued bonds < Financial activities | Cash | 7000.00 |
| 8 | 1 | 909876502-i-bond71 < Cash receipts from issued bonds < Financial activities | Cash | 6000.00 |
| 9 | 1 | 909876504-i-bond71 < Cash receipts from issued bonds < Financial activities | Cash | 5000.00 |
| 10 | 1 | 909876507-i-bond71 < Cash receipts from issued bonds < Financial activities | Cash | 6000.00 |
| 11 | 1 | 909876509-i-bond71 < Cash receipts from issued bonds < Financial activities | Cash | 6000.00 |
| 12 | 1 | 909876511-i-bond71 < Cash receipts from issued bonds < Financial activities | Cash | 5000.00 |
| 13 | 1 | 909876512-i-bond71 < Cash receipts from issued bonds < Financial activities | Cash | 4000.00 |
| 14 | 1 | 909876516-i-bond71 < Cash receipts from issued bonds < Financial activities | Cash | 7000.00 |
| 15 | 1 | 909876517-i-bond71 < Cash receipts from issued bonds < Financial activities | Cash | 5000.00 |
| 16 | 1 | 909876518-i-bond71 < Cash receipts from issued bonds < Financial activities | Cash | 6000.00 |
| 17 | 1 | 909876519-i-bond71 < Cash receipts from issued bonds < Financial activities | Cash | 5000.00 |
| 18 | 1 | 909876520-i-bond71 < Cash receipts from issued bonds < Financial activities | Cash | 8000.00 |
| 19 | 1 | 909876504-i-bond72 < Cash receipts from issued bonds < Financial activities | Cash | 4000.00 |
| 20 | 1 | 909876505-i-bond72 < Cash receipts from issued bonds < Financial activities | Cash | 5000.00 |

| 21 | 1 | 909876506-i-bond72 < Cash receipts from issued bonds < Financial activities | Cash | 6000.00 |
|---|---|---|---|---|
| 22 | 1 | 909876508-i-bond72 < Cash receipts from issued bonds < Financial activities | Cash | 5000.00 |
| 23 | 1 | 909876510-i-bond72 < Cash receipts from issued bonds < Financial activities | Cash | 6000.00 |
| 24 | 1 | 909876513-i-bond72 < Cash receipts from issued bonds < Financial activities | Cash | 4000.00 |
| 25 | 1 | 909876515-i-bond72 < Cash receipts from issued bonds < Financial activities | Cash | 5000.00 |
| 26 | 1 | 909876516-i-bond72 < Cash receipts from issued bonds < Financial activities | Cash | 6000.00 |
| 27 | 1 | 909876517-i-bond72 < Cash receipts from issued bonds < Financial activities | Cash | 5000.00 |
| 28 | 1 | 909876518-i-bond72 < Cash receipts from issued bonds < Financial activities | Cash | 4000.00 |
| 29 | 1 | 88-654306-t-truck2 < Cash payments for machinery < Operating activities | Cash | -40000.00 |
| 30 | 1 | 88-654306-t-computer server2 < Cash payments for machinery < Operating activities | Cash | -2700.00 |
| 31 | 1 | 88-654306-t-computer3 < Cash payments for machinery < Operating activities | Cash | -1400.00 |
| 32 | 1 | 88-654306-t-computer4 < Cash payments for machinery < Operating activities | Cash | -1300.00 |
| 33 | 1 | Cash payments for operating expenses < Operating activities | Cash | -101132.56 |
| 34 | 1 | Cash payments for operating expenses < Operating activities | Cash | -100637.18 |
| 35 | 1 | 88-654303-n-tax < Cash payments for operating expenses < Operating activities | Cash | -10079.23 |
| 36 | 1 | Cash payments to suppliers<Operating activities | Cash | 0 |
| 37 | 1 | 88-654304-n-investment bond12 < Cash payments for investments < Investing activities | Cash | -6000.00 |
| 38 | 1 | 88-654305-n-investment bond21 < Cash payments for investments < Investing activities | Cash | -7000.00 |
| 39 | 1 | 88-654305-n-investment bond22 < Cash payments for investments < Investing activities | Cash | -4000.00 |
| 40 | 1 | n | Supplies | 167.85 |
| 41 | 1 | 123456784 | Account receivable | 1000.00 |
| 42 | 1 | 123456783 | Account receivable | 300.00 |
| 43 | 1 | 123456782 | Account receivable | 800.00 |
| 44 | 1 | 123456781 | Account receivable | 300.00 |
| 45 | 1 | Inven411-P2-20151127-In411-1000T < Inven41 < Inven4 | Inventory | 3.00*1000 = 3000.00 |
| 46 | 1 | Inven412-P2-20151127-In412-1000T < Inven41 < Inven4 | Inventory | 11.10*1000 = 11100.00 |
| 47 | 1 | TTTCU parts-P2-20151127-TTP-1000T < TTT parts < Inven4 | Inventory | 12.00*1000 = 12000.00 |
| 48 | 1 | RRRHJK parts-P2-20151127-RRP-1000T < Inven4 | Inventory | 12.00*1000 = 12000.00 |
| 49 | 1 | Food411-P2-20151127-FO411-1000T < Food41 < Food4 | Inventory | 5.00*1000 = 5000.00 |
| 50 | 1 | Food412-P2-20151127-FO412-1000T < Food41 < Food4 | Inventory | 5.50*1000 = 5500.00 |
| 51 | 1 | Food421-P2-20151127-FO421-1000T < Food42 < Food4 | Inventory | 6.00*1000 = 6000.00 |
| 52 | 1 | Food422-P2-20151127-FO422-1000T < Food42 < Food4 | Inventory | 6.50*1000 = 6500.00 |
| 53 | 1 | Food43-P2-20151127-FO43-1000T < Food4 | Inventory | 7.00*1000 = 7000.00 |
| 54 | 1 | Food44-P2-20151127-FO44-1000T < Food4 | Inventory | 7.50*1000 = 7500.00 |
| 55 | 1 | Food511-P2-20151127-FO511-1000T < Food51 < Food5 | Inventory | 4.00*1000 = 4000.00 |
| 56 | 1 | Food512-P2-20151127-FO512-1000T < Food51 < Food5 | Inventory | 4.50*1000 = 4500.00 |

| 57 | 1 | Food513-P2-20151127-FO513-1000T < Food51 < Food5 | Inventory | 5.00*1000 = 5000.00 |
|---|---|---|---|---|
| 58 | 1 | Food514-P2-20151127-FO514-1000T < Food51 < Food5 | Inventory | 5.50*1000 = 5500.00 |
| 59 | 1 | Food521-P2-20151127-FO521-1000T < Food52 < Food5 | Inventory | 6.00*1000 = 6000.00 |
| 60 | 1 | Food522-P2-20151127-FO522-1000T < Food52 < Food5 | Inventory | 6.50*1000 = 6500.00 |
| 61 | 1 | Food53-P2-20151127-FO53-1000T < Food5 | Inventory | 8.00*1000 = 8000.00 |
| 62 | 1 | Food611-P2-20151127-FO611-200T < Food61 < Food6 | Inventory | 10.00*200 = 2000.00 |
| 63 | 1 | Food612-P2-20151127-FO612-200T < Food61 < Food6 | Inventory | 12.00*200 = 2400.00 |
| 64 | 1 | Food613-P2-20151127-FO613-200T < Food61 < Food6 | Inventory | 13.00*200 = 2600.00 |
| 65 | 1 | Food614-P2-20151127-FO614-200T < Food61 < Food6 | Inventory | 15.00*200 = 3000.00 |
| 66 | 1 | Food621-P2-20151127-FO621-200T < Food62 < Food6 | Inventory | 13.00*200 = 2600.00 |
| 67 | 1 | Food622-P2-20151127-FO622-200T < Food62 < Food6 | Inventory | 14.00*200 = 2800.00 |
| 68 | 1 | Supplies1-P2-20150920-SUP1-200T | Inventory | 7.00*200 = 1400.00 |
| 69 | 1 | Supplies2-P2-20150920-SUP2-200T | Inventory | 8.00*200 = 1600.00 |
| 70 | 1 | Inven31 < Inven3 | Inventory | 10.00*100 = 1000.00 |
| 71 | 1 | Inven32 < Inven3 | Inventory | 50.00*100 = 5000.00 |
| 72 | 1 | Inven331 < Inven33 < Inven3 | Inventory | 20.00*100 = 2000.00 |
| 73 | 1 | Inven332 < Inven33 < Inven3 | Inventory | 45.00*100 = 4500.00 |
| 74 | 1 | HGFCVB parts < QASXC parts < Inven3 | Inventory | 10.00*100 = 1000.00 |
| 75 | 1 | PPGHUP parts < ASDUP parts < Inven3 | Inventory | 20.00*100 = 2000.00 |
| 76 | 1 | Working-Inven411 < Working-Inven41 < Working-Inven4 | Working-in-process inventory | 2.00*1000 = 2000.00 |
| 77 | 1 | Working-Inven412 < Working-Inven41 < Working-Inven4 | Working-in-process inventory | 6.10*1000 = 6100.00 |
| 78 | 1 | Working-TTTCU parts < Working-TTT parts < Working-Inven4 | Working-in-process inventory | 6.50*1000 = 6500.00 |
| 79 | 1 | Working-RRRHJK parts < Working-Inven4 | Working-in-process inventory | 7.00*1000 = 7000.00 |
| 80 | 1 | Working-Food411 < Working-Food41 < Working-Food4 | Working-in-process inventory | 3.00*1000 = 3000.00 |
| 81 | 1 | Working-Food412 < Working-Food41 < Working-Food4 | Working-in-process inventory | 3.25*1000 = 3250.00 |
| 82 | 1 | Working-Food421 < Working-Food42 < Working-Food4 | Working-in-process inventory | 3.00*1000 = 3000.00 |
| 83 | 1 | Working-Food422 < Working-Food42 < Working-Food4 | Working-in-process inventory | 3.50*1000 = 3500.00 |
| 84 | 1 | Working-Food43 < Working-Food4 | Working-in-process inventory | 4.00*1000 = 4000.00 |
| 85 | 1 | Working-Food44 < Working-Food4 | Working-in-process inventory | 3.50*1000 = 3500.00 |
| 86 | 1 | Working-Food511 < Working-Food51 < Working-Food5 | Working-in-process inventory | 2.00*1000 = 2000.00 |
| 87 | 1 | Working-Food512 < Working-Food51 < Working-Food5 | Working-in-process inventory | 2.50*1000 = 2500.00 |
| 88 | 1 | Working-Food513 < Working-Food51 < Working-Food5 | Working-in-process inventory | 3.00*1000 = 3000.00 |
| 89 | 1 | Working-Food514 < Working-Food51 < Working-Food5 | Working-in-process inventory | 3.50*1000 = 3500.00 |
| 90 | 1 | Working-Food521 < Working-Food52 < Working-Food5 | Working-in-process inventory | 3.00*1000 = 3000.00 |
| 91 | 1 | Working-Food522 < Working-Food52 < Working-Food5 | Working-in-process inventory | 3.50*1000 = 3500.00 |
| 92 | 1 | Working-Food53 < Working-Food5 | Working-in-process inventory | 4.00*1000 = 4000.00 |
| 93 | 1 | Working-Food611 < Working-Food61 < Working-Food6 | Working-in-process inventory | 5.00*200 = 1000.00 |

| 94 | 1 | Working-Food612 < Working-Food61 < Working-Food6 | Working-in-process inventory | 6.00*200 = 1200.00 |
|---|---|---|---|---|
| 95 | 1 | Working-Food613 < Working-Food61 < Working-Food6 | Working-in-process inventory | 6.50*200 = 1300.00 |
| 96 | 1 | Working-Food614 < Working-Food61 < Working-Food6 | Working-in-process inventory | 7.50*200 = 1500.00 |
| 97 | 1 | Working-Food621 < Working-Food62 < Working-Food6 | Working-in-process inventory | 6.00*200 = 1200.00 |
| 98 | 1 | Working-Food622 < Working-Food62 < Working-Food6 | Working-in-process inventory | 7.00*200 = 1400.00 |
| 99 | 1 | Working-Supplies1 | Working-in-process inventory | 3.00*200 = 600.00 |
| 100 | 1 | Working-Supplies2 | Working-in-process inventory | 4.00*200 = 800.00 |
| 101 | 1 | Bond11 | Bonds | 0 |
| 102 | 1 | Bond12 | Bonds | 6000.00 |
| 103 | 1 | Bond21 | Bonds | 7000.00 |
| 104 | 1 | Bond22 | Bonds | 4000.00 |
| 105 | 1 | Truck21 < Truck2 < Truck | Vehicle | 40000.00 |
| 106 | 1 | Truck21-accumulated amortization < Truck2-accumulated amortization < Truck-accumulated amortization | Accumulated amortization: Vehicle | -13333.33 |
| 107 | 1 | Computer server21 < Computer server2 < Computer server | Computer | 2700.00 |
| 108 | 1 | Computer31 < Computer3 | Computer | 1400.00 |
| 109 | 1 | Computer41 < Computer4 | Computer | 1300.00 |
| 110 | 1 | Computer server21-accumulated amortization < Computer server2-accumulated amortization < Computer server-accumulated amortization | Accumulated amortization: Computer | -1462.50 |
| 111 | 1 | Computer31-accumulated amortization < Computer3-accumulated amortization | Accumulated amortization: Computer | -758.33 |
| 112 | 1 | Computer41-accumulated amortization < Computer4-accumulated amortization | Accumulated amortization: Computer | -704.17 |
| 113 | 2 | 123456084 | Account payable | 2000.00 |
| 114 | 2 | 123456083 | Account payable | 0 |
| 115 | 2 | 123456082 | Account payable | 200.00 |
| 116 | 2 | 123456081 | Account payable | 400.00 |
| 117 | 2 | Bond71-interest payable < Bonds-interest payable | Accrued interest payable | 0 |
| 118 | 2 | Bond72-interest payable < Bonds-interest payable | Accrued interest payable | 0 |
| 119 | 2 | Notes-interest payable | Accrued interest payable | 0 |
| 120 | 2 | Bond71-909876501 < Bond71 | Bonds payable | 7000.00 |
| 121 | 2 | Bond71-909876502 < Bond71 | Bonds payable | 6000.00 |
| 122 | 2 | Bond71-909876504 < Bond71 | Bonds payable | 5000.00 |
| 123 | 2 | Bond71-909876507 < Bond71 | Bonds payable | 6000.00 |
| 124 | 2 | Bond71-909876509 < Bond71 | Bonds payable | 6000.00 |
| 125 | 2 | Bond71-909876511 < Bond71 | Bonds payable | 5000.00 |
| 126 | 2 | Bond71-909876512 < Bond71 | Bonds payable | 4000.00 |
| 127 | 2 | Bond71-909876516 < Bond71 | Bonds payable | 7000.00 |
| 128 | 2 | Bond71-909876517 < Bond71 | Bonds payable | 5000.00 |

| | | | | |
|---|---|---|---|---|
| 129 | 2 | Bond71-909876518 < Bond71 | Bonds payable | 6000.00 |
| 130 | 2 | Bond71-909876519 < Bond71 | Bonds payable | 5000.00 |
| 131 | 2 | Bond71-909876520 < Bond71 | Bonds payable | 8000.00 |
| 132 | 2 | Bond72-909876504 < Bond72 | Bonds payable | 4000.00 |
| 133 | 2 | Bond72-909876505 < Bond72 | Bonds payable | 5000.00 |
| 134 | 2 | Bond72-909876506 < Bond72 | Bonds payable | 6000.00 |
| 135 | 2 | Bond72-909876508 < Bond72 | Bonds payable | 5000.00 |
| 136 | 2 | Bond72-909876510 < Bond72 | Bonds payable | 6000.00 |
| 137 | 2 | Bond72-909876513 < Bond72 | Bonds payable | 4000.00 |
| 138 | 2 | Bond72-909876515 < Bond72 | Bonds payable | 5000.00 |
| 139 | 2 | Bond72-909876516 < Bond72 | Bonds payable | 6000.00 |
| 140 | 2 | Bond72-909876517 < Bond72 | Bonds payable | 5000.00 |
| 141 | 2 | Bond72-909876518 < Bond72 | Bonds payable | 4000.00 |
| 142 | 3 | Capital-909876524 | Share capital | 150000.00 |
| 143 | 3 | n | Retained earnings (Conversion) | 6228.21 |
| 144 | 4 | Sales-909876525 | Sales | 0 |
| 145 | 5 | 909876524-travelling < Sales department-travelling | Travelling expenses | 0 |
| 146 | 5 | 909876525-travelling < Product department-travelling | Travelling expenses | 0 |
| 147 | 5 | 909876524-other < Sales department-other | Other expenses | 0 |
| 148 | 5 | 909876525-other < Product department-other | Other expenses | 0 |
| 149 | 5 | 909876524-salary < Sales department-salary | Salary expenses | 0 |
| 150 | 5 | Supplies expenses | Cost of goods mined | 0 |
| 151 | 5 | 909876525-salary < Product department-salary < Salary expenses | Cost of goods mined | 0 |
| 152 | 5 | General parts expenses | Cost of goods mined | 0 |
| 153 | 5 | Bond71-interest | Bond interest expenses | 0 |
| 154 | 5 | Bond72-interest | Bond interest expenses | 0 |
| 155 | 5 | Note25-interest | Note interest expenses | 0 |
| 156 | 5 | Truck21-amortization < Truck2-amortization < Vehicle-truck-amortization | Amortization expenses | 0 |
| 157 | 5 | Computer server21-amortization < Computer server2-amortization < Computer-amortization | Amortization expenses | 0 |
| 158 | 5 | Computer31-amortization < Computer3-amortization < Computer-amortization | Amortization expenses | 0 |
| 159 | 5 | Computer41-amortization < Computer4-amortization < Computer-amortization | Amortization expenses | 0 |
| 160 | 4 | Accrued interest income-bond12 < Bonds | Investment incomes | 0 |
| 161 | 4 | Accrued interest income-bond21 < Bonds | Investment incomes | 0 |
| 162 | 4 | Accrued interest income-bond22 < Bonds | Investment incomes | 0 |
| 163 | 4 | n | Deposits interest income | 0 |

Figure 2.4-25   Proprietorship2 Converting Multi-Subaccount Names Table

Just as said before, only the first products are added their product codes or their product batch to the lowest multi-subaccounts. For simplification, the product batch is used in all products of the Proprietorship2. These changes have been done in the Figure 2.4-26. They are the Inventory with the Other 45 to the Other 69.

After I first enter the two initialization sub-equations, all converting transaction sub-equations can be designed and written as the followings.

- I build a transaction sub-equation for the "Account receivable" and the "Account payable" accounts. The transaction sub-equation includes the "Account receivable" account with the Order 41 to the Order 44, the "Account payable" account with the Order 113 to the Order 116, and the part of the "Cash" account with the Order 3, The first transaction sub-equation is:

  Cash (1): 200 + Account receivable (1): 1000 + Account receivable (1): 300 + Account receivable (1): 800 + Account receivable (1): 300 = Account payable (2): 2000 + Account payable (2): 200 + Account payable (2): 400

  After entering this transaction, the new balance of the "Cash" account with the Order 3 is $11,800 (= $120,000 - $200).

- The transaction sub-equation includes the "Cash" account with the Order 1 and the Order 2, the rest ($11,800) of the "Cash" account with the Order 3, the part the "Cash" account with the Order 33, the "Cash" account with the Order 4 to the Order 6, and the "Share capital" account with the Order 142. Because the balance of the "Cash" with the Order 2 is zero, the second transaction sub-equation is:

  Cash (1): 150000 + Cash (1): 11800 + Cash (1): -12817.66 + Cash (1): 378 + Cash (1): 478.33 + Cash (1): 161.33 = Share capital (3): 150000

  After entering this transaction, the new balance of the "Cash" account with the Order 33 is -$88,314.90 (= -$101,132.56 + $12,817.66).

- The transaction sub-equation includes the "Cash" account with the Order 7 to the

Order 12 and the "Bonds payable" account with the Order 120 to the Order 125. The third transaction sub-equation is:

Cash (1): 7000 + Cash (1): 6000 + Cash (1): 5000 + Cash (1): 6000 + Cash (1): 6000 + Cash (1): 5000 = Bonds payable (2): 7000 + Bonds payable (2): 6000 + Bonds payable (2): 5000 + Bonds payable (2): 6000 + Bonds payable (2): 6000 + Bonds payable (2): 5000

- The transaction sub-equation includes the "Cash" account with the Order 13 to the Order 18 and the "Bonds payable" account with the Order 126 to the Order 131. The fourth transaction sub-equation is:

Cash (1): 4000 + Cash (1):7000 + Cash (1): 5000 + Cash (1): 6000 + Cash (1): 5000 + Cash (1): 8000 = Bonds payable (2): 4000 + Bonds payable (2): 7000 + Bonds payable (2): 5000 + Bonds payable (2): 6000 + Bonds payable (2): 5000 + Bonds payable (2): 8000

- The transaction sub-equation includes the "Cash" account with the Order 19 to the Order 24 and the "Bonds payable" account with the Order 132 and the Order 137. The fifth transaction sub-equation is:

Cash (1): 4000 + Cash (1):5000 + Cash (1): 6000 + Cash (1): 5000 + Cash (1): 6000 + Cash (1): 4000 = Bonds payable (2): 4000 + Bonds payable (2): 5000 + Bonds payable (2): 6000 + Bonds payable (2): 5000 + Bonds payable (2): 6000 + Bonds payable (2): 4000

- The transaction sub-equation includes the "Cash" account with the Order 25 to the Order 28 and the "Bonds" account with the Order 138 to the Order 141. The sixth transaction sub-equation is:

Cash (1): 5000 + Cash (1): 6000 + Cash (1): 5000 + Cash (1): 4000 = Bonds payable (2): 5000 + Bonds payable (2): 6000 + Bonds payable (2): 5000 + Bonds payable (2): 4000

- The transaction sub-equation includes the "Cash" account with the Order 29 to the Order 32, the "Vehicle" account with the Order 105, and the "Computer" account with the Order 107 to the Order 109. The seventh transaction sub-equation is:

  Cash (1): -40000 + Cash (1): -2700 + Cash (1): -1400 + Cash (1): -1300 + Vehicle (1): 40000 + Computer (1): 2700 + Computer (1): 1400 + Computer (1): 1300 = 0

- The transaction sub-equation includes the "Cash" account with the Order 37 to the Order 39 and the "Bonds" account with the Order 102 to the Order 104. The eighth transaction sub-equation is:

  Cash (1): -6000 + Cash (1): -7000 + Cash (1): -4000 + Bonds (1): 6000 + Bonds (1): 7000 + Bonds (1): 4000 = 0

- The transaction sub-equation includes the part of the "Cash" account with the Order 33, the "Supplies" account with the Order 40, and the "Inventory" account with the Order 45 to the Order 54. The ninth transaction sub-equation is:

  Cash (1): -75767.85 + Supplies (1): 167.85 + Inventory (1): 3000 + Inventory (1): 11100 + Inventory (1): 12000 + Inventory (1): 12000 + Inventory (1): 5000 + Inventory (1): 5500 + Inventory (1): 6000 + Inventory (1): 6500 + Inventory (1): 7000 + Inventory (1): 7500 = 0

  After entering this transaction, the new balance of the "Cash" account with the Order 33 is -$12,547.05 (= -$88,314.90 + $75,767.85).

- The transaction sub-equation includes the rest (-$12,547.05) of the "Cash" account with the Order 33, the part of the "Cash" account with the Order 34, and the "Inventory" account with the Order 55 to 64. The tenth transaction sub-equation is:

Cash (1): -12547.05 + Cash (1): -33952.95 + Inventory (1): 4000 + Inventory (1): 4500 + Inventory (1): 5000 + Inventory (1): 5500 + Inventory (1): 6000 + Inventory (1): 6500 + Inventory (1): 8000 + Inventory (1): 2000 + Inventory (1): 2400 + Inventory (1): 2600 = 0

After entering this transaction, the new balance of the "Cash" account with the Order 34 is -$66,684.23 (= -$100637.18 + $33,952.95).

- The transaction sub-equation includes the part of the "Cash" account with the Order 34 and the "Inventory" account with the Order 65 to the Order 75. The eleventh transaction sub-equation is:

Cash (1): -26900 + Inventory (1): 3000 + Inventory (1): 2600 + Inventory (1): 2800 + Inventory (1): 1400 + Inventory (1): 1600 + Inventory (1): 1000 + Inventory (1): 5000 + Inventory (1): 2000 + Inventory (1): 4500 + Inventory (1): 1000 + Inventory (1): 2000 = 0

After entering this transaction, the new balance of the "Cash" account with the Order 34 is -$39,784.23 (= -$66,684.23 + $26,900).

- The transaction sub-equation includes the rest (-$39,784.23) of the "Cash" account with the Order 34, the part of the "Accumulated amortization: Vehicle" account with the Order 106, and the "Working-in-process inventory" account with the Order 76 to the Order 85. The twelfth transaction sub-equation is:

Cash (1): -39784.23 + Accumulated amortization: Vehicle (1): -2065.77 + Working-in-process inventory (1): 2000 + Working-in-process inventory (1): 6100 + Working-in-process inventory (1): 6500 + Working-in-process inventory (1): 7000 + Working-in-process inventory (1): 3000 + Working-in-process inventory (1): 3250 + Working-in-process inventory (1): 3000 + Working-in-process inventory (1): 3500 + Working-in-process inventory (1): 4000 + Working-in-process inventory (1): 3500 = 0

After entering this transaction, the new balance of the "Accumulated amortization: Vehicle" account with the Order 106 is -$11,267.56 (= -$13,333.33 + $2,065.77).

- The transaction sub-equation includes the "Cash" account with the Order 35, the part of the "Accumulated amortization: Vehicle" account with the Order 106, the "Accumulated amortization: Computer" account with the Order 110 to the Order 112, and the "Working-in-process inventory" account with the Order 86 to the Order 91. The thirteenth transaction sub-equation is:

Cash (1): -10079.23 + Accumulated amortization: Vehicle (1): -4495.77 + Accumulated amortization: Computer (1): -1462.50 + Accumulated amortization: Computer (1): -758.33 + Accumulated amortization: Computer (1): -704.17 + Working-in-process inventory (1): 2000 + Working-in-process inventory (1): 2500 + Working-in-process inventory (1): 3000 + Working-in-process inventory (1): 3500 + Working-in-process inventory (1): 3000 + Working-in-process inventory (1): 3500 = 0

After entering this transaction, the new balance of the "Accumulated amortization: Vehicle" account with the Order 106 is -$6,771.79 (= -$11,267.56 + $4,495.77).

- The transaction sub-equation includes the rest (-$6,771.79) of the "Accumulated amortization: Vehicle" account with the Order 106, the "Working-in-process inventory" account with the Order 92 to the Order 100, and the "Retained earnings" account with the balance $12,574.23. The fourteenth transaction sub-equation is: Accumulated amortization: Vehicle (1): -6771.79 + Working-in-process inventory (1): 4000 + Working-in-process inventory (1): 1000 + Working-in-process inventory (1): 1200 + Working-in-process inventory (1): 1300 Working-in-process inventory (1): 1500 + Working-in-process inventory (1): 1200 + Working-in-process inventory (1): 1400 + Working-in-process inventory (1): 600 + Working-in-process inventory (1): 800 = Retained earnings (Conversion) (3): 6228.21

After completing this transaction, the dynamic accounting equation of the Proprietorship2

December 31, 2015 has entered into the database dcj211.

### 2.4.7.2 Brief Summary of the Proprietorship2

The Figure 2.4-26 on the next page shows the partial information of inventory purchased or inventory sold by other social members in the public database dcj200.

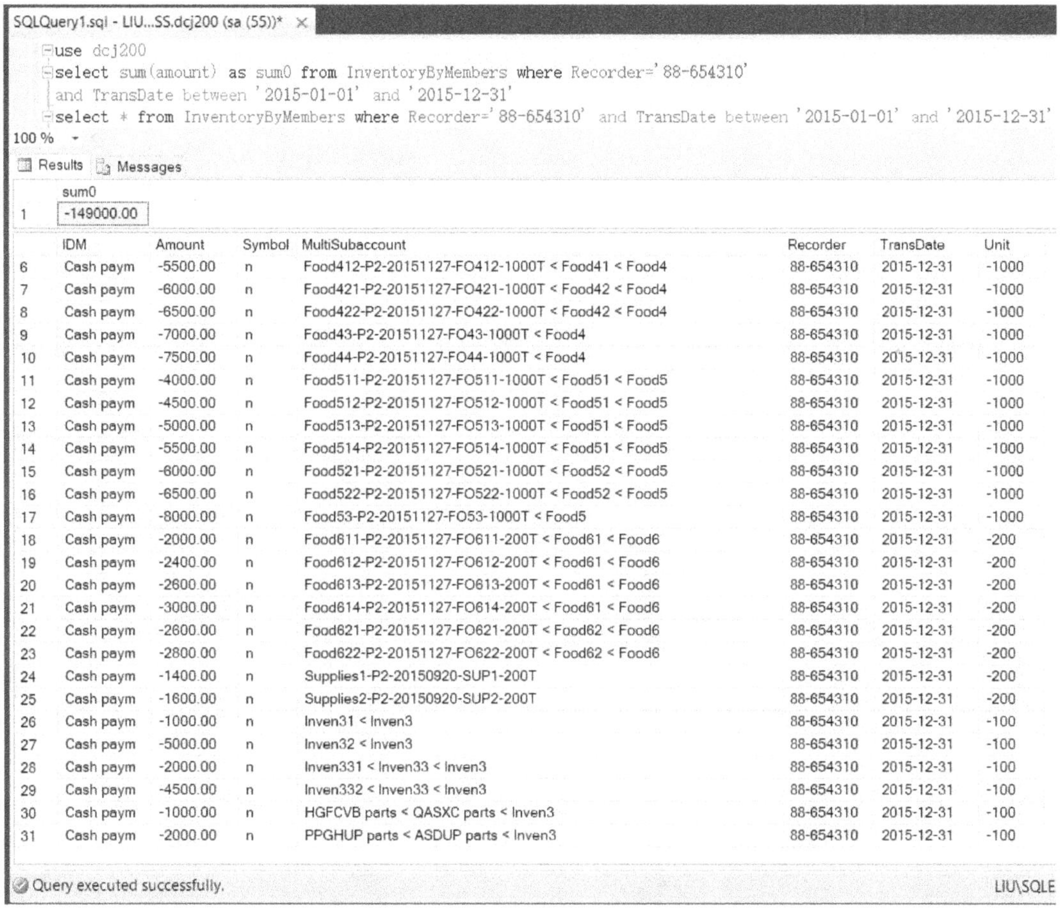
SQLQuery1.sql - LIU...SS.dcj200 (sa (55))*

```
use dcj200
select sum(amount) as sum0 from InventoryByMembers where Recorder='88-654310'
and TransDate between '2015-01-01' and '2015-12-31'
select * from InventoryByMembers where Recorder='88-654310' and TransDate between '2015-01-01' and '2015-12-31'
```

100 %

Results | Messages

| | sum0 |
|---|---|
| 1 | -149000.00 |

| | IDM | Amount | Symbol | MultiSubaccount | Recorder | TransDate | Unit |
|---|---|---|---|---|---|---|---|
| 6 | Cash paym | -5500.00 | n | Food412-P2-20151127-FO412-1000T < Food41 < Food4 | 88-654310 | 2015-12-31 | -1000 |
| 7 | Cash paym | -6000.00 | n | Food421-P2-20151127-FO421-1000T < Food42 < Food4 | 88-654310 | 2015-12-31 | -1000 |
| 8 | Cash paym | -6500.00 | n | Food422-P2-20151127-FO422-1000T < Food42 < Food4 | 88-654310 | 2015-12-31 | -1000 |
| 9 | Cash paym | -7000.00 | n | Food43-P2-20151127-FO43-1000T < Food4 | 88-654310 | 2015-12-31 | -1000 |
| 10 | Cash paym | -7500.00 | n | Food44-P2-20151127-FO44-1000T < Food4 | 88-654310 | 2015-12-31 | -1000 |
| 11 | Cash paym | -4000.00 | n | Food511-P2-20151127-FO511-1000T < Food51 < Food5 | 88-654310 | 2015-12-31 | -1000 |
| 12 | Cash paym | -4500.00 | n | Food512-P2-20151127-FO512-1000T < Food51 < Food5 | 88-654310 | 2015-12-31 | -1000 |
| 13 | Cash paym | -5000.00 | n | Food513-P2-20151127-FO513-1000T < Food51 < Food5 | 88-654310 | 2015-12-31 | -1000 |
| 14 | Cash paym | -5500.00 | n | Food514-P2-20151127-FO514-1000T < Food51 < Food5 | 88-654310 | 2015-12-31 | -1000 |
| 15 | Cash paym | -6000.00 | n | Food521-P2-20151127-FO521-1000T < Food52 < Food5 | 88-654310 | 2015-12-31 | -1000 |
| 16 | Cash paym | -6500.00 | n | Food522-P2-20151127-FO522-1000T < Food52 < Food5 | 88-654310 | 2015-12-31 | -1000 |
| 17 | Cash paym | -8000.00 | n | Food53-P2-20151127-FO53-1000T < Food5 | 88-654310 | 2015-12-31 | -1000 |
| 18 | Cash paym | -2000.00 | n | Food611-P2-20151127-FO611-200T < Food61 < Food6 | 88-654310 | 2015-12-31 | -200 |
| 19 | Cash paym | -2400.00 | n | Food612-P2-20151127-FO612-200T < Food61 < Food6 | 88-654310 | 2015-12-31 | -200 |
| 20 | Cash paym | -2600.00 | n | Food613-P2-20151127-FO613-200T < Food61 < Food6 | 88-654310 | 2015-12-31 | -200 |
| 21 | Cash paym | -3000.00 | n | Food614-P2-20151127-FO614-200T < Food61 < Food6 | 88-654310 | 2015-12-31 | -200 |
| 22 | Cash paym | -2600.00 | n | Food621-P2-20151127-FO621-200T < Food62 < Food6 | 88-654310 | 2015-12-31 | -200 |
| 23 | Cash paym | -2800.00 | n | Food622-P2-20151127-FO622-200T < Food62 < Food6 | 88-654310 | 2015-12-31 | -200 |
| 24 | Cash paym | -1400.00 | n | Supplies1-P2-20150920-SUP1-200T | 88-654310 | 2015-12-31 | -200 |
| 25 | Cash paym | -1600.00 | n | Supplies2-P2-20150920-SUP2-200T | 88-654310 | 2015-12-31 | -200 |
| 26 | Cash paym | -1000.00 | n | Inven31 < Inven3 | 88-654310 | 2015-12-31 | -100 |
| 27 | Cash paym | -5000.00 | n | Inven32 < Inven3 | 88-654310 | 2015-12-31 | -100 |
| 28 | Cash paym | -2000.00 | n | Inven331 < Inven33 < Inven3 | 88-654310 | 2015-12-31 | -100 |
| 29 | Cash paym | -4500.00 | n | Inven332 < Inven33 < Inven3 | 88-654310 | 2015-12-31 | -100 |
| 30 | Cash paym | -1000.00 | n | HGFCVB parts < QASXC parts < Inven3 | 88-654310 | 2015-12-31 | -100 |
| 31 | Cash paym | -2000.00 | n | PPGHUP parts < ASDUP parts < Inven3 | 88-654310 | 2015-12-31 | -100 |

Query executed successfully. LIU\SQLE

Figure 2.4-26 Proprietorship1 Inventory Purchased or Sold by Other Members

## 2.5 Button Rank of Social Members

The button rank of social members is all individuals. These individuals do not do business and there is no paper money in circulating process, so there is not any transaction to be recorded in this rank. Their employers and suppliers have recorded their transaction information while they get their salary and purchase various commodities by using of the various smart cards issued by different business bank. Of course, the children can use their parents' second card.

# Chapter 3

# Social Members Accounting Fiscal Years

In this chapter, the accounting fiscal years of ten organizations (plus an abstract organization of the Cash Management Center) will be discussed and entered into themselves databases. All individuals' information in this accounting fiscal year will be included in the organizations, so financial information of all social members will be recoded and discussed in detail. Of course, the information of the Inventory account will be focused on.

## 3.1 Central Bank

The Central Bank includes an abstract organization of the Cash Management Center, so the Central Bank has two financial statements which will be respectively discussed below.

### 3.1.1 Cash Management Center

### 3.1.1.1 An Accounting Fiscal Year of the Cash Management Center

In the new fiscal year, the Cash Management Center (CMC) occurs the following transactions.

- On January 2, 2016, the CMC pays the money to governments at all levels (including the Central Bank) according to the planned national budgets. Here, the three-level subaccount names of the Cash account all are the "ID-n-Budgets". There are the following four transaction sub-equations, seeing the table in the Figure 3.1-1.

| Order | Government Names | Amount | Sub-equations | Cash Multi-Subaccounts |
|-------|------------------|--------|---------------|------------------------|
| 1 | Central Bank | 85000 | Cash (1): -85000 = Tax receipts payable (2): -85000 | 88-654301-n-budgets < Cash payments of national budgets < Operating activities |
| 2 | Government1 | 90000 | Cash (1): -90000 = Tax receipts payable (2): -90000 | 88-654302-n-budgets < Cash payments of national budgets < Operating activities |

| | | | | |
|---|---|---|---|---|
| 3 | Tax Bureau | 95000 | Cash (1): -95000 = Tax receipts payable (2): -95000 | 88-654303-n-budgets < Cash payments of national budgets < Operating activities |
| 4 | Cash Management Center | 2062.66 | 0 = Tax receipts payable (2): -2062.66 + National capital (3): 2062.66 | - |
| 5 | **Total** | **272062.66** | - | - |

Figure 3.1-1  Detail Information of Planned National Budgets

- On January 31, 2016, the Cash Management Center records a transaction of the Accrued interest payable account ($200) and the Interest expenses account (one-level subaccount "Bond01-interest") about the Bond01.

- On February 28, 2016, the CMC records the above transaction repeatedly.

- On March 31, 2016, the CMC records the above transaction repeatedly.

- On April 30, 2016, the CMC records the above transaction repeatedly.

- On May 31, 2016, the CMC records the above transaction repeatedly.

- On June 1, 2016, the Cash Management Center purchases one Bond23 (three years, 4.5% annually, pay at the end of each year) for -$25,000 from the Business Bank2. The multi-subaccount name of the Cash account is:

  88-654305-n-investment bond23 < Cash payments for investments < Investing activities

- On June 30, 2016, the Cash Management Center records the transaction of the Accrued interest payable account and the Interest expenses account about the Bond01 repeatedly.

- On July 31, 2016, the CMC records the above transaction repeatedly.

- On August 31, 2016, the Cash Management Center records the transaction of the Accrued interest payable account and the Interest expenses account about the Bond01 repeatedly.

- On September 30, 2016, the CMC records the above transaction repeatedly.

- On October 31, 2016, the CMC records the above transaction repeatedly.

- On November 30, 2016, the CMC records the above transaction repeatedly.

- On December 31, 2016, the CMC records the above transaction repeatedly.

- On the same day, the Cash Management Center pays cash -$2,400 for the balance of the Accrued interest payable account for the Bond01 to the bond holders. Here, the transaction is put in the financial activities and the three-level sub-account names are different from other organizations or companies. Later, the same transactions for other organizations or companies are put in the operating activities. The twelve multi-subaccount names of the Cash account respectively are:

  909876501-t-interest expenses < Cash payments for issued bond interest < Financial activities

  (909865302, 909865303, 909865307, 909865309, 909865310, 909865311, 909865312, 909865315, 909865316, 909865321, 909865322)

- On the same day, the Cash Management Center pays -$2,500 cash to the Business Bank1 for the administrative fee (Bank fee expenses). The multi-subaccount name of the Cash account is:

  88-654304-t-bank fee expenses < Cash payments to Business banks < Operating activities

- On the same day, the Cash Management Center receives cash $656.25 (Investment incomes) from the Business Bank2 for investment interest of the Bond23. The multi-subaccount name of the Cash account is:

  88-654305-c-investment income < Cash receipts from investments < Investing activities

- On the same day, the Cash Management Center records the Tax expenses $0 and the Tax payable $0. Because tax rate is zero, the amount of the Tax expenses is also zero. The multi-subaccount name forms of the Tax expenses and the Tax payable accounts all are the 'n'.

So far, I have entered the CMC transactions to the database dcj2021 in the fiscal year 2016.

### 3.1.1.2 Brief Summary of Cash Management Center

Obviously, there is not any information of the Inventory account in these transaction sub-equations.

## 3.1.2 Central Bank

### 3.1.2.1 An Accounting Fiscal Year of the Central Bank

In the new fiscal year, the Central Bank occurs the following transactions.

- On January 2, 2016, the Central Bank receives cash $85,000 from the Cash Management Center for the planned national budgets. Here, I presume that the received cash is revenue (sales) of the Central Bank. Of course, you can set it as other account, such as the Budgets payable account and merge it into the Retained earnings or Budgets capital at the end of each fiscal year. The multi-subaccount name of the Cash account and the transaction sub-equation respectively are:

   88-654300-c-budgets < Cash receipts from national budgets < Financial activities

   Cash (1): 85000 = Sales (received budgets) (4): 85000

- On January 21, 2016, the Central Bank pays -$176.56 cash to A1 (SIN: 909876501) for the Travelling expenses -$137.56 and the Other expenses -$39. Because the Proprietorship2 has record the product batch of its product, I do not record the detail information of the meals. The two multi-subaccount names of the Cash, the Travelling expenses, and the Other expenses accounts respectively are:

   909876501-n-operating expenses < Cash payments for operating expenses < Operating activities
   909876501-n-travelling < Cash payments for operating expenses < Operating activities
   909876501-n-other < Cash payments for operating expenses < Operating activities

- On January 31, 2016, the Central Bank pays two employees' salary for cash -$5,650. The two multi-subaccount names of the Cash account respectively are:

   909876501-t-salary < Cash payments for operating expenses < Operating activities
   909876502-t-salary < Cash payments for operating expenses < Operating activities

- On February 13, 2016, the Central Bank pays -$800 cash to Company1 (phone number: 123456784) with the General ID 1 and pays $200 cash to Company3 (phone number: 123456782) with the General ID 1. The two multi-subaccount names of the Cash account respectively are:

88-654306-t-machinery < Cash payments for machinery < Operating activities

88-654308-t-operating expenses < Cash payments for operating expenses < Operating activities

- On February 22, 2016, the Central Bank purchases the following inventories $5,600 as the consumables from the Company3 (phone number: 123456782) with the General ID 9 for cash -$3,600 and other on credit. For simplification, the consumables will be recorded one time on December 31, 2016. Their multi-subaccount name are:

Inven111-C3-20150922-In111-1000T < Inven11 < Inven1: 10*40

Inven112-C3-20150922-In112-800T < Inven11 < Inven1: 40*40

Inven221-C3-20150922-In221-750T < Inven22 < Inven2: 30*40

Inven222-C3-20150922-In222-400T < Inven22 < Inven2: 50*40

PPGH parts-C3-20150922-PG-1600T < ASD parts < Inven2: 2*200

The multi-subaccount name of the Cash account and transaction sub-equation respectively are:

88-654308-t-supplies < Cash payments to suppliers < Operating activities

Cash (1): -3600 + Inventory (1): 10*40 + Inventory (1): 40*40 + Inventory (1): 30*40 + Inventory (1): 50*40 + Inventory (1): 2*200 = Account payable (2): 2000

- On February 28, 2016, the Central Bank pays two employees' salary for cash -$5,650.
- On March 25, 2016, the Central Bank pays -$600 cash to the Company1 (phone number: 123456784) with the General ID 1. The multi-subaccount name of the Cash account is:

88-654306-t-machinery < Cash payments for machinery < Operating activities

- On March 28, 2016, the Central Bank pays -$459.61 cash to A2 (SIN: 909876502)

for the Travelling expenses -$387.61 and the Other expenses -$72. The multi-subaccount name of the Cash account is:

909876502-n-operating expenses < Cash payments for operating expenses < Operating activities

- On March 31, 2016, the Central Bank pays two employees' salary for cash -$5,650.
- On April 19, 2016, the Central Bank pays -$159.78 cash to A2 (SIN: 909876502) for the Travelling expenses -$109.78 and the Other expenses -$50.
- On April 30, 2016, the Central Bank pays two employees' salary for cash -$5,650.
- On April 30, 2016, the Central Bank records the Amortization expenses -$983.34 of a computer server1 (-$466.67, four months), a computer1 (-$266.67, four months), and a computer2 (-$250, four months). The transaction sub-equation is:
- On April 30, 2016, the Central Bank cancels the balances of the Computer account and the Accumulated amortization: Computer account because these computers have used for two years. The transaction sub-equation is:
- On May 1, 2016, the Central Bank purchases a new computer server1, a new computer1, and a new computer2 for cash -$1,900 and other on credit $4,000 from the Company1 (phone number: 123456784) with the General ID 18. The multi-subaccount names of the Cash account and the Inventory account and the transaction sub-equation respectively are:

88-654306-t-machinery < Cash payments for machinery < Operating activities
Computer server1-C1-201501007-COMS1-039 < Computer server: 2800*1
Computer1-C1-201501008-COM1-055: 1600*1
Computer2-C1-201501008-COM2-065: 1500*1

Cash (1): -1900 + Inventory (1): 2800 + Inventory (1): 1600 + Inventory (1): 1500 = Account payable (2): 4000

Meanwhile, the purchased inventory transfers to the equipment by the interior transaction. For simplification, the Central Bank does not record the product codes in the equipment, so the multi-subaccount names of the Computer do not change.

The multi-subaccount names of the Computer account and the transaction sub-equation respectively are:

Computer server11 < Computer server1 < Computer server: 2800*1

Computer11 < Computer1: 1600*1

Computer21 < Computer2: 1500*1

Inventory (1): -2800 + Inventory (1): -1600 + Inventory (1): -1500 + Computer (1): 2800 + Computer (1): 1600 + Computer (1): 1500 = 0

- On May 16, 2016, the Central Bank purchases inventory as office supplies from the Proprietorship2 for cash -$316 ($14*10 + $16*11). The multi-subaccount names of the Cash and the Inventory accounts and the transaction sub-equation are:

  88-654310-t-supplies < Cash payments to supplies < Operating activities

  Supplies1-P2-20150920-SUP1-200T: 14*10

  Supplies2-P2-20150920-SUP2-200T: 16*11

  Cash (1): -316 + Inventory (1): 14*10 + Inventory (1): 16*11 = 0

- On May 31, 2016, the Central Bank pays two employees' salary for cash -$5,650.
- On June 1, 2016, the Central Bank purchases one Bond23 (three years, 4.5% annually, pay at end of each year) for -$5,000 from the Business Bank2. The multi-subaccount name of the Cash account is:

  88-654305-n-Bonds < Cash payments for investments < Investing activities

- On June 22, 2016, the Central Bank pays -$477.25 cash to A2 (SIN: 909876502) for the Travelling expenses -$341.25 and the Other expenses -$136.
- On June 30, 2016, the Central Bank pays two employees' salary for cash -$5,650.
- On July 31, 2016, the Central Bank pays two employees' salary for cash -$5,650.
- On August 14, 2016, the Central Bank purchases two service packages (Truck1-Service package1 < Truck-service < Vehicle-service for cash -$550 and Car1-Service package3 < Car-service < Vehicle-service for cash -$490) for cash -$1,040

from the Company1. The multi-subaccount name of the Cash account and the transaction sub-equation respectively are:

88-654306-t-service packages < Cash payments to suppliers < Operating activities

Cash (1): -1040 = Service package expenses (5): -550 + Service package expenses (5): -490

- On August 31, 2016, the Central Bank pays two employees' salary for cash -$5,650.
- On September 7, 2016, the Central Bank pays -$233.16 cash to A2 (SIN: 909876502) for the Travelling expenses -$174.16 and the Other expenses -$59.
- On September 30, 2016, the Central Bank pays two employees' salary -$5,650.
- On October 31, 2016, the Central Bank pays two employees' salary for cash -$5,650.
- On November 30, 2016, the Central Bank pays two employees' salary -$5,650.
- On December 11, 2016, Central Bank pays -$552.37 cash to A1 (SIN: 909876501) for the Travelling expenses -$432.37 and the Other expenses -$120.
- On December 31, 2016, the Central Bank pays two employees' salary -$5,650.
- On the same day, the Central Bank receives cash $131.25 (Investment incomes) from the Business Bank2 for investment interest of the Bond23. The multi-subaccount name of the Cash account is:

  88-654305-c-investment income < Cash receipts from investments < Investing activities

- On the same day, the Central Bank receives cash $120 (Deposit interest incomes) from the Business Bank2 for primary deposit interest. The multi-subaccount name of the Cash account is:

  88-654305-c-deposit interest income < Cash receipts from deposit interest < Financial activities

- On the same day, the Central Bank records the Vehicle's amortization expenses -$17,000 (-$9,000 -$8,000) one year (5 years, straight line).
- On the same day, the Central Bank records the Computer's amortization expenses

$1,966.66 eight months (2 years, straight line) which includes a new computer server1 ($933.33), a new computer1 ($533.33), and a new computer2 ($500).

- On the same day, the Central Bank records the Consumables expenses -$5,600. The multi-subaccount names of the Inventory account and transaction sub-equation respectively are:

Inven111-C3-20150922-In111-1000T < Inven11 < Inven1: -10*40

Inven112-C3-20150922-In112-800T < Inven11 < Inven1: -40*40

Inven221-C3-20150922-In221-750T < Inven22 < Inven2: -30*40

Inven222-C3-20150922-In222-400T < Inven22 < Inven2: -50*40

PPGH parts-C3-20150922-PG-1600T < ASD parts < Inven2: -2*200

Inventory (1): -10*40 + Inventory (1): -40*40 + Inventory (1): -30*40 + Inventory (1): -50*40 + Inventory (1): -2*200 = Consumables expenses (5): -5600

- On the same day, the Central Bank records the Office supplies expenses -$335.72. It is consisted of two parts of the Supplies -$169.72 and the Inventory -$166 (-$14*5 - $16*6). The multi-subaccount names of the Inventory account and transaction sub-equation respectively are:

Supplies1-P2-20150920-SUP1-200T: -14*5
Supplies2-P2-20150920-SUP2-200T: -16*6

Supplies (1): -169.72 + Inventory (1): -14*5 + Inventory (1): 16*6 = Office supplies expenses (5): -335.72

- On the same day, the Central Bank pays cash $3,500 to the Company1 (phone number: 123456784) with the General ID 18. The multi-subaccount name of the Cash account is:

88-654306-t-machinery < Cash payments for machinery < Operating activities

- On the same day, the Central Bank records the Tax expenses $0 and the Tax payable $0. The multi-subaccount names of the Tax expenses and the Tax payable accounts all are the 'n'.

So far, I have entered all transactions of the fiscal year 2016 to the database dcj2022.

### 3.1.2.2 Brief Summary of the Central Bank

The Figure 3.1-2 shows all inventory transactions of the Central Bank in the fiscal year 2016 by using of SQL Server query.

```
SQLQuery1.sql - LIU...SS.dcj200 (sa (52))*  ×
  use dcj200
  select * from InventoryByMembers where Recorder='88-654301' and TransDate between '2016-01-01' and '2016-12-31'
  order by TransDate
100 %  ▾
```

| | IDM | Amount | Symbol | MultiSubaccount | Recorder | TransDate | Unit |
|---|---|---|---|---|---|---|---|
| 1 | 88-654308 | -400.00 | t | Inven111-C3-20150922-In111-1000T < Inven11 < Inven1 | 88-654301 | 2016-02-22 | -40 |
| 2 | 88-654308 | -1600.00 | t | Inven112-C3-20150922-In112-800T < Inven11 < Inven1 | 88-654301 | 2016-02-22 | -40 |
| 3 | 88-654308 | -1200.00 | t | Inven221-C3-20150922-In221-750T < Inven22 < Inven2 | 88-654301 | 2016-02-22 | -40 |
| 4 | 88-654308 | -2000.00 | t | Inven222-C3-20150922-In222-400T < Inven22 < Inven2 | 88-654301 | 2016-02-22 | -40 |
| 5 | 88-654308 | -400.00 | t | PPGH parts-C3-20150922-PG-1600T < ASD parts < Inven2 | 88-654301 | 2016-02-22 | -200 |
| 6 | 88-654306 | -2800.00 | t | Computer server1-C1-201501007-COMS1-039 < Computer server | 88-654301 | 2016-05-01 | -1 |
| 7 | 88-654306 | -1600.00 | t | Computer1-C1-201501008-COM1-055 | 88-654301 | 2016-05-01 | -1 |
| 8 | 88-654306 | -1500.00 | t | Computer2-C1-201501008-COM2-065 | 88-654301 | 2016-05-01 | -1 |
| 9 | 88-654301 | 1500.00 | e | Computer2-C1-201501008-COM2-065 | 88-654301 | 2016-05-01 | 1 |
| 10 | 88-654301 | 2800.00 | e | Computer server1-C1-201501007-COMS1-039 < Computer server | 88-654301 | 2016-05-01 | 1 |
| 11 | 88-654301 | 1600.00 | e | Computer1-C1-201501008-COM1-055 | 88-654301 | 2016-05-01 | 1 |
| 12 | 88-654310 | -140.00 | t | Supplies1-P2-20150920-SUP1-200T | 88-654301 | 2016-05-16 | -10 |
| 13 | 88-654310 | -176.00 | t | Supplies2-P2-20150920-SUP2-200T | 88-654301 | 2016-05-16 | -11 |
| 14 | 88-654301 | 400.00 | s | Inven111-C3-20150922-In111-1000T < Inven11 < Inven1 | 88-654301 | 2016-12-31 | 40 |
| 15 | 88-654301 | 1200.00 | s | Inven221-C3-20150922-In221-750T < Inven22 < Inven2 | 88-654301 | 2016-12-31 | 40 |
| 16 | 88-654301 | 2000.00 | s | Inven222-C3-20150922-In222-400T < Inven22 < Inven2 | 88-654301 | 2016-12-31 | 40 |
| 17 | 88-654301 | 400.00 | s | PPGH parts-C3-20150922-PG-1600T < ASD parts < Inven2 | 88-654301 | 2016-12-31 | 200 |
| 18 | 88-654301 | 70.00 | s | Supplies1-P2-20150920-SUP1-200T | 88-654301 | 2016-12-31 | 5 |
| 19 | 88-654301 | 96.00 | s | Supplies2-P2-20150920-SUP2-200T | 88-654301 | 2016-12-31 | 6 |
| 20 | 88-654301 | 1600.00 | s | Inven112-C3-20150922-In112-800T < Inven11 < Inven1 | 88-654301 | 2016-12-31 | 40 |

Figure 3.1-2   Central Bank Inventory Purchased or Sold by Other Members

# 3.2 Government1

## 3.2.1 An Accounting Fiscal Year of the Government1

In the new fiscal year, the Government1 occurs the following transactions.

- On January 2, 2016, the Government1 receives cash $90,000 from the Cash Management Center for the planned national budgets. The multi-subaccount name of the Cash account and the transaction sub-equation respectively are:

    88-654300-c-budgets < Cash receipts from national budgets < Financial activities

Cash (1): 90000 = Sales (received budgets) (4): 90000

- On January 9, 2016, the Government1 pays -$307.23 cash to A3 (SIN: 909876503) for the Travelling expenses -$199.23 and the Other expenses -$108. The multi-subaccount name of the Cash account is:

  909876503-n-operating expenses < Cash payments for operating expenses < Operating activities

- On January 31, 2016, the Government1 pays two employees' salary expenses for cash -$5,660. The two multi-subaccount names of the Cash account respectively are:

  909876503-t-salary < Cash payments for operating expenses < Operating activities
  909876504-t-salary < Cash payments for operating expenses < Operating activities

- On February 21, 2016, the Government1 pays -$500 cash to Company2 (phone number: 123456783) with the General ID 1. The multi-subaccount name of the Cash account is:

  88-654307-t-machinery < Cash payments for machinery < Operating activities

- On February 28, 2016, the Government1 pays two employees' salary for cash -$5,660.

  On February 28, 2016, the Government1 pays -$295.17 cash to A3 (SIN: 909876503) for the Travelling expenses -$196.17 and the Other expenses -$99.

- On March 22, 2016, the Government1 pays -$558.34 cash to A4 (SIN: 909876504) for the Travelling expenses -$386.34 and the Other expenses -$172.

- On March 31, 2016, the Government1 pays two employees' salary for cash -$5,660.

- On April 24, 2016, the Government1 pays -$283.53 cash to A4 (SIN: 909876504) for the Travelling expenses -$183.53 and the Other expenses -$100.

- On April 30, 2016, the Government1 pays two employees' salary for cash -$5,660.

- On April 30, 2016, the Government1 purchases inventory (supplies) $330 ($14*11 + $16*11) from the Proprietorship2 (phone number: 123456780) for cash -$330. The multi-subaccount name of the Cash account and the transaction sub-equation respectively are:

88-654310-t-supplies<Cash payments for operating expenses<Operating activities

Cash (1): -330 + Inventory (1): 14*11 + Inventory (1): 16*11 = 0

- On April 30, 2016, the Government1 purchases one service packages (Computer server1- Service package6 < Computer server-service < Computer-service) for cash -$60 from the Company1. The multi-subaccount name of the Cash account is:

  88-654306-t-service packages < Cash payments for operating expenses <
  Operating activities

- On May 1, 2016, the Government1 purchases a new Car1 for cash -$8,000 and other on credit $32,000 from the Company1 (phone number: 123456784). The multi-subaccount names of the Cash account and the Inventory account and the transaction sub-equation respectively are:

  88-654306-t-machinery < Cash payments for machinery < Operating activities

  Car1-C1-20150921-C1-023 < Car < Vehicle: 40000*1

  Cash (1): -8000 + Inventory (1): 40000 = Account payable (2): 32000

  Meanwhile, the purchased inventory transfers to the equipment by the interior transaction. For simplification, the Central Bank does not record the product codes in the equipment, so the multi-subaccount name of the Vehicle do not change. The multi-subaccount name of the Vehicle account and the transaction sub-equation respectively are:

  Car12 < Car1 < Car: 40000*1

  Inventory (1): -40000 + Vehicle (1): 40000 = 0

- On May 16, 2016, the Government1 pays -$415.97 cash to A3 (SIN: 909876503) for the Travelling expenses -$310.97 and the Other expenses -$105.

- On May 31, 2016, the Government1 pays two employees' salary for cash -$5,660.

- On June 1, 2016, the Government1 purchases one Bond23 (three years, 4.5% annually, pay at end of each year) for cash -$5,000 from the Business Bank2. The multi-subaccount name of the Cash account is:

88-654305-n-bonds < Cash payments for investments < Investing activities

- On June 17, 2016, the Government1 pays -$272.59 cash to A3 (SIN: 909876503) for the Travelling expenses -$179.59 and the Other expenses -$93.

- On June 30, 2016, the Central Bank pays two employees' salary for cash -$5,660.

- On July 19, 2016, the Government1 pays -$336.87 cash to A4 (SIN: 909876504) for the Travelling expenses -$224.87 and the Other expenses -$112.

- On July 31, 2016, the Government1 pays two employees' salary for cash $5,660.

- On August 13, 2016, the Government1 pays -$481.11 cash to A3 (SIN: 909876503) for the Travelling expenses -$331.11 and the Other expenses -$150.

- On August 31, 2016, the Government1 pays two employees' salary for cash -$5,660.

- On September 7, 2016, the Government1 pays -$384.46 cash to A4 (SIN: 909876504) for the Travelling expenses -$298.46 and the Other expenses -$86.

- On September 25, 2016, the Government1 purchases the following inventories (consumables) $4,200 from the Company3 (phone number: 123456782) for cash - $3,200 and other on credit.

  Inven111-C3-20150922-In111-1000T < Inven11 < Inven1: 10*30

  Inven112-C3-20150922-In112-800T < Inven11 < Inven1: 40*30

  Inven221-C3-20150922-In221-750T < Inven22 < Inven2: 30*30

  Inven222-C3-20150922-In222-400T < Inven22 < Inven2: 50*30

  PPGH parts-C3-20150922-PG-1600T < ASD parts < Inven2: 2*150

  The multi-subaccount name of the Cash account and transaction sub-equation respectively are:

  88-654308-t-supplies < Cash payments to suppliers < Operating activities

  Cash (1): -3200 + Inventory (1): 10*30 + Inventory (1): 40*30 + Inventory (1): 30*30 + Inventory (1): 50*30 + Inventory (1): 2*150 = Account payable (2): 1000

- On September 30, 2016, the Government1 pays two employees' salary -$5,660.

- On October 3, 2016, the Government1 purchases two service packages (Truck2-Service package2 < Truck-service < Vehicle-service for cash -$500 and Car1-Service package3 < Car-service < Vehicle-service for cash -$490) for cash -$990 from the Company1. The multi-subaccount name of the Cash account is:

  88-654306-t-service packages < Cash payments for operating expenses < Operating activities

- On October 24, 2016, the Government1 pays -$377.77 cash to A3 (SIN: 909876503) for the Travelling expenses -$256.77 and the Other expenses -$121.

- On October 31, 2016, the Government1 pays two employees' salary -$5,660.

- On November 14, 2016, the Government1 pays -$375.39 cash to A4 (SIN: 909876504) for the Travelling expenses -$290.39 and the Other expenses -$85.

- On November 30, 2016, the Government1 pays two employees' salary -$5,660.

- On December 23, 2016, the Government1 pays -$514.62 cash to A3 (SIN: 909876503) for the Travelling expenses -$385.62 and the Other expenses -$129.

- On December 30, 2016, the Government1 pays cash -$2,000 to the Company1 (phone number: 123456784) with the General ID 18. The multi-subaccount name of the Cash account is:

  88-654306-t-machinery < Cash payments for machinery < Operating activities

- On December 31, 2016, the Government1 pays two employees' salary for cash -$5,660 repeatedly.

- On the same day, the Government1 receives cash $240 (Investment incomes) from the Business Bank1 for investment interest of the Bond11. The multi-subaccount name of the Cash account is:

  88-654304-c-investment income < Cash receipts from investments < Investing activities

- On the same day, the Government1 receives $500.25 (cash $369 for investment interest of the Bond21and cash $131.25 for investment interest of the Bond23) from the Business Bank2. The multi-subaccount name of the Cash account is:

88-654305-c-investment income < Cash receipts from investments < Investing activities

- On the same day, the Government1 receives cash $120 (Deposit interest incomes) from the Business Bank1 for primary deposit interest. The multi-subaccount name of the Cash account is:

  88-654304-c-deposit interest income < Cash receipts from deposit interest < Financial activities

- On the same day, the Government1 records the Consumables expenses -$4,200. The multi-subaccount names of the Inventory account and transaction sub-equation respectively are:

  Inven111-C3-20150922-In111-1000T < Inven11 < Inven1: -10*30

  Inven112-C3-20150922-In112-800T < Inven11 < Inven1: -40*30

  Inven221-C3-20150922-In221-750T < Inven22 < Inven2: -30*30

  Inven222-C3-20150922-In222-400T < Inven22 < Inven2: -50*30

  PPGH parts-C3-20150922-PG-1600T < ASD parts < Inven2: -2*150

  Inventory (1): -10*30 + Inventory (1): -40*30 + Inventory (1): -30*30 + Inventory (1): -50*30 + Inventory (1): -2*150 = Consumables expenses (5): -4200

- On the same day, the Government1 records the Office supplies expenses -$377.33. It is consisted of two parts of the Supplies -$61.33 and the Inventory -$316 (-$14*10 - $16*11). The multi-subaccount names of the Inventory account and transaction sub-equation respectively are:

  Supplies1-P2-20150920-SUP1-200T: -14*10

  Supplies2-P2-20150920-SUP2-200T: -16*11

  Supplies (1): -61.33 + Inventory (1): -14*10 + Inventory (1): -16*11 = Office supplies expenses (5): -377.33

- On the same day, the Government1 records the Vehicle's amortization expenses -

$17,000 (-\$8,000 - \$8,000 - \$5,333.33)$ one year (5 years, straight line).

- On the same day, the Government1 records the Computer's amortization expenses $2,950 eight months (2 years, straight line) which includes a new computer server1 ($1,400), a new computer1 ($800), and a new computer2 ($750).

- On the same day, the Government1 records the Tax expenses $0 and the Tax payable $0. The multi-subaccount names of the Tax expenses and the Tax payable accounts all are the 'n'.

So far, I have entered all transactions of the fiscal year 2016 to the database dcj203.

## 3.2.2 Brief Summary of the Government1

The Figure 3.2-1 on the next page shows all inventory transactions of the Government1 in the fiscal year 2016 by using of SQL Server query.

```
SQLQuery1.sql - LIU...SS.dcj200 (sa (52))*  ×
 use dcj200
 select * from InventoryByMembers where Recorder='88-654302' and TransDate between '2016-01-01' and '2016-12-31'
 order by TransDate
100 %  ▾
```

Results | Messages

|    | IDM | Amount | Symbol | MultiSubaccount | Recorder | TransDate | Unit |
|----|-----|--------|--------|-----------------|----------|-----------|------|
| 1  | 88-654310 | -154.00 | t | Supplies1-P2-20150920-SUP1-200T | 88-654302 | 2016-04-30 | -11 |
| 2  | 88-654310 | -176.00 | t | Supplies2-P2-20150920-SUP2-200T | 88-654302 | 2016-04-30 | -11 |
| 3  | 88-654308 | -40000.00 | t | Car1-C1-20150921-C1-023 < Car < Vehicle | 88-654302 | 2016-05-01 | -1 |
| 4  | 88-654302 | 40000.00 | e | Car1-C1-20150921-C1-023 < Car < Vehicle | 88-654302 | 2016-05-01 | 1 |
| 5  | 88-654308 | -300.00 | t | Inven111-C3-20150922-In111-1000T < Inven11 < Inven1 | 88-654302 | 2016-09-25 | -30 |
| 6  | 88-654308 | -1200.00 | t | Inven112-C3-20150922-In112-800T < Inven11 < Inven1 | 88-654302 | 2016-09-25 | -30 |
| 7  | 88-654308 | -900.00 | t | Inven221-C3-20150922-In221-750T < Inven22 < Inven2 | 88-654302 | 2016-09-25 | -30 |
| 8  | 88-654308 | -1500.00 | t | Inven222-C3-20150922-In222-400T < Inven22 < Inven2 | 88-654302 | 2016-09-25 | -30 |
| 9  | 88-654308 | -300.00 | t | PPGH parts-C3-20150922-PG-1600T < ASD parts < Inven2 | 88-654302 | 2016-09-25 | -150 |
| 10 | 88-654302 | 140.00 | s | Supplies1-P2-20150920-SUP1-200T | 88-654302 | 2016-12-31 | 10 |
| 11 | 88-654302 | 176.00 | s | Supplies2-P2-20150920-SUP2-200T | 88-654302 | 2016-12-31 | 11 |
| 12 | 88-654302 | 900.00 | s | Inven221-C3-20150922-In221-750T < Inven22 < Inven2 | 88-654302 | 2016-12-31 | 30 |
| 13 | 88-654302 | 1500.00 | s | Inven222-C3-20150922-In222-400T < Inven22 < Inven2 | 88-654302 | 2016-12-31 | 30 |
| 14 | 88-654302 | 300.00 | s | PPGH parts-C3-20150922-PG-1600T < ASD parts < Inven2 | 88-654302 | 2016-12-31 | 150 |
| 15 | 88-654302 | 300.00 | s | Inven111-C3-20150922-In111-1000T < Inven11 < Inven1 | 88-654302 | 2016-12-31 | 30 |
| 16 | 88-654302 | 1200.00 | s | Inven112-C3-20150922-In112-800T < Inven11 < Inven1 | 88-654302 | 2016-12-31 | 30 |

Figure 3.2-1   Government1 Inventory Received or Paid by Other Members

## 3.3 Tax Bureau

## 3.3.1 An Accounting Fiscal Year of the Tax Bureau

In the new fiscal year, the Tax Bureau occurs the following transactions.

- On January 2, 2016, the Tax Bureau receives cash $95,000 from the Cash Management Center for the planned national budgets. The multi-subaccount name of the Cash account and the transaction sub-equation respectively are:

  88-654303-c-budgets < Cash receipts from national budgets < Financial activities

- On January 12, 2016, the Tax Bureau pays -$283.71 cash to A5 (SIN: 909876505) for the Travelling expenses -$185.71 and the Other expenses -$98. The multi-subaccount name of the Cash account is:

  909876505-n-operating expenses < Cash payments for operating expenses < Operating activities

- On January 12, 2016, the Tax Bureau pays -$277.71 cash to A6 (SIN: 909876506) for the Travelling expenses -$185.71 and the Other expenses -$92. The multi-subaccount name of the Cash account is:

  909876506-n-operating expenses < Cash payments for operating expenses < Operating activities

- On January 13, 2016, the Tax Bureau purchases one service packages (Computer server1- Service package6 < Computer server-service < Computer-service) for cash -$60 from the Company1. The multi-subaccount name of the Cash account is:

  88-654306-t-service packages < Cash payments for operating expenses < Operating activities

- On January 31, 2016, the Tax Bureau pays two employees' salary expenses for cash -$5,670. The two multi-subaccount names of the Cash account are:

  909876505-t-salary < Cash payments for operating expenses < Operating activities
  909876506-t-salary < Cash payments for operating expenses < Operating activities

- On February 2, 2016, the Tax Bureau pays -$500 cash to Company1 (phone number: 123456784) with the General ID 1. The multi-subaccount name of the Cash is:

  88-654306-t-machinery < Cash payments for machinery < Operating activities

- On February 11, 2016, the Tax Bureau pays -$400 cash to Company2 (phone number: 123456783) with the General ID 1. The multi-subaccount name of the Cash is:

88-654307-t-machinery < Cash payments for machinery < Operating activities

- On February 23, 2016, the Tax Bureau pays -$300 cash to Company3 (phone number: 123456782) with the General ID 1. The multi-subaccount name of the Cash is: 88-654308-t-operating expenses < Cash payments for operating expenses < Operating activities

- On February 26, 2016, the Tax Bureau pays -$335.63 cash to A5 (SIN: 909876505) for the Travelling expenses -$225.63 and the Other expenses -$110.

- On February 28, 2016, the Tax Bureau pays two employees' salary for cash $5,670.

- On March 12, 2016, the Tax Bureau pays -$419.99 cash to A6 (SIN: 909876506) for the Travelling expenses -$296.99 and the Other expenses -$123.

- On March 31, 2016, the Tax Bureau pays two employees' salary for cash $5,670.

- On April 16, 2016, the Tax Bureau pays -$358.13 cash to A5 (SIN: 909876505) for the Travelling expenses -$246.13 and the Other expenses -$112.

- On April 30, 2016, the Tax Bureau pays two employees' salary for cash -$5,670.

- On May 8, 2016, the Tax Bureau purchases inventory $300 ($14*10 + $16*10) from the Proprietorship2 for cash -$300. The multi-subaccount name of the Cash account and the transaction sub-equation respectively are:

  88-654310-t-supplies < Cash payments for operating expenses < Operating activities

  Cash (1): -300 + Inventory (1): 14*10 + Inventory (1): 16*10 = 0

- On May 16, 2016, the Tax Bureau pays -$443.18 cash to A6 (SIN: 909876506) for the Travelling expenses -$331.18 and the Other expenses -$112.

- On May 31, 2016, the Tax Bureau pays two employees' salary for cash -$5,670.

- On June 1, 2016, the Tax Bureau purchases one Bond23 (three years, 4.5% annually, pay at end of each year) for -$5,000 from the Business Bank2. The multi-subaccount name of the Cash account is:

  88-654305-n-Bonds < Cash payments for investments < Investing activities

- On June 20, 2016, the Tax Bureau pays -$364.55 cash to A5 (SIN: 909876505) for the Travelling expenses -$271.55 and the Other expenses -$93.

- On June 20, 2016, the Tax Bureau pays -$361.55 cash to A6 (SIN: 909876506) for the Travelling expenses -$271.55 and the Other expenses -$90.

- On June 29, 2016, the Tax Bureau purchases the following inventories -$4,740 from the Company3 (phone number: 123456782) for cash -$2,000 and other on credit.

  Inven121-C3-20150922-In121-20000T < Inven12 < Inven1: 0.8*300

  Inven122-C3-20150922-In122-1000T < Inven12 < Inven1: 50*30

  Inven21-C3-20150922-In21-1250T < Inven2: 30*30

  Inven221-C3-20150922-In221-750T < Inven22 < Inven2: 30*30

  PPUK parts-C3-20150922-PU-500T < ASD parts < Inven2: 40*30

  The multi-subaccount name of the Cash account and transaction sub-equation respectively are:

  88-654308-t-supplies < Cash payments to suppliers < Operating activities

  Cash (1): -2000 + Inventory (1): 0.8*300 + Inventory (1): 50*30 + Inventory (1): 30*30 + Inventory (1): 30*30 + Inventory (1): 40*30 = Account payable (2): 2740

- On June 30, 2016, the Tax Bureau pays two employees' salary for cash $5,670.

- On July 24, 2016, the Tax Bureau pays -$317.22 cash to A5 (SIN: 909876505) for the Travelling expenses -$212.22 and the Other expenses -$105.

- On July 31, 2016, the Tax Bureau pays two employees' salary for cash -$5,670.

- On August 11, 2016, the Tax Bureau pays -$395.47 cash to A6 (SIN: 909876506) for the Travelling expenses -$281.47 and the Other expenses -$114.

- On August 31, 2016, the Tax Bureau pays two employees' salary for cash -$5,670.

- On September 17, 2016, the Tax Bureau pays -$399.36 cash to A6 (SIN: 909876506) for the Travelling expenses -$294.36 and the Other expenses -$105.

- On September 30, 2016, the Tax Bureau pays two employees' salary for cash -$5,670.

- On September 30, 2016, the Tax Bureau records the Amortization expenses $2,212.5

of a computer server1 ($1,050, nine months), a computer1 ($600, nine months), and a computer2 ($562.5, nine months). The transaction sub-equation is:

- On September 30, 2016, the Tax Bureau cancels the balances of the Computer account and the Accumulated amortization: Computer account because these computers have used for two years. The transaction sub-equation is:

- On October 1, 2016, the Tax Bureau purchases a new computer server1, a new computer1, and a new computer2 for cash -$2,400 and other on credit $3,500 with the General ID 37 from the Company1. The multi-subaccount names of the Cash account and the Inventory account and the transaction sub-equation respectively are:

  88-654306-t-computer < Cash payments for machinery < Operating activities
  Computer server1-C1-201501007-COMS1-040 < Computer server: 2800*1
  Computer1-C1-201501008-COM1-056: 1600*1
  Computer2-C1-201501008-COM2-066: 1500*1

  Cash (1): -2400 + Inventory (1): 2800 + Inventory (1): 1600 + Inventory (1): 1500
  = Account payable (2): 3500

  Meanwhile, the purchased inventory transfers to the equipment by the interior transaction. For simplification, the Tax Bureau does not record the product codes in the equipment, so the multi-subaccount name of the Computer do not change. The multi-subaccount name of the Computer account and the transaction sub-equation respectively are:
  Computer server11 < Computer server1 < Computer server: 2800*1
  Computer11 < Computer1: 1600*1
  Computer21 < Computer2: 1500*1

  Inventory (1): -2800 + Inventory (1): -1600 + Inventory (1): -1500 + Computer
  (1): 2800 + Computer (1): 1600 + Computer (1): 1500 = 0

- On October 3, 2016, the Tax Bureau purchases one Truck2 part1 for cash -$4,500 and other on credit $4,000 from the Company2 (123456783). Here, the parts are not as the equipment but as the Vehicle part expenses (Operating and administrative expenses) for simplification. The following similar transactions are the same as this. The multi-subaccount names of the Cash account and the Inventory account and the transaction sub-equation respectively are:

88-654307-t-parts supplier < Cash payments for operating activities < Operating activities

Truck2 part1-C2-20150728-T2P1-053 < Truck2 parts < Vehicle parts: 8500*1

Cash (1): -4500 + Inventory (1): 8500 = Account payable (2): 4000

Meanwhile, the purchased inventory transfers to the Vehicle part expenses account by the interior transaction. The multi-subaccount name of the Vehicle part expenses account is the "n" and the transaction sub-equation respectively is:

Inventory (1): -8500 = Vehicle part expenses (5): -8500

- On October 25, 2016, the Tax Bureau pays -$369.53 cash to A5 (SIN: 909876508) for the Travelling expenses -$253.53 and the Other expenses -$116.

- On October 31, 2016, the Tax Bureau pays two employees' salary for cash -$5,670.

- On November 18, 2016, the Tax Bureau pays -$388.19 cash to A6 (SIN: 909876506) for the Travelling expenses -$295.19 and the Other expenses -$93.

- On November 19, 2016, the Tax Bureau purchases three service packages (Truck2-Service package2 for cash -$500, Car1- Service package3 for cash -$490, and Car3-Service package5 for cash -$410) for cash -$1,400 from the Company1. The multi-subaccount name of the Cash account is:

88-654306-t-service packages < Cash payments for operating expenses < Operating activities

- On November 30, 2016, the Tax Bureau pays two employees' salary for cash -$5,670.

- On December 1, 2016, the Tax Bureau records the Computer2's amortization expenses -$125 two months (2 years, straight line) and transfers this Computer2 to the Inventory account for sale. The three transaction sub-equations are:

Accumulated amortization: Computer (1): -125 = Amortization expenses (5): -125

Accumulated amortization: Computer (1): 125 + Computer (1): -125 = 0

Inventory (1): 1375*1 + Computer (1): -1375 = 0

- On December 1, 2016, the Tax Bureau sells a used computer2 (Book value $1,375) on credit to the Proprietorship2 (phone number: 123456080). The multi-subaccount names of the Cash account and the Inventory account and the transaction sub-equation respectively are:

  88-654310-c-customers < Cash receipts from customers < Operating activities
  Computer2-C1-201501008-COM2-066: -1375*1

  Inventory (1): -1375*1 + Account receivable (1): 1375 = Sales (4): 1375 + Cost of goods sold (5): -1375

- On December 1, 2016, the Tax Bureau purchases a new computer1 ($1,600) on credit from the Company1. The multi-subaccount names of the Cash account and the Inventory account and the two transaction sub-equations respectively are:

  88-654306-t-computer < Cash payments for machinery < Operating activities
  Computer1-C1-20160430-COM1-068 < Computer

  Inventory (1): 1600*1 = Account payable (2): 1600

  Inventory (1): -1600*1 + Computer (1): 1600 = 0

- On December 28, 2016, the Tax Bureau pays -$664.58 cash to A5 (SIN: 909876505) for the Travelling expenses -$472.58 and the Other expenses -$192.
- On December 28, 2016, the Tax Bureau pays -$670.58 cash to A6 (SIN: 909876506) for the Travelling expenses -$472.58 and the Other expenses -$198.

- On December 28, 2016, the Tax Bureau pays -$2,500 cash to Company3 (phone number: 123456782) with the General ID 27.

- On December 29, 2016, the Tax Bureau pays -$2,400 cash to Company1 (phone number: 123456784) with the General ID 37. The multi-subaccount name of the Cash account is:

  88-654306-t-machinery < Cash payments for machinery < Operating activities

- On December 31, 2016, the Tax Bureau pays two employees' salary for cash -$5,670.

- On the same day, the Tax Bureau receives cash $200 (Investment incomes) from the Business Bank1 for investment interest of the Bond11. The multi-subaccount name of the Cash account is:

  88-654304-c-investment income < Cash receipts from investments < Investing activities

- On the same day, the Tax Bureau receives cash $459.25 ($328 for investment interest of the Bond21and cash $131.25 for investment interest of the Bond23) from the Business Bank2. The multi-subaccount name of the Cash account is:

  88-654305-c-investment income < Cash receipts from investments < Investing activities

- On the same day, the Tax Bureau receives cash $120 (Deposit interest incomes) from the Business Bank1 for primary deposit interest. The multi-subaccount name of the Cash account is:

  88-654304-c-deposit interest income < Cash receipts from deposit interest < Financial activities

- On the same day, the Tax Bureau records the Consumables expenses -$4,740. The multi-subaccount names of the Inventory account and transaction sub-equation respectively are:

  Inven121-C3-20150922-In121-20000T < Inven12 < Inven1: -0.8*300

  Inven122-C3-20150922-In122-1000T < Inven12 < Inven1: -50*30

  Inven21-C3-20150922-In21-1250T < Inven2: -30*30

  Inven221-C3-20150922-In221-750T < Inven22 < Inven2: -30*30

PPUK parts-C3-20150922-PU-500T < ASD parts < Inven2: -40*30

Inventory (1): -0.8*300 + Inventory (1): -50*30 + Inventory (1): -30*30 + Inventory (1): -30*30 + Inventory (1): -40*30 = Consumables expenses (5): -4740

- On the same day, the Tax Bureau records the Office supplies expenses -$431.46. It is consisted of two parts of the Supplies -$147.46 and the Inventory -$316 (-$14*10 - $16*9). The multi-subaccount names of the Inventory account and transaction sub-equation respectively are:

  Supplies1-P2-20150920-SUP1-200T: -14*10
  Supplies2-P2-20150920-SUP2-200T: -16*9

  Supplies (1): -147.46 + Inventory (1): -14*10 + Inventory (1): -16*9 = Office supplies expenses (5): -431.46

- On the same day, the Tax Bureau records the Vehicle's amortization expenses - $23,600 (-$8,000 - $8,000 - $7,600) one year (5 years, straight line).

- On the same day, the Tax Bureau records the Computer's amortization expenses - $616.67 which includes a new computer server1 (-$350, three months (2 years, straight line)), a new computer1 (-$200, three months (2 years, straight line)), and a new computer1 (-$-66.67, one months).

- On the same day, the Tax Bureau records the Tax expenses $0 and the Tax payable $0. The two accounts' multi-subaccount names all are the 'n'.

So far, I have entered all transactions of the fiscal year 2016 to the database dcj204.

## 3.3.2 Brief Summary of the Tax Bureau

The Figure 3.3-1 shows all inventory transactions of the Tax Bureau in the fiscal year 2016 by using of SQL Server query.

From the Figure 3.3-1, the Computer2 is purchased on September 30, 2016, seeing the Order 10. The negative unit means the Computer2 is sold by other member to the Tax Bureau.

Please pay attention of the IDM and the Symbol. The Computer2 is transferred to the Equipment on September 30, 2016, seeing the Order 13. Because this transaction is an interior transaction, it records itself IDM. Therefore, the positive unit means that the Computer2 is transferred to the Equipment and the negative unit means that the Computer2 is transferred to the Inventory account from the Equipment (seeing the Order 23).

```
SQLQuery1.sql - LIU...SS.dcj200 (sa (52))*  ×
  use dcj200
  select * from InventoryByMembers where Recorder='88-654303' and TransDate between '2016-01-01' and '2016-12-31'
  order by TransDate
100 %  ▼
```

Results | Messages

| | IDM | Amount | Symbol | MultiSubaccount | Recorder | TransDate | Unit |
|---|---|---|---|---|---|---|---|
| 1 | 88-654310 | -140.00 | t | Supplies1-P2-20150920-SUP1-200T | 88-654303 | 2016-05-08 | -10 |
| 2 | 88-654310 | -160.00 | t | Supplies2-P2-20150920-SUP2-200T | 88-654303 | 2016-05-08 | -10 |
| 3 | 88-654308 | -240.00 | t | Inven121-C3-20150922-In121-20000T < Inven12 < Inven1 | 88-654303 | 2016-06-29 | -300 |
| 4 | 88-654308 | -1500.00 | t | Inven122-C3-20150922-In122-1000T < Inven12 < Inven1 | 88-654303 | 2016-06-29 | -30 |
| 5 | 88-654308 | -900.00 | t | Inven21-C3-20150922-In21-1250T < Inven2 | 88-654303 | 2016-06-29 | -30 |
| 6 | 88-654308 | -900.00 | t | Inven221-C3-20150922-In221-750T < Inven22 < Inven2 | 88-654303 | 2016-06-29 | -30 |
| 7 | 88-654308 | -1200.00 | t | PPUK parts-C3-20150922-PU-500T < ASD parts < Inven2 | 88-654303 | 2016-06-29 | -30 |
| 8 | 88-654306 | -2800.00 | t | Computer server1-C1-201501007-COMS1-040 < Computer server | 88-654303 | 2016-09-30 | -1 |
| 9 | 88-654306 | -1600.00 | t | Computer1-C1-201501008-COM1-056 | 88-654303 | 2016-09-30 | -1 |
| 10 | 88-654303 | 2800.00 | e | Computer server1-C1-201501007-COMS1-040 < Computer server | 88-654303 | 2016-09-30 | 1 |
| 11 | 88-654303 | 1600.00 | e | Computer1-C1-201501008-COM1-056 | 88-654303 | 2016-09-30 | 1 |
| 12 | 88-654303 | 1500.00 | e | Computer2-C1-201501008-COM2-066 | 88-654303 | 2016-10-01 | 1 |
| 13 | 88-654306 | -1500.00 | t | Computer2-C1-201501008-COM2-066 | 88-654303 | 2016-10-01 | -1 |
| 14 | 88-654307 | -8500.00 | t | Truck2 part1-C2-20150728-T2P1-053 < Truck2 parts < Vehicle parts | 88-654303 | 2016-10-03 | -1 |
| 15 | 88-654303 | 8500.00 | s | Truck2 part1-C2-20150728-T2P1-053 < Truck2 parts < Vehicle parts | 88-654303 | 2016-10-03 | 1 |
| 16 | 88-654303 | -1375.00 | e | Computer2-C1-201501008-COM2-066 | 88-654303 | 2016-12-01 | -1 |
| 17 | 88-654310 | 1375.00 | c | Computer2-C1-201501008-COM2-066 | 88-654303 | 2016-12-01 | 1 |
| 18 | 88-654306 | -1600.00 | t | Computer1-C1-20160430-COM1-068 < Computer | 88-654303 | 2016-12-01 | -1 |
| 19 | 88-654303 | 1600.00 | e | Computer1-C1-20160430-COM1-068 < Computer | 88-654303 | 2016-12-01 | 1 |
| 20 | 88-654303 | 240.00 | s | Inven121-C3-20150922-In121-20000T < Inven12 < Inven1 | 88-654303 | 2016-12-31 | 300 |
| 21 | 88-654303 | 1500.00 | s | Inven122-C3-20150922-In122-1000T < Inven12 < Inven1 | 88-654303 | 2016-12-31 | 30 |
| 22 | 88-654303 | 900.00 | s | Inven21-C3-20150922-In21-1250T < Inven2 | 88-654303 | 2016-12-31 | 30 |
| 23 | 88-654303 | 900.00 | s | Inven221-C3-20150922-In221-750T < Inven22 < Inven2 | 88-654303 | 2016-12-31 | 30 |
| 24 | 88-654303 | 1200.00 | s | PPUK parts-C3-20150922-PU-500T < ASD parts < Inven2 | 88-654303 | 2016-12-31 | 30 |
| 25 | 88-654303 | 140.00 | s | Supplies1-P2-20150920-SUP1-200T | 88-654303 | 2016-12-31 | 10 |
| 26 | 88-654303 | 144.00 | s | Supplies2-P2-20150920-SUP2-200T | 88-654303 | 2016-12-31 | 9 |

Figure 3.3-1   Tax Bureau Inventory Purchased or Sold by Other Members

## 3.4 Business Bank1

The Business Bank1 has two class of transactions. One is itself transaction; another is only transaction of other organizations and individuals' deposit change. The transactions itself are first recorded. After that, the transactions of other organizations and individuals are recorded according to other organization's names. The customer deposit transactions are not the Business Bank1's transactions and are only an intermediate process between the customers of the Business Bank1. Therefore, the ID in three level subaccount of the Cash account is the customer itself. In fact, the transaction can be recorded by various bank cards and internet automatically. For simplification, the multi-subaccount name form of the Deposits payable account is the 'n'. All customer deposit transactions which are ordered by organizations or companies in the Business Bank1 are listed in the Appendixes A.

### 3.4.1 An Accounting Fiscal Year of the Business Bank1

In the new fiscal year, the Business Bank1 occurs the following the Business Bank1 itself transactions.

- On January 2, 2016, the Business Bank1 purchases the inventories $162 (supplies1 $14*7 and supplies2 $16*4) from the Proprietorship2 (phone number: 123456080) for cash -$162. The multi-subaccount names of the Cash account and the Inventory account and transaction sub-equation respectively are:

  88-654310-t-supplies < Cash payments for operating expenses < Operating activities

  Supplies1-P2-20150920-SUP1-200T: 14*7
  Supplies2-P2-20150920-SUP2-200T: 16*4

  Cash (1): -162 + Inventory (1): 14*7 + Inventory (1): 16*4 = 0

- On January 10, 2016, A1 transfers $10,000 to his or her second account in the Business Bank2. For simplification, the multi-subaccount name of the Deposits payable account is the "n". The multi-subaccount name of the Cash account is:

  909876501-d-deposits < Cash receipts from customers deposits < Operating activities

- On January 13, 2016, the Business Bank1 purchases the following inventories $4,660 from the Company3 (phone number: 123456782) for cash -$2,000 and other on credit. For simplification, the inventories will be transfer to the Consumables expenses account at the end of the fiscal year.

Inven121-C3-20150922-In121-20000T < Inven12 < Inven1: 0.8*200

Inven122-C3-20150922-In122-1000T < Inven12 < Inven1: 50*30

Inven21-C3-20150922-In21-1250T < Inven2: 30*30

Inven221-C3-20150922-In221-750T < Inven22 < Inven2: 30*30

PPUK parts-C3-20150922-PU-500T < ASD parts < Inven2: 40*30

The multi-subaccount name of the Cash account and transaction sub-equation respectively are:

88-654308-t-suppliers < Cash payments to suppliers < Operating activities

Cash (1): -2000 + Inventory (1): 0.8*200 + Inventory (1): 50*30 + Inventory (1): 30*30 + Inventory (1): 30*30 + Inventory (1): 40*30 = Account payable (2): 2660

- On January 18, 2016, the Business Bank1 pays -$148.78 cash to A8 (SIN: 909876508) for the Travelling expenses -$91.78 and the Other expenses -$57. The multi-subaccount name of the Cash account is:

909876508-n-operating expenses < Cash payments for operating expenses < Operating activities

The twin multi-subaccount name of the Cash account and the twin transaction sub-equation are respectively:

909876508-d-deposits < Cash receipts from customers deposits < Operating

Cash (1): 148.78 = Deposits payable (2): 148.78

- On January 23, 2016, the Business Bank1 pays -$179.59 cash to A7 (SIN: 909876507) for the Travelling expenses -$97.59 and the Other expenses -$82.

- On January 26, 2016, A12 receives cash $13,000 from his or her primary account in the Business Bank2. The multi-subaccount name of the Cash account is:

909876512-d-deposits<Cash receipts from customers deposits<Operating activities

- On January 26, 2016, the Business Bank1 purchases one Car1part2 from the

Company2 (phone number: 123456783) for cash -$5200 and other on credit. The multi-subaccount names of the Cash account and the Inventory account and transaction sub-equation respectively are:

88-654307-t-supplies<Cash payments for operating expenses<Operating activities
Car1 part2-C2-20150816-C1P2-068 < Car1 parts < Vehicle parts: 7200*1

Cash (1): -5200 + Inventory (1): 7200 = Account payable (2): 2000

Meanwhile, the purchased inventory transfers to the Vehicle part expenses account by the interior transaction. The multi-subaccount name of the Vehicle part expenses account is the "n" and the transaction sub-equation respectively is:

Inventory (1): -7200 = Vehicle part expenses (5): -7200

- On January 27, 2016, the Business Bank1 pays -$232.31 cash to A9 (SIN: 909876509) for the Travelling expenses -$132.31 and the Other expenses -$100.
- On January 31, 2016, the Business Bank1 pays three employees' salary for cash -$8,660. The three multi-subaccount names of the Cash account respectively are:
  909876507-t-salary< Cash payments for operating expenses < Operating activities
  909876508-t-salary< Cash payments for operating expenses < Operating activities
  909876509-t-salary< Cash payments for operating expenses < Operating activities

The twin three multi-subaccount names of the Cash account and the twin transaction sub-equation are respectively:
88-654307-d-deposits<Cash receipts from customers deposits<Operating activities (88-654308, 88-654309)

- On February 1, 2016, the Business Bank1 purchases one Car2 $39,000 from the Company1 (phone number: 123456784) for cash -$19,000 and other on credit. The multi-subaccount name of the Cash account and the Inventory account, and transaction sub-equation and the interior transaction sub-equation respectively are:
  88-654306-t-machinery < Cash payments for machinery < Operating activities

Car2-C1-20150925-C2-027 < Car-inventory < Vehicle-inventory: 39000*1

Cash (1): -19000 + Inventory (1): 39000*1 = Account payable (2): 20000

Inventory (1): -39000*1 + Vehicle (1): 39000 = 0

- On February 21, 2016, the Business Bank1 pays -$290.33 cash to A9 (SIN: 909876509) for the Travelling expenses -$178.33 and the Other expenses -$112.

- On February 24, 2016, the Business Bank1 pays -$226.44 cash to A8 (SIN: 909876508) for the Travelling expenses -$130.44 and the Other expenses -$96.

- On February 28, 2016, the Business Bank1 pays three employees' salary expenses for cash -$8,660 repeatedly.

- On March 20, 2016, the Business Bank1 pays -$252.59 cash to A9 (SIN: 909876509) for the Travelling expenses -$148.59 and the Other expenses -$104.

- On March 24, 2016, the Business Bank1 pays -$226.44 cash to A7 (SIN: 909876500) for the Travelling expenses -$130.44 and the Other expenses -$96.

- On March 29, 2016, the Business Bank1 pays -$148.93 cash to A8 (SIN: 909876508) for the Travelling expenses -$97.93 and the Other expenses -$51.

- On March 31, 2016, the Business Bank1 pays three employees' salary -$8,660.

- On April 8, 2016, the Business Bank1 pays -$255.17 cash to A9 (SIN: 909876509) for the Travelling expenses -$147.17 and the Other expenses -$108.

- On April 29, 2016, the Business Bank1 pays -$219.94 cash to A7 (SIN: 909876507) for the Travelling expenses -$117.94 and the Other expenses -$102.

- On April 30, 2016, the Business Bank1 pays three employees' salary -$8,660.

- On May 14, 2016, the Business Bank1 pays -$263.47 cash to A9 (SIN: 909876509) for the Travelling expenses -$151.47 and the Other expenses -$112.

- On May 31, 2016, the Business Bank1 pays three employees' salary -$8,660.

- On June 5, 2016, the Business Bank1 pays -$153.37 cash to A8 (SIN: 909876508) for the Travelling expenses -$99.37 and the Other expenses -$54.

- On June 16, 2016, the Business Bank1 pays -$229.58 cash to A9 (SIN: 909876509) for the Travelling expenses -$133.58 and the Other expenses -$96.

- On June 30, 2016, the Business Bank1 pays three employees' salary -$8,660.

- On July 4, 2016, the Business Bank1 pays -$279.41 cash to A9 (SIN: 909876509) for the Travelling expenses -$162.41 and the Other expenses -$117.

- On July 31, 2016, the Business Bank1 pays three employees' salary -$8,660.

- On July 31, 2016, the Business Bank1 records the Amortization expenses -$1,633.33 of a computer server2 (-$787.5, seven months), a computer2 (-$437.5, seven months), and a computer3 (-$408.33, seven months). The transaction sub-equation is:

- On July 31, 2016, the Business Bank1 cancels the balances of the Computer account and the Accumulated amortization: Computer account because these computers have used for two years. The transaction sub-equation is:

- On August 1, 2016, the Business Bank1 purchases one Computer server1 $2,800, one Computer1 $1,600, and one Computer2 $1,500 from the Company1 (phone number: 123456784) for cash -$5,000 and other on credit. The multi-subaccount names of the Cash account and the Inventory account, and transaction sub-equation and the interior transaction sub-equation respectively are:

  88-654306-t-machinery < Cash payments for machinery < Operating activities
  Computer server1-C1-201501008-COMS1-041 < Computer server-inventory < Computer-inventory: 2800*1
  Computer1-C1-201501008-COM1-057 < Computer-inventory: 1600*1
  Computer2-C1-201501008-COM2-067 < Computer-inventory: 1500*1

  Cash (1): -5000 + Inventory (1): 2800*1 + Inventory (1): 1600*1 + Inventory (1): 1500*1 = Account payable (2): 900

  Inventory (1): -2800 + Inventory (1): -1600 + Inventory (1): -1500 + Computer (1): 2800 + Computer (1): 1600 + Computer (1): 1500 = 0

- On August 14, 2016, the Business Bank1 pays -$284.33 cash to A9 (SIN: 909876509) for the Travelling expenses -$166.33 and the Other expenses -$118.

- On August 17, 2016, the Business Bank1 pays -$142.72 cash to A8 (SIN: 909876508) for the Travelling expenses -$90.72 and the Other expenses -$52.

- On August 31, 2016, the Business Bank1 pays three employees' salary -$8,660.

- On September 9, 2016, the Business Bank1 pays -$191.51 cash to A7 (SIN: 909876507) for the Travelling expenses -$101.51 and the Other expenses -$90.

- On September 12, 2016, the Business Bank1 pays -$18,000 cash to the Company1 (phone number: 123456784) with the General ID 33. The multi-subaccount name of the Cash account is:

  88-654306-t-machinery < Cash payments for machinery < Operating activities

- On September 19, 2016, the Business Bank1 pays -$261.35 cash to A9 (SIN: 909876509) for the Travelling expenses -$149.35 and the Other expenses -$112.

- On September 30 2016, the Business Bank1 pays three employees' salary -$8,660.

- On October 10, 2016, the Business Bank1 pays -$157.94 cash to A8 (SIN: 909876508) for the Travelling expenses -$101.94 and the Other expenses -$56.

- On October 18, 2016, the Business Bank1 pays -$2,660 cash to the Company3 (phone number: 123456782) with the General ID 21. The multi-subaccount name of the Cash account and transaction sub-equation respectively are:

  88-654308-t-suppliers < Cash payments to suppliers < Operating activities

- On October 25, 2016, the Business Bank1 pays -$268.73 cash to A9 (SIN: 909876509) for the Travelling expenses -$154.73 and the Other expenses -$114.

- On October 31, 2016, the Business Bank1 pays three employees' salary -$8,660.

- On November 18, 2016, the Business Bank1 pays -$286.66 cash to A9 (SIN: 909876509) for the Travelling expenses -$162.66 and the Other expenses -$124.

- On November 30, 2016, the Business Bank1 pays three employees' salary -$8,660.

- On December 11, 2016, the Business Bank1 pays -$1,500 cash to the Company1 (phone number: 123456784) with the General ID 33 (-$600) and the General ID 71 (-$900). The multi-subaccount name of the Cash account is:

  88-654306-t-machinery < Cash payments for machinery < Operating activities

- On December 17, 2016, the Business Bank1 pays -$220.85 cash to A9 (SIN:

909876509) for the Travelling expenses -$121.85 and the Other expenses -$99.

- On December 28, 2016, the Business Bank1 pays -$238.88 cash to A7 (SIN: 909876507) for the Travelling expenses -$130.88 and the Other expenses -$108.

- On December 30, 2016, the Business Bank1 pays -$1,400 cash to the Company1 (phone number: 123456784) with the General ID 33. The multi-subaccount name of the Cash account is:

  88-654306-t-machinery < Cash payments to suppliers < Operating activities

- On December 31, 2016, the Business Bank1 receives cash $38,650 from the Company1 for interest income $22,500 of the Note11 ($250,000, 9%) and interest income $16,150 of the Note15 ($170,000, 9.5%). Here, the interest incomes of the notes are recorded as the Sales (notes interest) account for the Business Banks. The multi-subaccount name of the Cash account is:

  88-654306-c-customers < Cash receipts from customers < Operating activities

- On December 31, 2016, the Business Bank1 receives cash $35,600 ($12,600 + $23,000) from the Company2 for interest income of the Note12 ($140,000, 9%) and the Note14 ($250,000, 9.2%). The multi-subaccount name of the Cash account is:

  88-654307-c-customers < Cash receipts from customers < Operating activities

- On December 31, 2016, the Business Bank1 receives cash $18,000 from the Company3 for interest income of the Note13 ($200,000, 9%). The multi-subaccount name of the Cash account is:

  88-654308-c-customers < Cash receipts from customers < Operating activities

- On December 31, 2016, the Business Bank1 receives cash $2,500 from the Cash Management Center for bank fee income. The multi-subaccount name of the Cash account is:

  88-654300-t-bank fee income< Cash receipts from customers< Operating activities

- On December 31, the Business Bank1 pays -$2,400 cash to the bond holders for the Bond interest expenses of the Bond11 (one-level subaccount "Bond11-interest expenses"). Here, there is some twin transactions for its individuals whose primary accounts (seeing the Figure 2.1-3 on the page 12) are opened in the Business Bank1, and other individuals are recorded in the Business Bank2. The twin transactions for its organization customers have been recorded by these related organizations. Therefore, the multi-subaccount names of the Cash account and the transaction sub-equations respectively are:

88-654302-t-bond interest < Cash payments to bond holders< Operating activities (88-654303, 88-654305, 88-654306, 88-654308, 88-654309, 909876507, 909876509, 909876513, 909876514)

Cash (1): -240 + Cash (1): -200 + Cash (1): -280 + Cash (1): -400 + Cash (1): -320 + Cash (1): -200 + Cash (1): -360 + Cash (1): -240 = Bond interest expenses (5): -2240

Cash (1): -120 + Cash (1): -40 = Bond interest expenses (5): -160

The twin transaction sub-equation for 909876507, 909876509, 909876513, and 909876514 individuals must be entered.

- On the same day, the Business Bank1 pays -$1,680 cash to the bond holders for the Bond interest expenses of the Bond12 (one-level subaccount "Bond12-interest expenses"). Here, there is some twin transactions for the individuals whose primary accounts (seeing the Figure 2.1-3 on the page 12) are opened in the Business Bank1, and other individuals are recorded in the Business Bank2. The multi-subaccount names of the Cash account and the transaction sub-equation respectively are:

88-654305-t-bond interest < Cash payments to bond holders< Operating activities (88-654307, 88-654309, 88-654310, 909876501, 909876502, 909876504, 909876521)

Cash (1): -126 + Cash (1): -336 + Cash (1): -126 + Cash (1): -252 + Cash (1): -210 + Cash (1): -84 + Cash (1): -294 + Cash (1): -252 = Bond interest expenses (5): -1680

The twin transaction sub-equation for 909876501, 909876502, and 909876504 must be entered.

- On the same day, the Business Bank1 pays -$2,250 cash to the bond holders for the Bond interest expenses of the Bond13 (one-level subaccount "Bond13-interest expenses"). Here, there is some twin transactions for the individuals whose primary accounts (seeing the Figure 2.1-3 on the page 12) are opened in the Business Bank1, and other individuals are recorded in the Business Bank2. Therefore, the multi-subaccount names of the Cash account and the transaction sub-equations respectively are:

  88-654305-t-bond interest < Cash payments to bond holders< Operating activities (88-654306, 88-654309, 909876503, 909876505, 909876506, 909876515, 909876517, 909876518, 909876519, 909876521)

  Cash (1): -270 + Cash (1): -135 + Cash (1): -90 + Cash (1): -270 + Cash (1): -180 + Cash (1): -315 + Cash (1): -180 + Cash (1): -225 + Cash (1): -135 = Bond interest expenses (5): -1800

  Cash (1): -270 + Cash (1): -180 = Bond interest expenses (5): -450

  The twin transaction sub-equation for the individual 909876503, 909876505, 909876506, 909876515, and 909876518 is:

  Cash (1): 270 + Cash (1): 180 + Cash (1): 315 + Cash (1): 180 + Cash (1): 135 = Deposits payable (2): 1080

- On the same day, the Business Bank1 pays cash -$2,400 to its customers (not including itself) for primary deposit interest (interest expenses). Here, the Deposit interest expenses are recorded as the one-level subaccount of the Cost of notes interest parent account for the Business Banks. In addition, there is some twin transactions for its individuals whose primary accounts (seeing the Figure 2.1-3 on the page 12) are opened in the Business Bank1, and other individuals are recorded in the Business Bank2. The twin transactions for its organization customers have been recorded by these related organizations. The multi-subaccount names of the Cash account respectively are:

88-654302-t-deposit interest expenses < Cash payments for operating expenses < Operating activities: -120

(88-654303, 88-654306, 88-654309, 909876501, 909876502, 909876503, 909876504, 909876505, 909876506, 909876507, 909876508, 909876509, 909876513, 909876514, 909876515, 909876516, 909876518, 909876524, 909876525)

The twin transaction sub-equations for the above individuals must be entered.

- On the same day, the Business Bank1 receives cash $466 (= $246 + $220) for investment interest of the Bond21 ($6,000) and the Bond22 ($5,000) from the Business Bank2. The multi-subaccount name of the Cash account is:

88-654305-c-investment income < Cash receipts from investments < Investing activities

- On December 31, 2016, the Business Bank1 pays three employees' salary expenses for cash -$8,660 repeatedly.

- On the same day, the Business Bank1 records the Office supplies expenses -$213.95. It is consisted of two parts of the Supplies -$61.33 and the Inventory -$118 (-$14*5 - $16*3). The multi-subaccount names of the Inventory account and transaction sub-equation respectively are:

Supplies1-P2-20150920-SUP1-200T: -14*5
Supplies2-P2-20150920-SUP2-200T: -16*3

Supplies (1): -95.95 + Inventory (1): -14*5 + Inventory (1): -16*3 = Office supplies expenses (5): -213.95

- On the same day, the Business Bank1 records the Office supplies expenses -$4,660. The multi-subaccount names of the Inventory account and transaction sub-equation respectively are:

Inven121-C3-20150922-In121-20000T < Inven12 < Inven1: -0.8*200

Inven122-C3-20150922-In122-1000T < Inven12 < Inven1: -50*30

Inven21-C3-20150922-In21-1250T < Inven2: -30*30

Inven221-C3-20150922-In221-750T < Inven22 < Inven2: -30*30

PPUK parts-C3-20150922-PU-500T < ASD parts < Inven2: -40*30

Inventory (1): -0.8*200 + Inventory (1): -50*30 + Inventory (1): -30*30 + Inventory (1): -30*30 + Inventory (1): -40*30 = Office supplies expenses (5): -4660

- On the same day, the Business Bank1 records the Vehicle's amortization expenses - $22,100 (5 years, straight line) which includes a Truck1 ($9,000, one year), a Car1($8,000, one year), and a new Car2 ($7,150, eleven months).

- On the same day, the Business Bank1 records the Computer's amortization expenses $1,229.16 five months (2 years, straight line) which includes a new computer server1 ($583.33), a new computer1 ($333.33), and a new computer2 ($312.5).

- On December 31, the Business Bank1 records the Tax expenses $0 and the Tax payable $0. The multi-subaccount name forms of the Tax expenses and the Tax payable accounts all are the 'n'.

So far, I have entered all transactions of the Business Bank1 itself to the database dcj206 in the fiscal year 2016.

## 3.4.2 Brief Summary of the Business Bank1

The Figure 3.4-1 shows all inventory transactions of the Business Bank1 in the fiscal year 2016 by using of SQL Server query.

```
SQLQuery1.sql - LIU...SS.dcj200 (sa (52))*  ×
  use dcj200
  select * from InventoryByMembers where Recorder='88-654304' and TransDate between '2016-01-01' and '2016-12-31'
  order by TransDate
```

100 %   ▾

Results  Messages

| | IDM | Amount | Symbol | MultiSubaccount | Recorder | TransDate | Unit |
|---|---|---|---|---|---|---|---|
| 1 | 88-654310 | -98.00 | t | Supplies1-P2-20150920-SUP1-200T | 88-654304 | 2016-01-02 | -7 |
| 2 | 88-654310 | -64.00 | t | Supplies2-P2-20150920-SUP2-200T | 88-654304 | 2016-01-02 | -4 |
| 3 | 88-654308 | -160.00 | t | Inven121-C3-20150922-In121-20000T < Inven12 < Inven1 | 88-654304 | 2016-01-13 | -200 |
| 4 | 88-654308 | -1500.00 | t | Inven122-C3-20150922-In122-1000T < Inven12 < Inven1 | 88-654304 | 2016-01-13 | -30 |
| 5 | 88-654308 | -900.00 | t | Inven21-C3-20150922-In21-1250T < Inven2 | 88-654304 | 2016-01-13 | -30 |
| 6 | 88-654308 | -900.00 | t | Inven221-C3-20150922-In221-750T < Inven22 < Inven2 | 88-654304 | 2016-01-13 | -30 |
| 7 | 88-654308 | -1200.00 | t | PPUK parts-C3-20150922-PU-500T < ASD parts < Inven2 | 88-654304 | 2016-01-13 | -30 |
| 8 | 88-654307 | -7200.00 | t | Car1 part2-C2-20150816-C1P2-068 < Car1 parts < Vehicle parts | 88-654304 | 2016-01-26 | -1 |
| 9 | 88-654304 | 7200.00 | s | Car1 part2-C2-20150816-C1P2-068 < Car1 parts < Vehicle parts | 88-654304 | 2016-01-26 | 1 |
| 10 | 88-654306 | -39000.00 | t | Car2-C1-20150925-C2-027 < Car-inventory < Vehicle-inventory | 88-654304 | 2016-02-01 | -1 |
| 11 | 88-654304 | 39000.00 | e | Car2-C1-20150925-C2-027 < Car-inventory < Vehicle-inventory | 88-654304 | 2016-02-01 | 1 |
| 12 | 88-654306 | -2800.00 | t | Computer server1-C1-201501008-COMS1-041 < Computer server-inventory < C... | 88-654304 | 2016-08-01 | -1 |
| 13 | 88-654306 | -1600.00 | t | Computer1-C1-201501008-COM1-057 < Computer-inventory | 88-654304 | 2016-08-01 | -1 |
| 14 | 88-654306 | -1500.00 | t | Computer2-C1-201501008-COM2-067 < Computer-inventory | 88-654304 | 2016-08-01 | -1 |
| 15 | 88-654304 | 2800.00 | e | Computer server1-C1-201501008-COMS1-041 < Computer server-inventory < C... | 88-654304 | 2016-08-01 | 1 |
| 16 | 88-654304 | 1600.00 | e | Computer1-C1-201501008-COM1-057 < Computer-inventory | 88-654304 | 2016-08-01 | 1 |
| 17 | 88-654304 | 1500.00 | e | Computer2-C1-201501008-COM2-067 < Computer-inventory | 88-654304 | 2016-08-01 | 1 |
| 18 | 88-654304 | 70.00 | s | Supplies1-P2-20150920-SUP1-200T | 88-654304 | 2016-12-31 | 5 |
| 19 | 88-654304 | 48.00 | s | Supplies2-P2-20150920-SUP2-200T | 88-654304 | 2016-12-31 | 3 |
| 20 | 88-654304 | 160.00 | s | Inven121-C3-20150922-In121-20000T < Inven12 < Inven1 | 88-654304 | 2016-12-31 | 200 |
| 21 | 88-654304 | 1500.00 | s | Inven122-C3-20150922-In122-1000T < Inven12 < Inven1 | 88-654304 | 2016-12-31 | 30 |
| 22 | 88-654304 | 900.00 | s | Inven21-C3-20150922-In21-1250T < Inven2 | 88-654304 | 2016-12-31 | 30 |
| 23 | 88-654304 | 900.00 | s | Inven221-C3-20150922-In221-750T < Inven22 < Inven2 | 88-654304 | 2016-12-31 | 30 |
| 24 | 88-654304 | 1200.00 | s | PPUK parts-C3-20150922-PU-500T < ASD parts < Inven2 | 88-654304 | 2016-12-31 | 30 |

Figure 3.4-1   Business Bank1 Inventory Purchased or Sold by Other Members

## 3.5 Business Bank2

The Business Bank2 has also two class of transactions. All customer deposit transactions which are ordered by organizations or companies in the Business Bank2 are listed in the Appendixes B.

### 3.5.1 An Accounting Fiscal Year of the Business Bank2

In the new fiscal year, the Business Bank2 occurs the following transactions.

- On January 2, 2016, the Business Bank2 purchases the inventories $186 (supplies1 $14*3 and supplies2 $16*9) from the Proprietorship2 (phone number: 123456780) for cash -$186. The multi-subaccount name of the Cash account and the Inventory account and the transaction sub-equation are respectively:

88-654310-t-supplies < Cash payments for operating expenses < Operating activities

Supplies1-P2-20150920-SUP1-200T: 14*3

Supplies2-P2-20150920-SUP2-200T: 16*9

Cash (1): -186 + Inventory (1): 14*3 + Inventory (1): 16*9 = 0

- On January 10, 2016, A1 receives cash $10,000 from A1's primary account in the Business Bank1. The multi-subaccount name of the Cash account is:

  909876501-d-deposits<Cash receipts from customers deposits<Operating activities

- On January 15, 2016, Government1 transfers $600 from the Business Bank2 to its primary account in the Business Bank1. The multi-subaccount name of the Cash account is:

  88-654302-d-deposits<Cash receipts from customers deposits<Operating activities

- On January 17, 2016, the Business Bank2 pays -$144.36 cash to A11 (SIN: 909876511) for the Travelling expenses -$90.36 and the Other expenses -$54. The multi-subaccount name of the Cash account is:

  909876511-n-operating expenses < Cash payments for operating expenses < Operating activities

  The twin multi-subaccount name of the Cash account is:

  909876511-d-deposits<Cash receipts from customers deposits<Operating activities

- On January 24, 2016, the Business Bank2 pays -$265.94 cash to A12 (SIN: 909876512) for the Travelling expenses -$145.94 and the Other expenses -$120.

- On January 26, 2016, A12 transfers $13,000 to his or her second account in the Business Bank1. The multi-subaccount name of the Cash account is:

  909876512-d-deposits < Cash receipts from customers deposits < Operating

- On January 29, 2016, the Business Bank2 pays -$158.67 cash to A10 (SIN: 909876510) for the Travelling expenses -$101.67 and the Other expenses -$57.

- On January 31, 2016, the Business Bank2 pays three employees' salary expenses for cash -$8,640. The multi-subaccount names of the Cash account respectively are:

909876510-t-salary < Cash payments for operating expenses< Operating activities

909876511-t-salary < Cash payments for operating expenses< Operating activities

909876512-t-salary < Cash payments for operating expenses< Operating activities

The twin three multi-subaccount names of the Cash account are respectively:

909876510-d-deposits<Cash receipts from customers deposits<Operating activities
(909876511, 909876512)

- On February 8, 2016, the Business Bank2 pays -$272.76 cash to A12 (SIN: 909876512) for the Travelling expenses -$156.76 and the Other expenses -$116.

- On February 28, 2016, the Business Bank2 pays three employees' salary $8,640.

- On March 1, 2016, the Business Bank2 purchases one Car2 $39,000 from the Company1 (phone number: 123456084) for cash -$19,000 and other on credit. The multi-subaccount names of the Cash account and the Inventory account and the two transaction sub-equations respectively are:

88-654306-t-machinery < Cash payments for machinery < Operating activities

Car2-C1-20150925-C2-028 < Car-inventory < Vehicle-inventory: 39000*1

Cash (1): -19000 + Inventory (1): 39000 = Account payable (2): 20000

Inventory (1): -39000 + Vehicle (1): 39000 = 0

- On March 9, 2016, the Business Bank2 pays -$247.59 cash to A12 (SIN: 909876512) for the Travelling expenses -$147.59 and the Other -$100.

- On March 13, 2016, the Business Bank2 pays -$149.61 cash to A11 (SIN: 909876511) for the Travelling expenses -$99.61 and the Other expenses -$50.

- On March 31, 2016, the Business Bank2 pays three employees' salary $8,640.

- On April 6, 2016, the Business Bank2 purchases the following inventories -$2,200 from the Company3 (phone number: 123456782) for cash -$1,500 and other on credit. Here, the inventories will be recorded as the Office supplies expenses at the end of the fiscal for simplification.

Inven111-C3-20150922-In111-1000T < Inven11 < Inven1: 10*10

Inven112-C3-20150922-In112-800T < Inven11 < Inven1: 40*10

Inven221-C3-20150922-In221-750T < Inven22 < Inven2: 30*20

Inven222-C3-20150922-In222-400T < Inven22 < Inven2: 50*20

PPGH parts-C3-20150922-PG-1600T < ASD parts < Inven2: 2*50

The multi-subaccount name of the Cash account and the transaction sub-equations respectively are:

88-654308-t-suppliers < Cash payments to suppliers < Operating activities

Cash (1): -1500 + Inventory (1): 10*10 + Inventory (1): 40*10 + Inventory (1): 30*20 + Inventory (1): 50*20 + Inventory (1): 2*50 = Account payable (2): 700

- On April 15, 2016, the Business Bank2 pays -$172.53 cash to A11 (SIN: 909876511) for the Travelling expenses -$103.53 and the Other expenses -$69.

- On April 19, 2016, the Business Bank2 pays -$288.24 cash to A12 (SIN: 909876512) for the Travelling expenses -$168.24 and the Other expenses -$120.

- On April 30, 2016, the Business Bank2 pays three employees' salary -$8,640.

- On May 22, 2016, the Business Bank2 pays -$159.22 cash to A11 (SIN: 909876511) for the Travelling expenses -$103.22 and the Other expenses -$56.

- On May 26, 2016, the Business Bank2 pays -$273.52 cash to A12 (SIN: 909876512) for the Travelling expenses -$165.52 and the Other expenses -$108.

- On May 31, 2016, the Business Bank2 pays three employees' salary -$8,640.

- On June 1, 2016, the Business Bank2 issues one Bond23 $40,000 (three years, 4.5% annually, pay at end of each year), seeing the following Figure 3.5-1.

| Order | Bond | Amount | Term | Purchaser Name | Identity |
|-------|------|--------|------|----------------|----------|
| 1 | Bond23 | 25000 | June 1, 2016, three years, 4.5% annually, pay at end of each year | Cash Management Center | 88-654300 |
| 2 | Bond23 | 5000 | June 1, 2016, three years, 4.5% annually, pay at end of each year | Central Bank | 88-654301 |
| 3 | Bond23 | 5000 | June 1, 2016, three years, 4.5% annually, pay at end of each year | Government1 | 88-654302 |
| 4 | Bond23 | 5000 | June 1, 2016, three years, 4.5% annually, pay at end of each year | Tax Bureau | 88-654303 |
| 9 | Total | 40000 | | | |

Figure 3.5-1   Business Bank2 Issued Bond Information Table

The multi-subaccount names of the Cash account and transaction sub-equation respectively are:

88-654300-i-bond23 < Cash receipts from issued bonds < Financial activities

88-654301-i-bond23 < Cash receipts from issued bonds < Financial activities

88-654302-i-bond23 < Cash receipts from issued bonds < Financial activities

88-654303-i-bond23 < Cash receipts from issued bonds < Financial activities

Cash (1): 25000 + Cash (1): 5000 + Cash (1): 5000 + Cash (1): 5000 = Bonds payable (2): 25000 + Bonds payable (2): 5000 + Bonds payable (2): 5000 + Bonds payable (2): 5000

- On June 21, 2016, the Business Bank2 pays -$278.54 cash to A12 (SIN: 909876512) for the Travelling expenses -$169.54 and the Other expenses -$109.

- On June 30, 2016, the Business Bank2 pays three employees' salary expenses for cash -$8,640 repeatedly.

- On July 11, 2016, the Business Bank2 pays -$187.57 cash to A11 (SIN: 909876511) for the Travelling expenses -$113.57 and the Other expenses -$74.

- On July 23, 2016, the Business Bank2 pays -$308.39 cash to A12 (SIN: 909876512) for the Travelling expenses -$183.39 and the Other expenses -$125.

- On July 31, 2016, the Business Bank2 pays three employees' -$8,640.

- On August 19, 2016, the Business Bank2 pays -$161.88 cash to A10 (SIN: 909876510) for the Travelling expenses -$98.88 and the Other expenses -$63.

- On August 24, 2016, the Business Bank2 pays -$267.61 cash to A12 (SIN: 909876512) for the Travelling expenses -$155.61 and the Other expenses -$112.

- On August 31, 2016, the Business Bank2 pays three employees' salary -$8,640.

- On September 19, 2016, the Business Bank2 pays -$251.18 cash to A12 (SIN: 909876512) for the Travelling expenses -$147.18 and the Other expenses -$104.

- On September 26, 2016, the Business Bank2 pays -$17,000 cash to the Company1 (phone number: 123456784) with the General ID 35. The multi-subaccount name of the Cash account is:

88-654306-t-machinery < Cash payments for machinery < Operating activities

- On September 30 2016, the Business Bank2 pays three employees' salary -$8,640.

- On September 30, 2016, the Business Bank2 records the Amortization expenses - $2,212.5 of a computer server1 (-$1,050, nine months), a computer1 (-$600, nine months), and a computer2 (-$562.5, nine months).

- On September 30, 2016, the Business Bank2 cancels the balances of the Computer account and the Accumulated amortization: Computer account because these computers have used for two years.

- On October 1, 2016, the Business Bank2 purchases one Computer server1 $2,800, one Computer1 $1,600, and one Computer2 $1,500 from the Company1 (phone number: 123456784) for cash -$5,000 and other on credit. The multi-subaccount names of the Cash account and the Inventory account, and the two transaction sub-equations respectively are:

88-654306-t-machinery < Cash payments for machinery < Operating activities

Computer server1-C1-20160430-COMS1-042 < Computer server-inventory < Computer-inventory

Computer1-C1-20160430-COM1-059 < Computer-inventory

Computer2-C1-20160430-COM2-069 < Computer-inventory

Cash (1): -5000 + Inventory (1): 2800 + Inventory (1): 1600 + Inventory (1): 1500 = Account payable (2): 900

Inventory (1): -2800 + Inventory (1): -1600 + Inventory (1): -1500 + Computer (1): 2800 + Computer (1): 1600 + Computer (1): 1500 = 0

- On October 18, 2016, the Business Bank2 pays -$260.75 cash to A12 (SIN: 909876512) for the Travelling expenses -$152.75 and the Other expenses -$108.

- On October 31, 2016, the Business Bank2 pays three employees' salary -$8,640.

- On November 3, 2016, the Business Bank2 pays -$161.42 cash to A11 (SIN:

909876511) for the Travelling expenses -$100.42 and the Other expenses -$61.

- On November 21, 2016, the Business Bank2 pays -$250.43 cash to A12 (SIN: 909876512) for the Travelling expenses -$150.43 and the Other expenses -$100.

- On November 30, 2016, the Business Bank2 pays three employees' salary -$8,640 repeatedly.

- On December 4, 2016, the Business Bank2 pays -$152.24 cash to A10 (SIN: 909876510) for the Travelling expenses -$76.24 and the Other expenses -$76.

- On December 19, 2016, the Business Bank2 pays -$2,800 cash to the Company1 (phone number: 123456784) with General ID 35. The multi-subaccount name of the Cash account is:

  88-654306-t-machinery < Cash payments for machinery < Operating activities

- On December 29, 2016, the Business Bank2 pays -$302.36 cash to A12 (SIN: 909876512) for the Travelling expenses -$177.36 and the Other expenses -$125.

- On December 31, 2016, the Business Bank2 receives cash $19,800 from the Company1 for interest income of the Note21 ($220,000, 9%). Here, the interest incomes of the notes are recorded as the Sales (notes interest) account for the Business Banks. The multi-subaccount name of the Cash account is:

  88-654306-c-customers < Cash receipts from customers < Operating activities

- On December 31, 2016, the Business Bank2 receives cash $21,600 from the Company2 for interest income of the Note22 ($240,000, 9%).

- On December 31, 2016, the Business Bank2 receives cash $34,400 ($16,200 + $18,200) from the Company3 for interest income of the Note23 ($180,000), 9% and Note24 ($200,000, 9.1%).

- On December 31, 2016, the Business Bank2 receives cash $11,280 from the Proprietorship1 for interest income of the Note25 ($120,000, 9.4%).

- On the same day, the Business Bank2 receives cash $676 ($280 + $126 + $270) for investment interest of the Bond11 ($7,000), Bond12 ($3,000), and the Bond13 ($6,000) from the Business Bank1. The Cash's multi-subaccount name is:

  88-654304-c-investment income < Cash receipts from investments < Investing activities

- On the same day, the Business Bank2 receives cash $230 for investment interest of the Bond31 ($5,000) from the Company1. The multi-subaccount name of the Cash account is:

  88-654306-c-investment income < Cash receipts from investments < Investing activities

- On the same day, the Business Bank2 receives cash $376 for investment interest of the Bond41 ($8,000) from the Company2. The multi-subaccount name of the Cash account is:

  88-654307-c-investment income < Cash receipts from investments < Investing activities

- On December 31, the Business Bank2 pays -$3,280 cash to the bond holders for the Bond interest expenses of the Bond21 (one-level subaccount "Bond21-interest expenses"). Here, there is some twin transactions for the individuals whose primary accounts (seeing the Figure 2.1-3 on the page 12) are opened in the Business Bank2, and other individuals are recorded in the Business Bank1. Therefore, the multi-subaccount names of the Cash account and the transaction sub-equations respectively are:

  88-654302-t-bond interest< Cash payments to bond holders< Operating activities
  (88-654303, 88-654304, 88-654306, 88-654308, 88-654310, 909876507, 909876509, 909876513, 909876514, 909876518, 909876520)

  Cash (1): -369 + Cash (1): -328 + Cash (1): -246 + Cash (1): -369 + Cash (1): -492 + Cash (1): -287 + Cash (1): -164 + Cash (1): -246 = Bond interest expenses (5): -2501

  Cash (1): -123 + Cash (1): -205 + Cash (1): -123 + Cash (1): -328 = Bond interest expenses (5): -779

  The twin transaction sub-equation for the A20 (SIN: 909876520) must be entered.

- On the same day, the Business Bank2 pays -$2,640 cash to the bond holders for the Bond interest expenses of the Bond22 (one-level subaccount "Bond22-interest expenses"). Here, there is some twin transactions for the individuals whose primary accounts (seeing the Figure 2.1-3 on the page 12) are opened in the Business Bank2, and other individuals are recorded in the Business Bank1. Therefore, the multi-subaccount names of the Cash account and the transaction sub-equations respectively are:

  88-654304-t-bond interest< Cash payments to bond holders< Operating activities
  (88-654307, 88-654309, 88-654310, 909876503, 909876504, 909876506,
  909876511, 909876519, 909876520)

  Cash (1): -220 + Cash (1): -264 + Cash (1): -352 + Cash (1): -176 + Cash (1): -264 + Cash (1): -308 + Cash (1): -264 + Cash (1): -352 + Cash (1): -132 + Cash (1): -308 = Bond interest expenses (5): -2640

  The twin transaction sub-equation for 909876511, 909876519, and 909876520 must be entered.

- On the same day, the Business Bank2 pays -$1,050 cash to the bond holders for the Bond interest expenses of the Bond23 (one-level subaccount "Bond23-interest expenses"). The multi-subaccount names of the Cash account and the transaction sub-equations respectively are:

  88-654300-t-bond interest < Cash payments to bond holders< Operating activities
  (88-654301, 88-654302, 88-654303)

  Cash (1): -656.25 + Cash (1): -131.25 + Cash (1): -131.25 + Cash (1): -131.25 = Bond interest expenses (5): -1050

- On the same day, the Business Bank2 pays cash -$1,560 to its customers (not including itself) for primary deposit interest (interest expenses). Here, the Deposit interest expenses are recorded as the one-level subaccount of the Cost of notes interest account for the Business Banks. In addition, there is some twin transactions for its individuals whose primary accounts (seeing the Figure 2.1-3 on the page 13) are opened in the Business Bank2, and other individuals are recorded in the Business Bank1. The twin transactions for its organization customers have been recorded by these organizations. The multi-subaccount names of the Cash account are:

88-654301-t-deposit interest expenses < Cash payments for operating expenses < Operating activities: -120

(88-654307, 88-654308, 88-654310, 909876510, 909876511, 909876512, 909876517, 909876519, 909876520, 909876521, 909876522, 909876523)

The twin transaction sub-equations for the above individuals (A10, A11, A12, A17, A19, A20, A21, A22, and A23) must be entered.

- On December 31, 2016, the Business Bank2 pays three employees' salary expenses for cash -$8,640 repeatedly.

- On the same day, the Business Bank2 records the Office supplies expenses -$215.77. It is consisted of two parts of the Supplies -$61.77 and the Inventory -$154 (-$14*3 - $16*7). The multi-subaccount names of the Inventory account and transaction sub-equation and the transaction sub-equation respectively are:

Supplies1-P2-20150920-SUP1-200T: -14*3
Supplies2-P2-20150920-SUP2-200T: -16*7

Supplies (1): -61.77 + Inventory (1): -14*3 + Inventory (1): -16*7 = Office supplies expenses (5): -215.77

- On the same day, the Business Bank2 records the Consumables expenses -$2,200. The multi-subaccount names of the Inventory account and transaction sub-equation respectively are:

Inven111-C3-20150922-In111-1000T < Inven11 < Inven1: -10*10
Inven112-C3-20150922-In112-800T < Inven11 < Inven1: -40*10
Inven221-C3-20150922-In221-750T < Inven22 < Inven2: -30*20
Inven222-C3-20150922-In222-400T < Inven22 < Inven2: -50*20

PPGH parts-C3-20150922-PG-1600T < ASD parts < Inven2: -2*50

Inventory (1): -10*10 + Inventory (1): -40*10 + Inventory (1): -30*20 + Inventory (1): -50*20 + Inventory (1): -2*50 = Consumables expenses (5): -2200

- On the same day, the Business Bank2 records the Vehicle's amortization expenses - $22,100 (5 years, straight line) which includes a Truck2 ($8,000, one year), a Car3($7,600, one year), and a new Car2 ($6,500, ten months).
- On the same day, the Business Bank2 records the Computer's amortization expenses $245.84 three months (2 years, straight line) which includes a new computer server1 ($350), a new computer1 ($200), and a new computer2 ($62.5).
- On December 31, the Business Bank2 records the Tax expenses $0 and the Tax payable $0. The two multi-subaccount names all are the 'n'.

So far, I have entered all transactions of the Business Bank2 to database dcj207 in the fiscal year 2016.

## 3.5.2 Brief Summary of the Business Bank2

The Figure 3.5-2 shows all inventory transactions of the Business Bank2 in the fiscal year 2016 by using of SQL Server query.

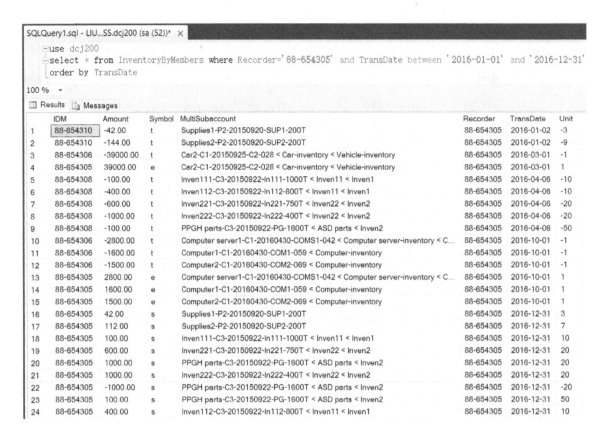

```
SQLQuery1.sql - LIU...SS.dcj200 (sa (52))* ×
use dcj200
select * from InventoryByMembers where Recorder='88-654305' and TransDate between '2016-01-01' and '2016-12-31'
order by TransDate
```

100 %  ▼

Results    Messages

| | IDM | Amount | Symbol | MultiSubaccount | Recorder | TransDate | Unit |
|---|---|---|---|---|---|---|---|
| 1 | 88-654310 | -42.00 | t | Supplies1-P2-20150920-SUP1-200T | 88-654305 | 2016-01-02 | -3 |
| 2 | 88-654310 | -144.00 | t | Supplies2-P2-20150920-SUP2-200T | 88-654305 | 2016-01-02 | -9 |
| 3 | 88-654306 | -39000.00 | t | Car2-C1-20150925-C2-028 < Car-inventory < Vehicle-inventory | 88-654305 | 2016-03-01 | -1 |
| 4 | 88-654305 | 39000.00 | e | Car2-C1-20150925-C2-028 < Car-inventory < Vehicle-inventory | 88-654305 | 2016-03-01 | 1 |
| 5 | 88-654308 | -100.00 | t | Inven111-C3-20150922-In111-1000T < Inven11 < Inven1 | 88-654305 | 2016-04-06 | -10 |
| 6 | 88-654308 | -400.00 | t | Inven112-C3-20150922-In112-800T < Inven11 < Inven1 | 88-654305 | 2016-04-06 | -10 |
| 7 | 88-654308 | -600.00 | t | Inven221-C3-20150922-In221-750T < Inven22 < Inven2 | 88-654305 | 2016-04-06 | -20 |
| 8 | 88-654308 | -1000.00 | t | Inven222-C3-20150922-In222-400T < Inven22 < Inven2 | 88-654305 | 2016-04-06 | -20 |
| 9 | 88-654308 | -100.00 | t | PPGH parts-C3-20150922-PG-1600T < ASD parts < Inven2 | 88-654305 | 2016-04-06 | -50 |
| 10 | 88-654306 | -2800.00 | t | Computer server1-C1-20160430-COMS1-042 < Computer server-inventory < C... | 88-654305 | 2016-10-01 | -1 |
| 11 | 88-654306 | -1600.00 | t | Computer1-C1-20160430-COM1-059 < Computer-inventory | 88-654305 | 2016-10-01 | -1 |
| 12 | 88-654306 | -1500.00 | t | Computer2-C1-20160430-COM2-069 < Computer-inventory | 88-654305 | 2016-10-01 | -1 |
| 13 | 88-654305 | 2800.00 | e | Computer server1-C1-20160430-COMS1-042 < Computer server-inventory < C... | 88-654305 | 2016-10-01 | 1 |
| 14 | 88-654305 | 1600.00 | e | Computer1-C1-20160430-COM1-059 < Computer-inventory | 88-654305 | 2016-10-01 | 1 |
| 15 | 88-654305 | 1500.00 | e | Computer2-C1-20160430-COM2-069 < Computer-inventory | 88-654305 | 2016-10-01 | 1 |
| 16 | 88-654305 | 42.00 | s | Supplies1-P2-20150920-SUP1-200T | 88-654305 | 2016-12-31 | 3 |
| 17 | 88-654305 | 112.00 | s | Supplies2-P2-20150920-SUP2-200T | 88-654305 | 2016-12-31 | 7 |
| 18 | 88-654305 | 100.00 | s | Inven111-C3-20150922-In111-1000T < Inven11 < Inven1 | 88-654305 | 2016-12-31 | 10 |
| 19 | 88-654305 | 600.00 | s | Inven221-C3-20150922-In221-750T < Inven22 < Inven2 | 88-654305 | 2016-12-31 | 20 |
| 20 | 88-654305 | 1000.00 | s | PPGH parts-C3-20150922-PG-1600T < ASD parts < Inven2 | 88-654305 | 2016-12-31 | 20 |
| 21 | 88-654305 | 1000.00 | s | Inven222-C3-20150922-In222-400T < Inven22 < Inven2 | 88-654305 | 2016-12-31 | 20 |
| 22 | 88-654305 | -1000.00 | s | PPGH parts-C3-20150922-PG-1600T < ASD parts < Inven2 | 88-654305 | 2016-12-31 | -20 |
| 23 | 88-654305 | 100.00 | s | PPGH parts-C3-20150922-PG-1600T < ASD parts < Inven2 | 88-654305 | 2016-12-31 | 50 |
| 24 | 88-654305 | 400.00 | s | Inven112-C3-20150922-In112-800T < Inven11 < Inven1 | 88-654305 | 2016-12-31 | 10 |

Figure 3.5-2  Business Bank2 Inventory Purchased or Sold by Other Members

## 3.6 Company1

### 3.6.1 An Accounting Fiscal Year of the Company1

In the new fiscal year, the Company1 occurs the following transactions.

- On January 2, 2016, the Company1 purchases the inventories $1,200 ($14*40 + $16*40) from the Proprietorship2 (phone number: 123456080) for cash -$200 and other on credit. The multi-subaccount name of the Cash account and transaction sub-equation respectively are:

    88-654310-t-supplies<Cash payments for operating expenses<Operating activities

    Cash (1): -200 + Inventory (1): 14*40 + Inventory (1): 16*40 = Account payable (2): 1000

- On January 2, 2016, the Company1 transfers the supplies $30 and the inventories $1,170 ($14*39 + $16*39) to the Cost of goods manufactured to satisfy the need of producing. The transaction sub-equation is:

  Supplies (1): -30 + Inventories (1): -14*39 + Inventories (1): -16*39 = Cost of goods manufactured (5): -1200

- On January 2, 2016, the Company1 transfers the following inventories $5,652 to the Cost of goods manufactured account to satisfy the need of producing.

  Inven111 < Inven11 < Inven1: -10*15

  Inven112 < Inven11 < Inven1: -40*20

  Inven121 < Inven12 < Inven1: -0.8*60

  Inven122 < Inven12 < Inven1: -50*6

  Inven21 < Inven2: -30*20

  Inven221 < Inven22 < Inven2: -30*10

  Inven222 < Inven22 < Inven2: -50*10

  PPUK parts < ASD parts < Inven2: -40*10

  PPGH parts < ASD parts < Inven2: -2*100

  Inven31 < Inven3: -10*10

  Inven32 < Inven3: -50*6

  Inven331 < Inven33 < Inven3: -20*10

  Inven332 < Inven33 < Inven3: -45*10

  HGFCVB parts < QASXC parts < Inven3: -10*2

  PPGHUP parts < ASDUP parts < Inven3: -20*10

  Inven411 < Inven41 < Inven4: -5*22

  Inven412 < Inven41 < Inven4: -18.5*4

  TTTCU parts < TTT parts < Inven4: -20*25

  RRRHJK parts < Inven4: -20*20

  The three transaction sub-equations are respectively:

Inventory (1): -10*15 + Inventory (1): -40*20 + Inventory (1): -0.8*60 + Inventory (1): -50*6 + Inventory (1): -30*20 + Inventory (1): -30*10 + Inventory (1): -50*10 + Inventory (1): -40*10 + Inventory (1): -2*100 = Cost of goods manufactured (5): -3298

Inventory (1): -10*10 + Inventory (1): -50*6 + Inventory (1): -20*10 + Inventory (1): -45*10 + Inventory (1): -10*2 + Inventory (1): -20*10 + Inventory (1): -5*22 + Inventory (1): -18.5*4 = Cost of goods manufactured (5): -1454

Inventory (1): -20*25 + Inventory (1): -20*20 = Cost of goods manufactured (5): -900

- On January 13, 2016, the Company1 sells one Computer server1- Service package6 to the Tax Bureau (phone number: 123456787) for cash $60. The multi-subaccount name of the Cash account is:

  88-654303-c-customers < Cash receipts from customers < Operating activities

- On January 14, 2016, the Company1 pays -$11,000 cash to the Company2 (phone number: 123456083) with the General ID 3. The multi-subaccount name of the Cash account is:

  88-654307-t-suppliers < Cash payments to suppliers < Operating activities

- On January 14, 2016, the Company1 pays -$8,000 cash to the Company3 (phone number: 123456082) with the General ID 3. The multi-subaccount name of the Cash account is:

  88-654308-t-suppliers < Cash payments to suppliers < Operating activities

- On January 15, 2016, the Company1 pays -$415.67 cash to A13 (SIN: 909876513) for the Travelling expenses -$207.67 and the Other expenses -$208. The multi-subaccount name of the Cash account is:

  909876513-n-operating expenses < Cash payments for operating expenses < Operating activities

- On January 16, 2016, the Company1 pays -$42.12 cash to A15 (SIN: 909876515) for the Travelling expenses -$22.12 and the Other expenses -$20.

- On January 31, 2016, the Company1 pays -$2,040 cash to the Proprietorship1 (phone number: 123456081) with the General ID 3. The multi-subaccount name of the Cash account is:

  88-654309-t-suppliers < Cash payments to suppliers < Operating activities

- On January 31, 2016, the Company1 pays -$1,000 cash to the Proprietorship2 (phone number: 123456080) with the General ID 3. The multi-subaccount name of the Cash account is:

  88-654310-t-suppliers < Cash payments to suppliers < Operating activities

- On January 31, 2016, the Company1 pays three employees' salary expenses for cash -$8,400. The multi-subaccount names of the Cash and the Cost of goods manufactured accounts and the transaction sub-equation respectively are:

  909876514-t-salary < Cash payments for operating expenses < Operating activities

  909876513-t-CGM < Cash payments for operating expenses < Operating activities

  909876515-t-CGM < Cash payments for operating expenses < Operating activities

  909876514-salary < Office department-salary

  909876513-CGM < Sales department-salary < Salary expenses-CGM

  909876515-CGM < Product department-salary < Salary expenses-CGM

  Cash (1): -2900 + Cash (1): -2600 + Cash (1): -2900 = Salary expenses (5): -2900 + Cost of goods manufactured (5): -2600 + Cost of goods manufactured (5): -2900

- On February 1, 2016, the Company1 sells one Car2 $39,000 (cost: $27,000) to the Business Bank1 (phone number: 123456786) for cash $19,000 and other on credit. The multi-subaccount names of the Cash account and the Inventory account and transaction sub-equation respectively are:

  88-654304-c-customers < Cash receipts from customers < Operating activities

  Car2-C1-20150925-C2-027 < Car-inventory < Vehicle-inventory: -27000*1

  Cash (1): 19000 + Account receivable (1): 20000 + Inventory (1): -27000*1 = Sales

(4): 39000 + Cost of goods sold (5): -27000

- On February 1, 2016, the Company1 sells one Car3 $38,000 (cost: $26,000) to the Proprietorship1 (phone number: 123456781) for cash $28,000 and other on credit. The multi-subaccount names of the Cash account and the Inventory account are:

    88-654309-c-customers < Cash receipts from customers < Operating activities

    Car3-C1-20150925-C3-028 < Car-inventory < Vehicle-inventory: -26000*1

- On February 1, 2016, the Company1 sells one Car3 $38,000 (cost: $26,000) to the Proprietorship2 (phone number: 123456780) for cash $30,000 and other on credit. The multi-subaccount names of the Cash account and the Inventory account are:

    88-654310-c-customers < Cash receipts from customers < Operating activities

    Car3-C1-20150925-C3-029 < Car-inventory < Vehicle-inventory: -26000*1

- On February 1, 2016, the Company1 pays -$49.68 cash to A14 (SIN: 909876514) for the Travelling expenses -$25.68 and the Other expenses -$24.

- On February 2, 2016, the Company1 receives $500 cash from the Tax Bureau (phone number: 123456787) with the General ID 3. The multi-subaccount name of the Cash account is:

    88-654303-c-customers < Cash receipts from customers < Operating activities

- On February 13, 2016, the Company1 receives $800 cash from the Central Bank (phone number: 123456789) with the General ID 3. The multi-subaccount name of the Cash account is:

    88-654301-c-customers < Cash receipts from customers < Operating activities

- On February 20, 2016, the Company1 pays -$557.83 cash to A13 (SIN: 909876513) for the Travelling expenses -$247.83 and the Other expenses -$310.

- On February 25, 2016, the Company1 receives $600 cash from the Company2 (phone number: 123456783) with the General ID 3. The multi-subaccount name of the Cash account is:

    88-654307-c-customers < Cash receipts from customers < Operating activities

- On February 27, 2016, the Company1 receives $900 cash from the Company3 (phone

number: 123456782) with the General ID 3. The multi-subaccount name of the Cash account is:

88-654308-c-customers < Cash receipts from customers < Operating activities

- On February 28, 2016, the Company1 pays three employees' salary for cash $8,400.

- On March 1, 2016, the Company1 sells one Car2 $39,000 to the Business Bank2 (phone number: 123456785) for cash $19000 and other on credit. The multi-subaccount names of the Cash account and the Inventory account respectively are:

88-654305-c-customers < Cash receipts from customers < Operating activities

Car2-C1-20150925-C2-028 < Car-inventory < Vehicle-inventory: -27000*1

- On March 4, 2016, the Company1 pays -$2,400 cash to the Company2 (phone number: 123456083) with the General ID 3. The multi-subaccount name of the Cash account is:

88-654307-t-suppliers < Cash payments to suppliers < Operating activities

- On March 4, 2016, the Company1 pays -$1,600 cash to the Company3 (phone number: 123456082) with the General ID 3. The multi-subaccount name of the Cash account is:

88-654308-t-suppliers < Cash payments to suppliers < Operating activities

- On March 4, 2016, the Company1 transfers the following inventories $2,010 to the Cost of goods manufactured account to satisfy the producing need.

Inven111 < Inven11 < Inven1: -10*40

Inven112 < Inven11 < Inven1: -40*20

Inven121 < Inven12 < Inven1: -0.8*100

Inven122 < Inven12 < Inven1: -50*8

Inven21 < Inven2: -30*5

Inven332 < Inven33 < Inven3: -45*2

HGFCVB parts < QASXC parts < Inven3: -10*3

PPGHUP parts < ASDUP parts < Inven3: -20*2

Inven411 < Inven41 < Inven4: -5*4

The transaction sub-equations is:

Inventory (1): -10*40 + Inventory (1): -40*20 + Inventory (1): -0.8*100 + Inventory (1): -50*8 + Inventory (1): -30*5 + Inventory (1): -45*2 + Inventory (1): -10*3 + Inventory (1): -20*2 + Inventory (1): -5*4 = Cost of goods manufactured (5): -2010

- On March 6, 2016, the Company1 receives $1,000 cash from the Proprietorship1 (phone number: 123456781) with the General ID 3. The multi-subaccount name of the Cash account is:

  88-654309-c-customers < Cash receipts from customers < Operating activities

- On March 9, 2016, the Company1 receives $2,000 cash from the Proprietorship2 (phone number: 123456780) with the General ID 3. The multi-subaccount name of the Cash account is:

  88-654310-c-customers < Cash receipts from customers < Operating activities

- On March 23, 2016, the Company1 pays -$516.37 cash to A13 (SIN: 909876513) for the Travelling expenses -$226.37 and the Other expenses -$290.

- On March 25, 2016, the Company1 receives $600 cash from the Central Bank (phone number: 123456789) with the General ID 3. The multi-subaccount name of the Cash account is:

  88-654301-c-customers < Cash receipts from customers < Operating activities

- On March 30, 2016, the Company1 pays -$239.73 cash to A14 (SIN: 909876514) for the Travelling expenses -$155.73 and the Other expenses -$84.

- On March 31, 2016, the Company1 pays three employees' salary expenses for cash -$8,400 repeatedly.

- On April 28, 2016, the Company1 pays -$717.38 cash to A13 (SIN: 909876513) for the Travelling expenses -$247.38 and the Other expenses -$470.

- On April 29, 2016, the Company1 pays -$1,000 cash to the Proprietorship2 (phone number: 123456080) with the General ID 21. The multi-subaccount name of the Cash account is:

  88-654310-t-suppliers < Cash payments to suppliers < Operating activities

- On April 30, 2016, the Company1 purchases the inventories $3,300 ($14*110 + $16*110) from the Proprietorship2 (phone number: 123456080) for cash -$1300 and other on credit. The multi-subaccount names of the Cash and the Inventory accounts respectively are:

  88-654310-t-supplies<Cash payments for operating expenses<Operating activities
  Supplies1-P2-20160430-Supp1-200T: 14*110
  Supplies2-P2-20160430-Supp2-200T: 16*110

- On April 30, 2016, the Company1 sells one Computer server1- Serving package6 to the Government1 (phone number: 123456788) for cash $60. The multi-subaccount name of the Cash account is:

  88-654302-c-customers < Cash receipts from customers < Operating activities

- On April 30, 2016, the Company1 pays three employees' salary expenses for cash -$8,400 repeatedly.

- On April 30, 2016, the Company1 has completed all products in the Working-in-process inventory account. If all general parts have just been consumed and the supplies has rest $148.65, the rest supplies must be returned to the Supplies account from the Cost of goods manufactured account. The transaction sub-equation is:

  Supplies (1): 4.65 + Inventory (1): 14*8 + Inventory (1): 16*2 = Cost of goods manufactured (5): 148.65

- On April 30, 2016, the Company1 transfers the balance of the Cost of goods manufactured account to the Working-in-process inventory account. The Cost of goods manufactured account has four subaccounts of the "Supplies expenses", the "909876513-salary < Sales department-salary < Salary expenses", the "909876515-salary < Product department-salary < Salary expenses", and the "General parts expenses". Their balances are -$1,051.35, -$10,400, -$11,600, and -$7,662 respectively. The two transaction sub-equations respectively are:

  Working-in-process inventory (1): 4127.09*2 + Working-in-process inventory (1):

2136.26\*3 + Working-in-process inventory (1): 1012.67\*2 + Working-in-process inventory (1): 2450.19\*2 + Working-in-process inventory (1): 1587.83\*3 = Cost of goods manufactured (5): 1051.35 + Cost of goods manufactured (5): 10400 + Cost of goods manufactured (5): 11600 + Cost of goods manufactured (5): 3300.82

Working-in-process inventory (1): 43.55\*4 + Working-in-process inventory (1): 23.71\*4 + Working-in-process inventory (1): 54.88\*10 + Working-in-process inventory (1): 102.88\*10 + Working-in-process inventory (1): 97.72\*12 + Working-in-process inventory (1): 89.46\*15 = Cost of goods manufactured (5): 4361.18

- On April 30, 2016, the Company1 transfers the balance of the Working-in-process inventory account to the Inventory account. The multi-subaccount names of the Inventory account respectively are:

Truck1-C1-20160430-T1-012 < Truck-inventory < Vehicle-inventory: 33700\*1
Truck1-C1-20160430-T1-013 < Truck-inventory < Vehicle-inventory: 33700\*1
Truck2-C1-20160430-T2-012 < Truck-inventory < Vehicle-inventory: 30000\*1
Truck2-C1-20160430-T2-013 < Truck-inventory < Vehicle-inventory: 30000\*1
Truck2-C1-20160430-T2-014 < Truck-inventory < Vehicle-inventory: 30000\*1
Car1-C1-20160430-C1-030 < Car-inventory < Vehicle-inventory: 28000\*1
Car1-C1-20160430-C1-031 < Car-inventory < Vehicle-inventory: 28000\*1
Car2-C1-20160430-C2-040 < Car-inventory < Vehicle-inventory: 27000\*1
Car2-C1-20160430-C2-041 < Car-inventory < Vehicle-inventory: 27000\*1
Car3-C1-20160430-C3-050 < Car-inventory < Vehicle-inventory: 26000\*1
Car3-C1-20160430-C3-051 < Car-inventory < Vehicle-inventory: 26000\*1
Car3-C1-20160430-C3-052 < Car-inventory < Vehicle-inventory: 26000\*1
Computer server1-C1-20160430-COMS1-042 < Computer server-inventory < Computer-inventory: 1600\*1
Computer server1-C1-20160430-COMS1-043 < Computer server-inventory <

Computer-inventory: 1600*1

Computer server1-C1-20160430-COMS1-044 < Computer server-inventory <
Computer-inventory: 1600*1

Computer server1-C1-20160430-COMS1-045 < Computer server-inventory <
Computer-inventory: 1600*1

Computer server2-C1-20160430-COMS2-047 < Computer server-inventory <
Computer-inventory: 1500*1

Computer server2-C1-20160430-COMS2-048 < Computer server-inventory <
Computer-inventory: 1500*1

Computer server2-C1-20160430-COMS2-049 < Computer server-inventory <
Computer-inventory: 1500*1

Computer server2-C1-20160430-COMS2-050 < Computer server-inventory <
Computer-inventory: 1500*1

Computer1-C1-20160430-COM1-059 < Computer-inventory: 1000*1

Computer1-C1-20160430-COM1-060 < Computer-inventory: 1000*1

Computer1-C1-20160430-COM1-061 < Computer-inventory: 1000*1

Computer1-C1-20160430-COM1-062 < Computer-inventory: 1000*1

Computer1-C1-20160430-COM1-063 < Computer-inventory: 1000*1

Computer1-C1-20160430-COM1-064 < Computer-inventory: 1000*1

Computer1-C1-20160430-COM1-065 < Computer-inventory: 1000*1

Computer1-C1-20160430-COM1-066 < Computer-inventory: 1000*1

Computer1-C1-20160430-COM1-067 < Computer-inventory: 1000*1

Computer1-C1-20160430-COM1-068 < Computer-inventory: 1000*1

Computer2-C1-20160430-COM2-069 < Computer-inventory: 920*1

Computer2-C1-20160430-COM2-070 < Computer-inventory: 920*1

Computer2-C1-20160430-COM2-071 < Computer-inventory: 920*1

Computer2-C1-20160430-COM2-072 < Computer-inventory: 920*1

Computer2-C1-20160430-COM2-073 < Computer-inventory: 920*1

Computer2-C1-20160430-COM2-074 < Computer-inventory: 920*1

Computer2-C1-20160430-COM2-075 < Computer-inventory: 920*1

Computer2-C1-20160430-COM2-076 < Computer-inventory: 920*1

Computer2-C1-20160430-COM2-077 < Computer-inventory: 920*1

Computer2-C1-20160430-COM2-078 < Computer-inventory: 920*1

Computer3-C1-20160430-COM3-103 < Computer-inventory: 830*1

Computer3-C1-20160430-COM3-104 < Computer-inventory: 830*1

Computer3-C1-20160430-COM3-105 < Computer-inventory: 830*1

Computer3-C1-20160430-COM3-106 < Computer-inventory: 830*1

Computer3-C1-20160430-COM3-107 < Computer-inventory: 830*1

Computer3-C1-20160430-COM3-108 < Computer-inventory: 830*1

Computer3-C1-20160430-COM3-109 < Computer-inventory: 830*1

Computer3-C1-20160430-COM3-110 < Computer-inventory: 830*1

Computer3-C1-20160430-COM3-111 < Computer-inventory: 830*1

Computer3-C1-20160430-COM3-112 < Computer-inventory: 830*1

Computer3-C1-20160430-COM3-113 < Computer-inventory: 830*1

Computer3-C1-20160430-COM3-114 < Computer-inventory: 830*1

Computer4-C1-20160430-COM4-103 < Computer-inventory: 770*1

Computer4-C1-20160430-COM4-104 < Computer-inventory: 770*1

Computer4-C1-20160430-COM4-105 < Computer-inventory: 770*1

Computer4-C1-20160430-COM4-106 < Computer-inventory: 770*1

Computer4-C1-20160430-COM4-107 < Computer-inventory: 770*1

Computer4-C1-20160430-COM4-108 < Computer-inventory: 770*1

Computer4-C1-20160430-COM4-109 < Computer-inventory: 770*1

Computer4-C1-20160430-COM4-110 < Computer-inventory: 770*1

Computer4-C1-20160430-COM4-111 < Computer-inventory: 770*1

Computer4-C1-20160430-COM4-112 < Computer-inventory: 770*1

Computer4-C1-20160430-COM4-113 < Computer-inventory: 770*1

Computer4-C1-20160430-COM4-114 < Computer-inventory: 770*1

Computer4-C1-20160430-COM4-115 < Computer-inventory: 770*1

Computer4-C1-20160430-COM4-116 < Computer-inventory: 770*1

Computer4-C1-20160430-COM4-117 < Computer-inventory: 770*1

The transaction sub-equations respectively are:

Working-in-process inventory (1): -33700*2 + Working-in-process inventory (1): -30000*3 + Working-in-process inventory (1): -28000*2 + Inventory (1): 33700*1 + Inventory (1): 33700*1 + Inventory (1): 30000*1 + Inventory (1): 30000*1 + Inventory (1): 30000*1 + Inventory (1): 28000*1 + Inventory (1): 28000*1 = 0

Working-in-process inventory (1): -27000*2 + Working-in-process inventory (1): -26000*3 + Inventory (1): 27000*1 + Inventory (1): 27000*1 + Inventory (1): 26000*2 + Inventory (1): 26000*1 + Inventory (1): 26000*1 = 0

Working-in-process inventory (1): -1600*4 + Working-in-process inventory (1): -1500*4 + Inventory (1): 1600*1 + Inventory (1): 1600*1+ Inventory (1): 1600*1+ Inventory (1): 1600*1 + Inventory (1): 1500*1 + Inventory (1): 1500*1 + Inventory (1): 1500*1 + Inventory (1): 1500*1 = 0

Working-in-process inventory (1): -1000*10 + Inventory (1): 1000*1 + Inventory (1): 1000*1 + Inventory (1): 1000*1 + Inventory (1): 1000*1 + Inventory (1): 1000*1 + Inventory (1): 1000*1 + Inventory (1): 1000*1 + Inventory (1): 1000*1 + Inventory (1): 1000*1 + Inventory (1): 1000*1 = 0

Working-in-process inventory (1): -920*10 + Inventory (1): 920*1 + Inventory (1): 920*1 + Inventory (1): 920*1 + Inventory (1): 920*1 + Inventory (1): 920*1 + Inventory (1): 920*1 + Inventory (1): 920*1 + Inventory (1): 920*1 + Inventory (1): 920*1 + Inventory (1): 920*1 = 0

Working-in-process inventory (1): -830*6 + Inventory (1): 830*1 + Inventory (1): 830*1 + Inventory (1): 830*1 + Inventory (1): 830*1 + Inventory (1): 830*1+ Inventory (1): 830*1 = 0

Working-in-process inventory (1): -830*6 + Inventory (1): 830*1 + Inventory (1): 830*1 + Inventory (1): 830*1 + Inventory (1): 830*1 + Inventory (1): 830*1+ Inventory (1): 830*1 = 0

Working-in-process inventory (1): -770*10 + Inventory (1): 770*1 + Inventory (1): 770*1 + Inventory (1): 770*1 + Inventory (1): 770*1 + Inventory (1): 770*1 + Inventory (1): 770*1 + Inventory (1): 770*1 + Inventory (1): 770*1 + Inventory (1): 770*1 + Inventory (1): 770*1 = 0

Working-in-process inventory (1): -770*5 + Inventory (1): 770*1 + Inventory (1): 770*1 + Inventory (1): 770*1 + Inventory (1): 770*1 + Inventory (1): 770*1= 0

- On May 1, 2016, the Company1 sells one Computer server1, one Computer1, and one Computer2 to the Central Bank (phone number: 123456789) for cash $1900 and other $4,000 on credit. The multi-subaccount names of the Cash account and the Inventory account and transaction sub-equation respectively are:

  88-654301-c-customers < Cash receipts from customers < Operating activities
  Computer server1-C1-201501007-COMS1-039 < Computer server-inventory < Computer-inventory: -1600*1
  Computer1-C1-201501008-COM1-055 < Computer-inventory: -1000*1
  Computer2-C1-201501008-COM2-065 < Computer-inventory: -920*1

  Cash (1): 1900 + Account receivable (1): 4000 + Inventory (1): -1600 + Inventory (1): -1000 + Inventory (1): -920 = Sales (4): 5900 + Cost of goods sold (5): -3520

- On May 1, 2016, the Company1 sells one Car1 $40,000 to the Government1 (phone number: 123456788) for cash $8,000 and other $32,000 on credit. The multi-subaccount names of the Cash account and the Inventory account respectively are:

  88-654302-c-customers < Cash receipts from customers < Operating activities

Car1-C1-20150921-C1-023 < Car-inventory < Vehicle-inventory: -28000*1

- On May 1, 2016, the Company1 plans to produce the following products in the following Figure 3.6-1.

| Order | Product (the Lowest-level Subaccount) Names | Multi-subaccount Names | Costs | Amount |
|---|---|---|---|---|
| 1 | Truck1 | Truck1 < Truck < Vehicle | 33700.00 | 1 |
| 2 | Truck2 | Truck2 < Truck < Vehicle | 30000.00 | 1 |
| 3 | Car1 | Car1 < Car < Vehicle | 28000.00 | 4 |
| 4 | Car2 | Car2 < Car < Vehicle | 27000.00 | 4 |
| 5 | Car3 | Car3 < Car < Vehicle | 26000.00 | 4 |
| 6 | Computer server1 | Computer server1 < Computer server < Computer | 1600.00 | 5 |
| 7 | Computer server2 | Computer server2 < Computer server < Computer | 1500.00 | 5 |
| 8 | Computer1 | Computer1 < Computer | 1000.00 | 15 |
| 9 | Computer2 | Computer2 < Computer | 920.00 | 15 |
| 10 | Computer3 | Computer3 < Computer | 830.00 | 15 |
| 11 | Computer4 | Computer4 < Computer | 770.00 | 15 |

Figure 3.6-1    Company1 Producing Plan Table

Therefore, the Company1 purchases following inventories $216,420 from the Company2 (phone number: 123456083) for -$15,000 cash and other on credit.

Car1 part1-C2-20150816-C1P1-061 < Car1 parts < Vehicle parts: 8300*1

Car1 part1-C2-20150816-C1P1-062 < Car1 parts < Vehicle parts: 8300*1

Car1 part1-C2-20150816-C1P1-063 < Car1 parts < Vehicle parts: 8300*1

Car1 part2-C2-20150816-C1P2-069 < Car1 parts < Vehicle parts: 7200*1

Car1 part2-C2-20150816-C1P2-070 < Car1 parts < Vehicle parts: 7200*1

Car1 part2-C2-20150816-C1P2-071 < Car1 parts < Vehicle parts: 7200*1

Car1 part3-C2-20150816-C1P3-070 < Car1 parts < Vehicle parts: 5100*1

Car1 part3-C2-20150816-C1P3-071 < Car1 parts < Vehicle parts: 5100*1

Car1 part3-C2-20150816-C1P3-072 < Car1 parts < Vehicle parts: 5100*1

Car2 part1-C2-20150902-C2P1-077 < Car2 parts < Vehicle parts: 7900*1

Car2 part1-C2-20150902-C2P1-078 < Car2 parts < Vehicle parts: 7900*1

Car2 part1-C2-20150902-C2P1-079 < Car2 parts < Vehicle parts: 7900*1

Car2 part2-C2-20150902-C2P2-081 < Car2 parts < Vehicle parts: 6800*1

Car2 part2-C2-20150902-C2P2-082 < Car2 parts < Vehicle parts: 6800*1

Car2 part2-C2-20150902-C2P2-083 < Car2 parts < Vehicle parts: 6800*1

Car2 part3-C2-20150902-C2P3-083 < Car2 parts < Vehicle parts: 4900*1

Car2 part3-C2-20150902-C2P3-084 < Car2 parts < Vehicle parts: 4900*1

Car2 part3-C2-20150902-C2P3-085 < Car2 parts < Vehicle parts: 4900*1

Car3 part1-C2-20150902-C3P1-084 < Car3 parts < Vehicle parts: 7500*1

Car3 part1-C2-20150902-C3P1-085 < Car3 parts < Vehicle parts: 7500*1

Car3 part1-C2-20150902-C3P1-086 < Car3 parts < Vehicle parts: 7500*1

Car3 part2-C2-20150902-C3P2-087 < Car3 parts < Vehicle parts: 6400*1

Car3 part2-C2-20150902-C3P2-088 < Car3 parts < Vehicle parts: 6400*1

Car3 part2-C2-20150902-C3P2-089 < Car3 parts < Vehicle parts: 6400*1

Car3 part3-C2-20150902-C3P3-094 < Car3 parts < Vehicle parts: 4700*1

Car3 part3-C2-20150902-C3P3-095 < Car3 parts < Vehicle parts: 4700*1

Car3 part3-C2-20150902-C3P3-096 < Car3 parts < Vehicle parts: 4700*1

Computer server1 part1-C2-20150709-COMS1P1-10T < Computer server parts < Computer parts: 600*4

Computer server1 part2-C2-20150709-COMS1P2-10T < Computer server parts < Computer parts: 400*4

Computer server2 part1-C2-20150709-COMS2P1-10T < Computer server parts < Computer parts: 540*4

Computer server2 part2-C2-20150709-COMS2P2-10T < Computer server parts < Computer parts: 380*4

Computer1 part1-C2-20150715-COM1P1-20T < Computer parts: 360*14

Computer1 part2-C2-20150715-COM1P2-20T < Computer parts: 310*14

Computer2 part1-C2-20150715-COM2P1-20T < Computer parts: 320*14

Computer2 part2-C2-20150715-COM2P2-20T < Computer parts: 290*14

Computer3 part1-C2-20150715-COM3P1-20T < Computer parts: 280*14

Computer3 part2-C2-20150715-COM3P2-20T < Computer parts: 260*14

Computer4 part1-C2-20150715-COM4P1-20T < Computer parts: 250*14

Computer4 part2-C2-20150715-COM4P2-20T < Computer parts: 240*14

The multi-subaccount name of the Cash account and the transaction sub-equations respectively are:

88-654307-t-suppliers < Cash payments to suppliers < Operating activities

Cash (1): -15000 + Inventory (1): 8300*1 + Inventory (1): 8300*1 + Inventory (1): 8300*1 + Inventory (1): 7200*1 + Inventory (1): 7200*1+ Inventory (1): 7200*1 + Inventory (1): 5100*1 + Inventory (1): 5100*1 + Inventory (1): 5100*1 = Account payable (2): 46800

Inventory (1): 7900*1 + Inventory (1): 7900*1 + Inventory (1): 7900*1 + Inventory (1): 6800*1 + Inventory (1): 6800*1 + Inventory (1): 6800*1 + Inventory (1): 4900*1 + Inventory (1): 4900*1 + Inventory (1): 4900*1 = Account payable (2): 58800

Inventory (1): 7500*1 + Inventory (1): 7500*1 + Inventory (1): 7500*1 + Inventory (1): 6400*1 + Inventory (1): 6400*1 + Inventory (1): 6400*1 + Inventory (1): 4700*1 + Inventory (1): 4700*1 + Inventory (1): 4700*1 = Account payable (2): 55800

Inventory (1): 600*4 + Inventory (1): 400*4 + Inventory (1): 540*4 + Inventory (1): 380*4 + Inventory (1): 360*14+ Inventory (1): 310*14 + Inventory (1): 320*14 + Inventory (1): 290*14 = Account payable (2): 25600

Inventory (1): 280*14 + Inventory (1): 260*14 + Inventory (1): 250*14 + Inventory (1): 240*14 = Account payable (2): 14420

- On May 1, 2016, the Company1 purchases following inventories $50,800 from the Company3 (phone number: 123456082) on credit.
Inven111-C3-20150922-In111-1000T < Inven11 < Inven1: 10*300

Inven112-C3-20150922-In112-800T < Inven11 < Inven1: 40*200

Inven121-C3-20150922-In121-20000T < Inven12 < Inven1: 0.8*6000

Inven122-C3-20150922-In122-1000T < Inven12 < Inven1: 50*200

Inven21-C3-20150922-In21-1250T < Inven2: 30*300

Inven221-C3-20150922-In221-750T < Inven22 < Inven2: 30*200

Inven222-C3-20150922-In222-400T < Inven22 < Inven2: 50*100

PPUK parts-C3-20150922-PU-500T < ASD parts < Inven2: 40*100

PPGH parts-C3-20150922-PG-1600T < ASD parts < Inven2: 2*500

The transaction sub-equation respectively is:

Inventory (1): 10*300 + Inventory (1): 40*200 + Inventory (1): 0.8*6000 + Inventory (1): 50*200 + Inventory (1): 30*300 + Inventory (1): 30*200 + Inventory (1): 50*100 + Inventory (1): 40*100 + Inventory (1): 2*500 = Account payable (2): 50800

- On May 1, 2016, the Company1 purchases following inventories $23,250 from the Proprietorship1 (phone number: 123456081) for -$3,250 cash and other on credit.

  Inven31-P1-20151125-In31-1000T < Inven3: 10*150

  Inven32-P1-20151125-In32-1000T < Inven3: 50*150

  Inven331-P1-20151125-In331-1000T < Inven33 < Inven3: 20*150

  Inven332-P1-20151125-In332-1000T < Inven33 < Inven3: 45*150

  HGFCVB parts-P1-20151125-HGP-1000T < QASXC parts < Inven3: 10*150

  PPGHUP parts-P1-20151125-PPP-1000T < ASDUP parts < Inven3: 20*150

  The multi-subaccount name of the Cash account and the transaction sub-equation respectively are:

  88-654309-t-suppliers < Cash payments to suppliers < Operating activities

  Cash (1): -3250 + Inventory (1): 10*150 + Inventory (1): 50*150 + Inventory (1): 20*150 + Inventory (1): 45*150 + Inventory (1): 10*150 + Inventory (1): 20*150 = Account payable (2): 20000

- On May 1, 2016, the Company1 purchases following inventories $6,350 from the Proprietorship2 (phone number: 123456080) for -$2,300 cash and other on credit.

  Inven411-P2-20151127-In411-1000T < Inven41 < Inven4: 5*100

  Inven412-P2-20151127-In412-1000T < Inven41 < Inven4: 18.5*100

  TTTCU parts-P2-20151127-TTP-1000T < TTT parts < Inven4: 20*100

  RRRHJK parts-P2-20151127-RRP-1000T < Inven4: 20*100

  The multi-subaccount name of the Cash account and the transaction sub-equation respectively are:

    88-654310-t-suppliers < Cash payments to suppliers < Operating activities

    Cash (1): -2300 + Inventory (1): 5*100 + Inventory (1): 18.5*100 + Inventory (1): 20*100 + Inventory (1): 20*100 = Account payable (2): 4050

- On May 2, 2016, the Company1 transfers the supplies $2,800 to the Cost of goods manufactured to satisfy the need of producing. The multi-subaccount names of the Inventory account and the transaction sub-equation respectively are:

  Supplies1-P2-20160430-Supp1-200T: -14*96

  Supplies2-P2-20160430-Supp2-200T: -16*91

    Inventory (1): -14*96 + Inventory (1): -16*91= Cost of goods manufactured (5): -2800

- On May 2, 2016, the Company1 transfers the following inventories $403,050 to the Cost of goods manufactured account (its subaccount: General parts expenses) to satisfy the producing need.

  Inven111-C3-20150922-In111-1000T < Inven11 < Inven1: -10*300

  Inven112-C3-20150922-In112-800T < Inven11 < Inven1: -40*200

  Inven121-C3-20150922-In121-20000T < Inven12 < Inven1: -0.8*6000

  Inven122-C3-20150922-In122-1000T < Inven12 < Inven1: -50*200

  Inven21-C3-20150922-In21-1250T < Inven2: -30*300

Inven221-C3-20150922-In221-750T < Inven22 < Inven2: -30*200

Inven222-C3-20150922-In222-400T < Inven22 < Inven2: -50*100

PPUK parts-C3-20150922-PU-500T < ASD parts < Inven2: -40*100

PPGH parts-C3-20150922-PG-1600T < ASD parts < Inven2: -2*500

Inven31-P1-20151125-In31-1000T < Inven3: -10*150

Inven32-P1-20151125-In32-1000T < Inven3: -50*150

Inven331-P1-20151125-In331-1000T < Inven33 < Inven3: -20*150

Inven332-P1-20151125-In332-1000T < Inven33 < Inven3: -45*150

HGFCVB parts-P1-20151125-HGP-1000T < QASXC parts < Inven3: -10*150

PPGHUP parts-P1-20151125-PPP-1000T < ASDUP parts < Inven3: -20*150

Inven411-P2-20151127-In411-1000T < Inven41 < Inven4: -5*100

Inven412-P2-20151127-In412-1000T < Inven41 < Inven4: -18.5*100

TTTCU parts-P2-20151127-TTP-1000T < TTT parts < Inven4: -20*100

RRRHJK parts-P2-20151127-RRP-1000T < Inven4: -20*100

Truck1 part1 < Truck1 parts < Vehicle parts: -8700*1

Truck1 part2 < Truck1 parts < Vehicle parts: -7600*1

Truck1 part3 < Truck1 parts < Vehicle parts: -5800*1

Truck2 part1 < Truck2 parts < Vehicle parts: -8500*1

Truck2 part2 < Truck2 parts < Vehicle parts: -7200*1

Truck2 part3 < Truck2 parts < Vehicle parts: -5400*1

Car1 part1 < Car1 parts < Vehicle parts: -8300*1

Car1 part1-C2-20150816-C1P1-061 < Car1 parts < Vehicle parts: -8300*1

Car1 part1-C2-20150816-C1P1-062 < Car1 parts < Vehicle parts: -8300*1

Car1 part1-C2-20150816-C1P1-063 < Car1 parts < Vehicle parts: -8300*1

Car1 part2 < Car1 parts < Vehicle parts: -7200*1

Car1 part2-C2-20150816-C1P2-069 < Car1 parts < Vehicle parts: -7200*1

Car1 part2-C2-20150816-C1P2-070 < Car1 parts < Vehicle parts: -7200*1

Car1 part2-C2-20150816-C1P2-071 < Car1 parts < Vehicle parts: -7200*1

Car1 part3 < Car1 parts < Vehicle parts: -5100*1

Car1 part3-C2-20150816-C1P3-070 < Car1 parts < Vehicle parts: -5100*1

Car1 part3-C2-20150816-C1P3-071 < Car1 parts < Vehicle parts: -5100*1

Car1 part3-C2-20150816-C1P3-072 < Car1 parts < Vehicle parts: -5100*1

Car2 part1 < Car2 parts < Vehicle parts: -7900*1

Car2 part1-C2-20150902-C2P1-077 < Car2 parts < Vehicle parts: -7900*1

Car2 part1-C2-20150902-C2P1-078 < Car2 parts < Vehicle parts: -7900*1

Car2 part1-C2-20150902-C2P1-079 < Car2 parts < Vehicle parts: -7900*1

Car2 part2 < Car2 parts < Vehicle parts: -6800*1

Car2 part2-C2-20150902-C2P2-081 < Car2 parts < Vehicle parts: -6800*1

Car2 part2-C2-20150902-C2P2-082 < Car2 parts < Vehicle parts: -6800*1

Car2 part2-C2-20150902-C2P2-083 < Car2 parts < Vehicle parts: -6800*1

Car2 part3 < Car2 parts < Vehicle parts: -4900*1

Car2 part3-C2-20150902-C2P3-083 < Car2 parts < Vehicle parts: -4900*1

Car2 part3-C2-20150902-C2P3-084 < Car2 parts < Vehicle parts: -4900*1

Car2 part3-C2-20150902-C2P3-085 < Car2 parts < Vehicle parts: -4900*1

Car3 part1 < Car3 parts < Vehicle parts: -7500*1

Car3 part1-C2-20150902-C3P1-084 < Car3 parts < Vehicle parts: -7500*1

Car3 part1-C2-20150902-C3P1-085 < Car3 parts < Vehicle parts: -7500*1

Car3 part1-C2-20150902-C3P1-086 < Car3 parts < Vehicle parts: -7500*1

Car3 part2 < Car3 parts < Vehicle parts: -6400*1

Car3 part2-C2-20150902-C3P2-087 < Car3 parts < Vehicle parts: -6400*1

Car3 part2-C2-20150902-C3P2-088 < Car3 parts < Vehicle parts: -6400*1

Car3 part2-C2-20150902-C3P2-089 < Car3 parts < Vehicle parts: -6400*1

Car3 part3 < Car3 parts < Vehicle parts: -4700*1

Car3 part3-C2-20150902-C3P3-094 < Car3 parts < Vehicle parts: -4700*1

Car3 part3-C2-20150902-C3P3-095 < Car3 parts < Vehicle parts: -4700*1

Car3 part3-C2-20150902-C3P3-096 < Car3 parts < Vehicle parts: -4700*1

Computer server1 part1 < Computer server parts < Computer parts: -600*1

Computer server1 part1-C2-20150709-COMS1P1-10T < Computer server parts <

Computer parts: -600*4

Computer server1 part2 < Computer server parts < Computer parts: -400*1

Computer server1 part2-C2-20150709-COMS1P2-10T < Computer server parts < Computer parts: -400*4

Computer server2 part1 < Computer server parts < Computer parts: -540*1

Computer server2 part1-C2-20150709-COMS2P1-10T < Computer server parts < Computer parts: -540*4

Computer server2 part2 < Computer server parts < Computer parts: -380*1

Computer server2 part2-C2-20150709-COMS2P2-10T < Computer server parts < Computer parts: -380*4

Computer1 part1 < Computer parts: -360*1

Computer1 part1-C2-20150715-COM1P1-20T < Computer parts: -360*14

Computer1 part2 < Computer parts: -310*1

Computer1 part2-C2-20150715-COM1P2-20T < Computer parts: -310*14

Computer2 part1 < Computer parts: -320*1

Computer2 part1-C2-20150715-COM2P1-20T < Computer parts: -320*14

Computer2 part2 < Computer parts: -290*1

Computer2 part2-C2-20150715-COM2P2-20T < Computer parts: -290*14

Computer3 part1 < Computer parts: -280*1

Computer3 part1-C2-20150715-COM3P1-20T < Computer parts: -280*14

Computer3 part2 < Computer parts: -260*1

Computer3 part2-C2-20150715-COM3P2-20T < Computer parts: -260*14

Computer4 part1 < Computer parts: -250*1

Computer4 part1-C2-20150715-COM4P1-20T < Computer parts: -250*14

Computer4 part2 < Computer parts: -240*1

Computer4 part2-C2-20150715-COM4P2-20T < Computer parts: -240*14

The ten transaction sub-equations are respectively:

Inventory (1): - 10*300 + Inventory (1): - 40*200 + Inventory (1): - 0.8*6000 +

Inventory (1): - 50*200 + Inventory (1): - 30*300 + Inventory (1): - 30*200 +

Inventory (1): - 50*100 + Inventory (1): - 40*100 + Inventory (1): - 2*500 = Cost of goods manufactured (5): -50800

Inventory (1): -10*150 + Inventory (1): -50*150 + Inventory (1): -20*150 + Inventory (1): -45*150 + Inventory (1): -10*150 + Inventory (1): -20*150 + Inventory (1): -5*100 + Inventory (1): -18.5*100 + Inventory (1): -20*100 = Cost of goods manufactured (5): -27600

Inventory (1): -20*100 + Inventory (1): -8700*1 + Inventory (1): -7600*1 + Inventory (1): -5800*1 + Inventory (1): -8500*1 + Inventory (1): -7200*1 + Inventory (1): -5400*1 + Inventory (1): -8300*1 + Inventory (1): -8300*1 + Inventory (1): -8300*1 + Inventory (1): -8300*1 = Cost of goods manufactured (5): -78400

Inventory (1): -7200*1 + Inventory (1): -7200*1 + Inventory (1): -7200*1 + Inventory (1): -7200*1 + Inventory (1): - 5100*1 + Inventory (1): - 5100*1 + Inventory (1): - 5100*1 + Inventory (1): - 5100*1 = Cost of goods manufactured (5): -49200

Inventory (1): - 7900*1 + Inventory (1): - 7900*1 + Inventory (1): - 7900*1 + Inventory (1): - 7900*1 + Inventory (1): - 6800*1 + Inventory (1): - 6800*1 + Inventory (1): - 6800*1 + Inventory (1): - 6800*1 = Cost of goods manufactured (5): -58800

Inventory (1): - 4900*1 + Inventory (1): - 4900*1 + Inventory (1): - 4900*1 + Inventory (1): - 4900*1 + Inventory (1): - 7500*1 + Inventory (1): - 7500*1 + Inventory (1): - 7500*1 + Inventory (1): - 7500*1 = Cost of goods manufactured (5): -49600

Inventory (1): - 6400*1 + Inventory (1): - 6400*1 + Inventory (1): - 6400*1 + Inventory (1): - 6400*1 + Inventory (1): - 4700*1 + Inventory (1): - 4700*1+

Inventory (1): - 4700*1 + Inventory (1): - 4700*1 = Cost of goods manufactured (5): -44400

Inventory (1): - 600*1 + Inventory (1): -600*4 + Inventory (1): - 400*1 + Inventory (1): -400*4 + Inventory (1): -540*1 + Inventory (1): -540*4 + Inventory (1): -380*1 + Inventory (1): -380*4 + Inventory (1): -360*1 + Inventory (1): -360*14 = Cost of goods manufactured (5): -15000

Inventory (1): -310*1 + Inventory (1): -310*14 + Inventory (1): -320*1 + Inventory (1): -320*14 + Inventory (1): -290*1 + Inventory (1): -290*14 + Inventory (1): -280*1 + Inventory (1): -280*14 + Inventory (1): -260*1 + Inventory (1): -260*14 = Cost of goods manufactured (5): -21900

Inventory (1): -250*1 + Inventory (1): -250*14 + Inventory (1): -240*1 + Inventory (1): -240*14 = Cost of goods manufactured (5): -7350

- On May 24, 2016, the Company1 pays -$623.75 cash to A13 (SIN: 909876513) for the Travelling expenses -$220.75 and the Other expenses -$403.

- On May 31, 2016, the Company1 pays three employees' salary expenses for cash - $8,400 repeatedly.

- On May 31, 2016, the Company1 records the Amortization expenses -$1,125 of a computer server2 (-$562.5, five months), a computer3 (-$291.67, five months), and a computer4 (-$270.83, five months).

- On May 31, 2016, the Company1 cancels the balances of the Computer account ($2,700 + $1,400 + $1,300) and the Accumulated amortization: Computer account because these computers have used for two years.

- On June 1, 2016, the Company1 purchases a new Computer server2, a new Computer1, and a new Computer1 from the Company1 itself, which means that the Company1 also sells these computers to the Company1 itself. The two transactions can be merged as a transaction. The balance of the Cash account does not change, so

The multi-subaccount names of the Inventory account and transaction sub-equation respectively are:

Computer server2-C1-201501008-COMS2-045 < Computer server-inventory < Computer-inventory: -1500*1

Computer1-C1-201501008-COM1-058 < Computer-inventory: -1000*1

Computer1-C1-20160430-COM1-066 < Computer-inventory: -1000*1

Computer (1): 2700 + Computer (1): 1600 + Computer (1): 1600 + Inventory (1): -1500*1 + Inventory (1): -1000*1 + Inventory (1): -1000*1 = Sale (4): 5900 + Cost of goods sold (5): -3500

- On June 1, 2016, the Company1 sells one Computer server1 $2,800, one Computer1 $1,600, and one Computer2 $1,500 for sales $5,900 to the Company3 (phone number: 123456782) for cash $3,000 and other on credit. The multi-subaccount names of the Cash and the Inventory accounts and transaction sub-equation respectively are:

  88-654308-c-customers < Cash receipts from customers < Operating activities

  Computer server1-C1-20160430-COMS1-044 < Computer server-inventory < Computer-inventory: -1600*1

  Computer1-C1-20160430-COM1-061 < Computer-inventory: -1000*1

  Computer2-C1-20160430-COM2-071 < Computer-inventory: -920*1

  Cash (1): 3000 + Account receivable (1): 2900 + Inventory (1): -1600*1 + Inventory (1): -1000*1 + Inventory (1): -920*1 = Sales (4): 5900 + Cost of goods sold (5): -3520

- On June 10, 2016, the Company1 pays -$15,000 cash to the Company3 (phone number: 123456082) with the General ID 67. The multi-subaccount name of the Cash account and transaction sub-equation respectively are:

  88-654308-t-suppliers < Cash payments to suppliers < Operating activities

- On June 12, 2016, the Company1 pays -$64,000 cash to the Company2 (phone

number: 123456083) with the General ID 64. The multi-subaccount name of the Cash account is:

88-654307-t-suppliers < Cash payments to suppliers < Operating activities

- On June 23, 2016, the Company1 pays -$580.91 cash to A13 (SIN: 909876513) for the Travelling expenses -$270.91 and the Other expenses -$310.

- On June 30, 2016, the Company1 pays three employees' salary expenses for cash -$8,400 repeatedly.

- On July 7, 2016, the Company1 pays -$442.56 cash to A14 (SIN: 909876514) for the Travelling expenses -$262.56 and the Other expenses -$180.

- On July 19, 2016, the Company1 sells one Computer4 to A8 (SIN: 909876508) for cash $1300. The multi-subaccount names of the Cash and the Inventory accounts are:
  909876508-c-customers < Cash receipts from customers < Operating activities
  Computer4-C1-20160430-COM4-117 < Computer-inventory: -770*1

- On July 25, 2016, the Company1 pays -$487.84 cash to A13 (SIN: 909876513) for the Travelling expenses -$185.84 and the Other expenses -$302.

- On July 31, 2016, the Company1 pays three employees' salary -$8,400 repeatedly.

- On August 1, 2016, the Company1 sells one Computer server1 $2,800 (cost: -$1,600), one Computer1 $1,600 (cost: $-1,000), and one Computer2 $1,500 (cost: -$920) for sales $5,900 to the Business Bank1 (phone number: 123456786) for cash $5,000 and other on credit. The multi-subaccount names of the Cash and the Inventory accounts and transaction sub-equation respectively are:
  88-654304-c-customers < Cash receipts from customers < Operating activities
  Computer server1-C1-201501008-COMS1-041 < Computer server-inventory < Computer-inventory: -1600*1
  Computer1-C1-201501008-COM1-057 < Computer-inventory: -1000*1
  Computer2-C1-201501008-COM2-067 < Computer-inventory: -920*1

  Cash (1): 5000 + Account receivable (1): 900 + Inventory (1): -1600*1 + Inventory (1): -1000*1 + Inventory (1): -920*1 = Sales (4): 5900 + Cost of goods

sold (5): -3520

- On August 1, 2016, the Company1 sells one Car3 $38,000 to A16 and A23 for cash $38,000. A16 pays cash -$10,000 with the primary account in the Business Bank1 and cash -$11,000 with the second account in the Business Bank2. A23 pays cash -$5,500 with the primary account in the Business Bank2 and cash -$11,500 with the second account in the Business Bank1. The multi-subaccount names of the Cash and the Inventory accounts and transaction sub-equation respectively are:

  909876516-c-customers < Cash receipts from customers < Operating activities

  909876523-c-customers < Cash receipts from customers < Operating activities

  Car3-C1-20160430-C3-052 < Car-inventory < Vehicle-inventory: -26000*1

  Cash (1): 10000 + Cash (1): 11000 + Cash (1): 5500 + Cash (1): 11500 + Inventory (1): -26000*1 = Sales (4): 38000 + Cost of goods sold (5): -26000

- On August 1, 2016, the Company1 sells one Computer server1 $2,800 (cost: $1,600), one Computer1 $1,600 (cost: $1,000), and one Computer2 $1,500 (cost: $920) for sales $5,900 to the Company2 (phone number: 123456783) for cash $3,000 and other on credit. The multi-subaccount names of the Cash and the Inventory accounts are:

  88-654307-c-customers < Cash receipts from customers < Operating activities

  Computer server1-C1-20160430-COMS1-043 < Computer server-inventory < Computer-inventory: -1600*1

  Computer1-C1-20160430-COM1-060 < Computer-inventory: -1000*1

  Computer2-C1-20160430-COM2-070 < Computer-inventory: -920*1

- On August 2, 2016, the Company1 sells one Computer1 to A1 (SIN: 909876501) for cash $1600. The multi-subaccount names of the Cash and the Inventory are:

  909876501-c-customers < Cash receipts from customers < Operating activities

  Computer1-C1-20160430-COM1-067 < Computer-inventory: -1000*1

- On August 3, 2016, the Company1 pays -$12,000 cash to the Company2 (phone number: 123456083) with the General ID 64. The multi-subaccount name of the

Cash account is:

88-654307-t-suppliers < Cash payments to suppliers < Operating activities

- On August 10, 2016, the Company1 sells one Computer2 to A11 (SIN: 909876511) for cash $1,500. The multi-subaccount names of the Cash and the Inventory accounts respectively are:

909876511-c-customers < Cash receipts from customers < Operating activities

Computer2-C1-20160430-COM2-073 < Computer-inventory: -920*1

- On August 14, 2016, the Company1 sells one Truck1- Service package1 $550 and one Car1- Service package3 $490 to the Central Bank (phone number: 123456789) for cash $1,040 (Service package incomes). The cash' s multi-subaccount name is:

88-654301-c-customers < Cash receipts from customers < Operating activities

- On August 17, 2016, the Company1 pays -$386.36 cash to A15 (SIN: 909876515) for the Travelling expenses -$263.36 and the Other expenses (meals: food522: $13*3 + food622: $28*3) -$123.

- On August 25, 2016, the Company1 pays -$501.22 cash to A13 (SIN: 909876513) for the Travelling expenses -$189.22 and the Other expenses -$312.

- On August 31, 2016, the Company1 pays three employees' salary expenses for cash -$8,400 repeatedly.

- On September 2, 2016, the Company1 sells one Car3 $38,000 to the Proprietorship2 (phone number: 123456780) for cash $18000 and other $20,000 on credit. The multi-subaccount names of the Cash and the Inventory accounts and transaction sub-equation respectively are:

88-654310-c-customers < Cash receipts from customers < Operating activities

Car3-C1-20150925-C3-029 < Car-inventory < Vehicle-inventory: -26000*1

Cash (1): 18000 + Account receivable (1): 20000 + Inventory (1): -26000 = Sales (4): 38000 + Cost of goods sold (5): -26000

- On September 12, 2016, the Company1 receives $18,000 cash from the Business Bank1 (phone number: 123456786) with the General ID 30.

- On September 13, 2016, the Company1 pays -$25,000 cash to the Company3 (phone number: 123456082) with General ID 3 ($1,000) and the General ID 67 ($24,000). The multi-subaccount name of the Cash account and transaction sub-equation respectively are:

  88-654308-t-suppliers < Cash payments to suppliers < Operating activities

- On September 14, 2016, the Company1 pays -$10,000 cash to the Company2 (phone number: 123456083) with the General ID 64.

- On September 26, 2016, the Company1 receives $17,000 cash from the Business Bank2 (phone number: 123456785) with the General ID 41.

- On September 26, 2016, the Company1 pays -$8,000 cash to the Company3 (phone number: 123456082) with the General ID 67.

- On September 28, 2016, the Company1 pays -$658.33 cash to A13 (SIN: 909876513) for the Travelling expenses -$207.33 and the Other expenses -$451.

- On September 30, 2016, the Company1 pays three employees' salary expenses for cash $8,400 repeatedly.

- On October 1, 2016, the Company1 sells one Computer server1 $2,800 (cost: -$1,600), one Computer1 $1,600 (cost: -$1,000), and one Computer2 $1,500 (cost: -$920) to the Tax Bureau (phone number: 123456787) for cash $2400 and other $3,500 on credit. The multi-subaccount names of the Cash and the Inventory accounts and transaction sub-equation respectively are:

  88-654303-c-customers < Cash receipts from customers < Operating activities
  Computer server1-C1-201501007-COMS1-040 < Computer server-inventory <
  Computer-inventory: -1600*1
  Computer1-C1-201501008-COM1-056 < Computer-inventory: -1000*1
  Computer2-C1-201501008-COM2-066 < Computer-inventory: -920*1

  Cash (1): 2400 + Account receivable (1): 3500 + Inventory (1): -1600*1 +
  Inventory (1): -1000*1 + Inventory (1): -920*1 = Sales (4): 5900 + Cost of goods
  sold (5): -3520

- On October 1, 2016, the Company1 sells one Computer server1 $2,800 (cost: -$1,600), one Computer1 $1,600 (cost: -$1,000), and one Computer2 $1,500 (cost: -$920) for sales $5,900 to the Business Bank2 (phone number: 123456785) for cash $5,000 and other $900 on credit. The multi-subaccount names of the Cash and the Inventory accounts respectively are:

  88-654305-c-customers < Cash receipts from customers < Operating activities

  Computer server1-C1-20160430-COMS1-042 < Computer server-inventory < Computer-inventory: -1600*1

  Computer1-C1-20160430-COM1-059 < Computer-inventory: -1000*1

  Computer2-C1-20160430-COM2-069 < Computer-inventory: -920*1

- On October 1, 2016, the Company1 sells one Computer server2 (-$1,500) and two Computer1s (-$1,000) to the Proprietorship1 (phone number: 123456781) for cash $5,500 and other $400 on credit. The multi-subaccount names of the Cash and the Inventory accounts respectively are:

  88-654309-c-customers < Cash receipts from customers < Operating activities

  Computer server2-C1-20160430-COMS2-047 < Computer server-inventory < Computer-inventory: -1500*1

  Computer1-C1-20160430-COM1-063 < Computer-inventory: -1000*1

  Computer1-C1-20160430-COM1-064 < Computer-inventory: -1000*1

- On October 3, 2016, the Company1 sells one Truck2-Service package2 $500 and one Car1-Service package3 $490 to the Governrmnt1 (phone number: 123456788) for cash $990. The multi-subaccount name of the Cash account is:

  88-654302-c-customers < Cash receipts from customers < Operating activities

- On October 5, 2016, the Company1 sells one Car2 $39,000 to A13 and A25 for cash $39,000. A13 pays cash -$10,000 with the primary account in the Business Bank1 and cash -$11,500 with the second account in the Business Bank2. A25 pays cash -$10,500 with the primary account in the Business Bank1 and cash -$7,000 with the second account in the Business Bank2. The multi-subaccount names of the Cash and the Inventory accounts and transaction sub-equation respectively are:

909876513-c-customers < Cash receipts from customers < Operating activities

909876525-c-customers < Cash receipts from customers < Operating activities

Car2-C1-20160430-C2-040 < Car-inventory < Vehicle-inventory: -27000*1

Cash (1): 10000 + Cash (1): 11500 + Cash (1): 10500 + Cash (1): 7000 + Inventory (1): -27000 = Sales (4): 39000 + Cost of goods sold (5): -27000

- On October 7, 2016, the Company1 pays -$392.36 cash to A15 (SIN: 909876515) for the Travelling expenses -$263.36 and the Other expenses -$129.

- On October 27, 2016, the Company1 pays -$607.57 cash to A13 (SIN: 909876513) for the Travelling expenses -$224.57 and the Other expenses -$383.

- On October 31, 2016, the Company1 pays three employees' salary -$8,400 repeatedly.

- On November 5, 2016, the Company1 receives $2,900 cash from the Company3 (phone number: 123456782) with the General ID 82. The multi-subaccount name of the Cash account is:

  88-654308-c-customers < Cash receipts from customers < Operating activities

- On November 19, 2016, the Company1 pays -$551.13 cash to A13 (SIN: 909876513) for the Travelling expenses -$190.13 and the Other expenses -$361.

- On November 19, 2016, the Company1 sells one Truck2-Service package2 ($500), one Car1-Service package3 ($490), and one Car3-Service package5 (410) to the Tax Bureau (phone number: 123456787) for cash $1400. The multi-subaccount name of the Cash account is:

  88-654303-c-customers < Cash receipts from customers < Operating activities

- On November 19, 2016, the Company1 pays -$401.13 cash to A15 (SIN: 909876515) for the Travelling expenses -$269.13 and the Other expenses -$132.

- On November 21, 2016, the Company1 completed all products ($68,300) of the Computer account and transfers the balance of the Cost of goods manufactured account to the Working-in-process inventory account and the Inventory account. The Cost of goods manufactured account has four subaccounts of the "Supplies expenses", the "909876513-salary < Sales department-salary < Salary expenses", the "909876515-salary < Product department-salary < Salary expenses", and the "General parts expenses". Their amounts, which are used in the products of the Computer, are estimated to be $800, $13,000, $5,000, and $49,500 respectively. The multi-subaccount names of the Inventory accounts, and one interior transaction and the eight transaction sub-equation respectively are:

Computer server1-C1-20161121-COMS1-080 < Computer server-inventory < Computer-inventory: 1600*1

Computer server1-C1-20161121-COMS1-081 < Computer server-inventory < Computer-inventory: 1600*1

Computer server1-C1-20161121-COMS1-082 < Computer server-inventory < Computer-inventory: 1600*1

Computer server1-C1-20161121-COMS1-083 < Computer server-inventory < Computer-inventory: 1600*1

Computer server1-C1-20161121-COMS1-084 < Computer server-inventory < Computer-inventory: 1600*1

Computer server2-C1-20161121-COMS2-091 < Computer server-inventory < Computer-inventory: 1500*1

Computer server2-C1-20161121-COMS2-092 < Computer server-inventory < Computer-inventory: 1500*1

Computer server2-C1-20161121-COMS2-093 < Computer server-inventory < Computer-inventory: 1500*1

Computer server2-C1-20161121-COMS2-094 < Computer server-inventory < Computer-inventory: 1500*1

Computer server2-C1-20161121-COMS2-095 < Computer server-inventory < Computer-inventory: 1500*1

Computer1-C1-20161121-COM1-081 < Computer-inventory: 1000*1

Computer1-C1-20161121-COM1-082 < Computer-inventory: 1000*1

Computer1-C1-20161121-COM1-083 < Computer-inventory: 1000*1

Computer1-C1-20161121-COM1-084 < Computer-inventory: 1000*1

Computer1-C1-20161121-COM1-085 < Computer-inventory: 1000*1

Computer1-C1-20161121-COM1-086 < Computer-inventory: 1000*1

Computer1-C1-20161121-COM1-087 < Computer-inventory: 1000*1

Computer1-C1-20161121-COM1-088 < Computer-inventory: 1000*1

Computer1-C1-20161121-COM1-089 < Computer-inventory: 1000*1

Computer1-C1-20161121-COM1-090 < Computer-inventory: 1000*1

Computer1-C1-20161121-COM1-091 < Computer-inventory: 1000*1

Computer1-C1-20161121-COM1-092 < Computer-inventory: 1000*1

Computer1-C1-20161121-COM1-093 < Computer-inventory: 1000*1

Computer1-C1-20161121-COM1-094 < Computer-inventory: 1000*1

Computer1-C1-20161121-COM1-095 < Computer-inventory: 1000*1

Computer2-C1-20161121-COM2-011 < Computer-inventory: 920*1

Computer2-C1-20161121-COM2-012 < Computer-inventory: 920*1

Computer2-C1-20161121-COM2-013 < Computer-inventory: 920*1

Computer2-C1-20161121-COM2-014 < Computer-inventory: 920*1

Computer2-C1-20161121-COM2-015 < Computer-inventory: 920*1

Computer2-C1-20161121-COM2-016 < Computer-inventory: 920*1

Computer2-C1-20161121-COM2-017 < Computer-inventory: 920*1

Computer2-C1-20161121-COM2-018 < Computer-inventory: 920*1

Computer2-C1-20161121-COM2-019 < Computer-inventory: 920*1

Computer2-C1-20161121-COM2-020 < Computer-inventory: 920*1

Computer2-C1-20161121-COM2-021 < Computer-inventory: 920*1

Computer2-C1-20161121-COM2-022 < Computer-inventory: 920*1

Computer2-C1-20161121-COM2-023 < Computer-inventory: 920*1

Computer2-C1-20161121-COM2-024 < Computer-inventory: 920*1

Computer2-C1-20161121-COM2-025 < Computer-inventory: 920*1

Computer3-C1-20161121-COM3-031 < Computer-inventory: 830*1

Computer3-C1-20161121-COM3-032 < Computer-inventory: 830*1

Computer3-C1-20161121-COM3-033 < Computer-inventory: 830*1

Computer3-C1-20161121-COM3-034< Computer-inventory: 830*1

Computer3-C1-20161121-COM3-035 < Computer-inventory: 830*1

Computer3-C1-20161121-COM3-036 < Computer-inventory: 830*1

Computer3-C1-20161121-COM3-037 < Computer-inventory: 830*1

Computer3-C1-20161121-COM3-038 < Computer-inventory: 830*1

Computer3-C1-20161121-COM3-039 < Computer-inventory: 830*1

Computer3-C1-20161121-COM3-040 < Computer-inventory: 830*1

Computer3-C1-20161121-COM3-041 < Computer-inventory: 830*1

Computer3-C1-20161121-COM3-042 < Computer-inventory: 830*1

Computer3-C1-20161121-COM3-043 < Computer-inventory: 830*1

Computer3-C1-20161121-COM3-044 < Computer-inventory: 830*1

Computer3-C1-20161121-COM3-045 < Computer-inventory: 830*1

Computer4-C1-20161121-COM4-141 < Computer-inventory: 770*1

Computer4-C1-20161121-COM4-142 < Computer-inventory: 770*1

Computer4-C1-20161121-COM4-143 < Computer-inventory: 770*1

Computer4-C1-20161121-COM4-144 < Computer-inventory: 770*1

Computer4-C1-20161121-COM4-145 < Computer-inventory: 770*1

Computer4-C1-20161121-COM4-146 < Computer-inventory: 770*1

Computer4-C1-20161121-COM4-147 < Computer-inventory: 770*1

Computer4-C1-20161121-COM4-148 < Computer-inventory: 770*1

Computer4-C1-20161121-COM4-149 < Computer-inventory: 770*1

Computer4-C1-20161121-COM4-150 < Computer-inventory: 770*1

Computer4-C1-20161121-COM4-151 < Computer-inventory: 770*1

Computer4-C1-20161121-COM4-152 < Computer-inventory: 770*1

Computer4-C1-20161121-COM4-153 < Computer-inventory: 770*1

Computer4-C1-20161121-COM4-154 < Computer-inventory: 770*1

Computer4-C1-20161121-COM4-155 < Computer-inventory: 770*1

Working-in-process inventory (1): 68300 = Cost of goods manufactured (5): 800 +

Cost of goods manufactured (5): 13000 + Cost of goods manufactured (5): 5000 + Cost of goods manufactured (5): 49500

Inventory (1): 1600*1 + Inventory (1): 1600*1 + Inventory (1): 1600*1 + Inventory (1): 1600*1 + Inventory (1): 1600*1 + Inventory (1): 1500*1 + Inventory (1): 1500*1 + Inventory (1): 1500*1 + Inventory (1): 1500*1 + Inventory (1): 1500*1 + Working-in-process inventory (1): -15500 = 0

Inventory (1): 1000*1 + Inventory (1): 1000*1 + Inventory (1): 1000*1 + Inventory (1): 1000*1 + Inventory (1): 1000*1 + Inventory (1): 1000*1 + Inventory (1): 1000*1 + Inventory (1): 1000*1 + Inventory (1): 1000*1 + Inventory (1): 1000*1 + Working-in-process inventory (1): -10000 = 0

Inventory (1): 1000*1 + Inventory (1): 1000*1 + Inventory (1): 1000*1 + Inventory (1): 1000*1 + Inventory (1): 1000*1 + Inventory (1): 920*1 + Inventory (1): 920*1 + Inventory (1): 920*1 + Inventory (1): 920*1 + Inventory (1): 920*1 + Working-in-process inventory (1): -9600 = 0

Inventory (1): 920*1 + Inventory (1): 920*1 + Inventory (1): 920*1 + Inventory (1): 920*1 + Inventory (1): 920*1 + Inventory (1): 920*1 + Inventory (1): 920*1 + Inventory (1): 920*1 + Inventory (1): 920*1 + Inventory (1): 920*1 + Working-in-process inventory (1): -9200 = 0

Inventory (1): 830*1 + Inventory (1): 830*1 + Inventory (1): 830*1 + Inventory (1): 830*1 + Inventory (1): 830*1 + Inventory (1): 830*1 + Inventory (1): 830*1 + Inventory (1): 830*1 + Inventory (1): 830*1 + Inventory (1): 830*1 + Working-in-process inventory (1): -8300 = 0

Inventory (1): 830*1 + Inventory (1): 830*1 + Inventory (1): 830*1 + Inventory (1): 830*1 + Inventory (1): 830*1 + Inventory (1): 770*1 + Inventory (1): 770*1 + Inventory (1): 770*1 + Inventory (1): 770*1 + Inventory (1): 770*1 +

Working-in-process inventory (1): -8000 = 0

Inventory (1): 770*1 + Inventory (1): 770*1 + Inventory (1): 770*1 + Inventory (1): 770*1 + Inventory (1): 770*1 + Inventory (1): 770*1 + Inventory (1): 770*1 + Inventory (1): 770*1 + Inventory (1): 770*1 + Inventory (1): 770*1 + Working-in-process inventory (1): -7700 = 0

- On November 29, 2016, the Company1 pays -$14,420 cash to the Company2 (phone number: 123456083) with the General ID 66. The multi-subaccount name of the Cash account and transaction sub-equation respectively are:

    88-654307-t-suppliers < Cash payments to suppliers < Operating activities

- On November 29, 2016, the Company1 pays -$3,000 cash to the Company3 (phone number: 123456082) with the General ID 67. The multi-subaccount name of the Cash account and transaction sub-equation respectively are:

    88-654308-t-suppliers < Cash payments to suppliers < Operating activities

- On November 29, 2016, the Company1 sells one Computer2 (-$920) to A4 (SIN: 909876504) for cash $1,500. The multi-subaccount names of the Cash and the Inventory accounts respectively are:

    909876504-c-customers < Cash receipts from customers < Operating activities
    Computer2-C1-20160430-COM2-074 < Computer-inventory: -920*1

- On November 30, 2016, the Company1 sells one Computer2 $1,500 (cost: -$920) to A18 (SIN: 909876518) for cash $1,500. The multi-subaccount names of the Cash and the Inventory accounts respectively are:

    909876518-c-customers < Cash receipts from customers < Operating activities
    Computer2-C1-20160430-COM2-075 < Computer-inventory: -920*1

- On November 30, 2016, the Company1 sells one Computer4 $1,300 (cost: -$770) to A6 (SIN: 909876506) for cash $1,300. The multi-subaccount names of the Cash and the Inventory accounts respectively are:

    909876506-c-customers < Cash receipts from customers < Operating activities
    Computer4-C1-20160430-COM4-116 < Computer-inventory: -770*1

- On November 30, 2016, the Company1 pays three employees' salary cash -$8,400.

- On December 1, 2016, the Company1 sells one Computer server1, one Computer1, and one Computer2 to the Proprietorship2 (phone number: 123456780) for cash $5,000 and other $900 on credit. The multi-subaccount names of the Cash and the Inventory accounts and transaction sub-equation respectively are:

  88-654310-c-customers < Cash receipts from customers < Operating activities

  Computer server1-C1-20160430-COMS1-045 < Computer server-inventory < Computer-inventory: -1600*1

  Computer1-C1-20160430-COM1-062 < Computer-inventory: -1000*1

  Computer2-C1-20160430-COM2-072 < Computer-inventory: -920*1

  Cash (1): 5000 + Account receivable (1): 900 + Inventory (1): -1600 + Inventory (1): -1000+ Inventory (1): -920 = Sales (4): 5900 + Cost of goods sold (5): -3520

- On December 1, 2016, the Company1 sells one Computer1 to the Tax Bureau (phone number: 123456787) on credit $1,600. The Inventory accounts is:

  Computer1-C1-20160430-COM1-068 < Computer-inventory: -1000*1

- On December 10, 2016, the Company1 sells one Computer1 $1,600 (cost: -$1,000) to A24 (SIN: 909876524) for cash $1,600. The multi-subaccount names of the Cash and the Inventory accounts respectively are:

  909876524-c-customers < Cash receipts from customers < Operating activities

  Computer1-C1-20161121-COM1-081 < Computer-inventory: -1000*1

- On December 11, 2016, the Company1 receives $1,500 cash from the Business Bank1 (phone number: 123456786) with the General ID 30. The multi-subaccount name of the Cash account is:

  88-654304-c-customers < Cash receipts from customers < Operating activities

- On December 16, 2016, the Company1 pays -$638.34 cash to A13 (SIN: 909876513) for the Travelling expenses -$225.34 and the Other expenses -$413.

- On December 19, 2016, the Company1 sells one Computer1 $1,600 (cost: -$1,000) to A22 (SIN: 909876522) for cash $1,600. The multi-subaccount names of the Cash and the Inventory accounts respectively are:

909876522-c-customers < Cash receipts from customers < Operating activities

Computer1-C1-20160430-COM1-065 < Computer-inventory: -1000*1

- On December 19, 2016, the Company1 receives $2,800 cash from the Business Bank2 (phone number: 123456785) with the General ID 41. The multi-subaccount name of the Cash account is:

88-654305-c-customers < Cash receipts from customers < Operating activities

- On December 22, 2016, the Company1 sells one Computer3 $1,400 (cost: -$830) to A2 (SIN: 909876502) for cash $1,400. The multi-subaccount names of the Cash and the Inventory accounts respectively are:

909876502-c-customers < Cash receipts from customers < Operating activities

Computer3-C1-20160430-COM3-103 < Computer-inventory: -830*1

- On December 23, 2016, the Company1 pays -$444.45 cash to A14 (SIN: 909876514) for the Travelling expenses -$282.45 and the Other expenses -$162.

- On December 23, 2016, the Company1 pays -$5,500 cash to the Proprietorship2 (phone number: 123456080) with the General ID 51 (-$2,000) and the General ID 69 (-$3,500). The multi-subaccount name of the Cash account and transaction sub-equation respectively are:

88-654310-t-suppliers < Cash payments to suppliers < Operating activities

- On December 23, 2016, the Company1 pays -$18,000 cash to the Proprietorship1 (phone number: 123456081) with the General ID 68. The multi-subaccount name of the Cash account and transaction sub-equation respectively are:

88-654309-t-suppliers < Cash payments to suppliers < Operating activities

- On December 29, 2016, the Company1 receives $2,400 cash from the Tax Bureau (phone number: 123456787) with the General ID 110. The multi-subaccount name of the Cash account is:

88-654303-c-customers < Cash receipts from customers < Operating activities

- On December 29, 2016, the Company1 receives $10,000 cash from the Proprietorship1 (phone number: 123456781) with the General ID 32. The multi-subaccount name of the Cash account is:

88-654309-c-customers < Cash receipts from customers < Operating activities

- On December 29, 2016, the Company1 receives $27,000 cash from the Proprietorship2 (phone number: 123456780) with the General ID 33 ($8,000) and General ID 102 ($19,000). The multi-subaccount name of the Cash account is:

88-654310-c-customers < Cash receipts from customers < Operating activities

- On December 29, 2016, the Company1 pays $39,700 cash to the Company2 (phone number: 123456083) with the General ID 65. The multi-subaccount name of the Cash account is:

88-654307-t-suppliers < Cash payments to suppliers < Operating activities

- On December 30, 2016, the Company1 receives $2,000 cash from the Government1 (phone number: 123456788) with the General ID 63. The multi-subaccount name of the Cash account is:

88-654302-c-customers < Cash receipts from customers < Operating activities

- On December 30, 2016, the Company1 receives $1,400 cash from the Business Bank1 (phone number: 123456786) with the General ID 30 ($500) the General ID 92 ($900). The multi-subaccount name of the Cash account is:

88-654304-c-customers < Cash receipts from customers < Operating activities

- On December 31, 2016, the Company1 receives $3,500 cash from the Central Bank (phone number: 123456789) with the General ID 62. The multi-subaccount name of the Cash account is:

88-654301-c-customers < Cash receipts from customers < Operating activities

- On December 31, 2016, the Company1 sells one Car1 $40,000 to A7 for cash $40,000. The multi-subaccount names of the Cash and the inventory accounts and transaction sub-equation respectively are:

909876507-c-customers < Cash receipts from customers < Operating activities

Car1-C1-20160430-C1-030 < Car-inventory < Vehicle-inventory: -28000*1

Cash (1): 40000 + Inventory (1): -28000*1 = Sales (4): 40000 + Cost of goods

sold (5): -28000

- On December 31, 2016, the Company1 sells one Car1 $40,000 (cost: -$28,000) to A10 for cash $40,000. The multi-subaccount names of the Cash and the inventory accounts respectively are:

    909876510-c-customers < Cash receipts from customers < Operating activities

    Car1-C1-20160430-C1-031 < Car-inventory < Vehicle-inventory: -28000*1

- On December 31, 2016, the Company1 pays three employees' salary -$8,400.

- On December 31, 2016, the Company1 transfers the balance of the Cost of goods manufactured account (products of vehicle) to the Working-in-process inventory account. The Cost of goods manufactured account has four subaccounts of the "Supplies expenses", the "909876513-salary < Sales department-salary < Salary expenses", the "909876515-salary < Product department-salary < Salary expenses", and the "General parts expenses". Their balances are -$2,000, -$7,800, -$18,200, and -$353,550 respectively. The transaction sub-equation is:

    Working-in-process inventory (1): 32650*1 + Working-in-process inventory (1): 29700*1 + Working-in-process inventory (1): 27600*4 + Working-in-process inventory (1): 26600*4 + Working-in-process inventory (1): 25600*4 = Cost of goods manufactured (5): 2000 + Cost of goods manufactured (5): 7800 + Cost of goods manufactured (5): 18200 + Cost of goods manufactured (5): 353550

- On the same day, 2016, the Company1 sells one Car3 $38,000 (cost: -$26,000) to A24 for cash $38,000. The multi-subaccount names of the Cash and the Inventory accounts respectively are:

    909876524-c-customers < Cash receipts from customers < Operating activities

    Car3-C1-20160430-C3-051 < Car-inventory < Vehicle-inventory: -26000*1

- On the same day, 2016, the Company1 pays -$55,000 cash to the Company2 (phone number: 123456083) with the General ID 64. The cash's multi-subaccount name is:

    88-654307-t-suppliers < Cash payments to suppliers < Operating activities

- On the same day, the Company1 pays -$38,650 cash to the Business Bank1 for the

Note interest expenses of the Note11 -$22,500 ($250,000, one-level subaccount "Note11-interest") and the Note15 -$16,150 ($170,000, one-level subaccount "Note15-interest"). The multi-subaccount name of the Cash account is:

88-654304-t-note interest < Cash payments to business banks < Operating activities

- On the same day, the Company1 pays -$19,800 cash to the Business Bank2 for the Note interest expenses of the Note21 ($140,000, one-level subaccount "Note21-interest"). The multi-subaccount name of the Cash account is:

88-654305-t-note interest < Cash payments to business banks < Operating activities

- On the same day, the Company1 pays -$2,300 cash to the bond holders for the Bond interest expenses of the Bond31 (one-level subaccount "Bond31-interest"). The multi-subaccount names of the Cash account and the two transaction sub-equations respectively are:

88-654305-t-bond interest < Cash payments to bond holders < Operating activities (909876501, 909876502, 909876508, 909876511, 909876514, 909876516, 909876518, 909876521, 909876522, 909876524, 909876525)

Cash (1): -230 + Cash (1): -138 + Cash (1): -276 + Cash (1): -230 + Cash (1): -322 + Cash (1): -92 = Bond interest expenses (5): -1288

Cash (1): -184 + Cash (1): -92 + Cash (1): -138 + Cash (1): -230 + Cash (1): -138 + Cash (1): -230 = Bond interest expenses (5): -1012

- On the same day, the Company1 receives cash $400 for investment interest (Investment incomes) of the Bond11and cash $135 for investment interest of the Bond13 from the Business Bank1. The Cash account's multi-subaccount name is:

88-654304-c-investment income < Cash receipts from investments < Investing activities

- On the same day, the Company1 receives cash $369 for investment interest (Investment incomes) of the Bond21 from the Business Bank2. The multi-subaccount name of the Cash account is:

88-654305-c-investment income < Cash receipts from investments < Investing activities

- On the same day, the Company1 receives cash $120 (Deposit interest incomes) from the Business Bank1 for primary deposit interest. The multi-subaccount name of the Cash account is:

  88-654304-c-deposit interest income < Cash receipts from deposit interest < Financial activities

- On the same day, the Company1 records the Office supplies expenses -$362.13. It is consisted of two parts of the Supplies -$48.13 and the Inventory -$316 (-$14*11 - $16*10). The Inventory account's multi-subaccount name are:

  Supplies1-P2-20160430-Supp1-200T: -14*11

  Supplies2-P2-20160430-Supp2-200T: -16*10

- On the same day, the Company1 records the Vehicle's amortization expenses - $24,200 (= -$9,000 - $8,000 - $7,200) one year (5 years, straight line).

- On the same day, the Company1 records the Computer's amortization expenses - $1,720.84 seven months (2 years, straight line) which includes a new computer server2 (-$787.5), a new computer1 (-$466.67), and a new computer1 (-$466.67). Please pay attention here. The new computers are different from the cancelled computers. The balance of the Amortization expenses account is equal to the sum of the cancelled computers' amortization expenses and the new computers' amortization expenses.

- On December 31, 2016, the Company1 records the Tax expenses -$9,477.39 and the Tax payable $9,477.39. The multi-subaccount name forms of the Tax expenses and the Tax payable accounts all are the 'n'.

So far, I have entered all transactions of the Company1 to the database dcj207 in the fiscal year 2016.

## 3.6.2 Brief Summary of the Company1

The Figure 3.6-2 on this page and next pages shows all inventory purchased or sold by other members in the fiscal year 2016 by using of SQL Server query.

```
use dcj200
select * from InventoryByMembers where Recorder='88-654306' and TransDate between '2016-01-01' and '2016-12-31'
order by TransDate
```

100 %   ▾

Results | Messages

| | IDM | Amount | Symbol | MultiSubaccount | Recorder | TransDate | Unit |
|---|---|---|---|---|---|---|---|
| 1 | 88-654310 | -560.00 | t | Supplies1-P2-20150920-SUP1-200T | 88-654306 | 2016-01-02 | -40 |
| 2 | 88-654310 | -640.00 | t | Supplies2-P2-20150920-SUP2-200T | 88-654306 | 2016-01-02 | -40 |
| 3 | 88-654306 | 546.00 | f | Supplies1-P2-20150920-SUP1-200T | 88-654306 | 2016-01-02 | 39 |
| 4 | 88-654306 | 624.00 | f | Supplies2-P2-20150920-SUP2-200T | 88-654306 | 2016-01-02 | 39 |
| 5 | 88-654306 | 150.00 | f | Inven111 < Inven11 < Inven1 | 88-654306 | 2016-01-02 | 15 |
| 6 | 88-654306 | 800.00 | f | Inven112 < Inven11 < Inven1 | 88-654306 | 2016-01-02 | 20 |
| 7 | 88-654306 | 48.00 | f | Inven121 < Inven12 < Inven1 | 88-654306 | 2016-01-02 | 60 |
| 8 | 88-654306 | 300.00 | f | Inven122 < Inven12 < Inven1 | 88-654306 | 2016-01-02 | 6 |
| 9 | 88-654306 | 600.00 | f | Inven21 < Inven2 | 88-654306 | 2016-01-02 | 20 |
| 10 | 88-654306 | 300.00 | f | Inven221 < Inven22 < Inven2 | 88-654306 | 2016-01-02 | 10 |
| 11 | 88-654306 | 500.00 | f | Inven222 < Inven22 < Inven2 | 88-654306 | 2016-01-02 | 10 |
| 12 | 88-654306 | 400.00 | f | PPUK parts < ASD parts < Inven2 | 88-654306 | 2016-01-02 | 10 |
| 13 | 88-654306 | 200.00 | f | PPGH parts < ASD parts < Inven2 | 88-654306 | 2016-01-02 | 100 |
| 14 | 88-654306 | 100.00 | f | Inven31 < Inven3 | 88-654306 | 2016-01-02 | 10 |
| 15 | 88-654306 | 300.00 | f | Inven32 < Inven3 | 88-654306 | 2016-01-02 | 6 |
| 16 | 88-654306 | 200.00 | f | Inven331 < Inven33 < Inven3 | 88-654306 | 2016-01-02 | 10 |
| 17 | 88-654306 | 450.00 | f | Inven332 < Inven33 < Inven3 | 88-654306 | 2016-01-02 | 10 |
| 18 | 88-654306 | 20.00 | f | HGFCVB parts < QASXC parts < Inven3 | 88-654306 | 2016-01-02 | 2 |
| 19 | 88-654306 | 200.00 | f | PPGHUP parts < ASDUP parts < Inven3 | 88-654306 | 2016-01-02 | 10 |
| 20 | 88-654306 | 110.00 | f | Inven411 < Inven41 < Inven4 | 88-654306 | 2016-01-02 | 22 |
| 21 | 88-654306 | 74.00 | f | Inven412 < Inven41 < Inven4 | 88-654306 | 2016-01-02 | 4 |
| 22 | 88-654306 | 500.00 | f | TTTCU parts < TTT parts < Inven4 | 88-654306 | 2016-01-02 | 25 |
| 23 | 88-654306 | 400.00 | f | RRRHJK parts < Inven4 | 88-654306 | 2016-01-02 | 20 |
| 24 | 88-654304 | 27000.00 | c | Car2-C1-20150925-C2-027 < Car-inventory < Vehicle-inventory | 88-654306 | 2016-02-01 | 1 |
| 25 | 88-654309 | 26000.00 | c | Car3-C1-20150925-C3-028 < Car-inventory < Vehicle-inventory | 88-654306 | 2016-02-01 | 1 |
| 26 | 88-654310 | 26000.00 | c | Car3-C1-20150925-C3-029 < Car-inventory < Vehicle-inventory | 88-654306 | 2016-02-01 | 1 |
| 27 | 88-654305 | 27000.00 | c | Car2-C1-20150925-C2-028 < Car-inventory < Vehicle-inventory | 88-654306 | 2016-03-01 | 1 |
| 28 | 88-654306 | 400.00 | f | Inven111 < Inven11 < Inven1 | 88-654306 | 2016-03-04 | 40 |
| 29 | 88-654306 | 800.00 | f | Inven112 < Inven11 < Inven1 | 88-654306 | 2016-03-04 | 20 |
| 30 | 88-654306 | 80.00 | f | Inven121 < Inven12 < Inven1 | 88-654306 | 2016-03-04 | 100 |
| 31 | 88-654306 | 400.00 | f | Inven122 < Inven12 < Inven1 | 88-654306 | 2016-03-04 | 8 |
| 32 | 88-654306 | 150.00 | f | Inven21 < Inven2 | 88-654306 | 2016-03-04 | 5 |
| 33 | 88-654306 | -90.00 | f | Inven332 < Inven33 < Inven3 | 88-654306 | 2016-03-04 | -2 |
| 34 | 88-654306 | 30.00 | f | HGFCVB parts < QASXC parts < Inven3 | 88-654306 | 2016-03-04 | 3 |
| 35 | 88-654306 | 40.00 | f | PPGHUP parts < ASDUP parts < Inven3 | 88-654306 | 2016-03-04 | 2 |
| 36 | 88-654306 | 20.00 | f | Inven411 < Inven41 < Inven4 | 88-654306 | 2016-03-04 | 4 |
| 37 | 88-654306 | 180.00 | f | Inven332 < Inven33 < Inven3 | 88-654306 | 2016-03-04 | 1 |
| 38 | 88-654310 | -1540.00 | t | Supplies1-P2-20150920-SUP1-200T | 88-654306 | 2016-04-30 | -110 |
| 39 | 88-654310 | -1760.00 | t | Supplies2-P2-20150920-SUP2-200T | 88-654306 | 2016-04-30 | -110 |
| 40 | 88-654306 | -112.00 | f | Supplies1-P2-20150920-SUP1-200T | 88-654306 | 2016-04-30 | -8 |
| 41 | 88-654306 | -32.00 | f | Supplies2-P2-20150920-SUP2-200T | 88-654306 | 2016-04-30 | -2 |
| 42 | 88-654306 | -33700.00 | p | Truck1-C1-20160430-T1-012 < Truck-inventory < Vehicle-inventory | 88-654306 | 2016-04-30 | -1 |
| 43 | 88-654306 | -33700.00 | p | Truck1-C1-20160430-T1-013 < Truck-inventory < Vehicle-inventory | 88-654306 | 2016-04-30 | -1 |
| 44 | 88-654306 | -30000.00 | p | Truck2-C1-20160430-T2-012 < Truck-inventory < Vehicle-inventory | 88-654306 | 2016-04-30 | -1 |
| 45 | 88-654306 | -30000.00 | p | Truck2-C1-20160430-T2-013 < Truck-inventory < Vehicle-inventory | 88-654306 | 2016-04-30 | -1 |
| 46 | 88-654306 | -30000.00 | p | Truck2-C1-20160430-T2-014 < Truck-inventory < Vehicle-inventory | 88-654306 | 2016-04-30 | -1 |
| 47 | 88-654306 | -28000.00 | p | Car1-C1-20160430-C1-030 < Car-inventory < Vehicle-inventory | 88-654306 | 2016-04-30 | -1 |
| 48 | 88-654306 | -28000.00 | p | Car1-C1-20160430-C1-031 < Car-inventory < Vehicle-inventory | 88-654306 | 2016-04-30 | -1 |
| 49 | 88-654306 | -27000.00 | p | Car2-C1-20160430-C2-040 < Car-inventory < Vehicle-inventory | 88-654306 | 2016-04-30 | -1 |
| 50 | 88-654306 | -27000.00 | p | Car2-C1-20160430-C2-041 < Car-inventory < Vehicle-inventory | 88-654306 | 2016-04-30 | -1 |
| 51 | 88-654306 | -26000.00 | p | Car3-C1-20160430-C3-050 < Car-inventory < Vehicle-inventory | Recorder | 2016-04-30 | -1 |
| 52 | 88-654306 | -26000.00 | p | Car3-C1-20160430-C3-051 < Car-inventory < Vehicle-inventory | 88-654306 | 2016-04-30 | -1 |
| 53 | 88-654306 | -26000.00 | p | Car3-C1-20160430-C3-052 < Car-inventory < Vehicle-inventory | 88-654306 | 2016-04-30 | -1 |
| 54 | 88-654306 | -1600.00 | p | Computer server1-C1-20160430-COMS1-042 < Computer server-invent... | 88-654306 | 2016-04-30 | -1 |
| 55 | 88-654306 | -1600.00 | p | Computer server1-C1-20160430-COMS1-043 < Computer server-invent... | 88-654306 | 2016-04-30 | -1 |
| 56 | 88-654306 | -1600.00 | p | Computer server1-C1-20160430-COMS1-044 < Computer server-invent... | 88-654306 | 2016-04-30 | -1 |
| 57 | 88-654306 | -1600.00 | p | Computer server1-C1-20160430-COMS1-045 < Computer server-invent... | 88-654306 | 2016-04-30 | -1 |
| 58 | 88-654306 | -1500.00 | p | Computer server2-C1-20160430-COMS2-047 < Computer server-invent... | 88-654306 | 2016-04-30 | -1 |
| 59 | 88-654306 | -1500.00 | p | Computer server2-C1-20160430-COMS2-048 < Computer server-invent... | 88-654306 | 2016-04-30 | -1 |
| 60 | 88-654306 | -1500.00 | p | Computer server2-C1-20160430-COMS2-049 < Computer server-invent... | 88-654306 | 2016-04-30 | -1 |
| 61 | 88-654306 | -1500.00 | p | Computer server2-C1-20160430-COMS2-050 < Computer server-invent... | 88-654306 | 2016-04-30 | -1 |
| 62 | 88-654306 | -1000.00 | p | Computer1-C1-20160430-COM1-059 < Computer-inventory | 88-654306 | 2016-04-30 | -1 |
| 63 | 88-654306 | -1000.00 | p | Computer1-C1-20160430-COM1-060 < Computer-inventory | 88-654306 | 2016-04-30 | -1 |

| | IDM | Amount | Symbol | MultiSubaccount | Recorder | TransDate | Unit |
|---|---|---|---|---|---|---|---|
| 64 | 88-654306 | -1000.00 | p | Computer1-C1-20160430-COM1-061 < Computer-inventory | 88-654306 | 2016-04-30 | -1 |
| 65 | 88-654306 | -1000.00 | p | Computer1-C1-20160430-COM1-062 < Computer-inventory | 88-654306 | 2016-04-30 | -1 |
| 66 | 88-654306 | -1000.00 | p | Computer1-C1-20160430-COM1-063 < Computer-inventory | 88-654306 | 2016-04-30 | -1 |
| 67 | 88-654306 | -1000.00 | p | Computer1-C1-20160430-COM1-064 < Computer-inventory | 88-654306 | 2016-04-30 | -1 |
| 68 | 88-654306 | -1000.00 | p | Computer1-C1-20160430-COM1-065 < Computer-inventory | 88-654306 | 2016-04-30 | -1 |
| 69 | 88-654306 | -1000.00 | p | Computer1-C1-20160430-COM1-066 < Computer-inventory | 88-654306 | 2016-04-30 | -1 |
| 70 | 88-654306 | -1000.00 | p | Computer1-C1-20160430-COM1-067 < Computer-inventory | 88-654306 | 2016-04-30 | -1 |
| 71 | 88-654306 | -1000.00 | p | Computer1-C1-20160430-COM1-068 < Computer-inventory | 88-654306 | 2016-04-30 | -1 |
| 72 | 88-654306 | -920.00 | p | Computer2-C1-20160430-COM2-069 < Computer-inventory | 88-654306 | 2016-04-30 | -1 |
| 73 | 88-654306 | -920.00 | p | Computer2-C1-20160430-COM2-070 < Computer-inventory | 88-654306 | 2016-04-30 | -1 |
| 74 | 88-654306 | -920.00 | p | Computer2-C1-20160430-COM2-071 < Computer-inventory | 88-654306 | 2016-04-30 | -1 |
| 75 | 88-654306 | -920.00 | p | Computer2-C1-20160430-COM2-072 < Computer-inventory | 88-654306 | 2016-04-30 | -1 |
| 76 | 88-654306 | -920.00 | p | Computer2-C1-20160430-COM2-073 < Computer-inventory | 88-654306 | 2016-04-30 | -1 |
| 77 | 88-654306 | -920.00 | p | Computer2-C1-20160430-COM2-074 < Computer-inventory | 88-654306 | 2016-04-30 | -1 |
| 78 | 88-654306 | -920.00 | p | Computer2-C1-20160430-COM2-075 < Computer-inventory | 88-654306 | 2016-04-30 | -1 |
| 79 | 88-654306 | -920.00 | p | Computer2-C1-20160430-COM2-076 < Computer-inventory | 88-654306 | 2016-04-30 | -1 |
| 80 | 88-654306 | -920.00 | p | Computer2-C1-20160430-COM2-077 < Computer-inventory | 88-654306 | 2016-04-30 | -1 |
| 81 | 88-654306 | -920.00 | p | Computer2-C1-20160430-COM2-078 < Computer-inventory | 88-654306 | 2016-04-30 | -1 |
| 82 | 88-654306 | -830.00 | p | Computer3-C1-20160430-COM3-103 < Computer-inventory | 88-654306 | 2016-04-30 | -1 |
| 83 | 88-654306 | -830.00 | p | Computer3-C1-20160430-COM3-104 < Computer-inventory | 88-654306 | 2016-04-30 | -1 |
| 84 | 88-654306 | -830.00 | p | Computer3-C1-20160430-COM3-105 < Computer-inventory | 88-654306 | 2016-04-30 | -1 |
| 85 | 88-654306 | -830.00 | p | Computer3-C1-20160430-COM3-106 < Computer-inventory | 88-654306 | 2016-04-30 | -1 |
| 86 | 88-654306 | -830.00 | p | Computer3-C1-20160430-COM3-107 < Computer-inventory | 88-654306 | 2016-04-30 | -1 |
| 87 | 88-654306 | -830.00 | p | Computer3-C1-20160430-COM3-108 < Computer-inventory | 88-654306 | 2016-04-30 | -1 |
| 88 | 88-654306 | -830.00 | p | Computer3-C1-20160430-COM3-109 < Computer-inventory | 88-654306 | 2016-04-30 | -1 |
| 89 | 88-654306 | -830.00 | p | Computer3-C1-20160430-COM3-110 < Computer-inventory | 88-654306 | 2016-04-30 | -1 |
| 90 | 88-654306 | -830.00 | p | Computer3-C1-20160430-COM3-111 < Computer-inventory | 88-654306 | 2016-04-30 | -1 |
| 91 | 88-654306 | -830.00 | p | Computer3-C1-20160430-COM3-112 < Computer-inventory | 88-654306 | 2016-04-30 | -1 |
| 92 | 88-654306 | -830.00 | p | Computer3-C1-20160430-COM3-113 < Computer-inventory | 88-654306 | 2016-04-30 | -1 |
| 93 | 88-654306 | -830.00 | p | Computer3-C1-20160430-COM3-114 < Computer-inventory | 88-654306 | 2016-04-30 | -1 |
| 94 | 88-654306 | -770.00 | p | Computer4-C1-20160430-COM4-103 < Computer-inventory | 88-654306 | 2016-04-30 | -1 |
| 95 | 88-654306 | -770.00 | p | Computer4-C1-20160430-COM4-104 < Computer-inventory | 88-654306 | 2016-04-30 | -1 |
| 96 | 88-654306 | -770.00 | p | Computer4-C1-20160430-COM4-105 < Computer-inventory | 88-654306 | 2016-04-30 | -1 |
| 97 | 88-654306 | -770.00 | p | Computer4-C1-20160430-COM4-106 < Computer-inventory | 88-654306 | 2016-04-30 | -1 |
| 98 | 88-654306 | -770.00 | p | Computer4-C1-20160430-COM4-107 < Computer-inventory | 88-654306 | 2016-04-30 | -1 |
| 99 | 88-654306 | -770.00 | p | Computer4-C1-20160430-COM4-108 < Computer-inventory | 88-654306 | 2016-04-30 | -1 |
| 100 | 88-654306 | -770.00 | p | Computer4-C1-20160430-COM4-109 < Computer-inventory | 88-654306 | 2016-04-30 | -1 |
| 101 | 88-654306 | -770.00 | p | Computer4-C1-20160430-COM4-110 < Computer-inventory | 88-654306 | 2016-04-30 | -1 |
| 102 | 88-654306 | -770.00 | p | Computer4-C1-20160430-COM4-111 < Computer-inventory | 88-654306 | 2016-04-30 | -1 |
| 103 | 88-654306 | -770.00 | p | Computer4-C1-20160430-COM4-112 < Computer-inventory | 88-654306 | 2016-04-30 | -1 |
| 104 | 88-654306 | -770.00 | p | Computer4-C1-20160430-COM4-113 < Computer-inventory | 88-654306 | 2016-04-30 | -1 |
| 105 | 88-654306 | -770.00 | p | Computer4-C1-20160430-COM4-114 < Computer-inventory | 88-654306 | 2016-04-30 | -1 |
| 106 | 88-654306 | -770.00 | p | Computer4-C1-20160430-COM4-115 < Computer-inventory | 88-654306 | 2016-04-30 | -1 |
| 107 | 88-654306 | -770.00 | p | Computer4-C1-20160430-COM4-116 < Computer-inventory | 88-654306 | 2016-04-30 | -1 |
| 108 | 88-654306 | -770.00 | p | Computer4-C1-20160430-COM4-117 < Computer-inventory | 88-654306 | 2016-04-30 | -1 |
| 109 | 88-654310 | 1540.00 | t | Supplies1-P2-20150920-SUP1-200T | 88-654306 | 2016-04-30 | 110 |
| 110 | 88-654310 | 1760.00 | t | Supplies2-P2-20150920-SUP2-200T | 88-654306 | 2016-04-30 | 110 |
| 111 | 88-654310 | -1540.00 | t | Supplies1-P2-20160430-Supp1-200T | 88-654306 | 2016-04-30 | -110 |
| 112 | 88-654310 | -1760.00 | t | Supplies2-P2-20160430-Supp2-200T | 88-654306 | 2016-04-30 | -110 |
| 113 | 88-654307 | -8300.00 | t | Car1 part1-C2-20150816-C1P1-061 < Car1 parts < Vehicle parts | 88-654306 | 2016-05-01 | -1 |
| 114 | 88-654307 | -8300.00 | t | Car1 part1-C2-20150816-C1P1-062 < Car1 parts < Vehicle parts | 88-654306 | 2016-05-01 | -1 |
| 115 | 88-654307 | -8300.00 | t | Car1 part1-C2-20150816-C1P1-063 < Car1 parts < Vehicle parts | 88-654306 | 2016-05-01 | -1 |
| 116 | 88-654307 | -7200.00 | t | Car1 part2-C2-20150816-C1P2-069 < Car1 parts < Vehicle parts | 88-654306 | 2016-05-01 | -1 |
| 117 | 88-654307 | -7200.00 | t | Car1 part2-C2-20150816-C1P2-070 < Car1 parts < Vehicle parts | 88-654306 | 2016-05-01 | -1 |
| 118 | 88-654307 | -7200.00 | t | Car1 part2-C2-20150816-C1P2-071 < Car1 parts < Vehicle parts | 88-654306 | 2016-05-01 | -1 |
| 119 | 88-654307 | -5100.00 | t | Car1 part3-C2-20150816-C1P3-070 < Car1 parts < Vehicle parts | 88-654306 | 2016-05-01 | -1 |
| 120 | 88-654307 | -5100.00 | t | Car1 part3-C2-20150816-C1P3-071 < Car1 parts < Vehicle parts | 88-654306 | 2016-05-01 | -1 |
| 121 | 88-654307 | -5100.00 | t | Car1 part3-C2-20150816-C1P3-072 < Car1 parts < Vehicle parts | 88-654306 | 2016-05-01 | -1 |
| 122 | 88-654307 | -7900.00 | t | Car2 part1-C2-20150902-C2P1-077 < Car2 parts < Vehicle parts | 88-654306 | 2016-05-01 | -1 |
| 123 | 88-654307 | -7900.00 | t | Car2 part1-C2-20150902-C2P1-078 < Car2 parts < Vehicle parts | 88-654306 | 2016-05-01 | -1 |
| 124 | 88-654307 | -7900.00 | t | Car2 part1-C2-20150902-C2P1-079 < Car2 parts < Vehicle parts | 88-654306 | 2016-05-01 | -1 |
| 125 | 88-654307 | -6800.00 | t | Car2 part2-C2-20150902-C2P2-081 < Car2 parts < Vehicle parts | 88-654306 | 2016-05-01 | -1 |
| 126 | 88-654307 | -6800.00 | t | Car2 part2-C2-20150902-C2P2-082 < Car2 parts < Vehicle parts | 88-654306 | 2016-05-01 | -1 |
| 127 | 88-654307 | -6800.00 | t | Car2 part2-C2-20150902-C2P2-083 < Car2 parts < Vehicle parts | 88-654306 | 2016-05-01 | -1 |
| 128 | 88-654307 | -4900.00 | t | Car2 part3-C2-20150902-C2P3-083 < Car2 parts < Vehicle parts | 88-654306 | 2016-05-01 | -1 |
| 129 | 88-654307 | -4900.00 | t | Car2 part3-C2-20150902-C2P3-084 < Car2 parts < Vehicle parts | 88-654306 | 2016-05-01 | -1 |

| | IDM | Amount | Symbol | MultiSubaccount | Recorder | TransDate | Unit |
|---|---|---|---|---|---|---|---|
| 130 | 88-654307 | -4900.00 | t | Car2 part3-C2-20150902-C2P3-085 < Car2 parts < Vehicle parts | 88-654306 | 2016-05-01 | -1 |
| 131 | 88-654307 | -7500.00 | t | Car3 part1-C2-20150902-C3P1-084 < Car3 parts < Vehicle parts | 88-654306 | 2016-05-01 | -1 |
| 132 | 88-654307 | -7500.00 | t | Car3 part1-C2-20150902-C3P1-085 < Car3 parts < Vehicle parts | 88-654306 | 2016-05-01 | -1 |
| 133 | 88-654307 | -7500.00 | t | Car3 part1-C2-20150902-C3P1-086 < Car3 parts < Vehicle parts | 88-654306 | 2016-05-01 | -1 |
| 134 | 88-654307 | -6400.00 | t | Car3 part2-C2-20150902-C3P2-087 < Car3 parts < Vehicle parts | 88-654306 | 2016-05-01 | -1 |
| 135 | 88-654307 | -6400.00 | t | Car3 part2-C2-20150902-C3P2-088 < Car3 parts < Vehicle parts | 88-654306 | 2016-05-01 | -1 |
| 136 | 88-654307 | -6400.00 | t | Car3 part2-C2-20150902-C3P2-089 < Car3 parts < Vehicle parts | 88-654306 | 2016-05-01 | -1 |
| 137 | 88-654307 | -4700.00 | t | Car3 part3-C2-20150902-C3P3-094 < Car3 parts < Vehicle parts | 88-654306 | 2016-05-01 | -1 |
| 138 | 88-654307 | -4700.00 | t | Car3 part3-C2-20150902-C3P3-095 < Car3 parts < Vehicle parts | 88-654306 | 2016-05-01 | -1 |
| 139 | 88-654307 | -4700.00 | t | Car3 part3-C2-20150902-C3P3-096 < Car3 parts < Vehicle parts | 88-654306 | 2016-05-01 | -1 |
| 140 | 88-654307 | -2400.00 | t | Computer server1 part1-C2-20150709-COMS1P1-10T < Computer serv... | 88-654306 | 2016-05-01 | -4 |
| 141 | 88-654307 | -1600.00 | t | Computer server1 part2-C2-20150709-COMS1P2-10T < Computer serv... | 88-654306 | 2016-05-01 | -4 |
| 142 | 88-654307 | -2160.00 | t | Computer server2 part1-C2-20150709-COMS2P1-10T < Computer serv... | 88-654306 | 2016-05-01 | -4 |
| 143 | 88-654307 | -1520.00 | t | Computer server2 part2-C2-20150709-COMS2P2-10T < Computer serv... | 88-654306 | 2016-05-01 | -4 |
| 144 | 88-654307 | -5040.00 | t | Computer1 part1-C2-20150715-COM1P1-20T < Computer parts | 88-654306 | 2016-05-01 | -14 |
| 145 | 88-654307 | -4340.00 | t | Computer1 part2-C2-20150715-COM1P2-20T < Computer parts | 88-654306 | 2016-05-01 | -14 |
| 146 | 88-654307 | -4480.00 | t | Computer2 part1-C2-20150715-COM2P1-20T < Computer parts | 88-654306 | 2016-05-01 | -14 |
| 147 | 88-654307 | -4060.00 | t | Computer2 part2-C2-20150715-COM2P2-20T < Computer parts | 88-654306 | 2016-05-01 | -14 |
| 148 | 88-654307 | -3920.00 | t | Computer3 part1-C2-20150715-COM3P1-20T < Computer parts | 88-654306 | 2016-05-01 | -14 |
| 149 | 88-654307 | -3640.00 | t | Computer3 part2-C2-20150715-COM3P2-20T < Computer parts | 88-654306 | 2016-05-01 | -14 |
| 150 | 88-654307 | -3500.00 | t | Computer4 part1-C2-20150715-COM4P1-20T < Computer parts | 88-654306 | 2016-05-01 | -14 |
| 151 | 88-654307 | -3360.00 | t | Computer4 part2-C2-20150715-COM4P2-20T < Computer parts | 88-654306 | 2016-05-01 | -14 |
| 152 | 88-654308 | -3000.00 | t | Inven111-C3-20150922-In111-1000T < Inven11 < Inven1 | 88-654306 | 2016-05-01 | -300 |
| 153 | 88-654308 | -8000.00 | t | Inven112-C3-20150922-In112-800T < Inven11 < Inven1 | 88-654306 | 2016-05-01 | -200 |
| 154 | 88-654308 | -4800.00 | t | Inven121-C3-20150922-In121-20000T < Inven12 < Inven1 | 88-654306 | 2016-05-01 | -60... |
| 155 | 88-654308 | -10000.00 | t | Inven122-C3-20150922-In122-1000T < Inven12 < Inven1 | 88-654306 | 2016-05-01 | -200 |
| 156 | 88-654308 | -9000.00 | t | Inven21-C3-20150922-In21-1250T < Inven2 | 88-654306 | 2016-05-01 | -300 |
| 157 | 88-654308 | -6000.00 | t | Inven221-C3-20150922-In221-750T < Inven22 < Inven2 | 88-654306 | 2016-05-01 | -200 |
| 158 | 88-654308 | -5000.00 | t | Inven222-C3-20150922-In222-400T < Inven22 < Inven2 | 88-654306 | 2016-05-01 | -100 |
| 159 | 88-654308 | -4000.00 | t | PPUK parts-C3-20150922-PU-500T < ASD parts < Inven2 | 88-654306 | 2016-05-01 | -100 |
| 160 | 88-654308 | -1000.00 | t | PPGH parts-C3-20150922-PG-1600T < ASD parts < Inven2 | 88-654306 | 2016-05-01 | -500 |
| 161 | 88-654309 | -1500.00 | t | Inven31-P1-20151125-In31-1000T < Inven3 | 88-654306 | 2016-05-01 | -150 |
| 162 | 88-654309 | -7500.00 | t | Inven32-P1-20151125-In32-1000T < Inven3 | 88-654306 | 2016-05-01 | -150 |
| 163 | 88-654309 | -3000.00 | t | Inven331-P1-20151125-In331-1000T < Inven33 < Inven3 | 88-654306 | 2016-05-01 | -150 |
| 164 | 88-654309 | -6750.00 | t | Inven332-P1-20151125-In332-1000T < Inven33 < Inven3 | 88-654306 | 2016-05-01 | -150 |
| 165 | 88-654309 | -1500.00 | t | HGFCVB parts-P1-20151125-HGP-1000T < QASXC parts < Inven3 | 88-654306 | 2016-05-01 | -150 |
| 166 | 88-654309 | -3000.00 | t | PPGHUP parts-P1-20151125-PPP-1000T < ASDUP parts < Inven3 | 88-654306 | 2016-05-01 | -150 |
| 167 | 88-654310 | -500.00 | t | Inven411-P2-20151127-In411-1000T < Inven41 < Inven4 | 88-654306 | 2016-05-01 | -100 |
| 168 | 88-654310 | -1850.00 | t | Inven412-P2-20151127-In412-1000T < Inven41 < Inven4 | 88-654306 | 2016-05-01 | -100 |
| 169 | 88-654310 | -2000.00 | t | TTTCU parts-P2-20151127-TTP-1000T < TTT parts < Inven4 | 88-654306 | 2016-05-01 | -100 |
| 170 | 88-654310 | -2000.00 | t | RRRHJK parts-P2-20151127-RRP-1000T < Inven4 | 88-654306 | 2016-05-01 | -100 |
| 171 | 88-654301 | 1600.00 | c | Computer server1-C1-201501007-COMS1-039 < Computer server-inven... | 88-654306 | 2016-05-01 | 1 |
| 172 | 88-654301 | 1000.00 | c | Computer1-C1-201501008-COM1-055 < Computer-inventory | 88-654306 | 2016-05-01 | 1 |
| 173 | 88-654301 | 920.00 | c | Computer2-C1-201501008-COM2-065 < Computer-inventory | 88-654306 | 2016-05-01 | 1 |
| 174 | 88-654302 | 28000.00 | c | Car1-C1-20150921-C1-023 < Car-inventory < Vehicle-inventory | 88-654306 | 2016-05-01 | 1 |
| 175 | 88-654306 | 3000.00 | f | Inven111-C3-20150922-In111-1000T < Inven11 < Inven1 | 88-654306 | 2016-05-02 | 300 |
| 176 | 88-654306 | 8000.00 | f | Inven112-C3-20150922-In112-800T < Inven11 < Inven1 | 88-654306 | 2016-05-02 | 200 |
| 177 | 88-654306 | 4800.00 | f | Inven121-C3-20150922-In121-20000T < Inven12 < Inven1 | 88-654306 | 2016-05-02 | 6000 |
| 178 | 88-654306 | 10000.00 | f | Inven122-C3-20150922-In122-1000T < Inven12 < Inven1 | 88-654306 | 2016-05-02 | 200 |
| 179 | 88-654306 | 9000.00 | f | Inven21-C3-20150922-In21-1250T < Inven2 | 88-654306 | 2016-05-02 | 300 |
| 180 | 88-654306 | 6000.00 | f | Inven221-C3-20150922-In221-750T < Inven22 < Inven2 | 88-654306 | 2016-05-02 | 200 |
| 181 | 88-654306 | 5000.00 | f | Inven222-C3-20150922-In222-400T < Inven22 < Inven2 | 88-654306 | 2016-05-02 | 100 |
| 182 | 88-654306 | 4000.00 | f | PPUK parts-C3-20150922-PU-500T < ASD parts < Inven2 | 88-654306 | 2016-05-02 | 100 |
| 183 | 88-654306 | 1000.00 | f | PPGH parts-C3-20150922-PG-1600T < ASD parts < Inven2 | 88-654306 | 2016-05-02 | 500 |
| 184 | 88-654306 | 1500.00 | f | Inven31-P1-20151125-In31-1000T < Inven3 | 88-654306 | 2016-05-02 | 150 |
| 185 | 88-654306 | 7500.00 | f | Inven32-P1-20151125-In32-1000T < Inven3 | 88-654306 | 2016-05-02 | 150 |
| 186 | 88-654306 | 3000.00 | f | Inven331-P1-20151125-In331-1000T < Inven33 < Inven3 | 88-654306 | 2016-05-02 | 150 |
| 187 | 88-654306 | 6750.00 | f | Inven332-P1-20151125-In332-1000T < Inven33 < Inven3 | 88-654306 | 2016-05-02 | 150 |
| 188 | 88-654306 | 1500.00 | f | HGFCVB parts-P1-20151125-HGP-1000T < QASXC parts < Inven3 | 88-654306 | 2016-05-02 | 150 |
| 189 | 88-654306 | 3000.00 | f | PPGHUP parts-P1-20151125-PPP-1000T < ASDUP parts < Inven3 | 88-654306 | 2016-05-02 | 150 |
| 190 | 88-654306 | 500.00 | f | Inven411-P2-20151127-In411-1000T < Inven41 < Inven4 | 88-654306 | 2016-05-02 | 100 |
| 191 | 88-654306 | 1850.00 | f | Inven412-P2-20151127-In412-1000T < Inven41 < Inven4 | 88-654306 | 2016-05-02 | 100 |
| 192 | 88-654306 | 2000.00 | f | TTTCU parts-P2-20151127-TTP-1000T < TTT parts < Inven4 | 88-654306 | 2016-05-02 | 100 |
| 193 | 88-654306 | 2000.00 | f | RRRHJK parts-P2-20151127-RRP-1000T < Inven4 | 88-654306 | 2016-05-02 | 100 |
| 194 | 88-654306 | 8700.00 | f | Truck1 part1 < Truck1 parts < Vehicle parts | 88-654306 | 2016-05-02 | 1 |
| 195 | 88-654306 | 7600.00 | f | Truck1 part2 < Truck1 parts < Vehicle parts | 88-654306 | 2016-05-02 | 1 |

| | IDM | Amount | Symbol | MultiSubaccount | Recorder | TransDate | Unit |
|---|---|---|---|---|---|---|---|
| 196 | 88-654306 | 5800.00 | f | Truck1 part3 < Truck1 parts < Vehicle parts | 88-654306 | 2016-05-02 | 1 |
| 197 | 88-654306 | 8500.00 | f | Truck2 part1 < Truck2 parts < Vehicle parts | 88-654306 | 2016-05-02 | 1 |
| 198 | 88-654306 | 7200.00 | f | Truck2 part2 < Truck2 parts < Vehicle parts | 88-654306 | 2016-05-02 | 1 |
| 199 | 88-654306 | 5400.00 | f | Truck2 part3 < Truck2 parts < Vehicle parts | 88-654306 | 2016-05-02 | 1 |
| 200 | 88-654306 | 8300.00 | f | Car1 part1 < Car1 parts < Vehicle parts | 88-654306 | 2016-05-02 | 1 |
| 201 | 88-654306 | 8300.00 | f | Car1 part1-C2-20150816-C1P1-061 < Car1 parts < Vehicle parts | 88-654306 | 2016-05-02 | 1 |
| 202 | 88-654306 | 8300.00 | f | Car1 part1-C2-20150816-C1P1-062 < Car1 parts < Vehicle parts | 88-654306 | 2016-05-02 | 1 |
| 203 | 88-654306 | 8300.00 | f | Car1 part1-C2-20150816-C1P1-063 < Car1 parts < Vehicle parts | 88-654306 | 2016-05-02 | 1 |
| 204 | 88-654306 | 7200.00 | f | Car1 part2 < Car1 parts < Vehicle parts | 88-654306 | 2016-05-02 | 1 |
| 205 | 88-654306 | 7200.00 | f | Car1 part2-C2-20150816-C1P2-069 < Car1 parts < Vehicle parts | 88-654306 | 2016-05-02 | 1 |
| 206 | 88-654306 | 7200.00 | f | Car1 part2-C2-20150816-C1P2-070 < Car1 parts < Vehicle parts | 88-654306 | 2016-05-02 | 1 |
| 207 | 88-654306 | 7200.00 | f | Car1 part2-C2-20150816-C1P2-071 < Car1 parts < Vehicle parts | 88-654306 | 2016-05-02 | 1 |
| 208 | 88-654306 | 5100.00 | f | Car1 part3 < Car1 parts < Vehicle parts | 88-654306 | 2016-05-02 | 1 |
| 209 | 88-654306 | 5100.00 | f | Car1 part3-C2-20150816-C1P3-070 < Car1 parts < Vehicle parts | 88-654306 | 2016-05-02 | 1 |
| 210 | 88-654306 | 5100.00 | f | Car1 part3-C2-20150816-C1P3-071 < Car1 parts < Vehicle parts | 88-654306 | 2016-05-02 | 1 |
| 211 | 88-654306 | 5100.00 | f | Car1 part3-C2-20150816-C1P3-072 < Car1 parts < Vehicle parts | 88-654306 | 2016-05-02 | 1 |
| 212 | 88-654306 | 7900.00 | f | Car2 part1 < Car2 parts < Vehicle parts | 88-654306 | 2016-05-02 | 1 |
| 213 | 88-654306 | 7900.00 | f | Car2 part1-C2-20150902-C2P1-077 < Car2 parts < Vehicle parts | 88-654306 | 2016-05-02 | 1 |
| 214 | 88-654306 | 7900.00 | f | Car2 part1-C2-20150902-C2P1-078 < Car2 parts < Vehicle parts | 88-654306 | 2016-05-02 | 1 |
| 215 | 88-654306 | 7900.00 | f | Car2 part1-C2-20150902-C2P1-079 < Car2 parts < Vehicle parts | 88-654306 | 2016-05-02 | 1 |
| 216 | 88-654306 | 6800.00 | f | Car2 part2 < Car2 parts < Vehicle parts | 88-654306 | 2016-05-02 | 1 |
| 217 | 88-654306 | 6800.00 | f | Car2 part2-C2-20150902-C2P2-081 < Car2 parts < Vehicle parts | 88-654306 | 2016-05-02 | 1 |
| 218 | 88-654306 | 6800.00 | f | Car2 part2-C2-20150902-C2P2-082 < Car2 parts < Vehicle parts | 88-654306 | 2016-05-02 | 1 |
| 219 | 88-654306 | 6800.00 | f | Car2 part2-C2-20150902-C2P2-083 < Car2 parts < Vehicle parts | 88-654306 | 2016-05-02 | 1 |
| 220 | 88-654306 | 4900.00 | f | Car2 part3 < Car2 parts < Vehicle parts | 88-654306 | 2016-05-02 | 1 |
| 221 | 88-654306 | 4900.00 | f | Car2 part3-C2-20150902-C2P3-083 < Car2 parts < Vehicle parts | 88-654306 | 2016-05-02 | 1 |
| 222 | 88-654306 | 4900.00 | f | Car2 part3-C2-20150902-C2P3-084 < Car2 parts < Vehicle parts | 88-654306 | 2016-05-02 | 1 |
| 223 | 88-654306 | 4900.00 | f | Car2 part3-C2-20150902-C2P3-085 < Car2 parts < Vehicle parts | 88-654306 | 2016-05-02 | 1 |
| 224 | 88-654306 | 7500.00 | f | Car3 part1 < Car3 parts < Vehicle parts | 88-654306 | 2016-05-02 | 1 |
| 225 | 88-654306 | 7500.00 | f | Car3 part1-C2-20150902-C3P1-084 < Car3 parts < Vehicle parts | 88-654306 | 2016-05-02 | 1 |
| 226 | 88-654306 | 7500.00 | f | Car3 part1-C2-20150902-C3P1-085 < Car3 parts < Vehicle parts | 88-654306 | 2016-05-02 | 1 |
| 227 | 88-654306 | 7500.00 | f | Car3 part1-C2-20150902-C3P1-086 < Car3 parts < Vehicle parts | 88-654306 | 2016-05-02 | 1 |
| 228 | 88-654306 | 6400.00 | f | Car3 part2 < Car3 parts < Vehicle parts | 88-654306 | 2016-05-02 | 1 |
| 229 | 88-654306 | 6400.00 | f | Car3 part2-C2-20150902-C3P2-087 < Car3 parts < Vehicle parts | 88-654306 | 2016-05-02 | 1 |
| 230 | 88-654306 | 6400.00 | f | Car3 part2-C2-20150902-C3P2-088 < Car3 parts < Vehicle parts | 88-654306 | 2016-05-02 | 1 |
| 231 | 88-654306 | 6400.00 | f | Car3 part2-C2-20150902-C3P2-089 < Car3 parts < Vehicle parts | 88-654306 | 2016-05-02 | 1 |
| 232 | 88-654306 | 4700.00 | f | Car3 part3 < Car3 parts < Vehicle parts | 88-654306 | 2016-05-02 | 1 |
| 233 | 88-654306 | 4700.00 | f | Car3 part3-C2-20150902-C3P3-094 < Car3 parts < Vehicle parts | 88-654306 | 2016-05-02 | 1 |
| 234 | 88-654306 | 4700.00 | f | Car3 part3-C2-20150902-C3P3-095 < Car3 parts < Vehicle parts | 88-654306 | 2016-05-02 | 1 |
| 235 | 88-654306 | 4700.00 | f | Car3 part3-C2-20150902-C3P3-096 < Car3 parts < Vehicle parts | 88-654306 | 2016-05-02 | 1 |
| 236 | 88-654306 | 600.00 | f | Computer server1 part1 < Computer server parts < Computer parts | 88-654306 | 2016-05-02 | 1 |
| 237 | 88-654306 | 2400.00 | f | Computer server1 part1-C2-20150709-COMS1P1-10T < Computer serv... | 88-654306 | 2016-05-02 | 4 |
| 238 | 88-654306 | 400.00 | f | Computer server1 part2 < Computer server parts < Computer parts | 88-654306 | 2016-05-02 | 1 |
| 239 | 88-654306 | 1600.00 | f | Computer server1 part2-C2-20150709-COMS1P2-10T < Computer serv... | 88-654306 | 2016-05-02 | 4 |
| 240 | 88-654306 | 540.00 | f | Computer server2 part1 < Computer server parts < Computer parts | 88-654306 | 2016-05-02 | 1 |
| 241 | 88-654306 | 2160.00 | f | Computer server2 part1-C2-20150709-COMS2P1-10T < Computer serv... | 88-654306 | 2016-05-02 | 4 |
| 242 | 88-654306 | 380.00 | f | Computer server2 part2 < Computer server parts < Computer parts | 88-654306 | 2016-05-02 | 1 |
| 243 | 88-654306 | 1520.00 | f | Computer server2 part2-C2-20150709-COMS2P2-10T < Computer serv... | 88-654306 | 2016-05-02 | 4 |
| 244 | 88-654306 | 360.00 | f | Computer1 part1 < Computer parts | 88-654306 | 2016-05-02 | 1 |
| 245 | 88-654306 | 5040.00 | f | Computer1 part1-C2-20150715-COM1P1-20T < Computer parts | 88-654306 | 2016-05-02 | 14 |
| 246 | 88-654306 | 310.00 | f | Computer1 part2 < Computer parts | 88-654306 | 2016-05-02 | 1 |
| 247 | 88-654306 | 4340.00 | f | Computer1 part2-C2-20150715-COM1P2-20T < Computer parts | 88-654306 | 2016-05-02 | 14 |
| 248 | 88-654306 | 320.00 | f | Computer2 part1 < Computer parts | 88-654306 | 2016-05-02 | 1 |
| 249 | 88-654306 | 4480.00 | f | Computer2 part1-C2-20150715-COM2P1-20T < Computer parts | 88-654306 | 2016-05-02 | 14 |
| 250 | 88-654306 | 290.00 | f | Computer2 part2 < Computer parts | 88-654306 | 2016-05-02 | 1 |
| 251 | 88-654306 | 4060.00 | f | Computer2 part2-C2-20150715-COM2P2-20T < Computer parts | 88-654306 | 2016-05-02 | 14 |
| 252 | 88-654306 | 280.00 | f | Computer3 part1 < Computer parts | 88-654306 | 2016-05-02 | 1 |
| 253 | 88-654306 | 3920.00 | f | Computer3 part1-C2-20150715-COM3P1-20T < Computer parts | 88-654306 | 2016-05-02 | 14 |
| 254 | 88-654306 | 260.00 | f | Computer3 part2 < Computer parts | 88-654306 | 2016-05-02 | 1 |
| 255 | 88-654306 | 3640.00 | f | Computer3 part2-C2-20150715-COM3P2-20T < Computer parts | 88-654306 | 2016-05-02 | 14 |
| 256 | 88-654306 | 250.00 | f | Computer4 part1 < Computer parts | 88-654306 | 2016-05-02 | 1 |
| 257 | 88-654306 | 3500.00 | f | Computer4 part1-C2-20150715-COM4P1-20T < Computer parts | 88-654306 | 2016-05-02 | 14 |
| 258 | 88-654306 | 240.00 | f | Computer4 part2 < Computer parts | 88-654306 | 2016-05-02 | 1 |
| 259 | 88-654306 | 3360.00 | f | Computer4 part2-C2-20150715-COM4P2-20T < Computer parts | 88-654306 | 2016-05-02 | 14 |
| 260 | 88-654306 | 1344.00 | f | Supplies1-P2-20160430-Supp1-200T | 88-654306 | 2016-05-20 | 96 |
| 261 | 88-654306 | 1456.00 | f | Supplies2-P2-20160430-Supp2-200T | 88-654306 | 2016-05-20 | 91 |

| | IDM | Amount | Symbol | MultiSubaccount | Recorder | TransDate | Unit |
|---|---|---|---|---|---|---|---|
| 262 | 88-654306 | 1500.00 | e | Computer server2-C1-201501008-COMS2-045 < Computer server-inven... | 88-654306 | 2016-06-01 | 1 |
| 263 | 88-654306 | 1000.00 | e | Computer1-C1-201501008-COM1-058 < Computer-inventory | 88-654306 | 2016-06-01 | 1 |
| 264 | 88-654306 | 1000.00 | e | Computer1-C1-20160430-COM1-066 < Computer-inventory | 88-654306 | 2016-06-01 | 1 |
| 265 | 88-654308 | 1600.00 | c | Computer server1-C1-20160430-COMS1-044 < Computer server-invent... | 88-654306 | 2016-06-01 | 1 |
| 266 | 88-654308 | 1000.00 | c | Computer1-C1-20160430-COM1-061 < Computer-inventory | 88-654306 | 2016-06-01 | 1 |
| 267 | 88-654308 | 920.00 | c | Computer2-C1-20160430-COM2-071 < Computer-inventory | 88-654306 | 2016-06-01 | 1 |
| 268 | 909876508 | 770.00 | c | Computer4-C1-20160430-COM4-117 < Computer-inventory | 88-654306 | 2016-07-19 | 1 |
| 269 | 88-654304 | 1600.00 | c | Computer server1-C1-201501008-COMS1-041 < Computer server-inven... | 88-654306 | 2016-08-01 | 1 |
| 270 | 88-654304 | 1000.00 | c | Computer1-C1-201501008-COM1-057 < Computer-inventory | 88-654306 | 2016-08-01 | 1 |
| 271 | 88-654304 | 920.00 | c | Computer2-C1-201501008-COM2-067 < Computer-inventory | 88-654306 | 2016-08-01 | 1 |
| 272 | 909876516 | 26000.00 | c | Car3-C1-20160430-C3-052 < Car-inventory < Vehicle-inventory | 88-654306 | 2016-08-01 | 1 |
| 273 | 88-654307 | 1600.00 | c | Computer server1-C1-20160430-COMS1-043 < Computer server-invent... | 88-654306 | 2016-08-01 | 1 |
| 274 | 88-654307 | 1000.00 | c | Computer1-C1-20160430-COM1-060 < Computer-inventory | 88-654306 | 2016-08-01 | 1 |
| 275 | 88-654307 | 920.00 | c | Computer2-C1-20160430-COM2-070 < Computer-inventory | 88-654306 | 2016-08-01 | 1 |
| 276 | 909876501 | 1000.00 | c | Computer1-C1-20160430-COM1-067 < Computer-inventory | 88-654306 | 2016-08-02 | 1 |
| 277 | 909876511 | 920.00 | c | Computer2-C1-20160430-COM2-073 < Computer-inventory | 88-654306 | 2016-08-10 | 1 |
| 278 | 88-654310 | 26000.00 | c | Car3-C1-20150925-C3-029 < Car-inventory < Vehicle-inventory | 88-654306 | 2016-09-02 | 1 |
| 279 | 88-654303 | 1600.00 | c | Computer server1-C1-201501007-COMS1-040 < Computer server-inven... | 88-654306 | 2016-10-01 | 1 |
| 280 | 88-654303 | 1000.00 | c | Computer1-C1-201501008-COM1-056 < Computer-inventory | 88-654306 | 2016-10-01 | 1 |
| 281 | 88-654303 | 920.00 | c | Computer2-C1-201501008-COM2-066 < Computer-inventory | 88-654306 | 2016-10-01 | 1 |
| 282 | 88-654305 | 1600.00 | c | Computer server1-C1-20160430-COMS1-042 < Computer server-invent... | 88-654306 | 2016-10-01 | 1 |
| 283 | 88-654305 | 1000.00 | c | Computer1-C1-20160430-COM1-059 < Computer-inventory | 88-654306 | 2016-10-01 | 1 |
| 284 | 88-654305 | 920.00 | c | Computer2-C1-20160430-COM2-069 < Computer-inventory | 88-654306 | 2016-10-01 | 1 |
| 285 | 88-654309 | 1500.00 | c | Computer server2-C1-20160430-COMS2-047 < Computer server-invent... | 88-654306 | 2016-10-01 | 1 |
| 286 | 88-654309 | 1000.00 | c | Computer1-C1-20160430-COM1-063 < Computer-inventory | 88-654306 | 2016-10-01 | 1 |
| 287 | 88-654309 | 1000.00 | c | Computer1-C1-20160430-COM1-064 < Computer-inventory | 88-654306 | 2016-10-01 | 1 |
| 288 | 909876513 | 27000.00 | c | Car2-C1-20160430-C2-040 < Car-inventory < Vehicle-inventory | 88-654306 | 2016-10-05 | 1 |
| 289 | 88-654306 | -1000.00 | p | Computer1-C1-20161121-COM1-085 < Computer-inventory | 88-654306 | 2016-11-21 | -1 |
| 290 | 88-654306 | -1000.00 | p | Computer1-C1-20161121-COM1-086 < Computer-inventory | 88-654306 | 2016-11-21 | -1 |
| 291 | 88-654306 | -1000.00 | p | Computer1-C1-20161121-COM1-087 < Computer-inventory | 88-654306 | 2016-11-21 | -1 |
| 292 | 88-654306 | -1000.00 | p | Computer1-C1-20161121-COM1-088 < Computer-inventory | 88-654306 | 2016-11-21 | -1 |
| 293 | 88-654306 | -1000.00 | p | Computer1-C1-20161121-COM1-089 < Computer-inventory | 88-654306 | 2016-11-21 | -1 |
| 294 | 88-654306 | -1000.00 | p | Computer1-C1-20161121-COM1-090 < Computer-inventory | 88-654306 | 2016-11-21 | -1 |
| 295 | 88-654306 | -1000.00 | p | Computer1-C1-20161121-COM1-091 < Computer-inventory | 88-654306 | 2016-11-21 | -1 |
| 296 | 88-654306 | -1000.00 | p | Computer1-C1-20161121-COM1-092 < Computer-inventory | 88-654306 | 2016-11-21 | -1 |
| 297 | 88-654306 | -1000.00 | p | Computer1-C1-20161121-COM1-093 < Computer-inventory | 88-654306 | 2016-11-21 | -1 |
| 298 | 88-654306 | -1000.00 | p | Computer1-C1-20161121-COM1-094 < Computer-inventory | 88-654306 | 2016-11-21 | -1 |
| 299 | 88-654306 | -1000.00 | p | Computer1-C1-20161121-COM1-095 < Computer-inventory | 88-654306 | 2016-11-21 | -1 |
| 300 | 88-654306 | -920.00 | p | Computer2-C1-20161121-COM2-011 < Computer-inventory | 88-654306 | 2016-11-21 | -1 |
| 301 | 88-654306 | -920.00 | p | Computer2-C1-20161121-COM2-012 < Computer-inventory | 88-654306 | 2016-11-21 | -1 |
| 302 | 88-654306 | -920.00 | p | Computer2-C1-20161121-COM2-013 < Computer-inventory | 88-654306 | 2016-11-21 | -1 |
| 303 | 88-654306 | -920.00 | p | Computer2-C1-20161121-COM2-014 < Computer-inventory | 88-654306 | 2016-11-21 | -1 |
| 304 | 88-654306 | -920.00 | p | Computer2-C1-20161121-COM2-015 < Computer-inventory | 88-654306 | 2016-11-21 | -1 |
| 305 | 88-654306 | -920.00 | p | Computer2-C1-20161121-COM2-016 < Computer-inventory | 88-654306 | 2016-11-21 | -1 |
| 306 | 88-654306 | -920.00 | p | Computer2-C1-20161121-COM2-017 < Computer-inventory | 88-654306 | 2016-11-21 | -1 |
| 307 | 88-654306 | -920.00 | p | Computer2-C1-20161121-COM2-018 < Computer-inventory | 88-654306 | 2016-11-21 | -1 |
| 308 | 88-654306 | -920.00 | p | Computer2-C1-20161121-COM2-019 < Computer-inventory | 88-654306 | 2016-11-21 | -1 |
| 309 | 88-654306 | -920.00 | p | Computer2-C1-20161121-COM2-020 < Computer-inventory | 88-654306 | 2016-11-21 | -1 |
| 310 | 88-654306 | -920.00 | p | Computer2-C1-20161121-COM2-021 < Computer-inventory | 88-654306 | 2016-11-21 | -1 |
| 311 | 88-654306 | -920.00 | p | Computer2-C1-20161121-COM2-022 < Computer-inventory | 88-654306 | 2016-11-21 | -1 |
| 312 | 88-654306 | -920.00 | p | Computer2-C1-20161121-COM2-023 < Computer-inventory | 88-654306 | 2016-11-21 | -1 |
| 313 | 88-654306 | -920.00 | p | Computer2-C1-20161121-COM2-024 < Computer-inventory | 88-654306 | 2016-11-21 | -1 |
| 314 | 88-654306 | -920.00 | p | Computer2-C1-20161121-COM2-025 < Computer-inventory | 88-654306 | 2016-11-21 | -1 |
| 315 | 88-654306 | -830.00 | p | Computer3-C1-20161121-COM3-031 < Computer-inventory | 88-654306 | 2016-11-21 | -1 |
| 316 | 88-654306 | -830.00 | p | Computer3-C1-20161121-COM3-032 < Computer-inventory | 88-654306 | 2016-11-21 | -1 |
| 317 | 88-654306 | -830.00 | p | Computer3-C1-20161121-COM3-033 < Computer-inventory | 88-654306 | 2016-11-21 | -1 |
| 318 | 88-654306 | -830.00 | p | Computer3-C1-20161121-COM3-034 < Computer-inventory | 88-654306 | 2016-11-21 | -1 |
| 319 | 88-654306 | -830.00 | p | Computer3-C1-20161121-COM3-035 < Computer-inventory | 88-654306 | 2016-11-21 | -1 |
| 320 | 88-654306 | -830.00 | p | Computer3-C1-20161121-COM3-036 < Computer-inventory | 88-654306 | 2016-11-21 | -1 |
| 321 | 88-654306 | -830.00 | p | Computer3-C1-20161121-COM3-037 < Computer-inventory | 88-654306 | 2016-11-21 | -1 |
| 322 | 88-654306 | -830.00 | p | Computer3-C1-20161121-COM3-038 < Computer-inventory | 88-654306 | 2016-11-21 | -1 |
| 323 | 88-654306 | -830.00 | p | Computer3-C1-20161121-COM3-039 < Computer-inventory | 88-654306 | 2016-11-21 | -1 |
| 324 | 88-654306 | -830.00 | p | Computer3-C1-20161121-COM3-040 < Computer-inventory | 88-654306 | 2016-11-21 | -1 |
| 325 | 88-654306 | -830.00 | p | Computer3-C1-20161121-COM3-041 < Computer-inventory | 88-654306 | 2016-11-21 | -1 |
| 326 | 88-654306 | -830.00 | p | Computer3-C1-20161121-COM3-042 < Computer-inventory | 88-654306 | 2016-11-21 | -1 |
| 327 | 88-654306 | -830.00 | p | Computer3-C1-20161121-COM3-043 < Computer-inventory | 88-654306 | 2016-11-21 | -1 |

| | IDM | Amount | Symbol | MultiSubaccount | Recorder | TransDate | Unit |
|---|---|---|---|---|---|---|---|
| 328 | 88-654306 | -830.00 | p | Computer3-C1-20161121-COM3-044 < Computer-inventory | 88-654306 | 2016-11-21 | -1 |
| 329 | 88-654306 | -830.00 | p | Computer3-C1-20161121-COM3-045 < Computer-inventory | 88-654306 | 2016-11-21 | -1 |
| 330 | 88-654306 | -770.00 | p | Computer4-C1-20161121-COM4-141 < Computer-inventory | 88-654306 | 2016-11-21 | -1 |
| 331 | 88-654306 | -770.00 | p | Computer4-C1-20161121-COM4-142 < Computer-inventory | 88-654306 | 2016-11-21 | -1 |
| 332 | 88-654306 | -770.00 | p | Computer4-C1-20161121-COM4-143 < Computer-inventory | 88-654306 | 2016-11-21 | -1 |
| 333 | 88-654306 | -770.00 | p | Computer4-C1-20161121-COM4-144 < Computer-inventory | 88-654306 | 2016-11-21 | -1 |
| 334 | 88-654306 | -770.00 | p | Computer4-C1-20161121-COM4-145 < Computer-inventory | 88-654306 | 2016-11-21 | -1 |
| 335 | 88-654306 | -770.00 | p | Computer4-C1-20161121-COM4-146 < Computer-inventory | 88-654306 | 2016-11-21 | -1 |
| 336 | 88-654306 | -770.00 | p | Computer4-C1-20161121-COM4-147 < Computer-inventory | 88-654306 | 2016-11-21 | -1 |
| 337 | 88-654306 | -770.00 | p | Computer4-C1-20161121-COM4-148 < Computer-inventory | 88-654306 | 2016-11-21 | -1 |
| 338 | 88-654306 | -770.00 | p | Computer4-C1-20161121-COM4-149 < Computer-inventory | 88-654306 | 2016-11-21 | -1 |
| 339 | 88-654306 | -770.00 | p | Computer4-C1-20161121-COM4-150 < Computer-inventory | 88-654306 | 2016-11-21 | -1 |
| 340 | 88-654306 | -770.00 | p | Computer4-C1-20161121-COM4-151 < Computer-inventory | 88-654306 | 2016-11-21 | -1 |
| 341 | 88-654306 | -770.00 | p | Computer4-C1-20161121-COM4-152 < Computer-inventory | 88-654306 | 2016-11-21 | -1 |
| 342 | 88-654306 | -770.00 | p | Computer4-C1-20161121-COM4-153 < Computer-inventory | 88-654306 | 2016-11-21 | -1 |
| 343 | 88-654306 | -770.00 | p | Computer4-C1-20161121-COM4-154 < Computer-inventory | 88-654306 | 2016-11-21 | -1 |
| 344 | 88-654306 | -770.00 | p | Computer4-C1-20161121-COM4-155 < Computer-inventory | 88-654306 | 2016-11-21 | -1 |
| 345 | 88-654306 | -1600.00 | p | Computer server1-C1-20161121-COMS1-080 < Computer server-invento... | 88-654306 | 2016-11-21 | -1 |
| 346 | 88-654306 | -1600.00 | p | Computer server1-C1-20161121-COMS1-081 < Computer server-invento... | 88-654306 | 2016-11-21 | -1 |
| 347 | 88-654306 | -1600.00 | p | Computer server1-C1-20161121-COMS1-082 < Computer server-invento... | 88-654306 | 2016-11-21 | -1 |
| 348 | 88-654306 | -1600.00 | p | Computer server1-C1-20161121-COMS1-083 < Computer server-invento... | 88-654306 | 2016-11-21 | -1 |
| 349 | 88-654306 | -1600.00 | p | Computer server1-C1-20161121-COMS1-084 < Computer server-invento... | 88-654306 | 2016-11-21 | -1 |
| 350 | 88-654306 | -1500.00 | p | Computer server2-C1-20161121-COMS2-091 < Computer server-invento... | 88-654306 | 2016-11-21 | -1 |
| 351 | 88-654306 | -1500.00 | p | Computer server2-C1-20161121-COMS2-092 < Computer server-invento... | 88-654306 | 2016-11-21 | -1 |
| 352 | 88-654306 | -1500.00 | p | Computer server2-C1-20161121-COMS2-093 < Computer server-invento... | 88-654306 | 2016-11-21 | -1 |
| 353 | 88-654306 | -1500.00 | p | Computer server2-C1-20161121-COMS2-094 < Computer server-invento... | 88-654306 | 2016-11-21 | -1 |
| 354 | 88-654306 | -1500.00 | p | Computer server2-C1-20161121-COMS2-095 < Computer server-invento... | 88-654306 | 2016-11-21 | -1 |
| 355 | 88-654306 | -1000.00 | p | Computer1-C1-20161121-COM1-081 < Computer-inventory | 88-654306 | 2016-11-21 | -1 |
| 356 | 88-654306 | -1000.00 | p | Computer1-C1-20161121-COM1-082 < Computer-inventory | 88-654306 | 2016-11-21 | -1 |
| 357 | 88-654306 | -1000.00 | p | Computer1-C1-20161121-COM1-083 < Computer-inventory | 88-654306 | 2016-11-21 | -1 |
| 358 | 88-654306 | -1000.00 | p | Computer1-C1-20161121-COM1-084 < Computer-inventory | 88-654306 | 2016-11-21 | -1 |
| 359 | 909876504 | 920.00 | c | Computer2-C1-20160430-COM2-074 < Computer-inventory | 88-654306 | 2016-11-29 | 1 |
| 360 | 909876518 | 920.00 | c | Computer2-C1-20160430-COM2-075 < Computer-inventory | 88-654306 | 2016-11-30 | 1 |
| 361 | 909876506 | 770.00 | c | Computer4-C1-20160430-COM4-116 < Computer-inventory | 88-654306 | 2016-11-30 | 1 |
| 362 | 88-654310 | 1600.00 | c | Computer server1-C1-20160430-COMS1-045 < Computer server-invento... | 88-654306 | 2016-12-01 | 1 |
| 363 | 88-654310 | 1000.00 | c | Computer1-C1-20160430-COM1-062 < Computer-inventory | 88-654306 | 2016-12-01 | 1 |
| 364 | 88-654310 | 920.00 | c | Computer2-C1-20160430-COM2-072 < Computer-inventory | 88-654306 | 2016-12-01 | 1 |
| 365 | 88-654303 | 1000.00 | c | Computer1-C1-201501008-COM1-056 < Computer-inventory | 88-654306 | 2016-12-01 | 1 |
| 366 | 909876524 | 1000.00 | c | Computer1-C1-20161121-COM1-081 < Computer-inventory | 88-654306 | 2016-12-10 | 1 |
| 367 | 909876522 | 1000.00 | c | Computer1-C1-20160430-COM1-065 < Computer-inventory | 88-654306 | 2016-12-19 | 1 |
| 368 | 909876502 | 830.00 | c | Computer3-C1-20160430-COM3-103 < Computer-inventory | 88-654306 | 2016-12-22 | 1 |
| 369 | 909876507 | 28000.00 | c | Car1-C1-20160430-C1-030 < Car-inventory < Vehicle-inventory | 88-654306 | 2016-12-31 | 1 |
| 370 | 909876510 | 28000.00 | c | Car1-C1-20160430-C1-031 < Car-inventory < Vehicle-inventory | 88-654306 | 2016-12-31 | 1 |
| 371 | 909876524 | 26000.00 | c | Car3-C1-20160430-C3-051 < Car-inventory < Vehicle-inventory | 88-654306 | 2016-12-31 | 1 |
| 372 | 88-654306 | 154.00 | s | Supplies1-P2-20160430-Supp1-200T | 88-654306 | 2016-12-31 | 11 |
| 373 | 88-654306 | 160.00 | s | Supplies2-P2-20160430-Supp2-200T | 88-654306 | 2016-12-31 | 10 |
| 374 | 88-654303 | 1000.00 | c | Computer1-C1-20160430-COM1-068 < Computer-inventory | 88-654306 | 2016-12-31 | 1 |
| 375 | 88-654303 | -1000.00 | c | Computer1-C1-201501008-COM1-056 < Computer-inventory | 88-654306 | 2016-12-31 | -1 |

Query executed successfully.　　　　　　　　　　　　　　　　　　LIU\SQLE

Figure 3.6-2   Company1 Inventory Purchased or Sold by Other Members

# 3.7 Company2

## 3.7.1 An Accounting Fiscal Year of the Company2

In the new fiscal year, the Company2 occurs the following transactions.

- On January 2, 2016, the Company2 purchases the inventories $880 ($14*40 + $16*20) from the Proprietorship2 (phone number: 123456080) for cash -$500 and other on credit. The multi-subaccount names of the Cash account and the Inventory account and transaction sub-equation respectively are:

  88-654310-t-supplies<Cash payments for operating expenses<Operating activities

  Supplies1-P2-20150920-SUP1-200T: 14*40

  Supplies2-P2-20150920-SUP2-200T: 16*20

  Cash (1): -500 + Inventory (1): 14*40 + Inventory (1): 16*20 = Account payable (2): 380

- On January 2, 2016, the Company2 transfers the supplies $1,000 to the Cost of goods manufactured to satisfy the need of producing. The transaction sub-equation is:

  Supplies (1): -120 + Inventory (1): -14*40 + Inventory (1): -16*20 = Cost of goods manufactured (5): -1000

- On January 2, 2016, the Company2 transfers the following inventories -$17,580 to the Cost of goods manufactured account to satisfy the need of producing.

  Inven111 < Inven11 < Inven1: -10*50

  Inven112 < Inven11 < Inven1: -40*40

  Inven121 < Inven12 < Inven1: -0.8*100

  Inven122 < Inven12 < Inven1: -50*30

  Inven21 < Inven2: -30*30

  Inven221 < Inven22 < Inven2: -30*50

  Inven222 < Inven22 < Inven2: -50*20

  PPUK parts < ASD parts < Inven2: -40*30

  PPGH parts < ASD parts < Inven2: -2*100

  Inven51 < Inven5: -10*75

  Inven52 < Inven5: -50*30

Inven531 < Inven53 < Inven5: -25*50

Inven532 < Inven53 < Inven5: -35*50

Inven541 < Inven54 < Inven5: -12*50

Inven542 < Inven54 < Inven5: -15*40

Inven611 < Inven61 < Inven6: -6.5*50

Inven612 < Inven61 < Inven6: -12.5*50

Inven621 < Inven62 < Inven6: -18*50

Inven63 < Inven6: -16*50

The two transaction sub-equations are respectively:

Inventory (1): -10*50 + Inventory (1): -40*40 + Inventory (1): -0.8*100 + Inventory (1): -50*30 + Inventory (1): -30*30 + Inventory (1): -30*50 + Inventory (1): -50*20 + Inventory (1): -40*30 + Inventory (1): -2*100 = Cost of goods manufactured (5): -8480

Inventory (1): -10*75 + Inventory (1): -50*30+ Inventory (1): -25*50 + Inventory (1): -35*50 + Inventory (1): -12*50+ Inventory (1): -15*40 + Inventory (1): -6.5*50 + Inventory (1): -12.5*50 + Inventory (1): -18*50 + Inventory (1): -16*50 = Cost of goods manufactured (5): -9100

- On January 12, 2016, the Company2 sells one Computer1 part1 (-$235*1) to A25 (SIN: 909876525) for cash $360. The multi-subaccount names of the Cash account and the Inventory account and transaction sub-equation respectively are:

  909876525-c-customers < Cash receipts from customers < Operating activities

  Computer1 part1-C2-20150715-COM1P1-20T < Computer parts: -235*1

- On January 14, 2016, the Company2 receives $11,000 cash from the Company1 (phone number: 123456784) with the General ID 3. The multi-subaccount name of the Cash account is:

  88-654306-c-customers < Cash receipts from customers < Operating activities

- On January 15, 2016, the Company2 pays -$5,000 cash to the Company3 (phone number: 123456082) with the General ID 3. The Cash's multi-subaccount name is:

88-654308-t-suppliers < Cash payments to suppliers < Operating activities

- On January 15, 2016, the Company2 pays -$411.32 cash to A16 (SIN: 909876516) for the Travelling expenses -$219.32 and the Other expenses -$192. The multi-subaccount name of the Cash account is:

909876516-n-operating expenses < Cash payments for operating expenses < Operating activities

- On January 18, 2016, the Company2 pays -$112.57 cash to A17 (SIN: 909876517) for the Travelling expenses -$68.57 and the Other expenses -$44.

- On January 24, 2016, the Company2 receives $600 cash from the Company3 (phone number: 123456782) with the General ID 3. The multi-subaccount name of the Cash account is:

88-654308-c-customers < Cash receipts from customers < Operating activities

- On January 27, 2016, the Company2 receives $250 cash from the Proprietorship1 (phone number: 123456781) with the General ID 3. The multi-subaccount name of the Cash account is:

88-654309-c-customers < Cash receipts from customers < Operating activities

- On January 28, 2016, the Company2 sells one Truck1part2 $7,600 (cost: -$4,950) and one Truck2part3 $5,400 (cost: -$3500) for sales $13,000 to the Company3 (phone number: 123456782) for cash $7,000 and other on credit. The multi-subaccount names of the Cash account and the Inventory account respectively are:

88-654308-c-customers < Cash receipts from customers < Operating activities

Truck1 part2-C2-20150721-T1P2-042 < Truck1 parts < Vehicle parts: -4950*1

Truck2 part3-C2-20150728-T2P3-053 < Truck2 parts < Vehicle parts: -3500*1

- On January 30, 2016, the Company2 pays -$379.78 cash to A18 (SIN: 909876518) for the Travelling expenses -$235.78 and the Other expenses -$144.

- On January 30, 2016, the Company2 pays -$500 cash to the Proprietorship1 (phone number: 123456081) with the General ID 3. The multi-subaccount name of the Cash account is:

88-654309-t-suppliers < Cash payments to suppliers < Operating activities

- On January 30, 2016, the Company2 pays -$300 cash to the Proprietorship2 (phone number: 123456080) with the General ID 3. The multi-subaccount name of the Cash account is:

  88-654310-t-suppliers < Cash payments to suppliers < Operating activities

- On January 31, 2016, the Company2 pays three employees' salary expenses for cash -$8,380. The two multi-subaccount names of the Cash account respectively are:
  909876517-t-salary < Cash payments for operating expenses < Operating activities
  909876516-t-CGM < Cash payments for operating expenses < Operating activities
  909876518-t-CGM < Cash payments for operating expenses < Operating activities

- On February 11, 2016, the Company2 receives $400 cash from the Tax Bureau (phone number: 123456787) with the General ID 3. The multi-subaccount name of the Cash account is:

  88-654303-c-customers < Cash receipts from customers < Operating activities

- On February 20, 2016, the Company2 pays -$557.83 cash to A16 (SIN: 909876516) for the Travelling expenses -$247.83 and the Other expenses -$310. The multi-subaccount name of the Cash account is:

  909876516-n-operating expenses < Cash payments for operating expenses < Operating activities

- On February 21, 2016, the Company2 receives $500 cash from the Government1 (phone number: 123456788) with the General ID 3. The multi-subaccount name of the Cash account is:

  88-654302-c-customers < Cash receipts from customers < Operating activities

- On February 25, 2016, the Company2 pays -$600 cash to the Company1 (phone number: 123456084) with the General ID 3. The multi-subaccount name of the Cash account is:

  88-654306-t-suppliers < Cash payments to suppliers < Operating activities

- On February 26, 2016, the Company2 sells one Car1part2 $7,200 to the Business Bank1 (phone number: 123456786) for cash $5,200 and other on credit. The multi-subaccount names of the Cash account and the Inventory account respectively are:

88-654304-c-customers < Cash receipts from customers < Operating activities

Car1 part2-C2-20150816-C1P2-068 < Car1 parts < Vehicle parts: -4650*1

- On February 28, 2016, the Company2 pays three employees' salary expenses for cash -$8,380.

- On March 1, 2016, the Company2 pays -$221.16 cash to A18 (SIN: 909876518) for the Travelling expenses -$119.16 and the Other expenses -$102.

- On March 4, 2016, the Company2 receives $2,400 cash from the Company1 (phone number: 123456784) with the General ID 3. The multi-subaccount name of the Cash account is:

88-654306-c-customers < Cash receipts from customers < Operating activities

- On March 23, 2016, the Company2 pays -$347.65 cash to A16 (SIN: 909876516) for the Travelling expenses -$216.65 and the Other expenses -$131.

- On March 26, 2016, the Company2 pays -$253.93 cash to A17 (SIN: 909876517) for the Travelling expenses -$166.93 and the Other expenses -$87.

- On March 30, 2016, the Company2 pays -$700 cash to the Company3 (phone number: 123456082) with the General ID 3. The Cash account's multi-subaccount name is:

88-654308-t-suppliers < Cash payments to suppliers < Operating activities

- On March 31, 2016, the Company2 pays three employees' salary -$8,380 repeatedly.

- On April 12, 2016, the Company2 sells one Computer1 part2 $310 to A1 (SIN: 909876501) for cash $310. The multi-subaccount names of the Cash account and the Inventory account respectively are:

909876501-c-customers < Cash receipts from customers < Operating activities

Computer1 part2-C2-20150715-COM1P2-20T < Computer parts: -202*1

- On April 26, 2016, the Company2 pays -$369.88 cash to A16 (SIN: 909876516) for the Travelling expenses -$213.88 and the Other expenses -$156.

- On April 29, 2016, the Company2 sells one Truck2 part2 $7,200 (Cost:-$4,660) to the Proprietorship1 (phone number: 123456781) for cash $5000 and other on credit. The multi-subaccount names of the Cash account and the Inventory account are:

88-654309-c-customers < Cash receipts from customers < Operating activities

Truck2 part2-C2-20150728-T2P2-053 < Truck2 parts < Vehicle parts: -4660*1

- On April 30, 2016, the Company2 pays three employees' salary -$8,380 repeatedly.

- On May 1, 2016, the Company2 sells the following inventories -$140,192 for sales $216,420 to the Company1 (phone number: 123456784) for $15,000 cash and other $125,192 on credit.

Car1 part1-C2-20150816-C1P1-061 < Car1 parts < Vehicle parts: -5380*1

Car1 part1-C2-20150816-C1P1-062 < Car1 parts < Vehicle parts: -5380*1

Car1 part1-C2-20150816-C1P1-063 < Car1 parts < Vehicle parts: -5380*1

Car1 part2-C2-20150816-C1P2-069 < Car1 parts < Vehicle parts: -4650*1

Car1 part2-C2-20150816-C1P2-070 < Car1 parts < Vehicle parts: -4650*1

Car1 part2-C2-20150816-C1P2-071 < Car1 parts < Vehicle parts: -4650*1

Car1 part3-C2-20150816-C1P3-070 < Car1 parts < Vehicle parts: -3300*1

Car1 part3-C2-20150816-C1P3-071 < Car1 parts < Vehicle parts: -3300*1

Car1 part3-C2-20150816-C1P3-072 < Car1 parts < Vehicle parts: -3300*1

Car2 part1-C2-20150902-C2P1-077 < Car2 parts < Vehicle parts: -5100*1

Car2 part1-C2-20150902-C2P1-078 < Car2 parts < Vehicle parts: -5100*1

Car2 part1-C2-20150902-C2P1-079 < Car2 parts < Vehicle parts: -5100*1

Car2 part2-C2-20150902-C2P2-081 < Car2 parts < Vehicle parts: -4400*1

Car2 part2-C2-20150902-C2P2-082 < Car2 parts < Vehicle parts: -4400*1

Car2 part2-C2-20150902-C2P2-083 < Car2 parts < Vehicle parts: -4400*1

Car2 part3-C2-20150902-C2P3-083 < Car2 parts < Vehicle parts: -3170*1

Car2 part3-C2-20150902-C2P3-084 < Car2 parts < Vehicle parts: -3170*1

Car2 part3-C2-20150902-C2P3-085 < Car2 parts < Vehicle parts: -3170*1

Car3 part1-C2-20150902-C3P1-084 < Car3 parts < Vehicle parts: -4850*1

Car3 part1-C2-20150902-C3P1-085 < Car3 parts < Vehicle parts: -4850*1

Car3 part1-C2-20150902-C3P1-086 < Car3 parts < Vehicle parts: -4850*1

Car3 part2-C2-20150902-C3P2-087 < Car3 parts < Vehicle parts: -4150*1

Car3 part2-C2-20150902-C3P2-088 < Car3 parts < Vehicle parts: -4150*1

Car3 part2-C2-20150902-C3P2-089 < Car3 parts < Vehicle parts: -4150*1

Car3 part3-C2-20150902-C3P3-094 < Car3 parts < Vehicle parts: -3050*1

Car3 part3-C2-20150902-C3P3-095 < Car3 parts < Vehicle parts: -3050*1

Car3 part3-C2-20150902-C3P3-096 < Car3 parts < Vehicle parts: -3050*1

Computer server1 part1-C2-20150709-COMS1P1-10T < Computer server parts < Computer parts: -390*4

Computer server1 part2-C2-20150709-COMS1P2-10T < Computer server parts < Computer parts: -260*4

Computer server2 part1-C2-20150709-COMS2P1-10T < Computer server parts < Computer parts: -350*4

Computer server2 part2-C2-20150709-COMS2P2-10T < Computer server parts < Computer parts: -250*4

Computer1 part1-C2-20150715-COM1P1-20T < Computer parts: -235*14

Computer1 part2-C2-20150715-COM1P2-20T < Computer parts: -202*14

Computer2 part1-C2-20150715-COM2P1-20T < Computer parts: -208*14

Computer2 part2-C2-20150715-COM2P2-20T < Computer parts: -189*14

Computer3 part1-C2-20150715-COM3P1-20T < Computer parts: -182*14

Computer3 part2-C2-20150715-COM3P2-20T < Computer parts: -169*14

Computer4 part1-C2-20150715-COM4P1-20T < Computer parts: -162*14

Computer4 part2-C2-20150715-COM4P2-20T < Computer parts: -156*14

The multi-subaccount name of the Cash account and the transaction sub-equations respectively are:

88-654306-c-customers < Cash receipts from customers < Operating activities

Cash (1): 15000 + Account receivable (1): 31500 + Inventory (1): -5380*1 + Inventory (1): -5380*1 + Inventory (1): -5380*1 + Inventory (1): -4650*1 + Inventory (1): -4650*1 + Inventory (1): -4650*1 = Sales (4): 46500 + Cost of goods sold (5): -30090

Account receivable (1): 59400 + Inventory (1): -3300*1 + Inventory (1): -3300*1

+ Inventory (1): -3300*1 + Inventory (1): -5100*1 + Inventory (1): -5100*1 + Inventory (1): -5100*1 + Inventory (1): -4400*1 + Inventory (1): -4400*1 + Inventory (1): -4400*1 = Sales (4): 59400 + Cost of goods sold (5): -38400

Account receivable (1): 56400 + Inventory (1): -3170*1 + Inventory (1): -3170*1 + Inventory (1): -3170*1 + Inventory (1): -4850*1 + Inventory (1): -4850*1 + Inventory (1): -4850*1 + Inventory (1): -4150*1 + Inventory (1): -4150*1 + Inventory (1): -4150*1 = Sales (4): 56400 + Cost of goods sold (5): -36510

Account receivable (1): 31160 + Inventory (1): -3050*1 + Inventory (1): -3050*1 + Inventory (1): -3050*1 + Inventory (1): -390*4 + Inventory (1): -260*4 + Inventory (1): -350*4 + Inventory (1): -250*4 + Inventory (1): -235*14 + Inventory (1): -202*14 = Sales (4): 31160 + Cost of goods sold (5): -20268

Account receivable (1): 22960 + Inventory (1): -208*14 + Inventory (1): -189*14 + Inventory (1): -182*14 + Inventory (1): -169*14 + Inventory (1): -162*14 + Inventory (1): -156*14 = Sales (4): 22960 + Cost of goods sold (5): -14924

- On May 2, 2016, the Company2 pays -$307.09 cash to A18 (SIN: 909876518) for the Travelling expenses -$217.09 and the Other expenses -$90.

- On May 3, 2016, the Company2 sells one Computer2 part2 (cost: $189) to A13 (SIN: 909876513) for cash $290. The multi-subaccount names of the Cash account and the Inventory account respectively are:

  909876513-c-customers < Cash receipts from customers < Operating activities
  Computer2 part2-C2-20150715-COM2P2-20T < Computer parts: -189*1

- On May 24, 2016, the Company2 pays -$366.59 cash to A16 (SIN: 909876516) for the Travelling expenses -$211.59 and the Other expenses -$155.

- On May 31, 2016, the Company2 pays three employees' salary -$8,380 repeatedly.

- On June 12, 2016, the Company2 receives $64,000 cash from the Company1 (phone number: 123456784) with the General ID 58. The Cash's multi-subaccount name is:

88-654306-c-customers < Cash receipts from customers < Operating activities

- On June 14, 2016, the Company2 pays -$255.54 cash to A17 (SIN: 909876517) for the Travelling expenses -$187.54 and the Other expenses -$68.

- On June 23, 2016, the Company2 pays -$362.81 cash to A16 (SIN: 909876516) for the Travelling expenses -$199.81 and the Other expenses -$163.

- On June 30, 2016, the Company2 pays three employees' salary -$8,380 repeatedly.

- On July 11, 2016, the Company2 sells one Computer2 part2 (cost: $189) for sales $290 to A5 (SIN: 909876505) for cash $290. The multi-subaccount names of the Cash account the Inventory account respectively are:

    909876505-c-customers < Cash receipts from customers < Operating activities

    Computer2 part2-C2-20150715-COM2P2-20T < Computer parts: -189*1

- On July 13, 2016, the Company2 sells one Computer2 part1 ($208) for sales $320 to A7 (SIN: 909876507) for cash $320. The multi-subaccount names of the Cash account and the Inventory account respectively are:

    909876507-c-customers < Cash receipts from customers < Operating activities

    Computer2 part1-C2-20150715-COM2P1-20T < Computer parts: -208*1

- On July 27, 2016, the Company2 pays -$307.41 cash to A16 (SIN: 909876516) for the Travelling expenses -$189.41 and the Other expenses -$118.

- On July 31, 2016, the Company2 records the Amortization expenses -$1,720.84 of a computer server1 (-$816.67, seven months), a computer1 (-$466.67, seven months), and a computer2 (-$437.5, seven months).

- On July 31, 2016, the Company2 cancels the balances of the Computer account (-$2,800 - $1,600 - $1,500) and the Accumulated amortization: Computer account because these computers have used for two years.

- On July 31, 2016, the Company2 pays three employees' salary -$8,380 repeatedly.

- On August 1, 2016, the Company2 purchases one Computer server1, one Computer1, and one Computer2 from the Company1 (phone number: 123456084) for cash -$3,000 and other $2,900 on credit. The multi-subaccount names of the Cash account and the Inventory account and the transaction sub-equations respectively are:

88-654306-t-suppliers < Cash payments to suppliers < Operating activities

Computer server1-C1-20160430-COMS1-043 < Computer server-inventory < Computer-inventory: 2800*1

Computer1-C1-20160430-COM1-060 < Computer-inventory: 1600*1

Computer2-C1-20160430-COM2-070 < Computer-inventory: 1500*1

Cash (1): -3000 + Inventory (1): 2800 + Inventory (1): 1600 + Inventory (1): 1500 = Account payable (2): 2900

Inventory (1): -2800 + Inventory (1): -1600 + Inventory (1): -1500 + Computer (1): 2800 + Computer (1): 1600 + Computer (1): 1500 = 0

- On August 3, 2016, the Company2 receives $12,000 cash from the Company1 (phone number: 123456784) with the General ID 58. The multi-subaccount name of the Cash account is:

  88-654306-c-customers < Cash receipts from customers < Operating activities

- On August 13, 2016, the Company2 sells one Computer1 part1 (cost: -$235) to A11 (SIN: 909876511) for cash $360. The multi-subaccount name of the Cash account and the Inventory account respectively are:

  909876511-c-customers < Cash receipts from customers < Operating activities

  Computer1 part1-C2-20150715-COM1P1-20T < Computer parts: -235*1

- On August 16, 2016, the Company2 pays -$373.77 cash to A17 (SIN: 909876517) for the Travelling expenses -$253.77 and the Other expenses -$120.

- On August 23, 2016, the Company2 pays -$392.33 cash to A16 (SIN: 909876516) for the Travelling expenses -$230.33 and the Other expenses -$162.

- On August 31, 2016, the Company2 pays three employees' salary -$8,380 repeatedly.

- On September 3, 2016, the Company2 sells one Computer1 part2 (cost: -$202) for sales $310 to A19 (SIN: 909876519) for cash $310. The multi-subaccount names of the Cash account and the Inventory account respectively:

  909876519-c-customers < Cash receipts from customers < Operating activities

Computer1 part2-C2-20150715-COM1P2-20T < Computer parts: -202*1

- On September 10, 2016, the Company2 sells one Computer2 part1 (cost: -$208) for sales $320 to A22 (SIN: 909876522) for cash $320. The multi-subaccount names of the Cash account and the Inventory account respectively:

  909876522-c-customers < Cash receipts from customers < Operating activities

  Computer2 part1-C2-20150715-COM2P1-20T < Computer parts: -208*1

- On September 12, 2016, the Company2 receives $4,000 cash from the Company3 (phone number: 123456782) with the General ID 37. The multi-subaccount name of the Cash account is:

  88-654308-c-customers < Cash receipts from customers < Operating activities

- On September 14, 2016, the Company2 pays -$380 cash to the Proprietorship2 (phone number: 123456080) with the General ID 26. The multi-subaccount name of the Cash account is:

  88-654310-t-suppliers < Cash payments to suppliers < Operating activities

- On September 14, 2016, the Company2 receives $10,000 cash from the Company1 (phone number: 123456784) with the General ID 58.

- On September 26, 2016, the Company2 receives $1,800 cash from the Proprietorship1 (phone number: 123456781) with the General ID 56. The multi-subaccount name of the Cash account is:

  88-654309-c-customers < Cash receipts from customers < Operating activities

- On September 28, 2016, the Company2 pays -$410.89 cash to A16 (SIN: 909876516) for the Travelling expenses -$227.89 and the Other expenses -$183.

- On September 30, 2016, the Company2 pays three employees' salary -$8,380.

- On October 3, 2016, the Company2 sells one Truck2 part1 (cost: -$5,500) for sales $8,500 to the Tax Bureau (phone number: 123456787) for cash $4500 and other $4,000 on credit. The multi-subaccount names of the Cash account and the Inventory account respectively are:

  88-654303-c-customers < Cash receipts from customers < Operating activities

  Truck2 part1-C2-20150728-T2P1-053 < Truck2 parts < Vehicle parts: -5500*1

- On October 6, 2016, the Company2 pays -$377.63 cash to A18 (SIN: 909876518) for the Travelling expenses -$260.63 and the Other expenses -$117.

- On October 27, 2016, the Company2 pays -$396.27 cash to A16 (SIN: 909876516) for the Travelling expenses -$222.27 and the Other expenses -$174.

- On October 31, 2016, the Company2 pays three employees' salary -$8,380 repeatedly.

- On November 19, 2016, the Company2 pays -$399.28 cash to A16 (SIN: 909876516) for the Travelling expenses -$215.28 and the Other expenses -$184.

- On November 20, 2016, the Company2 sells one Computer1 part1 (cost: -$235) for sales $360 to A18 (SIN: 909876518) for cash $360. The multi-subaccount names of the Cash account and the Inventory account respectively are:

    909876518-c-customers < Cash receipts from customers < Operating activities

    Computer1 part1-C2-20150715-COM1P1-20T < Computer parts: -235*1

- On November 20, 2016, the Company2 completed all computer products ($37,560) and transfers $6,444 of the Cost of goods manufactured account to the Working-in-process inventory account. The multi-subaccount names of the Cost of goods manufactured account and the two transaction sub-equations respectively are the "Supplies expenses" ($300) and the "General parts expenses" ($6,144). The two transaction sub-equations respectively are:

    Working-in-process inventory (1): 61*6 + Working-in-process inventory (1): 74*6 + Working-in-process inventory (1): 65*6 + Working-in-process inventory (1): 75*6 + Working-in-process inventory (1): 26.5*20 + Working-in-process inventory (1): 19.8*20 = Cost of goods manufactured (5): 300 + Cost of goods manufactured (5): 2276

    Working-in-process inventory (1): 29.2*20 + Working-in-process inventory (1): 31.1*20 + Working-in-process inventory (1): 31.8*20 + Working-in-process inventory (1): 33.1*20 + Working-in-process inventory (1): 33.8*20 + Working-in-process inventory (1): 34.4*20 = Cost of goods manufactured (5): 3868

- On November 20, 2016, the Company2 transfers the balance of the Working-in-process inventory account for all computer products ($37,560) to the Inventory account. The multi-subaccount names of the Inventory account and the two transaction sub-equations respectively are:

  Computer server1 part1-C2-20161120-COMS1P1-6T < Computer server parts < Computer parts: 390*6

  Computer server1 part2-C2-20161120-COMS1P2-6T < Computer server parts < Computer parts: 260*6

  Computer server2 part1-C2-20161120-COMS2P1-6T < Computer server parts < Computer parts: 350*6

  Computer server2 part2-C2-20161120-COMS2P2-6T < Computer server parts < Computer parts: 250*6

  Computer1 part1-C2-20161120-COM1P1-20T < Computer parts: 235*20

  Computer1 part2-C2-20161120-COM1P2-20T < Computer parts: 202*20

  Computer2 part1-C2-20161120-COM2P1-20T < Computer parts: 208*20

  Computer2 part2-C2-20161120-COM2P2-20T < Computer parts: 189*20

  Computer3 part1-C2-20161120-COM3P1-20T < Computer parts: 182*20

  Computer3 part2-C2-20161120-COM3P2-20T < Computer parts: 169*20

  Computer4 part1-C2-20161120-COM4P1-20T < Computer parts: 162*20

  Computer4 part2-C2-20161120-COM4P2-20T < Computer parts: 156*20

  Inventory (1): 390*6 + Inventory (1): 260*6 + Inventory (1): 350*6 + Inventory (1): 250*6 + Inventory (1): 235*20 + Inventory (1): 202*20 + Working-in-process inventory (1): -390*6 + Working-in-process inventory (1): -260*6 + Working-in-process inventory (1): -350*6 + Working-in-process inventory (1): -250*6 + Working-in-process inventory (1): -235*20 + Working-in-process inventory (1): -202*20 = 0

  Inventory (1): 208*20 + Inventory (1): 189*20 + Inventory (1): 182*20 +

Inventory (1): 169*20 + Inventory (1): 162*20 + Inventory (1): 156*20 + Working-in-process inventory (1): -208*20 + Working-in-process inventory (1): -189*20 + Working-in-process inventory (1): -182*20 + Working-in-process inventory (1): -169*20 + Working-in-process inventory (1): -162*20 + Working-in-process inventory (1): -156*20 = 0

- On November 28, 2016, the Company2 transfers the supplies $50 to the Cost of goods manufactured to satisfy the producing need.

- On November 29, 2016, the Company2 receives $14,420 cash from the Company1 (phone number: 123456784) with the General ID 58. The multi-subaccount name of the Cash account is:

  88-654306-c-customers < Cash receipts from customers < Operating activities

- On November 30, 2016, the Company2 pays three employees' salary expenses for cash -$8,380 repeatedly.

- On December 17, 2016, the Company2 pays -$395.88 cash to A16 (SIN: 909876516) for the Travelling expenses -$221.88 and the Other expenses (meals: food111: $10*6 + food123: $15*4 + food321: $27*2) -$174.

- On December 20, 2016, the Company2 pays -$424.37 cash to A18 (SIN: 909876518) for the Travelling expenses -$280.37 and the Other expenses (meals: food611: $20*3 + food622: $28*3) -$144.

- On December 29, 2016, the Company2 receives $39,700 cash from the Company1 (phone number: 123456784) with the General ID 58.

- On December 30, 2016, the Company2 purchases the Inven611 (Inven611< Inven61 < Inven6) $1300 ($6.5*200) from the Company3 (phone number: 123456082) for cash -$600 and other $700 on credit. The multi-subaccount names of the Cash account and the Inventory account respectively are:

  88-654308-t-supplies < Cash payments for operating expenses < Operating activities

  Inven611-C3-20151003-In611-1300T < Inven61 < Inven6: 6.5*200

- On December 31, 2016, the Company2 receives $55,000 cash from the Company1 (phone number: 123456784) with the General ID 58.

- On December 31, 2016, the Company2 pays three employees' salary expenses for cash -$8,380 repeatedly.

- On the same day, the Company2 pays -$35,600 cash to the Business Bank1 for the Note interest expenses of the Note12 -$12,600 ($140,000, one-level subaccount "Note12-interest") and the Note14 -$23,000 ($250,000, one-level subaccount "Note14-interest"). The multi-subaccount name of the Cash account is:

  88-654304-t-note interest < Cash payments to business banks < Operating activities

- On the same day, the Company2 pays -$21,600 cash to the Business Bank2 for the Note interest expenses of the Note22 ($240,000, one-level subaccount "Note22-interest"). The multi-subaccount name of the Cash account is:

  88-654305-t-note interest < Cash payments to business banks < Operating activities

- On the same day, the Company2 pays -$1,880 cash to the bond holders for the Bond interest expenses of the Bond41 (one-level subaccount "Bond41-interest"). The multi-subaccount names of the Cash account and the transaction sub-equations respectively are:

  88-654305-t-bond interest< Cash payments to bond holders < Operating activities
  (909876504, 909876505, 909876506, 909876510, 909876513, 909876515, 909876519, 909876520, 909876523, 909876524, 909876525)

  Cash (1): -376 + Cash (1): -188 + Cash (1): -94 + Cash (1): -47 + Cash (1): -141 + Cash (1): -235 = Bond interest expenses (5): -1081

  Cash (1): -94 + Cash (1): -141 + Cash (1): -94 + Cash (1): -141 + Cash (1): -235 + Cash (1): -94 = Bond interest expenses (5): -799

- On the same day, the Company2 receives cash $336 for investment interest (Investment incomes) of the Bond12 from the Business Bank1. The multi-subaccount name of the Cash account is:

88-654304-c-investment income < Cash receipts from investments < Investing activities

- On the same day, the Company2 receives cash $264 for investment interest (Investment incomes) of the Bond22 from the Business Bank2. The multi-subaccount name of the Cash account is:

  88-654305-c-investment income < Cash receipts from investments < Investing activities

- On the same day, the Company2 receives cash $120 from the Business Bank2 for primary deposit interest. The multi-subaccount name of the Cash account is:

  88-654305-c-deposit interest income < Cash receipts from deposit interest < Financial activities

- On the same day, the Company2 records the Office supplies expenses -$21.02.

- On the same day, the Company2 records the Vehicle's amortization expenses - $24,200 (-$9,000 - $8,000 - $8,000) one year (5 years, straight line).

- On the same day, the Company2 records the Computer's amortization expenses $1,229.16 five months (2 years, straight line) which includes a new computer server1 (-$583.33), a new computer1 (-$333.33), and a new computer2 (-$312.5).

- On December 31, 2016, due to some reasons, the Company2 does not complete the vehicle parts' products and transfers the amount $46,950 of the Cost of goods manufactured account to the Working-in-process inventory account. The Cost of goods manufactured account has four subaccounts of the "Supplies expenses", the "909876516-salary < Sales department-salary < Salary expenses", the "909876518-salary < Product department-salary < Salary expenses", and the "General parts expenses". Their amounts are -$750, -$31,320, -$3,444, and -$11,436 respectively. The balance of the Cost of goods manufactured account is -$31,116. Of course, the balance may be transferred to the Salary expenses account. The three transaction sub-equations respectively are:

  Working-in-process inventory (1): 600*5 + Working-in-process inventory (1):

600*5 + Working-in-process inventory (1): 600*5 + Working-in-process inventory (1): 600*5 + Working-in-process inventory (1): 600*5 = Cost of goods manufactured (5): 750 + Cost of goods manufactured (5): 10,806 + Cost of goods manufactured (5): 3444

Working-in-process inventory (1): 600*5+ Working-in-process inventory (1): 600*5+ Working-in-process inventory (1): 600*5 + Working-in-process inventory (1): 600*5 + Working-in-process inventory (1): 600*5 = Cost of goods manufactured (5): 15000

Working-in-process inventory (1): 600*5 + Working-in-process inventory (1): 600*5 + Working-in-process inventory (1): 600*6 + Working-in-process inventory (1): 600*6 + Working-in-process inventory (1): 625*6 = Cost of goods manufactured (5): 5514 + Cost of goods manufactured (5): 11436

- On December 31, 2016, the Company2 records the Tax expenses $0 and the Tax payable $0. The multi-subaccount names of the Tax expenses and the Tax payable accounts all are the 'n'.

So far, I have entered all transactions of the Company2 to database dcj208 in the fiscal year 2016.

## 3.7.2 Brief Summary of the Company2

The Figure 3.7-1 shows all inventory purchased or sold by other members in the Company2 by using of SQL Server query.

SQLQuery3.sql - LIU...SS.dcj200 (sa (52))* | SQLQuery2.sql - LIU...SS.dcj200 (sa (51))* ✕ | SQLQuery1.sql - LIU...SS.dcj200 (sa (55))*

```
use dcj200
select * from InventoryByMembers where Recorder='88-654307' and TransDate between '2016-01-01' and '2016-12-31'
order by TransDate
```

100 % ▾

▦ Results  ▤ Messages

| | IDM | Amount | Symbol | MultiSubaccount | Recorder | TransDate | Unit |
|---|---|---|---|---|---|---|---|
| 1 | 88-654310 | -560.00 | t | Supplies1-P2-20150920-SUP1-200T | 88-654307 | 2016-01-02 | -40 |
| 2 | 88-654310 | -320.00 | t | Supplies2-P2-20150920-SUP2-200T | 88-654307 | 2016-01-02 | -20 |
| 3 | 88-654307 | 560.00 | f | Supplies1-P2-20150920-SUP1-200T | 88-654307 | 2016-01-02 | 40 |
| 4 | 88-654307 | 320.00 | f | Supplies2-P2-20150920-SUP2-200T | 88-654307 | 2016-01-02 | 20 |
| 5 | 88-654307 | 500.00 | f | Inven111 < Inven11 < Inven1 | 88-654307 | 2016-01-02 | 50 |
| 6 | 88-654307 | 1600.00 | f | Inven112 < Inven11 < Inven1 | 88-654307 | 2016-01-02 | 40 |
| 7 | 88-654307 | 80.00 | f | Inven121 < Inven12 < Inven1 | 88-654307 | 2016-01-02 | 100 |
| 8 | 88-654307 | 1500.00 | f | Inven122 < Inven12 < Inven1 | 88-654307 | 2016-01-02 | 30 |
| 9 | 88-654307 | 900.00 | f | Inven21 < Inven2 | 88-654307 | 2016-01-02 | 30 |
| 10 | 88-654307 | 1500.00 | f | Inven221 < Inven22 < Inven2 | 88-654307 | 2016-01-02 | 50 |
| 11 | 88-654307 | 1000.00 | f | Inven222 < Inven22 < Inven2 | 88-654307 | 2016-01-02 | 20 |
| 12 | 88-654307 | 1200.00 | f | PPUK parts < ASD parts < Inven2 | 88-654307 | 2016-01-02 | 30 |
| 13 | 88-654307 | 200.00 | f | PPGH parts < ASD parts < Inven2 | 88-654307 | 2016-01-02 | 100 |
| 14 | 88-654307 | 750.00 | f | Inven51 < Inven5 | 88-654307 | 2016-01-02 | 75 |
| 15 | 88-654307 | 1500.00 | f | Inven52 < Inven5 | 88-654307 | 2016-01-02 | 30 |
| 16 | 88-654307 | 1250.00 | f | Inven531 < Inven53 < Inven5 | 88-654307 | 2016-01-02 | 50 |
| 17 | 88-654307 | 1750.00 | f | Inven532 < Inven53 < Inven5 | 88-654307 | 2016-01-02 | 50 |
| 18 | 88-654307 | 600.00 | f | Inven541 < Inven54 < Inven5 | 88-654307 | 2016-01-02 | 50 |
| 19 | 88-654307 | 600.00 | f | Inven542 < Inven54 < Inven5 | 88-654307 | 2016-01-02 | 40 |
| 20 | 88-654307 | 325.00 | f | Inven611 < Inven61 < Inven6 | 88-654307 | 2016-01-02 | 50 |
| 21 | 88-654307 | 625.00 | f | Inven612 < Inven61 < Inven6 | 88-654307 | 2016-01-02 | 50 |
| 22 | 88-654307 | 900.00 | f | Inven621 < Inven62 < Inven6 | 88-654307 | 2016-01-02 | 50 |
| 23 | 88-654307 | 800.00 | f | Inven63 < Inven6 | 88-654307 | 2016-01-02 | 50 |
| 24 | 909876525 | 235.00 | c | Computer1 part1-C2-20150715-COM1P1-20T < Computer parts | 88-654307 | 2016-01-12 | 1 |
| 25 | 88-654308 | 4950.00 | c | Truck1 part2-C2-20150721-T1P2-042 < Truck1 parts < Vehicle parts | 88-654307 | 2016-01-28 | 1 |
| 26 | 88-654308 | 3500.00 | c | Truck2 part3-C2-20150728-T2P3-053 < Truck2 parts < Vehicle parts | 88-654307 | 2016-01-28 | 1 |
| 27 | 88-654304 | 4650.00 | c | Car1 part2-C2-20150816-C1P2-068 < Car1 parts < Vehicle parts | 88-654307 | 2016-02-26 | 1 |
| 28 | 909876501 | 202.00 | c | Computer1 part2-C2-20150715-COM1P2-20T < Computer parts | 88-654307 | 2016-04-12 | 1 |
| 29 | 88-654309 | 4660.00 | c | Truck2 part2-C2-20150728-T2P2-053 < Truck2 parts < Vehicle parts | 88-654307 | 2016-04-29 | 1 |
| 30 | 88-654306 | 5380.00 | c | Car1 part1-C2-20150816-C1P1-061 < Car1 parts < Vehicle parts | 88-654307 | 2016-05-01 | 1 |
| 31 | 88-654306 | 5380.00 | c | Car1 part1-C2-20150816-C1P1-062 < Car1 parts < Vehicle parts | 88-654307 | 2016-05-01 | 1 |
| 32 | 88-654306 | 5380.00 | c | Car1 part1-C2-20150816-C1P1-063 < Car1 parts < Vehicle parts | 88-654307 | 2016-05-01 | 1 |
| 33 | 88-654306 | 4650.00 | c | Car1 part2-C2-20150816-C1P2-069 < Car1 parts < Vehicle parts | 88-654307 | 2016-05-01 | 1 |
| 34 | 88-654306 | 4650.00 | c | Car1 part2-C2-20150816-C1P2-070 < Car1 parts < Vehicle parts | 88-654307 | 2016-05-01 | 1 |
| 35 | 88-654306 | 4650.00 | c | Car1 part2-C2-20150816-C1P2-071 < Car1 parts < Vehicle parts | 88-654307 | 2016-05-01 | 1 |
| 36 | 88-654307 | 3300.00 | p | Car1 part3-C2-20150816-C1P3-070 < Car1 parts < Vehicle parts | 88-654307 | 2016-05-01 | 1 |
| 37 | 88-654307 | 3300.00 | p | Car1 part3-C2-20150816-C1P3-071 < Car1 parts < Vehicle parts | 88-654307 | 2016-05-01 | 1 |
| 38 | 88-654307 | 3300.00 | p | Car1 part3-C2-20150816-C1P3-072 < Car1 parts < Vehicle parts | 88-654307 | 2016-05-01 | 1 |
| 39 | 88-654307 | 5100.00 | p | Car2 part1-C2-20150902-C2P1-077 < Car2 parts < Vehicle parts | 88-654307 | 2016-05-01 | 1 |
| 40 | 88-654307 | 5100.00 | p | Car2 part1-C2-20150902-C2P1-078 < Car2 parts < Vehicle parts | 88-654307 | 2016-05-01 | 1 |
| 41 | 88-654307 | 5100.00 | p | Car2 part1-C2-20150902-C2P1-079 < Car2 parts < Vehicle parts | 88-654307 | 2016-05-01 | 1 |
| 42 | 88-654307 | 4400.00 | p | Car2 part2-C2-20150902-C2P2-081 < Car2 parts < Vehicle parts | 88-654307 | 2016-05-01 | 1 |
| 43 | 88-654307 | 4400.00 | p | Car2 part2-C2-20150902-C2P2-082 < Car2 parts < Vehicle parts | 88-654307 | 2016-05-01 | 1 |
| 44 | 88-654307 | 4400.00 | p | Car2 part2-C2-20150902-C2P2-083 < Car2 parts < Vehicle parts | 88-654307 | 2016-05-01 | 1 |
| 45 | 88-654307 | 3170.00 | p | Car2 part3-C2-20150902-C2P3-083 < Car2 parts < Vehicle parts | 88-654307 | 2016-05-01 | 1 |
| 46 | 88-654307 | 3170.00 | p | Car2 part3-C2-20150902-C2P3-084 < Car2 parts < Vehicle parts | 88-654307 | 2016-05-01 | 1 |
| 47 | 88-654307 | 3170.00 | p | Car2 part3-C2-20150902-C2P3-085 < Car2 parts < Vehicle parts | 88-654307 | 2016-05-01 | 1 |
| 48 | 88-654307 | 4850.00 | p | Car3 part1-C2-20150902-C3P1-084 < Car3 parts < Vehicle parts | 88-654307 | 2016-05-01 | 1 |
| 49 | 88-654307 | 4850.00 | p | Car3 part1-C2-20150902-C3P1-085 < Car3 parts < Vehicle parts | 88-654307 | 2016-05-01 | 1 |
| 50 | 88-654307 | 4850.00 | p | Car3 part1-C2-20150902-C3P1-086 < Car3 parts < Vehicle parts | Recorder | 2016-05-01 | 1 |
| 51 | 88-654307 | 4150.00 | p | Car3 part2-C2-20150902-C3P2-087 < Car3 parts < Vehicle parts | 88-654307 | 2016-05-01 | 1 |
| 52 | 88-654307 | 4150.00 | p | Car3 part2-C2-20150902-C3P2-088 < Car3 parts < Vehicle parts | 88-654307 | 2016-05-01 | 1 |
| 53 | 88-654307 | 4150.00 | p | Car3 part2-C2-20150902-C3P2-089 < Car3 parts < Vehicle parts | 88-654307 | 2016-05-01 | 1 |
| 54 | 88-654307 | 3050.00 | p | Car3 part3-C2-20150902-C3P3-094 < Car3 parts < Vehicle parts | 88-654307 | 2016-05-01 | 1 |
| 55 | 88-654307 | 3050.00 | p | Car3 part3-C2-20150902-C3P3-095 < Car3 parts < Vehicle parts | 88-654307 | 2016-05-01 | 1 |
| 56 | 88-654307 | 3050.00 | p | Car3 part3-C2-20150902-C3P3-096 < Car3 parts < Vehicle parts | 88-654307 | 2016-05-01 | 1 |
| 57 | 88-654307 | 1560.00 | p | Computer server1 part1-C2-20150709-COMS1P1-10T < Computer server p... | 88-654307 | 2016-05-01 | 4 |
| 58 | 88-654307 | 1040.00 | p | Computer server1 part2-C2-20150709-COMS1P2-10T < Computer server p... | 88-654307 | 2016-05-01 | 4 |
| 59 | 88-654307 | 1400.00 | p | Computer server2 part1-C2-20150709-COMS2P1-10T < Computer server p... | 88-654307 | 2016-05-01 | 4 |
| 60 | 88-654307 | 1000.00 | p | Computer server2 part2-C2-20150709-COMS2P2-10T < Computer server p... | 88-654307 | 2016-05-01 | 4 |
| 61 | 88-654307 | 3290.00 | p | Computer1 part1-C2-20150715-COM1P1-20T < Computer parts | 88-654307 | 2016-05-01 | 14 |
| 62 | 88-654307 | 2828.00 | p | Computer1 part2-C2-20150715-COM1P2-20T < Computer parts | 88-654307 | 2016-05-01 | 14 |
| 63 | 88-654307 | 2912.00 | p | Computer2 part1-C2-20150715-COM2P1-20T < Computer parts | 88-654307 | 2016-05-01 | 14 |

| | IDM | Amount | Symbol | MultiSubaccount | Recorder | TransDate | Unit |
|---|---|---|---|---|---|---|---|
| 64 | 88-654307 | 2646.00 | p | Computer2 part2-C2-20150715-COM2P2-20T < Computer parts | 88-654307 | 2016-05-01 | 14 |
| 65 | 88-654307 | 2548.00 | p | Computer3 part1-C2-20150715-COM3P1-20T < Computer parts | 88-654307 | 2016-05-01 | 14 |
| 66 | 88-654307 | 2366.00 | p | Computer2 part2-C2-20150715-COM3P2-20T < Computer parts | 88-654307 | 2016-05-01 | 14 |
| 67 | 88-654307 | 2268.00 | p | Computer4 part1-C2-20150715-COM4P1-20T < Computer parts | 88-654307 | 2016-05-01 | 14 |
| 68 | 88-654307 | 2184.00 | p | Computer4 part2-C2-20150715-COM4P2-20T < Computer parts | 88-654307 | 2016-05-01 | 14 |
| 69 | 909876513 | 189.00 | c | Computer2 part2-C2-20150715-COM2P2-20T < Computer parts | 88-654307 | 2016-05-03 | 1 |
| 70 | 909876505 | 189.00 | c | Computer2 part2-C2-20150715-COM2P2-20T < Computer parts | 88-654307 | 2016-07-11 | 1 |
| 71 | 909876507 | 208.00 | c | Computer2 part1-C2-20150715-COM2P1-20T < Computer parts | 88-654307 | 2016-07-13 | 1 |
| 72 | 88-654306 | -2800.00 | t | Computer server1-C1-20150430-COMS1-043 < Computer server-inventory ... | 88-654307 | 2016-08-01 | -1 |
| 73 | 88-654306 | -1600.00 | t | Computer1-C1-20160430-COM1-060 < Computer-inventory | 88-654307 | 2016-08-01 | -1 |
| 74 | 88-654306 | -1500.00 | t | Computer2-C1-20160430-COM2-070 < Computer-inventory | 88-654307 | 2016-08-01 | -1 |
| 75 | 88-654307 | 2800.00 | e | Computer server1-C1-20160430-COMS1-043 < Computer server-inventory ... | 88-654307 | 2016-08-01 | 1 |
| 76 | 88-654307 | 1600.00 | e | Computer1-C1-20160430-COM1-060 < Computer-inventory | 88-654307 | 2016-08-01 | 1 |
| 77 | 88-654307 | 1500.00 | e | Computer2-C1-20160430-COM2-070 < Computer-inventory | 88-654307 | 2016-08-01 | 1 |
| 78 | 909876511 | 235.00 | c | Computer1 part1-C2-20150715-COM1P1-20T < Computer parts | 88-654307 | 2016-08-13 | 1 |
| 79 | 909876519 | 202.00 | c | Computer1 part2-C2-20150715-COM1P2-20T < Computer parts | 88-654307 | 2016-09-03 | 1 |
| 80 | 909876522 | 208.00 | c | Computer2 part1-C2-20150715-COM2P1-20T < Computer parts | 88-654307 | 2016-09-10 | 1 |
| 81 | 88-654303 | 5500.00 | c | Truck2 part1-C2-20150728-T2P1-053 < Truck2 parts < Vehicle parts | 88-654307 | 2016-10-03 | 1 |
| 82 | 909876518 | 235.00 | c | Computer1 part1-C2-20150715-COM1P1-20T < Computer parts | 88-654307 | 2016-11-20 | 1 |
| 83 | 88-654307 | -2340.00 | p | Computer server1 part1-C2-20161120-COMS1P1-6T < Computer server pa... | 88-654307 | 2016-11-20 | -6 |
| 84 | 88-654307 | -1560.00 | p | Computer server1 part2-C2-20161120-COMS1P2-6T < Computer server pa... | 88-654307 | 2016-11-20 | -6 |
| 85 | 88-654307 | -2100.00 | p | Computer server2 part1-C2-20161120-COMS2P1-6T < Computer server pa... | 88-654307 | 2016-11-20 | -6 |
| 86 | 88-654307 | -1500.00 | p | Computer server2 part2-C2-20161120-COMS2P2-6T < Computer server pa... | 88-654307 | 2016-11-20 | -6 |
| 87 | 88-654307 | -4700.00 | p | Computer1 part1-C2-20161120-COM1P1-20T < Computer parts | 88-654307 | 2016-11-20 | -20 |
| 88 | 88-654307 | -4040.00 | p | Computer1 part2-C2-20161120-COM1P2-20T < Computer parts | 88-654307 | 2016-11-20 | -20 |
| 89 | 88-654307 | -4160.00 | p | Computer2 part1-C2-20161120-COM2P1-20T < Computer parts | 88-654307 | 2016-11-20 | -20 |
| 90 | 88-654307 | -3780.00 | p | Computer2 part2-C2-20161120-COM2P2-20T < Computer parts | 88-654307 | 2016-11-20 | -20 |
| 91 | 88-654307 | -3640.00 | p | Computer3 part1-C2-20161120-COM3P1-20T < Computer parts | 88-654307 | 2016-11-20 | -20 |
| 92 | 88-654307 | -3380.00 | p | Computer3 part2-C2-20161120-COM3P2-20T < Computer parts | 88-654307 | 2016-11-20 | -20 |
| 93 | 88-654307 | -3240.00 | p | Computer4 part1-C2-20161120-COM4P1-20T < Computer parts | 88-654307 | 2016-11-20 | -20 |
| 94 | 88-654307 | -3120.00 | p | Computer4 part2-C2-20161120-COM4P2-20T < Computer parts | 88-654307 | 2016-11-20 | -20 |
| 95 | 88-654308 | -1300.00 | t | Inven611-C3-20151003-In611-1300T < Inven61 < Inven6 | 88-654307 | 2016-12-30 | -200 |

Query executed successfully. LIU\SQLE

Figure 3.7-1　Company2 Inventory Purchased or Sold by Other Members

## 3.8 Company3

### 3.8.1 An Accounting Fiscal Year of the Company3

In the new fiscal year, the Company3 occurs the following transactions.

- On January 2, 2016, the Company3 purchases the inventories $976 ($14*24 + $16*40) from the Proprietorship2 (phone number: 123456080) for cash -$400 and other on credit. The multi-subaccount names of the Cash account and the Inventory account and transaction sub-equation respectively are:

  88-654310-t-supplies<Cash payments for operating expenses<Operating activities

  Supplies1-P2-20150920-SUP1-200T: 14*24

  Supplies2-P2-20150920-SUP2-200T: 16*40

Cash (1): -316 + Inventory (1): 14*24 + Inventory (1): 16*40 = Account payable (2): 660

- On January 2, 2016, the Company3 sells the following inventories $94,830 for sales $161,468 to the Proprietorship1 (phone number: 123456781) for $10,000 cash and other on credit.

Inven51-C3-20150922-In51-1000T < Inven5: -6*500

Inven52-C3-20150922-In52-500T < Inven5: -30*250

Inven531-C3-20150922-In531-1000T < Inven53 < Inven5: -15*500

Inven532-C3-20150922-In532-1000T < Inven53 < Inven5: -21*500

Inven541-C3-20150922-In541-1000T < Inven54 < Inven5: -7.2*500

Inven542-C3-20150922-In542-1000T < Inven54 < Inven5: -7.5*500

Inven611-C3-20151003-In611-1300T < Inven61 < Inven6: -4*600

Inven612-C3-20151003-In612-1100T < Inven61 < Inven6: -7.5*500

Inven621-C3-20151003-In621-900T < Inven62 < Inven6: -10*400

Inven63-C3-20151003-In63-1000T < Inven6: -8*500

Inven711-C3-20151003-In711-500T < Inven71 < Inven7: -21.6*200

Inven712-C3-20151003-In712-100T < Inven71 < Inven7: -18.6*50

Inven721-C3-20151003-In721-744T < Inven72 < Inven7: -12.5*344

Inven722-C3-20151003-In722-600T < Inven72 < Inven7: -12*300

Inven731-C3-20151003-In731-600T < Inven73 < Inven7: -10.8*300

Inven732-C3-20151003-In732-1000T < Inven73 < Inven7: -9.6*500

Inven811-C3-20151003-In811-600T < Inven81 < Inven8: -15*300

Inven812-C3-20151003-In812-600T < Inven81 < Inven8: -14.4*300

Inven813-C3-20151003-In813-600T < Inven81 < Inven8: -13.8*300

Inven82-C3-20151003-In82-600T < Inven8: -12*300

Inven831-C3-20151003-In831-600T < Inven83 < Inven8: -10.8*300

Inven832-C3-20151003-In832-800T < Inven83 < Inven8: -9.6*400

The multi-subaccount name of the Cash account and the four transaction sub-equations respectively are:

88-654309-c-customers < Cash receipts from customers < Operating activities

Cash (1): 10000 + Account receivable (1): 51000 + Inventory (1): -6*500 + Inventory (1): -30*250 + Inventory (1): -15*500 + Inventory (1): -21*500 + Inventory (1): -7.2*500 + Inventory (1): -7.5*500 = Sales (4): 61000 + Cost of goods sold (5): -35850

Account receivable (1): 34100 + Inventory (1): -4*600 + Inventory (1): -7.5*500 + Inventory (1): -10*400 + Inventory (1): -8*500 + Inventory (1): -21.6*200 + Inventory (1): -18.6*50 = Sales (4): 34100 + Cost of goods sold (5): -19400

Account receivable (1): 41668 + Inventory (1): -12.5*344 + Inventory (1): -12*300 + Inventory (1): -10.8*300 + Inventory (1): -9.6*500 + Inventory (1): -15*300 + Inventory (1): -14.4*300 = Sales (4): 41668 + Cost of goods sold (5): -24760

Account receivable (1): 24700 + Inventory (1): -13.8*300 + Inventory (1): -12*300 + Inventory (1): -10.8*300 + Inventory (1): -9.6*400 = Sales (4): 24700 + Cost of goods sold (5): -14820

- On January 2, 2016, the Company3 sells the following inventories $98,790 for sales $168,450 to the Proprietorship2 (phone number: 123456780) for $8,000 cash and other on credit.

  Inven121-C3-20150922-In121-20000T < Inven12 < Inven1: -0.4*1250
  Inven51-C3-20150922-In51-1000T < Inven5: -6*500
  Inven52-C3-20150922-In52-500T < Inven5: -30*250
  Inven531-C3-20150922-In531-1000T < Inven53 < Inven5: -15*500
  Inven532-C3-20150922-In532-1000T < Inven53 < Inven5: -21*500
  Inven541-C3-20150922-In541-1000T < Inven54 < Inven5: -7.2*500
  Inven542-C3-20150922-In542-1000T < Inven54 < Inven5: -7.5*500

Inven611-C3-20151003-In611-1300T < Inven61 < Inven6: -4*500

Inven612-C3-20151003-In612-1100T < Inven61 < Inven6: -7.5*500

Inven621-C3-20151003-In621-900T < Inven62 < Inven6: -10*500

Inven63-C3-20151003-In63-1000T < Inven6: -8*500

Inven711-C3-20151003-In711-500T < Inven71 < Inven7: -21.6*300

Inven712-C3-20151003-In712-100T < Inven71 < Inven7: -18.6*50

Inven721-C3-20151003-In721-744T < Inven72 < Inven7: -12.5*400

Inven722-C3-20151003-In722-600T < Inven72 < Inven7: -12*300

Inven731-C3-20151003-In731-600T < Inven73 < Inven7: -10.8*300

Inven732-C3-20151003-In732-1000T < Inven73 < Inven7: -9.6*500

Inven811-C3-20151003-In811-600T < Inven81 < Inven8: -15*300

Inven812-C3-20151003-In812-600T < Inven81 < Inven8: -14.4*300

Inven813-C3-20151003-In813-600T < Inven81 < Inven8: -13.8*300

Inven82-C3-20151003-In82-600T < Inven8: -12*300

Inven831-C3-20151003-In831-600T < Inven83 < Inven8: -10.8*300

Inven832-C3-20151003-In832-800T < Inven83 < Inven8: -9.6*400

The multi-subaccount name of the Cash account and four transaction sub-equations respectively are:

88-654310-c-customers < Cash receipts from customers < Operating activities

Cash (1): 8000 + Account receivable (1): 54000 + Inventory (1): -0.4*1250 + Inventory (1): -6*500 + Inventory (1): -30*250 + Inventory (1): -15*500 + Inventory (1): -21*500 + Inventory (1): -7.2*500 + Inventory (1): -7.5*500 = Sales (4): 62000 + Cost of goods sold (5): -36350

Account receivable (1): 38850 + Inventory (1): -4*500 + Inventory (1): -7.5*500 + Inventory (1): -10*500 + Inventory (1): -8*500 + Inventory (1): -21.6*300 + Inventory (1): -18.6*50 = Sales (4): 38850 + Cost of goods sold (5): -22160

Account receivable (1): 42900 + Inventory (1): -12.5*400 + Inventory (1): -

12*300 + Inventory (1): -10.8*300 + Inventory (1): -9.6*500 + Inventory (1): -15*300 + Inventory (1): -14.4*300 = Sales (4): 42900 + Cost of goods sold (5): -25460

Account receivable (1): 24700 + Inventory (1): -13.8*300 + Inventory (1): -12*300 + Inventory (1): -10.8*300 + Inventory (1): -9.6*400 = Sales (4): 24700 + Cost of goods sold (5): -14820

- On January 3, 2016, the Company3 purchases the following inventories $34,800 from the Proprietorship1 (phone number: 123456081) with the General ID 29 for cash -$9,300 and other $25,500 on credit.

  Inven31-P1-20151125-In31-1000T < Inven3: 10*260

  Inven32-P1-20151125-In32-1000T < Inven3: 50*150

  Inven331-P1-20151125-In331-1000T < Inven33 < Inven3: 20*260

  Inven332-P1-20151125-In332-1000T < Inven33 < Inven3: 45*260

  HGFCVB parts-P1-20151125-HGP-1000T < QASXC parts < Inven3: 10*260

  PPGHUP parts-P1-20151125-PPP-1000T < ASDUP parts < Inven3: 20*260

  The multi-subaccount name of the Cash account and transaction sub-equation respectively are:

  88-654309-t-suppliers < Cash payments to suppliers < Operating activities

  Cash (1): -9300 + Inventory (1): 10*260 + Inventory (1): 50*150 + Inventory (1): 20*260 + Inventory (1): 45*260 + Inventory (1): 10*260 + Inventory (1): 20*260 = Account payable (2): 25500

- On January 3, 2016, the Company3 purchases the following inventories $19,050 from the Proprietorship2 (phone number: 123456080) for cash -$6,000 and other $13,050 on credit.

  Inven411-P2-20151127-In411-1000T < Inven41 < Inven4: 5*300

  Inven412-P2-20151127-In412-1000T < Inven41 < Inven4: 18.5*300

TTTCU parts-P2-20151127-TTP-1000T < TTT parts < Inven4: 20*300

RRRHJK parts-P2-20151127-RRP-1000T < Inven4: 20*300

The multi-subaccount name of the Cash account is:

88-654310-t-suppliers < Cash payments to suppliers < Operating activities

- On January 3, 2016, the Company3 transfers the supplies $920 to the Cost of goods manufactured to satisfy the need of producing. It is consisted of two parts of the Supplies -$52 and the Inventory -$868 (-$14*22 - $16*35). The multi-subaccount names of the Inventory account respectively are:

Supplies1-P2-20150920-SUP1-200T: -14*22

Supplies2-P2-20150920-SUP2-200T: -16*35

- On January 3, 2016, the Company3 transfers the following inventories -$75,700 to the Cost of goods manufactured account to satisfy the need of producing. During these inventories, the inventories -$21,850 are the inventories purchased before the conversation on January 1, 2016.

Inven31 < Inven3: -10*100

Inven32 < Inven3: -50*100

Inven331 < Inven33 < Inven3: -20*100

Inven332 < Inven33 < Inven3: -45*100

HGFCVB parts < QASXC parts < Inven3: -10*100

PPGHUP parts < ASDUP parts < Inven3: -20*100

Inven411 < Inven41 < Inven4: -5*100

Inven412 < Inven41 < Inven4: -18.5*100

TTTCU parts < TTT parts < Inven4: -20*100

RRRHJK parts < Inven4: -20*100

Inven31-P1-20151125-In31-1000T < Inven3: -10*260

Inven32-P1-20151125-In32-1000T < Inven3: -50*150

Inven331-P1-20151125-In331-1000T < Inven33 < Inven3: -20*260

Inven332-P1-20151125-In332-1000T < Inven33 < Inven3: -45*260

HGFCVB parts-P1-20151125-HGP-1000T < QASXC parts < Inven3: -10*260

PPGHUP parts-P1-20151125-PPP-1000T < ASDUP parts < Inven3: -20*260

Inven411-P2-20151127-In411-1000T < Inven41 < Inven4: -5*300

Inven412-P2-20151127-In412-1000T < Inven41 < Inven4: -18.5*300

TTTCU parts-P2-20151127-TTP-1000T < TTT parts < Inven4: -20*300

RRRHJK parts-P2-20151127-RRP-1000T < Inven4: -20*300

The two transaction sub-equations are respectively:

Inventory (1): -10*100 + Inventory (1): -50*100 + Inventory (1): -20*100 +
Inventory (1): -45*100 + Inventory (1): -10*100 + Inventory (1): -20*100 +
Inventory (1): -5*100 + Inventory (1): -18.5*100 + Inventory (1): -20*100 +
Inventory (1): -20*100  = Cost of goods manufactured (5): -21850

Inventory (1): -10*260 + Inventory (1): -50*150 + Inventory (1): -20*260 +
Inventory (1): -45*260 + Inventory (1): -10*260 + Inventory (1): -20*260 +
Inventory (1): -5*300 + Inventory (1): -18.5*300 + Inventory (1): -20*300 +
Inventory (1): -20*300 = Cost of goods manufactured (5): -53850

- On January 13, 2016, the Company3 receives $150 cash from the Proprietorship1 (phone number: 123456781) with the General ID 4. The multi-subaccount name of the Cash account is:

  88-654309-c-customers < Cash receipts from customers < Operating activities

- On January 13, 2016, the Company3 sells the following inventories -$2,852 for sales $4,660 to the Business Bank1 (phone number: 123456786) with the General ID 35 for cash $2,000 and other $2,660 on credit.

  Inven121-C3-20150922-In121-20000T < Inven12 < Inven1: -0.4*200

  Inven122-C3-20150922-In122-1000T < Inven12 < Inven1: -30*30

  Inven21-C3-20150922-In21-1250T < Inven2: -20*30

  Inven221-C3-20150922-In221-750T < Inven22 < Inven2: -20*30

  PPUK parts-C3-20150922-PU-500T < ASD parts < Inven2: -22.4*30

  The multi-subaccount name of the Cash account is:

88-654304-c-customers < Cash receipts from customers < Operating activities

- On January 14, 2016, the Company3 receives $8,000 cash from the Company1 (phone number: 123456784) with the General ID 4. The multi-subaccount name of the Cash account is:

  88-654306-c-customers < Cash receipts from customers < Operating activities

- On January 15, 2016, the Company3 receives $5,000 cash from the Company2 (phone number: 123456783) with the General ID 4. The multi-subaccount name of the Cash account is:

  88-654307-c-customers < Cash receipts from customers < Operating activities

- On January 18, 2016, the Company3 pays -$261.26 cash to A19 (SIN: 909876519) for the Travelling expenses -$139.26 and the Other -$122. The multi-subaccount name of the Cash account and the transaction sub-equation respectively are:

  909876519-n-operating expenses < Cash payments for operating expenses < Operating activities

- On January 19, 2016, the Company3 pays -$143.68 cash to A20 (SIN: 909876520) for the Travelling expenses -$92.68 and the Other expenses -$51.

- On January 23, 2016, the Company3 sells two Inven112s (-$25*2) and three Inven222s (-$27*3) to A22 (SIN: 909876522) for cash $230 ($40*2 + $50*3). The multi-subaccount names of the Cash and the Inventory accounts respectively are:

  909876522-c-customers < Cash receipts from customers < Operating activities
  Inven112-C3-20150922-In112-800T < Inven11 < Inven1: -25*2
  Inven222-C3-20150922-In222-400T < Inven22 < Inven2: -27*3

- On January 24, 2016, the Company3 pays -$600 cash to the Company2 (phone number: 123456083) with the General ID 4. The multi-subaccount name of the Cash account is:

  88-654307-t-suppliers < Cash payments to suppliers < Operating activities

- On January 26, 2016, the Company3 pays -$1,300 cash to the Proprietorship1 (phone number: 123456081) with the General ID 4. The multi-subaccount name of the Cash account is:

88-654309-t-suppliers < Cash payments to suppliers < Operating activities

- On January 26, 2016, the Company3 pays -$800 cash to the Proprietorship2 (phone number: 123456080) with the General ID 4. The multi-subaccount name of the Cash account is:

  88-654310-t-suppliers < Cash payments to suppliers < Operating activities

- On January 28, 2016, the Company3 receives $200 cash from the Proprietorship2 (phone number: 123456780) with the General ID 4. The multi-subaccount name of the Cash account is:

  88-654310-c-customers < Cash receipts from customers < Operating activities

- On January 28, 2016, the Company3 purchases $13,000 parts (one Truck1 part2 $7,600 and Truck2 part3 $5,400) from the Company2 (phone number: 123456083) for cash -$7,000 and other on credit. Here, the parts are recorded as the Vehicle part expenses for simplification. The multi-subaccount names of the Cash account and the Inventory account and the two transaction sub-equations respectively are:

  88-654307-t-suppliers < Cash payments to suppliers < Operating activities

  Truck1 part2-C2-20150721-T1P2-042 < Truck1 parts < Vehicle parts: 7600*1

  Truck2 part3-C2-20150728-T2P3-053 < Truck2 parts < Vehicle parts: 5400*1

  Cash (1): -7000 + Inventory (1): 7600*1 + Inventory (1): 5400*1= Account payable (2): 6000

  Inventory (1): -7600*1 + Inventory (1): -5400*1 = Vehicle part expenses (5): -7600 + Vehicle part expenses (5): -5400

- On January 30, 2016, the Company3 pays -$143.33 cash to A21 (SIN: 909876521) for the Travelling expenses -$101.33 and the Other expenses (meals: Food 212: $9*2 + food312: $24*1) -$42.

- On January 31, 2016, the Company3 sells ten Inven111s (-$6*10) and five Inven122s (-$30*5) to A6 (SIN: 909876506) for cash $350 ($10*10 + $50*5). The multi-subaccount names of the Cash account and the Inventory account respectively are:

909876506-c-customers < Cash receipts from customers < Operating activities

Inven111-C3-20150922-In111-1000T < Inven11 < Inven1: -6*10

Inven122-C3-20150922-In122-1000T < Inven12 < Inven1: -30*5

- On January 31, 2016, the Company3 pays three employees' salary expenses for cash -$8,370. The three multi-subaccount names of the Cash account respectively are:

  909876520-t-salary < Cash payments for operating expenses < Operating activities: -2880

  909876519-t-CGM < Cash payments for operating expenses < Operating activities: -2700

  909876521-t-CGM < Cash payments for operating expenses < Operating activities: -2790

- On February 13, 2016, the Company3 receives $200 cash from the Central Bank (phone number: 123456789) with the General ID 4. The multi-subaccount name of the Cash account is:

  88-654301-c-customers < Cash receipts from customers < Operating activities

- On February 22, 2016, the Company3 sells the following inventories -$3,320 for sales $5,600 to the Central Bank (phone number: 123456789) for cash $3,600 and other $2,000 on credit.

  Inven111-C3-20150922-In111-1000T < Inven11 < Inven1: -6*40

  Inven112-C3-20150922-In112-800T < Inven11 < Inven1: -25*40

  Inven221-C3-20150922-In221-750T < Inven22 < Inven2: -20*40

  Inven222-C3-20150922-In222-400T < Inven22 < Inven2: -27*40

  PPGH parts-C3-20150922-PG-1600T < ASD parts < Inven2: -1*200

  The multi-subaccount name of the Cash account is:

  88-654301-c-customers < Cash receipts from customers < Operating activities

- On February 23, 2016, the Company3 receives $300 cash from the Tax Bureau (phone number: 123456787) with the General ID 4. The multi-subaccount name of the Cash account is:

  88-654303-c-customers < Cash receipts from customers < Operating activities

- On February 25, 2016, the Company3 pays -$339.49 cash to A19 (SIN: 909876519) for the Travelling expenses -$215.49 and the Other expenses -$124.

- On February 27, 2016, the Company3 pays -$900 cash to the Company1 (phone number: 123456084) with the General ID 4. The multi-subaccount name of the Cash account is:

  88-654306-t-suppliers < Cash payments to suppliers < Operating activities

- On February 27, 2016, the Company3 sells the Inven21s (-$20*15) and the Inven221s (-$20*20) to A23 (SIN: 909876523) for cash $1,050 ($30*15 + $30*20). The multi-subaccount names of the Cash account and the Inventory account respectively are:

  909876523-c-customers < Cash receipts from customers < Operating activities
  Inven21-C3-20150922-In21-1250T < Inven2: -20*15
  Inven221-C3-20150922-In221-750T < Inven22 < Inven2: -20*20

- On February 28, 2016, the Company3 pays three employees' salary -$8,370.

- On March 1, 2016, the Company3 pays -$225.64 cash to A21 (SIN: 909876521) for the Travelling expenses -$123.64 and the Other expenses -$102.

- On March 4, 2016, the Company3 receives $1,600 cash from the Company1 (phone number: 123456784) with the General ID 4. The multi-subaccount name of the Cash account and transaction sub-equation respectively are:

  88-654306-c-customers < Cash receipts from customers < Operating activities

- On March 23, 2016, the Company3 pays -$198.56 cash to A19 (SIN: 909876519) for the Travelling expenses -$125.56 and the Other expenses -$73.

- On March 24, 2016, the Company3 sells the Inven21s (-$20*50) and the Inven222s (-$27*40) to A2 (SIN: 909876502) for cash $3,500 ($30*50 + $50*40). The multi-subaccount names of the Cash account and the Inventory account respectively are:
  909876502-c-customers < Cash receipts from customers < Operating activities
  Inven21-C3-20150922-In21-1250T < Inven2: -20*50
  Inven222-C3-20150922-In222-400T < Inven22 < Inven2: -27*40

- On March 30, 2016, the Company3 receives $700 cash from the Company2 (phone

number: 123456783) with the General ID 4. The multi-subaccount name of the Cash account is:

   88-654307-c-customers < Cash receipts from customers < Operating activities

- On March 31, 2016, the Company3 pays three employees' salary expenses for cash -$8,370 repeatedly.

- On April 6, 2016, the Company3 sells the following inventories -$1,300 for sales $2,200 to the Business Bank2 (phone number: 123456785) for cash $1,500 and other on credit.

   Inven111-C3-20150922-In111-1000T < Inven11 < Inven1: -6*10

   Inven112-C3-20150922-In112-800T < Inven11 < Inven1: -25*10

   Inven221-C3-20150922-In221-750T < Inven22 < Inven2: -20*20

   Inven222-C3-20150922-In222-400T < Inven22 < Inven2: -27*20

   PPGH parts-C3-20150922-PG-1600T < ASD parts < Inven2: -1*50

   The multi-subaccount name of the Cash account is:

   88-654305-c-customers < Cash receipts from customers < Operating activities

- On April 14, 2016, the Company3 sells the Inven112s (-$25*50), the Inven121s (-$0.4*200), and the PPUK parts (-$22.4*50) to A10 (SIN: 909876510) for cash $4,160 ($40*50 + $0.8*200 + $40*50). The multi-subaccount names of the Cash account and the Inventory account respectively are:

   909876510-c-customers < Cash receipts from customers < Operating activities

   Inven112-C3-20150922-In112-800T < Inven11 < Inven1: -25*50

   Inven121-C3-20150922-In121-20000T < Inven12 < Inven1: -0.4*200

   PPUK parts-C3-20150922-PU-500T < ASD parts < Inven2: -22.4*50

- On April 26, 2016, the Company3 pays -$236.37 cash to A19 (SIN: 909876519) for the Travelling expenses -$158.37 and the Other expenses -$78.

- On April 30, 2016, the Company3 pays three employees' salary -$8,370 repeatedly.

- On May 1, 2016, the Company3 sells the following inventories -$30,640 (-$15,200 - $15,440) for sales $50,800 to the Company1 (phone number: 123456784) on credit.

   Inven111-C3-20150922-In111-1000T < Inven11 < Inven1: -6*300

Inven112-C3-20150922-In112-800T < Inven11 < Inven1: -25*200

Inven121-C3-20150922-In121-20000T < Inven12 < Inven1: -0.4*6000

Inven122-C3-20150922-In122-1000T < Inven12 < Inven1: -30*200

Inven21-C3-20150922-In21-1250T < Inven2: -20*300

Inven221-C3-20150922-In221-750T < Inven22 < Inven2: -20*200

Inven222-C3-20150922-In222-400T < Inven22 < Inven2: -27*100

PPUK parts-C3-20150922-PU-500T < ASD parts < Inven2: -22.4*100

PPGH parts-C3-20150922-PG-1600T < ASD parts < Inven2: -1*500

- On May 2, 2016, the Company3 pays -$167.19 cash to A21 (SIN: 909876521) for the Travelling expenses -$117.19 and the Other expenses -$50.

- On May 3, 2016, the Company3 sells the Inven112s (-$25*20) and the Inven121s (-$0.4*100) for sales $880 ($40*20 + $0.8*100) to A14 (SIN: 909876514) for cash $880. The multi-subaccount name of the Cash account and the Inventory account respectively are:

  909876514-c-customers < Cash receipts from customers < Operating activities

  Inven112-C3-20150922-In112-800T < Inven11 < Inven1: -25*20

  Inven121-C3-20150922-In121-20000T < Inven12 < Inven1: -0.4*100

- On May 24, 2016, the Company3 pays -$339.55 cash to A19 (SIN: 909876516) for the Travelling expenses -$201.55 and the Other expenses -$138.

- On May 31, 2016, the Company3 pays three employees' salary -$8,370 repeatedly.

- On May 31, 2016, the Company3 records the Amortization expenses -$1,125 of a computer server2 (-$562.5, five months), a computer3 (-$291.67, five months), and a computer4 (-$270.83, five months).

- On May 31, 2016, the Company3 cancels the balances of the Computer account (-$2,700 - $1,400 - $1,300) and the Accumulated amortization: Computer account because these computers have used for two years.

- On June 1, 2016, the Company3 purchases one Computer server1, one Computer1, and one Computer2 from the Company1 (phone number: 123456084) for cash -$3,000 and other on credit. The multi-subaccount names of the Cash account and the

Inventory account and the two transaction sub-equations respectively are:

88-654306-t-suppliers < Cash payments to suppliers < Operating activities

Computer server1-C1-20160430-COMS1-044 < Computer server-inventory < Computer-inventory: 2800*1

Computer1-C1-20160430-COM1-061 < Computer-inventory: 1600*1

Computer2-C1-20160430-COM2-071 < Computer-inventory: 1500*1

Cash (1): -3000 + Inventory (1): 2800 + Inventory (1): 1600 + Inventory (1): 1500 = Account payable (2): 2900

Inventory (1): -2800 + Inventory (1): -1600 + Inventory (1): -1500 + Computer (1): 2800 + Computer (1): 1600 + Computer (1): 1500 = 0

- On June 10, 2016, the Company3 receives $15,000 cash from the Company1 (phone number: 123456784) with the General ID 64.

- On June 14, 2016, the Company3 pays -$193.49 cash to A20 (SIN: 909876520) for the Travelling expenses -$125.49 and the Other expenses -$68.

- On June 15, 2016, the Company3 purchases the inventories $84 ($14*6) from the Proprietorship2 (phone number: 123456080) for cash -$84. The multi-subaccount names of the Cash account and the Inventory account respectively are:

88-654310-t-supplies < Cash payments for operating expenses < Operating activities

Supplies1-P2-20160430-Supp1-200T: 14*6

- On June 16, 2016, the Company3 pays -$300 cash to the Proprietorship1 (phone number: 123456081) with the General ID 4. The multi-subaccount name of the Cash account is:

88-654309-t-suppliers < Cash payments to suppliers < Operating activities

- On June 23, 2016, the Company3 pays -$254.33 cash to A19 (SIN: 909876519) for the Travelling expenses -$146.33 and the Other expenses -$108.

- On June 29, 2016, the Company3 sells the following inventories -$2,892 for sales

$4,740 to the Tax Bureau (phone number: 123456787) with the General ID 78 for cash $2,000 and other on credit.

Inven121-C3-20150922-In121-20000T < Inven12 < Inven1: -0.4*300

Inven122-C3-20150922-In122-1000T < Inven12 < Inven1: -30*30

Inven21-C3-20150922-In21-1250T < Inven2: -20*30

Inven221-C3-20150922-In221-750T < Inven22 < Inven2: -20*30

PPUK parts-C3-20150922-PU-500T < ASD parts < Inven2: -22.4*30

The multi-subaccount name of the Cash account is:

88-654303-c-customers < Cash receipts from customers < Operating activities

- On June 30, 2016, the Company3 pays three employees' salary -$8,370 repeatedly.

- On July 3, 2016, the Company3 receives $53,000 cash from the Proprietorship2 (phone number: 123456780) with the General ID 25. The multi-subaccount name of the Cash account and transaction sub-equation respectively are:

88-654310-c-customers < Cash receipts from customers < Operating activities

- On July 4, 2016, the Company3 receives $55,000 cash from the Proprietorship1 (phone number: 123456781) with the General ID 21 ($51,000) and the General ID 22 ($4,000). The multi-subaccount name of the Cash account and transaction sub-equation respectively are:

88-654309-c-customers < Cash receipts from customers < Operating activities

- On July 11, 2016, the Company3 sells the Inven111s (-$6*10) and the Inven221s (-$20*5) for sales $250 ($10*10 + $30*5) to A4 (SIN: 909876504) for cash $250. The multi-subaccount names of the Cash and the Inventory accounts respectively are:

909876504-c-customers < Cash receipts from customers < Operating activities

Inven111-C3-20150922-In111-1000T < Inven11 < Inven1: -6*10

Inven221-C3-20150922-In221-750T < Inven22 < Inven2: -20*5

- On July 13, 2016, the Company3 sells the Inven112s (-$25*12) and the Inven222s (-$27*6) for sales $780 ($40*12 + $50*6) to A21 (SIN: 909876521) for cash $780. The multi-subaccount names of the Cash and the Inventory accounts respectively are:

909876521-c-customers < Cash receipts from customers < Operating activities

Inven112-C3-20150922-In112-800T < Inven11 < Inven1: -25*12

Inven222-C3-20150922-In222-400T < Inven22 < Inven2: -27*6

- On July 16, 2016, the Company3 pays -$13,000 cash to the Proprietorship2 (phone number: 123456080) with the General ID 20 ($660) and the General ID 30 ($12,340). The multi-subaccount name of the Cash account is:

  88-654310-t-suppliers < Cash payments to suppliers < Operating activities

- On July 27, 2016, the Company3 pays -$221.14 cash to A19 (SIN: 909876519) for the Travelling expenses -$133.14 and the Other expenses -$88.

- On July 31, 2016, the Company3 pays three employees' salary -$8,370 repeatedly.

- On August 3, 2016, the Company3 sells the Inven112s (-$25*10) and the Inven221s (-$20*5) for sales $550 ($40*10 + $30*5) to A17 (SIN: 909876517) for cash $550. The multi-subaccount names of the Cash and the Inventory accounts respectively are:

  909876517-c-customers < Cash receipts from customers < Operating activities

  Inven112-C3-20150922-In112-800T < Inven11 < Inven1: -25*10

  Inven221-C3-20150922-In221-750T < Inven22 < Inven2: -20*5

- On August 13, 2016, the Company3 sells the Inven222s (-$27*10) and the PPGH parts (-$1*100) for sales $700 ($50*10 + $2*100) to A13 (SIN: 909876513) for cash $700. The multi-subaccount names of the Cash and the Inventory accounts are:

  909876513-c-customers < Cash receipts from customers < Operating activities

  Inven222-C3-20150922-In222-400T < Inven22 < Inven2: -27*10

  PPGH parts-C3-20150922-PG-1600T < ASD parts < Inven2: -1*100

- On August 15, 2016, the Company3 receives $66,000 cash from the Proprietorship2 (phone number: 123456780) with the General ID 25 (-$1,000), the General ID 26 (-$38,850), the General ID 27 (-$1,450) and the General ID 28 (-$24,700). The multi-subaccount name of the Cash account is:

  88-654310-c-customers < Cash receipts from customers < Operating activities

- On August 17, 2016, the Company3 receives $65,000 cash from the Proprietorship1 (phone number: 123456781) with the General ID 22 ($34,100) and the General ID 23 ($30,900). The multi-subaccount name of the Cash account is:

88-654309-c-customers < Cash receipts from customers < Operating activities

- On August 23, 2016, the Company3 pays -$208.31 cash to A19 (SIN: 909876519) for the Travelling expenses -$130.31 and the Other expenses -$78.

- On August 31, 2016, the Company3 pays three employees' salary -$8,370 repeatedly.

- On September 4, 2016, the Company3 sells the Inven121s (-$0.4*200) and the Inven221s (-$20*12) for sales $520 ($30*12 + $0.8*200) to A18 (SIN: 909876518) for cash $520. The multi-subaccount names of the Cash and Inventory accounts is:
  909876518-c-customers < Cash receipts from customers < Operating activities
  Inven121-C3-20150922-In121-20000T < Inven12 < Inven1: -0.4*200
  Inven221-C3-20150922-In221-750T < Inven22 < Inven2: -20*12

- On September 10, 2016, the Company3 sells the Inven111s (-$6*15) and the Inven112s (-$25*10) for sales $550 ($10*15 + $40*10) to A23 (SIN: 909876523) for cash $550. The multi-subaccount names of the Cash and the Inventory accounts respectively are:
  909876523-c-customers < Cash receipts from customers < Operating activities
  Inven111-C3-20150922-In111-1000T < Inven11 < Inven1: -6*15
  Inven112-C3-20150922-In112-800T < Inven11 < Inven1: -25*10

- On September 12, 2016, the Company3 pays -$4,000 cash to the Company2 (phone number: 123456083) with the General ID 44. The multi-subaccount name of the Cash account is:
  88-654307-t-suppliers < Cash payments to suppliers < Operating activities

- On September 13, 2016, the Company3 receives $25,000 cash from the Company1 (phone number: 123456784) with the General ID 64. The multi-subaccount name of the Cash account and transaction sub-equation respectively are:
  88-654306-c-customers < Cash receipts from customers < Operating activities

- On September 15, 2016, the Company3 pays -$300 cash to the Proprietorship1 (phone number: 123456081) with the General ID 29. The multi-subaccount name of the Cash account is:
  88-654309-t-suppliers < Cash payments to suppliers < Operating activities

- On September 25, 2016, the Company3 sells the following inventories -$2,490 for sales $4,200 to the Government1 (phone number: 123456788) for cash $3,200 and other $1,000 on credit.

  Inven111-C3-20150922-In111-1000T < Inven11 < Inven1: -6*30

  Inven112-C3-20150922-In112-800T < Inven11 < Inven1: -25*30

  Inven221-C3-20150922-In221-750T < Inven22 < Inven2: -20*30

  Inven222-C3-20150922-In222-400T < Inven22 < Inven2: -27*30

  PPGH parts-C3-20150922-PG-1600T < ASD parts < Inven2: -1*150

  The multi-subaccount name of the Cash account is:

  88-654302-c-customers < Cash receipts from customers < Operating activities

- On September 26, 2016, the Company3 receives $8,000 cash from the Company1 (phone number: 123456784) with the General ID 4 ($1,000) and the General ID 64 ($7,000). The multi-subaccount name of the Cash account is:

  88-654306-c-customers < Cash receipts from customers < Operating activities

- On September 28, 2016, the Company3 pays -$214.84 cash to A19 (SIN: 909876519) for the Travelling expenses -$127.84 and the Other expenses -$87.

- On September 30, 2016, the Company3 pays three employees' salary -$8,370.

- On October 3, 2016, the Company3 sells the Inven111s (-$6*15) and the Inven112s (-$25*10) for sales $550 ($10*15 + $40*10) to A15 (SIN: 909876515) for cash $550. The multi-subaccount names of the Cash and the Inventory accounts are:

  909876515-c-customers < Cash receipts from customers < Operating activities

  Inven111-C3-20150922-In111-1000T < Inven11 < Inven1: -6*15

  Inven112-C3-20150922-In112-800T < Inven11 < Inven1: -25*10

- On October 8, 2016, the Company3 pays -$218.66 cash to A21 (SIN: 909876521) for the Travelling expenses -$140.66 and the Other expenses -$78.

- On October 11, 2016, the Company3 receives $41,000 cash from the Proprietorship2 (phone number: 123456780) with the General ID 27 ($41,000). The multi-subaccount name of the Cash account and transaction sub-equation respectively are:

  88-654310-c-customers < Cash receipts from customers < Operating activities

- On October 12, 2016, the Company3 receives $31,000 cash from the Proprietorship1 (phone number: 123456781) with the General ID 24 ($31,000). The multi-subaccount name of the Cash account is:

  88-654309-c-customers < Cash receipts from customers < Operating activities

- On October 18, 2016, the Company3 receives $2,660 cash from the Business Bank1 (phone number: 123456786) with the General ID 35. The multi-subaccount name of the Cash account is:

  88-654304-c-customers < Cash receipts from customers < Operating activities

- On October 25, 2016, the Company3 pays -$25,000 cash to the Proprietorship1 (phone number: 123456081) with the General ID 29. The multi-subaccount name of the Cash account is:

  88-654309-t-suppliers < Cash payments to suppliers < Operating activities

- On October 27, 2016, the Company3 pays -$242.23 cash to A19 (SIN: 909876519) for the Travelling expenses -$152.23 and the Other expenses -$90.

- On October 31, 2016, the Company3 pays three employees' salary -$8,370 repeatedly.

- On November 5, 2016, the Company3 pays -$2,900 cash to the Company1 (phone number: 123456084) with the General ID 14. The multi-subaccount name of the Cash account is:

  88-654306-t-suppliers < Cash payments to suppliers < Operating activities

- On November 19, 2016, the Company3 pays -$223.61 cash to A19 (SIN: 909876519) for the Travelling expenses -$136.61 and the Other expenses -$87.

- On November 20, 2016, the Company3 sells the Inven111s (-$6*14) and the Inven222s (-$27*10) for sales $640 ($10*14 + $50*10) to A6 (SIN: 909876506) for cash $640. The multi-subaccount names of the Cash account and the Inventory account respectively are:

  909876506-c-customers < Cash receipts from customers < Operating activities
  Inven111-C3-20150922-In111-1000T < Inven11 < Inven1: -6*14
  Inven222-C3-20150922-In222-400T < Inven22 < Inven2: -27*10

- On November 29, 2016, the Company3 receives $3,000 cash from the Company1 (phone number: 123456784). The multi-subaccount name of the Cash account is:

  88-654306-c-customers < Cash receipts from customers < Operating activities

- On November 30, 2016, the Company3 pays three employees' salary -$8,370.

- On December 17, 2016, the Company3 pays -$272.78 cash to A19 (SIN: 909876519) for the Travelling expenses -$168.78 and the Other expenses -$104.

- On December 20, 2016, the Company3 pays -$248.53 cash to A21 (SIN: 909876521) for the Travelling expenses -$160.53 and the Other expenses -$88.

- On December 28, 2016, the Company3 receives $2,500 cash from the Tax Bureau (phone number: 123456787) with the General ID 78 ($2,500). The multi-subaccount name of the Cash account is:

  88-654303-c-customers < Cash receipts from customers < Operating activities

- On December 30, 2016, the Company3 sells the Inven611s -$800 (-$4*200) for sales $1,300 ($6.5*200) to the Company2 (phone number: 123456783) for cash $600 and other on credit. The multi-subaccount names of the Cash and the Inventory accounts are respectively:

  88-654307-c-customers < Cash receipts from customers < Operating activities
  Inven611-C3-20151003-In611-1300T < Inven61 < Inven6: -4*200

- On December 31, 2016, the Company3 pays three employees' salary expenses for cash -$8,370 repeatedly.

- On the same day, the Company3 pays -$18,000 cash to the Business Bank1 for the Note interest expenses of the Note13 ($200,000, one-level subaccount "Note13-interest"). The multi-subaccount name of the Cash account is:

  88-654304-t-note interest< Cash payments to business banks< Operating activities

- On the same day, the Company3 pays -$34,400 cash to the business Bank2 for the Note interest expenses of the Note23 -$16,200 ($180,000, one-level subaccount "Note23-interest") and Note24 -$18,200 ($200,000, one-level subaccount "Note24-interest"). The multi-subaccount name of the Cash account is:

  88-654305-t-note interest< Cash payments to business banks< Operating activities

- On the same day, the Company3 pays -$3,840 cash to the bond holders for the Bond interest expenses of the Bond51 (one-level subaccount "Bond51-interest"). The multi-subaccount names of the Cash account and the transaction sub-equations respectively are:

  909876501-t-bond interest < Cash payments to bond holders< Operating activities (909876502, 909876503, 909876507, 909876508,909876509, 909876511, 909876512, 909876514, 909876516, 909876517, 909876518, 909876521, 909876522)

  Cash (1): -288 + Cash (1): -192 + Cash (1): -336 + Cash (1): -288 + Cash (1): -336 + Cash (1): -240 + Cash (1): -192 + Cash (1): -384 = Bond interest expenses (5): -2256

  Cash (1): -240 + Cash (1): -336 + Cash (1): -240 + Cash (1): -288 + Cash (1): -192 + Cash (1): -288 = Bond interest expenses (5): -1584

- On the same day, the Company3 receives cash $320 for the Investment incomes of the Bond11 ($8,000) from the Business Bank1. The multi-subaccount name of the Cash account is:

  88-654304-c-investment income < Cash receipts from investments < Investing activities

- On the same day, the Company3 receives cash $492 for investment interest of the Bond21 ($12,000) from the Business Bank2. The multi-subaccount name of the Cash account is:

  88-654305-c-investment income < Cash receipts from investments < Investing activities

- On the same day, the Company3 receives cash $120 from the Business Bank2 for primary deposit interest (Deposit interest incomes). The multi-subaccount name of the Cash account is:

  88-654305-c-deposit interest income < Cash receipts from deposit interest <

Financial activities

- On the same day, the Company3 records the Office supplies expenses -$96.75.

- On the same day, the Company3 records the Vehicle's amortization expenses - $41,200 (-$9,000 - $9,000 - $8,000 - $7,600 - $7,600) one year (5 years, straight line).

- On the same day, the Company3 records the Computer's amortization expenses $1,720.84 seven months (2 years, straight line) which includes a new computer server1 ($816.67), a new computer1 ($466.67), and a new computer2 ($437.5).

- On December 31, 2016, the Company3 transfers the balance $142,500 of the Cost of goods manufactured account to the Working-in-process inventory account. The Cost of goods manufactured account has four subaccounts of the "Supplies expenses", the "909876519-salary < Sales department-salary < Salary expenses", the "909876521-salary < Product department-salary < Salary expenses", and the "General parts expenses". Their balances are -$920, -$32,400, -$33,480, and -$75,700 respectively. Here, the balance of the "General parts expenses" is divided to four parts. The four transaction sub-equations respectively are:

Working-in-process inventory (1): 1*1000 + Working-in-process inventory (1): 4*1000 + Working-in-process inventory (1): 0.19*10000 + Working-in-process inventory (1): 4.1*1000 + Working-in-process inventory (1): 5.5*1000 + Working-in-process inventory (1): 5.1*1000 + Working-in-process inventory (1): 1*1000 + Working-in-process inventory (1): 2*1000 = Cost of goods manufactured (5): 920 + Cost of goods manufactured (5): 23680

Working-in-process inventory (1): 0.1*6000 + Working-in-process inventory (1): 0.5*5000 + Working-in-process inventory (1): 5*1000 + Working-in-process inventory (1): 2*1000 + Working-in-process inventory (1): 3*1000 + Working-in-process inventory (1): 0.83*1000 + Working-in-process inventory (1): 0.29*1000 + Working-in-process inventory (1): 0.5*5000 = Cost of goods manufactured (5): 16720

Working-in-process inventory (1): 0.9*1000 + Working-in-process inventory (1): 1.1*1000 + Working-in-process inventory (1): 0.01*1000 + Working-in-process inventory (1): 10.87*1000 + Working-in-process inventory (1): 9.1*1000 + Working-in-process inventory (1): 5.5*1000 + Working-in-process inventory (1): 5*1000 + Working-in-process inventory (1): 5.3*1000 = Cost of goods manufactured (5): 32400 + Cost of goods manufactured (5): 5380

Working-in-process inventory (1): 3.7*1000 + Working-in-process inventory (1): 7*1000 + Working-in-process inventory (1): 7*1000 + Working-in-process inventory (1): 6.53*1000 + Working-in-process inventory (1): 6.17*1000 + Working-in-process inventory (1): 6*3000 + Working-in-process inventory (1): 5*3000 = Cost of goods manufactured (5): 33480 + Cost of goods manufactured (5): 29920

- On December 31, 2016, the Company3 records the Tax expenses -$3,613.03 and the Tax payable $3,613.03. The multi-subaccount name forms of the Tax expenses and the Tax payable accounts all are the 'n'.

So far, I have entered all transactions of the Company3 to the database dcj209 in the fiscal year 2016.

### 3.8.2 Brief Summary of the Company3

The Figure 3.8-1 shows all inventory of the Company3 purchased or sold by other members by using of SQL Server query.

```
use dcj200
select * from InventoryByMembers where Recorder='88-654308' and TransDate between '2016-01-01' and '2016-12-31'
order by TransDate
```

100 %  ▼

Results   Messages

| | IDM | Amount | Symbol | MultiSubaccount | Recorder | TransDate | Unit |
|---|---|---|---|---|---|---|---|
| 1 | 88-654310 | -336.00 | t | Supplies1-P2-20150920-SUP1-200T | 88-654308 | 2016-01-02 | -24 |
| 2 | 88-654310 | -640.00 | t | Supplies2-P2-20150920-SUP2-200T | 88-654308 | 2016-01-02 | -40 |
| 3 | 88-654309 | 3000.00 | c | Inven51-C3-20150922-In51-1000T < Inven5 | 88-654308 | 2016-01-02 | 500 |
| 4 | 88-654309 | 7500.00 | c | Inven52-C3-20150922-In52-500T < Inven5 | 88-654308 | 2016-01-02 | 250 |
| 5 | 88-654309 | 7500.00 | c | Inven531-C3-20150922-In531-1000T < Inven53 < Inven5 | 88-654308 | 2016-01-02 | 500 |
| 6 | 88-654309 | 10500.00 | c | Inven532-C3-20150922-In532-1000T < Inven53 < Inven5 | 88-654308 | 2016-01-02 | 500 |
| 7 | 88-654309 | 3600.00 | c | Inven541-C3-20150922-In541-1000T < Inven54 < Inven5 | 88-654308 | 2016-01-02 | 500 |
| 8 | 88-654309 | 3750.00 | c | Inven542-C3-20150922-In542-1000T < Inven54 < Inven5 | 88-654308 | 2016-01-02 | 500 |
| 9 | 88-654309 | 2400.00 | c | Inven611-C3-20151003-In611-1300T < Inven61 < Inven6 | 88-654308 | 2016-01-02 | 600 |
| 10 | 88-654309 | 3750.00 | c | Inven612-C3-20151003-In612-1100T < Inven61 < Inven6 | 88-654308 | 2016-01-02 | 500 |
| 11 | 88-654309 | 4000.00 | c | Inven621-C3-20151003-In621-900T < Inven62 < Inven6 | 88-654308 | 2016-01-02 | 400 |
| 12 | 88-654309 | 4000.00 | c | Inven63-C3-20151003-In63-1000T < Inven6 | 88-654308 | 2016-01-02 | 500 |
| 13 | 88-654309 | 4320.00 | c | Inven711-C3-20151003-In711-500T < Inven71 < Inven7 | 88-654308 | 2016-01-02 | 200 |
| 14 | 88-654309 | 930.00 | c | Inven712-C3-20151003-In712-100T < Inven71 < Inven7 | 88-654308 | 2016-01-02 | 50 |
| 15 | 88-654309 | 4300.00 | c | Inven721-C3-20151003-In721-744T < Inven72 < Inven7 | 88-654308 | 2016-01-02 | 344 |
| 16 | 88-654309 | 3600.00 | c | Inven722-C3-20151003-In722-600T < Inven72 < Inven7 | 88-654308 | 2016-01-02 | 300 |
| 17 | 88-654309 | 3240.00 | c | Inven731-C3-20151003-In731-600T < Inven73 < Inven7 | 88-654308 | 2016-01-02 | 300 |
| 18 | 88-654309 | 4800.00 | c | Inven732-C3-20151003-In732-1000T < Inven73 < Inven7 | 88-654308 | 2016-01-02 | 500 |
| 19 | 88-654309 | 4500.00 | c | Inven811-C3-20151003-In811-600T < Inven81 < Inven8 | 88-654308 | 2016-01-02 | 300 |
| 20 | 88-654309 | 4320.00 | c | Inven812-C3-20151003-In812-600T < Inven81 < Inven8 | 88-654308 | 2016-01-02 | 300 |
| 21 | 88-654309 | 4140.00 | c | Inven813-C3-20151003-In813-600T < Inven81 < Inven8 | 88-654308 | 2016-01-02 | 300 |
| 22 | 88-654309 | 3600.00 | c | Inven82-C3-20151003-In82-600T < Inven8 | 88-654308 | 2016-01-02 | 300 |
| 23 | 88-654309 | 3240.00 | c | Inven831-C3-20151003-In831-600T < Inven83 < Inven8 | 88-654308 | 2016-01-02 | 300 |
| 24 | 88-654309 | 3840.00 | c | Inven832-C3-20151003-In832-800T < Inven83 < Inven8 | 88-654308 | 2016-01-02 | 400 |
| 25 | 88-654310 | 500.00 | c | Inven121-C3-20150922-In121-20000T < Inven12 < Inven1 | 88-654308 | 2016-01-02 | 1250 |
| 26 | 88-654310 | 3000.00 | c | Inven51-C3-20150922-In51-1000T < Inven5 | 88-654308 | 2016-01-02 | 500 |
| 27 | 88-654310 | 7500.00 | c | Inven52-C3-20150922-In52-500T < Inven5 | 88-654308 | 2016-01-02 | 250 |
| 28 | 88-654310 | 7500.00 | c | Inven531-C3-20150922-In531-1000T < Inven53 < Inven5 | 88-654308 | 2016-01-02 | 500 |
| 29 | 88-654310 | 10500.00 | c | Inven532-C3-20150922-In532-1000T < Inven53 < Inven5 | 88-654308 | 2016-01-02 | 500 |
| 30 | 88-654310 | 3600.00 | c | Inven541-C3-20150922-In541-1000T < Inven54 < Inven5 | 88-654308 | 2016-01-02 | 500 |
| 31 | 88-654310 | 3750.00 | c | Inven542-C3-20150922-In542-1000T < Inven54 < Inven5 | 88-654308 | 2016-01-02 | 500 |
| 32 | 88-654310 | 2000.00 | c | Inven611-C3-20151003-In611-1300T < Inven61 < Inven6 | 88-654308 | 2016-01-02 | 500 |
| 33 | 88-654310 | 3750.00 | c | Inven612-C3-20151003-In612-1100T < Inven61 < Inven6 | 88-654308 | 2016-01-02 | 500 |
| 34 | 88-654310 | 5000.00 | c | Inven621-C3-20151003-In621-900T < Inven62 < Inven6 | 88-654308 | 2016-01-02 | 500 |
| 35 | 88-654310 | 4000.00 | c | Inven63-C3-20151003-In63-1000T < Inven6 | 88-654308 | 2016-01-02 | 500 |
| 36 | 88-654310 | 6480.00 | c | Inven711-C3-20151003-In711-500T < Inven71 < Inven7 | 88-654308 | 2016-01-02 | 300 |
| 37 | 88-654310 | 930.00 | c | Inven712-C3-20151003-In712-100T < Inven71 < Inven7 | 88-654308 | 2016-01-02 | 50 |
| 38 | 88-654310 | 5000.00 | c | Inven721-C3-20151003-In721-744T < Inven72 < Inven7 | 88-654308 | 2016-01-02 | 400 |
| 39 | 88-654310 | 3600.00 | c | Inven722-C3-20151003-In722-600T < Inven72 < Inven7 | 88-654308 | 2016-01-02 | 300 |
| 40 | 88-654310 | 3240.00 | c | Inven731-C3-20151003-In731-600T < Inven73 < Inven7 | 88-654308 | 2016-01-02 | 300 |
| 41 | 88-654310 | 4800.00 | c | Inven732-C3-20151003-In732-1000T < Inven73 < Inven7 | 88-654308 | 2016-01-02 | 500 |
| 42 | 88-654310 | 4500.00 | c | Inven811-C3-20151003-In811-600T < Inven81 < Inven8 | 88-654308 | 2016-01-02 | 300 |
| 43 | 88-654310 | 4320.00 | c | Inven812-C3-20151003-In812-600T < Inven81 < Inven8 | 88-654308 | 2016-01-02 | 300 |
| 44 | 88-654310 | 4140.00 | c | Inven813-C3-20151003-In813-600T < Inven81 < Inven8 | 88-654308 | 2016-01-02 | 300 |
| 45 | 88-654310 | 3600.00 | c | Inven82-C3-20151003-In82-600T < Inven8 | 88-654308 | 2016-01-02 | 300 |
| 46 | 88-654310 | 3240.00 | c | Inven831-C3-20151003-In831-600T < Inven83 < Inven8 | 88-654308 | 2016-01-02 | 300 |
| 47 | 88-654310 | 3840.00 | c | Inven832-C3-20151003-In832-800T < Inven83 < Inven8 | 88-654308 | 2016-01-02 | 400 |
| 48 | 88-654309 | -2600.00 | t | Inven31-P1-20151125-In31-1000T < Inven3 | 88-654308 | 2016-01-03 | -260 |
| 49 | 88-654309 | -7500.00 | t | Inven32-P1-20151125-In32-1000T < Inven3 | 88-654308 | 2016-01-03 | -150 |
| 50 | 88-654309 | -5200.00 | t | Inven331-P1-20151125-In331-1000T < Inven33 < Inven3 | 88-654308 | 2016-01-03 | -260 |
| 51 | 88-654309 | -11700.00 | t | Inven332-P1-20151125-In332-1000T < Inven33 < Inven3 | 88-654308 | 2016-01-03 | -260 |
| 52 | 88-654309 | -2600.00 | t | HGFCVB parts-P1-20151125-HGP-1000T < QASXC parts < Inven3 | 88-654308 | 2016-01-03 | -260 |
| 53 | 88-654309 | -5200.00 | t | PPGHUP parts-P1-20151125-PPP-1000T < ASDUP parts < Inven3 | 88-654308 | 2016-01-03 | -260 |
| 54 | 88-654310 | -1500.00 | t | Inven411-P2-20151127-In411-1000T < Inven41 < Inven4 | 88-654308 | 2016-01-03 | -300 |
| 55 | 88-654310 | -5550.00 | t | Inven412-P2-20151127-In412-1000T < Inven41 < Inven4 | 88-654308 | 2016-01-03 | -300 |
| 56 | 88-654310 | -6000.00 | t | TTTCU parts-P2-20151127-TTP-1000T < TTT parts < Inven4 | 88-654308 | 2016-01-03 | -300 |
| 57 | 88-654310 | -6000.00 | t | RRRHJK parts-P2-20151127-RRP-1000T < Inven4 | 88-654308 | 2016-01-03 | -300 |
| 58 | 88-654308 | 1500.00 | f | Inven411-P2-20151127-In411-1000T < Inven41 < Inven4 | 88-654308 | 2016-01-03 | 300 |
| 59 | 88-654308 | 5550.00 | f | Inven412-P2-20151127-In412-1000T < Inven41 < Inven4 | 88-654308 | 2016-01-03 | 300 |
| 60 | 88-654308 | 6000.00 | f | TTTCU parts-P2-20151127-TTP-1000T < TTT parts < Inven4 | 88-654308 | 2016-01-03 | 300 |
| 61 | 88-654308 | 6000.00 | f | RRRHJK parts-P2-20151127-RRP-1000T < Inven4 | 88-654308 | 2016-01-03 | 300 |

| | IDM | Amount | Symbol | MultiSubaccount | Recorder | TransDate | Unit |
|---|---|---|---|---|---|---|---|
| 62 | 88-654308 | 308.00 | f | Supplies1-P2-20150920-SUP1-200T | 88-654308 | 2016-01-03 | 22 |
| 63 | 88-654308 | 560.00 | f | Supplies2-P2-20150920-SUP2-200T | 88-654308 | 2016-01-03 | 35 |
| 64 | 88-654308 | 1000.00 | f | Inven31 < Inven3 | 88-654308 | 2016-01-03 | 100 |
| 65 | 88-654308 | 5000.00 | f | Inven32 < Inven3 | 88-654308 | 2016-01-03 | 100 |
| 66 | 88-654308 | 2000.00 | f | Inven331 < Inven33 < Inven3 | 88-654308 | 2016-01-03 | 100 |
| 67 | 88-654308 | 4500.00 | f | Inven332 < Inven33 < Inven3 | 88-654308 | 2016-01-03 | 100 |
| 68 | 88-654308 | 1000.00 | f | HGFCVB parts < QASXC parts < Inven3 | 88-654308 | 2016-01-03 | 100 |
| 69 | 88-654308 | 2000.00 | f | PPGHUP parts < ASDUP parts < Inven3 | 88-654308 | 2016-01-03 | 100 |
| 70 | 88-654308 | 500.00 | f | Inven411 < Inven41 < Inven4 | 88-654308 | 2016-01-03 | 100 |
| 71 | 88-654308 | 1850.00 | f | Inven412 < Inven41 < Inven4 | 88-654308 | 2016-01-03 | 100 |
| 72 | 88-654308 | 2000.00 | f | TTTCU parts < TTT parts < Inven4 | 88-654308 | 2016-01-03 | 100 |
| 73 | 88-654308 | 2000.00 | f | RRRHJK parts < Inven4 | 88-654308 | 2016-01-03 | 100 |
| 74 | 88-654308 | 2600.00 | f | Inven31-P1-20151125-In31-1000T < Inven3 | 88-654308 | 2016-01-03 | 260 |
| 75 | 88-654308 | 7500.00 | f | Inven32-P1-20151125-In32-1000T < Inven3 | 88-654308 | 2016-01-03 | 150 |
| 76 | 88-654308 | 5200.00 | f | Inven331-P1-20151125-In331-1000T < Inven33 < Inven3 | 88-654308 | 2016-01-03 | 260 |
| 77 | 88-654308 | 11700.00 | f | Inven332-P1-20151125-In332-1000T < Inven33 < Inven3 | 88-654308 | 2016-01-03 | 260 |
| 78 | 88-654308 | 2600.00 | f | HGFCVB parts-P1-20151125-HGP-1000T < QASXC parts < Inven3 | 88-654308 | 2016-01-03 | 260 |
| 79 | 88-654308 | 5200.00 | f | PPGHUP parts-P1-20151125-PPP-1000T < ASDUP parts < Inven3 | 88-654308 | 2016-01-03 | 260 |
| 80 | 88-654304 | 80.00 | c | Inven121-C3-20150922-In121-20000T < Inven12 < Inven1 | 88-654308 | 2016-01-13 | 200 |
| 81 | 88-654304 | 900.00 | c | Inven122-C3-20150922-In122-1000T < Inven12 < Inven1 | 88-654308 | 2016-01-13 | 30 |
| 82 | 88-654304 | 600.00 | c | Inven21-C3-20150922-In21-1250T < Inven2 | 88-654308 | 2016-01-13 | 30 |
| 83 | 88-654304 | 600.00 | c | Inven221-C3-20150922-In221-750T < Inven22 < Inven2 | 88-654308 | 2016-01-13 | 30 |
| 84 | 88-654304 | 672.00 | c | PPUK parts-C3-20150922-PU-500T < ASD parts < Inven2 | 88-654308 | 2016-01-13 | 30 |
| 85 | 909876522 | 50.00 | c | Inven112-C3-20150922-In112-800T < Inven11 < Inven1 | 88-654308 | 2016-01-23 | 2 |
| 86 | 909876522 | 81.00 | c | Inven222-C3-20150922-In222-400T < Inven22 < Inven2 | 88-654308 | 2016-01-23 | 3 |
| 87 | 88-654307 | -7600.00 | t | Truck1 part2-C2-20150721-T1P2-042 < Truck1 parts < Vehicle parts | 88-654308 | 2016-01-28 | -1 |
| 88 | 88-654307 | -5400.00 | t | Truck2 part3-C2-20150728-T2P3-053 < Truck2 parts < Vehicle parts | 88-654308 | 2016-01-28 | -1 |
| 89 | 88-654308 | 7600.00 | s | Truck1 part2-C2-20150721-T1P2-042 < Truck1 parts < Vehicle parts | 88-654308 | 2016-01-28 | 1 |
| 90 | 88-654308 | 5400.00 | s | Truck2 part3-C2-20150728-T2P3-053 < Truck2 parts < Vehicle parts | 88-654308 | 2016-01-28 | 1 |
| 91 | 909876506 | 60.00 | c | Inven111-C3-20150922-In111-1000T < Inven11 < Inven1 | 88-654308 | 2016-01-31 | 10 |
| 92 | 909876506 | 150.00 | c | Inven122-C3-20150922-In122-1000T < Inven12 < Inven1 | 88-654308 | 2016-01-31 | 5 |
| 93 | 88-654301 | 240.00 | c | Inven111-C3-20150922-In111-1000T < Inven11 < Inven1 | 88-654308 | 2016-02-22 | 40 |
| 94 | 88-654301 | 1000.00 | c | Inven112-C3-20150922-In112-800T < Inven11 < Inven1 | 88-654308 | 2016-02-22 | 40 |
| 95 | 88-654301 | 800.00 | c | Inven221-C3-20150922-In221-750T < Inven22 < Inven2 | 88-654308 | 2016-02-22 | 40 |
| 96 | 88-654301 | 1080.00 | c | Inven222-C3-20150922-In222-400T < Inven22 < Inven2 | 88-654308 | 2016-02-22 | 40 |
| 97 | 88-654301 | 200.00 | c | PPGH parts-C3-20150922-PG-1600T < ASD parts < Inven2 | 88-654308 | 2016-02-22 | 200 |
| 98 | 909876523 | 300.00 | c | Inven21-C3-20150922-In21-1250T < Inven2 | 88-654308 | 2016-02-27 | 15 |
| 99 | 909876523 | 400.00 | c | Inven221-C3-20150922-In221-750T < Inven22 < Inven2 | 88-654308 | 2016-02-27 | 20 |
| 100 | 909876502 | 1000.00 | c | Inven21-C3-20150922-In21-1250T < Inven2 | 88-654308 | 2016-03-24 | 50 |
| 101 | 909876502 | 1080.00 | c | Inven222-C3-20150922-In222-400T < Inven22 < Inven2 | 88-654308 | 2016-03-24 | 40 |
| 102 | 88-654305 | 60.00 | c | Inven111-C3-20150922-In111-1000T < Inven11 < Inven1 | 88-654308 | 2016-04-06 | 10 |
| 103 | 88-654305 | 250.00 | c | Inven112-C3-20150922-In112-800T < Inven11 < Inven1 | 88-654308 | 2016-04-06 | 10 |
| 104 | 88-654305 | 400.00 | c | Inven221-C3-20150922-In221-750T < Inven22 < Inven2 | 88-654308 | 2016-04-06 | 20 |
| 105 | 88-654305 | 540.00 | c | Inven222-C3-20150922-In222-400T < Inven22 < Inven2 | 88-654308 | 2016-04-06 | 20 |
| 106 | 88-654305 | 50.00 | c | PPGH parts-C3-20150922-PG-1600T < ASD parts < Inven2 | 88-654308 | 2016-04-06 | 50 |
| 107 | 909876510 | 1250.00 | c | Inven112-C3-20150922-In112-800T < Inven11 < Inven1 | 88-654308 | 2016-04-14 | 50 |
| 108 | 909876510 | 80.00 | c | Inven121-C3-20150922-In121-20000T < Inven12 < Inven1 | 88-654308 | 2016-04-14 | 200 |
| 109 | 909876510 | 1120.00 | c | PPUK parts-C3-20150922-PU-500T < ASD parts < Inven2 | 88-654308 | 2016-04-14 | 50 |
| 110 | 88-654306 | 2400.00 | c | Inven121-C3-20150922-In121-20000T < Inven12 < Inven1 | 88-654308 | 2016-05-01 | 6000 |
| 111 | 88-654306 | 6000.00 | c | Inven122-C3-20150922-In122-1000T < Inven12 < Inven1 | 88-654308 | 2016-05-01 | 200 |
| 112 | 88-654306 | 6000.00 | c | Inven21-C3-20150922-In21-1250T < Inven2 | 88-654308 | 2016-05-01 | 300 |
| 113 | 88-654306 | 4000.00 | c | Inven221-C3-20150922-In221-750T < Inven22 < Inven2 | 88-654308 | 2016-05-01 | 200 |
| 114 | 88-654306 | 2700.00 | c | Inven222-C3-20150922-In222-400T < Inven22 < Inven2 | 88-654308 | 2016-05-01 | 100 |
| 115 | 88-654306 | 2240.00 | c | PPUK parts-C3-20150922-PU-500T < ASD parts < Inven2 | 88-654308 | 2016-05-01 | 100 |
| 116 | 88-654306 | 500.00 | c | PPGH parts-C3-20150922-PG-1600T < ASD parts < Inven2 | 88-654308 | 2016-05-01 | 500 |
| 117 | 88-654306 | 1800.00 | c | Inven111-C3-20150922-In111-1000T < Inven11 < Inven1 | 88-654308 | 2016-05-01 | 300 |
| 118 | 88-654306 | 5000.00 | c | Inven112-C3-20150922-In112-800T < Inven11 < Inven1 | 88-654308 | 2016-05-01 | 200 |
| 119 | 909876514 | 500.00 | c | Inven112-C3-20150922-In112-800T < Inven11 < Inven1 | 88-654308 | 2016-05-03 | 20 |
| 120 | 909876514 | 40.00 | c | Inven121-C3-20150922-In121-20000T < Inven12 < Inven1 | 88-654308 | 2016-05-03 | 100 |
| 121 | 88-654306 | -2800.00 | t | Computer server1-C1-20160430-COMS1-044 < Computer server-inventory... | 88-654308 | 2016-06-01 | -1 |
| 122 | 88-654306 | -1600.00 | t | Computer1-C1-20160430-COM1-061 < Computer-inventory | 88-654308 | 2016-06-01 | -1 |
| 123 | 88-654306 | -1500.00 | t | Computer2-C1-20160430-COM2-071 < Computer-inventory | 88-654308 | 2016-06-01 | -1 |

| | IDM | Amount | Symbol | MultiSubaccount | Recorder | TransDate | Unit |
|---|---|---|---|---|---|---|---|
| 124 | 88-654308 | 2800.00 | e | Computer server1-C1-20160430-COMS1-044 < Computer server-inventory... | 88-654308 | 2016-06-01 | 1 |
| 125 | 88-654308 | 1600.00 | e | Computer1-C1-20160430-COM1-061 < Computer-inventory | 88-654308 | 2016-06-01 | 1 |
| 126 | 88-654308 | 1500.00 | e | Computer2-C1-20160430-COM2-071 < Computer-inventory | 88-654308 | 2016-06-01 | 1 |
| 127 | 88-654310 | -84.00 | t | Supplies1-P2-20160430-Supp1-200T | 88-654308 | 2016-06-15 | -6 |
| 128 | 88-654303 | 120.00 | c | Inven121-C3-20150922-In121-20000T < Inven12 < Inven1 | 88-654308 | 2016-06-29 | 300 |
| 129 | 88-654303 | 900.00 | c | Inven122-C3-20150922-In122-1000T < Inven12 < Inven1 | 88-654308 | 2016-06-29 | 30 |
| 130 | 88-654303 | 600.00 | c | Inven21-C3-20150922-In21-1250T < Inven2 | 88-654308 | 2016-06-29 | 30 |
| 131 | 88-654303 | 600.00 | c | Inven221-C3-20150922-In221-750T < Inven22 < Inven2 | 88-654308 | 2016-06-29 | 30 |
| 132 | 88-654303 | 672.00 | c | PPUK parts-C3-20150922-PU-500T < ASD parts < Inven2 | 88-654308 | 2016-06-29 | 30 |
| 133 | 909876504 | 60.00 | c | Inven111-C3-20150922-In111-1000T < Inven11 < Inven1 | 88-654308 | 2016-07-11 | 10 |
| 134 | 909876504 | 100.00 | c | Inven221-C3-20150922-In221-750T < Inven22 < Inven2 | 88-654308 | 2016-07-11 | 5 |
| 135 | 909876521 | 300.00 | c | Inven112-C3-20150922-In112-800T < Inven11 < Inven1 | 88-654308 | 2016-07-13 | 12 |
| 136 | 909876521 | 162.00 | c | Inven222-C3-20150922-In222-400T < Inven22 < Inven2 | 88-654308 | 2016-07-13 | 6 |
| 137 | 909876517 | 250.00 | c | Inven112-C3-20150922-In112-800T < Inven11 < Inven1 | 88-654308 | 2016-08-03 | 10 |
| 138 | 909876517 | 100.00 | c | Inven221-C3-20150922-In221-750T < Inven22 < Inven2 | 88-654308 | 2016-08-03 | 5 |
| 139 | 909876513 | 270.00 | c | Inven222-C3-20150922-In222-400T < Inven22 < Inven2 | 88-654308 | 2016-08-13 | 10 |
| 140 | 909876513 | 100.00 | c | PPGH parts-C3-20150922-PG-1600T < ASD parts < Inven2 | 88-654308 | 2016-08-13 | 100 |
| 141 | 909876518 | 80.00 | c | Inven121-C3-20150922-In121-20000T < Inven12 < Inven1 | 88-654308 | 2016-09-04 | 200 |
| 142 | 909876518 | 240.00 | c | Inven221-C3-20150922-In221-750T < Inven22 < Inven2 | 88-654308 | 2016-09-04 | 12 |
| 143 | 909876523 | 90.00 | c | Inven111-C3-20150922-In111-1000T < Inven11 < Inven1 | 88-654308 | 2016-09-10 | 15 |
| 144 | 909876523 | 250.00 | c | Inven112-C3-20150922-In112-800T < Inven11 < Inven1 | 88-654308 | 2016-09-10 | 10 |
| 145 | 88-654302 | 180.00 | c | Inven111-C3-20150922-In111-1000T < Inven11 < Inven1 | 88-654308 | 2016-09-25 | 30 |
| 146 | 88-654302 | 750.00 | c | Inven112-C3-20150922-In112-800T < Inven11 < Inven1 | 88-654308 | 2016-09-25 | 30 |
| 147 | 88-654302 | 600.00 | c | Inven221-C3-20150922-In221-750T < Inven22 < Inven2 | 88-654308 | 2016-09-25 | 30 |
| 148 | 88-654302 | 810.00 | c | Inven222-C3-20150922-In222-400T < Inven22 < Inven2 | 88-654308 | 2016-09-25 | 30 |
| 149 | 88-654302 | 150.00 | c | PPGH parts-C3-20150922-PG-1600T < ASD parts < Inven2 | 88-654308 | 2016-09-25 | 150 |
| 150 | 909876515 | 90.00 | c | Inven111-C3-20150922-In111-1000T < Inven11 < Inven1 | 88-654308 | 2016-10-03 | 15 |
| 151 | 909876515 | 250.00 | c | Inven112-C3-20150922-In112-800T < Inven11 < Inven1 | 88-654308 | 2016-10-03 | 10 |
| 152 | 909876506 | 84.00 | c | Inven111-C3-20150922-In111-1000T < Inven11 < Inven1 | 88-654308 | 2016-11-20 | 14 |
| 153 | 909876506 | 270.00 | c | Inven222-C3-20150922-In222-400T < Inven22 < Inven2 | 88-654308 | 2016-11-20 | 10 |
| 154 | 88-654307 | 800.00 | c | Inven611-C3-20151003-In611-1300T < Inven61 < Inven6 | 88-654308 | 2016-12-30 | 200 |

Query executed successfully. LIU\SQLE

Figure 3.8-1　Company3 Inventory Received or Sold by Other Members

# 3.9 Proprietorship1

## 3.9.1 An Accounting Fiscal Year of the Proprietorship1

Because the Proprietorship1 mainly sells foods to individuals, it has many transactions every day. For simplification, I assume that an individual only buy foods (exception of business meal foods) three times for one year. Therefore, in the new fiscal year, the Proprietorship1 occurs the following transactions.

- On January 2, 2016, the Proprietorship1 purchases the inventory (supplies) $1,050 ($14\*35 + $16\*35) from the Proprietorship2 (phone number: 123456080) for cash - $450 and other on credit. The multi-subaccount names of the Cash account and the Inventory account are:

88-654310-t-supplies<Cash payments for operating expenses<Operating activities

Supplies1-P2-20150920-SUP1-200T: 14*35

Supplies2-P2-20150920-SUP2-200T: 16*35

- On January 2, 2016, the Proprietorship1 purchases the following inventories $161,468 from the Company3 (phone number: 123456082) for -$10,000 cash and other on credit.

Inven51-C3-20150922-In51-1000T < Inven5: 10*500

Inven52-C3-20150922-In52-500T < Inven5: 50*250

Inven531-C3-20150922-In531-1000T < Inven53 < Inven5: 25*500

Inven532-C3-20150922-In532-1000T < Inven53 < Inven5: 35*500

Inven541-C3-20150922-In541-1000T < Inven54 < Inven5: 12*500

Inven542-C3-20150922-In542-1000T < Inven54 < Inven5: 15*500

Inven611-C3-20151003-In611-1300T < Inven61 < Inven6: 6.5*600

Inven612-C3-20151003-In612-1100T < Inven61 < Inven6: 12.5*500

Inven621-C3-20151003-In621-900T < Inven62 < Inven6: 18*400

Inven63-C3-20151003-In63-1000T < Inven6: 16*500

Inven711-C3-20151003-In711-500T < Inven71 < Inven7: 36*200

Inven712-C3-20151003-In712-100T < Inven71 < Inven7: 31*50

Inven721-C3-20151003-In721-744T < Inven72 < Inven7: 22*344

Inven722-C3-20151003-In722-600T < Inven72 < Inven7: 20*300

Inven731-C3-20151003-In731-600T < Inven73 < Inven7: 18*300

Inven732-C3-20151003-In732-1000T < Inven73 < Inven7: 16*500

Inven811-C3-20151003-In811-600T < Inven81 < Inven8: 25*300

Inven812-C3-20151003-In812-600T < Inven81 < Inven8: 24*300

Inven813-C3-20151003-In813-600T < Inven81 < Inven8: 23*300

Inven82-C3-20151003-In82-600T < Inven8: 20*300

Inven831-C3-20151003-In831-600T < Inven83 < Inven8: 18*300

Inven832-C3-20151003-In832-800T < Inven83 < Inven8: 16*400

The multi-subaccount name of the Cash account and three transaction sub-equations respectively are:

88-654308-t-suppliers < Cash payments to suppliers < Operating activities

Cash (1): -10000 + Inventory (1): 10*500 + Inventory (1): 50*250 + Inventory (1): 25*500 + Inventory (1): 35*500 + Inventory (1): 12*500 + Inventory (1): 15*500 + Inventory (1): 6.5*600 + Inventory (1): 12.5*500 = Account Payable (2): 61150

Inventory (1): 18*400 + Inventory (1): 16*500 + Inventory (1): 36*200 + Inventory (1): 31*50 + Inventory (1): 22*344 + Inventory (1): 20*300 + Inventory (1): 18*300 + Inventory (1): 16*500 + Inventory (1): 25*300 = Account Payable (2): 58418

Inventory (1): 24*300 + Inventory (1): 23*300 + Inventory (1): 20*300 + Inventory (1): 18*300 + Inventory (1): 16*400 = Account Payable (2): 31900

- On January 3, 2016, the Proprietorship1 sells the following inventories -$20,360 for sales $34,800 to the Company3 (phone number: 123456782) for cash $9,300 and other on credit.

Inven31-P1-20151125-In31-1000T < Inven3: -6*260

Inven32-P1-20151125-In32-1000T < Inven3: -30*150

Inven331-P1-20151125-In331-1000T < Inven33 < Inven3: -10*260

Inven332-P1-20151125-In332-1000T < Inven33 < Inven3: -27*260

HGFCVB parts-P1-20151125-HGP-1000T < QASXC parts < Inven3: -6*260

PPGHUP parts-P1-20151125-PPP-1000T < ASDUP parts < Inven3: -12*260

The multi-subaccount name of the Cash account and transaction sub-equation respectively are:

88-654308-c-customers < Cash receipts from customers < Operating activities

Cash (1): 9300 + Account receivable (1): 25500 + Inventory (1): -6*260 +

Inventory (1): -30*150 + Inventory (1): -10*260 + Inventory (1): -27*260 + Inventory (1): -6*260 + Inventory (1): -12*260 = Sales (4): 34800 + Cost of goods sold (5): -20360

- On January 3, 2016, the Proprietorship1 transfers the inventories (supplies) -$860 to the Cost of goods manufactured account to satisfy the need of producing. It is consisted of two parts of the Supplies -$6 and the Inventory -$854 (-$14*29 - $16*28).The multi-subaccount names of the Inventory account respectively are:
  Supplies1-P2-20150920-SUP1-200T: -14*29
  Supplies2-P2-20150920-SUP2-200T: -16*28

- On January 3, 2016, the Proprietorship1 transfers the following inventories $6,350 to the Cost of goods manufactured account to satisfy the need of producing.
  Inven411 < Inven41 < Inven4: -5*100
  Inven412 < Inven41 < Inven4: -18.5*100
  TTTCU parts < TTT parts < Inven4: -20*100
  RRRHJK parts < Inven4: -20*100
  The transaction sub-equations is:

  Inventory (1): -5*100 + Inventory (1): -18.5*100 + Inventory (1): -20*100 + Inventory (1): -20*100 = Cost of goods manufactured (5): -6350

- On January 3, 2016, the Proprietorship1 transfers the following inventories $48,370 to the Cost of goods manufactured account to satisfy the need of producing.
  Inven51-C3-20150922-In51-1000T < Inven5: -10*150
  Inven52-C3-20150922-In52-500T < Inven5: -50*75
  Inven531-C3-20150922-In531-1000T < Inven53 < Inven5: -25*150
  Inven532-C3-20150922-In532-1000T < Inven53 < Inven5: -35*150
  Inven541-C3-20150922-In541-1000T < Inven54 < Inven5: -12*150
  Inven542-C3-20150922-In542-1000T < Inven54 < Inven5: -15*150
  Inven611-C3-20151003-In611-1300T < Inven61 < Inven6: -6.5*180

Inven612-C3-20151003-In612-1100T < Inven61 < Inven6: -12.5*150

Inven621-C3-20151003-In621-900T < Inven62 < Inven6: -18*120

Inven63-C3-20151003-In63-1000T < Inven6: -16*150

Inven711-C3-20151003-In711-500T < Inven71 < Inven7: -36*60

Inven712-C3-20151003-In712-100T < Inven71 < Inven7: -31*15

Inven721-C3-20151003-In721-744T < Inven72 < Inven7: -22*100

Inven722-C3-20151003-In722-600T < Inven72 < Inven7: -20*90

Inven731-C3-20151003-In731-600T < Inven73 < Inven7: -18*90

Inven732-C3-20151003-In732-1000T < Inven73 < Inven7: -16*150

Inven811-C3-20151003-In811-600T < Inven81 < Inven8: -25*90

Inven812-C3-20151003-In812-600T < Inven81 < Inven8: -24*90

Inven813-C3-20151003-In813-600T < Inven81 < Inven8: -23*90

Inven82-C3-20151003-In82-600T < Inven8: -20*90

Inven831-C3-20151003-In831-600T < Inven83 < Inven8: -18*90

Inven832-C3-20151003-In832-800T < Inven83 < Inven8: -16*120

The three transaction sub-equations are respectively:

Inventory (1): -10*150 + Inventory (1): -50*75 + Inventory (1): -25*150 + Inventory (1): -35*150 + Inventory (1): -12*150 + Inventory (1): -15*150 + Inventory (1): -6.5*180 + Inventory (1): -12.5*150 + Inventory (1): -18*120 = Cost of goods manufactured (5): -23505

Inventory (1): -16*150 + Inventory (1): -36*60 + Inventory (1): -31*15 + Inventory (1): -22*100 + Inventory (1): -20*90 + Inventory (1): -18*90 + Inventory (1): -16*150 + Inventory (1): -25*90 + Inventory (1): -24*90 = Cost of goods manufactured (5): -17455

Inventory (1): -23*90 + Inventory (1): -20*90 + Inventory (1): -18*90 + Inventory (1): -16*120 = Cost of goods manufactured (5): -7410

- On January 6, 2016, the Proprietorship1 sells the Food113 $12*4 (cost: -$6*4) and the Food 322 $30*2 (cost: -$13*2) to A3 (SIN: 909876503) for cash $108. The multi-subaccount names of the Cash account and the Inventory account respectively are:

  909876503-c-customers < Cash receipts from customers < Operating activities

  Food113-P1-20151203-F113-1000T < Food11 < Food1: -6*4

  Food322-P1-20151203-F322-1000T < Food32 < Food3: -13*2

- On January 10, 2016, the Proprietorship1 sells the Food214 $11*4 (cost: -$5.5*4) and the Food321 $27*2 (cost: -$12*2) to A5 (SIN: 909876505) for cash $98. The multi-subaccount names of the Cash and the Inventory accounts respectively are:

  909876505-c-customers < Cash receipts from customers < Operating activities

  Food214-P1-20151203-F214-1000T < Food21 < Food2: -5.5*4

  Food321-P1-20151203-F321-1000T < Food32 < Food3: -12*2

- On January 10, 2016, the Proprietorship1 sells the Food112 $11*4 (cost: -$5.5*4) and the Food23 $16*3 (cost: -$7.5*3) to A6 (SIN: 909876506) for cash $92. The multi-subaccount names of the Cash and the Inventory accounts respectively are:

  909876506-c-customers < Cash receipts from customers < Operating activities

  Food112-P1-20151203-F112-1000T < Food11 < Food1: -5.5*4

  Food23-P1-20151203-F23-1000T < Food2: -7.5*3

- On January 13, 2016, the Proprietorship1 pays -$150 cash to the Company3 (phone number: 123456082) with the General ID 3. The multi-subaccount name of the Cash account is:

  88-654308-t-supplier<Cash payments for operating expenses<Operating activities

- On January 13, 2016, the Proprietorship1 sells the Food311: $20*1 (cost: -$8.5*1) to A15 (SIN: 909876515) for cash $20. The multi-subaccount names of the Cash account and the Inventory account respectively are:

  909876515-c-customers < Cash receipts from customers < Operating activities

  Food311-P1-20151203-F311-1000T < Food31 < Food3: -8.5*1

- On January 13, 2016, the Proprietorship1 sells the Food221 $12*8 (cost: -$6*8) and the Food312 $24*4 (cost: -$11*4) to A16 (SIN: 909876516) for cash $192. The

multi-subaccount names of the Cash and the Inventory accounts respectively are:

909876516-c-customers < Cash receipts from customers < Operating activities

Food221-P1-20151203-F221-1000T < Food22 < Food2: -6*8

Food312-P1-20151203-F312-1000T < Food31 < Food3: -11*4

- On January 16, 2016, the Proprietorship1 sells the Food321 $27*1 (cost: -$12*1) and the Food322 $30*1 (cost: -$13*1) to A8 (SIN: 909876508) for cash $57. The multi-subaccount names of the Cash account and the Inventory account respectively are:

909876508-c-customers < Cash receipts from customers < Operating activities

Food321-P1-20151203-F321-1000T < Food32 < Food3: -12*1

Food322-P1-20151203-F322-1000T < Food32 < Food3: -13*1

- On January 16, 2016, the Proprietorship1 sells the Food311 $20*1 (cost: -$8.5*1) and the Food312 $24*1 (cost: -$11*1) to A17 (SIN: 909876517) for cash $44. The multi-subaccount names of the Cash and the Inventory accounts respectively are:

909876517-c-customers < Cash receipts from customers < Operating activities

Food311-P1-20151203-F311-1000T < Food31 < Food3: -8.5*1

Food312-P1-20151203-F312-1000T < Food31 < Food3: -11*1

- On January 18, 2016, the Proprietorship1 sells the Food312 $24*1 (cost: -$11*1) and the Food321 $27*1 (cost: -$12*1) to A20 (SIN: 909876520) for cash $51. The multi-subaccount names of the Cash account and the Inventory account respectively are:

909876520-c-customers < Cash receipts from customers < Operating activities

Food312-P1-20151203-F312-1000T < Food31 < Food3: -11*1

Food321-P1-20151203-F321-1000T < Food32 < Food3: -12*1

- On January 18, 2016, the Proprietorship1 pays -$153.87 cash to A22 (SIN: 909876522) for the Travelling expenses -$105.87 and the Other expenses -$48. The multi-subaccount name of the Cash account is:

909876522-n-operating expenses < Cash payments for operating expenses < Operating activities

- On January 19, 2016, the Proprietorship1 sells the Food321 $27*1 (cost: -$12*1) and the Food322 $30*1 (cost: -$13*1) to A25 (SIN: 909876525) for cash $57. The multi-subaccount names of the Cash account and the Inventory account respectively are:

909876525-c-customers < Cash receipts from customers < Operating activities

Food321-P1-20151203-F321-1000T < Food32 < Food3: -12*1

Food322-P1-20151203-F322-1000T < Food32 < Food3: -13*1

- On January 25, 2016, the Proprietorship1 sells the Food311 $20*2 (cost: -$8.5*2) and the Food322 $30*2 (cost: -$13*2) to A9 (SIN: 909876509) for cash $100. The multi-subaccount names of the Cash and the Inventory accounts respectively are:

909876509-c-customers < Cash receipts from customers < Operating activities

Food311-P1-20151203-F311-1000T < Food31 < Food3: -8.5*2

Food322-P1-20151203-F322-1000T < Food32 < Food3: -13*2

- On January 26, 2016, the Proprietorship1 receives $1,300 cash from the Company3 (phone number: 123456782) with the General ID 3. The multi-subaccount name of the Cash account is:

88-654308-c-customers < Cash receipts from customers < Operating activities

- On January 27, 2016, the Proprietorship1 pays -$250 cash to the Company2 (phone number: 123456083) with the General ID 3. The multi-subaccount name of the Cash account is:

88-654307-t-suppliers < Cash payments to suppliers < Operating activities

- On January 27, 2016, the Proprietorship1 sells the Food321 $27*1 (cost: -$12*1) and the Food322 $30*1 (cost: -$13*1) to A10 (SIN: 909876510) for cash $57. The multi-subaccount names of the Cash and the Inventory accounts respectively are:

909876510-c-customers < Cash receipts from customers < Operating activities

Food321-P1-20151203-F321-1000T < Food32 < Food3: -12*1

Food322-P1-20151203-F322-1000T < Food32 < Food3: -13*1

- On January 28, 2016, the Proprietorship1 sells the Food312 $24*6 (cost: -$11*6) to A18 (SIN: 909876518) for cash $144. The multi-subaccount names of the Cash and the Inventory accounts respectively are:

909876518-c-customers < Cash receipts from customers < Operating activities

Food312-P1-20151203-F312-1000T < Food31 < Food3: -11*6

- On January 28, 2016, the Proprietorship1 sells the Food212 $9*2 (cost: -$4.5*2) and the Food312 $24*1 (cost: -$11*1) to A21 (SIN: 909876521) for cash $42. The multi-subaccount names of the Cash and the Inventory accounts respectively are:

  909876521-c-customers < Cash receipts from customers < Operating activities

  Food212-P1-20151203-F212-1000T < Food21 < Food2: -4.5*2

  Food312-P1-20151203-F312-1000T < Food31 < Food3: -11*1

- On January 28, 2016, the Proprietorship1 sells the Food213 $10*2 (cost: -$5*2) and the Food312 $24*1 (cost: -$11*1) to A23 (SIN: 909876523) for cash $44. The multi-subaccount names of the Cash and the Inventory accounts respectively are:

  909876523-c-customers < Cash receipts from customers < Operating activities

  Food213-P1-20151203-F213-1000T < Food21 < Food2: -5*2

  Food312-P1-20151203-F312-1000T < Food31 < Food3: -11*1

- On January 30, 2016, the Proprietorship1 receives $500 cash from the Company2 (phone number: 123456783) with the General ID 3. The multi-subaccount name of the Cash account is:

  88-654307-c-customers < Cash receipts from customers < Operating activities

- On January 30, 2016, the Proprietorship1 pays -$145.54 cash to A23 (SIN: 909876523) for the Travelling expenses -$101.54 and the Other expenses -$44.

- On January 31, 2016, the Proprietorship1 receives $2,040 cash from the Company1 (phone number: 123456784) with the General ID 3. The multi-subaccount name of the Cash account is:

  88-654306-c-customers < Cash receipts from customers < Operating activities

- On January 31, 2016, the Proprietorship1 pays two employees' salary expenses for cash -$5,670 ($2,870 + $2,800). The two multi-subaccount names of the Cash account respectively are:

  909876522-t-salary < Cash payments for operating expenses< Operating activities

  909876523-t-CGM < Cash payments for operating expenses< Operating activities

- On January 31, 2016, the Proprietorship1 sells the following inventories -$5,200 for sales $10,400 to A12A20 (SIN: 909876528), who uses his (or her) father A12's (or mother A12's) secondary card of the Business Bank1, for cash $10,400.

Food111-P1-20151203-F111-1000T < Food11 < Food1: -5*130

Food121-P1-20151203-F121-1000T < Food12 < Food1: -6.5*130

Food122-P1-20151203-F122-1000T < Food12 < Food1: -7*130

Food211-P1-20151203-F211-1000T < Food21 < Food2: -4*130

Food213-P1-20151203-F213-1000T < Food21 < Food2: -5*130

Food221-P1-20151203-F221-1000T < Food22 < Food2: -6*130

Food222-P1-20151203-F222-1000T < Food22 < Food2: -6.5*130

The multi-subaccount name of the Cash account is:

909876512-c-customers < Cash receipts from customers < Operating activities

- On January 31, 2016, the Proprietorship1 sells the following inventories -$6,890 for sales $14,560 to A1 (SIN: 909876501) for cash $14,560.

Food112-P1-20151203-F112-1000T < Food11 < Food1: -5.5*130

Food121-P1-20151203-F121-1000T < Food12 < Food1: -6.5*130

Food122-P1-20151203-F122-1000T < Food12 < Food1: -7*40

Food123-P1-20151203-F123-1000T < Food12 < Food1: -7.5*130

Food212-P1-20151203-F212-1000T < Food21 < Food2: -4.5*140

Food221-P1-20151203-F221-1000T < Food22 < Food2: -6*130

Food311-P1-20151203-F311-1000T < Food31 < Food3: -8.5*130

Food321-P1-20151203-F321-1000T < Food32 < Food3: -12*130

The multi-subaccount name of the Cash account is:

909876501-c-customers < Cash receipts from customers < Operating activities

- On January 31, 2016, the Proprietorship1 sells the following inventories -$6,370 for sales $13,000 to A2 (SIN: 909876502) for cash $13,000.

Food112-P1-20151203-F112-1000T < Food11 < Food1: -5.5*130

Food121-P1-20151203-F121-1000T < Food12 < Food1: -6.5*130

Food122-P1-20151203-F122-1000T < Food12 < Food1: -7*40

Food123-P1-20151203-F123-1000T < Food12 < Food1: -7.5*130

Food212-P1-20151203-F212-1000T < Food21 < Food2: -4.5*140

Food214-P1-20151203-F214-1000T < Food21 < Food2: -5.5*130

Food221-P1-20151203-F221-1000T < Food22 < Food2: -6*130

Food312-P1-20151203-F312-1000T < Food31 < Food3: -11*130

The multi-subaccount name of the Cash account is:

 909876502-c-customers < Cash receipts from customers < Operating activities

- On January 31, 2016, the Proprietorship1 sells the following inventories -$6,305 for sales $13,130 to A3 (SIN: 909876503) for cash $13,130.

Food111-P1-20151203-F111-1000T < Food11 < Food1: -5*130

Food112-P1-20151203-F112-1000T < Food11 < Food1: -5.5*130

Food213-P1-20151203-F213-1000T < Food21 < Food2: -5*156

Food221-P1-20151203-F221-1000T < Food22 < Food2: -6*130

Food222-P1-20151203-F222-1000T < Food22 < Food2: -6.5*130

Food23-P1-20151203-F23-1000T < Food2: -7.5*130

Food321-P1-20151203-F321-1000T < Food32 < Food3: -12*130

The multi-subaccount name of the Cash account is:

 909876503-c-customers < Cash receipts from customers < Operating activities

- On January 31, 2016, the Proprietorship1 sells the following inventories -$6,825 for sales $14,430 to A4 (SIN: 909876504) for cash $14,430.

Food111-P1-20151203-F111-1000T < Food11 < Food1: -5*130

Food113-P1-20151203-F113-1000T < Food11 < Food1: -6*130

Food121-P1-20151203-F121-1000T < Food12 < Food1: -6.5*130

Food122-P1-20151203-F122-1000T < Food12 < Food1: -7*130

Food123-P1-20151203-F123-1000T < Food12 < Food1: -7.5*50

Food211-P1-20151203-F211-1000T < Food21 < Food2: -4*150

Food311-P1-20151203-F311-1000T < Food31 < Food3: -8.5*130

Food321-P1-20151203-F321-1000T < Food32 < Food3: -12*130

The multi-subaccount name of the Cash account is:

 909876504-c-customers < Cash receipts from customers < Operating activities

- On January 31, 2016, the Proprietorship1 sells the following inventories -$6,955 for sales $14,170 to A5 (SIN: 909876505) for cash $14,170.

Food111-P1-20151203-F111-1000T < Food11 < Food1: -5*169

Food112-P1-20151203-F112-1000T < Food11 < Food1: -5.5*130

Food113-P1-20151203-F113-1000T < Food11 < Food1: -6*130

Food122-P1-20151203-F122-1000T < Food12 < Food1: -7*130

Food123-P1-20151203-F123-1000T < Food12 < Food1: -7.5*130

Food213-P1-20151203-F213-1000T < Food21 < Food2: -5*260

Food312-P1-20151203-F312-1000T < Food31 < Food3: -11*130

The multi-subaccount name of the Cash account is:

909876505-c-customers < Cash receipts from customers < Operating activities

- On January 31, 2016, the Proprietorship1 sells the following inventories -$6,045 for sales $12,610 to A6 (SIN: 909876506) for cash $12,610.

Food111-P1-20151203-F111-1000T < Food11 < Food1: -5*130

Food113-P1-20151203-F113-1000T < Food11 < Food1: -6*130

Food121-P1-20151203-F121-1000T < Food12 < Food1: -6.5*40

Food122-P1-20151203-F122-1000T < Food12 < Food1: -7*130

Food211-P1-20151203-F211-1000T < Food21 < Food2: -4*130

Food212-P1-20151203-F212-1000T < Food21 < Food2: -4.5*130

Food213-P1-20151203-F213-1000T < Food21 < Food2: -5*130

Food322-P1-20151203-F322-1000T < Food32 < Food3: -13*130

The multi-subaccount name of the Cash account is:

909876506-c-customers < Cash receipts from customers < Operating activities

- On January 31, 2016, the Proprietorship1 sells the following inventories -$5,930 for sales $12,400 to A7 (SIN: 909876507) for cash $12,400.

Food112-P1-20151203-F112-1000T < Food11 < Food1: -5.5*130

Food113-P1-20151203-F113-1000T < Food11 < Food1: -6*130

Food121-P1-20151203-F121-1000T < Food12 < Food1: -6.5*40

Food122-P1-20151203-F122-1000T < Food12 < Food1: -7*130

Food123-P1-20151203-F123-1000T < Food12 < Food1: -7.5*130

Food212-P1-20151203-F212-1000T < Food21 < Food2: -4.5*130

Food311-P1-20151203-F311-1000T < Food31 < Food3: -8.5*130

Food321-P1-20151203-F321-1000T < Food32 < Food3: -12*50

The multi-subaccount name of the Cash account is:

909876507-c-customers < Cash receipts from customers < Operating activities

- On January 31, 2016, the Proprietorship1 sells the following inventories -$6,305 for sales $13,000 to A8 (SIN: 909876508) for cash $13,000.

Food112-P1-20151203-F112-1000T < Food11 < Food1: -5.5*130

Food113-P1-20151203-F113-1000T < Food11 < Food1: -6*130

Food121-P1-20151203-F121-1000T < Food12 < Food1: -6.5*40

Food122-P1-20151203-F122-1000T < Food12 < Food1: -7*130

Food123-P1-20151203-F123-1000T < Food12 < Food1: -7.5*130

Food211-P1-20151203-F211-1000T < Food21 < Food2: -4*130

Food212-P1-20151203-F212-1000T < Food21 < Food2: -4.5*130

Food321-P1-20151203-F321-1000T < Food32 < Food3: -12*130

The multi-subaccount name of the Cash account is:

909876508-c-customers < Cash receipts from customers < Operating activities

- On January 31, 2016, the Proprietorship1 sells the following inventories -$8,550 for sales $18,460 to A9 (SIN: 909876509) for cash $18,460.

Food214-P1-20151203-F214-1000T < Food21 < Food2: -5.5*270

Food221-P1-20151203-F221-1000T < Food22 < Food2: -6*130

Food222-P1-20151203-F222-1000T < Food22 < Food2: -6.5*130

Food23-P1-20151203-F23-1000T < Food2: -7.5*130

Food311-P1-20151203-F311-1000T < Food31 < Food3: -8.5*130

Food312-P1-20151203-F312-1000T < Food31 < Food3: -11*130

Food321-P1-20151203-F321-1000T < Food32 < Food3: -12*20

Food322-P1-20151203-F322-1000T < Food32 < Food3: -13*130

The multi-subaccount name of the Cash account is:

909876509-c-customers < Cash receipts from customers < Operating activities

- On January 31, 2016, the Proprietorship1 sells the following inventories -$6,580 for sales $13,900 to A10 (SIN: 909876510) for cash $13,900.

  Food213-P1-20151203-F213-1000T < Food21 < Food2: -5*260

  Food221-P1-20151203-F221-1000T < Food22 < Food2: -6*130

  Food222-P1-20151203-F222-1000T < Food22 < Food2: -6.5*130

  Food23-P1-20151203-F23-1000T < Food2: -7.5*130

  Food312-P1-20151203-F312-1000T < Food31 < Food3: -11*130

  Food321-P1-20151203-F321-1000T < Food32 < Food3: -12*50

  Food322-P1-20151203-F322-1000T < Food32 < Food3: -13*50

  The multi-subaccount name of the Cash account is:

  909876510-c-customers < Cash receipts from customers < Operating activities

- On January 31, 2016, the Proprietorship1 sells the following inventories -$6,825 for sales $14,430 to A11 (SIN: 909876511) for cash $14,430.

  Food111-P1-20151203-F111-1000T < Food11 < Food1: -5*130

  Food113-P1-20151203-F113-1000T < Food11 < Food1: -6*130

  Food121-P1-20151203-F121-1000T < Food12 < Food1: -6.5*130

  Food122-P1-20151203-F122-1000T < Food12 < Food1: -7*40

  Food123-P1-20151203-F123-1000T < Food12 < Food1: -7.5*130

  Food212-P1-20151203-F212-1000T < Food21 < Food2: -4.5*140

  Food311-P1-20151203-F311-1000T < Food31 < Food3: -8.5*130

  Food321-P1-20151203-F321-1000T < Food32 < Food3: -12*130

  The multi-subaccount name of the Cash account is:

  909876511-c-customers < Cash receipts from customers < Operating activities

- On January 31, 2016, the Proprietorship1 sells the following inventories -$6,890 for sales $14,560 to A12 (SIN: 909876512) for cash $14,560.

  Food112-P1-20151203-F112-1000T < Food11 < Food1: -5.5*130

  Food113-P1-20151203-F113-1000T < Food11 < Food1: -6*130

  Food121-P1-20151203-F121-1000T < Food12 < Food1: -6.5*130

  Food122-P1-20151203-F122-1000T < Food12 < Food1: -7*40

Food123-P1-20151203-F123-1000T < Food12 < Food1: -7.5*130

Food212-P1-20151203-F212-1000T < Food21 < Food2: -4.5*140

Food311-P1-20151203-F311-1000T < Food31 < Food3: -8.5*130

Food321-P1-20151203-F321-1000T < Food32 < Food3: -12*130

The multi-subaccount name of the Cash account is:

909876512-c-customers < Cash receipts from customers < Operating activities

- On January 31, 2016, the Proprietorship1 sells the following inventories -$8,550 for sales $18,460 to A13 (SIN: 909876513) for cash $18,460.

Food214-P1-20151203-F214-1000T < Food21 < Food2: -5.5*270

Food221-P1-20151203-F221-1000T < Food22 < Food2: -6*130

Food222-P1-20151203-F222-1000T < Food22 < Food2: -6.5*130

Food23-P1-20151203-F23-1000T < Food2: -7.5*130

Food311-P1-20151203-F311-1000T < Food31 < Food3: -8.5*130

Food312-P1-20151203-F312-1000T < Food31 < Food3: -11*130

Food321-P1-20151203-F321-1000T < Food32 < Food3: -12*20

Food322-P1-20151203-F322-1000T < Food32 < Food3: -13*130

The multi-subaccount name of the Cash account is:

909876513-c-customers < Cash receipts from customers < Operating activities

- On February 1, 2016, the Proprietorship1 purchases one Car3 $38,000 from the Company1 (phone number: 123456084) for cash -$28,000 and other $10,000on credit. The multi-subaccount names of the Cash and the Inventory accounts and the two transaction sub-equations are respectively:

88-654306-t-machinery < Cash payments for machinery < Operating activities

Car3-C1-20150925-C3-028 < Car-inventory < Vehicle-inventory: 38000*1

Cash (1): -28000 + Inventory (1): 38000 = Account payable (2): 10000

Vehicle (1): 38000 + Inventory (1): -38000 = 0

- On February 17, 2016, the Proprietorship1 sells the Food23 $16*10 (cost: -$7.5*10)

and the Food 322 $30*5 (cost: -$13*5) to A13 (SIN: 909876513) for cash $310. The multi-subaccount names of the Cash and the Inventory accounts respectively are:

909876513-c-customers < Cash receipts from customers < Operating activities

Food23-P1-20151203-F23-1000T < Food2: -7.5*10

Food322-P1-20151203-F322-1000T < Food32 < Food3: -13*5

- On February 20, 2016, the Proprietorship1 receives $400 cash from the Proprietorship2 (phone number: 123456780) with the General ID 3. The multi-subaccount name of the Cash account is:

  88-654310-c-customers < Cash receipts from customers < Operating activities

- On February 21, 2016, the Proprietorship1 pays -$300 cash to the Proprietorship2 (phone: 123456080) with the General ID 3. The multi-subaccount name of the Cash account is:

  88-654310-t-suppliers < Cash payments to suppliers < Operating activities

- On February 23, 2016, the Proprietorship1 sells the Food23 $16*4 (cost: -$7.5*4) and the Food322 $30*2 (cost: -$13*2) to A19 (SIN: 909876519) for cash $124. The multi-subaccount names of the Cash and the Inventory accounts respectively are:

  909876519-c-customers < Cash receipts from customers < Operating activities

  Food23-P1-20151203-F23-1000T < Food2: -7.5*4

  Food322-P1-20151203-F322-1000T < Food32 < Food3: -13*2

- On February 24, 2016, the Proprietorship1 sells the Food122 $ 14*4 (cost: -$7*4) and the Food321 $27*2 (cost: -$12*2) to A5 (SIN: 909876505) for cash $110. The multi-subaccount names of the Cash and the Inventory accounts respectively are:

  909876505-c-customers < Cash receipts from customers < Operating activities

  Food122-P1-20151203-F122-1000T < Food12 < Food1: -7*4

  Food321-P1-20151203-F321-1000T < Food32 < Food3: -12*2

- On February 25, 2016, the Proprietorship1 sells the Food123 $15*3 (cost: -$7.5*3) and the Food321 $27*2 (cost: -$12*2) to A3 (SIN: 909876503) for cash $99. The multi-subaccount names of the Cash and the Inventory accounts respectively are:

  909876503-c-customers < Cash receipts from customers < Operating activities

Food123-P1-20151203-F123-1000T < Food12 < Food1: -7.5*3

Food321-P1-20151203-F321-1000T < Food32 < Food3: -12*2

- On February 28, 2016, the Proprietorship1 sells the Food312 $24*2 (cost: -$11*2) and the Food321 $27*2 (cost: -$12*2) to A18 (SIN: 909876518) for cash $102. The multi-subaccount names of the Cash and the Inventory accounts respectively are:

  909876518-c-customers < Cash receipts from customers < Operating activities

  Food312-P1-20151203-F312-1000T < Food31 < Food3: -11*2

  Food321-P1-20151203-F321-1000T < Food32 < Food3: -12*2

- On February 28, 2016, the Proprietorship1 sells the Food312 $24*2 (cost: -$11*2) and the Food321 $27*2 (cost: -$12*2) to A21 (SIN: 909876521) for cash $102. The multi-subaccount names of the Cash and the Inventory accounts respectively are:

  909876521-c-customers < Cash receipts from customers < Operating activities

  Food312-P1-20151203-F312-1000T < Food31 < Food3: -11*2

  Food321-P1-20151203-F321-1000T < Food32 < Food3: -12*2

- On February 28, 2016, the Proprietorship1 pays two employees' salary -$5,670.

- On March 6, 2016, the Proprietorship1 pays -$1,000 cash to the Company1 (phone number: 123456084) with the General ID 3. The Cash's multi-subaccount name is:

  88-654306-t-suppliers < Cash payments to suppliers < Operating activities

- On March 7, 2016, the Proprietorship1 sells the Food312 $24*2 (cost: -$11*2) and the Food322 $30*1 (cost: -$13*1) to A25 (SIN: 909876525) for cash $78. The multi-subaccount names of the Cash and the Inventory accounts respectively are:

  909876525-c-customers < Cash receipts from customers < Operating activities

  Food312-P1-20151203-F312-1000T < Food31 < Food3: -11*2

  Food322-P1-20151203-F322-1000T < Food32 < Food3: -13*1

- On March 10, 2016, the Proprietorship1 sells the Food214 $11*3 (cost: -$5.5*3) and the Food322 $30*3 (cost: -$13*3) to A6 (SIN: 909876506) for cash $123. The multi-subaccount names of the Cash and the Inventory accounts respectively are:

  909876506-c-customers < Cash receipts from customers < Operating activities

  Food214-P1-20151203-F214-1000T < Food21 < Food2: -5.5*3

Food322-P1-20151203-F322-1000T < Food32 < Food3: -13*3

- On March 11, 2016, the Proprietorship1 sells the Food111 $10*2 (cost: -$5*2) and the Food322 $30*1 (cost: -$13*1) to A11 (SIN: 909876511) for cash $50. The multi-subaccount names of the Cash and the Inventory accounts respectively are:

  909876511-c-customers < Cash receipts from customers < Operating activities

  Food111-P1-20151203-F111-1000T < Food11 < Food1: -5*2

  Food322-P1-20151203-F322-1000T < Food32 < Food3: -13*1

- On March 19, 2016, the Proprietorship1 sells the Food112 $11*2 (cost: -$5.5*2), the Food213 $10*3 (cost: -$5*3), and the Food 322 $30*4 (cost: -$13*4) to A4 (SIN: 909876504) for cash $172. The multi-subaccount names of the Cash and the Inventory accounts respectively are:

  909876504-c-customers < Cash receipts from customers < Operating activities

  Food112-P1-20151203-F112-1000T < Food11 < Food1: -5.5*2

  Food213-P1-20151203-F213-1000T < Food21 < Food2: -5*3

- On March 23, 2016, the Proprietorship1 pays -$159.45 cash to A22 (SIN: 909876522) for the Travelling expenses -$101.45 and the Other expenses -$58.

- On March 26, 2016, the Proprietorship1 sells the Food111 $10*1 (cost: -$5*1), the Food214 $11*1 (cost: -$5.5*1), the Food312 $24*1 (cost: -$11*1), and the Food 321 $27*1 (cost: -$12*1) to A2 (SIN: 909876502) for cash $72. The multi-subaccount names of the Cash and the Inventory accounts respectively are:

  909876502-c-customers < Cash receipts from customers < Operating activities

  Food111-P1-20151203-F111-1000T < Food11 < Food1: -5*1

  Food214-P1-20151203-F214-1000T < Food21 < Food2: -5.5*1

  Food312-P1-20151203-F312-1000T < Food31 < Food3: -11*1

  Food321-P1-20151203-F321-1000T < Food32 < Food3: -12*1

- On March 27, 2016, the Proprietorship1 sells the Food312 $24*1 (cost: -$11*1) and the Food321 $27*1 (cost: -$12*1) to A8 (SIN: 909876508) for cash $51. The multi-subaccount names of the Cash and the Inventory accounts respectively are:

  909876508-c-customers < Cash receipts from customers < Operating activities

Food312-P1-20151203-F312-1000T < Food31 < Food3: -11*1

Food321-P1-20151203-F321-1000T < Food32 < Food3: -12*1

- On March 31, 2016, the Proprietorship1 pays two employees' salary -$5,670.

- On April 13, 2016, the Proprietorship1 sells the Food222 $13*3 (cost: -$6.5*3) and the Food322 $30*1 (cost: -$13*1) to A11 (SIN: 909876511) for cash $69. The multi-subaccount names of the Cash and the Inventory accounts respectively are:

    909876511-c-customers < Cash receipts from customers < Operating activities

    Food222-P1-20151203-F222-1000T < Food22 < Food2: -6.5*3

    Food322-P1-20151203-F322-1000T < Food32 < Food3: -13*1

- On April 22, 2016, the Proprietorship1 sells the Food312 $24*2 (cost: -$11*2) and the Food321 $27*1 (cost: -$12*1) to A24 (SIN: 909876524) for cash $75. The multi-subaccount names of the Cash and the Inventory accounts respectively are:

    909876524-c-customers < Cash receipts from customers < Operating activities

    Food312-P1-20151203-F312-1000T < Food31 < Food3: -11*2

    Food321-P1-20151203-F321-1000T < Food32 < Food3: -12*1

- On April 24, 2016, the Proprietorship1 sells the Food312 $24*3 (cost: -$11*3), the Food321 $27*2 (cost: -$12*2), and the Food322 $30*1 (cost: -$13*1) to A16 (SIN: 909876516) for cash $156. The multi-subaccount names of the Cash and the Inventory accounts respectively are:

    909876516-c-customers < Cash receipts from customers < Operating activities

    Food312-P1-20151203-F312-1000T < Food31 < Food3: -11*3

    Food321-P1-20151203-F321-1000T < Food32 < Food3: -12*2

    Food322-P1-20151203-F322-1000T < Food32 < Food3: -13*1

- On April 24, 2016, the Proprietorship1 sells the Food312 $24*2 (cost: -$11*2) and the Food322 $30*1 (cost: -$13*1) to A19 (SIN: 909876519) for cash $78. The multi-subaccount names of the Cash and the Inventory accounts respectively are:

    909876519-c-customers < Cash receipts from customers < Operating activities

    Food312-P1-20151203-F312-1000T < Food31 < Food3: -11*2

    Food322-P1-20151203-F322-1000T < Food32 < Food3: -13*1

- On April 27, 2016, the Proprietorship1 sells the Food312 $24*2 (cost: -$11*2) and the Food321 $27*2 (cost: -$12*2) to A7 (SIN: 909876507) for cash $102. The multi-subaccount names of the Cash and the Inventory accounts respectively are:

  909876507-c-customers < Cash receipts from customers < Operating activities

  Food312-P1-20151203-F312-1000T < Food31 < Food3: -11*2

  Food321-P1-20151203-F321-1000T < Food32 < Food3: -12*2

- On April 29, 2016, the Proprietorship1 purchases one Truck2 part2 $7,200 from the Company2 for cash -$5,000 and other on credit. The multi-subaccount names of the Cash and the Inventory accounts and the transaction sub-equations are respectively:

  88-654307-t-supplies<Cash payments for operating expenses<Operating activities

  Truck2 part2-C2-20150728-T2P2-053 < Truck2 parts < Vehicle parts: 7200*1

  Cash (1): -5000 + Inventory (1): 7200 = Account payable (2): 2200

  Inventory (1): -7200 = Vehicle parts expenses (5): 7200

- On April 30, 2016, the Proprietorship1 pays two employees' salary -$5,670.

- On April 30, 2016, the Proprietorship1 has completed all products of the Working-in-process inventory account. If the all general parts and supplies have just been consumed, then the Proprietorship1 transfers the balance of the Cost of goods manufactured account to the Working-in-process inventory account. The Cost of goods manufactured account has three subaccounts of the "Supplies expenses", the "909876523-salary < Product department-salary < Salary expenses", and the "General parts expenses". Their balances are -$860, -$11,200, and -$54,720 (-$48,370 - $6,350) respectively. Here, the balance of the subaccount "General parts expenses" will be divided to three parts which are used in three transaction sub-equations respectively. The three transaction sub-equations are respectively:

  Working-in-process inventory (1): 3*600 + Working-in-process inventory (1): 16*600 + Working-in-process inventory (1): 5*600 + Working-in-process inventory (1): 14*600 + Working-in-process inventory (1): 3*600 + Working-in-process inventory (1): 6*600 + Working-in-process inventory (1): 2.6*600 = Cost of goods manufactured (5): 860 + Cost of goods manufactured (5): 11200 + Cost of goods manufactured (5): 17700

Working-in-process inventory (1): 3*600 + Working-in-process inventory (1): 3*600 + Working-in-process inventory (1): 3.6*600 + Working-in-process inventory (1): 4*600 + Working-in-process inventory (1): 4*600 + Working-in-process inventory (1): 2*600 + Working-in-process inventory (1): 2.5*600 + Working-in-process inventory (1): 2.8*600 = Cost of goods manufactured (5): 14940

Working-in-process inventory (1): 3*600 + Working-in-process inventory (1): 3*600 + Working-in-process inventory (1): 3.4*600 + Working-in-process inventory (1): 4*600 + Working-in-process inventory (1): 4.4*600 + Working-in-process inventory (1): 6*600 + Working-in-process inventory (1): 6*600 + Working-in-process inventory (1): 7*600 = Cost of goods manufactured (5): 22080

- On April 30, 2016, the Proprietorship1 transfers the balance of the Working-in-process inventory account to the Inventory account. The multi-subaccount names of the Inventory account and the five transaction sub-equations respectively are:
  Inven31-P1-20160430-In31-600T < Inven3: 6*600
  Inven32-P1-20160430-In32-600T < Inven3: 30*600
  Inven331-P1-20160430-In331-600T < Inven33 < Inven3: 10*600
  Inven332-P1-20160430-In332-600T < Inven33 < Inven3: 27*600
  HGFCVB parts-P1-20160430-HGP-600T < QASXC parts < Inven3: 6*600
  PPGHUP parts-P1-20160430-PPP-600T < ASDUP parts < Inven3: 12*600
  Food111-P1-20160430-F111-600T < Food11 < Food1: 5*600
  Food112-P1-20160430-F112-600T < Food11 < Food1: 5.5*600

Food113-P1-20160430-F113-600T < Food11 < Food1: 6*600

Food121-P1-20160430-F121-600T < Food12 < Food1: 6.5*600

Food122-P1-20160430-F122-600T < Food12 < Food1: 7*600

Food123-P1-20160430-F123-600T < Food12 < Food1: 7.5*600

Food211-P1-20160430-F211-600T < Food21 < Food2: 4*600

Food212-P1-20160430-F212-600T < Food21 < Food2: 4.5*600

Food213-P1-20160430-F213-600T < Food21 < Food2: 5*600

Food214-P1-20160430-F214-600T < Food21 < Food2: 5.5*600

Food221-P1-20160430-F221-600T < Food22 < Food2: 6*600

Food222-P1-20160430-F222-600T < Food22 < Food2: 6.5*600

Food23-P1-20160430-F23-600T < Food2: 7.5*600

Food311-P1-20160430-F311-600T < Food31 < Food3: 8.5*600

Food312-P1-20160430-F312-600T < Food31 < Food3: 11*600

Food321-P1-20160430-F321-600T < Food32 < Food3: 12*600

Food322-P1-20160430-F322-600T < Food32 < Food3: 13*600

Working-in-process inventory (1): -6*600 + Working-in-process inventory (1): -30*600 + Working-in-process inventory (1): -10*600 + Working-in-process inventory (1): -27*600 + Working-in-process inventory (1): -6*600 + Inventory (1): 30*600 + Inventory (1): 10*600 + Inventory (1): 27*600 + Inventory (1): 6*600 = 0

Working-in-process inventory (1): -12*600 + Working-in-process inventory (1): -5*600 + Working-in-process inventory (1): -5.5*600 + Working-in-process inventory (1): -6*600 + Working-in-process inventory (1): -6.5*600 + Inventory (1): 12*600 + Inventory (1): 5*600 + Inventory (1): 5.5*600 + Inventory (1): 6*600 + Inventory (1): 6.5*600 = 0

Working-in-process inventory (1): -7*600 + Working-in-process inventory (1): -7.5*600 + Working-in-process inventory (1): -4*600 + Working-in-process inventory (1): -4.5*600 + Working-in-process inventory (1): -5*600 + Inventory (1): 7*600 + Inventory (1): 7.5*600 + Inventory (1): 4*600 + Inventory (1): 4.5*600 + Inventory (1): 5*600 = 0

Working-in-process inventory (1): -5.5*600 + Working-in-process inventory (1): -6*600 + Working-in-process inventory (1): -6.5*600 + Working-in-process inventory (1): -7.5*600 + Working-in-process inventory (1): -8.5*600 + Inventory (1): 5.5*600 + Inventory (1): 6*600 + Inventory (1): 6.5*600 + Inventory (1): 7.5*600 + Inventory (1): 8.5*600 = 0

Working-in-process inventory (1): -11*600 + Working-in-process inventory (1): -12*600 + Working-in-process inventory (1): -13*600 + Inventory (1): 11*600 + Inventory (1): 12*600 + Inventory (1): 13*600 = 0

- On May 1, 2016, the Proprietorship 1 plans to produce the following products in the Figure 3.9-1.

| Order | Product (the Lowest-level Subaccount) Names | Multi-subaccount Names | Costs | Amount |
|-------|---------------------------------------------|------------------------|-------|--------|
| 1 | Food111 | Food111 < Food11 < Food1 | 5.00 | 1200 |
| 2 | Food112 | Food112 < Food11 < Food1 | 5.50 | 1200 |
| 3 | Food113 | Food113 < Food11 < Food1 | 6.00 | 1200 |
| 4 | Food121 | Food121 < Food12 < Food1 | 6.50 | 1200 |
| 5 | Food122 | Food122 < Food12 < Food1 | 7.00 | 1200 |
| 6 | Food123 | Food123 < Food12 < Food1 | 7.50 | 1200 |
| 7 | Food211 | Food211 < Food21 < Food2 | 4.00 | 1200 |
| 8 | Food212 | Food212 < Food21 < Food2 | 4.50 | 1200 |
| 9 | Food213 | Food213 < Food21 < Food2 | 5.00 | 1200 |
| 10 | Food214 | Food214 < Food21 < Food2 | 5.50 | 1200 |
| 11 | Food221 | Food221 < Food22 < Food2 | 6.00 | 1200 |
| 12 | Food222 | Food222 < Food22 < Food2 | 6.50 | 1200 |
| 13 | Food23 | Food23 < Food2 | 7.50 | 1200 |
| 14 | Food311 | Food311 < Food31 < Food3 | 8.50 | 1200 |
| 15 | Food312 | Food312 < Food31 < Food3 | 11.00 | 1200 |
| 16 | Food321 | Food321 < Food32 < Food3 | 12.00 | 1200 |
| 17 | Food322 | Food322 < Food32 < Food3 | 13.00 | 1200 |

Figure 3.9-1    Producing Plan Table

Therefore, the Proprietorship1 purchases the inventories (supplies) $1,500 ($14*50 + $16*50) from the Proprietorship2 (phone number: 123456080) for cash -$800 and other on credit. The multi-subaccount names of the Cash account and the Inventory account and transaction sub-equations respectively are:

88-654310-t-supplies < Cash payments for operating expenses < Operating activities

Supplies1-P2-20160430-Supp1-200T: 14*50

Supplies2-P2-20160430-Supp2-200T: 16*50

Cash (1): -800 + Inventory (1): 14*50 + Inventory (1): 16*50= Account payable (2): 700

- On May 1, 2016, the Proprietorship1 purchases the following inventories $8,255 from the Proprietorship2 (phone number: 123456080) for -$5,000 cash and other $3,255 on credit.

Inven411-P2-20151127-In411-1000T < Inven41 < Inven4: 5*130

Inven412-P2-20151127-In412-1000T < Inven41 < Inven4: 18.5*130

TTTCU parts-P2-20151127-TTP-1000T < TTT parts < Inven4: 20*130

RRRHJK parts-P2-20151127-RRP-1000T < Inven4: 20*130

The multi-subaccount name of the Cash account and the four transaction sub-equations respectively are:

88-654310-t-suppliers < Cash payments to suppliers < Operating activities

Cash (1): -5000 + Inventory (1): 5*130 + Inventory (1): 18.5*130 + Inventory (1): 20*130 + Inventory (1): 20*130 = Account Payable (2): 3255

- On May 1, 2016, the Proprietorship1 sells the following inventories -$13,650 for sales $23,250 to the Company1 (phone number: 123456784) for cash $3,250 and other on credit.

Inven31-P1-20151125-In31-1000T < Inven3: -6*150

Inven32-P1-20151125-In32-1000T < Inven3: -30*150

Inven331-P1-20151125-In331-1000T < Inven33 < Inven3: -10*150

Inven332-P1-20151125-In332-1000T < Inven33 < Inven3: -27*150

HGFCVB parts-P1-20151125-HGP-1000T < QASXC parts < Inven3: -6*150

PPGHUP parts-P1-20151125-PPP-1000T < ASDUP parts < Inven3: -12*150

The multi-subaccount name of the Cash account and the transaction sub-equation respectively are:

88-654306-c-customers < Cash receipts from customers < Operating activities

Cash (1): 3250 + Account receivable (1): 20000 + Inventory (1): -6*150 + Inventory (1): -30*150 + Inventory (1): -10*150 + Inventory (1): -27*150 + Inventory (1): -12*150 + Inventory (1): = Sales (4): 23250 + Cost of goods sold (5): -13650

- On May 1, 2016, the Proprietorship1 sells the following inventories -$14,250 for sales $24,250 to the Proprietorship2 (phone number: 123456780) for cash $9,000 and other on credit.

Inven31-P1-20160430-In31-600T < Inven3: -6*250

Inven32-P1-20160430-In32-600T < Inven3: -30*150

Inven331-P1-20160430-In331-600T < Inven33 < Inven3: -10*150

Inven332-P1-20160430-In332-600T < Inven33 < Inven3: -27*150

HGFCVB parts-P1-20160430-HGP-600T < QASXC parts < Inven3: -6*150

PPGHUP parts-P1-20160430-PPP-600T < ASDUP parts < Inven3: -12*150

The multi-subaccount name of the Cash account and the transaction sub-equation respectively are:

88-654310-c-customers < Cash receipts from customers < Operating activities

Cash (1): 9000 + Account receivable (1): 15250 + Inventory (1): -6*250 + Inventory (1): -30*150 + Inventory (1): -10*150 + Inventory (1): -27*150 + Inventory (1): -6*150 + Inventory (1): -12*150 = Sales (4): 24250 + Cost of goods sold (5): -14250

- On May 1, 2016, the Proprietorship1 sells the Food213 $10*3 (cost: -$5*3) and the Food311 $20*3 (cost: -$8.5*3) to A18 (SIN: 909876518) for cash $90. The multi-subaccount names of the Cash and the Inventory accounts respectively are:

  909876518-c-customers < Cash receipts from customers < Operating activities

  Food213-P1-20151203-F213-1000T < Food21 < Food2: -5*3

  Food311-P1-20151203-F311-1000T < Food31 < Food3: -8.5*3

- On May 1, 2016, the Proprietorship1 sells the Food213 $10*3 (cost: -$5*3) and the Food311 $20*1 (cost: -$8.5*1) to A21 (SIN: 909876521) for cash $50. The multi-subaccount names of the Cash and the Inventory accounts respectively are:

  909876521-c-customers < Cash receipts from customers < Operating activities

  Food213-P1-20151203-F213-1000T < Food21 < Food2: -5*3

  Food311-P1-20151203-F311-1000T < Food31 < Food3: -8.5*1

- On May 2, 2016, the Proprietorship1 transfers the Inventory (supplies) $1,500 to the Cost of goods manufactured account to satisfy the need of producing. It is consisted of two parts of the Supplies -$60 and the Inventory -$1,440 (-$14*48 - $16*48). The multi-subaccount names of the Inventory accounts respectively are:

  Supplies1-P2-20160430-Supp1-200T: -14*48

  Supplies2-P2-20160430-Supp2-200T: -16*48

- On May 2, 2016, the Proprietorship1 transfers the following inventories -$8,255 to the Cost of goods manufactured account to satisfy the need of producing.

  Inven411-P2-20151127-In411-1000T < Inven41 < Inven4: -5*130

  Inven412-P2-20151127-In412-1000T < Inven41 < Inven4: -18.5*130

  TTTCU parts-P2-20151127-TTP-1000T < TTT parts < Inven4: -20*130

  RRRHJK parts-P2-20151127-RRP-1000T < Inven4: -20*130

  The transaction sub-equations is:

  Inventory (1): -5*130 + Inventory (1): -18.5*130 + Inventory (1): -20*130 + Inventory (1): -20*130 = Cost of goods manufactured (5): -8255

- On May 2, 2016, the Proprietorship1 transfers the following inventories -$113,098 to the Cost of goods manufactured account to satisfy the need of producing.

  Inven51-C3-20150922-In51-1000T < Inven5: -10*350

  Inven52-C3-20150922-In52-500T < Inven5: -50*175

  Inven531-C3-20150922-In531-1000T < Inven53 < Inven5: -25*350

  Inven532-C3-20150922-In532-1000T < Inven53 < Inven5: -35*350

  Inven541-C3-20150922-In541-1000T < Inven54 < Inven5: -12*350

  Inven542-C3-20150922-In542-1000T < Inven54 < Inven5: -15*350

  Inven611-C3-20151003-In611-1300T < Inven61 < Inven6: -6.5*420

  Inven612-C3-20151003-In612-1100T < Inven61 < Inven6: -12.5*350

  Inven621-C3-20151003-In621-900T < Inven62 < Inven6: -18*280

  Inven63-C3-20151003-In63-1000T < Inven6: -16*350

  Inven711-C3-20151003-In711-500T < Inven71 < Inven7: -36*140

  Inven712-C3-20151003-In712-100T < Inven71 < Inven7: -31*35

  Inven721-C3-20151003-In721-744T < Inven72 < Inven7: -22*244

  Inven722-C3-20151003-In722-600T < Inven72 < Inven7: -20*210

  Inven731-C3-20151003-In731-600T < Inven73 < Inven7: -18*210

  Inven732-C3-20151003-In732-1000T < Inven73 < Inven7: -16*350

  Inven811-C3-20151003-In811-600T < Inven81 < Inven8: -25*210

  Inven812-C3-20151003-In812-600T < Inven81 < Inven8: -24*210

  Inven813-C3-20151003-In813-600T < Inven81 < Inven8: -23*210

  Inven82-C3-20151003-In82-600T < Inven8: -20*210

  Inven831-C3-20151003-In831-600T < Inven83 < Inven8: -18*210

  Inven832-C3-20151003-In832-800T < Inven83 < Inven8: -16*280

  The three transaction sub-equations are respectively:

  Inventory (1): -10*350 + Inventory (1): -50*175 + Inventory (1): -25*350 +
  Inventory (1): -35*350 + Inventory (1): -12*350 + Inventory (1): -15*350 +
  Inventory (1): -6.5*420 + Inventory (1): -12.5*350 + Inventory (1): 18*280 =

Cost of goods manufactured (5): -54845

Inventory (1): -16*350 + Inventory (1): -36*140 + Inventory (1): -31*35 + Inventory (1): -22*244 + Inventory (1): -20*210 + Inventory (1): -18*210 + Inventory (1): -16*350 + Inventory (1): -25*210 + Inventory (1): -24*210 = Cost of goods manufactured (5): -40963

Inventory (1): -23*210 + Inventory (1): -20*210 + Inventory (1): -18*210 + Inventory (1): -16*280 = Cost of goods manufactured (5): -17290

- On May 12, 2016, the Proprietorship1 sells the Food222 $13*4 (cost: -$6.5*4) and the Food311 $20*3 (cost: -$8.5*3) to A9 (SIN: 909876509) for cash $112. The multi-subaccount names of the Cash and the Inventory accounts respectively are:
  909876509-c-customers < Cash receipts from customers < Operating activities
  Food222-P1-20151203-F222-1000T < Food22 < Food2: -6.5*4
  Food311-P1-20151203-F311-1000T < Food31 < Food3: -8.5*3

- On May 12, 2016, the Proprietorship1 sells the Food213 $10*3 (cost: -$5*3) and the Food311 $20*1 (cost: -$8.5*1) to A23 (SIN: 909876523) for cash $50. The multi-subaccount names of the Cash and the Inventory accounts respectively are:
  909876523-c-customers < Cash receipts from customers < Operating activities
  Food213-P1-20151203-F213-1000T < Food21 < Food2: -5*3
  Food311-P1-20151203-F311-1000T < Food31 < Food3: -8.5*1

- On May 13, 2016, the Proprietorship1 sells the Food121 $13*4 (cost: -$6.5*3) and the Food311 $20*3 (cost: -$8.5*3) to A6 (SIN: 909876506) for cash $112. The multi-subaccount names of the Cash and the Inventory accounts respectively are:
  909876506-c-customers < Cash receipts from customers < Operating activities
  Food121-P1-20151203-F112-1000T < Food11 < Food1: -6.5*3
  Food311-P1-20151203-F311-1000T < Food31 < Food3: -8.5*3

- On May 14, 2016, the Proprietorship1 pays -$166.23 cash to A23 (SIN: 909876523) for the Travelling expenses -$116.23 and the Other expenses -$50.

- On May 14, 2016, the Proprietorship1 sells the Food123 $15*3 (cost: -$7.5*3) and the Food311 $20*3 (cost: -$8.5*3) to A3 (SIN: 909876503) for cash $105. The multi-subaccount names of the Cash and the Inventory accounts respectively are:

    909876503-c-customers < Cash receipts from customers < Operating activities

    Food123-P1-20151203-F123-1000T < Food12 < Food1: -7.5*3

    Food311-P1-20151203-F311-1000T < Food31 < Food3: -8.5*3

- On May 20, 2016, the Proprietorship1 sells the Food121 $13*2 (cost: -$6.5*2) and the Food322 $30*1 (cost: -$13*1) to A11 (SIN: 909876511) for cash $56. The multi-subaccount names of the Cash and the Inventory accounts respectively are:

    909876511-c-customers < Cash receipts from customers < Operating activities

    Food121-P1-20151203-F121-1000T < Food12 < Food1: -6.5*2

    Food322-P1-20151203-F322-1000T < Food32 < Food3: -13*1

- On May 22, 2016, the Proprietorship1 sells the Food111 $10*10 (cost: -$5*10), the Food123 $15*10 (cost: -$7.5*10), the Food312 $24*3 (cost: -$11*3), and the Food321 $27*3 (cost: -$12*3) to A13 (SIN: 909876513) for cash $403. The multi-subaccount names of the Cash and the Inventory accounts respectively are:

    909876513-c-customers < Cash receipts from customers < Operating activities

    Food111-P1-20160430-F111-600T < Food11 < Food1: -5*10

    Food123-P1-20160430-F123-600T < Food12 < Food1: -7.5*10

    Food312-P1-20151203-F312-1000T < Food31 < Food3: -11*3

    Food321-P1-20151203-F321-1000T < Food32 < Food3: -12*3

- On May 22, 2016, the Proprietorship1 sells the Food111 $10*8 (cost: -$5*8), the Food312 $24*2 (cost: -$11*2), and the Food321 $27*1 (cost: -$12*1) to A16 (SIN: 909876516) for cash $155. The multi-subaccount names of the Cash and the Inventory accounts respectively are:

    909876516-c-customers < Cash receipts from customers < Operating activities

    Food111-P1-20151203-F111-1000T < Food11 < Food1: -5*8

    Food312-P1-20151203-F312-1000T < Food31 < Food3: -11*2

    Food321-P1-20151203-F321-1000T < Food32 < Food3: -12*1

- On May 22, 2016, the Proprietorship1 sells the Food111 $10*6 (cost: -$5*6), the Food312 $24*2 (cost: -$11*2), and the Food322 $30*1 (cost: -$13*1) to A19 (SIN: 909876519) for cash $138. The multi-subaccount names of the Cash and the Inventory accounts respectively are:

  909876519-c-customers < Cash receipts from customers < Operating activities

  Food111-P1-20151203-F111-1000T < Food11 < Food1: -5*6

  Food312-P1-20151203-F312-1000T < Food31 < Food3: -11*2

  Food322-P1-20151203-F322-1000T < Food32 < Food3: -13*1

- On May 24, 2016, the Proprietorship1 pays -$176.95 cash to A22 (SIN: 909876522) for the Travelling expenses -$120.95 and the Other expenses -$56.

- On May 31, 2016, the Proprietorship1 pays two employees' salary expenses for cash $5,670 repeatedly.

- On June 14, 2016, the Proprietorship1 sells the Food23 $16*3 (cost: -$7.5*3) and the Food312 $24*2 (cost: -$11*2) to A9 (SIN: 909876509) for cash $96. The multi-subaccount names of the Cash and the Inventory accounts respectively are:

  909876509-c-customers < Cash receipts from customers < Operating activities

  Food23-P1-20151203-F23-1000T < Food2: -7.5*3

  Food312-P1-20151203-F312-1000T < Food31 < Food3: -11*2

- On June 16, 2016, the Proprietorship1 receives cash $300 from the Company3 (phone number: 123456782) with the General ID 3. The multi-subaccount name of the Cash account is:

  88-654308-c-customers < Cash receipts from customers < Operating activities

- On June 18, 2016, the Proprietorship1 sells the Food214 $11*5 (cost: -$5.5*5) and the Food321 $27*2 (cost: -$12*2) to A12 (SIN: 909876512) for cash $109. The multi-subaccount names of the Cash and the Inventory accounts respectively are:

  909876512-c-customers < Cash receipts from customers < Operating activities

  Food214-P1-20151203-F214-1000T < Food21 < Food2: -5.5*5

  Food321-P1-20151203-F321-1000T < Food32 < Food3: -12*2

- On June 20, 2016, the Proprietorship1 sells the Food112 $11*10 (cost: -$5.5*10), the Food211 $8*10 (cost: -$4*10), and the Food311 $20*6 (cost: -$8.5*6) to A13 (SIN: 909876513) for cash $310. The multi-subaccount names of the Cash and the Inventory accounts respectively are:

  909876513-c-customers < Cash receipts from customers < Operating activities

  Food112-P1-20151203-F112-1000T < Food11 < Food1: -5.5*10

  Food211-P1-20151203-F211-1000T < Food21 < Food2: -4*10

  Food311-P1-20151203-F311-1000T < Food31 < Food3: -8.5*6

- On June 20, 2016, the Proprietorship1 sells the Food113 $12*5 (cost: -$6*5), the Food214 $11*5 (cost: -$5.5*5), and the Food312 $24*2 (cost: -$11*2) to A16 (SIN: 909876516) for cash $163. The multi-subaccount names of the Cash and the Inventory accounts respectively are:

  909876516-c-customers < Cash receipts from customers < Operating activities

  Food113-P1-20151203-F113-1000T < Food11 < Food1: -6*5

  Food214-P1-20151203-F214-1000T < Food21 < Food2: -5.5*5

  Food312-P1-20151203-F312-1000T < Food31 < Food3: -11*2

- On June 21, 2016, the Proprietorship1 sells the Food113 $12*5 (cost: -$6*5) and the Food312 $24*2 (cost: -$11*2) to A19 (SIN: 909876519) for cash $108. The multi-subaccount names of the Cash and the Inventory accounts respectively are:

  909876519-c-customers < Cash receipts from customers < Operating activities

  Food113-P1-20151203-F113-1000T < Food11 < Food1: -6*5

  Food312-P1-20151203-F312-1000T < Food31 < Food3: -11*2

- On June 23, 2016, the Proprietorship1 pays -$157.37 cash to A22 (SIN: 909876522) for the Travelling expenses -$109.37 and the Other expenses -$48.

- On June 30, 2016, the Proprietorship1 pays two employees' salary -$5,670 repeatedly.

- On July 4, 2016, the Proprietorship1 pays -$55,000 cash to the Company3 (phone number: 123456082) with the General ID 16. The multi-subaccount name of the Cash account and transaction sub-equation respectively are:

  88-654308-t-suppliers < Cash payments to suppliers < Operating activities

- On July 5, 2016, the Proprietorship1 sells the Food123 $15*6 (cost: -$7.5*6) and the Food322 $30*3 (cost: -$13*3) to A14 (SIN: 909876514) for cash $180. The multi-subaccount names of the Cash and the Inventory accounts respectively are:

    909876514-c-customers < Cash receipts from customers < Operating activities

    Food123-P1-20151203-F123-1000T < Food12 < Food1: -7.5*6

    Food322-P1-20151203-F322-1000T < Food32 < Food3: -13*3

- On July 16, 2016, the Proprietorship1 sells the Food211 $8*6 (cost: -$4*6) and the Food 23 $16*4 (cost: -$7.5*4) to A4 (SIN: 909876504) for cash $112. The multi-subaccount names of the Cash and the Inventory accounts respectively are:

    909876504-c-customers < Cash receipts from customers < Operating activities

    Food211-P1-20151203-F211-1000T < Food21 < Food2: -4*6

    Food23-P1-20151203-F23-1000T < Food2: -7.5*4

- On July 21, 2016, the Proprietorship1 sells the Food222 $13*5 (cost: -$6.5*5) and the Food322 $30*2 (cost: -$13*2) to A12 (SIN: 909876512) for cash $125. The multi-subaccount names of the Cash and the Inventory accounts respectively are:

    909876512-c-customers < Cash receipts from customers < Operating activities

    Food222-P1-20151203-F222-1000T < Food22 < Food2: -6.5*5

    Food322-P1-20151203-F322-1000T < Food32 < Food3: -13*2

- On July 22, 2016, the Proprietorship1 sells the Food211 $8*10 (cost: -$4*10), the Food212 $9*10 (cost: -$4.5*10), the Food311 $20*3 (cost: -$8.5*3), and the Food312 $24*3 (cost: -$11*3) to A13 (SIN: 909876513) for cash $302. The multi-subaccount names of the Cash and the Inventory accounts respectively are:

    909876513-c-customers < Cash receipts from customers < Operating activities

    Food211-P1-20151203-F211-1000T < Food21 < Food2: -4*10

    Food212-P1-20151203-F212-1000T < Food21 < Food2: -4.5*10

    Food311-P1-20151203-F311-1000T < Food31 < Food3: -8.5*3

    Food312-P1-20151203-F312-1000T < Food31 < Food3: -11*3

- On July 22, 2016, the Proprietorship1 sells the Food212 $9*5 (cost: -$4.5*5) and the Food311 $20*3 (cost: -$8.5*3) to A5 (SIN: 909876505) for cash $105. The multi-

subaccount names of the Cash and the Inventory accounts respectively are:

909876505-c-customers < Cash receipts from customers < Operating activities

Food212-P1-20151203-F212-1000T < Food21 < Food2: -4.5*5

Food311-P1-20151203-F311-1000T < Food31 < Food3: -8.5*3

- On July 25, 2016, the Proprietorship1 sells the Food212 $9*6 (cost: -$4.5*6), the Food311 $20*2 (cost: -$8.5*2), and the Food312 $24*1 (cost: -$11*1) to A16 (SIN: 909876516) for cash $118. The multi-subaccount names of the Cash and the Inventory accounts respectively are:

909876516-c-customers < Cash receipts from customers < Operating activities

Food212-P1-20151203-F212-1000T < Food21 < Food2: -4.5*6

Food311-P1-20151203-F311-1000T < Food31 < Food3: -8.5*2

Food312-P1-20151203-F312-1000T < Food31 < Food3: -11*1

- On July 25, 2016, the Proprietorship1 sells the Food311 $20*2 (cost: -$8.5*2) and the Food312 $24*2 (cost: -$11*2) to A19 (SIN: 909876519) for cash $88. The multi-subaccount names of the Cash and the Inventory accounts respectively are:

909876519-c-customers < Cash receipts from customers < Operating activities

Food311-P1-20151203-F311-1000T < Food31 < Food3: -8.5*2

Food312-P1-20151203-F312-1000T < Food31 < Food3: -11*2

- On July 25, 2016, the Proprietorship1 sells the Food311 $20*2 (cost: -$8.5*2) and the Food312 $24*1 (cost: -$11*1) to A23 (SIN: 909876523) for cash $64. The multi-subaccount names of the Cash and the Inventory accounts respectively are:

909876523-c-customers < Cash receipts from customers < Operating activities

Food311-P1-20151203-F311-1000T < Food31 < Food3: -8.5*2

Food312-P1-20151203-F312-1000T < Food31 < Food3: -11*1

- On July 27, 2016, the Proprietorship1 pays -$187.55 cash to A23 (SIN: 909876523) for the Travelling expenses -$123.55 and the Other expenses -$64.

- On July 31, 2016, the Proprietorship1 pays two employees' salary $5,670 repeatedly.

- On July 31, 2016, the Proprietorship1 sells the following inventories -$5,135 for sales $10,270 to A1A8 (SIN: 909876526), who uses his (or her) father A1's (or motherA1's) secondary card of the Business Bank2, for cash $10,270.

Food111-P1-20160430-F111-600T < Food11 < Food1: -5*10

Food112-P1-20160430-F112-600T < Food11 < Food1: -5.5*130

Food113-P1-20160430-F113-600T < Food11 < Food1: -6*130

Food121-P1-20160430-F121-600T < Food12 < Food1: -6.5*10

Food122-P1-20160430-F122-600T < Food12 < Food1: -7*130

Food123-P1-20160430-F123-600T < Food12 < Food1: -7.5*80

Food211-P1-20160430-F211-600T < Food21 < Food2: -4*130

Food213-P1-20160430-F213-600T < Food21 < Food2: -5*130

Food222-P1-20160430-F222-600T < Food22 < Food2: -6.5*130

The multi-subaccount name of the Cash account is:

909876501-c-customers < Cash receipts from customers < Operating activities

- On July 31, 2016, the Proprietorship1 sells the following inventories -$8,385 for sales $18,460 to A14 (SIN: 909876514) for cash $18,460.

Food112-P1-20160430-F112-600T < Food11 < Food1: -5.5*130

Food221-P1-20160430-F221-600T < Food22 < Food2: -6*130

Food222-P1-20160430-F222-600T < Food22 < Food2: -6.5*20

Food23-P1-20160430-F23-600T < Food2: -7.5*130

Food311-P1-20160430-F311-600T < Food31 < Food3: -8.5*130

Food312-P1-20160430-F312-600T < Food31 < Food3: -11*130

Food321-P1-20160430-F321-600T < Food32 < Food3: -12*130

Food322-P1-20160430-F322-600T < Food32 < Food3: -13*130

The multi-subaccount name of the Cash account is:

909876514-c-customers < Cash receipts from customers < Operating activities

- On July 31, 2016, the Proprietorship1 sells the following inventories -$8,255 for sales $18,200 to A15 (SIN: 909876515) for cash $18,200.

Food111-P1-20160430-F111-600T < Food11 < Food1: -5*130

Food112-P1-20160430-F112-600T < Food11 < Food1: -5.5*130

Food222-P1-20160430-F222-600T < Food22 < Food2: -6.5*20

Food23-P1-20160430-F23-600T < Food2: -7.5*130

Food311-P1-20160430-F311-600T < Food31 < Food3: -8.5*130

Food312-P1-20160430-F312-600T < Food31 < Food3: -11*130

Food321-P1-20160430-F321-600T < Food32 < Food3: -12*130

Food322-P1-20160430-F322-600T < Food32 < Food3: -13*130

The multi-subaccount name of the Cash account is:

   909876515-c-customers < Cash receipts from customers < Operating activities

- On July 31, 2016, the Proprietorship1 sells the following inventories -$1,463 for sales $3,510 to A16 (SIN: 909876516) for cash $3,510.

Food112-P1-20160430-F112-600T < Food11 < Food1: -5.5*130

Food122-P1-20160430-F122-600T < Food12 < Food1: -7*10

Food222-P1-20160430-F222-600T < Food22 < Food2: -6.5*20

Food322-P1-20160430-F322-600T < Food32 < Food3: -13*56

The multi-subaccount name of the Cash account is:

   909876516-c-customers < Cash receipts from customers < Operating activities

- On July 31, 2016, the Proprietorship1 sells the following inventories -$1,365 for sales $2,730 to A17 (SIN: 909876517) for cash $2,730.

Food111-P1-20160430-F111-600T < Food11 < Food1: -5*130

Food211-P1-20160430-F211-600T < Food21 < Food2: -4*130

Food222-P1-20160430-F222-600T < Food22 < Food2: -6.5*30

The multi-subaccount name of the Cash account is:

   909876517-c-customers < Cash receipts from customers < Operating activities

- On July 31, 2016, the Proprietorship1 sells the following inventories -$1,625 for sales $3,250 to A18 (SIN: 909876518) for cash $3,250.

Food111-P1-20160430-F111-600T < Food11 < Food1: -5*130

Food113-P1-20160430-F113-600T < Food11 < Food1: -6*130

Food222-P1-20160430-F222-600T < Food22 < Food2: -6.5*30

The multi-subaccount name of the Cash account is:

   909876518-c-customers < Cash receipts from customers < Operating activities

- On July 31, 2016, the Proprietorship1 sells the following inventories -$8,450 for sales $18,590 to A19 (SIN: 909876519) for cash $18,590.

  Food113-P1-20160430-F113-600T < Food11 < Food1: -6*130

  Food121-P1-20160430-F121-600T < Food12 < Food1: -6.5*10

  Food222-P1-20160430-F222-600T < Food22 < Food2: -6.5*130

  Food23-P1-20160430-F23-600T < Food2: -7.5*130

  Food311-P1-20160430-F311-600T < Food31 < Food3: -8.5*130

  Food312-P1-20160430-F312-600T < Food31 < Food3: -11*130

  Food321-P1-20160430-F321-600T < Food32 < Food3: -12*130

  Food322-P1-20160430-F322-600T < Food32 < Food3: -13*130

  The multi-subaccount name of the Cash account is:

  909876519-c-customers < Cash receipts from customers < Operating activities

- On July 31, 2016, the Proprietorship1 sells the following inventories -$5,200 for sales $10,400 to A20 (SIN: 909876520) for cash $10,400.

  Food113-P1-20160430-F113-600T < Food11 < Food1: -6*130

  Food121-P1-20160430-F121-600T < Food12 < Food1: -6.5*10

  Food122-P1-20160430-F122-600T < Food12 < Food1: -7*130

  Food123-P1-20160430-F123-600T < Food12 < Food1: -7.5*10

  Food211-P1-20160430-F211-600T < Food21 < Food2: -4*130

  Food212-P1-20160430-F212-600T < Food21 < Food2: -4.5*130

  Food213-P1-20160430-F213-600T < Food21 < Food2: -5*130

  Food214-P1-20160430-F214-600T < Food21 < Food2: -5.5*130

  Food221-P1-20160430-F221-600T < Food22 < Food2: -6*150

  The multi-subaccount name of the Cash account is:

  909876520-c-customers < Cash receipts from customers < Operating activities

- On July 31, 2016, the Proprietorship1 sells the following inventories -$5,330 for sales $10,660 to A21 (SIN: 909876521) for cash $10,660.

  Food111-P1-20160430-F111-600T < Food11 < Food1: -5*169

  Food122-P1-20160430-F122-600T < Food12 < Food1: -7*130

Food123-P1-20160430-F123-600T < Food12 < Food1: -7.5*20

Food211-P1-20160430-F211-600T < Food21 < Food2: -4*10

Food212-P1-20160430-F212-600T < Food21 < Food2: -4.5*130

Food213-P1-20160430-F213-600T < Food21 < Food2: -5*130

Food214-P1-20160430-F214-600T < Food21 < Food2: -5.5*150

Food221-P1-20160430-F221-600T < Food22 < Food2: -6*80

Food222-P1-20160430-F222-600T < Food22 < Food2: -6.5*130

The multi-subaccount name of the Cash account is:

  909876521-c-customers < Cash receipts from customers < Operating activities

- On July 31, 2016, the Proprietorship1 sells the following inventories -$5,265 for sales $10,530 to A22 (SIN: 909876522) for cash $10,530.

    Food121-P1-20160430-F121-600T < Food12 < Food1: -6.5*130

    Food122-P1-20160430-F122-600T < Food12 < Food1: -7*130

    Food123-P1-20160430-F123-600T < Food12 < Food1: -7.5*20

    Food211-P1-20160430-F211-600T < Food21 < Food2: -4*130

    Food212-P1-20160430-F212-600T < Food21 < Food2: -4.5*130

    Food213-P1-20160430-F213-600T < Food21 < Food2: -5*130

    Food214-P1-20160430-F214-600T < Food21 < Food2: -5.5*150

    Food221-P1-20160430-F221-600T < Food22 < Food2: -6*130

The multi-subaccount name of the Cash account is:

  909876522-c-customers < Cash receipts from customers < Operating activities

- On July 31, 2016, the Proprietorship1 sells the following inventories -$3,593 for sales $7,540 to A23 (SIN: 909876523) for cash $7,540.

    Food121-P1-20160430-F121-600T < Food12 < Food1: -6.5*130

    Food122-P1-20160430-F122-600T < Food12 < Food1: -7*10

    Food123-P1-20160430-F123-600T < Food12 < Food1: -7.5*130

    Food23-P1-20160430-F23-600T < Food2: -7.5*130

    Food322-P1-20160430-F322-600T < Food32 < Food3: -13*56

The multi-subaccount name of the Cash account is:

909876523-c-customers < Cash receipts from customers < Operating activities

- On July 31, 2016, the Proprietorship1 sells the following inventories -$3,835 for sales $8,060 to A24 (SIN: 909876524) for cash $8,060.

  Food121-P1-20160430-F121-600T < Food12 < Food1: -6.5*130

  Food122-P1-20160430-F122-600T < Food12 < Food1: -7*10

  Food123-P1-20160430-F123-600T < Food12 < Food1: -7.5*130

  Food311-P1-20160430-F311-600T < Food31 < Food3: -8.5*130

  Food322-P1-20160430-F322-600T < Food32 < Food3: -13*56

  The multi-subaccount name of the Cash account is:

  909876524-c-customers < Cash receipts from customers < Operating activities

- On July 31, 2016, the Proprietorship1 sells the following inventories -$4,160 for sales $8,580 to A25 (SIN: 909876525) for cash $8,580.

  Food121-P1-20160430-F121-600T < Food12 < Food1: -6.5*130

  Food122-P1-20160430-F122-600T < Food12 < Food1: -7*40

  Food123-P1-20160430-F123-600T < Food12 < Food1: -7.5*130

  Food212-P1-20160430-F212-600T < Food21 < Food2: -4.5*140

  Food312-P1-20160430-F312-600T < Food31 < Food3: -11*130

  The multi-subaccount name of the Cash account is:

  909876525-c-customers < Cash receipts from customers < Operating activities

- On August 10, 2016, the Proprietorship1 sells the Food212 $9*6 (cost: -$4.5*6) and the Food312 $24*4 (cost: -$11*4) to A3 (SIN: 909876503) for cash $150. The multi-subaccount names of the Cash and the Inventory accounts respectively are:

  909876503-c-customers < Cash receipts from customers < Operating activities

  Food212-P1-20160430-F212-600T < Food21 < Food2: -4.5*6

  Food312-P1-20160430-F312-600T < Food31 < Food3: -11*4

- On August 14, 2016, the Proprietorship1 sells the Food123 $15*4 (cost: -$7.5*4) and the Food322 $30*2 (cost: -$13*2) to A17 (SIN: 909876517) for cash $120. The multi-subaccount names of the Cash and the Inventory accounts respectively are:

  909876517-c-customers < Cash receipts from customers < Operating activities

Food123-P1-20160430-F123-600T < Food12 < Food1: -7.5*4

Food322-P1-20160430-F322-600T < Food32 < Food3: -13*2

- On August 17, 2016, the Proprietorship1 pays -$65,000 cash to the Company3 (phone number: 123456082) with the General ID 16 (-$6,150), the General ID 17 (-$26,950), and the General ID 18 (-$31,900). The multi-subaccount name of the Cash account and transaction sub-equation respectively are:

  88-654308-t-suppliers < Cash payments to suppliers < Operating activities

- On August 17, 2016, the Proprietorship1 sells the Food221 $12*3 (cost: -$6*3) and the Food321 $27*1 (cost: -$12*1) to A10 (SIN: 909876510) for cash $63. The multi-subaccount names of the Cash and the Inventory accounts respectively are:

  909876510-c-customers < Cash receipts from customers < Operating activities

  Food221-P1-20160430-F221-600T < Food22 < Food2: -6*3

  Food321-P1-20160430-F321-600T < Food32 < Food3: -12*1

- On August 20, 2016, the Proprietorship1 sells the Food213 $10*6 (cost: -$5*6), the Food312 $24*3 (cost: -$11*3), and the Food322 $30*1 (cost: -$13*1) to A16 (SIN: 909876516) for cash $162. The multi-subaccount names of the Cash and the Inventory accounts respectively are:

  909876516-c-customers < Cash receipts from customers < Operating activities

  Food213-P1-20160430-F213-600T < Food21 < Food2: -5*6

  Food312-P1-20160430-F312-600T < Food31 < Food3: -11*3

  Food322-P1-20160430-F322-600T < Food32 < Food3: -13*1

- On August 21, 2016, the Proprietorship1 sells the Food312 $24*2 (cost: -$11*2) and the Food322 $30*1 (cost: -$13*1) to A19 (SIN: 909876519) for cash $78. The multi-subaccount names of the Cash and the Inventory accounts respectively are:

  909876519-c-customers < Cash receipts from customers < Operating activities

  Food312-P1-20160430-F312-600T < Food31 < Food3: -11*2

  Food322-P1-20160430-F322-600T < Food32 < Food3: -13*1

- On August 22, 2016, the Proprietorship1 sells the Food23 $16*4 (cost: -$7.5*4) and the Food312 $24*2 (cost: -$11*2) to A12 (SIN: 909876512) for cash $112. The

multi-subaccount names of the Cash and the Inventory accounts respectively are:

909876512-c-customers < Cash receipts from customers < Operating activities

Food23-P1-20160430-F23-600T < Food2: -7.5*4

Food312-P1-20160430-F312-600T < Food31 < Food3: -11*2

- On August 22, 2016, the Proprietorship1 sells the Food211 $8*10 (cost: -$4*10), the Food213 $10*10 (cost: -$5*10), the Food311 $20*3 (cost: -$8.5*3), and the Food312 $24*3 (cost: -$11*3) to A13 (SIN: 909876513) for cash $312. The multi-subaccount names of the Cash and the Inventory accounts respectively are:

  909876513-c-customers < Cash receipts from customers < Operating activities

  Food211-P1-20160430-F211-600T < Food21 < Food2: -4*10

  Food213-P1-20160430-F213-600T < Food21 < Food2: -5*10

  Food311-P1-20160430-F311-600T < Food31 < Food3: -8.5*3

  Food312-P1-20160430-F312-600T < Food31 < Food3: -11*3

- On August 23, 2016, the Proprietorship1 pays -$166.18 cash to A22 (SIN: 909876522) for the Travelling expenses -$110.18 and the Other expenses -$56.

- On August 31, 2016, the Proprietorship1 pays two employees' salary expenses for cash -$5,670 repeatedly.

- On September 15, 2016, the Proprietorship1 receives $300 cash from the Company3 (phone number: 123456782) with the General ID 19. The multi-subaccount name of the Cash account is:

  88-654302-c-customers < Cash receipts from customers < Operating activities

- On September 17, 2016, the Proprietorship1 sells the Food222 $13*4 (cost: -$6.5*4) and the Food322 $30*2 (cost: -$13*2) to A9 (SIN: 909876509) for cash $112. The multi-subaccount names of the Cash and the Inventory accounts respectively are:

  909876509-c-customers < Cash receipts from customers < Operating activities

  Food222-P1-20160430-F222-600T < Food22 < Food2: -6.5*4

  Food322-P1-20160430-F322-600T < Food32 < Food3: -13*2

- On September 17, 2016, the Proprietorship1 sells the Food213 $10*5 (cost: -$5*5) and the Food321 $27*2 (cost: -$12*2) to A12 (SIN: 909876512) for cash $104. The

multi-subaccount names of the Cash and the Inventory accounts respectively are:

909876512-c-customers < Cash receipts from customers < Operating activities

Food213-P1-20160430-F213-600T < Food21 < Food2: -5*5

Food321-P1-20160430-F321-600T < Food32 < Food3: -12*2

- On September 19, 2016, the Proprietorship1 sells the Food312 $24*3 (cost: -$11*3) and the Food321 $27*1 (cost: -$12*1) to A24 (SIN: 909876524) for cash $99. The multi-subaccount names of the Cash and the Inventory accounts respectively are:

909876524-c-customers < Cash receipts from customers < Operating activities

Food312-P1-20160430-F312-600T < Food31 < Food3: -11*3

Food321-P1-20160430-F321-600T < Food32 < Food3: -12*1

- On September 26, 2016, the Proprietorship1 sells the Food221 $12*10 (cost: -$6*10), the Food23 $16*10 (cost: -$7.5*10), the Food321 $27*3 (cost: -$12*3), and the Food322 $30*3 (cost: -$13*3) to A13 (SIN: 909876513) for cash $451. The multi-subaccount names of the Cash and the Inventory accounts respectively are:

909876513-c-customers < Cash receipts from customers < Operating activities

Food221-P1-20160430-F221-600T < Food22 < Food2: -6*10

Food23-P1-20160430-F23-600T < Food2: -7.5*10

Food321-P1-20160430-F321-600T < Food32 < Food3: -12*3

Food322-P1-20160430-F322-600T < Food32 < Food3: -13*3

- On September 26, 2016, the Proprietorship1 pays -$1,800 cash to the Company2 (phone number: 123456083) with the General ID 80. The multi-subaccount name of the Cash account is:

88-654307-t-suppliers < Cash payments to suppliers < Operating activities

- On September 26, 2016, the Proprietorship1 sells the Food23 $16*6 (cost: -$7.5*6), the Food311 $20*3 (cost: -$8.5*3), and the Food321 $27*1 (cost: -$12*1) to A16 (SIN: 909876516) for cash $183. The multi-subaccount names of the Cash and the Inventory accounts respectively are:

909876516-c-customers < Cash receipts from customers < Operating activities

Food23-P1-20160430-F23-600T < Food2: -7.5*6

Food311-P1-20160430-F311-600T < Food31 < Food3: -8.5*3

Food321-P1-20160430-F321-600T < Food32 < Food3: -12*1

- On September 26, 2016, the Proprietorship1 sells the Food311 $20*3 (cost: -$8.5*3) and the Food321 $27*1 (cost: -$12*1) to A19 (SIN: 909876519) for cash $87. The multi-subaccount names of the Cash and the Inventory accounts respectively are:

  909876519-c-customers < Cash receipts from customers < Operating activities

  Food311-P1-20160430-F311-600T < Food31 < Food3: -8.5*3

  Food321-P1-20160430-F321-600T < Food32 < Food3: -12*1

- On September 30, 2016, the Proprietorship1 pays two employees' salary -$5,670.

- On September 30, 2016, the Proprietorship1 records the Amortization expenses - $2,025 of a computer server2 (-$1,012.5, nine months), a computer3 (-$525, nine months), and a computer4 (-$487.5, nine months).

- On September 30, 2016, the Proprietorship1 cancels the balances (-$2,700 - $1,400 - $1,300) of the Computer account and the Accumulated amortization: Computer account because these computers have used for two years.

- On October 1, 2016, the Proprietorship1 purchases one Computer server2 and two Computer1s from the Company1 (phone number: 123456084) for cash $5,500 and other $400 on credit. The multi-subaccount names of the Cash and the Inventory accounts and the two transaction sub-equation respectively are:

  88-654306-t-machinery < Cash payments for machinery < Operating activities

  Computer server2-C1-20160430-COMS2-047 < Computer server-inventory < Computer-inventory: 2700*1

  Computer1-C1-20160430-COM1-063 < Computer-inventory: 1600*1

  Computer1-C1-20160430-COM1-064 < Computer-inventory: 1600*1

  Cash (1): -5500 + Inventory (1): 2700*1 + Inventory (1): 1600*1 + Inventory (1): 1600*1 = Account payable (2): 400

  Inventory (1): -2700*1 + Inventory (1): -1600*1 + Inventory (1): -1600*1 + Computer (1): 2700*1 + Computer (1): 1600*1 + Computer (1): 1600*1 = 0

- On October 8, 2016, the Proprietorship1 pays -$168.73 cash to A22 (SIN: 909876522) for the Travelling expenses -$114.73 and the Other expenses -$54.

- On October 12, 2016, the Proprietorship1 pays -$31,000 cash to the Company3 (phone number: 123456082) with the General ID 17. The multi-subaccount name of the Cash account is:

  88-654308-t-suppliers < Cash payments to suppliers < Operating activities

- On October 16, 2016, the Proprietorship1 sells the Food123 $15*4 (cost: -$7.5*4) and the Food23 $16*3 (cost: -$7.5*3) to A12 (SIN: 909876512) for cash $108. The multi-subaccount names of the Cash and the Inventory accounts respectively are:

  909876512-c-customers < Cash receipts from customers < Operating activities
  Food123-P1-20160430-F123-600T < Food12 < Food1: -7.5*4
  Food23-P1-20160430-F23-600T < Food2: -7.5*3

- On October 21, 2016, the Proprietorship1 sells the Food213 $ 10*4 (cost: -$5*4) and the Food321 $27*3 (cost: -$12*3) to A3 (SIN: 909876503) for cash $121. The multi-subaccount names of the Cash and the Inventory accounts respectively are:

  909876503-c-customers < Cash receipts from customers < Operating activities
  Food213-P1-20160430-F213-600T < Food21 < Food2: -5*4
  Food321-P1-20160430-F321-600T < Food32 < Food3: -12*3

- On October 22, 2016, the Proprietorship1 sells the Food214 $11*4 (cost: -$5.5*4) and the Food312 $24*3 (cost: -$11*3) to A5 (SIN: 909876505) for cash $116. The multi-subaccount names of the Cash and the Inventory accounts respectively are:

  909876505-c-customers < Cash receipts from customers < Operating activities
  Food214-P1-20160430-F214-600T < Food21 < Food2: -5.5*4
  Food312-P1-20160430-F312-600T < Food31 < Food3: -11*3

- On October 22, 2016, the Proprietorship1 sells the Food123 $15*4 (cost: -$7.5*4) and the Food321 $27*2 (cost: -$12*2) to A9 (SIN: 909876509) for cash $114. The multi-subaccount names of the Cash and the Inventory accounts respectively are:

  909876509-c-customers < Cash receipts from customers < Operating activities
  Food123-P1-20160430-F123-600T < Food12 < Food1: -7.5*4

Food321-P1-20160430-F321-600T < Food32 < Food3: -12*2

- On October 24, 2016, the Proprietorship1 sells the Food113 $12*10 (cost: -$6*10), the Food214 $11*10 (cost: -$5.5*10), the Food312 $24*3 (cost: -$11*3), and the Food321 $27*3 (cost: -$12*3) to A13 (SIN: 909876513) for cash $383. The multi-subaccount names of the Cash and the Inventory accounts respectively are:

   909876513-c-customers < Cash receipts from customers < Operating activities
   Food113-P1-20151203-F113-1000T < Food11 < Food1: -6*10
   Food214-P1-20151203-F214-1000T < Food21 < Food2: -5.5*10
   Food312-P1-20160430-F312-600T < Food31 < Food3: -11*3
   Food321-P1-20160430-F321-600T < Food32 < Food3: -12*3

- On October 25, 2016, the Proprietorship1 receives $25,000 cash from the Company3 (phone number: 123456782) with the General ID 19. The multi-subaccount name of the Cash account is:

   88-654308-c-customers < Cash receipts from customers < Operating activities

- On October 25, 2016, the Proprietorship1 sells the Food113 $12*6 (cost: -$6*6), the Food312 $24*3 (cost: -$11*3), and the Food322 $30*1 (cost: -$13*1) to A16 (SIN: 909876516) for cash $174. The multi-subaccount names of the Cash and the Inventory accounts respectively are:

   909876516-c-customers < Cash receipts from customers < Operating activities
   Food113-P1-20160430-F113-600T < Food11 < Food1: -6*6
   Food312-P1-20160430-F312-600T < Food31 < Food3: -11*3
   Food322-P1-20160430-F322-600T < Food32 < Food3: -13*1

- On October 25, 2016, the Proprietorship1 sells the Food113 $12*5 (cost: -$6*5) and the Food322 $30*1 (cost: -$13*1) to A19 (SIN: 909876519) for cash $90. The multi-subaccount names of the Cash and the Inventory accounts respectively are:

   909876519-c-customers < Cash receipts from customers < Operating activities
   Food113-P1-20160430-F113-600T < Food11 < Food1: -6*5
   Food322-P1-20160430-F322-600T < Food32 < Food3: -13*1

- On October 31, 2016, the Proprietorship1 pays two employees' salary -$5,670.

- On November 15, 2016, the Proprietorship1 sells the Food121 $13*3 (cost: -$6.5*3) and the Food321 $27*2 (cost: -$12*2) to A6 (SIN: 909876506) for cash $93. The multi-subaccount names of the Cash and the Inventory accounts respectively are:

  909876506-c-customers < Cash receipts from customers < Operating activities

  Food121-P1-20160430-F121-600T < Food12 < Food1: -6.5*3

  Food321-P1-20160430-F321-600T < Food32 < Food3: -12*2

- On November 15, 2016, the Proprietorship1 sells the Food111 $10*10 (cost: -$5*10), the Food113 $12*10 (cost: -$6*10), the Food311 $20*3 (cost: -$8.5*3), and the Food321 $27*3 (cost: -$12*3) to A13 (SIN: 909876513) for cash $361. The multi-subaccount names of the Cash and the Inventory accounts respectively are:

  909876513-c-customers < Cash receipts from customers < Operating activities

  Food111-P1-20151203-F111-1000T < Food11 < Food1: -5*10

  Food113-P1-20160430-F113-600T < Food11 < Food1: -6*10

  Food311-P1-20160430-F311-600T < Food31 < Food3: -8.5*3

  Food321-P1-20160430-F321-600T < Food32 < Food3: -12*3

- On November 17, 2016, the Proprietorship1 sells the Food111 $10*7 (cost: -$5*7), the Food311 $20*3 (cost: -$8.5*3), and the Food321 $27*2 (cost: -$12*2) to A16 (SIN: 909876516) for cash $184. The multi-subaccount names of the Cash and the Inventory accounts respectively are:

  909876516-c-customers < Cash receipts from customers < Operating activities

  Food111-P1-20151203-F111-1000T < Food11 < Food1: -5*7

  Food311-P1-20160430-F311-600T < Food31 < Food3: -8.5*3

  Food321-P1-20160430-F321-600T < Food32 < Food3: -12*2

- On November 17, 2016, the Proprietorship1 sells the Food311 $20*3 (cost: -$8.5*3) and the Food321 $27*1 (cost: -$12*1) to A19 (SIN: 909876519) for cash $87. The multi-subaccount names of the Cash and the Inventory accounts respectively are:

  909876519-c-customers < Cash receipts from customers < Operating activities

  Food311-P1-20160430-F311-600T < Food31 < Food3: -8.5*3

  Food321-P1-20160430-F321-600T < Food32 < Food3: -12*1

- On November 19, 2016, the Proprietorship1 sells the Food113 $12*5 (cost: -$6*5) and the Food311 $20*2 (cost: -$8.5*2) to A12 (SIN: 909876512) for cash $100. The multi-subaccount names of the Cash and the Inventory accounts respectively are:

    909876512-c-customers < Cash receipts from customers < Operating activities

    Food113-P1-20160430-F113-600T < Food11 < Food1: -6*5

    Food311-P1-20160430-F311-600T < Food31 < Food3: -8.5*2

- On November 19, 2016, the Proprietorship1 pays -$177.16 cash to A22 (SIN: 909876522) for the Travelling expenses -$120.16 and the Other expenses -$57.

- On November 30, 2016, the Proprietorship1 pays two employees' salary expenses for cash -$5,670 repeatedly.

- On November 30, 2016, the Proprietorship1 has completed all products of the Working-in-process inventory account. If the all general parts have just been consumed and the supplies has the rest $53, then the rest supplies must be returned to the Supplies account from the Cost of goods manufactured account. It is consisted of two parts of the Supplies $9 and the Inventory $44 ($14*2 + $16*1). The multi-subaccount names of the Inventory accounts respectively are:

    Supplies1-P2-20160430-Supp1-200T: 14*2

    Supplies2-P2-20160430-Supp2-200T: 16*1

- On November 30, 2016, the Proprietorship1 transfers the balance of the Cost of goods manufactured account to the Working-in-process inventory account. The Cost of goods manufactured account has three subaccounts of the "Supplies expenses", the "909876523-salary < Product department-salary < Salary expenses", and the "General parts expenses". Their balances are -$1,447, -$22,400, and -$113,098 respectively. Here, the balance of the subaccount "909876523-salary < Product department-salary < Salary expenses" is the sum of the eight months' salary expenses because the Proprietorship1 will not produce any product and only do some maintenance of the equipment in December 2016. In addition, the balance of the subaccount "General parts expenses" will be divided to two parts which are used in three transaction sub-equations respectively. The two transaction sub-equations are:

Working-in-process inventory (1): 5*1200 + Working-in-process inventory (1): 5.5*1200 + Working-in-process inventory (1): 6*1200 + Working-in-process inventory (1): 6.5*1200 + Working-in-process inventory (1): 7*1200 + Working-in-process inventory (1): 7.5*1200 + Working-in-process inventory (1): 4*1200 = Cost of goods manufactured (5): 1447 + Cost of goods manufactured (5): 22400 + Cost of goods manufactured (5): 25953

Working-in-process inventory (1): 4.5*1200 + Working-in-process inventory (1): 5*1200 + Working-in-process inventory (1): 5.5*1200 + Working-in-process inventory (1): 6*1200 + Working-in-process inventory (1): 6.5*1200 + Working-in-process inventory (1): 7.5*1200 + Working-in-process inventory (1): 8.5*1200 + Working-in-process inventory (1): 11*1200 + Working-in-process inventory (1): 12*1200 + Working-in-process inventory (1): 13*1200 = Cost of goods manufactured (5): 95400

- On November 30, 2016, the proprietorship1 transfers the balance of the Working-in-process inventory account to the Inventory account. The multi-subaccount names of the Inventory account and the four transaction sub-equations respectively are:
Food111-P1-20161130-F111-1200T < Food11 < Food1: 5*1200
Food112-P1-20161130-F112-1200T < Food11 < Food1: 5.5*1200
Food113-P1-20161130-F113-1200T < Food11 < Food1: 6*1200
Food121-P1-20161130-F121-1200T < Food12 < Food1: 6.5*1200
Food122-P1-20161130-F122-1200T < Food12 < Food1: 7*1200
Food123-P1-20161130-F123-1200T < Food12 < Food1: 7.5*1200
Food211-P1-20160110-F211-1200T < Food21 < Food2: 4*1200
Food212-P1-20161130-F212-1200T < Food21 < Food2: 4.5*1200
Food213-P1-20161130-F213-1200T < Food21 < Food2: 5*1200
Food214-P1-20161130-F214-1200T < Food21 < Food2: 5.5*1200
Food221-P1-20161130-F221-1200T < Food22 < Food2: 6*1200
Food222-P1-20161130-F222-1200T < Food22 < Food2: 6.5*1200

Food23-P1-20161130-F23-1200T < Food2: 7.5*1200

Food311-P1-20161130-F311-1200T < Food31 < Food3: 8.5*1200

Food312-P1-20161130-F312-1200T < Food31 < Food3: 11*1200

Food321-P1-20161130-F321-1200T < Food32 < Food3: 12*1200

Food322-P1-20161130-F322-1200T < Food32 < Food3: 13*1200

Working-in-process inventory (1): -5*1200 + Working-in-process inventory (1): -5.5*1200 + Working-in-process inventory (1): -6*1200 + Working-in-process inventory (1): -6.5*1200 + Working-in-process inventory (1): -7*1200 + Inventory (1): 5*1200 + Inventory (1): 5.5*1200 + Inventory (1): 6*1200 + Inventory (1): 6.5*1200 + Inventory (1): 7*1200 = 0

Working-in-process inventory (1): -7.5*1200 + Working-in-process inventory (1): -4*1200 + Working-in-process inventory (1): -4.5*1200 + Working-in-process inventory (1): -5*1200 + Working-in-process inventory (1): -5.5*1200 + Inventory (1): 7.5*1200 + Inventory (1): 4*1200 + Inventory (1): 4.5*1200 + Inventory (1): 5*1200 + Inventory (1): 5.5*1200 = 0

Working-in-process inventory (1): -6*1200 + Working-in-process inventory (1): -6.5*1200 + Working-in-process inventory (1): -7.5*1200 + Working-in-process inventory (1): -8.5*1200 + Working-in-process inventory (1): -11*1200 + Inventory (1): 6*1200 + Inventory (1): 6.5*1200 + Inventory (1): 7.5*1200 + Inventory (1): 8.5*1200 + Inventory (1): 11*1200 = 0

Working-in-process inventory (1): -12*1200 + Working-in-process inventory (1): -13*1200 + Inventory (1): 12*1200 + Inventory (1): 13*1200 = 0

- On December 1, 2016, the Proprietorship1 sells the following inventories -$6,760 for sales $15,210 to A16 (SIN: 909876516) for cash $15,210.
  Food23-P1-20161130-F23-1200T < Food2: -7.5*130

Food311-P1-20161130-F311-1200T < Food31 < Food3: -8.5*130

Food312-P1-20161130-F312-1200T < Food31 < Food3: -11*130

Food321-P1-20161130-F321-1200T < Food32 < Food3: -12*130

Food322-P1-20161130-F322-1200T < Food32 < Food3: -13*130

The multi-subaccount name of the Cash account is:

  909876516-c-customers < Cash receipts from customers < Operating activities

- On December 1, 2016, the Proprietorship1 sells the following inventories -$6,760 for sales $15,210 to A17 (SIN: 909876517) for cash $15,210.

  Food23-P1-20161130-F23-1200T < Food2: -7.5*130

  Food311-P1-20161130-F311-1200T < Food31 < Food3: -8.5*130

  Food312-P1-20161130-F312-1200T < Food31 < Food3: -11*130

  Food321-P1-20161130-F321-1200T < Food32 < Food3: -12*130

  Food322-P1-20161130-F322-1200T < Food32 < Food3: -13*130

  The multi-subaccount name of the Cash account is:

    909876517-c-customers < Cash receipts from customers < Operating activities

- On December 1, 2016, the Proprietorship1 sells the following inventories -$6,760 for sales $15,210 to A18 (SIN: 909876518) for cash $15,210.

  Food23-P1-20161130-F23-1200T < Food2: -7.5*130

  Food311-P1-20161130-F311-1200T < Food31 < Food3: -8.5*130

  Food312-P1-20161130-F312-1200T < Food31 < Food3: -11*130

  Food321-P1-20161130-F321-1200T < Food32 < Food3: -12*130

  Food322-P1-20161130-F322-1200T < Food32 < Food3: -13*130

  The multi-subaccount name of the Cash account is:

    909876518-c-customers < Cash receipts from customers < Operating activities

- On December 1, 2016, the Proprietorship1 sells the following inventories -$1,755 for sales $3,510 to A23 (SIN: 909876523) for cash $3,510.

  Food211-P1-20160110-F211-1200T < Food21 < Food2: -4*130

  Food212-P1-20161130-F212-1200T < Food21 < Food2: -4.5*130

  Food213-P1-20161130-F213-1200T < Food21 < Food2: -5*130

The multi-subaccount name of the Cash account is:

　909876523-c-customers < Cash receipts from customers < Operating activities

- On December 1, 2016, the Proprietorship1 sells the following inventories -$1,755 for sales $3,510 to A24 (SIN: 909876524) for cash $3,510.

　Food211-P1-20160110-F211-1200T < Food21 < Food2: -4*130

　Food212-P1-20161130-F212-1200T < Food21 < Food2: -4.5*130

　Food213-P1-20161130-F213-1200T < Food21 < Food2: -5*130

　The multi-subaccount name of the Cash account is:

　909876524-c-customers < Cash receipts from customers < Operating activities

- On December 1, 2016, the Proprietorship1 sells the following inventories -$1,755 for sales $3,510 to A25 (SIN: 909876525) for cash $3,510.

　Food211-P1-20160110-F211-1200T < Food21 < Food2: -4*130

　Food212-P1-20161130-F212-1200T < Food21 < Food2: -4.5*130

　Food213-P1-20161130-F213-1200T < Food21 < Food2: -5*130

　The multi-subaccount name of the Cash account is:

　909876525-c-customers < Cash receipts from customers < Operating activities

- On December 13, 2016, the Proprietorship1 sells the Food112 $11*10 (cost: -$5.5*10), the Food123 $15*10 (cost: -$7.5*10), the Food312 $24*3 (cost: -$11*3), and the Food321 $27*3 (cost: -$12*3) to A13 (SIN: 909876513) for cash $413. The multi-subaccount names of the Cash and the Inventory accounts respectively are:

　909876513-c-customers < Cash receipts from customers < Operating activities

　Food112-P1-20161130-F112-1200T < Food11 < Food1: -5.5*10

　Food123-P1-20161130-F123-1200T < Food12 < Food1: -7.5*10

　Food312-P1-20161130-F312-1200T < Food31 < Food3: -11*3

　Food321-P1-20161130-F321-1200T < Food32 < Food3: -12*3

- On December 15, 2016, the Proprietorship1 sells the Food222 $13*3 (cost: -$6.5*3) and the Food311 $20*3 (cost: -$8.5*3) to A9 (SIN: 909876509) for cash $99. The multi-subaccount names of the Cash and the Inventory accounts respectively are:

　909876509-c-customers < Cash receipts from customers < Operating activities

Food222-P1-20161130-F222-1200T < Food22 < Food2: -6.5*3

Food311-P1-20161130-F311-1200T < Food31 < Food3: -8.5*3

- On December 15, 2016, the Proprietorship1 sells the Food111 $10*5 (cost: -$5*5) and the Food321 $27*2 (cost: -$12*2) to A19 (SIN: 909876519) for cash $104. The multi-subaccount names of the Cash and the Inventory accounts respectively are:

    909876519-c-customers < Cash receipts from customers < Operating activities

    Food111-P1-20161130-F111-1200T < Food11 < Food1: -5*5

    Food321-P1-20161130-F321-1200T < Food32 < Food3: -12*2

- On December 15, 2016, the Proprietorship1 sells the Food111 $10*2 (cost: -$5*2) and the Food321 $27*2 (cost: -$12*2) to A23 (SIN: 909876523) for cash $74. The multi-subaccount names of the Cash and the Inventory accounts respectively are:

    909876523-c-customers < Cash receipts from customers < Operating activities

    Food111-P1-20161130-F111-1200T < Food11 < Food1: -5*2

    Food321-P1-20161130-F321-1200T < Food32 < Food3: -12*2

- On December 15, 2016, the Proprietorship1 sells the Food111 $10*6 (cost: -$5*6), the Food123 $15*4 (cost: -$7.5*4), and the Food321 $27*2 (cost: -$12*2) to A16 (SIN: 909876516) for cash $174. The multi-subaccount names of the Cash and the Inventory accounts respectively are:

    909876516-c-customers < Cash receipts from customers < Operating activities

    Food111-P1-20161130-F111-1200T < Food11 < Food1: -5*6

    Food123-P1-20161130-F123-1200T < Food12 < Food1: -7.5*4

    Food321-P1-20161130-F321-1200T < Food32 < Food3: -12*2

- On December 17, 2016, the Proprietorship1 pays -$207.52 cash to A23 (SIN: 909876523) for the Travelling expenses -$133.52 and the Other expenses -$74.

- On December 19, 2016, the Proprietorship1 pays -$198.35 cash to A22 (SIN: 909876522) for the Travelling expenses -$130.35 and the Other expenses -$68.

- On December 20, 2016, the Proprietorship1 sells the Food221 $12*3 (cost: -$6*3), Food222 $13*3 (cost: -$6.5*3), and the Food321 $27*2 (cost: -$12*2) to A3 (SIN:

909876503) for cash \$129. The multi-subaccount names of the Cash and the Inventory accounts respectively are:

909876503-c-customers < Cash receipts from customers < Operating activities

Food221-P1-20161130-F221-1200T < Food22 < Food2: -6*3

Food222-P1-20161130-F222-1200T < Food22 < Food2: -6.5*3

Food321-P1-20161130-F321-1200T < Food32 < Food3: -12*2

- On December 23, 2016, the Proprietorship1 receives \$18,000 cash from the Company1 (phone number: 123456784) with the General ID 93. The multi-subaccount name of the Cash account is:

88-654306-c-customers < Cash receipts from customers < Operating activities

- On December 26, 2016, the Proprietorship1 sells the Food111 \$10*6 (cost: -\$5*6), Food213 \$10*6 (cost: -\$5*6), and the Food312 \$24*3 (cost: -\$11*3) to A5 (SIN: 909876505) for cash \$192. The multi-subaccount names of the Cash and the Inventory accounts respectively are:

909876505-c-customers < Cash receipts from customers < Operating activities

Food111-P1-20161130-F111-1200T < Food11 < Food1: -5*6

Food213-P1-20161130-F213-1200T < Food21 < Food2: -5*6

Food312-P1-20161130-F312-1200T < Food31 < Food3: -11*3

- On December 26, 2016, the Proprietorship1 sells the Food113 \$12*6 (cost: -\$6*6), Food214 \$11*6 (cost: -\$5.5*6), and the Food311 \$20*3 (cost: -\$8.5*3) to A6 (SIN: 909876506) for cash \$198. The multi-subaccount names of the Cash and the Inventory accounts respectively are:

909876506-c-customers < Cash receipts from customers < Operating activities

Food113-P1-20161130-F113-1200T < Food11 < Food1: -6*6

Food214-P1-20161130-F214-1200T < Food21 < Food2: -5.5*6

Food311-P1-20161130-F311-1200T < Food31 < Food3: -8.5*3

- On December 27, 2016, the Proprietorship1 sells the Food222 \$13*5 (cost: -\$6.5*5) and the Food322 \$30*2 (cost: -\$13*2) to A12 (SIN: 909876512) for cash \$125. The multi-subaccount name of the Cash account is:

909876512-c-customers < Cash receipts from customers < Operating activities

Food222-P1-20161130-F222-1200T < Food22 < Food2: -6.5*5

Food322-P1-20161130-F322-1200T < Food32 < Food3: -13*2

- On December 29, 2016, the Proprietorship1 pays -$10,000 cash to the Company1 (phone number: 123456084) with the General ID 60. The multi-subaccount name of the Cash account is:

  88-654306-t-suppliers < Cash payments to suppliers < Operating activities

- On December 31, 2016, the Proprietorship1 pays -$4,300 cash to the Proprietorship2 (phone number: 123456080) with the General ID 15 ($600), the General ID 91 ($700), and the General ID 92 ($3,000). The multi-subaccount name of the Cash account is:

  88-654310-t-suppliers < Cash payments to suppliers < Operating activities

- On December 31, 2016, the Proprietorship1 pays two employees' salary expenses for cash -$5,670 repeatedly.

- On the same day, the Proprietorship1 pays -$11,280 cash to the business Bank2 for the Note interest expenses of the Note25 ($120,000, one-level subaccount "Note25-interest"). The multi-subaccount name of the Cash account is:

  88-654305-t-note interest < Cash payments to business banks < Operating activities

- On the same day, the Proprietorship1 pays -$2,500 cash to the bond holders for the Bond interest expenses of the Bond61 (one-level subaccount "Bond61-interest"). The multi-subaccount names of the Cash account and the transaction sub-equations respectively are:

  909876504-t-bond interest < Cash payments to bond holder< Operating activities
  (909876505, 909876506, 909876508, 909876510, 909876513, 909876515,
  909876516, 909876517, 909876518, 909876519, 909876520, 909876521,
  909876522)

  Cash (1): -150 + Cash (1): -200 + Cash (1): -250 + Cash (1): -100 + Cash (1): -

150 + Cash (1): -250 + Cash (1): -200 + Cash (1): -100 = Bond interest expenses (5): -1400

Cash (1): -250 + Cash (1): -150 + Cash (1): -250 + Cash (1): -150 + Cash (1): -200 + Cash (1): -100 = Bond interest expenses (5): -1100

- On the same day, the Proprietorship1 receives cash $416 ($200 + $126 + $90) for investment interest (Investment incomes) of the Bond11 ($5,000), the Bond12 ($3,000), and the Bond13 ($2,000) from the Business Bank1. The multi-subaccount name of the Cash account is:

  88-654304-c-investment income < Cash receipts from investments < Investing activities

- On the same day, the Proprietorship1 receives cash $352 for investment interest (Investment incomes) of the Bond22 ($8,000) from the Business Bank2. The multi-subaccount name of the Cash account is:

  88-654305-c-investment income < Cash receipts from investments < Investing activities

- On the same day, the Proprietorship1 receives cash $120 from the Business Bank1 for primary deposit interest (Deposit interest incomes). The multi-subaccount name of the Cash account and transaction sub-equation respectively are:

  88-654304-c-deposit interest income < Cash receipts from deposit interest < Financial activities

- On the same day, the Proprietorship1 records the Office supplies expenses -$321.57. It is consisted of two parts of the Supplies -$21.57 and the Inventory -$300 (-$14*10 - $16*10). The multi-subaccount names of the Inventory account respectively are:

  Supplies1-P2-20150920-SUP1-200T: -14*6
  Supplies2-P2-20150920-SUP2-200T: -16*7
  Supplies1-P2-20160430-Supp1-200T: -14*4
  Supplies2-P2-20160430-Supp2-200T: -16*3

- On the same day, the Proprietorship1 records the Vehicle's amortization expenses -

$14,966.67 (-$8,000 - $6,966.67) one year (5 years, straight line).

- On the same day, the Proprietorship1 records the Computer's amortization expenses -$737.5 three months (2 years, straight line) which includes a new computer server1 (-$337.5), a new computer1 (-$200), and a new computer1 (-$200).

- On December 31, 2016, the Proprietorship1 records the Tax expenses -$33,638.77 and the Tax payable $33,638.77. The multi-subaccount name forms of the Tax expenses and the Tax payable accounts all are the 'n'.

So far, I have entered all transactions of the Proprietorship1 to the database dcj210 in the fiscal year 2016.

## 3.9.2 Brief Summary of the Proprietorship1

The Figure 3.9-2 all inventory purchased or sold by other members in the Proprietorship1 by using of SQL Server query.

```
use dcj200
select * from InventoryByMembers where Recorder='88-654309' and TransDate between '2016-01-01' and '2016-12-31'
order by TransDate
```

100 %  ▾

Results | Messages

| | IDM | Amount | Symbol | MultiSubaccount | Recorder | TransDate | Unit |
|---|---|---|---|---|---|---|---|
| 1 | 88-654308 | -12500.00 | t | Inven52-C3-20150922-In52-500T < Inven5 | 88-654309 | 2016-01-02 | -250 |
| 2 | 88-654310 | -490.00 | t | Supplies1-P2-20150920-SUP1-200T | 88-654309 | 2016-01-02 | -35 |
| 3 | 88-654310 | -560.00 | t | Supplies2-P2-20150920-SUP2-200T | 88-654309 | 2016-01-02 | -35 |
| 4 | 88-654308 | -5000.00 | t | Inven51-C3-20150922-In51-1000T < Inven5 | 88-654309 | 2016-01-02 | -500 |
| 5 | 88-654308 | -7200.00 | t | Inven621-C3-20151003-In621-900T < Inven62 < Inven6 | 88-654309 | 2016-01-02 | -400 |
| 6 | 88-654308 | -8000.00 | t | Inven63-C3-20151003-In63-1000T < Inven6 | 88-654309 | 2016-01-02 | -500 |
| 7 | 88-654308 | -7200.00 | t | Inven711-C3-20151003-In711-500T < Inven71 < Inven7 | 88-654309 | 2016-01-02 | -200 |
| 8 | 88-654308 | -1550.00 | t | Inven712-C3-20151003-In712-100T < Inven71 < Inven7 | 88-654309 | 2016-01-02 | -50 |
| 9 | 88-654308 | -7568.00 | t | Inven721-C3-20151003-In721-744T < Inven72 < Inven7 | 88-654309 | 2016-01-02 | -344 |
| 10 | 88-654308 | -6000.00 | t | Inven722-C3-20151003-In722-600T < Inven72 < Inven7 | 88-654309 | 2016-01-02 | -300 |
| 11 | 88-654308 | -5400.00 | t | Inven731-C3-20151003-In731-600T < Inven73 < Inven7 | 88-654309 | 2016-01-02 | -300 |
| 12 | 88-654308 | -8000.00 | t | Inven732-C3-20151003-In732-1000T < Inven73 < Inven7 | 88-654309 | 2016-01-02 | -500 |
| 13 | 88-654308 | -7500.00 | t | Inven811-C3-20151003-In811-600T < Inven81 < Inven8 | 88-654309 | 2016-01-02 | -300 |
| 14 | 88-654308 | -7200.00 | t | Inven812-C3-20151003-In812-600T < Inven81 < Inven8 | 88-654309 | 2016-01-02 | -300 |
| 15 | 88-654308 | -6900.00 | t | Inven813-C3-20151003-In813-600T < Inven81 < Inven8 | 88-654309 | 2016-01-02 | -300 |
| 16 | 88-654308 | -6000.00 | t | Inven82-C3-20151003-In82-600T < inven8 | 88-654309 | 2016-01-02 | -300 |
| 17 | 88-654308 | -5400.00 | t | Inven831-C3-20151003-In831-600T < Inven83 < Inven8 | 88-654309 | 2016-01-02 | -300 |
| 18 | 88-654308 | -6400.00 | t | Inven832-C3-20151003-In832-800T < Inven83 < Inven8 | 88-654309 | 2016-01-02 | -400 |
| 19 | 88-654308 | -12500.00 | t | Inven531-C3-20150922-In531-1000T < Inven53 < Inven5 | 88-654309 | 2016-01-02 | -500 |
| 20 | 88-654308 | -17500.00 | t | Inven532-C3-20150922-In532-1000T < Inven53 < Inven5 | 88-654309 | 2016-01-02 | -500 |
| 21 | 88-654308 | -6000.00 | t | Inven541-C3-20150922-In541-1000T < Inven54 < Inven5 | 88-654309 | 2016-01-02 | -500 |
| 22 | 88-654308 | -7500.00 | t | Inven542-C3-20150922-In542-1000T < Inven54 < Inven5 | 88-654309 | 2016-01-02 | -500 |
| 23 | 88-654308 | -3900.00 | t | Inven611-C3-20151003-In611-1300T < Inven61 < Inven6 | 88-654309 | 2016-01-02 | -600 |
| 24 | 88-654308 | -6250.00 | t | Inven612-C3-20151003-In612-1100T < Inven61 < Inven6 | 88-654309 | 2016-01-02 | -500 |
| 25 | 88-654308 | 1560.00 | c | Inven31-P1-20151125-In31-1000T < Inven3 | 88-654309 | 2016-01-03 | 260 |
| 26 | 88-654308 | 4500.00 | c | Inven32-P1-20151125-In32-1000T < Inven3 | 88-654309 | 2016-01-03 | 150 |
| 27 | 88-654308 | 2600.00 | c | Inven331-P1-20151125-In331-1000T < Inven33 < Inven3 | 88-654309 | 2016-01-03 | 260 |
| 28 | 88-654308 | 7020.00 | c | Inven332-P1-20151125-In332-1000T < Inven33 < Inven3 | 88-654309 | 2016-01-03 | 260 |
| 29 | 88-654308 | 1560.00 | c | HGFCVB parts-P1-20151125-HGP-1000T < QASXC parts < Inven3 | 88-654309 | 2016-01-03 | 260 |
| 30 | 88-654308 | 3120.00 | c | PPGHUP parts-P1-20151125-PPP-1000T < ASDUP parts < Inven3 | 88-654309 | 2016-01-03 | 260 |

| | IDM | Amount | Symbol | MultiSubaccount | Recorder | TransDate | Unit |
|---|---|---|---|---|---|---|---|
| 31 | 88-654309 | 406.00 | f | Supplies1-P2-20150920-SUP1-200T | 88-654309 | 2016-01-03 | 29 |
| 32 | 88-654309 | 448.00 | f | Supplies2-P2-20150920-SUP2-200T | 88-654309 | 2016-01-03 | 28 |
| 33 | 88-654309 | 500.00 | f | Inven411 < Inven41 < Inven4 | 88-654309 | 2016-01-03 | 100 |
| 34 | 88-654309 | 1850.00 | f | Inven412 < Inven41 < Inven4 | 88-654309 | 2016-01-03 | 100 |
| 35 | 88-654309 | 2000.00 | f | TTTCU parts < TTT parts < Inven4 | 88-654309 | 2016-01-03 | 100 |
| 36 | 88-654309 | 2000.00 | f | RRRHJK parts < Inven4 | 88-654309 | 2016-01-03 | 100 |
| 37 | 88-654309 | 1500.00 | f | Inven51-C3-20150922-In51-1000T < Inven5 | 88-654309 | 2016-01-03 | 150 |
| 38 | 88-654309 | 3750.00 | f | Inven52-C3-20150922-In52-500T < Inven5 | 88-654309 | 2016-01-03 | 75 |
| 39 | 88-654309 | 3750.00 | f | Inven531-C3-20150922-In531-1000T < Inven53 < Inven5 | 88-654309 | 2016-01-03 | 150 |
| 40 | 88-654309 | 5250.00 | f | Inven532-C3-20150922-In532-1000T < Inven53 < Inven5 | 88-654309 | 2016-01-03 | 150 |
| 41 | 88-654309 | 1800.00 | f | Inven541-C3-20150922-In541-1000T < Inven54 < Inven5 | 88-654309 | 2016-01-03 | 150 |
| 42 | 88-654309 | 2250.00 | f | Inven542-C3-20150922-In542-1000T < Inven54 < Inven5 | 88-654309 | 2016-01-03 | 150 |
| 43 | 88-654309 | 1170.00 | f | Inven611-C3-20151003-In611-1300T < Inven61 < Inven6 | 88-654309 | 2016-01-03 | 180 |
| 44 | 88-654309 | 1875.00 | f | Inven612-C3-20151003-In612-1100T < Inven61 < Inven6 | 88-654309 | 2016-01-03 | 150 |
| 45 | 88-654309 | 2160.00 | f | Inven621-C3-20151003-In621-900T < Inven62 < Inven6 | 88-654309 | 2016-01-03 | 120 |
| 46 | 88-654309 | 2400.00 | f | Inven63-C3-20151003-In63-1000T < Inven6 | 88-654309 | 2016-01-03 | 150 |
| 47 | 88-654309 | 2160.00 | f | Inven711-C3-20151003-In711-500T < Inven71 < Inven7 | 88-654309 | 2016-01-03 | 60 |
| 48 | 88-654309 | 465.00 | f | Inven712-C3-20151003-In712-100T < Inven71 < Inven7 | 88-654309 | 2016-01-03 | 15 |
| 49 | 88-654309 | 2200.00 | f | Inven721-C3-20151003-In721-744T < Inven72 < Inven7 | 88-654309 | 2016-01-03 | 100 |
| 50 | 88-654309 | 1800.00 | f | Inven722-C3-20151003-In722-600T < Inven72 < Inven7 | 88-654309 | 2016-01-03 | 90 |
| 51 | 88-654309 | 1620.00 | f | Inven731-C3-20151003-In731-600T < Inven73 < Inven7 | 88-654309 | 2016-01-03 | 90 |
| 52 | 88-654309 | 2400.00 | f | Inven732-C3-20151003-In732-1000T < Inven73 < Inven7 | 88-654309 | 2016-01-03 | 150 |
| 53 | 88-654309 | 2250.00 | f | Inven811-C3-20151003-In811-600T < Inven81 < Inven8 | 88-654309 | 2016-01-03 | 90 |
| 54 | 88-654309 | 2160.00 | f | Inven812-C3-20151003-In812-600T < Inven81 < Inven8 | 88-654309 | 2016-01-03 | 90 |
| 55 | 88-654309 | 2070.00 | f | Inven813-C3-20151003-In813-600T < Inven81 < Inven8 | 88-654309 | 2016-01-03 | 90 |
| 56 | 88-654309 | 1800.00 | f | Inven82-C3-20151003-In82-600T < Inven8 | 88-654309 | 2016-01-03 | 90 |
| 57 | 88-654309 | 1620.00 | f | Inven831-C3-20151003-In831-600T < Inven83 < Inven8 | 88-654309 | 2016-01-03 | 90 |
| 58 | 88-654309 | 1920.00 | f | Inven832-C3-20151003-In832-800T < Inven83 < Inven8 | 88-654309 | 2016-01-03 | 120 |
| 59 | 909876503 | 24.00 | c | Food113-P1-20151203-F113-1000T < Food11 < Food1 | 88-654309 | 2016-01-06 | 4 |
| 60 | 909876503 | 26.00 | c | Food322-P1-20151203-F322-1000T < Food32 < Food3 | 88-654309 | 2016-01-06 | 2 |
| 61 | 909876505 | 22.00 | c | Food214-P1-20151203-F214-1000T < Food21 < Food2 | 88-654309 | 2016-01-10 | 4 |
| 62 | 909876505 | 24.00 | c | Food321-P1-20151203-F321-1000T < Food32 < Food3 | 88-654309 | 2016-01-10 | 2 |
| 63 | 909876506 | 22.00 | c | Food112-P1-20151203-F112-1000T < Food11 < Food1 | 88-654309 | 2016-01-10 | 4 |
| 64 | 909876506 | 22.50 | c | Food23-P1-20151203-F23-1000T < Food2 | 88-654309 | 2016-01-10 | 3 |
| 65 | 909876515 | 8.50 | c | Food311-P1-20151203-F311-1000T < Food31 < Food3 | 88-654309 | 2016-01-13 | 1 |
| 66 | 909876516 | 48.00 | c | Food221-P1-20151203-F221-1000T < Food22 < Food2 | 88-654309 | 2016-01-13 | 8 |
| 67 | 909876516 | 44.00 | c | Food312-P1-20151203-F312-1000T < Food31 < Food3 | 88-654309 | 2016-01-13 | 4 |
| 68 | 909876508 | 12.00 | c | Food321-P1-20151203-F321-1000T < Food32 < Food3 | 88-654309 | 2016-01-16 | 1 |
| 69 | 909876508 | 13.00 | c | Food322-P1-20151203-F322-1000T < Food32 < Food3 | 88-654309 | 2016-01-16 | 1 |
| 70 | 909876517 | 8.50 | c | Food311-P1-20151203-F311-1000T < Food31 < Food3 | 88-654309 | 2016-01-16 | 1 |
| 71 | 909876517 | 11.00 | c | Food312-P1-20151203-F312-1000T < Food31 < Food3 | 88-654309 | 2016-01-16 | 1 |
| 72 | 909876520 | 11.00 | c | Food312-P1-20151203-F312-1000T < Food31 < Food3 | 88-654309 | 2016-01-18 | 1 |
| 73 | 909876520 | 12.00 | c | Food321-P1-20151203-F321-1000T < Food32 < Food3 | 88-654309 | 2016-01-18 | 1 |
| 74 | 909876525 | 12.00 | c | Food321-P1-20151203-F321-1000T < Food32 < Food3 | 88-654309 | 2016-01-19 | 1 |
| 75 | 909876525 | 13.00 | c | Food322-P1-20151203-F322-1000T < Food32 < Food3 | 88-654309 | 2016-01-19 | 1 |
| 76 | 909876509 | 17.00 | c | Food311-P1-20151203-F311-1000T < Food31 < Food3 | 88-654309 | 2016-01-25 | 2 |
| 77 | 909876509 | 26.00 | c | Food322-P1-20151203-F322-1000T < Food32 < Food3 | 88-654309 | 2016-01-25 | 2 |
| 78 | 909876510 | 12.00 | c | Food321-P1-20151203-F321-1000T < Food32 < Food3 | 88-654309 | 2016-01-27 | 1 |
| 79 | 909876510 | 13.00 | c | Food322-P1-20151203-F322-1000T < Food32 < Food3 | 88-654309 | 2016-01-27 | 1 |
| 80 | 909876518 | 66.00 | c | Food312-P1-20151203-F312-1000T < Food31 < Food3 | 88-654309 | 2016-01-28 | 6 |
| 81 | 909876521 | 9.00 | c | Food212-P1-20151203-F212-1000T < Food21 < Food2 | 88-654309 | 2016-01-28 | 2 |
| 82 | 909876521 | 11.00 | c | Food312-P1-20151203-F312-1000T < Food31 < Food3 | 88-654309 | 2016-01-28 | 1 |
| 83 | 909876523 | 10.00 | c | Food213-P1-20151203-F213-1000T < Food21 < Food2 | 88-654309 | 2016-01-28 | 2 |
| 84 | 909876523 | 11.00 | c | Food312-P1-20151203-F312-1000T < Food31 < Food3 | 88-654309 | 2016-01-28 | 1 |
| 85 | 909876512 | 650.00 | c | Food111-P1-20151203-F111-1000T < Food11 < Food1 | 88-654309 | 2016-01-31 | 130 |
| 86 | 909876512 | 780.00 | c | Food113-P1-20151203-F113-1000T < Food11 < Food1 | 88-654309 | 2016-01-31 | 130 |
| 87 | 909876512 | 845.00 | c | Food121-P1-20151203-F121-1000T < Food12 < Food1 | 88-654309 | 2016-01-31 | 130 |
| 88 | 909876512 | 910.00 | c | Food122-P1-20151203-F122-1000T < Food12 < Food1 | 88-654309 | 2016-01-31 | 130 |
| 89 | 909876512 | 520.00 | c | Food211-P1-20151203-F211-1000T < Food21 < Food2 | 88-654309 | 2016-01-31 | 130 |
| 90 | 909876512 | 650.00 | c | Food213-P1-20151203-F213-1000T < Food21 < Food2 | 88-654309 | 2016-01-31 | 130 |
| 91 | 909876512 | 845.00 | c | Food222-P1-20151203-F222-1000T < Food22 < Food2 | 88-654309 | 2016-01-31 | 130 |
| 92 | 909876501 | 715.00 | c | Food112-P1-20151203-F112-1000T < Food11 < Food1 | 88-654309 | 2016-01-31 | 130 |
| 93 | 909876501 | 780.00 | c | Food113-P1-20151203-F113-1000T < Food11 < Food1 | 88-654309 | 2016-01-31 | 130 |
| 94 | 909876501 | 845.00 | c | Food121-P1-20151203-F121-1000T < Food12 < Food1 | 88-654309 | 2016-01-31 | 130 |
| 95 | 909876501 | 910.00 | c | Food122-P1-20151203-F122-1000T < Food12 < Food1 | 88-654309 | 2016-01-31 | 130 |
| 96 | 909876501 | 975.00 | c | Food123-P1-20151203-F123-1000T < Food12 < Food1 | 88-654309 | 2016-01-31 | 130 |

| | IDM | Amount | Symbol | MultiSubaccount | Recorder | TransDate | Unit |
|---|---|---|---|---|---|---|---|
| 97 | 909876501 | 1105.00 | c | Food311-P1-20151203-F311-1000T < Food31 < Food3 | 88-654309 | 2016-01-31 | 130 |
| 98 | 909876501 | 1560.00 | c | Food321-P1-20151203-F321-1000T < Food32 < Food3 | 88-654309 | 2016-01-31 | 130 |
| 99 | 909876502 | 715.00 | c | Food112-P1-20151203-F112-1000T < Food11 < Food1 | 88-654309 | 2016-01-31 | 130 |
| 100 | 909876502 | 780.00 | c | Food113-P1-20151203-F113-1000T < Food11 < Food1 | 88-654309 | 2016-01-31 | 130 |
| 101 | 909876502 | 845.00 | c | Food121-P1-20151203-F121-1000T < Food12 < Food1 | 88-654309 | 2016-01-31 | 130 |
| 102 | 909876502 | 910.00 | c | Food122-P1-20151203-F122-1000T < Food12 < Food1 | 88-654309 | 2016-01-31 | 130 |
| 103 | 909876502 | 975.00 | c | Food123-P1-20151203-F123-1000T < Food12 < Food1 | 88-654309 | 2016-01-31 | 130 |
| 104 | 909876502 | 715.00 | c | Food214-P1-20151203-F214-1000T < Food21 < Food2 | 88-654309 | 2016-01-31 | 130 |
| 105 | 909876502 | 1430.00 | c | Food312-P1-20151203-F312-1000T < Food31 < Food3 | 88-654309 | 2016-01-31 | 130 |
| 106 | 909876503 | 650.00 | c | Food111-P1-20151203-F111-1000T < Food11 < Food1 | 88-654309 | 2016-01-31 | 130 |
| 107 | 909876503 | 715.00 | c | Food112-P1-20151203-F112-1000T < Food11 < Food1 | 88-654309 | 2016-01-31 | 130 |
| 108 | 909876503 | 780.00 | c | Food113-P1-20151203-F113-1000T < Food11 < Food1 | 88-654309 | 2016-01-31 | 130 |
| 109 | 909876503 | 780.00 | c | Food221-P1-20151203-F221-1000T < Food22 < Food2 | 88-654309 | 2016-01-31 | 130 |
| 110 | 909876503 | 845.00 | c | Food222-P1-20151203-F222-1000T < Food22 < Food2 | 88-654309 | 2016-01-31 | 130 |
| 111 | 909876503 | 975.00 | c | Food23-P1-20151203-F23-1000T < Food2 | 88-654309 | 2016-01-31 | 130 |
| 112 | 909876503 | 1560.00 | c | Food321-P1-20151203-F321-1000T < Food32 < Food3 | 88-654309 | 2016-01-31 | 130 |
| 113 | 909876504 | 650.00 | c | Food111-P1-20151203-F111-1000T < Food11 < Food1 | 88-654309 | 2016-01-31 | 130 |
| 114 | 909876504 | 780.00 | c | Food113-P1-20151203-F113-1000T < Food11 < Food1 | 88-654309 | 2016-01-31 | 130 |
| 115 | 909876504 | 845.00 | c | Food121-P1-20151203-F121-1000T < Food12 < Food1 | 88-654309 | 2016-01-31 | 130 |
| 116 | 909876504 | 910.00 | c | Food122-P1-20151203-F122-1000T < Food12 < Food1 | 88-654309 | 2016-01-31 | 130 |
| 117 | 909876504 | 975.00 | c | Food123-P1-20151203-F123-1000T < Food12 < Food1 | 88-654309 | 2016-01-31 | 130 |
| 118 | 909876504 | 1105.00 | c | Food311-P1-20151203-F311-1000T < Food31 < Food3 | 88-654309 | 2016-01-31 | 130 |
| 119 | 909876504 | 1560.00 | c | Food321-P1-20151203-F321-1000T < Food32 < Food3 | 88-654309 | 2016-01-31 | 130 |
| 120 | 909876505 | 715.00 | c | Food112-P1-20151203-F112-1000T < Food11 < Food1 | 88-654309 | 2016-01-31 | 130 |
| 121 | 909876505 | 780.00 | c | Food113-P1-20151203-F113-1000T < Food11 < Food1 | 88-654309 | 2016-01-31 | 130 |
| 122 | 909876505 | 845.00 | c | Food121-P1-20151203-F121-1000T < Food12 < Food1 | 88-654309 | 2016-01-31 | 130 |
| 123 | 909876505 | 910.00 | c | Food122-P1-20151203-F122-1000T < Food12 < Food1 | 88-654309 | 2016-01-31 | 130 |
| 124 | 909876505 | 975.00 | c | Food123-P1-20151203-F123-1000T < Food12 < Food1 | 88-654309 | 2016-01-31 | 130 |
| 125 | 909876505 | 1105.00 | c | Food311-P1-20151203-F311-1000T < Food31 < Food3 | 88-654309 | 2016-01-31 | 130 |
| 126 | 909876505 | 1430.00 | c | Food312-P1-20151203-F312-1000T < Food31 < Food3 | 88-654309 | 2016-01-31 | 130 |
| 127 | 909876506 | 650.00 | c | Food111-P1-20151203-F111-1000T < Food11 < Food1 | 88-654309 | 2016-01-31 | 130 |
| 128 | 909876506 | 780.00 | c | Food113-P1-20151203-F113-1000T < Food11 < Food1 | 88-654309 | 2016-01-31 | 130 |
| 129 | 909876506 | 845.00 | c | Food121-P1-20151203-F121-1000T < Food12 < Food1 | 88-654309 | 2016-01-31 | 130 |
| 130 | 909876506 | 910.00 | c | Food122-P1-20151203-F122-1000T < Food12 < Food1 | 88-654309 | 2016-01-31 | 130 |
| 131 | 909876506 | 520.00 | c | Food211-P1-20151203-F211-1000T < Food21 < Food2 | 88-654309 | 2016-01-31 | 130 |
| 132 | 909876506 | 650.00 | c | Food213-P1-20151203-F213-1000T < Food21 < Food2 | 88-654309 | 2016-01-31 | 130 |
| 133 | 909876506 | 1690.00 | c | Food322-P1-20151203-F322-1000T < Food32 < Food3 | 88-654309 | 2016-01-31 | 130 |
| 134 | 909876507 | 715.00 | c | Food112-P1-20151203-F112-1000T < Food11 < Food1 | 88-654309 | 2016-01-31 | 130 |
| 135 | 909876507 | 780.00 | c | Food113-P1-20151203-F113-1000T < Food11 < Food1 | 88-654309 | 2016-01-31 | 130 |
| 136 | 909876507 | 845.00 | c | Food121-P1-20151203-F121-1000T < Food12 < Food1 | 88-654309 | 2016-01-31 | 130 |
| 137 | 909876507 | 910.00 | c | Food122-P1-20151203-F122-1000T < Food12 < Food1 | 88-654309 | 2016-01-31 | 130 |
| 138 | 909876507 | 975.00 | c | Food123-P1-20151203-F123-1000T < Food12 < Food1 | 88-654309 | 2016-01-31 | 130 |
| 139 | 909876507 | 1105.00 | c | Food311-P1-20151203-F311-1000T < Food31 < Food3 | 88-654309 | 2016-01-31 | 130 |
| 140 | 909876507 | 600.00 | c | Food321-P1-20151203-F321-1000T < Food32 < Food3 | 88-654309 | 2016-01-31 | 50 |
| 141 | 909876508 | 715.00 | c | Food112-P1-20151203-F112-1000T < Food11 < Food1 | 88-654309 | 2016-01-31 | 130 |
| 142 | 909876508 | 780.00 | c | Food113-P1-20151203-F113-1000T < Food11 < Food1 | 88-654309 | 2016-01-31 | 130 |
| 143 | 909876508 | 845.00 | c | Food121-P1-20151203-F121-1000T < Food12 < Food1 | 88-654309 | 2016-01-31 | 130 |
| 144 | 909876508 | 910.00 | c | Food122-P1-20151203-F122-1000T < Food12 < Food1 | 88-654309 | 2016-01-31 | 130 |
| 145 | 909876508 | 975.00 | c | Food123-P1-20151203-F123-1000T < Food12 < Food1 | 88-654309 | 2016-01-31 | 130 |
| 146 | 909876508 | 520.00 | c | Food211-P1-20151203-F211-1000T < Food21 < Food2 | 88-654309 | 2016-01-31 | 130 |
| 147 | 909876508 | 1560.00 | c | Food321-P1-20151203-F321-1000T < Food32 < Food3 | 88-654309 | 2016-01-31 | 130 |
| 148 | 909876509 | 780.00 | c | Food221-P1-20151203-F221-1000T < Food22 < Food2 | 88-654309 | 2016-01-31 | 130 |
| 149 | 909876509 | 845.00 | c | Food222-P1-20151203-F222-1000T < Food22 < Food2 | 88-654309 | 2016-01-31 | 130 |
| 150 | 909876509 | 975.00 | c | Food23-P1-20151203-F23-1000T < Food2 | 88-654309 | 2016-01-31 | 130 |
| 151 | 909876509 | 1105.00 | c | Food311-P1-20151203-F311-1000T < Food31 < Food3 | 88-654309 | 2016-01-31 | 130 |
| 152 | 909876509 | 1430.00 | c | Food312-P1-20151203-F312-1000T < Food31 < Food3 | 88-654309 | 2016-01-31 | 130 |
| 153 | 909876509 | 1560.00 | c | Food321-P1-20151203-F321-1000T < Food32 < Food3 | 88-654309 | 2016-01-31 | 130 |
| 154 | 909876509 | 1690.00 | c | Food322-P1-20151203-F322-1000T < Food32 < Food3 | 88-654309 | 2016-01-31 | 130 |
| 155 | 909876510 | 780.00 | c | Food221-P1-20151203-F221-1000T < Food22 < Food2 | 88-654309 | 2016-01-31 | 130 |
| 156 | 909876510 | 845.00 | c | Food222-P1-20151203-F222-1000T < Food22 < Food2 | 88-654309 | 2016-01-31 | 130 |
| 157 | 909876510 | 975.00 | c | Food23-P1-20151203-F23-1000T < Food2 | 88-654309 | 2016-01-31 | 130 |
| 158 | 909876510 | 1105.00 | c | Food311-P1-20151203-F311-1000T < Food31 < Food3 | 88-654309 | 2016-01-31 | 130 |
| 159 | 909876510 | 1430.00 | c | Food312-P1-20151203-F312-1000T < Food31 < Food3 | 88-654309 | 2016-01-31 | 130 |
| 160 | 909876510 | 600.00 | c | Food321-P1-20151203-F321-1000T < Food32 < Food3 | 88-654309 | 2016-01-31 | 50 |
| 161 | 909876510 | 650.00 | c | Food322-P1-20151203-F322-1000T < Food32 < Food3 | 88-654309 | 2016-01-31 | 50 |
| 162 | 909876511 | 650.00 | c | Food111-P1-20151203-F111-1000T < Food11 < Food1 | 88-654309 | 2016-01-31 | 130 |

| | IDM | Amount | Symbol | MultiSubaccount | Recorder | TransDate | Unit |
|---|---|---|---|---|---|---|---|
| 163 | 909876511 | 780.00 | c | Food113-P1-20151203-F113-1000T < Food11 < Food1 | 88-654309 | 2016-01-31 | 130 |
| 164 | 909876511 | 845.00 | c | Food121-P1-20151203-F121-1000T < Food12 < Food1 | 88-654309 | 2016-01-31 | 130 |
| 165 | 909876511 | 910.00 | c | Food122-P1-20151203-F122-1000T < Food12 < Food1 | 88-654309 | 2016-01-31 | 130 |
| 166 | 909876511 | 975.00 | c | Food123-P1-20151203-F123-1000T < Food12 < Food1 | 88-654309 | 2016-01-31 | 130 |
| 167 | 909876511 | 1105.00 | c | Food311-P1-20151203-F311-1000T < Food31 < Food3 | 88-654309 | 2016-01-31 | 130 |
| 168 | 909876511 | 1560.00 | c | Food321-P1-20151203-F321-1000T < Food32 < Food3 | 88-654309 | 2016-01-31 | 130 |
| 169 | 909876512 | 715.00 | c | Food112-P1-20151203-F112-1000T < Food11 < Food1 | 88-654309 | 2016-01-31 | 130 |
| 170 | 909876512 | 780.00 | c | Food113-P1-20151203-F113-1000T < Food11 < Food1 | 88-654309 | 2016-01-31 | 130 |
| 171 | 909876512 | 845.00 | c | Food121-P1-20151203-F121-1000T < Food12 < Food1 | 88-654309 | 2016-01-31 | 130 |
| 172 | 909876512 | 910.00 | c | Food122-P1-20151203-F122-1000T < Food12 < Food1 | 88-654309 | 2016-01-31 | 130 |
| 173 | 909876512 | 975.00 | c | Food123-P1-20151203-F123-1000T < Food12 < Food1 | 88-654309 | 2016-01-31 | 130 |
| 174 | 909876512 | 1105.00 | c | Food311-P1-20151203-F311-1000T < Food31 < Food3 | 88-654309 | 2016-01-31 | 130 |
| 175 | 909876512 | 1560.00 | c | Food321-P1-20151203-F321-1000T < Food32 < Food3 | 88-654309 | 2016-01-31 | 130 |
| 176 | 909876513 | 780.00 | c | Food221-P1-20151203-F221-1000T < Food22 < Food2 | 88-654309 | 2016-01-31 | 130 |
| 177 | 909876513 | 845.00 | c | Food222-P1-20151203-F222-1000T < Food22 < Food2 | 88-654309 | 2016-01-31 | 130 |
| 178 | 909876513 | 975.00 | c | Food23-P1-20151203-F23-1000T < Food2 | 88-654309 | 2016-01-31 | 130 |
| 179 | 909876513 | 1105.00 | c | Food311-P1-20151203-F311-1000T < Food31 < Food3 | 88-654309 | 2016-01-31 | 130 |
| 180 | 909876513 | 1430.00 | c | Food312-P1-20151203-F312-1000T < Food31 < Food3 | 88-654309 | 2016-01-31 | 130 |
| 181 | 909876513 | 1560.00 | c | Food321-P1-20151203-F321-1000T < Food32 < Food3 | 88-654309 | 2016-01-31 | 130 |
| 182 | 909876513 | 1690.00 | c | Food322-P1-20151203-F322-1000T < Food32 < Food3 | 88-654309 | 2016-01-31 | 130 |
| 183 | 909876512 | 630.00 | c | Food212-P1-20151203-F212-1000T < Food21 < Food2 | 88-654309 | 2016-01-31 | 140 |
| 184 | 909876501 | 630.00 | c | Food212-P1-20151203-F212-1000T < Food21 < Food2 | 88-654309 | 2016-01-31 | 140 |
| 185 | 909876501 | -630.00 | c | Food122-P1-20151203-F122-1000T < Food12 < Food1 | 88-654309 | 2016-01-31 | -90 |
| 186 | 909876502 | -630.00 | c | Food122-P1-20151203-F122-1000T < Food12 < Food1 | 88-654309 | 2016-01-31 | -90 |
| 187 | 909876502 | 630.00 | c | Food212-P1-20151203-F212-1000T < Food21 < Food2 | 88-654309 | 2016-01-31 | 140 |
| 188 | 909876513 | 1485.00 | c | Food214-P1-20151203-F214-1000T < Food21 < Food2 | 88-654309 | 2016-01-31 | 270 |
| 189 | 909876513 | -1320.00 | c | Food321-P1-20151203-F321-1000T < Food32 < Food3 | 88-654309 | 2016-01-31 | -110 |
| 190 | 909876509 | 1485.00 | c | Food214-P1-20151203-F214-1000T < Food21 < Food2 | 88-654309 | 2016-01-31 | 270 |
| 191 | 909876509 | -1320.00 | c | Food321-P1-20151203-F321-1000T < Food32 < Food3 | 88-654309 | 2016-01-31 | -110 |
| 192 | 909876510 | -1105.00 | c | Food311-P1-20151203-F311-1000T < Food31 < Food3 | 88-654309 | 2016-01-31 | -130 |
| 193 | 909876510 | 1300.00 | c | Food213-P1-20151203-F213-1000T < Food21 < Food2 | 88-654309 | 2016-01-31 | 260 |
| 194 | 909876505 | 1300.00 | c | Food213-P1-20151203-F213-1000T < Food21 < Food2 | 88-654309 | 2016-01-31 | 260 |
| 195 | 909876505 | -1105.00 | c | Food311-P1-20151203-F311-1000T < Food31 < Food3 | 88-654309 | 2016-01-31 | -130 |
| 196 | 909876512 | -630.00 | c | Food122-P1-20151203-F122-1000T < Food12 < Food1 | 88-654309 | 2016-01-31 | -90 |
| 197 | 909876512 | 780.00 | c | Food221-P1-20151203-F221-1000T < Food22 < Food2 | 88-654309 | 2016-01-31 | 130 |
| 198 | 909876512 | -780.00 | c | Food113-P1-20151203-F113-1000T < Food11 < Food1 | 88-654309 | 2016-01-31 | -130 |
| 199 | 909876501 | 780.00 | c | Food221-P1-20151203-F221-1000T < Food22 < Food2 | 88-654309 | 2016-01-31 | 130 |
| 200 | 909876501 | -780.00 | c | Food113-P1-20151203-F113-1000T < Food11 < Food1 | 88-654309 | 2016-01-31 | -130 |
| 201 | 909876502 | 780.00 | c | Food221-P1-20151203-F221-1000T < Food22 < Food2 | 88-654309 | 2016-01-31 | 130 |
| 202 | 909876502 | -780.00 | c | Food113-P1-20151203-F113-1000T < Food11 < Food1 | 88-654309 | 2016-01-31 | -130 |
| 203 | 909876503 | 780.00 | c | Food213-P1-20151203-F213-1000T < Food21 < Food2 | 88-654309 | 2016-01-31 | 156 |
| 204 | 909876503 | -780.00 | c | Food113-P1-20151203-F113-1000T < Food11 < Food1 | 88-654309 | 2016-01-31 | -130 |
| 205 | 909876504 | -600.00 | c | Food123-P1-20151203-F123-1000T < Food12 < Food1 | 88-654309 | 2016-01-31 | -80 |
| 206 | 909876504 | 600.00 | c | Food211-P1-20151203-F211-1000T < Food21 < Food2 | 88-654309 | 2016-01-31 | 150 |
| 207 | 909876505 | 845.00 | c | Food111-P1-20151203-F111-1000T < Food11 < Food1 | 88-654309 | 2016-01-31 | 169 |
| 208 | 909876505 | -845.00 | c | Food121-P1-20151203-F121-1000T < Food12 < Food1 | 88-654309 | 2016-01-31 | -130 |
| 209 | 909876506 | 585.00 | c | Food212-P1-20151203-F212-1000T < Food21 < Food2 | 88-654309 | 2016-01-31 | 130 |
| 210 | 909876506 | -585.00 | c | Food121-P1-20151203-F121-1000T < Food12 < Food1 | 88-654309 | 2016-01-31 | -90 |
| 211 | 909876507 | 585.00 | c | Food212-P1-20151203-F212-1000T < Food21 < Food2 | 88-654309 | 2016-01-31 | 130 |
| 212 | 909876507 | -585.00 | c | Food121-P1-20151203-F121-1000T < Food12 < Food1 | 88-654309 | 2016-01-31 | -90 |
| 213 | 909876508 | 585.00 | c | Food212-P1-20151203-F212-1000T < Food21 < Food2 | 88-654309 | 2016-01-31 | 130 |
| 214 | 909876508 | -585.00 | c | Food121-P1-20151203-F121-1000T < Food12 < Food1 | 88-654309 | 2016-01-31 | -90 |
| 215 | 909876511 | 630.00 | c | Food212-P1-20151203-F212-1000T < Food21 < Food2 | 88-654309 | 2016-01-31 | 140 |
| 216 | 909876511 | -630.00 | c | Food122-P1-20151203-F122-1000T < Food12 < Food1 | 88-654309 | 2016-01-31 | -90 |
| 217 | 88-654306 | -38000.00 | t | Car3-C1-20150925-C3-028 < Car-inventory < Vehicle-inventory: 38000*1 | 88-654309 | 2016-02-01 | -1 |
| 218 | 88-654309 | 38000.00 | e | Car3-C1-20150925-C3-028 < Car-inventory < Vehicle-inventory: 38000*1 | 88-654309 | 2016-02-01 | 1 |
| 219 | 909876513 | 75.00 | c | Food23-P1-20151203-F23-1000T < Food2 | 88-654309 | 2016-02-17 | 10 |
| 220 | 909876513 | 65.00 | c | Food322-P1-20151203-F322-1000T < Food32 < Food3 | 88-654309 | 2016-02-17 | 5 |
| 221 | 909876519 | 30.00 | c | Food23-P1-20151203-F23-1000T < Food2 | 88-654309 | 2016-02-23 | 4 |
| 222 | 909876519 | 26.00 | c | Food322-P1-20151203-F322-1000T < Food32 < Food3 | 88-654309 | 2016-02-23 | 2 |
| 223 | 909876505 | 28.00 | c | Food122-P1-20151203-F122-1000T < Food12 < Food1 | 88-654309 | 2016-02-24 | 4 |
| 224 | 909876505 | 24.00 | c | Food321-P1-20151203-F321-1000T < Food32 < Food3 | 88-654309 | 2016-02-24 | 2 |
| 225 | 909876503 | 22.50 | c | Food123-P1-20151203-F123-1000T < Food12 < Food1 | 88-654309 | 2016-02-25 | 3 |
| 226 | 909876503 | 24.00 | c | Food321-P1-20151203-F321-1000T < Food32 < Food3 | 88-654309 | 2016-02-25 | 2 |
| 227 | 909876518 | 22.00 | c | Food312-P1-20151203-F312-1000T < Food31 < Food3 | 88-654309 | 2016-02-28 | 2 |
| 228 | 909876518 | 24.00 | c | Food321-P1-20151203-F321-1000T < Food32 < Food3 | 88-654309 | 2016-02-28 | 2 |

| | IDM | Amount | Symbol | MultiSubaccount | Recorder | TransDate | Unit |
|---|---|---|---|---|---|---|---|
| 229 | 909876521 | 22.00 | c | Food312-P1-20151203-F312-1000T < Food31 < Food3 | 88-654309 | 2016-02-28 | 2 |
| 230 | 909876521 | 24.00 | c | Food321-P1-20151203-F321-1000T < Food32 < Food3 | 88-654309 | 2016-02-28 | 2 |
| 231 | 909876525 | 22.00 | c | Food312-P1-20151203-F312-1000T < Food31 < Food3 | 88-654309 | 2016-03-07 | 2 |
| 232 | 909876525 | 13.00 | c | Food322-P1-20151203-F322-1000T < Food32 < Food3 | 88-654309 | 2016-03-07 | 1 |
| 233 | 909876506 | 16.50 | c | Food214-P1-20151203-F214-1000T < Food21 < Food2 | 88-654309 | 2016-03-10 | 3 |
| 234 | 909876506 | 39.00 | c | Food322-P1-20151203-F322-1000T < Food32 < Food3 | 88-654309 | 2016-03-10 | 3 |
| 235 | 909876511 | 10.00 | c | Food111-P1-20151203-F111-1000T < Food11 < Food1 | 88-654309 | 2016-03-11 | 2 |
| 236 | 909876511 | 13.00 | c | Food322-P1-20151203-F322-1000T < Food32 < Food3 | 88-654309 | 2016-03-11 | 1 |
| 237 | 909876504 | 11.00 | c | Food112-P1-20151203-F112-1000T < Food11 < Food1 | 88-654309 | 2016-03-19 | 2 |
| 238 | 909876504 | 15.00 | c | Food213-P1-20151203-F213-1000T < Food21 < Food2 | 88-654309 | 2016-03-19 | 3 |
| 239 | 909876502 | 5.00 | c | Food111-P1-20151203-F111-1000T < Food11 < Food1 | 88-654309 | 2016-03-26 | 1 |
| 240 | 909876502 | 5.50 | c | Food214-P1-20151203-F214-1000T < Food21 < Food2 | 88-654309 | 2016-03-26 | 1 |
| 241 | 909876502 | 12.00 | c | Food321-P1-20151203-F321-1000T < Food32 < Food3 | 88-654309 | 2016-03-26 | 1 |
| 242 | 909876502 | 11.00 | c | Food312-P1-20151203-F312-1000T < Food31 < Food3 | 88-654309 | 2016-03-26 | 1 |
| 243 | 909876508 | 11.00 | c | Food312-P1-20151203-F312-1000T < Food31 < Food3 | 88-654309 | 2016-03-27 | 1 |
| 244 | 909876508 | 12.00 | c | Food321-P1-20151203-F321-1000T < Food32 < Food3 | 88-654309 | 2016-03-27 | 1 |
| 245 | 909876511 | 19.50 | c | Food222-P1-20151203-F222-1000T < Food22 < Food2 | 88-654309 | 2016-04-13 | 3 |
| 246 | 909876511 | 13.00 | c | Food322-P1-20151203-F322-1000T < Food32 < Food3 | 88-654309 | 2016-04-13 | 1 |
| 247 | 909876524 | 22.00 | c | Food312-P1-20151203-F312-1000T < Food31 < Food3 | 88-654309 | 2016-04-22 | 2 |
| 248 | 909876524 | 12.00 | c | Food321-P1-20151203-F321-1000T < Food32 < Food3 | 88-654309 | 2016-04-22 | 1 |
| 249 | 909876516 | 33.00 | c | Food312-P1-20151203-F312-1000T < Food31 < Food3 | 88-654309 | 2016-04-24 | 3 |
| 250 | 909876516 | 24.00 | c | Food321-P1-20151203-F321-1000T < Food32 < Food3 | 88-654309 | 2016-04-24 | 1 |
| 251 | 909876516 | 13.00 | c | Food322-P1-20151203-F322-1000T < Food32 < Food3 | 88-654309 | 2016-04-24 | 1 |
| 252 | 909876519 | 22.00 | c | Food312-P1-20151203-F312-1000T < Food31 < Food3 | 88-654309 | 2016-04-24 | 2 |
| 253 | 909876519 | 13.00 | c | Food322-P1-20151203-F322-1000T < Food32 < Food3 | 88-654309 | 2016-04-24 | 1 |
| 254 | 909876507 | 22.00 | c | Food312-P1-20151203-F312-1000T < Food31 < Food3 | 88-654309 | 2016-04-27 | 2 |
| 255 | 909876507 | 24.00 | c | Food321-P1-20151203-F321-1000T < Food32 < Food3 | 88-654309 | 2016-04-27 | 2 |
| 256 | 88-654307 | -7200.00 | t | Truck2 part2-C2-20150728-T2P2-053 < Truck2 parts < Vehicle parts: 72... | 88-654309 | 2016-04-29 | -1 |
| 257 | 88-654309 | 7200.00 | s | Truck2 part2-C2-20150728-T2P2-053 < Truck2 parts < Vehicle parts: 72... | 88-654309 | 2016-04-29 | 1 |
| 258 | 88-654309 | -3600.00 | p | Inven31-P1-20160430-In31-600T < Inven3 | 88-654309 | 2016-04-30 | -600 |
| 259 | 88-654309 | -18000.00 | p | Inven32-P1-20160430-In32-600T < Inven3 | 88-654309 | 2016-04-30 | -600 |
| 260 | 88-654309 | -6000.00 | p | Inven331-P1-20160430-In331-600T < Inven33 < Inven3 | 88-654309 | 2016-04-30 | -600 |
| 261 | 88-654309 | -16200.00 | p | Inven332-P1-20160430-In332-600T < Inven33 < Inven3 | 88-654309 | 2016-04-30 | -600 |
| 262 | 88-654309 | -3600.00 | p | HGFCVB parts-P1-20160430-HGP-600T < QASXC parts < Inven3 | 88-654309 | 2016-04-30 | -600 |
| 263 | 88-654309 | -7200.00 | p | PPGHUP parts-P1-20160430-PPP-600T < ASDUP parts < Inven3 | 88-654309 | 2016-04-30 | -600 |
| 264 | 88-654309 | -4500.00 | p | Food23-P1-20160430-F23-600T < Food2 | 88-654309 | 2016-04-30 | -600 |
| 265 | 88-654309 | -5100.00 | p | Food311-P1-20160430-F311-600T < Food31 < Food3 | 88-654309 | 2016-04-30 | -600 |
| 266 | 88-654309 | -6600.00 | p | Food312-P1-20160430-F312-600T < Food31 < Food3 | 88-654309 | 2016-04-30 | -600 |
| 267 | 88-654309 | -7200.00 | p | Food321-P1-20160430-F321-600T < Food32 < Food3 | 88-654309 | 2016-04-30 | -600 |
| 268 | 88-654309 | -7800.00 | p | Food322-P1-20160430-F322-600T < Food32 < Food3 | 88-654309 | 2016-04-30 | -600 |
| 269 | 88-654309 | -2400.00 | p | Food211-P1-20160430-F211-600T < Food21 < Food2 | 88-654309 | 2016-04-30 | -600 |
| 270 | 88-654309 | -2700.00 | p | Food212-P1-20160430-F212-600T < Food21 < Food2 | 88-654309 | 2016-04-30 | -600 |
| 271 | 88-654309 | -3000.00 | p | Food213-P1-20160430-F213-600T < Food21 < Food2 | 88-654309 | 2016-04-30 | -600 |
| 272 | 88-654309 | -3300.00 | p | Food214-P1-20160430-F214-600T < Food21 < Food2 | 88-654309 | 2016-04-30 | -600 |
| 273 | 88-654309 | -3600.00 | p | Food221-P1-20160430-F221-600T < Food22 < Food2 | 88-654309 | 2016-04-30 | -600 |
| 274 | 88-654309 | -3900.00 | p | Food222-P1-20160430-F222-600T < Food22 < Food2 | 88-654309 | 2016-04-30 | -600 |
| 275 | 88-654309 | -3000.00 | p | Food111-P1-20160430-F111-600T < Food11 < Food1 | 88-654309 | 2016-04-30 | -600 |
| 276 | 88-654309 | -3300.00 | p | Food112-P1-20160430-F112-600T < Food11 < Food1 | 88-654309 | 2016-04-30 | -600 |
| 277 | 88-654309 | -3600.00 | p | Food113-P1-20160430-F113-600T < Food11 < Food1 | 88-654309 | 2016-04-30 | -600 |
| 278 | 88-654309 | -3900.00 | p | Food121-P1-20160430-F121-600T < Food12 < Food1 | 88-654309 | 2016-04-30 | -600 |
| 279 | 88-654309 | -4200.00 | p | Food122-P1-20160430-F122-600T < Food12 < Food1 | 88-654309 | 2016-04-30 | -600 |
| 280 | 88-654309 | -4500.00 | p | Food123-P1-20160430-F123-600T < Food12 < Food1 | 88-654309 | 2016-04-30 | -600 |
| 281 | 88-654310 | -700.00 | t | Supplies1-P2-20160430-Supp1-200T | 88-654309 | 2016-05-01 | -50 |
| 282 | 88-654310 | -800.00 | t | Supplies2-P2-20160430-Supp2-200T | 88-654309 | 2016-05-01 | -50 |
| 283 | 88-654310 | -650.00 | t | Inven411-P2-20151127-In411-1000T < Inven41 < Inven4 | 88-654309 | 2016-05-01 | -130 |
| 284 | 88-654310 | -2405.00 | t | Inven412-P2-20151127-In412-1000T < Inven41 < Inven4 | 88-654309 | 2016-05-01 | -130 |
| 285 | 88-654310 | -2600.00 | t | TTTCU parts-P2-20151127-TTP-1000T < TTT parts < Inven4 | 88-654309 | 2016-05-01 | -130 |
| 286 | 88-654310 | -2600.00 | t | RRRHJK parts-P2-20151127-RRP-1000T < Inven4 | 88-654309 | 2016-05-01 | -130 |
| 287 | 88-654306 | 900.00 | c | Inven31-P1-20151125-In31-1000T < Inven3 | 88-654309 | 2016-05-01 | 150 |
| 288 | 88-654306 | 4500.00 | c | Inven32-P1-20151125-In32-1000T < Inven3 | 88-654309 | 2016-05-01 | 150 |
| 289 | 88-654306 | 1500.00 | c | Inven331-P1-20151125-In331-1000T < Inven33 < Inven3 | 88-654309 | 2016-05-01 | 150 |
| 290 | 88-654306 | 4050.00 | c | Inven332-P1-20151125-In332-1000T < Inven33 < Inven3 | 88-654309 | 2016-05-01 | 150 |
| 291 | 88-654306 | 900.00 | c | HGFCVB parts-P1-20151125-HGP-1000T < QASXC parts < Inven3 | 88-654309 | 2016-05-01 | 150 |
| 292 | 88-654306 | 1800.00 | c | PPGHUP parts-P1-20151125-PPP-1000T < ASDUP parts < Inven3 | 88-654309 | 2016-05-01 | 150 |
| 293 | 88-654310 | 1500.00 | c | Inven31-P1-20160430-In31-600T < Inven3 | 88-654309 | 2016-05-01 | 250 |
| 294 | 88-654310 | 4500.00 | c | Inven32-P1-20160430-In32-600T < Inven3 | 88-654309 | 2016-05-01 | 150 |

| | IDM | Amount | Symbol | MultiSubaccount | Recorder | TransDate | Unit |
|---|---|---|---|---|---|---|---|
| 295 | 88-654310 | 1500.00 | c | Inven331-P1-20160430-In331-600T < Inven33 < Inven3 | 88-654309 | 2016-05-01 | 150 |
| 296 | 88-654310 | 4050.00 | c | Inven332-P1-20160430-In332-600T < Inven33 < Inven3 | 88-654309 | 2016-05-01 | 150 |
| 297 | 88-654310 | 900.00 | c | HGFCVB parts-P1-20160430-HGP-600T < QASXC parts < Inven3 | 88-654309 | 2016-05-01 | 150 |
| 298 | 88-654310 | 1800.00 | c | PPGHUP parts-P1-20160430-PPP-600T < ASDUP parts < Inven3 | 88-654309 | 2016-05-01 | 150 |
| 299 | 909876518 | 15.00 | c | Food213-P1-20151203-F213-1000T < Food21 < Food2 | 88-654309 | 2016-05-01 | 3 |
| 300 | 909876518 | 25.50 | c | Food311-P1-20151203-F311-1000T < Food31 < Food3 | 88-654309 | 2016-05-01 | 3 |
| 301 | 909876521 | 15.00 | c | Food213-P1-20151203-F213-1000T < Food21 < Food2 | 88-654309 | 2016-05-01 | 3 |
| 302 | 909876521 | 8.50 | c | Food311-P1-20151203-F311-1000T < Food31 < Food3 | 88-654309 | 2016-05-01 | 1 |
| 303 | 88-654309 | 672.00 | f | Supplies1-P2-20160430-Supp1-200T | 88-654309 | 2016-05-02 | 48 |
| 304 | 88-654309 | 768.00 | f | Supplies2-P2-20160430-Supp2-200T | 88-654309 | 2016-05-02 | 48 |
| 305 | 88-654309 | 650.00 | f | Inven411-P2-20151127-In411-1000T < Inven41 < Inven4 | 88-654309 | 2016-05-02 | 130 |
| 306 | 88-654309 | 2405.00 | f | Inven412-P2-20151127-In412-1000T < Inven41 < Inven4 | 88-654309 | 2016-05-02 | 130 |
| 307 | 88-654309 | 2600.00 | f | TTTCU parts-P2-20151127-TTP-1000T < TTT parts < Inven4 | 88-654309 | 2016-05-02 | 130 |
| 308 | 88-654309 | 2600.00 | f | RRRHJK parts-P2-20151127-RRP-1000T < Inven4 | 88-654309 | 2016-05-02 | 130 |
| 309 | 88-654309 | 3500.00 | f | Inven51-C3-20150922-In51-1000T < Inven5 | 88-654309 | 2016-05-02 | 350 |
| 310 | 88-654309 | 8750.00 | f | Inven52-C3-20150922-In52-500T < Inven5 | 88-654309 | 2016-05-02 | 175 |
| 311 | 88-654309 | 8750.00 | f | Inven531-C3-20150922-In531-1000T < Inven53 < Inven5 | 88-654309 | 2016-05-02 | 350 |
| 312 | 88-654309 | 12250.00 | f | Inven532-C3-20150922-In532-1000T < Inven53 < Inven5 | 88-654309 | 2016-05-02 | 350 |
| 313 | 88-654309 | 4200.00 | f | Inven541-C3-20150922-In541-1000T < Inven54 < Inven5 | 88-654309 | 2016-05-02 | 350 |
| 314 | 88-654309 | 5250.00 | f | Inven542-C3-20150922-In542-1000T < Inven54 < Inven5 | 88-654309 | 2016-05-02 | 350 |
| 315 | 88-654309 | 2730.00 | f | Inven611-C3-20151003-In611-1300T < Inven61 < Inven6 | 88-654309 | 2016-05-02 | 420 |
| 316 | 88-654309 | 4375.00 | f | Inven612-C3-20151003-In612-1100T < Inven61 < Inven6 | 88-654309 | 2016-05-02 | 350 |
| 317 | 88-654309 | 5040.00 | f | Inven621-C3-20151003-In621-900T < Inven62 < Inven6 | 88-654309 | 2016-05-02 | 280 |
| 318 | 88-654309 | 5600.00 | f | Inven63-C3-20151003-In63-1000T < Inven6 | 88-654309 | 2016-05-02 | 350 |
| 319 | 88-654309 | 5040.00 | f | Inven711-C3-20151003-In711-500T < Inven71 < Inven7 | 88-654309 | 2016-05-02 | 140 |
| 320 | 88-654309 | 1085.00 | f | Inven712-C3-20151003-In712-100T < Inven71 < Inven7 | 88-654309 | 2016-05-02 | 35 |
| 321 | 88-654309 | 5368.00 | f | Inven721-C3-20151003-In721-744T < Inven72 < Inven7 | 88-654309 | 2016-05-02 | 244 |
| 322 | 88-654309 | 4200.00 | f | Inven722-C3-20151003-In722-600T < Inven72 < Inven7 | 88-654309 | 2016-05-02 | 210 |
| 323 | 88-654309 | 3780.00 | f | Inven731-C3-20151003-In731-600T < Inven73 < Inven7 | 88-654309 | 2016-05-02 | 210 |
| 324 | 88-654309 | 5600.00 | f | Inven732-C3-20151003-In732-1000T < Inven73 < Inven7 | 88-654309 | 2016-05-02 | 350 |
| 325 | 88-654309 | 5250.00 | f | Inven811-C3-20151003-In811-600T < Inven81 < Inven8 | 88-654309 | 2016-05-02 | 210 |
| 326 | 88-654309 | 5040.00 | f | Inven812-C3-20151003-In812-600T < Inven81 < Inven8 | 88-654309 | 2016-05-02 | 210 |
| 327 | 88-654309 | 4830.00 | f | Inven813-C3-20151003-In813-600T < Inven81 < Inven8 | 88-654309 | 2016-05-02 | 210 |
| 328 | 88-654309 | 4200.00 | f | Inven82-C3-20151003-In82-600T < Inven8 | 88-654309 | 2016-05-02 | 210 |
| 329 | 88-654309 | 3780.00 | f | Inven831-C3-20151003-In831-600T < Inven83 < Inven8 | 88-654309 | 2016-05-02 | 210 |
| 330 | 88-654309 | 4480.00 | f | Inven832-C3-20151003-In832-800T < Inven83 < Inven8 | 88-654309 | 2016-05-02 | 280 |
| 331 | 909876509 | 26.00 | c | Food222-P1-20151203-F222-1000T < Food22 < Food2 | 88-654309 | 2016-05-12 | 4 |
| 332 | 909876509 | 25.50 | c | Food311-P1-20151203-F311-1000T < Food31 < Food3 | 88-654309 | 2016-05-12 | 3 |
| 333 | 909876523 | 15.00 | c | Food213-P1-20151203-F213-1000T < Food21 < Food2 | 88-654309 | 2016-05-12 | 3 |
| 334 | 909876523 | 8.50 | c | Food311-P1-20151203-F311-1000T < Food31 < Food3 | 88-654309 | 2016-05-12 | 1 |
| 335 | 909876506 | 19.50 | c | Food121-P1-20151203-F121-1000T < Food12 < Food1 | 88-654309 | 2016-05-13 | 3 |
| 336 | 909876506 | 25.50 | c | Food311-P1-20151203-F311-1000T < Food31 < Food3 | 88-654309 | 2016-05-13 | 3 |
| 337 | 909876503 | 22.50 | c | Food123-P1-20151203-F123-1000T < Food12 < Food1 | 88-654309 | 2016-05-14 | 3 |
| 338 | 909876503 | 25.50 | c | Food311-P1-20151203-F311-1000T < Food31 < Food3 | 88-654309 | 2016-05-14 | 3 |
| 339 | 909876511 | 13.00 | c | Food121-P1-20151203-F121-1000T < Food12 < Food1 | 88-654309 | 2016-05-20 | 2 |
| 340 | 909876511 | 13.00 | c | Food322-P1-20151203-F322-1000T < Food32 < Food3 | 88-654309 | 2016-05-20 | 1 |
| 341 | 909876513 | 33.00 | c | Food312-P1-20160430-F312-600T < Food31 < Food3 | 88-654309 | 2016-05-22 | 3 |
| 342 | 909876513 | 50.00 | c | Food111-P1-20151203-F111-1000T < Food11 < Food1 | 88-654309 | 2016-05-22 | 10 |
| 343 | 909876513 | 75.00 | c | Food123-P1-20151203-F123-1000T < Food12 < Food1 | 88-654309 | 2016-05-22 | 10 |
| 344 | 909876513 | 36.00 | c | Food321-P1-20151203-F321-1000T < Food32 < Food3 | 88-654309 | 2016-05-22 | 3 |
| 345 | 909876516 | 40.00 | c | Food111-P1-20151203-F111-1000T < Food11 < Food1 | 88-654309 | 2016-05-22 | 8 |
| 346 | 909876516 | 22.00 | c | Food312-P1-20160430-F312-600T < Food31 < Food3 | 88-654309 | 2016-05-22 | 2 |
| 347 | 909876516 | 12.00 | c | Food321-P1-20151203-F321-1000T < Food32 < Food3 | 88-654309 | 2016-05-22 | 1 |
| 348 | 909876519 | 30.00 | c | Food111-P1-20151203-F111-1000T < Food11 < Food1 | 88-654309 | 2016-05-22 | 6 |
| 349 | 909876519 | 22.00 | c | Food312-P1-20151203-F312-1000T < Food31 < Food3 | 88-654309 | 2016-05-22 | 2 |
| 350 | 909876519 | 13.00 | c | Food322-P1-20151203-F322-1000T < Food32 < Food3 | 88-654309 | 2016-05-22 | 1 |
| 351 | 909876509 | 22.50 | c | Food23-P1-20151203-F23-1000T < Food2 | 88-654309 | 2016-06-14 | 3 |
| 352 | 909876509 | 22.00 | c | Food312-P1-20151203-F312-1000T < Food31 < Food3 | 88-654309 | 2016-06-14 | 2 |
| 353 | 909876512 | 27.50 | c | Food214-P1-20151203-F214-1000T < Food21 < Food2 | 88-654309 | 2016-06-18 | 5 |
| 354 | 909876512 | 24.00 | c | Food321-P1-20151203-F321-1000T < Food32 < Food3 | 88-654309 | 2016-06-18 | 2 |
| 355 | 909876513 | 55.00 | c | Food112-P1-20151203-F112-1000T < Food11 < Food1 | 88-654309 | 2016-06-20 | 10 |
| 356 | 909876513 | 40.00 | c | Food211-P1-20151203-F211-1000T < Food21 < Food2 | 88-654309 | 2016-06-20 | 10 |
| 357 | 909876513 | 51.00 | c | Food311-P1-20151203-F311-1000T < Food31 < Food3 | 88-654309 | 2016-06-20 | 6 |
| 358 | 909876516 | 30.00 | c | Food113-P1-20151203-F113-1000T < Food11 < Food1 | 88-654309 | 2016-06-20 | 5 |
| 359 | 909876516 | 11.00 | c | Food214-P1-20151203-F214-1000T < Food21 < Food2 | 88-654309 | 2016-06-20 | 2 |
| 360 | 909876516 | 22.00 | c | Food312-P1-20151203-F312-1000T < Food31 < Food3 | 88-654309 | 2016-06-20 | 2 |

| | IDM | Amount | Symbol | MultiSubaccount | Recorder | TransDate | Unit |
|---|---|---|---|---|---|---|---|
| 361 | 909876516 | 16.50 | c | Food214-P1-20151203-F214-1000T < Food21 < Food2 | 88-654309 | 2016-06-20 | 3 |
| 362 | 909876519 | 30.00 | c | Food113-P1-20151203-F113-1000T < Food11 < Food1 | 88-654309 | 2016-06-21 | 5 |
| 363 | 909876519 | 22.00 | c | Food312-P1-20151203-F312-1000T < Food31 < Food3 | 88-654309 | 2016-06-21 | 2 |
| 364 | 909876514 | 45.00 | c | Food123-P1-20151203-F123-1000T < Food12 < Food1 | 88-654309 | 2016-07-05 | 6 |
| 365 | 909876514 | 39.00 | c | Food322-P1-20151203-F322-1000T < Food32 < Food3 | 88-654309 | 2016-07-05 | 3 |
| 366 | 909876504 | 24.00 | c | Food211-P1-20151203-F211-1000T < Food21 < Food2 | 88-654309 | 2016-07-16 | 6 |
| 367 | 909876504 | 30.00 | c | Food23-P1-20151203-F23-1000T < Food2 | 88-654309 | 2016-07-16 | 4 |
| 368 | 909876512 | 32.50 | c | Food222-P1-20151203-F222-1000T < Food22 < Food2 | 88-654309 | 2016-07-21 | 5 |
| 369 | 909876512 | 26.00 | c | Food322-P1-20151203-F322-1000T < Food32 < Food3 | 88-654309 | 2016-07-21 | 2 |
| 370 | 909876513 | 40.00 | c | Food211-P1-20151203-F211-1000T < Food21 < Food2 | 88-654309 | 2016-07-22 | 10 |
| 371 | 909876513 | 45.00 | c | Food212-P1-20151203-F212-1000T < Food21 < Food2 | 88-654309 | 2016-07-22 | 10 |
| 372 | 909876513 | 25.50 | c | Food311-P1-20151203-F311-1000T < Food31 < Food3 | 88-654309 | 2016-07-22 | 3 |
| 373 | 909876513 | 33.00 | c | Food312-P1-20151203-F312-1000T < Food31 < Food3 | 88-654309 | 2016-07-22 | 3 |
| 374 | 909876505 | 22.50 | c | Food212-P1-20151203-F212-1000T < Food21 < Food2 | 88-654309 | 2016-07-22 | 5 |
| 375 | 909876505 | 25.50 | c | Food311-P1-20151203-F311-1000T < Food31 < Food3 | 88-654309 | 2016-07-22 | 3 |
| 376 | 909876516 | 27.00 | c | Food212-P1-20151203-F212-1000T < Food21 < Food2 | 88-654309 | 2016-07-25 | 6 |
| 377 | 909876516 | 17.00 | c | Food311-P1-20151203-F311-1000T < Food31 < Food3 | 88-654309 | 2016-07-25 | 2 |
| 378 | 909876516 | 11.00 | c | Food312-P1-20151203-F312-1000T < Food31 < Food3 | 88-654309 | 2016-07-25 | 1 |
| 379 | 909876519 | 17.00 | c | Food311-P1-20151203-F311-1000T < Food31 < Food3 | 88-654309 | 2016-07-25 | 2 |
| 380 | 909876519 | 22.00 | c | Food312-P1-20151203-F312-1000T < Food31 < Food3 | 88-654309 | 2016-07-25 | 2 |
| 381 | 909876523 | 17.00 | c | Food311-P1-20151203-F311-1000T < Food31 < Food3 | 88-654309 | 2016-07-25 | 2 |
| 382 | 909876523 | 11.00 | c | Food312-P1-20151203-F312-1000T < Food31 < Food3 | 88-654309 | 2016-07-25 | 1 |
| 383 | 909876501 | 650.00 | c | Food111-P1-20160430-F111-600T < Food11 < Food1 | 88-654309 | 2016-07-31 | 130 |
| 384 | 909876501 | 715.00 | c | Food112-P1-20160430-F112-600T < Food11 < Food1 | 88-654309 | 2016-07-31 | 130 |
| 385 | 909876501 | 780.00 | c | Food113-P1-20160430-F113-600T < Food11 < Food1 | 88-654309 | 2016-07-31 | 130 |
| 386 | 909876501 | 65.00 | c | Food121-P1-20160430-F121-600T < Food12 < Food1 | 88-654309 | 2016-07-31 | 10 |
| 387 | 909876501 | 910.00 | c | Food122-P1-20160430-F122-600T < Food12 < Food1 | 88-654309 | 2016-07-31 | 130 |
| 388 | 909876501 | 520.00 | c | Food211-P1-20160430-F211-600T < Food21 < Food2 | 88-654309 | 2016-07-31 | 130 |
| 389 | 909876501 | 650.00 | c | Food213-P1-20160430-F213-600T < Food21 < Food2 | 88-654309 | 2016-07-31 | 130 |
| 390 | 909876501 | 845.00 | c | Food222-P1-20160430-F222-600T < Food22 < Food2 | 88-654309 | 2016-07-31 | 130 |
| 391 | 909876514 | 715.00 | c | Food112-P1-20160430-F112-600T < Food11 < Food1 | 88-654309 | 2016-07-31 | 130 |
| 392 | 909876514 | 780.00 | c | Food221-P1-20160430-F221-600T < Food22 < Food2 | 88-654309 | 2016-07-31 | 130 |
| 393 | 909876514 | 130.00 | c | Food222-P1-20160430-F222-600T < Food22 < Food2 | 88-654309 | 2016-07-31 | 20 |
| 394 | 909876514 | 975.00 | c | Food23-P1-20160430-F23-600T < Food2 | 88-654309 | 2016-07-31 | 130 |
| 395 | 909876514 | 1105.00 | c | Food311-P1-20160430-F311-600T < Food31 < Food3 | 88-654309 | 2016-07-31 | 130 |
| 396 | 909876514 | 1430.00 | c | Food312-P1-20160430-F312-600T < Food31 < Food3 | 88-654309 | 2016-07-31 | 130 |
| 397 | 909876514 | 1560.00 | c | Food321-P1-20160430-F321-600T < Food32 < Food3 | 88-654309 | 2016-07-31 | 130 |
| 398 | 909876514 | 1690.00 | c | Food322-P1-20160430-F322-600T < Food32 < Food3 | 88-654309 | 2016-07-31 | 130 |
| 399 | 909876515 | 650.00 | c | Food111-P1-20160430-F111-600T < Food11 < Food1 | 88-654309 | 2016-07-31 | 130 |
| 400 | 909876515 | 715.00 | c | Food112-P1-20160430-F112-600T < Food11 < Food1 | 88-654309 | 2016-07-31 | 130 |
| 401 | 909876515 | 130.00 | c | Food222-P1-20160430-F222-600T < Food22 < Food2 | 88-654309 | 2016-07-31 | 20 |
| 402 | 909876515 | 975.00 | c | Food23-P1-20160430-F23-600T < Food2 | 88-654309 | 2016-07-31 | 130 |
| 403 | 909876515 | 1105.00 | c | Food311-P1-20160430-F311-600T < Food31 < Food3 | 88-654309 | 2016-07-31 | 130 |
| 404 | 909876515 | 1430.00 | c | Food312-P1-20160430-F312-600T < Food31 < Food3 | 88-654309 | 2016-07-31 | 130 |
| 405 | 909876515 | 1560.00 | c | Food321-P1-20160430-F321-600T < Food32 < Food3 | 88-654309 | 2016-07-31 | 130 |
| 406 | 909876515 | 1690.00 | c | Food322-P1-20160430-F322-600T < Food32 < Food3 | 88-654309 | 2016-07-31 | 130 |
| 407 | 909876516 | 715.00 | c | Food112-P1-20160430-F112-600T < Food11 < Food1 | 88-654309 | 2016-07-31 | 130 |
| 408 | 909876516 | 910.00 | c | Food122-P1-20160430-F122-600T < Food12 < Food1 | 88-654309 | 2016-07-31 | 130 |
| 409 | 909876516 | 130.00 | c | Food222-P1-20160430-F222-600T < Food22 < Food2 | 88-654309 | 2016-07-31 | 20 |
| 410 | 909876517 | 650.00 | c | Food111-P1-20160430-F111-600T < Food11 < Food1 | 88-654309 | 2016-07-31 | 130 |
| 411 | 909876517 | 520.00 | c | Food211-P1-20160430-F211-600T < Food21 < Food2 | 88-654309 | 2016-07-31 | 130 |
| 412 | 909876517 | 195.00 | c | Food222-P1-20160430-F222-600T < Food22 < Food2 | 88-654309 | 2016-07-31 | 30 |
| 413 | 909876518 | 650.00 | c | Food111-P1-20160430-F111-600T < Food11 < Food1 | 88-654309 | 2016-07-31 | 130 |
| 414 | 909876518 | 780.00 | c | Food113-P1-20160430-F113-600T < Food11 < Food1 | 88-654309 | 2016-07-31 | 130 |
| 415 | 909876518 | 195.00 | c | Food222-P1-20160430-F222-600T < Food22 < Food2 | 88-654309 | 2016-07-31 | 30 |
| 416 | 909876519 | 780.00 | c | Food113-P1-20160430-F113-600T < Food11 < Food1 | 88-654309 | 2016-07-31 | 130 |
| 417 | 909876519 | 65.00 | c | Food121-P1-20160430-F121-600T < Food12 < Food1 | 88-654309 | 2016-07-31 | 10 |
| 418 | 909876519 | 845.00 | c | Food222-P1-20160430-F222-600T < Food22 < Food2 | 88-654309 | 2016-07-31 | 130 |
| 419 | 909876519 | 975.00 | c | Food23-P1-20160430-F23-600T < Food2 | 88-654309 | 2016-07-31 | 130 |
| 420 | 909876519 | 1105.00 | c | Food311-P1-20160430-F311-600T < Food31 < Food3 | 88-654309 | 2016-07-31 | 130 |
| 421 | 909876519 | 1430.00 | c | Food312-P1-20160430-F312-600T < Food31 < Food3 | 88-654309 | 2016-07-31 | 130 |
| 422 | 909876519 | 1560.00 | c | Food321-P1-20160430-F321-600T < Food32 < Food3 | 88-654309 | 2016-07-31 | 130 |
| 423 | 909876519 | 1690.00 | c | Food322-P1-20160430-F322-600T < Food32 < Food3 | 88-654309 | 2016-07-31 | 130 |
| 424 | 909876520 | 780.00 | c | Food113-P1-20160430-F113-600T < Food11 < Food1 | 88-654309 | 2016-07-31 | 130 |
| 425 | 909876520 | 65.00 | c | Food121-P1-20160430-F121-600T < Food12 < Food1 | 88-654309 | 2016-07-31 | 10 |
| 426 | 909876520 | 910.00 | c | Food122-P1-20160430-F122-600T < Food12 < Food1 | 88-654309 | 2016-07-31 | 130 |

| | IDM | Amount | Symbol | MultiSubaccount | Recorder | TransDate | Unit |
|---|---|---|---|---|---|---|---|
| 427 | 909876520 | 75.00 | c | Food123-P1-20160430-F123-600T < Food12 < Food1 | 88-654309 | 2016-07-31 | 10 |
| 428 | 909876520 | 520.00 | c | Food211-P1-20160430-F211-600T < Food21 < Food2 | 88-654309 | 2016-07-31 | 130 |
| 429 | 909876520 | 585.00 | c | Food212-P1-20160430-F212-600T < Food21 < Food2 | 88-654309 | 2016-07-31 | 130 |
| 430 | 909876520 | 650.00 | c | Food213-P1-20160430-F213-600T < Food21 < Food2 | 88-654309 | 2016-07-31 | 130 |
| 431 | 909876520 | 715.00 | c | Food214-P1-20160430-F214-600T < Food21 < Food2 | 88-654309 | 2016-07-31 | 130 |
| 432 | 909876520 | 900.00 | c | Food221-P1-20160430-F221-600T < Food22 < Food2 | 88-654309 | 2016-07-31 | 150 |
| 433 | 909876521 | 845.00 | c | Food111-P1-20160430-F111-600T < Food11 < Food1 | 88-654309 | 2016-07-31 | 169 |
| 434 | 909876521 | 910.00 | c | Food122-P1-20160430-F122-600T < Food12 < Food1 | 88-654309 | 2016-07-31 | 130 |
| 435 | 909876521 | 150.00 | c | Food123-P1-20160430-F123-600T < Food12 < Food1 | 88-654309 | 2016-07-31 | 20 |
| 436 | 909876521 | 520.00 | c | Food211-P1-20160430-F211-600T < Food21 < Food2 | 88-654309 | 2016-07-31 | 130 |
| 437 | 909876521 | 585.00 | c | Food212-P1-20160430-F212-600T < Food21 < Food2 | 88-654309 | 2016-07-31 | 130 |
| 438 | 909876521 | 650.00 | c | Food213-P1-20160430-F213-600T < Food21 < Food2 | 88-654309 | 2016-07-31 | 130 |
| 439 | 909876521 | 825.00 | c | Food214-P1-20160430-F214-600T < Food21 < Food2 | 88-654309 | 2016-07-31 | 150 |
| 440 | 909876521 | 845.00 | c | Food222-P1-20160430-F222-600T < Food22 < Food2 | 88-654309 | 2016-07-31 | 130 |
| 441 | 909876522 | 845.00 | c | Food121-P1-20160430-F121-600T < Food12 < Food1 | 88-654309 | 2016-07-31 | 130 |
| 442 | 909876522 | 910.00 | c | Food122-P1-20160430-F122-600T < Food12 < Food1 | 88-654309 | 2016-07-31 | 130 |
| 443 | 909876522 | 150.00 | c | Food123-P1-20160430-F123-600T < Food12 < Food1 | 88-654309 | 2016-07-31 | 20 |
| 444 | 909876522 | 520.00 | c | Food211-P1-20160430-F211-600T < Food21 < Food2 | 88-654309 | 2016-07-31 | 130 |
| 445 | 909876522 | 585.00 | c | Food212-P1-20160430-F212-600T < Food21 < Food2 | 88-654309 | 2016-07-31 | 130 |
| 446 | 909876522 | 650.00 | c | Food213-P1-20160430-F213-600T < Food21 < Food2 | 88-654309 | 2016-07-31 | 130 |
| 447 | 909876522 | 825.00 | c | Food214-P1-20160430-F214-600T < Food21 < Food2 | 88-654309 | 2016-07-31 | 150 |
| 448 | 909876522 | 780.00 | c | Food221-P1-20160430-F221-600T < Food22 < Food2 | 88-654309 | 2016-07-31 | 130 |
| 449 | 909876523 | 845.00 | c | Food121-P1-20160430-F121-600T < Food12 < Food1 | 88-654309 | 2016-07-31 | 130 |
| 450 | 909876523 | 910.00 | c | Food122-P1-20160430-F122-600T < Food12 < Food1 | 88-654309 | 2016-07-31 | 130 |
| 451 | 909876523 | 975.00 | c | Food123-P1-20160430-F123-600T < Food12 < Food1 | 88-654309 | 2016-07-31 | 130 |
| 452 | 909876523 | 975.00 | c | Food23-P1-20160430-F23-600T < Food2 | 88-654309 | 2016-07-31 | 130 |
| 453 | 909876524 | 845.00 | c | Food121-P1-20160430-F121-600T < Food12 < Food1 | 88-654309 | 2016-07-31 | 130 |
| 454 | 909876524 | 910.00 | c | Food122-P1-20160430-F122-600T < Food12 < Food1 | 88-654309 | 2016-07-31 | 130 |
| 455 | 909876524 | 975.00 | c | Food123-P1-20160430-F123-600T < Food12 < Food1 | 88-654309 | 2016-07-31 | 130 |
| 456 | 909876524 | 1105.00 | c | Food311-P1-20160430-F311-600T < Food31 < Food3 | 88-654309 | 2016-07-31 | 130 |
| 457 | 909876525 | 845.00 | c | Food121-P1-20160430-F121-600T < Food12 < Food1 | 88-654309 | 2016-07-31 | 130 |
| 458 | 909876525 | 910.00 | c | Food122-P1-20160430-F122-600T < Food12 < Food1 | 88-654309 | 2016-07-31 | 130 |
| 459 | 909876525 | 975.00 | c | Food123-P1-20160430-F123-600T < Food12 < Food1 | 88-654309 | 2016-07-31 | 130 |
| 460 | 909876525 | 1430.00 | c | Food312-P1-20160430-F312-600T < Food31 < Food3 | 88-654309 | 2016-07-31 | 130 |
| 461 | 909876501 | -600.00 | c | Food111-P1-20160430-F111-600T < Food11 < Food1 | 88-654309 | 2016-07-31 | -120 |
| 462 | 909876501 | 600.00 | c | Food123-P1-20160430-F123-600T < Food12 < Food1 | 88-654309 | 2016-07-31 | 80 |
| 463 | 909876521 | -480.00 | c | Food211-P1-20160430-F211-600T < Food21 < Food2 | 88-654309 | 2016-07-31 | -120 |
| 464 | 909876521 | 480.00 | c | Food221-P1-20160430-F221-600T < Food22 < Food2 | 88-654309 | 2016-07-31 | 80 |
| 465 | 909876525 | -630.00 | c | Food122-P1-20160430-F122-600T < Food12 < Food1 | 88-654309 | 2016-07-31 | -90 |
| 466 | 909876525 | 630.00 | c | Food212-P1-20160430-F212-600T < Food21 < Food2 | 88-654309 | 2016-07-31 | 140 |
| 467 | 909876524 | -840.00 | c | Food122-P1-20160430-F122-600T < Food12 < Food1 | 88-654309 | 2016-07-31 | -120 |
| 468 | 909876524 | 728.00 | c | Food322-P1-20160430-F322-600T < Food32 < Food3 | 88-654309 | 2016-07-31 | 56 |
| 469 | 909876523 | -840.00 | c | Food122-P1-20160430-F122-600T < Food12 < Food1 | 88-654309 | 2016-07-31 | -120 |
| 470 | 909876523 | 728.00 | c | Food322-P1-20160430-F322-600T < Food32 < Food3 | 88-654309 | 2016-07-31 | 56 |
| 471 | 909876516 | -840.00 | c | Food122-P1-20160430-F122-600T < Food12 < Food1 | 88-654309 | 2016-07-31 | -120 |
| 472 | 909876516 | 728.00 | c | Food322-P1-20160430-F322-600T < Food32 < Food3 | 88-654309 | 2016-07-31 | 56 |
| 473 | 909876503 | 27.00 | c | Food212-P1-20160430-F212-600T < Food21 < Food2 | 88-654309 | 2016-08-10 | 6 |
| 474 | 909876503 | 44.00 | c | Food312-P1-20160430-F312-600T < Food31 < Food3 | 88-654309 | 2016-08-10 | 4 |
| 475 | 909876517 | 30.00 | c | Food123-P1-20160430-F123-600T < Food12 < Food1 | 88-654309 | 2016-08-14 | 4 |
| 476 | 909876517 | 26.00 | c | Food322-P1-20160430-F322-600T < Food32 < Food3 | 88-654309 | 2016-08-14 | 2 |
| 477 | 909876510 | 18.00 | c | Food221-P1-20160430-F221-600T < Food22 < Food2 | 88-654309 | 2016-08-17 | 3 |
| 478 | 909876510 | 12.00 | c | Food321-P1-20160430-F321-600T < Food32 < Food3 | 88-654309 | 2016-08-17 | 1 |
| 479 | 909876516 | 30.00 | c | Food213-P1-20160430-F213-600T < Food21 < Food2 | 88-654309 | 2016-08-20 | 6 |
| 480 | 909876516 | 33.00 | c | Food312-P1-20160430-F312-600T < Food31 < Food3 | 88-654309 | 2016-08-20 | 3 |
| 481 | 909876516 | 13.00 | c | Food322-P1-20160430-F322-600T < Food32 < Food3 | 88-654309 | 2016-08-20 | 1 |
| 482 | 909876519 | 22.00 | c | Food312-P1-20160430-F312-600T < Food31 < Food3 | 88-654309 | 2016-08-21 | 2 |
| 483 | 909876519 | 13.00 | c | Food322-P1-20160430-F322-600T < Food32 < Food3 | 88-654309 | 2016-08-21 | 1 |
| 484 | 909876512 | 30.00 | c | Food23-P1-20160430-F23-600T < Food2 | 88-654309 | 2016-08-22 | 4 |
| 485 | 909876512 | 22.00 | c | Food312-P1-20160430-F312-600T < Food31 < Food3 | 88-654309 | 2016-08-22 | 2 |
| 486 | 909876513 | 40.00 | c | Food211-P1-20160430-F211-600T < Food21 < Food2 | 88-654309 | 2016-08-22 | 10 |
| 487 | 909876513 | 33.00 | c | Food312-P1-20160430-F312-600T < Food31 < Food3 | 88-654309 | 2016-08-22 | 3 |
| 488 | 909876513 | 25.50 | c | Food311-P1-20160430-F311-600T < Food31 < Food3 | 88-654309 | 2016-08-22 | 3 |
| 489 | 909876513 | -50.00 | c | Food213-P1-20160430-F213-600T < Food21 < Food2 | 88-654309 | 2016-08-22 | -10 |
| 490 | 909876513 | 100.00 | c | Food213-P1-20160430-F213-600T < Food21 < Food2 | 88-654309 | 2016-08-22 | 20 |
| 491 | 909876509 | 26.00 | c | Food222-P1-20160430-F222-600T < Food22 < Food2 | 88-654309 | 2016-09-17 | 4 |
| 492 | 909876509 | 26.00 | c | Food322-P1-20160430-F322-600T < Food32 < Food3 | 88-654309 | 2016-09-17 | 2 |

| | IDM | Amount | Symbol | MultiSubaccount | Recorder | TransDate | Unit |
|---|---|---|---|---|---|---|---|
| 493 | 909876512 | 25.00 | c | Food213-P1-20160430-F213-600T < Food21 < Food2 | 88-654309 | 2016-09-17 | 5 |
| 494 | 909876512 | 24.00 | c | Food321-P1-20160430-F321-600T < Food32 < Food3 | 88-654309 | 2016-09-17 | 2 |
| 495 | 909876524 | 33.00 | c | Food312-P1-20160430-F312-600T < Food31 < Food3 | 88-654309 | 2016-09-19 | 3 |
| 496 | 909876524 | 12.00 | c | Food321-P1-20160430-F321-600T < Food32 < Food3 | 88-654309 | 2016-09-19 | 1 |
| 497 | 909876513 | 60.00 | c | Food221-P1-20160430-F221-600T < Food22 < Food2 | 88-654309 | 2016-09-26 | 10 |
| 498 | 909876513 | 75.00 | c | Food23-P1-20160430-F23-600T < Food2 | 88-654309 | 2016-09-26 | 10 |
| 499 | 909876513 | 36.00 | c | Food321-P1-20160430-F321-600T < Food32 < Food3 | 88-654309 | 2016-09-26 | 3 |
| 500 | 909876513 | 39.00 | c | Food322-P1-20160430-F322-600T < Food32 < Food3 | 88-654309 | 2016-09-26 | 3 |
| 501 | 909876516 | 45.00 | c | Food23-P1-20160430-F23-600T < Food2 | 88-654309 | 2016-09-26 | 6 |
| 502 | 909876516 | 25.50 | c | Food311-P1-20160430-F311-600T < Food31 < Food3 | 88-654309 | 2016-09-26 | 3 |
| 503 | 909876516 | 12.00 | c | Food321-P1-20160430-F321-600T < Food32 < Food3 | 88-654309 | 2016-09-26 | 1 |
| 504 | 909876519 | 25.50 | c | Food311-P1-20160430-F311-600T < Food31 < Food3 | 88-654309 | 2016-09-26 | 3 |
| 505 | 909876519 | 12.00 | c | Food321-P1-20160430-F321-600T < Food32 < Food3 | 88-654309 | 2016-09-26 | 1 |
| 506 | 88-654306 | -2700.00 | t | Computer server2-C1-20160430-COMS2-047 < Computer server-inventor... | 88-654309 | 2016-10-01 | -1 |
| 507 | 88-654306 | -1600.00 | t | Computer1-C1-20160430-COM1-063 < Computer-inventory | 88-654309 | 2016-10-01 | -1 |
| 508 | 88-654306 | -1600.00 | t | Computer1-C1-20160430-COM1-064 < Computer-inventory | 88-654309 | 2016-10-01 | -1 |
| 509 | 88-654309 | 2700.00 | e | Computer server2-C1-20160430-COMS2-047 < Computer server-inventor... | 88-654309 | 2016-10-01 | 1 |
| 510 | 88-654309 | 1600.00 | e | Computer1-C1-20160430-COM1-063 < Computer-inventory | 88-654309 | 2016-10-01 | 1 |
| 511 | 88-654309 | 1600.00 | e | Computer1-C1-20160430-COM1-064 < Computer-inventory | 88-654309 | 2016-10-01 | 1 |
| 512 | 909876512 | 30.00 | c | Food123-P1-20160430-F123-600T < Food12 < Food1 | 88-654309 | 2016-10-16 | 4 |
| 513 | 909876512 | 22.50 | c | Food23-P1-20160430-F23-600T < Food2 | 88-654309 | 2016-10-16 | 3 |
| 514 | 909876503 | 20.00 | c | Food213-P1-20160430-F213-600T < Food21 < Food2 | 88-654309 | 2016-10-21 | 4 |
| 515 | 909876503 | 36.00 | c | Food321-P1-20160430-F321-600T < Food32 < Food3 | 88-654309 | 2016-10-21 | 3 |
| 516 | 909876505 | 22.00 | c | Food214-P1-20160430-F214-600T < Food21 < Food2 | 88-654309 | 2016-10-22 | 4 |
| 517 | 909876505 | 33.00 | c | Food312-P1-20160430-F312-600T < Food31 < Food3 | 88-654309 | 2016-10-22 | 3 |
| 518 | 909876509 | 30.00 | c | Food123-P1-20160430-F123-600T < Food12 < Food1 | 88-654309 | 2016-10-22 | 4 |
| 519 | 909876509 | 24.00 | c | Food321-P1-20160430-F321-600T < Food32 < Food3 | 88-654309 | 2016-10-22 | 2 |
| 520 | 909876513 | 60.00 | c | Food113-P1-20160430-F113-600T < Food11 < Food1 | 88-654309 | 2016-10-24 | 10 |
| 521 | 909876513 | 55.00 | c | Food214-P1-20160430-F214-600T < Food21 < Food2 | 88-654309 | 2016-10-24 | 10 |
| 522 | 909876513 | 33.00 | c | Food312-P1-20160430-F312-600T < Food31 < Food3 | 88-654309 | 2016-10-24 | 3 |
| 523 | 909876513 | 36.00 | c | Food321-P1-20160430-F321-600T < Food32 < Food3 | 88-654309 | 2016-10-24 | 3 |
| 524 | 909876516 | 36.00 | c | Food113-P1-20160430-F113-600T < Food11 < Food1 | 88-654309 | 2016-10-25 | 6 |
| 525 | 909876516 | 33.00 | c | Food312-P1-20160430-F312-600T < Food31 < Food3 | 88-654309 | 2016-10-25 | 3 |
| 526 | 909876516 | 13.00 | c | Food322-P1-20160430-F322-600T < Food32 < Food3 | 88-654309 | 2016-10-25 | 1 |
| 527 | 909876519 | 30.00 | c | Food113-P1-20160430-F113-600T < Food11 < Food1 | 88-654309 | 2016-10-25 | 5 |
| 528 | 909876519 | 13.00 | c | Food322-P1-20160430-F322-600T < Food32 < Food3 | 88-654309 | 2016-10-25 | 1 |
| 529 | 909876506 | 19.50 | c | Food121-P1-20160430-F121-600T < Food12 < Food1 | 88-654309 | 2016-11-15 | 3 |
| 530 | 909876506 | 24.00 | c | Food321-P1-20160430-F321-600T < Food32 < Food3 | 88-654309 | 2016-11-15 | 2 |
| 531 | 909876513 | 50.00 | c | Food111-P1-20151203-F111-1000T < Food11 < Food1 | 88-654309 | 2016-11-15 | 10 |
| 532 | 909876513 | 60.00 | c | Food113-P1-20160430-F113-600T < Food11 < Food1 | 88-654309 | 2016-11-15 | 10 |
| 533 | 909876513 | 25.50 | c | Food311-P1-20160430-F311-600T < Food31 < Food3 | 88-654309 | 2016-11-15 | 3 |
| 534 | 909876513 | 36.00 | c | Food321-P1-20160430-F321-600T < Food32 < Food3 | 88-654309 | 2016-11-15 | 3 |
| 535 | 909876516 | 35.00 | c | Food111-P1-20151203-F111-1000T < Food11 < Food1 | 88-654309 | 2016-11-17 | 7 |
| 536 | 909876516 | 25.50 | c | Food311-P1-20160430-F311-600T < Food31 < Food3 | 88-654309 | 2016-11-17 | 3 |
| 537 | 909876516 | 24.00 | c | Food321-P1-20160430-F321-600T < Food32 < Food3 | 88-654309 | 2016-11-17 | 2 |
| 538 | 909876519 | 25.50 | c | Food311-P1-20160430-F311-600T < Food31 < Food3 | 88-654309 | 2016-11-17 | 3 |
| 539 | 909876519 | 12.00 | c | Food321-P1-20160430-F321-600T < Food32 < Food3 | 88-654309 | 2016-11-17 | 1 |
| 540 | 909876512 | 30.00 | c | Food113-P1-20160430-F113-600T < Food11 < Food1 | 88-654309 | 2016-11-19 | 5 |
| 541 | 909876512 | 17.00 | c | Food311-P1-20160430-F311-600T < Food31 < Food3 | 88-654309 | 2016-11-19 | 2 |
| 542 | 88-654309 | -28.00 | f | Supplies1-P2-20160430-Supp1-200T | 88-654309 | 2016-11-30 | -2 |
| 543 | 88-654309 | -16.00 | f | Supplies2-P2-20160430-Supp2-200T | 88-654309 | 2016-11-30 | -1 |
| 544 | 88-654309 | -6000.00 | p | Food111-P1-20161130-F111-1200T < Food11 < Food1 | 88-654309 | 2016-11-30 | -1200 |
| 545 | 88-654309 | -6600.00 | p | Food112-P1-20161130-F112-1200T < Food11 < Food1 | 88-654309 | 2016-11-30 | -1200 |
| 546 | 88-654309 | -7200.00 | p | Food113-P1-20161130-F113-1200T < Food11 < Food1 | 88-654309 | 2016-11-30 | -1200 |
| 547 | 88-654309 | -7800.00 | p | Food121-P1-20161130-F121-1200T < Food12 < Food1 | 88-654309 | 2016-11-30 | -1200 |
| 548 | 88-654309 | -8400.00 | p | Food122-P1-20161130-F122-1200T < Food12 < Food1 | 88-654309 | 2016-11-30 | -1200 |
| 549 | 88-654309 | -9000.00 | p | Food123-P1-20161130-F123-1200T < Food12 < Food1 | 88-654309 | 2016-11-30 | -1200 |
| 550 | 88-654309 | -4800.00 | p | Food211-P1-20160110-F211-1200T < Food21 < Food2 | 88-654309 | 2016-11-30 | -1200 |
| 551 | 88-654309 | -5400.00 | p | Food212-P1-20161130-F212-1200T < Food21 < Food2 | 88-654309 | 2016-11-30 | -1200 |
| 552 | 88-654309 | -6000.00 | p | Food213-P1-20161130-F213-1200T < Food21 < Food2 | 88-654309 | 2016-11-30 | -1200 |
| 553 | 88-654309 | -6600.00 | p | Food214-P1-20161130-F214-1200T < Food21 < Food2 | 88-654309 | 2016-11-30 | -1200 |
| 554 | 88-654309 | -7200.00 | p | Food221-P1-20161130-F221-1200T < Food22 < Food2 | 88-654309 | 2016-11-30 | -1200 |
| 555 | 88-654309 | -7800.00 | p | Food222-P1-20161130-F222-1200T < Food22 < Food2 | 88-654309 | 2016-11-30 | -1200 |
| 556 | 88-654309 | -9000.00 | p | Food23-P1-20161130-F23-1200T < Food2 | 88-654309 | 2016-11-30 | -1200 |
| 557 | 88-654309 | -10200.00 | p | Food311-P1-20161130-F311-1200T < Food31 < Food3 | 88-654309 | 2016-11-30 | -1200 |
| 558 | 88-654309 | -13200.00 | p | Food312-P1-20161130-F312-1200T < Food31 < Food3 | 88-654309 | 2016-11-30 | -1200 |

| | IDM | Amount | Symbol | MultiSubaccount | Recorder | TransDate | Unit |
|---|---|---|---|---|---|---|---|
| 559 | 88-654309 | -14400.00 | p | Food321-P1-20161130-F321-1200T < Food32 < Food3 | 88-654309 | 2016-11-30 | -1200 |
| 560 | 88-654309 | -15600.00 | p | Food322-P1-20161130-F322-1200T < Food32 < Food3 | 88-654309 | 2016-11-30 | -1200 |
| 561 | 909876516 | 975.00 | c | Food23-P1-20161130-F23-1200T < Food2 | 88-654309 | 2016-12-01 | 130 |
| 562 | 909876516 | 1105.00 | c | Food311-P1-20161130-F311-1200T < Food31 < Food3 | 88-654309 | 2016-12-01 | 130 |
| 563 | 909876516 | 1430.00 | c | Food312-P1-20161130-F312-1200T < Food31 < Food3 | 88-654309 | 2016-12-01 | 130 |
| 564 | 909876516 | 1560.00 | c | Food321-P1-20161130-F321-1200T < Food32 < Food3 | 88-654309 | 2016-12-01 | 130 |
| 565 | 909876516 | 1690.00 | c | Food322-P1-20161130-F322-1200T < Food32 < Food3 | 88-654309 | 2016-12-01 | 130 |
| 566 | 909876517 | 975.00 | c | Food23-P1-20161130-F23-1200T < Food2 | 88-654309 | 2016-12-01 | 130 |
| 567 | 909876517 | 1105.00 | c | Food311-P1-20161130-F311-1200T < Food31 < Food3 | 88-654309 | 2016-12-01 | 130 |
| 568 | 909876517 | 1430.00 | c | Food312-P1-20161130-F312-1200T < Food31 < Food3 | 88-654309 | 2016-12-01 | 130 |
| 569 | 909876517 | 1560.00 | c | Food321-P1-20161130-F321-1200T < Food32 < Food3 | 88-654309 | 2016-12-01 | 130 |
| 570 | 909876517 | 1690.00 | c | Food322-P1-20161130-F322-1200T < Food32 < Food3 | 88-654309 | 2016-12-01 | 130 |
| 571 | 909876518 | 975.00 | c | Food23-P1-20161130-F23-1200T < Food2 | 88-654309 | 2016-12-01 | 130 |
| 572 | 909876518 | 1105.00 | c | Food311-P1-20161130-F311-1200T < Food31 < Food3 | 88-654309 | 2016-12-01 | 130 |
| 573 | 909876518 | 1430.00 | c | Food312-P1-20161130-F312-1200T < Food31 < Food3 | 88-654309 | 2016-12-01 | 130 |
| 574 | 909876518 | 1560.00 | c | Food321-P1-20161130-F321-1200T < Food32 < Food3 | 88-654309 | 2016-12-01 | 130 |
| 575 | 909876518 | 1690.00 | c | Food322-P1-20161130-F322-1200T < Food32 < Food3 | 88-654309 | 2016-12-01 | 130 |
| 576 | 909876523 | 520.00 | c | Food211-P1-20160110-F211-1200T < Food21 < Food2 | 88-654309 | 2016-12-01 | 130 |
| 577 | 909876523 | 585.00 | c | Food212-P1-20161130-F212-1200T < Food21 < Food2 | 88-654309 | 2016-12-01 | 130 |
| 578 | 909876523 | 650.00 | c | Food213-P1-20161130-F213-1200T < Food21 < Food2 | 88-654309 | 2016-12-01 | 130 |
| 579 | 909876524 | 520.00 | c | Food211-P1-20160110-F211-1200T < Food21 < Food2 | 88-654309 | 2016-12-01 | 130 |
| 580 | 909876524 | 585.00 | c | Food212-P1-20161130-F212-1200T < Food21 < Food2 | 88-654309 | 2016-12-01 | 130 |
| 581 | 909876524 | 650.00 | c | Food213-P1-20161130-F213-1200T < Food21 < Food2 | 88-654309 | 2016-12-01 | 130 |
| 582 | 909876525 | 520.00 | c | Food211-P1-20160110-F211-1200T < Food21 < Food2 | 88-654309 | 2016-12-01 | 130 |
| 583 | 909876525 | 585.00 | c | Food212-P1-20161130-F212-1200T < Food21 < Food2 | 88-654309 | 2016-12-01 | 130 |
| 584 | 909876525 | 650.00 | c | Food213-P1-20161130-F213-1200T < Food21 < Food2 | 88-654309 | 2016-12-01 | 130 |
| 585 | 909876513 | 55.00 | c | Food112-P1-20161130-F112-1200T < Food11 < Food1 | 88-654309 | 2016-12-13 | 10 |
| 586 | 909876513 | 75.00 | c | Food123-P1-20161130-F123-1200T < Food12 < Food1 | 88-654309 | 2016-12-13 | 10 |
| 587 | 909876513 | 33.00 | c | Food312-P1-20161130-F312-1200T < Food31 < Food3 | 88-654309 | 2016-12-13 | 3 |
| 588 | 909876513 | 36.00 | c | Food321-P1-20161130-F321-1200T < Food32 < Food3 | 88-654309 | 2016-12-13 | 3 |
| 589 | 909876509 | 19.50 | c | Food222-P1-20161130-F222-1200T < Food22 < Food2 | 88-654309 | 2016-12-15 | 3 |
| 590 | 909876509 | 25.50 | c | Food311-P1-20161130-F311-1200T < Food31 < Food3 | 88-654309 | 2016-12-15 | 3 |
| 591 | 909876519 | 25.00 | c | Food111-P1-20161130-F111-1200T < Food11 < Food1 | 88-654309 | 2016-12-15 | 5 |
| 592 | 909876519 | 24.00 | c | Food321-P1-20161130-F321-1200T < Food32 < Food3 | 88-654309 | 2016-12-15 | 2 |
| 593 | 909876523 | 10.00 | c | Food111-P1-20161130-F111-1200T < Food11 < Food1 | 88-654309 | 2016-12-15 | 2 |
| 594 | 909876523 | 24.00 | c | Food321-P1-20161130-F321-1200T < Food32 < Food3 | 88-654309 | 2016-12-15 | 2 |
| 595 | 909876516 | 30.00 | c | Food111-P1-20161130-F111-1200T < Food11 < Food1 | 88-654309 | 2016-12-15 | 6 |
| 596 | 909876516 | 30.00 | c | Food123-P1-20161130-F123-1200T < Food12 < Food1 | 88-654309 | 2016-12-15 | 4 |
| 597 | 909876516 | 24.00 | c | Food321-P1-20161130-F321-1200T < Food32 < Food3 | 88-654309 | 2016-12-15 | 2 |
| 598 | 909876503 | 18.00 | c | Food221-P1-20161130-F221-1200T < Food22 < Food2 | 88-654309 | 2016-12-20 | 3 |
| 599 | 909876503 | 19.50 | c | Food222-P1-20161130-F222-1200T < Food22 < Food2 | 88-654309 | 2016-12-20 | 3 |
| 600 | 909876503 | 24.00 | c | Food321-P1-20161130-F321-1200T < Food32 < Food3 | 88-654309 | 2016-12-20 | 2 |
| 601 | 909876505 | 30.00 | c | Food111-P1-20161130-F111-1200T < Food11 < Food1 | 88-654309 | 2016-12-26 | 6 |
| 602 | 909876505 | 30.00 | c | Food213-P1-20161130-F213-1200T < Food21 < Food2 | 88-654309 | 2016-12-26 | 6 |
| 603 | 909876505 | 33.00 | c | Food312-P1-20161130-F312-1200T < Food31 < Food3 | 88-654309 | 2016-12-26 | 3 |
| 604 | 909876506 | 36.00 | c | Food113-P1-20161130-F113-1200T < Food11 < Food1 | 88-654309 | 2016-12-26 | 6 |
| 605 | 909876506 | 33.00 | c | Food214-P1-20161130-F214-1200T < Food21 < Food2 | 88-654309 | 2016-12-26 | 6 |
| 606 | 909876506 | 25.50 | c | Food311-P1-20161130-F311-1200T < Food31 < Food3 | 88-654309 | 2016-12-26 | 3 |
| 607 | 909876512 | 32.50 | c | Food222-P1-20161130-F222-1200T < Food22 < Food2 | 88-654309 | 2016-12-27 | 5 |
| 608 | 909876512 | 26.00 | c | Food322-P1-20161130-F322-1200T < Food32 < Food3 | 88-654309 | 2016-12-27 | 2 |
| 609 | 88-654309 | 112.00 | s | Supplies2-P2-20150920-SUP2-200T | 88-654309 | 2016-12-31 | 7 |
| 610 | 88-654309 | 56.00 | s | Supplies1-P2-20160430-Supp1-200T | 88-654309 | 2016-12-31 | 4 |
| 611 | 88-654309 | 48.00 | s | Supplies2-P2-20160430-Supp2-200T | 88-654309 | 2016-12-31 | 3 |
| 612 | 88-654309 | 84.00 | s | Supplies1-P2-20150920-SUP1-200T | 88-654309 | 2016-12-31 | 6 |

Query executed successfully.

LIU\SQLEX

Figure 3.9-2   Proprietorship1 Inventory Purchased or sold by Other Members

# 3.10 Proprietorship2

## 3.10.1 An Accounting Fiscal Year of the Proprietorship2

Because the Proprietorship2 mainly sells foods to individuals, it has many transactions every day. For simplification, I assume that an individual only buy foods (exception of business foods) two times for one year. Therefore, in the new fiscal year, the Proprietorship2 occurs the following transactions.

- On January 2, 2016, the Proprietorship2 sells the Inventory (-$7*7 - $8*4) for sales $162 to the Business Bank1 (phone number: 123456786) for cash $162. The multi-subaccount names of the Cash account and the Inventory account respectively are:

   88-654304-c-customers < Cash receipts from customers < Operating activities

   Supplies1-P2-20150920-SUP1-200T: -7*7

   Supplies2-P2-20150920-SUP2-200T: -8*4

- On January 2, 2016, the Proprietorship2 sells the Inventory (-$7*3 - $8*9) for sales $186 to the Business Bank2 (phone number: 123456785) for cash $186. The multi-subaccount names of the Cash and the Inventory accounts respectively are:

   88-654305-c-customers < Cash receipts from customers < Operating activities

   Supplies1-P2-20150920-SUP1-200T: -7*3

   Supplies2-P2-20150920-SUP2-200T: -8*9

- On January 2, 2016, the Proprietorship2 sells the Inventory (-$7*24 - $8*40) for sales $976 to the Company3 (phone number: 123456782) for cash $316 and other $660 on credit. The multi-subaccount names of the Cash and the Inventory accounts are:

   88-654308-c-customers < Cash receipts from customers < Operating activities

   Supplies1-P2-20150920-SUP1-200T: -7*24

   Supplies2-P2-20150920-SUP2-200T: -8*40

- On January 2, 2016, the Proprietorship2 sells the Inventory (-$7*40 - $8*20) for sales $880 to the Company2 (phone number: 123456783) for cash $500 and other $380 on credit. The multi-subaccount names of the Cash and the Inventory accounts are:

   88-654307-c-customers < Cash receipts from customers < Operating activities

   Supplies1-P2-20150920-SUP1-200T: -7*40

Supplies2-P2-20150920-SUP2-200T: -8*20

- On January 2, 2016, the Proprietorship2 sells the Inventory (-$7*35 - $8*35) for sales $1,050 to the Proprietorship 1 (phone number: 123456781) for cash $450 and $600 other on credit. The multi-subaccount names of the Cash and the Inventory accounts respectively are:

  88-654309-c-customers < Cash receipts from customers < Operating activities

  Supplies1-P2-20150920-SUP1-200T: -7*35

  Supplies2-P2-20150920-SUP2-200T: -8*35

- On January 2, 2016, the Proprietorship2 purchases the following inventories $168,450 From the Company3 (phone number: 123456082) for -$8,000 cash and other on credit.

  Inven121-C3-20150922-In121-20000T < Inven12 < Inven1: 0.8*1250

  Inven51-C3-20150922-In51-1000T < Inven5: 10*500

  Inven52-C3-20150922-In52-500T < Inven5: 50*250

  Inven531-C3-20150922-In531-1000T < Inven53 < Inven5: 25*500

  Inven532-C3-20150922-In532-1000T < Inven53 < Inven5: 35*500

  Inven541-C3-20150922-In541-1000T < Inven54 < Inven5: 12*500

  Inven542-C3-20150922-In542-1000T < Inven54 < Inven5: 15*500

  Inven611-C3-20151003-In611-1300T < Inven61 < Inven6: 6.5*500

  Inven612-C3-20151003-In612-1100T < Inven61 < Inven6: 12.5*500

  Inven621-C3-20151003-In621-900T < Inven62 < Inven6: 18*500

  Inven63-C3-20151003-In63-1000T < Inven6: 16*500

  Inven711-C3-20151003-In711-500T < Inven71 < Inven7: 36*300

  Inven712-C3-20151003-In712-100T < Inven71 < Inven7: 31*50

  Inven721-C3-20151003-In721-744T < Inven72 < Inven7: 22*400

  Inven722-C3-20151003-In722-600T < Inven72 < Inven7: 20*300

  Inven731-C3-20151003-In731-600T < Inven73 < Inven7: 18*300

  Inven732-C3-20151003-In732-1000T < Inven73 < Inven7: 16*500

  Inven811-C3-20151003-In811-600T < Inven81 < Inven8: 25*300

Inven812-C3-20151003-In812-600T < Inven81 < Inven8: 24*300

Inven813-C3-20151003-In813-600T < Inven81 < Inven8: 23*300

Inven82-C3-20151003-In82-600T < Inven8: 20*300

Inven831-C3-20151003-In831-600T < Inven83 < Inven8: 18*300

Inven832-C3-20151003-In832-800T < Inven83 < Inven8: 16*400

The multi-subaccount name of the Cash account and four transaction sub-equations respectively are:

88-654308-t-suppliers < Cash payments to suppliers < Operating activities

Cash (1): -8000 + Inventory (1): 0.8*1250 + Inventory (1): 10*500 + Inventory (1): 50*250 + Inventory (1): 25*500 + Inventory (1): 35*500 + Inventory (1): 12*500 + Inventory (1): 15*500 + Inventory (1): 6.5*500 + Inventory (1): 12.5*500 = Account Payable (2): 63500

Inventory (1): 18*500 + Inventory (1): 16*500 + Inventory (1): 36*300 + Inventory (1): 31*50 + Inventory (1): 22*400 + Inventory (1): 20*300 + Inventory (1): 18*300 + Inventory (1): 16*500 + Inventory (1): 25*300 = Account Payable (2): 65050

Inventory (1): 24*300 + Inventory (1): 23*300 + Inventory (1): 20*300 + Inventory (1): 18*300 + Inventory (1): 16*400 = Account Payable (2): 31900

- On January 2, 2016, the Proprietorship2 sells the Inventory (-$7*40 - $8*40) for sales $1,200 to the Company1 (phone number: 123456784) for cash $200 and other $1,000 on credit. The multi-subaccount names of the Cash account and the Inventory account respectively are:

  88-654306-c-customers < Cash receipts from customers < Operating activities

  Supplies1-P2-20150920-SUP1-200T: -7*40

  Supplies2-P2-20150920-SUP2-200T: -8*40

- On January 3, 2016, the Proprietorship2 sells the following inventories -$11,430 for sales $19,050 to the Company3 (phone number: 123456782) for cash $6,000 and other $13,050 on credit.

Inven411-P2-20151127-In411-1000T < Inven41 < Inven4: -3*300

Inven412-P2-20151127-In412-1000T < Inven41 < Inven4: -11.1*300

TTTCU parts-P2-20151127-TTP-1000T < TTT parts < Inven4: -12*300

RRRHJK parts-P2-20151127-RRP-1000T < Inven4: -12*300

The multi-subaccount name of the Cash account and transaction sub-equation are:

88-654308-c-customers < Cash receipts from customers < Operating activities

Cash (1): 6000 + Account receivable (1): 13050 + Inventory (1): -3*300 + Inventory (1): -11.1*300 + Inventory (1): -12*300 + Inventory (1): -12*300 = Sales (4): 19050 + Cost of goods sold (5): -11430

- On January 3, 2016, the Proprietorship2 transfers the inventories (supplies) -$440 (-$140 - $7*20 - $8*20) to the Cost of goods manufactured to satisfy the need of producing. The multi-subaccount names of the Cash and the Inventory accounts and the transaction sub-equation respectively are:

  Supplies1-P2-20150920-SUP1-200T: -7*20

  Supplies2-P2-20150920-SUP2-200T: -8*20

  Supplies (1): -140 + Inventory (1): -7*20 + Inventory (1): -8*20 = Cost of goods manufactured (5): -440

- On January 3, 2016, the Proprietorship2 transfers the following inventories $15,500 to the Cost of goods manufactured account to satisfy the need of producing.

  Inven31 < Inven3: -10*100

  Inven32 < Inven3: -50*100

  Inven331 < Inven33 < Inven3: -20*100

  Inven332 < Inven33 < Inven3: -45*100

  HGFCVB parts < QASXC parts < Inven3: -10*100

PPGHUP parts < ASDUP parts < Inven3: -20*100

The transaction sub-equations is:

Inventory (1): -10*100 + Inventory (1): -50*100 + Inventory (1): -20*100 +
Inventory (1): -45*100 + Inventory (1): -10*100 + Inventory (1): -20*100 = Cost
of goods manufactured (5): -15500

- On January 3, 2016, the Proprietorship2 transfers the following inventories -$34,050
  to the Cost of goods manufactured account to satisfy the need of producing.
  Inven121-C3-20150922-In121-20000T < Inven12 < Inven1: -0.8*375
  Inven51-C3-20150922-In51-1000T < Inven5: -10*100
  Inven52-C3-20150922-In52-500T < Inven5: -50*50
  Inven531-C3-20150922-In531-1000T < Inven53 < Inven5: -25*100
  Inven532-C3-20150922-In532-1000T < Inven53 < Inven5: -35*100
  Inven541-C3-20150922-In541-1000T < Inven54 < Inven5: -12*100
  Inven542-C3-20150922-In542-1000T < Inven54 < Inven5: -15*100
  Inven611-C3-20151003-In611-1300T < Inven61 < Inven6: -6.5*140
  Inven612-C3-20151003-In612-1100T < Inven61 < Inven6: -12.5*100
  Inven621-C3-20151003-In621-900T < Inven62 < Inven6: -18*100
  Inven63-C3-20151003-In63-1000T < Inven6: -16*100
  Inven711-C3-20151003-In711-500T < Inven71 < Inven7: -36*60
  Inven712-C3-20151003-In712-100T < Inven71 < Inven7: -31*10
  Inven721-C3-20151003-In721-744T < Inven72 < Inven7: -22*80
  Inven722-C3-20151003-In722-600T < Inven72 < Inven7: -20*60
  Inven731-C3-20151003-In731-600T < Inven73 < Inven7: -18*60
  Inven732-C3-20151003-In732-1000T < Inven73 < Inven7: -16*100
  Inven811-C3-20151003-In811-600T < Inven81 < Inven8: -25*60
  Inven812-C3-20151003-In812-600T < Inven81 < Inven8: -24*60
  Inven813-C3-20151003-In813-600T < Inven81 < Inven8: -23*60
  Inven82-C3-20151003-In82-600T < Inven8: -20*60

Inven831-C3-20151003-In831-600T < Inven83 < Inven8: -18*60

Inven832-C3-20151003-In832-800T < Inven83 < Inven8: -16*80

The three transaction sub-equations are respectively:

Inventory (1): -0.8*375 + Inventory (1): -10*100 + Inventory (1): -50*50 + Inventory (1): -25*100 + Inventory (1): -35*100 + Inventory (1): -12*100 + Inventory (1): -15*100 + Inventory (1): -6.5*140 + Inventory (1): -12.5*100 + Inventory (1): -18*100 = Cost of goods manufactured (5): -16460

Inventory (1): -16*100 + Inventory (1): -36*60 + Inventory (1): -31*10 + Inventory (1): -22*80 + Inventory (1): -20*60 + Inventory (1): -18*60 + Inventory (1): -16*100 + Inventory (1): -25*60 + Inventory (1): -24*60 = Cost of goods manufactured (5): -12650

Inventory (1): -23*60 + Inventory (1): -20*60 + Inventory (1): -18*60 + Inventory (1): -16*80 = Cost of goods manufactured (5): -4940

- On January 12, 2016, the Proprietorship2 sells the Food513 $10*4 (cost: -$5*4) and the Food613 $26*3 (cost: -$13*3) to A24 (SIN: 909876524) for cash $118. The multi-subaccount names of the Cash and the Inventory accounts respectively are:
  909876524-c-customers < Cash receipts from customers < Operating activities
  Food513-P2-20151127-FO513-1000T < Food51 < Food5: -5*4
  Food613-P2-20151127-FO613-200T < Food61 < Food6: -13*3

- On January 13, 2016, the Proprietorship2 sells the Food514 $11*8 (cost: -$5.5*8) and the Food614 $30*4 (cost: -$15*4) to A13 (SIN: 909876513) for cash $208. The multi-subaccount names of the Cash and the Inventory accounts respectively are:
  909876513-c-customers < Cash receipts from customers < Operating activities
  Food514-P2-20151127-FO514-1000T < Food51 < Food5: -5.5*8
  Food614-P2-20151127-FO614-200T < Food61 < Food6: -15*4

- On January 14, 2016, the Proprietorship2 pays -$255.37 cash to A24 (SIN:

909876524) for the Travelling expenses -$133.37 and the Other expenses -$122. The multi-subaccount name of the Cash account is:

909876524-n-operating expenses < Cash payments for operating expenses < Operating activities

- On January 15, 2016, the Proprietorship2 sells the Food621 $26*1 (cost: -$13*1) and the Food622 $28*1 (cost: -$14*1) to A11 (SIN: 909876511) for cash $54. The multi-subaccount names of the Cash and the Inventory accounts respectively are:

909876511-c-customers < Cash receipts from customers < Operating activities

Food621-P2-20151127-FO621-200T < Food62 < Food6: -13*1

Food622-P2-20151127-FO622-200T < Food62 < Food6: -14*1

- On January 16, 2016, the Proprietorship2 sells the Food514 $11*4 (cost: -$5.5*4) and the Food613 $26*3 (cost: -$13*3) to A19 (SIN: 909876519) for cash $122. The multi-subaccount names of the Cash and the Inventory accounts respectively are:

909876519-c-customers < Cash receipts from customers < Operating activities

Food514-P2-20151127-FO514-1000T < Food51 < Food5: -5.5*4

Food613-P2-20151127-FO613-200T < Food61 < Food6: -13*3

- On January 16, 2016, the Proprietorship2 sells the Food514 $11*2 (cost: -$5.5*2) and the Food613 $26*1 (cost: -$13*1) to A22 (SIN: 909876522) for cash $48. The multi-subaccount names of the Cash and the Inventory accounts respectively are:

909876522-c-customers < Cash receipts from customers < Operating activities

Food514-P2-20151127-FO514-1000T < Food51 < Food5: -5.5*2

Food613-P2-20151127-FO613-200T < Food61 < Food6: -13*1

- On January 18, 2016, the Proprietorship2 sells the Food422 $13*1 (cost: -$6.5*1) and the Food613 $26*1 (cost: -$13*1) to A1 (SIN: 909876501) for cash $39. The multi-subaccount names of the Cash and the Inventory accounts respectively are:

909876501-c-customers < Cash receipts from customers < Operating activities

Food422-P2-20151127-FO422-1000T < Food42 < Food4: -6.5*1

Food613-P2-20151127-FO613-200T < Food61 < Food6: -13*1

- On January 20, 2016, the Proprietorship2 sells the Food613 $26*2 (cost: -$13*2) and

the Food614 $30*1 (cost: -$15*1) to A7 (SIN: 909876507) for cash $82. The multi-subaccount names of the Cash and the Inventory accounts respectively are:

909876507-c-customers < Cash receipts from customers < Operating activities

Food613-P2-20151127-FO613-200T < Food61 < Food6: -13*2

Food614-P2-20151127-FO614-200T < Food61 < Food6: -15*1

- On January 21, 2016, the Proprietorship2 pays -$149.65 cash to A25 (SIN: 909876525) for the Travelling expenses -$92.65 and the Other expenses -$57.

- On January 22, 2016, the Proprietorship2 sells the Food53 $16*4 (cost: -$8*4) and the Food622 $28*2 (cost: -$14*2) to A12 (SIN: 909876512) for cash $120. The multi-subaccount names of the Cash and the Inventory accounts respectively are:

909876512-c-customers < Cash receipts from customers < Operating activities

Food53-P2-20151127-FO53-1000T < Food5: -8*4

Food622-P2-20151127-FO622-200T < Food62 < Food6: -14*2

- On January 26, 2016, the Proprietorship2 receives $800 cash from the Company3 (phone number: 123456782) with the General ID 3. The multi-subaccount name of the Cash account is:

88-654308-c-customers < Cash receipts from customers < Operating activities

- On January 28, 2016, the Proprietorship2 pays -$200 cash to the Company3 (phone number: 123456082) with the General ID 3. The multi-subaccount name of the Cash account is:

88-654308-t-suppliers < Cash payments to suppliers < Operating activities

- On January 30 2016, the Proprietorship2 receives $300 cash from the Company2 (phone number: 123456783) with the General ID 3. The multi-subaccount name of the Cash account is:

88-654307-c-customers < Cash receipts from customers < Operating activities

- On January 31, 2016, the Proprietorship2 receives $1,000 cash from the Company1 (phone number: 123456784) with the General ID 3. The multi-subaccount name of the Cash account is:

88-654306-c-customers < Cash receipts from customers < Operating activities

- On January 31, 2016, the Proprietorship2 sells the Food612 $24*1 (cost: -$12*1) to A14 (SIN: 909876514) for cash $24. The multi-subaccount names of the Cash and the Inventory accounts respectively are:

  909876514-c-customers < Cash receipts from customers < Operating activities

  Food612-P2-20151127-FO612-200T < Food61 < Food6: -12*1

- On January 31, 2016, the Proprietorship2 pays two employees' salary expenses for cash -$5,660 (-$2,870 - $2,790). The multi-subaccount names of the Cash account is:

  909876524-t-salary < Cash payments for operating expenses< Operating activities

  909876525-t-CGM < Cash payments for operating expenses< Operating activities

- On January 31, 2016, the Proprietorship2 sells the following inventories -$5,395 for sales $10,790 to A1A8 (SIN: 909876526), who uses his (or her) father A1's (or mother A1's) secondary card of the Business Bank2, for cash $10,790.

  Food411-P2-20151127-FO411-1000T < Food41 < Food4: -5*130

  Food412-P2-20151127-FO412-1000T < Food41 < Food4: -5.5*130

  Food421-P2-20151127-FO421-1000T < Food42 < Food4: -6*130

  Food422-P2-20151127-FO422-1000T < Food42 < Food4: -6.5*130

  Food43-P2-20151127-FO43-1000T < Food4: -7*130

  Food44-P2-20151127-FO44-1000T < Food4: -7.5*130

  Food511-P2-20151127-FO511-1000T < Food51 < Food5: -4*130

  The multi-subaccount name of the Cash account is:

  909876501-c-customers < Cash receipts from customers < Operating activities

- On January 31, 2016, the Proprietorship2 sells the following inventories -$5,460 for sales $10,920 to A14 (SIN: 909876514) for cash $10,920.

  Food411-P2-20151127-FO411-1000T < Food41 < Food4: -5*130

  Food412-P2-20151127-FO412-1000T < Food41 < Food4: -5.5*130

  Food421-P2-20151127-FO421-1000T < Food42 < Food4: -6*130

  Food422-P2-20151127-FO422-1000T < Food42 < Food4: -6.5*130

  Food43-P2-20151127-FO43-1000T < Food4: -7*130

  Food44-P2-20151127-FO44-1000T < Food4: -7.5*130

Food512-P2-20151127-FO512-1000T < Food51 < Food5: -4.5*130

The multi-subaccount name of the Cash account is:

909876514-c-customers < Cash receipts from customers < Operating activities

- On January 31, 2016, the Proprietorship2 sells the following inventories -$5,525 for sales $11,050 to A15 (SIN: 909876515) for cash $11,050.

Food411-P2-20151127-FO411-1000T < Food41 < Food4: -5*130

Food412-P2-20151127-FO412-1000T < Food41 < Food4: -5.5*130

Food421-P2-20151127-FO421-1000T < Food42 < Food4: -6*130

Food422-P2-20151127-FO422-1000T < Food42 < Food4: -6.5*130

Food43-P2-20151127-FO43-1000T < Food4: -7*130

Food44-P2-20151127-FO44-1000T < Food4: -7.5*130

Food513-P2-20151127-FO513-1000T < Food51 < Food5: -5*130

The multi-subaccount name of the Cash account is:

909876515-c-customers < Cash receipts from customers < Operating activities

- On January 31, 2016, the Proprietorship2 sells the following inventories -$5,590 for sales $11,180 to A16 (SIN: 909876516) for cash $11,180.

Food411-P2-20151127-FO411-1000T < Food41 < Food4: -5*130

Food412-P2-20151127-FO412-1000T < Food41 < Food4: -5.5*130

Food421-P2-20151127-FO421-1000T < Food42 < Food4: -6*130

Food422-P2-20151127-FO422-1000T < Food42 < Food4: -6.5*130

Food43-P2-20151127-FO43-1000T < Food4: -7*130

Food44-P2-20151127-FO44-1000T < Food4: -7.5*130

Food514-P2-20151127-FO514-1000T < Food51 < Food5: -5.5*130

The multi-subaccount name of the Cash account is:

909876516-c-customers < Cash receipts from customers < Operating activities

- On January 31, 2016, the Proprietorship2 sells the following inventories -$5,135 for sales $10,270 to A17 (SIN: 909876517) for cash $10,270.

Food511-P2-20151127-FO511-1000T < Food51 < Food5: -4*130

Food512-P2-20151127-FO512-1000T < Food51 < Food5: -4.5*130

Food513-P2-20151127-FO513-1000T < Food51 < Food5: -5*130

Food514-P2-20151127-FO514-1000T < Food51 < Food5: -5.5*130

Food521-P2-20151127-FO521-1000T < Food52 < Food5: -6*130

Food522-P2-20151127-FO522-1000T < Food52 < Food5: -6.5*130

Food53-P2-20151127-FO53-1000T < Food5: -8*130

The multi-subaccount name of the Cash account is:

909876517-c-customers < Cash receipts from customers < Operating activities

- On January 31, 2016, the Proprietorship2 sells the following inventories -$5,915 for sales $11,830 to A18 (SIN: 909876518) for cash $11,830.

Food511-P2-20151127-FO511-1000T < Food51 < Food5: -4*130

Food512-P2-20151127-FO512-1000T < Food51 < Food5: -4.5*130

Food513-P2-20151127-FO513-1000T < Food51 < Food5: -5*130

Food514-P2-20151127-FO514-1000T < Food51 < Food5: -5.5*130

Food521-P2-20151127-FO521-1000T < Food52 < Food5: -6*130

Food522-P2-20151127-FO522-1000T < Food52 < Food5: -6.5*130

Food622-P2-20151127-FO622-200T < Food62 < Food6: -14*130

The multi-subaccount name of the Cash account is:

909876518-c-customers < Cash receipts from customers < Operating activities

- On January 31, 2016, the Proprietorship2 sells the following inventories -$5,785 for sales $11,570 to A19 (SIN: 909876519) for cash $11,570.

Food511-P2-20151127-FO511-1000T < Food51 < Food5: -4*130

Food512-P2-20151127-FO512-1000T < Food51 < Food5: -4.5*130

Food513-P2-20151127-FO513-1000T < Food51 < Food5: -5*130

Food514-P2-20151127-FO514-1000T < Food51 < Food5: -5.5*130

Food521-P2-20151127-FO521-1000T < Food52 < Food5: -6*130

Food522-P2-20151127-FO522-1000T < Food52 < Food5: -6.5*130

Food621-P2-20151127-FO621-200T < Food62 < Food6: -13*130

The multi-subaccount name of the Cash account is:

909876519-c-customers < Cash receipts from customers < Operating activities

- On January 31, 2016, the Proprietorship2 sells the following inventories -$6,045 for sales $12,090 to A20 (SIN: 909876520) for cash $12,090.

  Food511-P2-20151127-FO511-1000T < Food51 < Food5: -4*130

  Food512-P2-20151127-FO512-1000T < Food51 < Food5: -4.5*130

  Food513-P2-20151127-FO513-1000T < Food51 < Food5: -5*130

  Food514-P2-20151127-FO514-1000T < Food51 < Food5: -5.5*130

  Food521-P2-20151127-FO521-1000T < Food52 < Food5: -6*130

  Food522-P2-20151127-FO522-1000T < Food52 < Food5: -6.5*130

  Food614-P2-20151127-FO614-200T < Food61 < Food6: -15*130

  The multi-subaccount name of the Cash account is:

  909876520-c-customers < Cash receipts from customers < Operating activities

- On January 31, 2016, the Proprietorship2 sells the following inventories -$6,435 for sales $12,870 to A21 (SIN: 909876521) for cash $12,870.

  Food411-P2-20151127-FO411-1000T < Food41 < Food4: -5*130

  Food412-P2-20151127-FO412-1000T < Food41 < Food4: -5.5*130

  Food421-P2-20151127-FO421-1000T < Food42 < Food4: -6*130

  Food422-P2-20151127-FO422-1000T < Food42 < Food4: -6.5*130

  Food43-P2-20151127-FO43-1000T < Food4: -7*130

  Food44-P2-20151127-FO44-1000T < Food4: -7.5*130

  Food612-P2-20151127-FO612-200T < Food61 < Food6: -12*130

  The multi-subaccount name of the Cash account is:

  909876521-c-customers < Cash receipts from customers < Operating activities

- On January 31, 2016, the Proprietorship2 sells the following inventories -$5,395 for sales $10,790 to A22 (SIN: 909876522) for cash $10,790.

  Food511-P2-20151127-FO511-1000T < Food51 < Food5: -4*130

  Food512-P2-20151127-FO512-1000T < Food51 < Food5: -4.5*130

  Food513-P2-20151127-FO513-1000T < Food51 < Food5: -5*130

  Food514-P2-20151127-FO514-1000T < Food51 < Food5: -5.5*130

  Food521-P2-20151127-FO521-1000T < Food52 < Food5: -6*130

Food522-P2-20151127-FO522-1000T < Food52 < Food5: -6.5*130

Food611-P2-20151127-FO611-200T < Food61 < Food6: -10*130

The multi-subaccount name of the Cash account is:

909876522-c-customers < Cash receipts from customers < Operating activities

- On January 31, 2016, the Proprietorship2 sells the following inventories -$6,175 for sales $12,350 to A23 (SIN: 909876523) for cash $12,350.

  Food411-P2-20151127-FO411-1000T < Food41 < Food4: -5*130

  Food412-P2-20151127-FO412-1000T < Food41 < Food4: -5.5*130

  Food421-P2-20151127-FO421-1000T < Food42 < Food4: -6*130

  Food44-P2-20151127-FO44-1000T < Food4: -7.5*64

  Food511-P2-20151127-FO511-1000T < Food51 < Food5: -4*10

  Food521-P2-20151127-FO521-1000T < Food52 < Food5: -6*130

  Food53-P2-20151127-FO53-1000T < Food5: -8*130

  Food613-P2-20151127-FO613-200T < Food61 < Food6: -13*130

  The multi-subaccount name of the Cash account is:

  909876523-c-customers < Cash receipts from customers < Operating activities

- On January 31, 2016, the Proprietorship2 sells the following inventories -$5,005 for sales $10,010 to A24 (SIN: 909876524) for cash $10,010.

  Food43-P2-20151127-FO43-1000T < Food4: -7*130

  Food44-P2-20151127-FO44-1000T < Food4: -7.5*78

  Food511-P2-20151127-FO511-1000T < Food51 < Food5: -4*130

  Food513-P2-20151127-FO513-1000T < Food51 < Food5: -5*130

  Food514-P2-20151127-FO514-1000T < Food51 < Food5: -5.5*130

  Food521-P2-20151127-FO521-1000T < Food52 < Food5: -6*130

  Food522-P2-20151127-FO522-1000T < Food52 < Food5: -6.5*130

  The multi-subaccount name of the Cash account is:

  909876524-c-customers < Cash receipts from customers < Operating activities

- On January 31, 2016, the Proprietorship2 sells the following inventories -$5,135 for sales $10,270 to A25 (SIN: 909876525) for cash $10,270.

Food411-P2-20151127-FO411-1000T < Food41 < Food4: -5*130

Food412-P2-20151127-FO412-1000T < Food41 < Food4: -5.5*130

Food421-P2-20151127-FO421-1000T < Food42 < Food4: -6*130

Food422-P2-20151127-FO422-1000T < Food42 < Food4: -6.5*130

Food512-P2-20151127-FO512-1000T < Food51 < Food5: -4.5*130

Food53-P2-20151127-FO53-1000T < Food5: -8*195

The multi-subaccount name of the Cash account is:

   909876525-c-customers < Cash receipts from customers < Operating activities

- On February 1, 2016, the Proprietorship2 purchases one Car3 $38,000 from the Company1 (phone number: 123456084) for cash -$30,000 and other on credit. The multi-subaccount names of the Cash and the Inventory accounts and the two transaction sub-equations respectively are:

   88-654306-t-machinery < Cash payments for machinery < Operating activities

   Car3-C1-20150925-C3-029 < Car-inventory < Vehicle-inventory: 38000*1

   Cash (1): -30000 + Inventory (1): 38000 = Account payable (2): 8000

   Inventory (1): -30000 + Vehicle (1): 38000 = Account payable (2): 8000

- On February 6, 2016, the Proprietorship2 sells the Food611 $20*3 (cost: -$10*3) and the Food622 $28*2 (cost: -$14*2) to A12 (SIN: 909876512, using secondary card of the Business Bank1) for cash $116. The multi-subaccount names of the Cash and the Inventory accounts respectively are:

   909876512-c-customers < Cash receipts from customers < Operating activities

   Food611-P2-20151127-FO611-200T < Food61 < Food6: -10*3

   Food622-P2-20151127-FO622-200T < Food62 < Food6: -14*2

- On February 17, 2016, the Proprietorship2 sells the Food53 $16*10 (cost: -$8*10) and the Food614 $30*5 (cost: -$15*5) to A16 (SIN: 909876516) for cash $310. The multi-subaccount names of the Cash and the Inventory accounts respectively are:

   909876516-c-customers < Cash receipts from customers < Operating activities

Food53-P2-20151127-FO53-1000T < Food5: -8*10

Food614-P2-20151127-FO614-200T < Food61 < Food6: -15*5

- On February 19, 2016, the Proprietorship2 sells the Food611 $20*3 (cost: -$10*3) and the Food621 $26*2 (cost: -$13*2) to A9 (SIN: 909876509) for cash $112. The multi-subaccount names of the Cash and the Inventory accounts respectively are:

    909876509-c-customers < Cash receipts from customers < Operating activities

    Food611-P2-20151127-FO611-200T < Food61 < Food6: -10*3

    Food621-P2-20151127-FO621-200T < Food62 < Food6: -13*2

- On February 20, 2016, the Proprietorship2 pays -$400 cash to the Proprietorship1 (phone number: 123456081) with the General ID 3. The multi-subaccount name of the Cash account is:

    88-654309-t-suppliers < Cash payments to suppliers < Operating activities

- On February 21, 2016, the Proprietorship2 receives $300 cash from the Proprietorship1 (phone number: 123456781) with the General ID 3. The multi-subaccount name of the Cash account is:

    88-654309-c-customers < Cash receipts from customers < Operating activities

- On February 22, 2016, the Proprietorship2 sells the Food611 $20*2 (cost: -$10*2) and the Food622 $28*2 (cost: -$14*2) to A8 (SIN: 909876508) for cash $96. The multi-subaccount names of the Cash and the Inventory accounts respectively are:

    909876508-c-customers < Cash receipts from customers < Operating activities

    Food611-P2-20151127-FO611-200T < Food61 < Food6: -10*2

    Food622-P2-20151127-FO622-200T < Food62 < Food6: -14*2

- On February 23, 2016, the Proprietorship2 sells the Food53 $16*2 (cost: -$8*2) and the Food614 $30*1 (cost: -$15*1) to A24 (SIN: 909876524) for cash $62. The multi-subaccount names of the Cash and the Inventory accounts respectively are:

    909876524-c-customers < Cash receipts from customers < Operating activities

    Food53-P2-20151127-FO53-1000T < Food5: -8*2

    Food614-P2-20151127-FO614-200T < Food61 < Food6: -15*1

- On February 25, 2016, the Proprietorship2 pays -$187.84 cash to A24 (SIN:

909876524) for the Travelling expenses -$125.84 and the Other expenses -$62.

- On February 28, 2016, the Proprietorship2 pays two employees' salary -$5,660.

- On March 7, 2016, the Proprietorship2 sells the Food521 $12*4 (cost: -$6*4) and the Food621 $26*2 (cost: -$13*2) to A12 (SIN: 909876512) for cash $100. The multi-subaccount names of the Cash and the Inventory accounts respectively are:

    909876512-c-customers < Cash receipts from customers < Operating activities

    Food521-P2-20151127-FO521-1000T < Food52 < Food5: -6*4

    Food621-P2-20151127-FO621-200T < Food62 < Food6: -13*2

- On March 7, 2016, the Proprietorship2 pays -$201.66 cash to A25 (SIN: 909876525) for the Travelling expenses -$123.66 and the Other expenses -$78.

- On March 9, 2016, the Proprietorship2 pays -$2,000 cash to the Company1 (phone number: 123456084) with the General ID 3. The multi-subaccount name of the Cash account is:

    88-654306-t-suppliers < Cash payments to suppliers < Operating activities

- On March 18, 2016, the Proprietorship2 sells the Food53 $16*3 (cost: -$8*3) and the Food622 $28*2 (cost: -$14*2) to A9 (SIN: 909876509) for cash $104. The multi-subaccount names of the Cash and the Inventory accounts respectively are:

    909876509-c-customers < Cash receipts from customers < Operating activities

    Food53-P2-20151127-FO53-1000T < Food5: -8*3

    Food622-P2-20151127-FO622-200T < Food62 < Food6: -14*2

- On March 20, 2016, the Proprietorship2 sells the Food44 $15*10 (cost: -$7.5*10) and the Food622 $28*5 (cost: -$14*5) to A13 (SIN: 909876513) for cash $290. The multi-subaccount names of the Cash and the Inventory accounts respectively are:

    909876513-c-customers < Cash receipts from customers < Operating activities

    Food44-P2-20151127-FO44-1000T < Food4: -7.5*10

    Food622-P2-20151127-FO622-200T < Food62 < Food6: -14*5

- On March 20, 2016, the Proprietorship2 sells the Food44 $15*5 (cost: -$7.5*5) and the Food622 $28*2 (cost: -$14*2) to A16 (SIN: 909876516) for cash $131. The multi-subaccount names of the Cash and the Inventory accounts respectively are:

909876516-c-customers < Cash receipts from customers < Operating activities

Food44-P2-20151127-FO44-1000T < Food4: -7.5*5

Food622-P2-20151127-FO622-200T < Food62 < Food6: -14*2

- On March 21, 2016, the Proprietorship2 sells the Food44 $15*3 (cost: -$7.5*3) and the Food622 $28*1 (cost: -$14*1) to A19 (SIN: 909876519) for cash $73. The multi-subaccount names of the Cash and the Inventory accounts respectively are:

  909876519-c-customers < Cash receipts from customers < Operating activities

  Food44-P2-20151127-FO44-1000T < Food4: -7.5*3

  Food622-P2-20151127-FO622-200T < Food62 < Food6: -14*1

- On March 21, 2016, the Proprietorship2 sells the Food44 $15*2 (cost: -$7.5*2) and the Food622 $28*1 (cost: -$14*1) to A22 (SIN: 909876522) for cash $58. The multi-subaccount names of the Cash and the Inventory accounts respectively are:

  909876522-c-customers < Cash receipts from customers < Operating activities

  Food44-P2-20151127-FO44-1000T < Food4: -7.5*2

  Food622-P2-20151127-FO622-200T < Food62 < Food6: -14*1

- On March 22, 2016, the Proprietorship2 sells the Food611 $20*2 (cost: -$10*2) and the Food622 $28*2 (cost: -$14*2) to A7 (SIN: 909876507) for cash $96. The multi-subaccount names of the Cash and the Inventory accounts respectively are:

  909876507-c-customers < Cash receipts from customers < Operating activities

  Food611-P2-20151127-FO611-200T < Food61 < Food6: -10*2

  Food622-P2-20151127-FO622-200T < Food62 < Food6: -14*2

- On March 24, 2016, the Proprietorship2 sells the Food522 $13*3 (cost: -$6.5*3) and the Food612 $24*2 (cost: -$12*2) to A17 (SIN: 909876517) for cash $87. The multi-subaccount names of the Cash and the Inventory accounts respectively are:

  909876517-c-customers < Cash receipts from customers < Operating activities

  Food522-P2-20151127-FO522-1000T < Food52 < Food5: -6.5*3

  Food612-P2-20151127-FO612-200T < Food61 < Food6: -12*2

- On March 25, 2016, the Proprietorship2 sells the Food43 $14*3 (cost: -$7*3) and the Food622 $28*1 (cost: -$14*1) to A25 (SIN: 909876525) for cash $70. The multi-

subaccount names of the Cash and the Inventory accounts respectively are:

909876525-c-customers < Cash receipts from customers < Operating activities

Food43-P2-20151127-FO43-1000T < Food4: -7*3

Food622-P2-20151127-FO622-200T < Food62 < Food6: -14*1

- On March 27, 2016, the Proprietorship2 pays -$191.43 cash to A25 (SIN: 909876525) for the Travelling expenses -$121.43 and the Other expenses -$70.

- On March 28, 2016, the Proprietorship2 sells the Food521 $12*3 (cost: -$6*3) and the Food612 $24*2 (cost: -$12*2) to A14 (SIN: 909876514) for cash $84. The multi-subaccount names of the Cash and the Inventory accounts respectively are:

909876514-c-customers < Cash receipts from customers < Operating activities

Food521-P2-20151127-FO521-1000T < Food52 < Food5: -6*3

Food612-P2-20151127-FO612-200T < Food61 < Food6: -12*2

- On March 31, 2016, the Proprietorship2 pays two employees' salary $5,660.

- On April 6, 2016, the Proprietorship2 sells the Food613 $26*2 (cost: -$13*2) and the Food622 $28*2 (cost: -$14*2) to A9 (SIN: 909876509) for cash $108. The multi-subaccount names of the Cash and the Inventory accounts respectively are:

909876509-c-customers < Cash receipts from customers < Operating activities

Food613-P2-20151127-FO613-200T < Food61 < Food6: -13*2

Food622-P2-20151127-FO622-200T < Food62 < Food6: -14*2

- On April 13, 2016, the Proprietorship2 sells the Food613 $26*2 (cost: -$13*2) and the Food614 $30*2 (cost: -$15*2) to A5 (SIN: 909876505) for cash $112. The multi-subaccount names of the Cash and the Inventory accounts respectively are:

909876505-c-customers < Cash receipts from customers < Operating activities

Food613-P2-20151127-FO613-200T < Food61 < Food6: -13*2

Food614-P2-20151127-FO614-200T < Food61 < Food6: -15*2

- On April 15, 2016, the Proprietorship2 sells the Food611 $20*1 (cost: -$10*1) and the Food614 $30*1 (cost: -$15*1) to A2 (SIN: 909876502) for cash $50. The multi-subaccount names of the Cash and the Inventory accounts respectively are:

909876502-c-customers < Cash receipts from customers < Operating activities

Food611-P2-20151127-FO611-200T < Food61 < Food6: -10*1

Food614-P2-20151127-FO614-200T < Food61 < Food6: -15*1

- On April 17, 2016, the Proprietorship2 sells the Food53 $16*4 (cost: -$8*4) and the Food622 $28*2 (cost: -$14*2) to A12 (SIN: 909876512) for cash $120. The multi-subaccount names of the Cash and the Inventory accounts respectively are:

  909876512-c-customers < Cash receipts from customers < Operating activities

  Food53-P2-20151127-FO53-1000T < Food5: -8*4

  Food622-P2-20151127-FO622-200T < Food62 < Food6: -14*2

- On April 20, 2016, the Proprietorship2 sells the Food612 $24*2 (cost: -$12*2) and the Food621 $26*2 (cost: -$13*2) to A4 (SIN: 909876502) for cash $100. The multi-subaccount names of the Cash and the Inventory accounts respectively are:

  909876504-c-customers < Cash receipts from customers < Operating activities

  Food612-P2-20151127-FO612-200T < Food61 < Food6: -12*2

  Food621-P2-20151127-FO621-200T < Food62 < Food6: -13*2

- On April 24, 2016, the Proprietorship2 pays -$236.37 cash to A24 (SIN: 909876524) for the Travelling expenses -$161.37 and the Other expenses -$75.

- On April 26, 2016, the Proprietorship2 sells the Food422 $13*10 (cost: -$6.5*10), the Food612 $24*5 (cost: -$12*5), the Food613 $26*5 (cost: -$13*5), and the Food614 $30*3 (cost: -$15*3) to A13 (SIN: 909876513) for cash $470. The multi-subaccount names of the Cash and the Inventory accounts respectively are:

  909876513-c-customers < Cash receipts from customers < Operating activities

  Food422-P2-20151127-FO422-1000T < Food42 < Food4: -6.5*10

  Food612-P2-20151127-FO612-200T < Food61 < Food6: -12*5

  Food613-P2-20151127-FO613-200T < Food61 < Food6: -13*5

  Food614-P2-20151127-FO614-200T < Food61 < Food6: -15*3

- On April 29, 2016, the Proprietorship2 receives $1,000 cash from the Company1 (phone number: 123456784) with the General ID 24. The multi-subaccount name of the Cash account is:

  88-654306-c-customers < Cash receipts from customers < Operating activities

- On April 30, 2016, the Proprietorship2 sells the Inventory (-$7*11 - $8*11) for sales $330 to the Government1 (phone number: 123456788) for cash $330. The multi-subaccount names of the Cash and the Inventory accounts respectively are:

    88-654302-c-customers < Cash receipts from customers < Operating activities

    Supplies1-P2-20150920-SUP1-200T: -7*11

    Supplies2-P2-20150920-SUP2-200T: -8*11

- On April 30, 2016, the Proprietorship2 pays three employees' salary -$5,660.

- On April 30, 2016, the Proprietorship2 has completed all products of the Working-in-process inventory account. If the supplies and the all general parts have just been consumed, then the Proprietorship2 transfers the balance of the Cost of goods manufactured account to the Working-in-process inventory account. The Cost of goods manufactured account has three subaccounts of the "Supplies expenses", the "909876525-salary < Product department-salary < Salary expenses", and the "General parts expenses". Their balances are -$440, -$11,160, and -$49,550 (-$34,050 - $15,500) respectively. Here, the balance of the subaccount "General parts expenses" will be divided to three parts which are used in three transaction sub-equations respectively. The three transaction sub-equations are:

    Working-in-process inventory (1): 1*1000 + Working-in-process inventory (1): 5*1000 + Working-in-process inventory (1): 5.5*1000 + Working-in-process inventory (1): 5*1000 + Working-in-process inventory (1): 2*1000 + Working-in-process inventory (1): 2.25*1000 + Working-in-process inventory (1): 3*1000 = Cost of goods manufactured (5): 440 + Cost of goods manufactured (5): 11160 + Cost of goods manufactured (5): 12150

    Working-in-process inventory (1): 3*1000 + Working-in-process inventory (1): 3*1000 + Working-in-process inventory (1): 4*1000 + Working-in-process inventory (1): 2*1000 + Working-in-process inventory (1): 2*1000 + Working-in-process inventory (1): 2*1000 + Working-in-process inventory (1): 2*1000 + Working-in-process inventory (1): 3*1000 + Working-in-process inventory (1):

3*1000 = Cost of goods manufactured (5): 24000

Working-in-process inventory (1): 4*1000 + Working-in-process inventory (1): 5*200 + Working-in-process inventory (1): 6*200 + Working-in-process inventory (1): 6.5*200 + Working-in-process inventory (1): 7.5*200 + Working-in-process inventory (1): 7*200 + Working-in-process inventory (1): 7*200 + Working-in-process inventory (1): 4*200 + Working-in-process inventory (1): 4*200 = Cost of goods manufactured (5): 13400

- On April 30, 2016, the Proprietorship2 transfers the balance of the Working-in-process inventory account to the Inventory account. The multi-subaccount names of the Inventory accounts and the five transaction sub-equations respectively are:

  Inven411-P2-20151127-In411-1000T < Inven41 < Inven4: 3*1000

  Inven412-P2-20151127-In412-1000T < Inven41 < Inven4: 11.1*1000

  TTTCU parts-P2-20151127-TTP-1000T < TTT parts < Inven4: 12*1000

  RRRHJK parts-P2-20151127-RRP-1000T < Inven4: 12*1000

  Food411-P2-20151127-FO411-1000T < Food41 < Food4: 5*1000

  Food412-P2-20151127-FO412-1000T < Food41 < Food4: 5.5*1000

  Food421-P2-20151127-FO421-1000T < Food42 < Food4: 6*1000

  Food422-P2-20151127-FO422-1000T < Food42 < Food4: 6.5*1000

  Food43-P2-20151127-FO43-1000T < Food4: 7*1000

  Food44-P2-20151127-FO44-1000T < Food4: -7.5*130: 7.5*1000

  Food511-P2-20151127-FO511-1000T < Food51 < Food5: 4*1000

  Food512-P2-20151127-FO512-1000T < Food51 < Food5: 4.5*1000

  Food513-P2-20151127-FO513-1000T < Food51 < Food5: 5*1000

  Food514-P2-20151127-FO514-1000T < Food51 < Food5: 5.5*1000

  Food521-P2-20151127-FO521-1000T < Food52 < Food5: 6*1000

  Food522-P2-20151127-FO522-1000T < Food52 < Food5: 6.5*1000

  Food53-P2-20151127-FO53-1000T < Food5: 8*1000

  Food611-P2-20151127-FO611-200T < Food61 < Food6: 10*200

Food612-P2-20151127-FO612-200T < Food61 < Food6: 12*200

Food613-P2-20151127-FO613-200T < Food61 < Food6: 13*200

Food614-P2-20151127-FO614-200T < Food61 < Food6: 15*200

Food621-P2-20151127-FO621-200T < Food62 < Food6: 13*200

Food622-P2-20151127-FO622-200T < Food62 < Food6: 14*200

Supplies1-P2-20150920-SUP1-200T: 7*200

Supplies2-P2-20150920-SUP2-200T: 8*200

Working-in-process inventory (1): -3*1000 + Working-in-process inventory (1): -11.1*1000 + Working-in-process inventory (1): -12*1000 + Working-in-process inventory (1): -12*1000 + Working-in-process inventory (1): -5*1000 + Inventory (1): 3*1000 + Inventory (1): 11.1*1000 + Inventory (1): 12*1000 + Inventory (1): 12*1000 + Inventory (1): 5*1000 = 0

Working-in-process inventory (1): -5.5*1000 + Working-in-process inventory (1): -6*1000 + Working-in-process inventory (1): -6.5*1000 + Working-in-process inventory (1): -7*1000 + Working-in-process inventory (1): -7.5*1000 + Inventory (1): 5.5*1000 + Inventory (1): 6*1000 + Inventory (1): 6.5*1000 + Inventory (1): 7*1000 + Inventory (1): 7.5*1000 = 0

Working-in-process inventory (1): -4*1000 + Working-in-process inventory (1): -4.5*1000 + Working-in-process inventory (1): -5*1000 + Working-in-process inventory (1): -5.5*1000 + Working-in-process inventory (1): -6*1000 + Inventory (1): 4*1000 + Inventory (1): 4.5*1000 + Inventory (1): 5*1000 + Inventory (1): 5.5*1000 + Inventory (1): 6*1000 = 0

Working-in-process inventory (1): -6.5*1000 + Working-in-process inventory (1): -8*1000 + Working-in-process inventory (1): -10*200 + Working-in-process inventory (1): -12*200 + Working-in-process inventory (1): -13*200 + Inventory (1): 6.5*1000 + Inventory (1): 8*1000 + Inventory (1): 10*200 + Inventory (1): 12*200 + Inventory (1): 13*200 = 0

Working-in-process inventory (1): -15*200 + Working-in-process inventory (1): -13*200 + Working-in-process inventory (1): -14*200 + Working-in-process inventory (1): -7*200 + Working-in-process inventory (1): -8*200 + Inventory (1): 15*200 + Inventory (1): 13*200 + Inventory (1): 14*200 + Inventory (1): 7*200 + Inventory (1): 8*200 = 0

- On April 30, 2016, the Proprietorship2 sells the Inventory (-$7*110 - $8*110) for sales $3300 to the Company1 (phone number: 123456784) for cash $1,300 and other $2,000 on credit. The multi-subaccount names of the Cash and the Inventory accounts respectively are:

    88-654306-c-customers < Cash receipts from customers < Operating activities
    Supplies1-P2-20150920-SUP1-200T: -7*110
    Supplies2-P2-20150920-SUP2-200T: -8*110

- On May 1, 2016, the Proprietorship2 plans to produce the following products in the Figure 3.10-1.

| Order | Product (the Lowest-level Subaccount) Names | Multi-subaccount Names | Costs | Amounts |
|---|---|---|---|---|
| 1 | Food411 | Food411 < Food41 < Food4 | 5.00 | 1200 |
| 2 | Food412 | Food412 < Food41 < Food4 | 5.50 | 1200 |
| 3 | Food421 | Food421 < Food42 < Food4 | 6.00 | 1200 |
| 4 | Food422 | Food422 < Food42 < Food4 | 6.50 | 1200 |
| 5 | Food43 | Food43 < Food4 | 7.00 | 1200 |
| 6 | Food44 | Food44 < Food4 | 7.50 | 1200 |
| 7 | Food511 | Food511 < Food51 < Food5 | 4.00 | 1200 |
| 8 | Food512 | Food512 < Food51 < Food5 | 4.50 | 1200 |
| 9 | Food513 | Food513 < Food51 < Food5 | 5.00 | 1200 |
| 10 | Food514 | Food514 < Food51 < Food5 | 5.50 | 1200 |
| 11 | Food521 | Food521 < Food52 < Food5 | 6.00 | 1200 |
| 12 | Food522 | Food522 < Food52 < Food5 | 6.50 | 1200 |
| 13 | Food53 | Food53 < Food5 | 8.00 | 1200 |
| 14 | Food611 | Food611 < Food61 < Food6 | 10.00 | 1000 |
| 15 | Food612 | Food612 < Food61 < Food6 | 12.00 | 1000 |
| 16 | Food613 | Food613 < Food61 < Food6 | 13.00 | 1000 |
| 17 | Food614 | Food614 < Food61 < Food6 | 15.00 | 1000 |

| 18 | Food621 | Food621 < Food62 < Food6 | 13.00 | 1000 |
|---|---|---|---|---|
| 19 | Food622 | Food622 < Food62 < Food6 | 14.00 | 1000 |
| 20 | Supplies1 | Supplies1 | 7.00 | 800 |
| 21 | Supplies2 | Supplies2 | 8.00 | 800 |

Figure 3.10-1    Producing Plan Table

Therefore, the Proprietorship2 transfers the inventories (supplies) -$430 (-$17-$7*27-$8*28) to the Cost of goods manufactured account to satisfy the need of producing. The multi-subaccount names of the Inventory account respectively are:

Supplies1-P2-20160430-Supp1-200T: -7*27

Supplies2-P2-20160430-Supp2-200T: -8*28

Supplies (1): -17 + Inventory (1): -7*27 + Inventory (1): -8*28 = Cost of goods manufactured (5): -430

- On May 1, 2016, the Proprietorship2 purchases the following inventories $24,250 from the Proprietorship1 (phone number: 123456081) for -$9,000 cash and other $15,250 on credit.

Inven31-P1-20160430-In31-600T < Inven3: 10*250

Inven32-P1-20160430-In32-600T < Inven3: 50*150

Inven331-P1-20160430-In331-600T < Inven33 < Inven3: 20*150

Inven332-P1-20160430-In332-600T < Inven33 < Inven3: 45*150

HGFCVB parts-P1-20160430-HGP-600T < QASXC parts < Inven3: 10*150

PPGHUP parts-P1-20160430-PPP-600T < ASDUP parts < Inven3: 20*150

The multi-subaccount name of the Cash account and the transaction sub-equation respectively are:

88-654309-t-suppliers < Cash payments to suppliers < Operating activities

Cash (1): -9000 + Inventory (1): 10*250 + Inventory (1): 50*150 + Inventory (1): 20*150 + Inventory (1): 45*150 + Inventory (1): 10*150 + Inventory (1): 20*150 = Account Payable (2): 15250

- On May 1, 2016, the Proprietorship2 sells the following inventories -$3,810 for sales $6,350 to the Company1 (phone number: 123456784) for cash $2,300 and other $4,050 on credit.

  Inven411-P2-20160430-In411-1000T < Inven41 < Inven4: -3*100

  Inven412-P2-20160430-In412-1000T < Inven41 < Inven4: -11.1*100

  TTTCU parts-P2-20160430-TTP-1000T < TTT parts < Inven4: -12*100

  RRRHJK parts-P2-20160430-RRP-1000T < Inven4: -12*100

  The multi-subaccount name of the Cash account and the transaction sub-equation respectively are:

  88-654306-c-customers < Cash receipts from customers < Operating activities

  Cash (1): 2300 + Account receivable (1): 4050 + Inventory (1): -3*100 + Inventory (1): -11.1*100 + Inventory (1): -12*100 + Inventory (1): -12*100 = Sales (4): 6350 + Cost of goods sold (5): -3810

- On May 1, 2016, the Proprietorship2 sells the following inventories -$4,953 for sales $8,255 to the Proprietorship1 (phone number: 123456781) for cash $5,000 and other $3,255 on credit.

  Inven411-P2-20160430-In411-1000T < Inven41 < Inven4: -3*130

  Inven412-P2-20160430-In412-1000T < Inven41 < Inven4: -11.1*130

  TTTCU parts-P2-20160430-TTP-1000T < TTT parts < Inven4: -12*130

  RRRHJK parts-P2-20160430-RRP-1000T < Inven4: -12*130

  The multi-subaccount name of the Cash account and the transaction sub-equation respectively are:

  88-654309-c-customers < Cash receipts from customers < Operating activities

  Cash (1): 5000 + Account receivable (1): 3255 + Inventory (1): -3*130 + Inventory (1): -11.1*130 + Inventory (1): -12*130 + Inventory (1): -12*130 = Sales (4): 8255 + Cost of goods sold (5): -4953

- On May 1, 2016, the Proprietorship2 sells the Inventory (-$7*50 - $8*50) for sales $1,500 to the Proprietorship1 (phone number: 123456781) for cash $800 and other $700 on credit. The multi-subaccount names of the Cash and the Inventory accounts respectively are:

  88-654309-c-customers < Cash receipts from customers < Operating activities

  Supplies1-P2-20160430-Supp1-200T: -7*50

  Supplies2-P2-20160430-Supp2-200T: -8*50

- On May 2, 2016, the Proprietorship2 transfers the following inventories -$24,250 to the Cost of goods manufactured account to satisfy the need of producing.

  Inven31-P1-20160430-In31-600T < Inven3: -10*250

  Inven32-P1-20160430-In32-600T < Inven3: -50*150

  Inven331-P1-20160430-In331-600T < Inven33 < Inven3: -20*150

  Inven332-P1-20160430-In332-600T < Inven33 < Inven3: -45*150

  HGFCVB parts-P1-20160430-HGP-600T < QASXC parts < Inven3: -10*150

  PPGHUP parts-P1-20160430-PPP-600T < ASDUP parts < Inven3: -20*150

  The transaction sub-equations is:

  Inventory (1): -10*250 + Inventory (1): -50*150 + Inventory (1): -20*150 + Inventory (1): -45*150 + Inventory (1): 10*150 + Inventory (1): 20*150 = Cost of goods manufactured (5): -24250

- On May 2, 2016, the Proprietorship2 transfers the following inventories -$134,400 to the Cost of goods manufactured account to satisfy the need of producing.

  Inven121-C3-20150922-In121-20000T < Inven12 < Inven1: -0.8*875

  Inven51-C3-20150922-In51-1000T < Inven5: -10*400

  Inven52-C3-20150922-In52-500T < Inven5: -50*200

  Inven531-C3-20150922-In531-1000T < Inven53 < Inven5: -25*400

  Inven532-C3-20150922-In532-1000T < Inven53 < Inven5: -35*400

  Inven541-C3-20150922-In541-1000T < Inven54 < Inven5: -12*400

  Inven542-C3-20150922-In542-1000T < Inven54 < Inven5: -15*400

Inven611-C3-20151003-In611-1300T < Inven61 < Inven6: -6.5*360

Inven612-C3-20151003-In612-1100T < Inven61 < Inven6: -12.5*400

Inven621-C3-20151003-In621-900T < Inven62 < Inven6: -18*400

Inven63-C3-20151003-In63-1000T < Inven6: -16*400

Inven711-C3-20151003-In711-500T < Inven71 < Inven7: -36*240

Inven712-C3-20151003-In712-100T < Inven71 < Inven7: -31*40

Inven721-C3-20151003-In721-744T < Inven72 < Inven7: -22*320

Inven722-C3-20151003-In722-600T < Inven72 < Inven7: -20*240

Inven731-C3-20151003-In731-600T < Inven73 < Inven7: -18*240

Inven732-C3-20151003-In732-1000T < Inven73 < Inven7: -16*400

Inven811-C3-20151003-In811-600T < Inven81 < Inven8: -25*240

Inven812-C3-20151003-In812-600T < Inven81 < Inven8: -24*240

Inven813-C3-20151003-In813-600T < Inven81 < Inven8: -23*240

Inven82-C3-20151003-In82-600T < Inven8: -20*240

Inven831-C3-20151003-In831-600T < Inven83 < Inven8: -18*240

Inven832-C3-20151003-In832-800T < Inven83 < Inven8: -16*320

The three transaction sub-equations are respectively:

Inventory (1): -0.8*875 + Inventory (1): -10*400 + Inventory (1): -50*200 + Inventory (1): -25*400 + Inventory (1): -35*400 + Inventory (1): -12*400 + Inventory (1): -15*400 + Inventory (1): -6.5*360 + Inventory (1): -12.5*400 + Inventory (1): 18*400 = Cost of goods manufactured (5): -64040

Inventory (1): -16*400 + Inventory (1): -36*240 + Inventory (1): -31*40 + Inventory (1): -22*320 + Inventory (1): -20*240 + Inventory (1): -18*240 + Inventory (1): -16*400 + Inventory (1): -25*240 + Inventory (1): -24*240 = Cost of goods manufactured (5): -50600

Inventory (1): -23*240 + Inventory (1): -20*240 + Inventory (1): -18*240 + Inventory (1): -16*320 = Cost of goods manufactured (5): -19760

- On May 8, 2016, the Proprietorship2 sells the Inventory (-$7*10 - $8*10) for sales $300 to the Tax Bureau (phone number: 123456787) for cash $300. The multi-subaccount names of the Cash and the Inventory accounts respectively are:

  88-654303-c-customers < Cash receipts from customers < Operating activities

  Supplies1-P2-20150920-SUP1-200T: -7*10

  Supplies2-P2-20150920-SUP2-200T: -8*10

- On May 15, 2016, the Proprietorship2 sells the Food613 $26*2 (cost: -$13*2) and the Food621 $26*1 (cost: -$13*1) to A24 (SIN: 909876524) for cash $78. The multi-subaccount names of the Cash and the Inventory accounts respectively are:

  909876524-c-customers < Cash receipts from customers < Operating activities

  Food613-P2-20151127-FO613-200T < Food61 < Food6: -13*2

  Food621-P2-20151127-FO621-200T < Food62 < Food6: -13*1

- On May 16, 2016, the Proprietorship2 sells the Inventory (-$7*10 -$ 8*11) for sales $316 to the Central Bank (phone number: 123456789) for cash $316. The multi-subaccount names of the Cash and the Inventory accounts respectively are:

  88-654301-c-customers < Cash receipts from customers < Operating activities

  Supplies1-P2-20150920-SUP1-200T: -7*10

  Supplies2-P2-20150920-SUP2-200T: -8*11

- On May 17, 2016, the Proprietorship2 pays -$210.77 cash to A24 (SIN: 909876524) for the Travelling expenses -$132.77 and the Other expenses -$78.

- On May 22, 2016, the Proprietorship2 sells the Food513 $10*3 (cost: -$5*3) and the Food621 $26*1 (cost: -$13*1) to A22 (SIN: 909876522) for cash $56. The multi-subaccount names of the Cash and the Inventory accounts respectively are:

  909876522-c-customers < Cash receipts from customers < Operating activities

  Food513-P2-20151127-FO513-1000T < Food51 < Food5: -5*3

  Food621-P2-20151127-FO621-200T < Food62 < Food6: -13*1

- On May 24, 2016, the Proprietorship2 sells the Food522 $13*4 (cost: -$6.5*4) and the Food622 $28*2 (cost: -$14*2) to A12 (SIN: 909876512) for cash $108. The multi-subaccount names of the Cash and the Inventory accounts respectively are:

909876512-c-customers < Cash receipts from customers < Operating activities

Food522-P2-20151127-FO522-1000T < Food52 < Food5: -6.5*4

Food622-P2-20151127-FO622-200T < Food62 < Food6: -14*2

- On May 31, 2016, the Proprietorship2 pays two employees' salary -$5,660 repeatedly.

- On June 3, 2016, the Proprietorship2 sells the Food613 $26*1 (cost: -$13*1) and the Food622 $28*1 (cost: -$14*1) to A8 (SIN: 909876508) for cash $54. The multi-subaccount names of the Cash and the Inventory accounts respectively are:

  909876508-c-customers < Cash receipts from customers < Operating activities

  Food613-P2-20151127-FO613-200T < Food61 < Food6: -13*1

  Food622-P2-20151127-FO622-200T < Food62 < Food6: -14*1

- On June 12, 2016, the Proprietorship2 sells the Food611 $20*2 (cost: -$10*2) and the Food622 $28*1 (cost: -$14*1) to A17 (SIN: 909876517) for cash $68. The multi-subaccount names of the Cash and the Inventory accounts respectively are:

  909876517-c-customers < Cash receipts from customers < Operating activities

  Food611-P2-20151127-FO611-200T < Food61 < Food6: -10*2

  Food622-P2-20151127-FO622-200T < Food62 < Food6: -14*1

- On June 12, 2016, the Proprietorship2 sells the Food611 $20*2 (cost: -$10*2) and the Food622 $28*1 (cost: -$14*1) to A20 (SIN: 909876520) for cash $68. The multi-subaccount names of the Cash and the Inventory accounts respectively are:

  909876520-c-customers < Cash receipts from customers < Operating activities

  Food611-P2-20151127-FO611-200T < Food61 < Food6: -10*2

  Food622-P2-20151127-FO622-200T < Food62 < Food6: -14*1

- On June 15, 2016, the Proprietorship2 sells the Inventory (cost: -$7*6) for sales $84 to the Company3 (phone number: 123456782) for cash $84 The multi-subaccount name of the Cash account and the Inventory account respectively are:

  88-654308-c-customers < Cash receipts from customers < Operating activities

  Supplies1-P2-20160430-Supp1-200T: -7*6

- On June 15, 2016, the Proprietorship2 sells the Food44 $15*3 (cost: -$7.5*3) and the Food53 $16*3 (cost: -$8*3) to A3 (SIN: 909876503) for cash $93. The multi-

subaccount names of the Cash and the Inventory accounts respectively are:

909876503-c-customers < Cash receipts from customers < Operating activities

Food44-P2-20151127-FO44-1000T < Food4: -7.5*3

Food53-P2-20151127-FO53-1000T < Food5: -8*3

- On June 17, 2016, the Proprietorship2 sells the Food514 $11*3 (cost: -$5.5*3) and the Food611 $20*3 (cost: -$10*3) to A5 (SIN: 909876505) for cash $93. The multi-subaccount names of the Cash and the Inventory accounts respectively are:

  909876505-c-customers < Cash receipts from customers < Operating activities

  Food514-P2-20151127-FO514-1000T < Food51 < Food5: -5.5*3

  Food611-P2-20151127-FO611-200T < Food61 < Food6: -10*3

- On June 17, 2016, the Proprietorship2 sells the Food513 $10*3 (cost: -$5*3) and the Food611 $20*3 (cost: -$10*3) to A6 (SIN: 909876506) for cash $90. The multi-subaccount names of the Cash and the Inventory accounts respectively are:

  909876506-c-customers < Cash receipts from customers < Operating activities

  Food513-P2-20151127-FO513-1000T < Food51 < Food5: -5*3

  Food611-P2-20151127-FO611-200T < Food61 < Food6: -10*3

- On June 17, 2016, the Proprietorship2 sells the Food612 $24*2 (cost: -$12*2) and the Food613 $26*1 (cost: -$13*1) to A24 (SIN: 909876524) for cash $74. The multi-subaccount names of the Cash and the Inventory accounts respectively are:

  909876524-c-customers < Cash receipts from customers < Operating activities

  Food612-P2-20151127-FO612-200T < Food61 < Food6: -12*2

  Food613-P2-20151127-FO613-200T < Food61 < Food6: -13*1

- On June 18, 2016, the Proprietorship2 sells the Food522 $13*4 (cost: -$6.5*4) and the Food622 $28*3 (cost: -$14*3) to A2 (SIN: 909876502) for cash $136. The multi-subaccount names of the Cash and the Inventory accounts respectively are:

  909876502-c-customers < Cash receipts from customers < Operating activities

  Food522-P2-20151127-FO522-1000T < Food52 < Food5: -6.5*4

  Food622-P2-20151127-FO622-200T < Food62 < Food6: -14*3

- On June 19, 2016, the Proprietorship2 pays -$196.83 cash to A24 (SIN: 909876524)

for the Travelling expenses -$122.83 and the Other expenses -$74.

- On June 21, 2016, the Proprietorship2 sells the Food521 $12*2 (cost: -$6*2) and the Food612 $24*1 (cost: -$12*1) to A22 (SIN: 909876522) for cash $48. The multi-subaccount names of the Cash and the Inventory accounts respectively are:

  909876522-c-customers < Cash receipts from customers < Operating activities

  Food521-P2-20151127-FO521-1000T < Food52 < Food5: -6*2

  Food612-P2-20151127-FO612-200T < Food61 < Food6: -12*1

- On June 30, 2016, the Proprietorship2 pays two employees' salary expenses for cash -$5,660 repeatedly.

- On July 2, 2016, the Proprietorship2 sells the Food44 $15*3 (cost: -$7.5*3) and the Food612 $24*3 (cost: -$12*3) to A9 (SIN: 909876509) for cash $117. The multi-subaccount names of the Cash and the Inventory accounts respectively are:

  909876509-c-customers < Cash receipts from customers < Operating activities

  Food44-P2-20151127-FO44-1000T < Food4: -7.5*3

  Food612-P2-20151127-FO612-200T < Food61 < Food6: -12*3

- On July 3, 2016, the Proprietorship2 pays -$53,000 cash to the Company3 (phone number: 123456082) with the General ID 21 (-$21,100) and the General ID 23(-$31,900). The multi-subaccount name of the Cash account is:

  88-654308-t-suppliers < Cash payments to suppliers < Operating activities

- On July 9, 2016, the Proprietorship2 sells the Food612 $24*2 (cost: -$12*2) and the Food621 $26*1 (cost: -$13*1) to A11 (SIN: 909876511) for cash $74. The multi-subaccount names of the Cash and the Inventory accounts respectively are:

  909876511-c-customers < Cash receipts from customers < Operating activities

  Food612-P2-20151127-FO612-200T < Food61 < Food6: -12*2

  Food621-P2-20151127-FO621-200T < Food62 < Food6: -13*1

- On July 16, 2016, the Proprietorship2 receives $13,000 cash from the Company3 (phone number: 123456782) with the General ID 18 (-$660) and the General ID 25 (-$12,340). The multi-subaccount name of the Cash account is:

  88-654308-c-customers < Cash receipts from customers < Operating activities

- On July 21, 2016, the Proprietorship2 sells the Food621 $26*2 (cost: -$13*2) and the Food622 $28*2 (cost: -$14*2) to A25 (SIN: 909876525) for cash $108. The multi-subaccount names of the Cash and the Inventory accounts respectively are:

  909876525-c-customers < Cash receipts from customers < Operating activities

  Food621-P2-20151127-FO621-200T < Food62 < Food6: -13*2

  Food622-P2-20151127-FO622-200T < Food62 < Food6: -14*2

- On July 23, 2016, the Proprietorship2 pays -$251.19 cash to A25 (SIN: 909876525) for the Travelling expenses -$143.19 and the Other expenses -$108.

- On July 31, 2016, the Proprietorship2 pays two employees' salary -$5,660 repeatedly.

- On July 31, 2016, the Proprietorship2 sells the following inventories -$5,460 for sales $10,920 to A12A20 (SIN: 909876528), who uses his (or her) father A12's (or mother A12's) secondary card of the Business Bank1, for cash $10,920.

  Food411-P2-20160430-FO411-1000T < Food41 < Food4: -5*130

  Food412-P2-20160430-FO412-1000T < Food41 < Food4: -5.5*130

  Food421-P2-20160430-FO421-1000T < Food42 < Food4: -6*130

  Food422-P2-20160430-FO422-1000T < Food42 < Food4: -6.5*130

  Food43-P2-20160430-FO43-1000T < Food4: -7*130

  Food44-P2-20160430-FO44-1000T < Food4: -7.5*130

  Food512-P2-20160430-FO512-1000T < Food51 < Food5: -4.5*130

  The multi-subaccount name of the Cash account is:

  909876512-c-customers < Cash receipts from customers < Operating activities

- On July 31, 2016, the Proprietorship2 sells the following inventories -$5,525 for sales $11,050 to A1 (SIN: 909876501) for cash $11,050.

  Food411-P2-20160430-FO411-1000T < Food41 < Food4: -5*130

  Food412-P2-20160430-FO412-1000T < Food41 < Food4: -5.5*50

  Food421-P2-20160430-FO421-1000T < Food42 < Food4: -6*130

  Food422-P2-20160430-FO422-1000T < Food42 < Food4: -6.5*130

  Food43-P2-20160430-FO43-1000T < Food4: -7*130

  Food44-P2-20160430-FO44-1000T < Food4: -7.5*130

Food513-P2-20160430-FO513-1000T < Food51 < Food5: -5*130

Food53-P2-20160430-FO53-1000T < Food5: -8*55

The multi-subaccount name of the Cash account is:

909876501-c-customers < Cash receipts from customers < Operating activities

- On July 31, 2016, the Proprietorship2 sells the following inventories -$5,590 for sales $11,180 to A2 (SIN: 909876502) for cash $11,180.

  Food411-P2-20160430-FO411-1000T < Food41 < Food4: -5*130

  Food412-P2-20160430-FO412-1000T < Food41 < Food4: -5.5*130

  Food421-P2-20160430-FO421-1000T < Food42 < Food4: -6*130

  Food422-P2-20160430-FO422-1000T < Food42 < Food4: -6.5*130

  Food43-P2-20160430-FO43-1000T < Food4: -7*130

  Food44-P2-20160430-FO44-1000T < Food4: -7.5*130

  Food514-P2-20160430-FO514-1000T < Food51 < Food5: -5.5*130

  The multi-subaccount name of the Cash account is:

  909876502-c-customers < Cash receipts from customers < Operating activities

- On July 31, 2016, the Proprietorship2 sells the following inventories -$5,655 for sales $11,310 to A3 (SIN: 909876503) for cash $11,310.

  Food411-P2-20160430-FO411-1000T < Food41 < Food4: -5*130

  Food412-P2-20160430-FO412-1000T < Food41 < Food4: -5.5*130

  Food421-P2-20160430-FO421-1000T < Food42 < Food4: -6*130

  Food422-P2-20160430-FO422-1000T < Food42 < Food4: -6.5*130

  Food43-P2-20160430-FO43-1000T < Food4: -7*130

  Food44-P2-20160430-FO44-1000T < Food4: -7.5*130

  Food521-P2-20160430-FO521-1000T < Food52 < Food5: -6*130

  The multi-subaccount name of the Cash account is:

  909876503-c-customers < Cash receipts from customers < Operating activities

- On July 31, 2016, the Proprietorship2 sells the following inventories -$5,720 for sales $11,440 to A4 (SIN: 909876504) for cash $11,440.

  Food411-P2-20160430-FO411-1000T < Food41 < Food4: -5*130

Food412-P2-20160430-FO412-1000T < Food41 < Food4: -5.5*130

Food421-P2-20160430-FO421-1000T < Food42 < Food4: -6*130

Food422-P2-20160430-FO422-1000T < Food42 < Food4: -6.5*130

Food43-P2-20160430-FO43-1000T < Food4: -7*130

Food44-P2-20160430-FO44-1000T < Food4: -7.5*130

Food522-P2-20160430-FO522-1000T < Food52 < Food5: -6.5*130

The multi-subaccount name of the Cash account is:

909876504-c-customers < Cash receipts from customers < Operating activities

- On July 31, 2016, the Proprietorship2 sells the following inventories -$5,915 for sales $11,830 to A5 (SIN: 909876505) for cash $11,830.

Food411-P2-20160430-FO411-1000T < Food41 < Food4: -5*130

Food412-P2-20160430-FO412-1000T < Food41 < Food4: -5.5*130

Food421-P2-20160430-FO421-1000T < Food42 < Food4: -6*130

Food422-P2-20160430-FO422-1000T < Food42 < Food4: -6.5*130

Food43-P2-20160430-FO43-1000T < Food4: -7*130

Food44-P2-20160430-FO44-1000T < Food4: -7.5*130

Food53-P2-20160430-FO53-1000T < Food5: -8*130

The multi-subaccount name of the Cash account is:

909876505-c-customers < Cash receipts from customers < Operating activities

- On July 31, 2016, the Proprietorship2 sells the following inventories -$5,395 for sales $10,790 to A6 (SIN: 909876506) for cash $10,790.

Food511-P2-20160430-FO511-1000T < Food51 < Food5: -4*130

Food512-P2-20160430-FO512-1000T < Food51 < Food5: -4.5*130

Food513-P2-20160430-FO513-1000T < Food51 < Food5: -5*130

Food514-P2-20160430-FO514-1000T < Food51 < Food5: -5.5*130

Food521-P2-20160430-FO521-1000T < Food52 < Food5: -6*130

Food522-P2-20160430-FO522-1000T < Food52 < Food5: -6.5*130

Food611-P2-20160430-FO611-200T < Food61 < Food6: -10*130

The multi-subaccount name of the Cash account is:

909876506-c-customers < Cash receipts from customers < Operating activities

- On July 31, 2016, the Proprietorship2 sells the following inventories -$5,655 for sales $11,310 to A7 (SIN: 909876507) for cash $11,310.

  Food511-P2-20160430-FO511-1000T < Food51 < Food5: -4*130

  Food512-P2-20160430-FO512-1000T < Food51 < Food5: -4.5*130

  Food513-P2-20160430-FO513-1000T < Food51 < Food5: -5*130

  Food514-P2-20160430-FO514-1000T < Food51 < Food5: -5.5*130

  Food521-P2-20160430-FO521-1000T < Food52 < Food5: -6*130

  Food522-P2-20160430-FO522-1000T < Food52 < Food5: -6.5*130

  Food612-P2-20160430-FO612-200T < Food61 < Food6: -12*130

  The multi-subaccount name of the Cash account is:

  909876507-c-customers < Cash receipts from customers < Operating activities

- On July 31, 2016, the Proprietorship2 sells the following inventories -$5,785 for sales $11,570 to A8 (SIN: 909876508) for cash $11,570.

  Food511-P2-20160430-FO511-1000T < Food51 < Food5: -4*130

  Food512-P2-20160430-FO512-1000T < Food51 < Food5: -4.5*130

  Food513-P2-20160430-FO513-1000T < Food51 < Food5: -5*130

  Food514-P2-20160430-FO514-1000T < Food51 < Food5: -5.5*130

  Food521-P2-20160430-FO521-1000T < Food52 < Food5: -6*130

  Food522-P2-20160430-FO522-1000T < Food52 < Food5: -6.5*130

  Food613-P2-20160430-FO613-200T < Food61 < Food6: -13*130

  The multi-subaccount name of the Cash account is:

  909876508-c-customers < Cash receipts from customers < Operating activities

- On July 31, 2016, the Proprietorship2 sells the following inventories -$6,045 for sales $12,090 to A9 (SIN: 909876509) for cash $12,090.

  Food511-P2-20160430-FO511-1000T < Food51 < Food5: -4*130

  Food512-P2-20160430-FO512-1000T < Food51 < Food5: -4.5*50

  Food513-P2-20160430-FO513-1000T < Food51 < Food5: -5*50

  Food514-P2-20160430-FO514-1000T < Food51 < Food5: -5.5*130

Food521-P2-20160430-FO521-1000T < Food52 < Food5: -6*130

Food522-P2-20160430-FO522-1000T < Food52 < Food5: -6.5*130

Food53-P2-20160430-FO53-1000T < Food5: -8*95

Food614-P2-20160430-FO614-200T < Food61 < Food6: -15*130

The multi-subaccount name of the Cash account is:

  909876509-c-customers < Cash receipts from customers < Operating activities

- On July 31, 2016, the Proprietorship2 sells the following inventories -$5,785 for sales $11,570 to A10 (SIN: 909876510) for cash $11,570.

    Food511-P2-20160430-FO511-1000T < Food51 < Food5: -4*130

    Food512-P2-20160430-FO512-1000T < Food51 < Food5: -4.5*130

    Food513-P2-20160430-FO513-1000T < Food51 < Food5: -5*130

    Food514-P2-20160430-FO514-1000T < Food51 < Food5: -5.5*130

    Food521-P2-20160430-FO521-1000T < Food52 < Food5: -6*130

    Food522-P2-20160430-FO522-1000T < Food52 < Food5: -6.5*130

    Food621-P2-20160430-FO621-200T < Food62 < Food6: -13*130

  The multi-subaccount name of the Cash account is:

    909876510-c-customers < Cash receipts from customers < Operating activities

- On July 31, 2016, the Proprietorship2 sells the following inventories -$5,135 for sales $10,270 to A11 (SIN: 909876511) for cash $10,270.

    Food412-P2-20160430-FO412-1000T < Food41 < Food4: -5.5*130

    Food511-P2-20160430-FO511-1000T < Food51 < Food5: -4*130

    Food512-P2-20160430-FO512-1000T < Food51 < Food5: -4.5*130

    Food513-P2-20160430-FO513-1000T < Food51 < Food5: -5*130

    Food521-P2-20160430-FO521-1000T < Food52 < Food5: -6*130

    Food522-P2-20160430-FO522-1000T < Food52 < Food5: -6.5*130

    Food53-P2-20160430-FO53-1000T < Food5: -8*130

  The multi-subaccount name of the Cash account is:

    909876511-c-customers < Cash receipts from customers < Operating activities

- On July 31, 2016, the Proprietorship2 sells the following inventories -$5,915 for sales \$11,830 to A12 (SIN: 909876512) for cash \$11,830.

Food511-P2-20160430-FO511-1000T < Food51 < Food5: -4*130

Food512-P2-20160430-FO512-1000T < Food51 < Food5: -4.5*130

Food513-P2-20160430-FO513-1000T < Food51 < Food5: -5*130

Food514-P2-20160430-FO514-1000T < Food51 < Food5: -5.5*130

Food521-P2-20160430-FO521-1000T < Food52 < Food5: -6*30

Food522-P2-20160430-FO522-1000T < Food52 < Food5: -6.5*50

Food53-P2-20160430-FO53-1000T < Food5: -8*140

Food622-P2-20160430-FO622-200T < Food62 < Food6: -14*130

The multi-subaccount name of the Cash account is:

  909876512-c-customers < Cash receipts from customers < Operating activities

- On July 31, 2016, the Proprietorship2 sells the following inventories -\$5,915 for sales \$11,830 to A13 (SIN: 909876513) for cash \$11,830.

Food411-P2-20160430-FO411-1000T < Food41 < Food4: -5*130

Food412-P2-20160430-FO412-1000T < Food41 < Food4: -5.5*130

Food421-P2-20160430-FO421-1000T < Food42 < Food4: -6*130

Food422-P2-20160430-FO422-1000T < Food42 < Food4: -6.5*130

Food43-P2-20160430-FO43-1000T < Food4: -7*130

Food44-P2-20160430-FO44-1000T < Food4: -7.5*130

Food53-P2-20160430-FO53-1000T < Food5: -8*130

The multi-subaccount name of the Cash account is:

  909876513-c-customers < Cash receipts from customers < Operating activities

- On August 9, 2016, the Proprietorship2 sells the Food513 \$10*5 (cost: -\$5*5) and the Food53 \$16*4 (cost: -\$8*4) to A6 (SIN: 909876506) for cash \$114. The multi-subaccount names of the Cash and the Inventory accounts respectively are:

  909876506-c-customers < Cash receipts from customers < Operating activities

  Food513-P2-20151127-FO513-1000T < Food51 < Food5: -5*5

  Food53-P2-20151127-FO53-1000T < Food5: -8*4

- On August 12, 2016, the Proprietorship2 sells the Food611 \$20*2 (cost: -\$10*2) and

the Food621 $26*3 (cost: -$13*3) to A9 (SIN: 909876509) for cash $118. The multi-subaccount names of the Cash and the Inventory accounts respectively are:

909876509-c-customers < Cash receipts from customers < Operating activities

Food611-P2-20151127-FO611-200T < Food61 < Food6: -10*2

Food621-P2-20151127-FO621-200T < Food62 < Food6: -13*3

- On August 14, 2016, the Proprietorship2 sells the Food522 $13*3 (cost: -$6.5*3) and the Food622 $28*3 (cost: -$14*3) to A15 (SIN: 909876515) for cash $123. The multi-subaccount names of the Cash and the Inventory accounts respectively are:

909876515-c-customers < Cash receipts from customers < Operating activities

Food522-P2-20151127-FO522-1000T < Food52 < Food5: -6.5*3

Food622-P2-20151127-FO622-200T < Food62 < Food6: -14*3

- On August 15, 2016, the Proprietorship2 pays -$66,000 cash to the Company3 (phone number: 123456082) with the General ID 21 (-$950) and the General ID 22 (-$65,050). The multi-subaccount name of the Cash account is:

88-654308-t-suppliers < Cash payments to suppliers < Operating activities

- On August 15, 2016, the Proprietorship2 sells the Food514 $11*2 (cost: -$5.5*2) and the Food614 $30*1 (cost: -$15*1) to A8 (SIN: 909876508) for cash $52. The multi-subaccount names of the Cash and the Inventory accounts respectively are:

909876508-c-customers < Cash receipts from customers < Operating activities

Food514-P2-20151127-FO514-1000T < Food51 < Food5: -5.5*2

Food614-P2-20151127-FO614-200T < Food61 < Food6: -15*1

- On August 16, 2016, the Proprietorship2 sells the Food612 $24*2 (cost: -$12*2) and the Food621 $26*1 (cost: -$13*1) to A24 (SIN: 909876524) for cash $74. The multi-subaccount names of the Cash and the Inventory accounts respectively are:

909876524-c-customers < Cash receipts from customers < Operating activities

Food612-P2-20151127-FO612-200T < Food61 < Food6: -12*2

Food621-P2-20151127-FO621-200T < Food62 < Food6: -13*1

- On August 18, 2016, the Proprietorship2 pays -$203.47 cash to A24 (SIN: 909876524) for the Travelling expenses -$129.47 and the Other expenses (meals:

food612: $24*2 + food621: $26*1) -$74.

- On August 21, 2016, the Proprietorship2 sells the Food522 $13*2 (cost: -$6.5*2) and the Food614 $30*1 (cost: -$15*1) to A22 (SIN: 909876522) for cash $56. The multi-subaccount names of the Cash and the Inventory accounts respectively are:

  909876522-c-customers < Cash receipts from customers < Operating activities

  Food522-P2-20151127-FO522-1000T < Food52 < Food5: -6.5*2

  Food614-P2-20151127-FO614-200T < Food61 < Food6: -15*1

- On August 31, 2016, the Proprietorship2 pays two employees' salary -$5,660.

- On September 2, 2016, the Proprietorship2 purchases one Car3 $38,000 from the Company1 (phone number: 123456084) for cash -$18,000 and other $20,000 on credit. The multi-subaccount names of the Cash and the Inventory accounts and the two transaction sub-equations respectively are:

  88-654306-t-machinery < Cash payments for machinery < Operating activities

  Car3-C1-20160430-C3-050 < Car-inventory < Vehicle-inventory: 38000*1

  Cash (1): -18000 + Inventory (1): 38000 = Account payable (2): 20000

  Vehicle (1): 38000 + Inventory (1): -38000 = 0

- On September 5, 2016, the Proprietorship2 sells the Food514 $11*3 (cost: -$5.5*3) and the Food621 $26*1 (cost: -$13*1) to A2 (SIN: 909876502) for cash $59. The multi-subaccount names of the Cash and the Inventory accounts respectively are:

  909876502-c-customers < Cash receipts from customers < Operating activities

  Food514-P2-20151127-FO514-1000T < Food51 < Food5: -5.5*3

  Food621-P2-20151127-FO621-200T < Food62 < Food6: -13*1

- On September 5, 2016, the Proprietorship2 sells the Food513 $10*3 (cost: -$5*3) and the Food622 $28*2 (cost: -$14*2) to A4 (SIN: 909876504) for cash $86. The multi-subaccount names of the Cash and the Inventory accounts respectively are:

  909876504-c-customers < Cash receipts from customers < Operating activities

  Food513-P2-20151127-FO513-1000T < Food51 < Food5: -5*3

Food622-P2-20151127-FO622-200T < Food62 < Food6: -14*2

- On September 7, 2016, the Proprietorship2 sells the Food43 $14*3 (cost: -$7*3) and the Food612 $24*2 (cost: -$12*2) to A7 (SIN: 909876507) for cash $90. The multi-subaccount names of the Cash and the Inventory accounts respectively are:

  909876507-c-customers < Cash receipts from customers < Operating activities

  Food43-P2-20151127-FO43-1000T < Food4: -7*3

  Food612-P2-20151127-FO612-200T < Food61 < Food6: -12*2

- On September 14, 2016, the Proprietorship2 receives $380 cash from the Company2 (phone number: 123456783) with the General ID 19. The multi-subaccount name of the Cash account is:

  88-654307-c-customers < Cash receipts from customers < Operating activities

- On September 15, 2016, the Proprietorship2 sells the Food514 $11*3 (cost: -$5.5*3) and the Food612 $24*3 (cost: -$12*3) to A6 (SIN: 909876506) for cash $105. The multi-subaccount names of the Cash and the Inventory accounts respectively are:

  909876506-c-customers < Cash receipts from customers < Operating activities

  Food514-P2-20151127-FO514-1000T < Food51 < Food5: -5.5*3

  Food612-P2-20151127-FO612-200T < Food61 < Food6: -12*3

- On September 21, 2016, the Proprietorship2 pays -$256.18 cash to A24 (SIN: 909876524) for the Travelling expenses -$157.18 and the Other expenses -$99.

- On September 30, 2016, the Proprietorship2 pays two employees' salary -$5,660.

- On October 3, 2016, the Proprietorship2 sells the Food522 $13*3 (cost: -$6.5*3) and the Food614 $30*3 (cost: -$15*3) to A15 (SIN: 909876515) for cash $129. The multi-subaccount names of the Cash and the Inventory accounts respectively are:

  909876515-c-customers < Cash receipts from customers < Operating activities

  Food522-P2-20151127-FO522-1000T < Food52 < Food5: -6.5*3

  Food614-P2-20151127-FO614-200T < Food61 < Food6: -15*3

- On October 4, 2016, the Proprietorship2 sells the Food522 $13*3 (cost: -$6.5*3) and the Food613 $26*3 (cost: -$13*3) to A18 (SIN: 909876518) for cash $117. The multi-subaccount names of the Cash and the Inventory accounts respectively are:

909876518-c-customers < Cash receipts from customers < Operating activities

Food522-P2-20151127-FO522-1000T < Food52 < Food5: -6.5*3

Food613-P2-20151127-FO613-200T < Food61 < Food6: -13*3

- On October 6, 2016, the Proprietorship2 sells the Food522 $13*2 (cost: -$6.5*2) and the Food613 $26*2 (cost: -$13*2) to A21 (SIN: 909876521) for cash $78. The multi-subaccount names of the Cash and the Inventory accounts respectively are:

  909876521-c-customers < Cash receipts from customers < Operating activities

  Food522-P2-20151127-FO522-1000T < Food52 < Food5: -6.5*2

  Food613-P2-20151127-FO613-200T < Food61 < Food6: -13*2

- On October 6, 2016, the Proprietorship2 sells the Food521 $12*2 (cost: -$6*2) and the Food614 $30*1 (cost: -$15*1) to A22 (SIN: 909876522) for cash $54. The multi-subaccount names of the Cash and the Inventory accounts respectively are:

  909876522-c-customers < Cash receipts from customers < Operating activities

  Food521-P2-20151127-FO521-1000T < Food52 < Food5: -6*2

  Food614-P2-20151127-FO614-200T < Food61 < Food6: -15*1

- On October 8, 2016, the Proprietorship2 sells the Food511 $8*3 (cost: -$4*3) and the Food53 $16*2 (cost: -$8*2) to A8 (SIN: 909876508) for cash $56. The multi-subaccount names of the Cash and the Inventory accounts respectively are:

  909876508-c-customers < Cash receipts from customers < Operating activities

  Food511-P2-20151127-FO511-1000T < Food51 < Food5: -4*3

  Food53-P2-20151127-FO53-1000T < Food5: -8*2

- On October 11, 2016, the Proprietorship2 pays -$41,000 cash to the Company3 (phone number: 123456082) with the General ID 21. The multi-subaccount name of the Cash account is:

  88-654308-t-suppliers < Cash payments to suppliers < Operating activities

- On October 16, 2016, the Proprietorship2 sells the Food522 $13*2 (cost: -$6.5*2) and the Food614 $30*2 (cost: -$15*2) to A24 (SIN: 909876524) for cash $86. The multi-subaccount names of the Cash and the Inventory accounts respectively are:

  909876524-c-customers < Cash receipts from customers < Operating activities

Food522-P2-20151127-FO522-1000T < Food52 < Food5: -6.5*2

Food614-P2-20151127-FO614-200T < Food61 < Food6: -15*2

- On October 18, 2016, the Proprietorship2 pays -$228.66 cash to A24 (SIN: 909876524) for the Travelling expenses -$142.66 and the Other expenses -$86.

- On October 31, 2016, the Proprietorship2 pays two employees' salary -$5,660.

- On November 1, 2016, the Proprietorship2 sells the Food514 $11*3 (cost: -$5.5*3) and the Food622 $28*1 (cost: -$14*1) to A11 (SIN: 909876511) for cash $61. The multi-subaccount names of the Cash and the Inventory accounts respectively are:

  909876511-c-customers < Cash receipts from customers < Operating activities

  Food514-P2-20151127-FO514-1000T < Food51 < Food5: -5.5*3

  Food622-P2-20151127-FO622-200T < Food62 < Food6: -14*1

- On November 11, 2016, the Proprietorship2 sells the Food514 $11*3 (cost: -$5.5*3) and the Food613 $26*2 (cost: -$13*2) to A4 (SIN: 909876504) for cash $85. The multi-subaccount names of the Cash and the Inventory accounts respectively are:

  909876504-c-customers < Cash receipts from customers < Operating activities

  Food514-P2-20151127-FO514-1000T < Food51 < Food5: -5.5*3

  Food613-P2-20151127-FO613-200T < Food61 < Food6: -13*2

- On November 16, 2016, the Proprietorship2 sells the Food53 $16*4 (cost: -$8*4) and the Food614 $30*2 (cost: -$15*2) to A9 (SIN: 909876509) for cash $124. The multi-subaccount names of the Cash and the Inventory accounts respectively are:

  909876509-c-customers < Cash receipts from customers < Operating activities

  Food53-P2-20151127-FO53-1000T < Food5: -8*4

  Food614-P2-20151127-FO614-200T < Food61 < Food6: -15*2

- On November 16, 2016, the Proprietorship2 sells the Food53 $16*3 (cost: -$8*3) and the Food622 $28*3 (cost: -$14*3) to A15 (SIN: 909876515) for cash $132. The multi-subaccount names of the Cash and the Inventory accounts respectively are:

  909876515-c-customers < Cash receipts from customers < Operating activities

  Food53-P2-20151127-FO53-1000T < Food5: -8*3

  Food622-P2-20151127-FO622-200T < Food62 < Food6: -14*3

- On November 18, 2016, the Proprietorship2 sells the Food611 $20*3 (cost: -$10*3) and the Food621 $26*1 (cost: -$13*1) to A24 (SIN: 909876524) for cash $86. The multi-subaccount names of the Cash and the Inventory accounts respectively are:

  909876524-c-customers < Cash receipts from customers < Operating activities

  Food611-P2-20151127-FO611-200T < Food61 < Food6: -10*3

  Food621-P2-20151127-FO621-200T < Food62 < Food6: -13*1

- On November 20, 2016, the Proprietorship2 pays -$204.61 cash to A24 (SIN: 909876524) for the Travelling expenses -$118.61 and the Other expenses -$86.

- On November 30, 2016, the Proprietorship2 pays two employees' salary cash -$5,660.

- On November 30, 2016, the Proprietorship2 records the Amortization expenses -$2,475 of a computer server2 (-$1,237.5, eleven months), a computer3 (-$641.67, eleven months), and a computer4 (-$595.83, eleven months).

- On November 30, 2016, the Proprietorship2 cancels the balances of the Computer account (-$2,700 - $1,400 - $1,300) and the Accumulated amortization: Computer account because these computers have used for two years.

- On November 30, 2016, the Proprietorship2 has completed all products of the Working-in-process inventory account. If the supplies and the all general parts have just been consumed, then the Proprietorship2 transfers the balance of the Cost of goods manufactured account to the Working-in-process inventory account. The Cost of goods manufactured account has three subaccounts of the "Supplies expenses", the "909876525-salary < Product department-salary < Salary expenses", and the "General parts expenses". Their balances are -$430, -$22,320, and -$158,650 (-$134,400 - $24,250) respectively. Here, the balance of the subaccount "909876525-salary < Product department-salary < Salary expenses" is the sum of the eight months' salary expenses because the Proprietorship2 will not produce any product and only do some maintenance of the equipment in December 2016. In addition, the balance of the subaccount "General parts expenses" will be divided to three parts which are used in three transaction sub-equations respectively. The three transaction sub-equations respectively are:

Working-in-process inventory (1): 5*1200 + Working-in-process inventory (1): 5.5*1200 + Working-in-process inventory (1): 6*1200 + Working-in-process inventory (1): 6.5*1200 + Working-in-process inventory (1): 7*1200 + Working-in-process inventory (1): 7.5*1200 + Working-in-process inventory (1): 4*1200 = Cost of goods manufactured (5): 430 + Cost of goods manufactured (5): 22320 + Cost of goods manufactured (5): 27050

Working-in-process inventory (1): 4.5*1200 + Working-in-process inventory (1): 5*1200 + Working-in-process inventory (1): 5.5*1200 + Working-in-process inventory (1): 6*1200 + Working-in-process inventory (1): 6.5*1200 + Working-in-process inventory (1): 8*1200 + Working-in-process inventory (1): 10*1000 + Working-in-process inventory (1): 12*1000 + Working-in-process inventory (1): 13*1000 = Cost of goods manufactured (5): 77600

Working-in-process inventory (1): 15*1000 + Working-in-process inventory (1): 13*1000 + Working-in-process inventory (1): 14*1000 + Working-in-process inventory (1): 7*800 + Working-in-process inventory (1): 8*800 = Cost of goods manufactured (5): 54000

- On November 30, 2016, the proprietorship2 transfers the balance of the Working-in-process inventory account to the Inventory account. The multi-subaccount names of the Inventory accounts and the five transaction sub-equations respectively are:
  Food411-P2-20161130-FO411-1200T < Food41 < Food4: 5*1200
  Food412-P2-20161130-FO412-1200T < Food41 < Food4: 5.5*1200
  Food421-P2-20161130-FO421-1200T < Food42 < Food4: 6*1200
  Food422-P2-20161130-FO422-1200T < Food42 < Food4: 6.5*1200
  Food43-P2-20161130-FO43-1200T < Food4: 7*1200
  Food44-P2-20161130-FO44-1200T < Food4: 7.5*1200
  Food511-P2-20161130-FO511-1200T < Food51 < Food5: 4*1200
  Food512-P2-20161130-FO512-1200T < Food51 < Food5: 4.5*1200

Food513-P2-20161130-FO513-1200T < Food51 < Food5: 5*1200

Food514-P2-20161130-FO514-1200T < Food51 < Food5: 5.5*1200

Food521-P2-20161130-FO521-1200T < Food52 < Food5: 6*1200

Food522-P2-20161130-FO522-1200T < Food52 < Food5: 6.5*1200

Food53-P2-20161130-FO53-1200T < Food5: 8*1200

Food611-P2-20161130-FO611-1000T < Food61 < Food6: 10*1000

Food612-P2-20161130-FO612-1000T < Food61 < Food6: 12*1000

Food613-P2-20161130-FO613-1000T < Food61 < Food6: 13*1000

Food614-P2-20161130-FO614-1000T < Food61 < Food6: 15*1000

Food621-P2-20161130-FO621-1000T < Food62 < Food6: 13*1000

Food622-P2-20161130-FO622-1000T < Food62 < Food6: 14*1000

Supplies1-P2-20161130-Supp1-800T: 7*800

Supplies2-P2-20161130-Supp2-800T: 8*800


Working-in-process inventory (1): -5*1200 + Working-in-process inventory (1): -5.5*1200 + Working-in-process inventory (1): -6*1200 + Working-in-process inventory (1): -6.5*1200 + Working-in-process inventory (1): -7*1200 + Inventory (1): 5*1200 + Inventory (1): 5.5*1200 + Inventory (1): 6*1200 + Inventory (1): 6.5*1200 + Inventory (1): 7*1200 = 0


Working-in-process inventory (1): -7.5*1200 + Working-in-process inventory (1): -4*1200 + Working-in-process inventory (1): -4.5*1200 + Working-in-process inventory (1): -5*1200 + Working-in-process inventory (1): -5.5*1200 + Inventory (1): 7.5*1200 + Inventory (1): 4*1200 + Inventory (1): 4.5*1200 + Inventory (1): 5*1200 + Inventory (1): 5.5*1200 = 0


Working-in-process inventory (1): -6*1200 + Working-in-process inventory (1): -6.5*1200 + Working-in-process inventory (1): -8*1200 + Working-in-process inventory (1): -10*1000 + Working-in-process inventory (1): -12*1000 + Inventory (1): 6*1200 + Inventory (1): 6.5*1200 + Inventory (1): 8*1200 +

Inventory (1): 10*1000 + Inventory (1): 12*1000 = 0

Working-in-process inventory (1): -13*1000 + Working-in-process inventory (1): -15*1000 + Working-in-process inventory (1): -13*1000 + Working-in-process inventory (1): -14*1000 + Inventory (1): 13*1000 + Inventory (1): 15*1000 + Inventory (1): 13*1000 + Inventory (1): 14*1000 = 0

Working-in-process inventory (1): -7*800 + Working-in-process inventory (1): -8*800 + Inventory (1): 7*800 + Inventory (1): 8*800 = 0

- On December 1, 2016, the Proprietorship2 purchases one Computer server1, one Computer1, and one Computer2 from the Company1 (phone number: 123456084) for cash -$5,000 and other $900 on credit. The multi-subaccount names of the Cash and the Inventory accounts and the two transaction sub-equation respectively are:

    88-654306-t-machinery < Cash payments for machinery < Operating activities

    Computer server1-C1-20160430-COMS1-045 < Computer server-inventory < Computer-inventory: 2800*1

    Computer1-C1-20160430-COM1-062 < Computer-inventory: 1600*1

    Computer2-C1-20160430-COM2-072 < Computer-inventory: 1500*1

    Cash (1): -5000 + Inventory (1): 2800*1 + Inventory (1): 1600*1 + Inventory (1): 1500*1 = Account payable (2): 900

    Inventory (1): -2800*1 + Inventory (1): -1600*1 + Inventory (1): -1500*1 + Computer (1): 2800 + Computer (1): 1600 + Computer (1): 1500 = 0

- On December 1, 2016, the Proprietorship2 purchases a used Computer2 $1,375 from the Tax Bureau (phone number: 123456087) on credit. The multi-subaccount name of the Inventory account is:

    Computer2-C1-201501008-COM2-066: 1375*1

- On December 2, 2016, the Proprietorship2 sells the Food612 $24*2 (cost: -$12*2) and the Food622 $28*1 (cost: -$14*1) to A10 (SIN: 909876510) for cash $76. The multi-subaccount names of the Cash and the Inventory accounts respectively are:

909876510-c-customers < Cash receipts from customers < Operating activities

Food612-P2-20151127-FO612-200T < Food61 < Food6: -12*2

Food622-P2-20151127-FO622-200T < Food62 < Food6: -14*1

- On December 8, 2016, the Proprietorship2 sells the Food43 $14*3 (cost: -$7*3), the Food44 $15*2 (cost: -$7.5*2), and the Food612 $24*2 (cost: -$12*2) to A1 (SIN: 909876501) for cash $120. The multi-subaccount names of the Cash and the Inventory accounts respectively are:

909876501-c-customers < Cash receipts from customers < Operating activities

Food43-P2-20151127-FO43-1000T < Food4: -7*3

Food44-P2-20151127-FO44-1000T < Food4: -7.5*2

Food612-P2-20151127-FO612-200T < Food61 < Food6: -12*2

- On December 15, 2016, the Proprietorship2 sells the Food613 $26*3 (cost: -$13*3) and the Food614 $30*1 (cost: -$15*1) to A24 (SIN: 909876524) for cash $108. The multi-subaccount names of the Cash and the Inventory accounts respectively are:

909876524-c-customers < Cash receipts from customers < Operating activities

Food613-P2-20151127-FO613-200T < Food61 < Food6: -13*3

Food614-P2-20151127-FO614-200T < Food61 < Food6: -15*1

- On December 17, 2016, the Proprietorship2 pays -$277.93 cash to A24 (SIN: 909876524) for the Travelling expenses -$169.93 and the Other expenses -$108.

- On December 17, 2016, the Proprietorship2 sells the Food611 $20*2 (cost: -$10*2) and the Food622 $28*1 (cost: -$14*1) to A22 (SIN: 909876522) for cash $68. The multi-subaccount names of the Cash and the Inventory accounts respectively are:

909876522-c-customers < Cash receipts from customers < Operating activities

Food611-P2-20151127-FO611-200T < Food61 < Food6: -10*2

Food622-P2-20151127-FO622-200T < Food62 < Food6: -14*1

- On December 18, 2016, the Proprietorship2 sells the Food611 $20*3 (cost: -$10*3) and the Food622 $28*3 (cost: -$14*3) to A18 (SIN: 909876518) for cash $144. The

multi-subaccount names of the Cash and the Inventory accounts respectively are:

909876518-c-customers < Cash receipts from customers < Operating activities

Food611-P2-20151127-FO611-200T < Food61 < Food6: -10*3

Food622-P2-20151127-FO622-200T < Food62 < Food6: -14*3

- On December 18, 2016, the Proprietorship2 sells the Food611 $20*3 (cost: -$10*3) and the Food622 $28*1 (cost: -$14*1) to A21 (SIN: 909876521) for cash $88. The multi-subaccount names of the Cash and the Inventory accounts respectively are:

909876521-c-customers < Cash receipts from customers < Operating activities

Food611-P2-20151127-FO611-200T < Food61 < Food6: -10*3

Food622-P2-20151127-FO622-200T < Food62 < Food6: -14*1

- On December 18, 2016, the Proprietorship2 sells the Food612 $24*3 (cost: -$12*3) and the Food613 $26*1 (cost: -$13*1) to A25 (SIN: 909876525) for cash $98. The multi-subaccount names of the Cash and the Inventory accounts respectively are:

909876525-c-customers < Cash receipts from customers < Operating activities

Food612-P2-20151127-FO612-200T < Food61 < Food6: -12*3

Food613-P2-20151127-FO613-200T < Food61 < Food6: -13*1

- On December 20, 2016, the Proprietorship2 sells the Food621 $26*3 (cost: -$13*3) and the Food622 $28*3 (cost: -$14*3) to A14 (SIN: 909876514) for cash $162. The multi-subaccount names of the Cash and the Inventory accounts respectively are:

909876514-c-customers < Cash receipts from customers < Operating activities

Food621-P2-20151127-FO621-200T < Food62 < Food6: -13*3

Food622-P2-20151127-FO622-200T < Food62 < Food6: -14*3

- On December 20, 2016, the Proprietorship2 pays -$249.51 cash to A25 (SIN: 909876525) for the Travelling expenses -$151.51 and the Other expenses -$98.

- On December 23, 2016, the Proprietorship2 receives $5,500 cash from the Company1 (phone number: 123456784) with the General ID 85 ($2,000) and the General ID 110 ($3,500). The multi-subaccount name of the Cash account is:

88-654306-c-customers < Cash receipts from customers < Operating activities

- On December 26, 2016, the Proprietorship2 sells the Food53 $16*3 (cost: -$8*3) and

the Food614 $30*2 (cost: -$15*2) to A7 (SIN: 909876507) for cash $108. The multi-subaccount names of the Cash and the Inventory accounts respectively are:

909876507-c-customers < Cash receipts from customers < Operating activities

Food53-P2-20151127-FO53-1000T < Food5: -8*3

Food614-P2-20151127-FO614-200T < Food61 < Food6: -15*2

- On December 29, 2016, the Proprietorship2 pays -$27,000 cash to the Company1 (phone number: 123456084) with the General ID 8 (-$8,000) and the General ID 165 (-$19,000). The multi-subaccount name of the Cash account is:

  88-654306-t-machinery < Cash payments for machinery < Operating activities

- On December 31, 2016, the Proprietorship2 receives $4,300 cash from the Proprietorship1 (phone number: 123456781) with the General ID 111 ($3,600) and the General ID 112 ($700). The multi-subaccount name of the Cash account is:

  88-654309-c-customers < Cash receipts from customers < Operating activities

- On December 31, 2016, the Proprietorship2 pays two employees' salary cash -$5,660.

- On the same day, the Proprietorship2 pays -$3,640 cash to the bond holders for the Bond interest expenses of the Bond71 (one-level subaccount "Bond71-interest"). The multi-subaccount names of the Cash account and the transaction sub-equations respectively are:

  909876501-t-bond interest < Cash payments to bond holders< Operating activities (909876502, 909876504, 909876507, 909876509, 909876511, 909876512, 909876516, 909876517, 909876518, 909876519, 909876520)

  Cash (1): -364 + Cash (1): -312 + Cash (1): -260 + Cash (1): -312 + Cash (1): -312 + Cash (1): -260 + Cash (1): -208 + Cash (1): -364 + Cash (1): -260 + Cash (1): -312 = Bond interest expenses (5): -2964

  Cash (1): -260 + Cash (1): -416 = Bond interest expenses (5): -676

- On the same day, the Proprietorship2 pays -$2,750 cash to the bond holders for the Bond interest expenses of the Bond72 (one-level subaccount "Bond72-interest").

The Cash's multi-subaccount names and the transaction sub-equations are:

909876504-t-bond interest < Cash payments to bond holders< Operating activities (909876505, 909876506, 909876508, 909876510, 909876513, 909876515, 909876516, 909876517, and 909876518)

Cash (1): -220 + Cash (1): -275 + Cash (1): -330 + Cash (1): -275 + Cash (1): -330 + Cash (1): -220 + Cash (1): -275 + Cash (1): -330 + Cash (1): -275 + Cash (1): -220 = Bond interest expenses (5): -2750

- On the same day, the Proprietorship2 receives cash $252 (Investment incomes) for investment interest of the Bond12 ($6,000) from the Business Bank1. The multi-subaccount name of the Cash account is:

  88-654304-c-investment income < Cash receipts from investments < Investing activities

- On the same day, the Proprietorship2 receives cash $463 (Investment incomes: $287 + $176) for investment interest of the Bond21 ($7,000) and the Bond22 ($4,000) from the Business Bank2. The multi-subaccount name of the Cash account is:

  88-654305-c-investment income < Cash receipts from investments < Investing activities

- On the same day, the Proprietorship2 receives cash $120 from the Business Bank2 for primary deposit interest (Deposit interest incomes). The multi-subaccount name of the Cash account is:

  88-654305-c-deposit interest income < Cash receipts from deposit interest < Financial activities

- On the same day, the Proprietorship2 records the Office supplies expenses -$180.53. It is consisted of two parts of the Supplies -$1.53 and the Inventory -$179 (-$7*13 - $8*11). The multi-subaccount names of the Inventory account respectively are:

  Supplies1-P2-20161130-Supp1-800T: -7*13

  Supplies2-P2-20161130-Supp2-800T: -8*11

- On the same day, the Proprietorship2 records the Vehicle's amortization expenses -

$14,966.67 (-$8,000 - $6,966.67 - $2,533.33) one year (5 years, straight line).

- On the same day, the Proprietorship2 records the Computer's amortization expenses -$245.84 (one months, 2 years, straight line). They are a computer server1 (-$116.67), a computer1 (-$66.67), a computer2 (-$62.5), and a used computer2 (-$57.29).

- On December 31, 2016, the Proprietorship2 records the Tax expenses -$22,236.37 and the Tax payable $22,236.37. The multi-subaccount name forms of the Tax expenses and the Tax payable accounts all are the 'n'.

So far, I have entered all inventory purchased or sold by other members in the Proprietorship2 in the fiscal year 2016.

## 3.10.2 Brief Summary of the Proprietorship2

The Figure 3.10-2 on this page and next pages shows all inventories purchased or sold by other members in the Proprietorship2 by using of SQL Server query.

SQLQuery1.sql - LIU...SS.dcj200 (sa (51))*  ×

```
use dcj200
select * from InventoryByMembers where Recorder='88-654310' and TransDate between '2016-01-01' and '2016-12-31'
order by TransDate
```

100 %  ▾

Results  Messages

| | IDM | Amount | Symbol | MultiSubaccount | Recorder | TransDate | Unit |
|---|---|---|---|---|---|---|---|
| 1 | 88-654308 | -1000.00 | t | Inven121-C3-20150922-In121-20000T < Inven12 < Inven1 | 88-654310 | 2016-01-02 | -1250 |
| 2 | 88-654308 | -5000.00 | t | Inven51-C3-20150922-In51-1000T < Inven5 | 88-654310 | 2016-01-02 | -500 |
| 3 | 88-654308 | -12500.00 | t | Inven52-C3-20150922-In52-500T < Inven5 | 88-654310 | 2016-01-02 | -250 |
| 4 | 88-654308 | -12500.00 | t | Inven531-C3-20150922-In531-1000T < Inven53 < Inven5 | 88-654310 | 2016-01-02 | -500 |
| 5 | 88-654308 | -17500.00 | t | Inven532-C3-20150922-In532-1000T < Inven53 < Inven5 | 88-654310 | 2016-01-02 | -500 |
| 6 | 88-654308 | -6000.00 | t | Inven541-C3-20150922-In541-1000T < Inven54 < Inven5 | 88-654310 | 2016-01-02 | -500 |
| 7 | 88-654308 | -7500.00 | t | Inven542-C3-20150922-In542-1000T < Inven54 < Inven5 | 88-654310 | 2016-01-02 | -500 |
| 8 | 88-654308 | -3250.00 | t | Inven611-C3-20151003-In611-1300T < Inven61 < Inven6 | 88-654310 | 2016-01-02 | -500 |
| 9 | 88-654308 | -6250.00 | t | Inven612-C3-20151003-In612-1100T < Inven61 < Inven6 | 88-654310 | 2016-01-02 | -500 |
| 10 | 88-654308 | -9000.00 | t | Inven621-C3-20151003-In621-900T < Inven62 < Inven6 | 88-654310 | 2016-01-02 | -500 |
| 11 | 88-654308 | -8000.00 | t | Inven63-C3-20151003-In63-1000T < Inven6 | 88-654310 | 2016-01-02 | -500 |
| 12 | 88-654308 | -10800.00 | t | Inven711-C3-20151003-In711-500T < Inven71 < Inven7 | 88-654310 | 2016-01-02 | -300 |
| 13 | 88-654308 | -1550.00 | t | Inven712-C3-20151003-In712-100T < Inven71 < Inven7 | 88-654310 | 2016-01-02 | -50 |
| 14 | 88-654308 | -8800.00 | t | Inven721-C3-20151003-In721-744T < Inven72 < Inven7 | 88-654310 | 2016-01-02 | -400 |
| 15 | 88-654308 | -6000.00 | t | Inven722-C3-20151003-In722-600T < Inven72 < Inven7 | 88-654310 | 2016-01-02 | -300 |
| 16 | 88-654308 | -5400.00 | t | Inven731-C3-20151003-In731-600T < Inven73 < Inven7 | 88-654310 | 2016-01-02 | -300 |
| 17 | 88-654308 | -8000.00 | t | Inven732-C3-20151003-In732-1000T < Inven73 < Inven7 | 88-654310 | 2016-01-02 | -500 |
| 18 | 88-654308 | -7500.00 | t | Inven811-C3-20151003-In811-600T < Inven81 < Inven8 | 88-654310 | 2016-01-02 | -300 |
| 19 | 88-654308 | -7200.00 | t | Inven812-C3-20151003-In812-600T < Inven81 < Inven8 | 88-654310 | 2016-01-02 | -300 |
| 20 | 88-654308 | -6900.00 | t | Inven813-C3-20151003-In813-600T < Inven81 < Inven8 | 88-654310 | 2016-01-02 | -300 |
| 21 | 88-654308 | -6000.00 | t | Inven82-C3-20151003-In82-600T < Inven8 | 88-654310 | 2016-01-02 | -300 |
| 22 | 88-654308 | -5400.00 | t | Inven831-C3-20151003-In831-600T < Inven83 < Inven8 | 88-654310 | 2016-01-02 | -300 |
| 23 | 88-654308 | -6400.00 | t | Inven832-C3-20151003-In832-800T < Inven83 < Inven8 | 88-654310 | 2016-01-02 | -400 |
| 24 | 88-654306 | 280.00 | c | Supplies1-P2-20150920-SUP1-200T | 88-654310 | 2016-01-02 | 40 |
| 25 | 88-654306 | 320.00 | c | Supplies2-P2-20150920-SUP2-200T | 88-654310 | 2016-01-02 | 40 |
| 26 | 88-654304 | 49.00 | c | Supplies1-P2-20150920-SUP1-200T | 88-654310 | 2016-01-02 | 7 |
| 27 | 88-654304 | 32.00 | c | Supplies2-P2-20150920-SUP2-200T | 88-654310 | 2016-01-02 | 4 |
| 28 | 88-654305 | 21.00 | c | Supplies1-P2-20150920-SUP1-200T | 88-654310 | 2016-01-02 | 3 |
| 29 | 88-654305 | 72.00 | c | Supplies2-P2-20150920-SUP2-200T | 88-654310 | 2016-01-02 | 9 |
| 30 | 88-654308 | 168.00 | c | Supplies1-P2-20150920-SUP1-200T | 88-654310 | 2016-01-02 | 24 |

| | IDM | Amount | Symbol | MultiSubaccount | Recorder | TransDate | Unit |
|---|---|---|---|---|---|---|---|
| 31 | 88-654308 | 320.00 | c | Supplies2-P2-20150920-SUP2-200T | 88-654310 | 2016-01-02 | 40 |
| 32 | 88-654307 | 280.00 | c | Supplies1-P2-20150920-SUP1-200T | 88-654310 | 2016-01-02 | 40 |
| 33 | 88-654307 | 160.00 | c | Supplies2-P2-20150920-SUP2-200T | 88-654310 | 2016-01-02 | 20 |
| 34 | 88-654309 | 245.00 | c | Supplies1-P2-20150920-SUP1-200T | 88-654310 | 2016-01-02 | 35 |
| 35 | 88-654309 | 280.00 | c | Supplies2-P2-20150920-SUP2-200T | 88-654310 | 2016-01-02 | 35 |
| 36 | 88-654310 | 1000.00 | f | Inven31 < Inven3 | 88-654310 | 2016-01-03 | 100 |
| 37 | 88-654310 | 5000.00 | f | Inven32 < Inven3 | 88-654310 | 2016-01-03 | 100 |
| 38 | 88-654310 | 2000.00 | f | Inven331 < Inven33 < Inven3 | 88-654310 | 2016-01-03 | 100 |
| 39 | 88-654310 | 4500.00 | f | Inven332 < Inven33 < Inven3 | 88-654310 | 2016-01-03 | 100 |
| 40 | 88-654310 | 1000.00 | f | HGFCVB parts < QASXC parts < Inven3 | 88-654310 | 2016-01-03 | 100 |
| 41 | 88-654310 | 2000.00 | f | PPGHUP parts < ASDUP parts < Inven3 | 88-654310 | 2016-01-03 | 100 |
| 42 | 88-654310 | 300.00 | f | Inven121-C3-20150922-In121-20000T < Inven12 < Inven1 | 88-654310 | 2016-01-03 | 375 |
| 43 | 88-654310 | 1000.00 | f | Inven51-C3-20150922-In51-1000T < Inven5 | 88-654310 | 2016-01-03 | 100 |
| 44 | 88-654310 | 2500.00 | f | Inven52-C3-20150922-In52-500T < Inven5 | 88-654310 | 2016-01-03 | 50 |
| 45 | 88-654310 | 2500.00 | f | Inven531-C3-20150922-In531-1000T < Inven53 < Inven5 | 88-654310 | 2016-01-03 | 100 |
| 46 | 88-654310 | 3500.00 | f | Inven532-C3-20150922-In532-1000T < Inven53 < Inven5 | 88-654310 | 2016-01-03 | 100 |
| 47 | 88-654310 | 1200.00 | f | Inven541-C3-20150922-In541-1000T < Inven54 < Inven5 | 88-654310 | 2016-01-03 | 100 |
| 48 | 88-654310 | 1500.00 | f | Inven542-C3-20150922-In542-1000T < Inven54 < Inven5 | 88-654310 | 2016-01-03 | 100 |
| 49 | 88-654310 | 910.00 | f | Inven611-C3-20151003-In611-1300T < Inven61 < Inven6 | 88-654310 | 2016-01-03 | 140 |
| 50 | 88-654310 | 1250.00 | f | Inven612-C3-20151003-In612-1100T < Inven61 < Inven6 | 88-654310 | 2016-01-03 | 100 |
| 51 | 88-654310 | 1800.00 | f | Inven621-C3-20151003-In621-900T < Inven62 < Inven6 | 88-654310 | 2016-01-03 | 100 |
| 52 | 88-654310 | 1600.00 | f | Inven63-C3-20151003-In63-1000T < Inven6 | 88-654310 | 2016-01-03 | 100 |
| 53 | 88-654310 | 2160.00 | f | Inven711-C3-20151003-In711-500T < Inven71 < Inven7 | 88-654310 | 2016-01-03 | 60 |
| 54 | 88-654310 | 310.00 | f | Inven712-C3-20151003-In712-100T < Inven71 < Inven7 | 88-654310 | 2016-01-03 | 10 |
| 55 | 88-654310 | 1760.00 | f | Inven721-C3-20151003-In721-744T < Inven72 < Inven7 | 88-654310 | 2016-01-03 | 80 |
| 56 | 88-654310 | 1200.00 | f | Inven722-C3-20151003-In722-600T < Inven72 < Inven7 | 88-654310 | 2016-01-03 | 60 |
| 57 | 88-654310 | 1080.00 | f | Inven731-C3-20151003-In731-600T < Inven73 < Inven7 | 88-654310 | 2016-01-03 | 60 |
| 58 | 88-654310 | 1600.00 | f | Inven732-C3-20151003-In732-1000T < Inven73 < Inven7 | 88-654310 | 2016-01-03 | 100 |
| 59 | 88-654310 | 1500.00 | f | Inven811-C3-20151003-In811-600T < Inven81 < Inven8 | 88-654310 | 2016-01-03 | 60 |
| 60 | 88-654310 | 1440.00 | f | Inven812-C3-20151003-In812-600T < Inven81 < Inven8 | 88-654310 | 2016-01-03 | 60 |
| 61 | 88-654310 | 1380.00 | f | Inven813-C3-20151003-In813-600T < Inven81 < Inven8 | 88-654310 | 2016-01-03 | 60 |
| 62 | 88-654310 | 1200.00 | f | Inven82-C3-20151003-In82-600T < Inven8 | 88-654310 | 2016-01-03 | 60 |
| 63 | 88-654310 | 1080.00 | f | Inven831-C3-20151003-In831-600T < Inven83 < Inven8 | 88-654310 | 2016-01-03 | 60 |
| 64 | 88-654310 | 1280.00 | f | Inven832-C3-20151003-In832-800T < Inven83 < Inven8 | 88-654310 | 2016-01-03 | 80 |
| 65 | 88-654308 | 900.00 | c | Inven411-P2-20151127-In411-1000T < Inven41 < Inven4 | 88-654310 | 2016-01-03 | 300 |
| 66 | 88-654308 | 3330.00 | c | Inven412-P2-20151127-In412-1000T < Inven41 < Inven4 | 88-654310 | 2016-01-03 | 300 |
| 67 | 88-654308 | 3600.00 | c | TTTCU parts-P2-20151127-TTP-1000T < TTT parts < Inven4 | 88-654310 | 2016-01-03 | 300 |
| 68 | 88-654308 | 3600.00 | c | RRRHJK parts-P2-20151127-RRP-1000T < Inven4 | 88-654310 | 2016-01-03 | 300 |
| 69 | 88-654310 | 140.00 | f | Supplies1-P2-20150920-SUP1-200T | 88-654310 | 2016-01-03 | 20 |
| 70 | 88-654310 | 160.00 | f | Supplies2-P2-20150920-SUP2-200T | 88-654310 | 2016-01-03 | 20 |
| 71 | 909876524 | 20.00 | c | Food513-P2-20151127-FO513-1000T < Food51 < Food5 | 88-654310 | 2016-01-12 | 4 |
| 72 | 909876524 | 39.00 | c | Food613-P2-20151127-FO613-200T < Food61 < Food6 | 88-654310 | 2016-01-12 | 3 |
| 73 | 909876513 | 44.00 | c | Food514-P2-20151127-FO514-1000T < Food51 < Food5 | 88-654310 | 2016-01-13 | 8 |
| 74 | 909876513 | 60.00 | c | Food614-P2-20151127-FO614-200T < Food61 < Food6 | 88-654310 | 2016-01-13 | 4 |
| 75 | 909876511 | 13.00 | c | Food621-P2-20151127-FO621-200T < Food62 < Food6 | 88-654310 | 2016-01-15 | 1 |
| 76 | 909876511 | 14.00 | c | Food622-P2-20151127-FO622-200T < Food62 < Food6 | 88-654310 | 2016-01-15 | 1 |
| 77 | 909876519 | 22.00 | c | Food514-P2-20151127-FO514-1000T < Food51 < Food5 | 88-654310 | 2016-01-16 | 4 |
| 78 | 909876519 | 39.00 | c | Food613-P2-20151127-FO613-200T < Food61 < Food6 | 88-654310 | 2016-01-16 | 3 |
| 79 | 909876522 | 11.00 | c | Food514-P2-20151127-FO514-1000T < Food51 < Food5 | 88-654310 | 2016-01-16 | 2 |
| 80 | 909876522 | 13.00 | c | Food613-P2-20151127-FO613-200T < Food61 < Food6 | 88-654310 | 2016-01-16 | 1 |
| 81 | 909876501 | 6.50 | c | Food422-P2-20151127-FO422-1000T < Food42 < Food4 | 88-654310 | 2016-01-18 | 1 |
| 82 | 909876501 | 13.00 | c | Food613-P2-20151127-FO613-200T < Food61 < Food6 | 88-654310 | 2016-01-18 | 1 |
| 83 | 909876507 | 26.00 | c | Food613-P2-20151127-FO613-200T < Food61 < Food6 | 88-654310 | 2016-01-20 | 2 |
| 84 | 909876507 | 15.00 | c | Food614-P2-20151127-FO614-200T < Food61 < Food6 | 88-654310 | 2016-01-20 | 1 |
| 85 | 909876512 | 32.00 | c | Food53-P2-20151127-FO53-1000T < Food5 | 88-654310 | 2016-01-22 | 4 |
| 86 | 909876512 | 28.00 | c | Food622-P2-20151127-FO622-200T < Food62 < Food6 | 88-654310 | 2016-01-22 | 2 |
| 87 | 909876514 | 12.00 | c | Food612-P2-20151127-FO612-200T < Food61 < Food6 | 88-654310 | 2016-01-31 | 1 |
| 88 | 909876501 | 650.00 | c | Food411-P2-20151127-FO411-1000T < Food41 < Food4 | 88-654310 | 2016-01-31 | 130 |
| 89 | 909876501 | 715.00 | c | Food412-P2-20151127-FO412-1000T < Food41 < Food4 | 88-654310 | 2016-01-31 | 130 |
| 90 | 909876501 | 780.00 | c | Food421-P2-20151127-FO421-1000T < Food42 < Food4 | 88-654310 | 2016-01-31 | 130 |
| 91 | 909876501 | 845.00 | c | Food422-P2-20151127-FO422-1000T < Food42 < Food4 | 88-654310 | 2016-01-31 | 130 |
| 92 | 909876501 | 910.00 | c | Food43-P2-20151127-FO43-1000T < Food4 | 88-654310 | 2016-01-31 | 130 |
| 93 | 909876501 | 975.00 | c | Food44-P2-20151127-FO44-1000T < Food4 | 88-654310 | 2016-01-31 | 130 |
| 94 | 909876501 | 520.00 | c | Food511-P2-20151127-FO511-1000T < Food51 < Food5 | 88-654310 | 2016-01-31 | 130 |
| 95 | 909876514 | 650.00 | c | Food411-P2-20151127-FO411-1000T < Food41 < Food4 | 88-654310 | 2016-01-31 | 130 |
| 96 | 909876514 | 715.00 | c | Food412-P2-20151127-FO412-1000T < Food41 < Food4 | 88-654310 | 2016-01-31 | 130 |

| | IDM | Amount | Symbol | MultiSubaccount | Recorder | TransDate | Unit |
|---|---|---|---|---|---|---|---|
| 97 | 909876514 | 780.00 | c | Food421-P2-20151127-FO421-1000T < Food42 < Food4 | 88-654310 | 2016-01-31 | 130 |
| 98 | 909876514 | 845.00 | c | Food422-P2-20151127-FO422-1000T < Food42 < Food4 | 88-654310 | 2016-01-31 | 130 |
| 99 | 909876514 | 910.00 | c | Food43-P2-20151127-FO43-1000T < Food4 | 88-654310 | 2016-01-31 | 130 |
| 100 | 909876514 | 975.00 | c | Food44-P2-20151127-FO44-1000T < Food4 | 88-654310 | 2016-01-31 | 130 |
| 101 | 909876514 | 585.00 | c | Food512-P2-20151127-FO512-1000T < Food51 < Food5 | 88-654310 | 2016-01-31 | 130 |
| 102 | 909876515 | 650.00 | c | Food411-P2-20151127-FO411-1000T < Food41 < Food4 | 88-654310 | 2016-01-31 | 130 |
| 103 | 909876515 | 715.00 | c | Food412-P2-20151127-FO412-1000T < Food41 < Food4 | 88-654310 | 2016-01-31 | 130 |
| 104 | 909876515 | 780.00 | c | Food421-P2-20151127-FO421-1000T < Food42 < Food4 | 88-654310 | 2016-01-31 | 130 |
| 105 | 909876515 | 845.00 | c | Food422-P2-20151127-FO422-1000T < Food42 < Food4 | 88-654310 | 2016-01-31 | 130 |
| 106 | 909876515 | 910.00 | c | Food43-P2-20151127-FO43-1000T < Food4 | 88-654310 | 2016-01-31 | 130 |
| 107 | 909876515 | 975.00 | c | Food44-P2-20151127-FO44-1000T < Food4 | 88-654310 | 2016-01-31 | 130 |
| 108 | 909876515 | 650.00 | c | Food513-P2-20151127-FO513-1000T < Food51 < Food5 | 88-654310 | 2016-01-31 | 130 |
| 109 | 909876516 | 650.00 | c | Food411-P2-20151127-FO411-1000T < Food41 < Food4 | 88-654310 | 2016-01-31 | 130 |
| 110 | 909876516 | 715.00 | c | Food412-P2-20151127-FO412-1000T < Food41 < Food4 | 88-654310 | 2016-01-31 | 130 |
| 111 | 909876516 | 780.00 | c | Food421-P2-20151127-FO421-1000T < Food42 < Food4 | 88-654310 | 2016-01-31 | 130 |
| 112 | 909876516 | 845.00 | c | Food422-P2-20151127-FO422-1000T < Food42 < Food4 | 88-654310 | 2016-01-31 | 130 |
| 113 | 909876516 | 910.00 | c | Food43-P2-20151127-FO43-1000T < Food4 | 88-654310 | 2016-01-31 | 130 |
| 114 | 909876516 | 975.00 | c | Food44-P2-20151127-FO44-1000T < Food4 | 88-654310 | 2016-01-31 | 130 |
| 115 | 909876516 | 715.00 | c | Food514-P2-20151127-FO514-1000T < Food51 < Food5 | 88-654310 | 2016-01-31 | 130 |
| 116 | 909876517 | 520.00 | c | Food511-P2-20151127-FO511-1000T < Food51 < Food5 | 88-654310 | 2016-01-31 | 130 |
| 117 | 909876517 | 585.00 | c | Food512-P2-20151127-FO512-1000T < Food51 < Food5 | 88-654310 | 2016-01-31 | 130 |
| 118 | 909876517 | 650.00 | c | Food513-P2-20151127-FO513-1000T < Food51 < Food5 | 88-654310 | 2016-01-31 | 130 |
| 119 | 909876517 | 715.00 | c | Food514-P2-20151127-FO514-1000T < Food51 < Food5 | 88-654310 | 2016-01-31 | 130 |
| 120 | 909876517 | 780.00 | c | Food521-P2-20151127-FO521-1000T < Food52 < Food5 | 88-654310 | 2016-01-31 | 130 |
| 121 | 909876517 | 845.00 | c | Food522-P2-20151127-FO522-1000T < Food52 < Food5 | 88-654310 | 2016-01-31 | 130 |
| 122 | 909876517 | 1040.00 | c | Food53-P2-20151127-FO53-1000T < Food5 | 88-654310 | 2016-01-31 | 130 |
| 123 | 909876518 | 520.00 | c | Food511-P2-20151127-FO511-1000T < Food51 < Food5 | 88-654310 | 2016-01-31 | 130 |
| 124 | 909876518 | 585.00 | c | Food512-P2-20151127-FO512-1000T < Food51 < Food5 | 88-654310 | 2016-01-31 | 130 |
| 125 | 909876518 | 650.00 | c | Food513-P2-20151127-FO513-1000T < Food51 < Food5 | 88-654310 | 2016-01-31 | 130 |
| 126 | 909876518 | 715.00 | c | Food514-P2-20151127-FO514-1000T < Food51 < Food5 | 88-654310 | 2016-01-31 | 130 |
| 127 | 909876518 | 780.00 | c | Food521-P2-20151127-FO521-1000T < Food52 < Food5 | 88-654310 | 2016-01-31 | 130 |
| 128 | 909876518 | 845.00 | c | Food522-P2-20151127-FO522-1000T < Food52 < Food5 | 88-654310 | 2016-01-31 | 130 |
| 129 | 909876518 | 1820.00 | c | Food622-P2-20151127-FO622-200T < Food62 < Food6 | 88-654310 | 2016-01-31 | 130 |
| 130 | 909876519 | 520.00 | c | Food511-P2-20151127-FO511-1000T < Food51 < Food5 | 88-654310 | 2016-01-31 | 130 |
| 131 | 909876519 | 585.00 | c | Food512-P2-20151127-FO512-1000T < Food51 < Food5 | 88-654310 | 2016-01-31 | 130 |
| 132 | 909876519 | 650.00 | c | Food513-P2-20151127-FO513-1000T < Food51 < Food5 | 88-654310 | 2016-01-31 | 130 |
| 133 | 909876519 | 715.00 | c | Food514-P2-20151127-FO514-1000T < Food51 < Food5 | 88-654310 | 2016-01-31 | 130 |
| 134 | 909876519 | 780.00 | c | Food521-P2-20151127-FO521-1000T < Food52 < Food5 | 88-654310 | 2016-01-31 | 130 |
| 135 | 909876519 | 845.00 | c | Food522-P2-20151127-FO522-1000T < Food52 < Food5 | 88-654310 | 2016-01-31 | 130 |
| 136 | 909876519 | 1690.00 | c | Food621-P2-20151127-FO621-200T < Food62 < Food6 | 88-654310 | 2016-01-31 | 130 |
| 137 | 909876520 | 520.00 | c | Food511-P2-20151127-FO511-1000T < Food51 < Food5 | 88-654310 | 2016-01-31 | 130 |
| 138 | 909876520 | 585.00 | c | Food512-P2-20151127-FO512-1000T < Food51 < Food5 | 88-654310 | 2016-01-31 | 130 |
| 139 | 909876520 | 650.00 | c | Food513-P2-20151127-FO513-1000T < Food51 < Food5 | 88-654310 | 2016-01-31 | 130 |
| 140 | 909876520 | 715.00 | c | Food514-P2-20151127-FO514-1000T < Food51 < Food5 | 88-654310 | 2016-01-31 | 130 |
| 141 | 909876520 | 780.00 | c | Food521-P2-20151127-FO521-1000T < Food52 < Food5 | 88-654310 | 2016-01-31 | 130 |
| 142 | 909876520 | 845.00 | c | Food522-P2-20151127-FO522-1000T < Food52 < Food5 | 88-654310 | 2016-01-31 | 130 |
| 143 | 909876520 | 1950.00 | c | Food614-P2-20151127-FO614-200T < Food61 < Food6 | 88-654310 | 2016-01-31 | 130 |
| 144 | 909876521 | 650.00 | c | Food411-P2-20151127-FO411-1000T < Food41 < Food4 | 88-654310 | 2016-01-31 | 130 |
| 145 | 909876521 | 715.00 | c | Food412-P2-20151127-FO412-1000T < Food41 < Food4 | 88-654310 | 2016-01-31 | 130 |
| 146 | 909876521 | 780.00 | c | Food421-P2-20151127-FO421-1000T < Food42 < Food4 | 88-654310 | 2016-01-31 | 130 |
| 147 | 909876521 | 845.00 | c | Food422-P2-20151127-FO422-1000T < Food42 < Food4 | 88-654310 | 2016-01-31 | 130 |
| 148 | 909876521 | 910.00 | c | Food43-P2-20151127-FO43-1000T < Food4 | 88-654310 | 2016-01-31 | 130 |
| 149 | 909876521 | 975.00 | c | Food44-P2-20151127-FO44-1000T < Food4 | 88-654310 | 2016-01-31 | 130 |
| 150 | 909876521 | 1560.00 | c | Food612-P2-20151127-FO612-200T < Food61 < Food6 | 88-654310 | 2016-01-31 | 130 |
| 151 | 909876522 | 520.00 | c | Food511-P2-20151127-FO511-1000T < Food51 < Food5 | 88-654310 | 2016-01-31 | 130 |
| 152 | 909876522 | 585.00 | c | Food512-P2-20151127-FO512-1000T < Food51 < Food5 | 88-654310 | 2016-01-31 | 130 |
| 153 | 909876522 | 650.00 | c | Food513-P2-20151127-FO513-1000T < Food51 < Food5 | 88-654310 | 2016-01-31 | 130 |
| 154 | 909876522 | 715.00 | c | Food514-P2-20151127-FO514-1000T < Food51 < Food5 | 88-654310 | 2016-01-31 | 130 |
| 155 | 909876522 | 780.00 | c | Food521-P2-20151127-FO521-1000T < Food52 < Food5 | 88-654310 | 2016-01-31 | 130 |
| 156 | 909876522 | 845.00 | c | Food522-P2-20151127-FO522-1000T < Food52 < Food5 | 88-654310 | 2016-01-31 | 130 |
| 157 | 909876522 | 1300.00 | c | Food611-P2-20151127-FO611-200T < Food61 < Food6 | 88-654310 | 2016-01-31 | 130 |
| 158 | 909876523 | 650.00 | c | Food411-P2-20151127-FO411-1000T < Food41 < Food4 | 88-654310 | 2016-01-31 | 130 |
| 159 | 909876523 | 715.00 | c | Food412-P2-20151127-FO412-1000T < Food41 < Food4 | 88-654310 | 2016-01-31 | 130 |
| 160 | 909876523 | 780.00 | c | Food421-P2-20151127-FO421-1000T < Food42 < Food4 | 88-654310 | 2016-01-31 | 130 |
| 161 | 909876523 | 480.00 | c | Food44-P2-20151127-FO44-1000T < Food4 | 88-654310 | 2016-01-31 | 64 |
| 162 | 909876523 | 40.00 | c | Food511-P2-20151127-FO511-1000T < Food51 < Food5 | 88-654310 | 2016-01-31 | 10 |

| | IDM | Amount | Symbol | MultiSubaccount | Recorder | TransDate | Unit |
|---|---|---|---|---|---|---|---|
| 163 | 909876523 | 780.00 | c | Food521-P2-20151127-FO521-1000T < Food52 < Food5 | 88-654310 | 2016-01-31 | 130 |
| 164 | 909876523 | 1040.00 | c | Food53-P2-20151127-FO53-1000T < Food5 | 88-654310 | 2016-01-31 | 130 |
| 165 | 909876523 | 1690.00 | c | Food613-P2-20151127-FO613-200T < Food61 < Food6 | 88-654310 | 2016-01-31 | 130 |
| 166 | 909876524 | 910.00 | c | Food43-P2-20151127-FO43-1000T < Food4 | 88-654310 | 2016-01-31 | 130 |
| 167 | 909876524 | 585.00 | c | Food44-P2-20151127-FO44-1000T < Food4 | 88-654310 | 2016-01-31 | 78 |
| 168 | 909876524 | 520.00 | c | Food511-P2-20151127-FO511-1000T < Food51 < Food5 | 88-654310 | 2016-01-31 | 130 |
| 169 | 909876524 | 650.00 | c | Food513-P2-20151127-FO513-1000T < Food51 < Food5 | 88-654310 | 2016-01-31 | 130 |
| 170 | 909876524 | 715.00 | c | Food514-P2-20151127-FO514-1000T < Food51 < Food5 | 88-654310 | 2016-01-31 | 130 |
| 171 | 909876524 | 780.00 | c | Food521-P2-20151127-FO521-1000T < Food52 < Food5 | 88-654310 | 2016-01-31 | 130 |
| 172 | 909876524 | 845.00 | c | Food522-P2-20151127-FO522-1000T < Food52 < Food5 | 88-654310 | 2016-01-31 | 130 |
| 173 | 909876525 | 650.00 | c | Food411-P2-20151127-FO411-1000T < Food41 < Food4 | 88-654310 | 2016-01-31 | 130 |
| 174 | 909876525 | 715.00 | c | Food412-P2-20151127-FO412-1000T < Food41 < Food4 | 88-654310 | 2016-01-31 | 130 |
| 175 | 909876525 | 780.00 | c | Food421-P2-20151127-FO421-1000T < Food42 < Food4 | 88-654310 | 2016-01-31 | 130 |
| 176 | 909876525 | 845.00 | c | Food422-P2-20151127-FO422-1000T < Food42 < Food4 | 88-654310 | 2016-01-31 | 130 |
| 177 | 909876525 | 585.00 | c | Food512-P2-20151127-FO512-1000T < Food51 < Food5 | 88-654310 | 2016-01-31 | 130 |
| 178 | 909876525 | 1560.00 | c | Food53-P2-20151127-FO53-1000T < Food5 | 88-654310 | 2016-01-31 | 195 |
| 179 | 88-654306 | -38000.00 | t | Car3-C1-20150925-C3-029 < Car-inventory < Vehicle-inventory | 88-654310 | 2016-02-01 | -1 |
| 180 | 88-654310 | 38000.00 | e | Car3-C1-20150925-C3-029 < Car-inventory < Vehicle-inventory | 88-654310 | 2016-02-01 | 1 |
| 181 | 909876512 | 30.00 | c | Food611-P2-20151127-FO611-200T < Food61 < Food6 | 88-654310 | 2016-02-06 | 3 |
| 182 | 909876512 | 28.00 | c | Food622-P2-20151127-FO622-200T < Food62 < Food6 | 88-654310 | 2016-02-06 | 2 |
| 183 | 909876516 | 80.00 | c | Food53-P2-20151127-FO53-1000T < Food5 | 88-654310 | 2016-02-17 | 10 |
| 184 | 909876516 | 75.00 | c | Food614-P2-20151127-FO614-200T < Food61 < Food6 | 88-654310 | 2016-02-17 | 5 |
| 185 | 909876509 | 30.00 | c | Food611-P2-20151127-FO611-200T < Food61 < Food6 | 88-654310 | 2016-02-19 | 3 |
| 186 | 909876509 | 26.00 | c | Food621-P2-20151127-FO621-200T < Food62 < Food6 | 88-654310 | 2016-02-19 | 2 |
| 187 | 909876508 | 20.00 | c | Food611-P2-20151127-FO611-200T < Food61 < Food6 | 88-654310 | 2016-02-22 | 2 |
| 188 | 909876508 | 28.00 | c | Food622-P2-20151127-FO622-200T < Food62 < Food6 | 88-654310 | 2016-02-22 | 2 |
| 189 | 909876524 | 16.00 | c | Food53-P2-20151127-FO53-1000T < Food5 | 88-654310 | 2016-02-23 | 2 |
| 190 | 909876524 | 15.00 | c | Food614-P2-20151127-FO614-200T < Food61 < Food6 | 88-654310 | 2016-02-23 | 1 |
| 191 | 909876512 | 24.00 | c | Food521-P2-20151127-FO521-1000T < Food52 < Food5 | 88-654310 | 2016-03-07 | 4 |
| 192 | 909876512 | 26.00 | c | Food621-P2-20151127-FO621-200T < Food62 < Food6 | 88-654310 | 2016-03-07 | 2 |
| 193 | 909876509 | 24.00 | c | Food53-P2-20151127-FO53-1000T < Food5 | 88-654310 | 2016-03-18 | 3 |
| 194 | 909876509 | 28.00 | c | Food622-P2-20151127-FO622-200T < Food62 < Food6 | 88-654310 | 2016-03-18 | 2 |
| 195 | 909876513 | 75.00 | c | Food44-P2-20151127-FO44-1000T < Food4 | 88-654310 | 2016-03-20 | 10 |
| 196 | 909876513 | 70.00 | c | Food622-P2-20151127-FO622-200T < Food62 < Food6 | 88-654310 | 2016-03-20 | 5 |
| 197 | 909876516 | 37.50 | c | Food44-P2-20151127-FO44-1000T < Food4 | 88-654310 | 2016-03-20 | 5 |
| 198 | 909876516 | 28.00 | c | Food622-P2-20151127-FO622-200T < Food62 < Food6 | 88-654310 | 2016-03-20 | 2 |
| 199 | 909876519 | 22.50 | c | Food44-P2-20151127-FO44-1000T < Food4 | 88-654310 | 2016-03-21 | 3 |
| 200 | 909876519 | 14.00 | c | Food622-P2-20151127-FO622-200T < Food62 < Food6 | 88-654310 | 2016-03-21 | 1 |
| 201 | 909876522 | 15.00 | c | Food44-P2-20151127-FO44-1000T < Food4 | 88-654310 | 2016-03-21 | 2 |
| 202 | 909876522 | 14.00 | c | Food622-P2-20151127-FO622-200T < Food62 < Food6 | 88-654310 | 2016-03-21 | 1 |
| 203 | 909876507 | 20.00 | c | Food611-P2-20151127-FO611-200T < Food61 < Food6 | 88-654310 | 2016-03-22 | 2 |
| 204 | 909876507 | 28.00 | c | Food622-P2-20151127-FO622-200T < Food62 < Food6 | 88-654310 | 2016-03-22 | 2 |
| 205 | 909876517 | 19.50 | c | Food522-P2-20151127-FO522-1000T < Food52 < Food5 | 88-654310 | 2016-03-24 | 3 |
| 206 | 909876517 | 24.00 | c | Food612-P2-20151127-FO612-200T < Food61 < Food6 | 88-654310 | 2016-03-24 | 2 |
| 207 | 909876525 | 14.00 | c | Food43-P2-20151127-FO43-1000T < Food4 | 88-654310 | 2016-03-25 | 2 |
| 208 | 909876525 | 14.00 | c | Food622-P2-20151127-FO622-200T < Food62 < Food6 | 88-654310 | 2016-03-25 | 1 |
| 209 | 909876525 | 7.00 | c | Food43-P2-20151127-FO43-1000T < Food4 | 88-654310 | 2016-03-25 | 1 |
| 210 | 909876514 | 18.00 | c | Food521-P2-20151127-FO521-1000T < Food52 < Food5 | 88-654310 | 2016-03-28 | 3 |
| 211 | 909876514 | 24.00 | c | Food612-P2-20151127-FO612-200T < Food61 < Food6 | 88-654310 | 2016-03-28 | 2 |
| 212 | 909876509 | 26.00 | c | Food613-P2-20151127-FO613-200T < Food61 < Food6 | 88-654310 | 2016-04-06 | 2 |
| 213 | 909876509 | 28.00 | c | Food622-P2-20151127-FO622-200T < Food62 < Food6 | 88-654310 | 2016-04-06 | 2 |
| 214 | 909876505 | 26.00 | c | Food613-P2-20151127-FO613-200T < Food61 < Food6 | 88-654310 | 2016-04-13 | 2 |
| 215 | 909876505 | 30.00 | c | Food614-P2-20151127-FO614-200T < Food61 < Food6 | 88-654310 | 2016-04-13 | 2 |
| 216 | 909876502 | 10.00 | c | Food611-P2-20151127-FO611-200T < Food61 < Food6 | 88-654310 | 2016-04-15 | 1 |
| 217 | 909876502 | 15.00 | c | Food614-P2-20151127-FO614-200T < Food61 < Food6 | 88-654310 | 2016-04-15 | 1 |
| 218 | 909876512 | 32.00 | c | Food53-P2-20151127-FO53-1000T < Food5 | 88-654310 | 2016-04-17 | 4 |
| 219 | 909876512 | 28.00 | c | Food622-P2-20151127-FO622-200T < Food62 < Food6 | 88-654310 | 2016-04-17 | 2 |
| 220 | 909876504 | 24.00 | c | Food612-P2-20151127-FO612-200T < Food61 < Food6 | 88-654310 | 2016-04-20 | 2 |
| 221 | 909876504 | 26.00 | c | Food621-P2-20151127-FO621-200T < Food62 < Food6 | 88-654310 | 2016-04-20 | 2 |
| 222 | 909876513 | 65.00 | c | Food422-P2-20151127-FO422-1000T < Food42 < Food4 | 88-654310 | 2016-04-26 | 10 |
| 223 | 909876513 | 60.00 | c | Food612-P2-20151127-FO612-200T < Food61 < Food6 | 88-654310 | 2016-04-26 | 5 |
| 224 | 909876513 | 65.00 | c | Food613-P2-20151127-FO613-200T < Food61 < Food6 | 88-654310 | 2016-04-26 | 5 |
| 225 | 909876513 | 45.00 | c | Food614-P2-20151127-FO614-200T < Food61 < Food6 | 88-654310 | 2016-04-26 | 3 |
| 226 | 88-654302 | 77.00 | c | Supplies1-P2-20150920-SUP1-200T | 88-654310 | 2016-04-30 | 11 |
| 227 | 88-654302 | 88.00 | c | Supplies2-P2-20150920-SUP2-200T | 88-654310 | 2016-04-30 | 11 |
| 228 | 88-654310 | -3000.00 | p | Inven411-P2-20160430-In411-1000T < Inven41 < Inven4 | 88-654310 | 2016-04-30 | -1000 |

| | IDM | Amount | Symbol | MultiSubaccount | Recorder | TransDate | Unit |
|---|---|---|---|---|---|---|---|
| 229 | 88-654310 | -11100.00 | p | Inven412-P2-20160430-In412-1000T < Inven41 < Inven4 | 88-654310 | 2016-04-30 | -1000 |
| 230 | 88-654310 | -12000.00 | p | TTTCU parts-P2-20160430-TTP-1000T < TTT parts < Inven4 | 88-654310 | 2016-04-30 | -1000 |
| 231 | 88-654310 | -12000.00 | p | RRRHJK parts-P2-20160430-RRP-1000T < Inven4 | 88-654310 | 2016-04-30 | -1000 |
| 232 | 88-654310 | -5000.00 | p | Food411-P2-20160430-FO411-1000T < Food41 < Food4 | 88-654310 | 2016-04-30 | -1000 |
| 233 | 88-654310 | -5500.00 | p | Food412-P2-20160430-FO412-1000T < Food41 < Food4 | 88-654310 | 2016-04-30 | -1000 |
| 234 | 88-654306 | 770.00 | c | Supplies1-P2-20160430-Supp1-200T | 88-654310 | 2016-04-30 | 110 |
| 235 | 88-654306 | 880.00 | c | Supplies2-P2-20160430-Supp2-200T | 88-654310 | 2016-04-30 | 110 |
| 236 | 88-654310 | -6000.00 | p | Food421-P2-20160430-FO421-1000T < Food42 < Food4 | 88-654310 | 2016-04-30 | -1000 |
| 237 | 88-654310 | -6500.00 | p | Food422-P2-20160430-FO422-1000T < Food42 < Food4 | 88-654310 | 2016-04-30 | -1000 |
| 238 | 88-654310 | -7000.00 | p | Food43-P2-20160430-FO43-1000T < Food4 | 88-654310 | 2016-04-30 | -1000 |
| 239 | 88-654310 | -7500.00 | p | Food44-P2-20160430-FO44-1000T < Food4 | 88-654310 | 2016-04-30 | -1000 |
| 240 | 88-654310 | -4000.00 | p | Food511-P2-20160430-FO511-1000T < Food51 < Food5 | 88-654310 | 2016-04-30 | -1000 |
| 241 | 88-654310 | -4500.00 | p | Food512-P2-20160430-FO512-1000T < Food51 < Food5 | 88-654310 | 2016-04-30 | -1000 |
| 242 | 88-654310 | -5000.00 | p | Food513-P2-20160430-FO513-1000T < Food51 < Food5 | 88-654310 | 2016-04-30 | -1000 |
| 243 | 88-654310 | -5500.00 | p | Food514-P2-20160430-FO514-1000T < Food51 < Food5 | 88-654310 | 2016-04-30 | -1000 |
| 244 | 88-654310 | -6000.00 | p | Food521-P2-20160430-FO521-1000T < Food52 < Food5 | 88-654310 | 2016-04-30 | -1000 |
| 245 | 88-654310 | -6500.00 | p | Food522-P2-20160430-FO522-1000T < Food52 < Food5 | 88-654310 | 2016-04-30 | -1000 |
| 246 | 88-654310 | -8000.00 | p | Food53-P2-20160430-FO53-1000T < Food5 | 88-654310 | 2016-04-30 | -1000 |
| 247 | 88-654310 | -2000.00 | p | Food611-P2-20160430-FO611-200T < Food61 < Food6 | 88-654310 | 2016-04-30 | -200 |
| 248 | 88-654310 | -2400.00 | p | Food612-P2-20160430-FO612-200T < Food61 < Food6 | 88-654310 | 2016-04-30 | -200 |
| 249 | 88-654310 | -2600.00 | p | Food613-P2-20160430-FO613-200T < Food61 < Food6 | 88-654310 | 2016-04-30 | -200 |
| 250 | 88-654310 | -3000.00 | p | Food614-P2-20160430-FO614-200T < Food61 < Food6 | 88-654310 | 2016-04-30 | -200 |
| 251 | 88-654310 | -2600.00 | p | Food621-P2-20160430-FO621-200T < Food62 < Food6 | 88-654310 | 2016-04-30 | -200 |
| 252 | 88-654310 | -2800.00 | p | Food622-P2-20160430-FO622-200T < Food62 < Food6 | 88-654310 | 2016-04-30 | -200 |
| 253 | 88-654310 | -1400.00 | p | Supplies1-P2-20160430-Supp1-200T | 88-654310 | 2016-04-30 | -200 |
| 254 | 88-654310 | -1600.00 | p | Supplies2-P2-20160430-Supp2-200T | 88-654310 | 2016-04-30 | -200 |
| 255 | 88-654309 | 350.00 | c | Supplies1-P2-20160430-Supp1-200T | 88-654310 | 2016-05-01 | 50 |
| 256 | 88-654309 | 400.00 | c | Supplies2-P2-20160430-Supp2-200T | 88-654310 | 2016-05-01 | 50 |
| 257 | 88-654310 | 189.00 | f | Supplies1-P2-20160430-Supp1-200T | 88-654310 | 2016-05-01 | 27 |
| 258 | 88-654310 | 224.00 | f | Supplies2-P2-20160430-Supp2-200T | 88-654310 | 2016-05-01 | 28 |
| 259 | 88-654309 | -2500.00 | t | Inven31-P1-20160430-In31-600T < Inven3 | 88-654310 | 2016-05-01 | -250 |
| 260 | 88-654309 | -7500.00 | t | Inven32-P1-20160430-In32-600T < Inven3 | 88-654310 | 2016-05-01 | -150 |
| 261 | 88-654309 | -3000.00 | t | Inven331-P1-20160430-In331-600T < Inven33 < Inven3 | 88-654310 | 2016-05-01 | -150 |
| 262 | 88-654309 | -6750.00 | t | Inven332-P1-20160430-In332-600T < Inven33 < Inven3 | 88-654310 | 2016-05-01 | -150 |
| 263 | 88-654309 | -1500.00 | t | HGFCVB parts-P1-20160430-HGP-600T < QASXC parts < Inven3 | 88-654310 | 2016-05-01 | -150 |
| 264 | 88-654309 | -3000.00 | t | PPGHUP parts-P1-20160430-PPP-600T < ASDUP parts < Inven3 | 88-654310 | 2016-05-01 | -150 |
| 265 | 88-654306 | 300.00 | c | Inven411-P2-20160430-In411-1000T < Inven41 < Inven4 | 88-654310 | 2016-05-01 | 100 |
| 266 | 88-654306 | 1110.00 | c | Inven412-P2-20160430-In412-1000T < Inven41 < Inven4 | 88-654310 | 2016-05-01 | 100 |
| 267 | 88-654306 | 1200.00 | c | TTTCU parts-P2-20160430-TTP-1000T < TTT parts < Inven4 | 88-654310 | 2016-05-01 | 100 |
| 268 | 88-654306 | 1200.00 | c | RRRHJK parts-P2-20160430-RRP-1000T < Inven4 | 88-654310 | 2016-05-01 | 100 |
| 269 | 88-654309 | 390.00 | c | Inven411-P2-20160430-In411-1000T < Inven41 < Inven4 | 88-654310 | 2016-05-01 | 130 |
| 270 | 88-654309 | 1443.00 | c | Inven412-P2-20160430-In412-1000T < Inven41 < Inven4 | 88-654310 | 2016-05-01 | 130 |
| 271 | 88-654309 | 1560.00 | c | TTTCU parts-P2-20160430-TTP-1000T < TTT parts < Inven4 | 88-654310 | 2016-05-01 | 130 |
| 272 | 88-654309 | 1560.00 | c | RRRHJK parts-P2-20160430-RRP-1000T < Inven4 | 88-654310 | 2016-05-01 | 130 |
| 273 | 88-654310 | 2500.00 | f | Inven31-P1-20160430-In31-600T < Inven3 | 88-654310 | 2016-05-02 | 250 |
| 274 | 88-654310 | 7500.00 | f | Inven32-P1-20160430-In32-600T < Inven3 | 88-654310 | 2016-05-02 | 150 |
| 275 | 88-654310 | 3000.00 | f | Inven331-P1-20160430-In331-600T < Inven33 < Inven3 | 88-654310 | 2016-05-02 | 150 |
| 276 | 88-654310 | 6750.00 | f | Inven332-P1-20160430-In332-600T < Inven33 < Inven3 | 88-654310 | 2016-05-02 | 150 |
| 277 | 88-654310 | 1500.00 | f | HGFCVB parts-P1-20160430-HGP-600T < QASXC parts < Inven3 | 88-654310 | 2016-05-02 | 150 |
| 278 | 88-654310 | 3000.00 | f | PPGHUP parts-P1-20160430-PPP-600T < ASDUP parts < Inven3 | 88-654310 | 2016-05-02 | 150 |
| 279 | 88-654310 | 700.00 | f | Inven121-C3-20150922-In121-20000T < Inven12 < Inven1 | 88-654310 | 2016-05-02 | 875 |
| 280 | 88-654310 | 4000.00 | f | Inven51-C3-20150922-In51-1000T < Inven5 | 88-654310 | 2016-05-02 | 400 |
| 281 | 88-654310 | 10000.00 | f | Inven52-C3-20150922-In52-500T < Inven5 | 88-654310 | 2016-05-02 | 200 |
| 282 | 88-654310 | 10000.00 | f | Inven531-C3-20150922-In531-1000T < Inven53 < Inven5 | 88-654310 | 2016-05-02 | 400 |
| 283 | 88-654310 | 14000.00 | f | Inven532-C3-20150922-In532-1000T < Inven53 < Inven5 | 88-654310 | 2016-05-02 | 400 |
| 284 | 88-654310 | 4000.00 | f | Inven541-C3-20150922-In541-1000T < Inven54 < Inven5 | 88-654310 | 2016-05-02 | 400 |
| 285 | 88-654310 | 6000.00 | f | Inven542-C3-20150922-In542-1000T < Inven54 < Inven5 | 88-654310 | 2016-05-02 | 400 |
| 286 | 88-654310 | 2340.00 | f | Inven611-C3-20151003-In611-1300T < Inven61 < Inven6 | 88-654310 | 2016-05-02 | 360 |
| 287 | 88-654310 | 5000.00 | f | Inven612-C3-20151003-In612-1100T < Inven61 < Inven6 | 88-654310 | 2016-05-02 | 400 |
| 288 | 88-654310 | 7200.00 | f | Inven621-C3-20151003-In621-900T < Inven62 < Inven6 | 88-654310 | 2016-05-02 | 400 |
| 289 | 88-654310 | 6400.00 | f | Inven63-C3-20151003-In63-1000T < Inven6 | 88-654310 | 2016-05-02 | 400 |
| 290 | 88-654310 | 8640.00 | f | Inven711-C3-20151003-In711-500T < Inven71 < Inven7 | 88-654310 | 2016-05-02 | 240 |
| 291 | 88-654310 | 1240.00 | f | Inven712-C3-20151003-In712-100T < Inven71 < Inven7 | 88-654310 | 2016-05-02 | 40 |
| 292 | 88-654310 | 7040.00 | f | Inven721-C3-20151003-In721-744T < Inven72 < Inven7 | 88-654310 | 2016-05-02 | 320 |
| 293 | 88-654310 | 4800.00 | f | Inven722-C3-20151003-In722-600T < Inven72 < Inven7 | 88-654310 | 2016-05-02 | 240 |
| 294 | 88-654310 | 4320.00 | f | Inven731-C3-20151003-In731-600T < Inven73 < Inven7 | 88-654310 | 2016-05-02 | 240 |

| | IDM | Amount | Symbol | MultiSubaccount | Recorder | TransDate | Unit |
|---|---|---|---|---|---|---|---|
| 295 | 88-654310 | 6400.00 | f | Inven732-C3-20151003-In732-1000T < Inven73 < Inven7 | 88-654310 | 2016-05-02 | 400 |
| 296 | 88-654310 | 6000.00 | f | Inven811-C3-20151003-In811-600T < Inven81 < Inven8 | 88-654310 | 2016-05-02 | 240 |
| 297 | 88-654310 | 5760.00 | f | Inven812-C3-20151003-In812-600T < Inven81 < Inven8 | 88-654310 | 2016-05-02 | 240 |
| 298 | 88-654310 | 5520.00 | f | Inven813-C3-20151003-In813-600T < Inven81 < Inven8 | 88-654310 | 2016-05-02 | 240 |
| 299 | 88-654310 | 4800.00 | f | Inven82-C3-20151003-In82-600T < Inven8 | 88-654310 | 2016-05-02 | 240 |
| 300 | 88-654310 | 4320.00 | f | Inven831-C3-20151003-In831-600T < Inven83 < Inven8 | 88-654310 | 2016-05-02 | 240 |
| 301 | 88-654310 | 5120.00 | f | Inven832-C3-20151003-In832-800T < Inven83 < Inven8 | 88-654310 | 2016-05-02 | 320 |
| 302 | 88-654303 | 70.00 | c | Supplies1-P2-20150920-SUP1-200T | 88-654310 | 2016-05-08 | 10 |
| 303 | 88-654303 | 80.00 | c | Supplies2-P2-20150920-SUP2-200T | 88-654310 | 2016-05-08 | 10 |
| 304 | 909876524 | 26.00 | c | Food613-P2-20151127-FO613-200T < Food61 < Food6 | 88-654310 | 2016-05-15 | 2 |
| 305 | 909876524 | 13.00 | c | Food621-P2-20151127-FO621-200T < Food62 < Food6 | 88-654310 | 2016-05-15 | 1 |
| 306 | 88-654301 | 70.00 | c | Supplies1-P2-20150920-SUP1-200T | 88-654310 | 2016-05-16 | 10 |
| 307 | 88-654301 | 88.00 | c | Supplies2-P2-20150920-SUP2-200T | 88-654310 | 2016-05-16 | 11 |
| 308 | 909876522 | 15.00 | c | Food513-P2-20151127-FO513-1000T < Food51 < Food5 | 88-654310 | 2016-05-22 | 3 |
| 309 | 909876522 | 13.00 | c | Food621-P2-20151127-FO621-200T < Food62 < Food6 | 88-654310 | 2016-05-22 | 1 |
| 310 | 909876512 | 26.00 | c | Food522-P2-20151127-FO522-1000T < Food52 < Food5 | 88-654310 | 2016-05-24 | 4 |
| 311 | 909876512 | 28.00 | c | Food622-P2-20151127-FO622-200T < Food62 < Food6 | 88-654310 | 2016-05-24 | 2 |
| 312 | 909876508 | 13.00 | c | Food613-P2-20151127-FO613-200T < Food61 < Food6 | 88-654310 | 2016-06-03 | 1 |
| 313 | 909876508 | 14.00 | c | Food622-P2-20151127-FO622-200T < Food62 < Food6 | 88-654310 | 2016-06-03 | 1 |
| 314 | 909876517 | 20.00 | c | Food611-P2-20151127-FO611-200T < Food61 < Food6 | 88-654310 | 2016-06-12 | 2 |
| 315 | 909876517 | 14.00 | c | Food622-P2-20151127-FO622-200T < Food62 < Food6 | 88-654310 | 2016-06-12 | 1 |
| 316 | 909876520 | 20.00 | c | Food611-P2-20151127-FO611-200T < Food61 < Food6 | 88-654310 | 2016-06-12 | 2 |
| 317 | 909876520 | 14.00 | c | Food622-P2-20151127-FO622-200T < Food62 < Food6 | 88-654310 | 2016-06-12 | 1 |
| 318 | 88-654308 | 42.00 | c | Supplies1-P2-20160430-Supp1-200T | 88-654310 | 2016-06-15 | 6 |
| 319 | 909876503 | 22.50 | c | Food44-P2-20151127-FO44-1000T < Food4 | 88-654310 | 2016-06-15 | 3 |
| 320 | 909876503 | 24.00 | c | Food53-P2-20151127-FO53-1000T < Food5 | 88-654310 | 2016-06-15 | 3 |
| 321 | 909876505 | 16.50 | c | Food514-P2-20151127-FO514-1000T < Food51 < Food5 | 88-654310 | 2016-06-17 | 3 |
| 322 | 909876505 | 30.00 | c | Food611-P2-20151127-FO611-200T < Food61 < Food6 | 88-654310 | 2016-06-17 | 3 |
| 323 | 909876506 | 15.00 | c | Food513-P2-20151127-FO513-1000T < Food51 < Food5 | 88-654310 | 2016-06-17 | 3 |
| 324 | 909876506 | 30.00 | c | Food611-P2-20151127-FO611-200T < Food61 < Food6 | 88-654310 | 2016-06-17 | 3 |
| 325 | 909876524 | 24.00 | c | Food612-P2-20151127-FO612-200T < Food61 < Food6 | 88-654310 | 2016-06-17 | 2 |
| 326 | 909876524 | 13.00 | c | Food613-P2-20151127-FO613-200T < Food61 < Food6 | 88-654310 | 2016-06-17 | 1 |
| 327 | 909876502 | 26.00 | c | Food522-P2-20151127-FO522-1000T < Food52 < Food5 | 88-654310 | 2016-06-18 | 4 |
| 328 | 909876502 | 42.00 | c | Food622-P2-20151127-FO622-200T < Food62 < Food6 | 88-654310 | 2016-06-18 | 3 |
| 329 | 909876522 | 12.00 | c | Food521-P2-20151127-FO521-1000T < Food52 < Food5 | 88-654310 | 2016-06-21 | 2 |
| 330 | 909876522 | 12.00 | c | Food612-P2-20151127-FO612-200T < Food61 < Food6 | 88-654310 | 2016-06-21 | 1 |
| 331 | 909876512 | 650.00 | c | Food411-P2-20160430-FO411-1000T < Food41 < Food4 | 88-654310 | 2016-07-01 | 130 |
| 332 | 909876512 | 715.00 | c | Food412-P2-20160430-FO412-1000T < Food41 < Food4 | 88-654310 | 2016-07-01 | 130 |
| 333 | 909876512 | 780.00 | c | Food421-P2-20160430-FO421-1000T < Food42 < Food4 | 88-654310 | 2016-07-01 | 130 |
| 334 | 909876512 | 845.00 | c | Food422-P2-20160430-FO422-1000T < Food42 < Food4 | 88-654310 | 2016-07-01 | 130 |
| 335 | 909876512 | 910.00 | c | Food43-P2-20160430-FO43-1000T < Food4 | 88-654310 | 2016-07-01 | 130 |
| 336 | 909876512 | 975.00 | c | Food44-P2-20160430-FO44-1000T < Food4 | 88-654310 | 2016-07-01 | 130 |
| 337 | 909876512 | 585.00 | c | Food512-P2-20160430-FO512-1000T < Food51 < Food5 | 88-654310 | 2016-07-01 | 130 |
| 338 | 909876501 | 650.00 | c | Food411-P2-20160430-FO411-1000T < Food41 < Food4 | 88-654310 | 2016-07-01 | 130 |
| 339 | 909876501 | 275.00 | c | Food412-P2-20160430-FO412-1000T < Food41 < Food4 | 88-654310 | 2016-07-01 | 50 |
| 340 | 909876501 | 780.00 | c | Food421-P2-20160430-FO421-1000T < Food42 < Food4 | 88-654310 | 2016-07-01 | 130 |
| 341 | 909876501 | 845.00 | c | Food422-P2-20160430-FO422-1000T < Food42 < Food4 | 88-654310 | 2016-07-01 | 130 |
| 342 | 909876501 | 910.00 | c | Food43-P2-20160430-FO43-1000T < Food4 | 88-654310 | 2016-07-01 | 130 |
| 343 | 909876501 | 975.00 | c | Food44-P2-20160430-FO44-1000T < Food4 | 88-654310 | 2016-07-01 | 130 |
| 344 | 909876501 | 650.00 | c | Food513-P2-20160430-FO513-1000T < Food51 < Food5 | 88-654310 | 2016-07-01 | 130 |
| 345 | 909876501 | 440.00 | c | Food53-P2-20160430-FO53-1000T < Food5 | 88-654310 | 2016-07-01 | 55 |
| 346 | 909876502 | 650.00 | c | Food411-P2-20160430-FO411-1000T < Food41 < Food4 | 88-654310 | 2016-07-01 | 130 |
| 347 | 909876502 | 715.00 | c | Food412-P2-20160430-FO412-1000T < Food41 < Food4 | 88-654310 | 2016-07-01 | 130 |
| 348 | 909876502 | 780.00 | c | Food421-P2-20160430-FO421-1000T < Food42 < Food4 | 88-654310 | 2016-07-01 | 130 |
| 349 | 909876502 | 845.00 | c | Food422-P2-20160430-FO422-1000T < Food42 < Food4 | 88-654310 | 2016-07-01 | 130 |
| 350 | 909876502 | 910.00 | c | Food43-P2-20160430-FO43-1000T < Food4 | 88-654310 | 2016-07-01 | 130 |
| 351 | 909876502 | 975.00 | c | Food44-P2-20151127-FO44-1000T < Food4 | 88-654310 | 2016-07-01 | 130 |
| 352 | 909876502 | 715.00 | c | Food514-P2-20160430-FO514-1000T < Food51 < Food5 | 88-654310 | 2016-07-01 | 130 |
| 353 | 909876503 | 650.00 | c | Food411-P2-20160430-FO411-1000T < Food41 < Food4 | 88-654310 | 2016-07-01 | 130 |
| 354 | 909876503 | 715.00 | c | Food412-P2-20160430-FO412-1000T < Food41 < Food4 | 88-654310 | 2016-07-01 | 130 |
| 355 | 909876503 | 780.00 | c | Food421-P2-20160430-FO421-1000T < Food42 < Food4 | 88-654310 | 2016-07-01 | 130 |
| 356 | 909876503 | 845.00 | c | Food422-P2-20160430-FO422-1000T < Food42 < Food4 | 88-654310 | 2016-07-01 | 130 |
| 357 | 909876503 | 910.00 | c | Food43-P2-20160430-FO43-1000T < Food4 | 88-654310 | 2016-07-01 | 130 |
| 358 | 909876503 | 975.00 | c | Food44-P2-20160430-FO44-1000T < Food4 | 88-654310 | 2016-07-01 | 130 |
| 359 | 909876503 | 780.00 | c | Food521-P2-20160430-FO521-1000T < Food52 < Food5 | 88-654310 | 2016-07-01 | 130 |
| 360 | 909876504 | 650.00 | c | Food411-P2-20160430-FO411-1000T < Food41 < Food4 | 88-654310 | 2016-07-01 | 130 |

| | IDM | Amount | Symbol | MultiSubaccount | Recorder | TransDate | Unit |
|---|---|---|---|---|---|---|---|
| 361 | 909876504 | 715.00 | c | Food412-P2-20160430-FO412-1000T < Food41 < Food4 | 88-654310 | 2016-07-01 | 130 |
| 362 | 909876504 | 780.00 | c | Food421-P2-20160430-FO421-1000T < Food42 < Food4 | 88-654310 | 2016-07-01 | 130 |
| 363 | 909876504 | 845.00 | c | Food422-P2-20160430-FO422-1000T < Food42 < Food4 | 88-654310 | 2016-07-01 | 130 |
| 364 | 909876504 | 910.00 | c | Food43-P2-20160430-FO43-1000T < Food4 | 88-654310 | 2016-07-01 | 130 |
| 365 | 909876504 | 975.00 | c | Food44-P2-20160430-FO44-1000T < Food4 | 88-654310 | 2016-07-01 | 130 |
| 366 | 909876504 | 845.00 | c | Food522-P2-20160430-FO522-1000T < Food52 < Food5 | 88-654310 | 2016-07-01 | 130 |
| 367 | 909876505 | 650.00 | c | Food411-P2-20160430-FO411-1000T < Food41 < Food4 | 88-654310 | 2016-07-01 | 130 |
| 368 | 909876505 | 715.00 | c | Food412-P2-20160430-FO412-1000T < Food41 < Food4 | 88-654310 | 2016-07-01 | 130 |
| 369 | 909876505 | 780.00 | c | Food421-P2-20160430-FO421-1000T < Food42 < Food4 | 88-654310 | 2016-07-01 | 130 |
| 370 | 909876505 | 845.00 | c | Food422-P2-20160430-FO422-1000T < Food42 < Food4 | 88-654310 | 2016-07-01 | 130 |
| 371 | 909876505 | 910.00 | c | Food43-P2-20160430-FO43-1000T < Food4 | 88-654310 | 2016-07-01 | 130 |
| 372 | 909876505 | 975.00 | c | Food44-P2-20160430-FO44-1000T < Food4 | 88-654310 | 2016-07-01 | 130 |
| 373 | 909876505 | 1040.00 | c | Food53-P2-20160430-FO53-1000T < Food5 | 88-654310 | 2016-07-01 | 130 |
| 374 | 909876506 | 520.00 | c | Food511-P2-20160430-FO511-1000T < Food51 < Food5 | 88-654310 | 2016-07-01 | 130 |
| 375 | 909876506 | 585.00 | c | Food512-P2-20160430-FO512-1000T < Food51 < Food5 | 88-654310 | 2016-07-01 | 130 |
| 376 | 909876506 | 650.00 | c | Food513-P2-20160430-FO513-1000T < Food51 < Food5 | 88-654310 | 2016-07-01 | 130 |
| 377 | 909876506 | 715.00 | c | Food514-P2-20160430-FO514-1000T < Food51 < Food5 | 88-654310 | 2016-07-01 | 130 |
| 378 | 909876506 | 780.00 | c | Food521-P2-20160430-FO521-1000T < Food52 < Food5 | 88-654310 | 2016-07-01 | 130 |
| 379 | 909876506 | 845.00 | c | Food522-P2-20160430-FO522-1000T < Food52 < Food5 | 88-654310 | 2016-07-01 | 130 |
| 380 | 909876506 | 1300.00 | c | Food611-P2-20160430-FO611-200T < Food61 < Food6 | 88-654310 | 2016-07-01 | 130 |
| 381 | 909876507 | 520.00 | c | Food511-P2-20160430-FO511-1000T < Food51 < Food5 | 88-654310 | 2016-07-01 | 130 |
| 382 | 909876507 | 585.00 | c | Food512-P2-20160430-FO512-1000T < Food51 < Food5 | 88-654310 | 2016-07-01 | 130 |
| 383 | 909876507 | 650.00 | c | Food513-P2-20160430-FO513-1000T < Food51 < Food5 | 88-654310 | 2016-07-01 | 130 |
| 384 | 909876507 | 715.00 | c | Food514-P2-20160430-FO514-1000T < Food51 < Food5 | 88-654310 | 2016-07-01 | 130 |
| 385 | 909876507 | 780.00 | c | Food521-P2-20160430-FO521-1000T < Food52 < Food5 | 88-654310 | 2016-07-01 | 130 |
| 386 | 909876507 | 845.00 | c | Food522-P2-20160430-FO522-1000T < Food52 < Food5 | 88-654310 | 2016-07-01 | 130 |
| 387 | 909876507 | 1560.00 | c | Food612-P2-20160430-FO612-200T < Food61 < Food6 | 88-654310 | 2016-07-01 | 130 |
| 388 | 909876508 | 520.00 | c | Food511-P2-20160430-FO511-1000T < Food51 < Food5 | 88-654310 | 2016-07-01 | 130 |
| 389 | 909876508 | 585.00 | c | Food512-P2-20160430-FO512-1000T < Food51 < Food5 | 88-654310 | 2016-07-01 | 130 |
| 390 | 909876508 | 650.00 | c | Food513-P2-20160430-FO513-1000T < Food51 < Food5 | 88-654310 | 2016-07-01 | 130 |
| 391 | 909876508 | 715.00 | c | Food514-P2-20160430-FO514-1000T < Food51 < Food5 | 88-654310 | 2016-07-01 | 130 |
| 392 | 909876508 | 780.00 | c | Food521-P2-20160430-FO521-1000T < Food52 < Food5 | 88-654310 | 2016-07-01 | 130 |
| 393 | 909876508 | 845.00 | c | Food522-P2-20160430-FO522-1000T < Food52 < Food5 | 88-654310 | 2016-07-01 | 130 |
| 394 | 909876508 | 1690.00 | c | Food613-P2-20160430-FO613-200T < Food61 < Food6 | 88-654310 | 2016-07-01 | 130 |
| 395 | 909876509 | 520.00 | c | Food511-P2-20160430-FO511-1000T < Food51 < Food5 | 88-654310 | 2016-07-01 | 130 |
| 396 | 909876509 | 225.00 | c | Food512-P2-20160430-FO512-1000T < Food51 < Food5 | 88-654310 | 2016-07-01 | 50 |
| 397 | 909876509 | 250.00 | c | Food513-P2-20160430-FO513-1000T < Food51 < Food5 | 88-654310 | 2016-07-01 | 50 |
| 398 | 909876509 | 715.00 | c | Food514-P2-20160430-FO514-1000T < Food51 < Food5 | 88-654310 | 2016-07-01 | 130 |
| 399 | 909876509 | 780.00 | c | Food521-P2-20160430-FO521-1000T < Food52 < Food5 | 88-654310 | 2016-07-01 | 130 |
| 400 | 909876509 | 845.00 | c | Food522-P2-20160430-FO522-1000T < Food52 < Food5 | 88-654310 | 2016-07-01 | 130 |
| 401 | 909876509 | 760.00 | c | Food53-P2-20160430-FO53-1000T < Food5 | 88-654310 | 2016-07-01 | 95 |
| 402 | 909876509 | 1950.00 | c | Food614-P2-20160430-FO614-200T < Food61 < Food6 | 88-654310 | 2016-07-01 | 130 |
| 403 | 909876510 | 520.00 | c | Food511-P2-20160430-FO511-1000T < Food51 < Food5 | 88-654310 | 2016-07-01 | 130 |
| 404 | 909876510 | 585.00 | c | Food512-P2-20160430-FO512-1000T < Food51 < Food5 | 88-654310 | 2016-07-01 | 130 |
| 405 | 909876510 | 650.00 | c | Food513-P2-20160430-FO513-1000T < Food51 < Food5 | 88-654310 | 2016-07-01 | 130 |
| 406 | 909876510 | 715.00 | c | Food514-P2-20160430-FO514-1000T < Food51 < Food5 | 88-654310 | 2016-07-01 | 130 |
| 407 | 909876510 | 780.00 | c | Food521-P2-20160430-FO521-1000T < Food52 < Food5 | 88-654310 | 2016-07-01 | 130 |
| 408 | 909876510 | 845.00 | c | Food522-P2-20160430-FO522-1000T < Food52 < Food5 | 88-654310 | 2016-07-01 | 130 |
| 409 | 909876510 | 1690.00 | c | Food621-P2-20160430-FO621-200T < Food62 < Food6 | 88-654310 | 2016-07-01 | 130 |
| 410 | 909876511 | 715.00 | c | Food412-P2-20160430-FO412-1000T < Food41 < Food4 | 88-654310 | 2016-07-01 | 130 |
| 411 | 909876511 | 520.00 | c | Food511-P2-20160430-FO511-1000T < Food51 < Food5 | 88-654310 | 2016-07-01 | 130 |
| 412 | 909876511 | 585.00 | c | Food512-P2-20160430-FO512-1000T < Food51 < Food5 | 88-654310 | 2016-07-01 | 130 |
| 413 | 909876511 | 650.00 | c | Food513-P2-20160430-FO513-1000T < Food51 < Food5 | 88-654310 | 2016-07-01 | 130 |
| 414 | 909876511 | 780.00 | c | Food521-P2-20160430-FO521-1000T < Food52 < Food5 | 88-654310 | 2016-07-01 | 130 |
| 415 | 909876511 | 845.00 | c | Food522-P2-20160430-FO522-1000T < Food52 < Food5 | 88-654310 | 2016-07-01 | 130 |
| 416 | 909876511 | 1040.00 | c | Food53-P2-20160430-FO53-1000T < Food5 | 88-654310 | 2016-07-01 | 130 |
| 417 | 909876512 | 520.00 | c | Food511-P2-20160430-FO511-1000T < Food51 < Food5 | 88-654310 | 2016-07-01 | 130 |
| 418 | 909876512 | 585.00 | c | Food512-P2-20160430-FO512-1000T < Food51 < Food5 | 88-654310 | 2016-07-01 | 130 |
| 419 | 909876512 | 650.00 | c | Food513-P2-20160430-FO513-1000T < Food51 < Food5 | 88-654310 | 2016-07-01 | 130 |
| 420 | 909876512 | 715.00 | c | Food514-P2-20160430-FO514-1000T < Food51 < Food5 | 88-654310 | 2016-07-01 | 130 |
| 421 | 909876512 | 180.00 | c | Food521-P2-20160430-FO521-1000T < Food52 < Food5 | 88-654310 | 2016-07-01 | 30 |
| 422 | 909876512 | 325.00 | c | Food522-P2-20160430-FO522-1000T < Food52 < Food5 | 88-654310 | 2016-07-01 | 50 |
| 423 | 909876512 | 1120.00 | c | Food53-P2-20160430-FO53-1000T < Food5 | 88-654310 | 2016-07-01 | 140 |
| 424 | 909876512 | 1820.00 | c | Food622-P2-20160430-FO622-200T < Food62 < Food6 | 88-654310 | 2016-07-01 | 130 |
| 425 | 909876513 | 650.00 | c | Food411-P2-20160430-FO411-1000T < Food41 < Food4 | 88-654310 | 2016-07-01 | 130 |
| 426 | 909876513 | 715.00 | c | Food412-P2-20160430-FO412-1000T < Food41 < Food4 | 88-654310 | 2016-07-01 | 130 |

| | IDM | Amount | Symbol | MultiSubaccount | Recorder | TransDate | Unit |
|---|---|---|---|---|---|---|---|
| 427 | 909876513 | 780.00 | c | Food421-P2-20160430-FO421-1000T < Food42 < Food4 | 88-654310 | 2016-07-01 | 130 |
| 428 | 909876513 | 845.00 | c | Food422-P2-20160430-FO422-1000T < Food42 < Food4 | 88-654310 | 2016-07-01 | 130 |
| 429 | 909876513 | 910.00 | c | Food43-P2-20160430-FO43-1000T < Food4 | 88-654310 | 2016-07-01 | 130 |
| 430 | 909876513 | 975.00 | c | Food44-P2-20160430-FO44-1000T < Food4 | 88-654310 | 2016-07-01 | 130 |
| 431 | 909876513 | 1040.00 | c | Food53-P2-20160430-FO53-1000T < Food5 | 88-654310 | 2016-07-01 | 130 |
| 432 | 909876509 | 22.50 | c | Food44-P2-20151127-FO44-1000T < Food4 | 88-654310 | 2016-07-02 | 3 |
| 433 | 909876509 | 36.00 | c | Food612-P2-20151127-FO612-200T < Food61 < Food6 | 88-654310 | 2016-07-02 | 3 |
| 434 | 909876511 | 24.00 | c | Food612-P2-20151127-FO612-200T < Food61 < Food6 | 88-654310 | 2016-07-09 | 2 |
| 435 | 909876511 | 13.00 | c | Food621-P2-20151127-FO621-200T < Food62 < Food6 | 88-654310 | 2016-07-09 | 1 |
| 436 | 909876525 | 26.00 | c | Food621-P2-20151127-FO621-200T < Food62 < Food6 | 88-654310 | 2016-07-21 | 2 |
| 437 | 909876525 | 28.00 | c | Food622-P2-20151127-FO622-200T < Food62 < Food6 | 88-654310 | 2016-07-21 | 2 |
| 438 | 909876506 | 25.00 | c | Food513-P2-20151127-FO513-1000T < Food51 < Food5 | 88-654310 | 2016-08-09 | 5 |
| 439 | 909876506 | 32.00 | c | Food53-P2-20151127-FO53-1000T < Food5 | 88-654310 | 2016-08-09 | 4 |
| 440 | 909876509 | 20.00 | c | Food611-P2-20151127-FO611-200T < Food61 < Food6 | 88-654310 | 2016-08-12 | 2 |
| 441 | 909876509 | 39.00 | c | Food621-P2-20151127-FO621-200T < Food62 < Food6 | 88-654310 | 2016-08-12 | 3 |
| 442 | 909876515 | 19.50 | c | Food522-P2-20151127-FO522-1000T < Food52 < Food5 | 88-654310 | 2016-08-14 | 3 |
| 443 | 909876515 | 42.00 | c | Food622-P2-20151127-FO622-200T < Food62 < Food6 | 88-654310 | 2016-08-14 | 3 |
| 444 | 909876508 | 11.00 | c | Food514-P2-20151127-FO514-1000T < Food51 < Food5 | 88-654310 | 2016-08-15 | 2 |
| 445 | 909876508 | 15.00 | c | Food614-P2-20151127-FO614-200T < Food61 < Food6 | 88-654310 | 2016-08-15 | 1 |
| 446 | 909876524 | 24.00 | c | Food612-P2-20151127-FO612-200T < Food61 < Food6 | 88-654310 | 2016-08-16 | 2 |
| 447 | 909876524 | 13.00 | c | Food621-P2-20151127-FO621-200T < Food62 < Food6 | 88-654310 | 2016-08-16 | 1 |
| 448 | 909876522 | 13.00 | c | Food522-P2-20151127-FO522-1000T < Food52 < Food5 | 88-654310 | 2016-08-21 | 2 |
| 449 | 909876522 | 15.00 | c | Food614-P2-20151127-FO614-200T < Food61 < Food6 | 88-654310 | 2016-08-21 | 1 |
| 450 | 88-654306 | -38000.00 | t | Car3-C1-20160430-C3-050 < Car-inventory < Vehicle-inventory | 88-654310 | 2016-09-02 | -1 |
| 451 | 88-654310 | 38000.00 | e | Car3-C1-20160430-C3-050 < Car-inventory < Vehicle-inventory | 88-654310 | 2016-09-02 | 1 |
| 452 | 909876502 | 16.50 | c | Food514-P2-20151127-FO514-1000T < Food51 < Food5 | 88-654310 | 2016-09-05 | 3 |
| 453 | 909876502 | 13.00 | c | Food621-P2-20151127-FO621-200T < Food62 < Food6 | 88-654310 | 2016-09-05 | 1 |
| 454 | 909876504 | 15.00 | c | Food513-P2-20151127-FO513-1000T < Food51 < Food5 | 88-654310 | 2016-09-05 | 3 |
| 455 | 909876504 | 28.00 | c | Food622-P2-20151127-FO622-200T < Food62 < Food6 | 88-654310 | 2016-09-05 | 2 |
| 456 | 909876507 | 21.00 | c | Food43-P2-20151127-FO43-1000T < Food4 | 88-654310 | 2016-09-07 | 3 |
| 457 | 909876507 | 24.00 | c | Food612-P2-20151127-FO612-200T < Food61 < Food6 | 88-654310 | 2016-09-07 | 2 |
| 458 | 909876506 | 16.50 | c | Food514-P2-20151127-FO514-1000T < Food51 < Food5 | 88-654310 | 2016-09-15 | 3 |
| 459 | 909876506 | 36.00 | c | Food612-P2-20151127-FO612-200T < Food61 < Food6 | 88-654310 | 2016-09-15 | 3 |
| 460 | 909876515 | 19.50 | c | Food522-P2-20151127-FO522-1000T < Food52 < Food5 | 88-654310 | 2016-10-03 | 3 |
| 461 | 909876515 | 45.00 | c | Food614-P2-20151127-FO614-200T < Food61 < Food6 | 88-654310 | 2016-10-03 | 3 |
| 462 | 909876518 | 19.50 | c | Food522-P2-20151127-FO522-1000T < Food52 < Food5 | 88-654310 | 2016-10-04 | 3 |
| 463 | 909876518 | 39.00 | c | Food613-P2-20151127-FO613-200T < Food61 < Food6 | 88-654310 | 2016-10-04 | 3 |
| 464 | 909876521 | 13.00 | c | Food522-P2-20151127-FO522-1000T < Food52 < Food5 | 88-654310 | 2016-10-06 | 2 |
| 465 | 909876521 | 26.00 | c | Food613-P2-20151127-FO613-200T < Food61 < Food6 | 88-654310 | 2016-10-06 | 2 |
| 466 | 909876522 | 12.00 | c | Food621-P2-20151127-FO621-200T < Food62 < Food6 | 88-654310 | 2016-10-06 | 2 |
| 467 | 909876522 | 15.00 | c | Food614-P2-20151127-FO614-200T < Food61 < Food6 | 88-654310 | 2016-10-06 | 1 |
| 468 | 909876508 | 12.00 | c | Food511-P2-20151127-FO511-1000T < Food51 < Food5 | 88-654310 | 2016-10-08 | 3 |
| 469 | 909876508 | 16.00 | c | Food53-P2-20151127-FO53-1000T < Food5 | 88-654310 | 2016-10-08 | 2 |
| 470 | 909876524 | 13.00 | c | Food522-P2-20151127-FO522-1000T < Food52 < Food5 | 88-654310 | 2016-10-16 | 2 |
| 471 | 909876524 | 30.00 | c | Food614-P2-20151127-FO614-200T < Food61 < Food6 | 88-654310 | 2016-10-16 | 2 |
| 472 | 909876511 | 16.50 | c | Food514-P2-20151127-FO514-1000T < Food51 < Food5 | 88-654310 | 2016-11-01 | 3 |
| 473 | 909876511 | 14.00 | c | Food622-P2-20151127-FO622-200T < Food62 < Food6 | 88-654310 | 2016-11-01 | 1 |
| 474 | 909876504 | 16.50 | c | Food514-P2-20151127-FO514-1000T < Food51 < Food5 | 88-654310 | 2016-11-11 | 3 |
| 475 | 909876504 | 26.00 | c | Food613-P2-20151127-FO613-200T < Food61 < Food6 | 88-654310 | 2016-11-11 | 2 |
| 476 | 909876509 | 32.00 | c | Food53-P2-20151127-FO53-1000T < Food5 | 88-654310 | 2016-11-16 | 4 |
| 477 | 909876509 | 30.00 | c | Food614-P2-20151127-FO614-200T < Food61 < Food6 | 88-654310 | 2016-11-16 | 2 |
| 478 | 909876515 | 24.00 | c | Food53-P2-20151127-FO53-1000T < Food5 | 88-654310 | 2016-11-16 | 3 |
| 479 | 909876515 | 42.00 | c | Food622-P2-20151127-FO622-200T < Food62 < Food6 | 88-654310 | 2016-11-16 | 3 |
| 480 | 909876524 | 30.00 | c | Food611-P2-20151127-FO611-200T < Food61 < Food6 | 88-654310 | 2016-11-18 | 3 |
| 481 | 909876524 | 13.00 | c | Food621-P2-20151127-FO621-200T < Food62 < Food6 | 88-654310 | 2016-11-18 | 1 |
| 482 | 88-654310 | -6000.00 | p | Food411-P2-20161130-FO411-1200T < Food41 < Food4 | 88-654310 | 2016-11-30 | -1200 |
| 483 | 88-654310 | -6600.00 | p | Food412-P2-20161130-FO412-1200T < Food41 < Food4 | 88-654310 | 2016-11-30 | -1200 |
| 484 | 88-654310 | -7200.00 | p | Food421-P2-20161130-FO421-1200T < Food42 < Food4 | 88-654310 | 2016-11-30 | -1200 |
| 485 | 88-654310 | -7800.00 | p | Food422-P2-20161130-FO422-1200T < Food42 < Food4 | 88-654310 | 2016-11-30 | -1200 |
| 486 | 88-654310 | -8400.00 | p | Food43-P2-20161130-FO43-1200T < Food4 | 88-654310 | 2016-11-30 | -1200 |
| 487 | 88-654310 | -9000.00 | p | Food44-P2-20161130-FO44-1200T < Food4 | 88-654310 | 2016-11-30 | -1200 |
| 488 | 88-654310 | -4800.00 | p | Food511-P2-20161130-FO511-1200T < Food51 < Food5 | 88-654310 | 2016-11-30 | -1200 |
| 489 | 88-654310 | -5400.00 | p | Food512-P2-20161130-FO512-1200T < Food51 < Food5 | 88-654310 | 2016-11-30 | -1200 |
| 490 | 88-654310 | -6000.00 | p | Food513-P2-20161130-FO513-1200T < Food51 < Food5 | 88-654310 | 2016-11-30 | -1200 |
| 491 | 88-654310 | -6600.00 | p | Food514-P2-20161130-FO514-1200T < Food51 < Food5 | 88-654310 | 2016-11-30 | -1200 |
| 492 | 88-654310 | -7200.00 | p | Food521-P2-20161130-FO521-1200T < Food52 < Food5 | 88-654310 | 2016-11-30 | -1200 |

| | IDM | Amount | Symbol | MultiSubaccount | Recorder | TransDate | Unit |
|---|---|---|---|---|---|---|---|
| 493 | 88-654310 | -7800.00 | p | Food522-P2-20161130-FO522-1200T < Food52 < Food5 | 88-654310 | 2016-11-30 | -1200 |
| 494 | 88-654310 | -9600.00 | p | Food53-P2-20161130-FO53-1200T < Food5 | 88-654310 | 2016-11-30 | -1200 |
| 495 | 88-654310 | -10000.00 | p | Food611-P2-20161130-FO611-1000T < Food61 < Food6 | 88-654310 | 2016-11-30 | -1000 |
| 496 | 88-654310 | -12000.00 | p | Food612-P2-20161130-FO612-1000T < Food61 < Food6 | 88-654310 | 2016-11-30 | -1000 |
| 497 | 88-654310 | -13000.00 | p | Food613-P2-20161130-FO613-1000T < Food61 < Food6 | 88-654310 | 2016-11-30 | -1000 |
| 498 | 88-654310 | -15000.00 | p | Food614-P2-20161130-FO614-1000T < Food61 < Food6 | 88-654310 | 2016-11-30 | -1000 |
| 499 | 88-654310 | -13000.00 | p | Food621-P2-20161130-FO621-1000T < Food62 < Food6 | 88-654310 | 2016-11-30 | -1000 |
| 500 | 88-654310 | -14000.00 | p | Food622-P2-20161130-FO622-1000T < Food62 < Food6 | 88-654310 | 2016-11-30 | -1000 |
| 501 | 88-654310 | -5600.00 | p | Supplies1-P2-20161130-Supp1-800T | 88-654310 | 2016-11-30 | -800 |
| 502 | 88-654310 | -6400.00 | p | Supplies2-P2-20161130-Supp2-800T | 88-654310 | 2016-11-30 | -800 |
| 503 | 88-654306 | -2800.00 | t | Computer server1-C1-20160430-COMS1-045 < Computer server-inv... | 88-654310 | 2016-12-01 | -1 |
| 504 | 88-654306 | -1600.00 | t | Computer1-C1-20160430-COM1-062 < Computer-inventory | 88-654310 | 2016-12-01 | -1 |
| 505 | 88-654306 | -1500.00 | t | Computer2-C1-20160430-COM2-072 < Computer-inventory | 88-654310 | 2016-12-01 | -1 |
| 506 | 88-654310 | 2800.00 | e | Computer server1-C1-20160430-COMS1-045 < Computer server-inv... | 88-654310 | 2016-12-01 | 1 |
| 507 | 88-654310 | 1600.00 | e | Computer1-C1-20160430-COM1-062 < Computer-inventory | 88-654310 | 2016-12-01 | 1 |
| 508 | 88-654310 | 1500.00 | e | Computer2-C1-20160430-COM2-072 < Computer-inventory | 88-654310 | 2016-12-01 | 1 |
| 509 | 88-654303 | -1375.00 | t | Computer2-C1-201501008-COM2-066 | 88-654310 | 2016-12-01 | -1 |
| 510 | 88-654310 | 1375.00 | e | Computer2-C1-201501008-COM2-066 | 88-654310 | 2016-12-01 | 1 |
| 511 | 909876510 | 24.00 | c | Food612-P2-20151127-FO612-200T < Food61 < Food6 | 88-654310 | 2016-12-02 | 2 |
| 512 | 909876510 | 14.00 | c | Food622-P2-20151127-FO622-200T < Food62 < Food6 | 88-654310 | 2016-12-02 | 1 |
| 513 | 909876501 | 21.00 | c | Food43-P2-20151127-FO43-1000T < Food4 | 88-654310 | 2016-12-08 | 3 |
| 514 | 909876501 | 15.00 | c | Food44-P2-20151127-FO44-1000T < Food4 | 88-654310 | 2016-12-08 | 2 |
| 515 | 909876501 | 24.00 | c | Food612-P2-20151127-FO612-200T < Food61 < Food6 | 88-654310 | 2016-12-08 | 2 |
| 516 | 909876524 | 39.00 | c | Food613-P2-20151127-FO613-200T < Food61 < Food6 | 88-654310 | 2016-12-15 | 3 |
| 517 | 909876524 | 15.00 | c | Food614-P2-20151127-FO614-200T < Food61 < Food6 | 88-654310 | 2016-12-15 | 1 |
| 518 | 909876522 | 20.00 | c | Food611-P2-20151127-FO611-200T < Food61 < Food6 | 88-654310 | 2016-12-17 | 2 |
| 519 | 909876522 | 14.00 | c | Food622-P2-20151127-FO622-200T < Food62 < Food6 | 88-654310 | 2016-12-17 | 1 |
| 520 | 909876518 | 30.00 | c | Food611-P2-20151127-FO611-200T < Food61 < Food6 | 88-654310 | 2016-12-18 | 3 |
| 521 | 909876518 | 42.00 | c | Food622-P2-20151127-FO622-200T < Food62 < Food6 | 88-654310 | 2016-12-18 | 3 |
| 522 | 909876521 | 30.00 | c | Food611-P2-20151127-FO611-200T < Food61 < Food6 | 88-654310 | 2016-12-18 | 3 |
| 523 | 909876521 | 14.00 | c | Food622-P2-20151127-FO622-200T < Food62 < Food6 | 88-654310 | 2016-12-18 | 1 |
| 524 | 909876525 | 36.00 | c | Food612-P2-20151127-FO612-200T < Food61 < Food6 | 88-654310 | 2016-12-18 | 3 |
| 525 | 909876525 | 13.00 | c | Food613-P2-20151127-FO613-200T < Food61 < Food6 | 88-654310 | 2016-12-18 | 1 |
| 526 | 909876514 | 39.00 | c | Food621-P2-20151127-FO621-200T < Food62 < Food6 | 88-654310 | 2016-12-20 | 3 |
| 527 | 909876514 | 42.00 | c | Food622-P2-20151127-FO622-200T < Food62 < Food6 | 88-654310 | 2016-12-20 | 3 |
| 528 | 909876507 | 24.00 | c | Food53-P2-20151127-FO53-1000T < Food5 | 88-654310 | 2016-12-26 | 3 |
| 529 | 909876507 | 30.00 | c | Food614-P2-20151127-FO614-200T < Food61 < Food6 | 88-654310 | 2016-12-26 | 2 |
| 530 | 88-654310 | 91.00 | s | Supplies1-P2-20160430-Supp1-200T | 88-654310 | 2016-12-31 | 13 |
| 531 | 88-654310 | 88.00 | s | Supplies2-P2-20161130-Supp2-800T | 88-654310 | 2016-12-31 | 11 |
| 532 | 88-654310 | 91.00 | s | Supplies1-P2-20161130-Supp1-800T | 88-654310 | 2016-12-31 | 13 |
| 533 | 88-654310 | -91.00 | s | Supplies1-P2-20160430-Supp1-200T | 88-654310 | 2016-12-31 | -13 |

Query executed successfully.　　　　　　　　　　　　　　　　　　　　　　　　　　LIU\SQLE

Figure 3.10-2　Proprietorship2 Inventories Purchased or Sold by Other Members

# Chapter 4

# Analysis and Conclusion

## 4.1 Inventory Flows

Inventory flows is similar to the Cash flows. It shows that the changes of all two-level and one-level the subaccounts of the Inventory account during a fiscal year. Therefore, designing the different multi-subaccounts of the Inventory can get the different Inventory flows. The Figure 4.1-1 shows the Inventory flows of the Company1 in the fiscal year 2016.

Inventory Flows Statement

| Inventory Flows Statement Year Ended 2016-12-31 | |
|---|---|
| Vehicle-inventory | |
| Car-inventory | -$107,000.00 |
| Truck-inventory | $157,400.00 |
| Net Inventory provided by Vehicle-inventory | $50,400.00 |
| | |
| Computer-inventory | |
| Computer server-inventory | $13,700.00 |
| Computer1-C1-201501008-COM1-055 | -$1,000.00 |
| Computer1-C1-201501008-COM1-056 | -$1,000.00 |
| Computer1-C1-201501008-COM1-057 | -$1,000.00 |
| Computer1-C1-201501008-COM1-058 | -$1,000.00 |
| Computer1-C1-20160430-COM1-059 | $0.00 |
| Computer1-C1-20160430-COM1-060 | $0.00 |
| Computer1-C1-20160430-COM1-061 | $0.00 |
| Computer1-C1-20160430-COM1-062 | $0.00 |
| Computer1-C1-20160430-COM1-063 | $0.00 |
| Computer1-C1-20160430-COM1-064 | $0.00 |
| Computer1-C1-20160430-COM1-065 | $0.00 |
| Computer1-C1-20160430-COM1-066 | $0.00 |
| Computer1-C1-20160430-COM1-067 | $0.00 |
| Computer1-C1-20160430-COM1-068 | $0.00 |
| Computer1-C1-20161121-COM1-081 | $0.00 |
| Computer1-C1-20161121-COM1-082 | $1,000.00 |
| Computer1-C1-20161121-COM1-083 | $1,000.00 |
| Computer1-C1-20161121-COM1-084 | $1,000.00 |

| Inventory Flows Statement Year Ended 2016-12-31 | |
|---|---:|
| Computer1-C1-20161121-COM1-085 | $1,000.00 |
| Computer1-C1-20161121-COM1-086 | $1,000.00 |
| Computer1-C1-20161121-COM1-087 | $1,000.00 |
| Computer1-C1-20161121-COM1-088 | $1,000.00 |
| Computer1-C1-20161121-COM1-089 | $1,000.00 |
| Computer1-C1-20161121-COM1-090 | $1,000.00 |
| Computer1-C1-20161121-COM1-091 | $1,000.00 |
| Computer1-C1-20161121-COM1-092 | $1,000.00 |
| Computer1-C1-20161121-COM1-093 | $1,000.00 |
| Computer1-C1-20161121-COM1-094 | $1,000.00 |
| Computer1-C1-20161121-COM1-095 | $1,000.00 |
| Computer2-C1-201501008-COM2-065 | -$920.00 |
| Computer2-C1-201501008-COM2-066 | -$920.00 |
| Computer2-C1-201501008-COM2-067 | -$920.00 |
| Computer2-C1-20160430-COM2-069 | $0.00 |
| Computer2-C1-20160430-COM2-070 | $0.00 |
| Computer2-C1-20160430-COM2-071 | $0.00 |
| Computer2-C1-20160430-COM2-072 | $0.00 |
| Computer2-C1-20160430-COM2-073 | $0.00 |
| Computer2-C1-20160430-COM2-074 | $0.00 |
| Computer2-C1-20160430-COM2-075 | $0.00 |
| Computer2-C1-20160430-COM2-076 | $920.00 |
| Computer2-C1-20160430-COM2-077 | $920.00 |
| Computer2-C1-20160430-COM2-078 | $920.00 |
| Computer2-C1-20161121-COM2-011 | $920.00 |
| Computer2-C1-20161121-COM2-012 | $920.00 |
| Computer2-C1-20161121-COM2-013 | $920.00 |
| Computer2-C1-20161121-COM2-014 | $920.00 |
| Computer2-C1-20161121-COM2-015 | $920.00 |
| Computer2-C1-20161121-COM2-016 | $920.00 |
| Computer2-C1-20161121-COM2-017 | $920.00 |
| Computer2-C1-20161121-COM2-018 | $920.00 |
| Computer2-C1-20161121-COM2-019 | $920.00 |
| Computer2-C1-20161121-COM2-020 | $920.00 |
| Computer2-C1-20161121-COM2-021 | $920.00 |
| Computer2-C1-20161121-COM2-022 | $920.00 |
| Computer2-C1-20161121-COM2-023 | $920.00 |
| Computer2-C1-20161121-COM2-024 | $920.00 |
| Computer2-C1-20161121-COM2-025 | $920.00 |
| Computer3-C1-20160430-COM3-103 | $0.00 |
| Computer3-C1-20160430-COM3-104 | $830.00 |
| Computer3-C1-20160430-COM3-105 | $830.00 |
| Computer3-C1-20160430-COM3-106 | $830.00 |
| Computer3-C1-20160430-COM3-107 | $830.00 |
| Computer3-C1-20160430-COM3-108 | $830.00 |
| Computer3-C1-20160430-COM3-109 | $830.00 |
| Computer3-C1-20160430-COM3-110 | $830.00 |
| Computer3-C1-20160430-COM3-111 | $830.00 |
| Computer3-C1-20160430-COM3-112 | $830.00 |
| Computer3-C1-20160430-COM3-113 | $830.00 |

| | |
|---|---|
| Computer3-C1-20160430-COM3-114 | $830.00 |
| Computer3-C1-20161121-COM3-031 | $830.00 |
| Computer3-C1-20161121-COM3-032 | $830.00 |
| Computer3-C1-20161121-COM3-033 | $830.00 |
| Computer3-C1-20161121-COM3-034 | $830.00 |
| Computer3-C1-20161121-COM3-035 | $830.00 |
| Computer3-C1-20161121-COM3-036 | $830.00 |
| Computer3-C1-20161121-COM3-037 | $830.00 |
| Computer3-C1-20161121-COM3-038 | $830.00 |
| Computer3-C1-20161121-COM3-039 | $830.00 |
| Computer3-C1-20161121-COM3-040 | $830.00 |
| Computer3-C1-20161121-COM3-041 | $830.00 |
| Computer3-C1-20161121-COM3-042 | $830.00 |
| Computer3-C1-20161121-COM3-043 | $830.00 |
| Computer3-C1-20161121-COM3-044 | $830.00 |
| Computer3-C1-20161121-COM3-045 | $830.00 |
| Computer4-C1-20160430-COM4-103 | $770.00 |
| Computer4-C1-20160430-COM4-104 | $770.00 |
| Computer4-C1-20160430-COM4-105 | $770.00 |
| Computer4-C1-20160430-COM4-106 | $770.00 |
| Computer4-C1-20160430-COM4-107 | $770.00 |
| Computer4-C1-20160430-COM4-108 | $770.00 |
| Computer4-C1-20160430-COM4-109 | $770.00 |
| Computer4-C1-20160430-COM4-110 | $770.00 |
| Computer4-C1-20160430-COM4-111 | $770.00 |
| Computer4-C1-20160430-COM4-112 | $770.00 |
| Computer4-C1-20160430-COM4-113 | $770.00 |
| Computer4-C1-20160430-COM4-114 | $770.00 |
| Computer4-C1-20160430-COM4-115 | $770.00 |
| Computer4-C1-20160430-COM4-116 | $0.00 |
| Computer4-C1-20160430-COM4-117 | $0.00 |
| Computer4-C1-20161121-COM4-141 | $770.00 |
| Computer4-C1-20161121-COM4-142 | $770.00 |
| Computer4-C1-20161121-COM4-143 | $770.00 |
| Computer4-C1-20161121-COM4-144 | $770.00 |
| Computer4-C1-20161121-COM4-145 | $770.00 |
| Computer4-C1-20161121-COM4-146 | $770.00 |
| Computer4-C1-20161121-COM4-147 | $770.00 |
| Computer4-C1-20161121-COM4-148 | $770.00 |
| Computer4-C1-20161121-COM4-149 | $770.00 |
| Computer4-C1-20161121-COM4-150 | $770.00 |
| Computer4-C1-20161121-COM4-151 | $770.00 |
| Computer4-C1-20161121-COM4-152 | $770.00 |
| Computer4-C1-20161121-COM4-153 | $770.00 |
| Computer4-C1-20161121-COM4-154 | $770.00 |
| Computer4-C1-20161121-COM4-155 | $770.00 |
| Net Inventory provided by Computer-inventory | $80,640.00 |
| | |
| Inven2 | |
| ASD parts | -$600.00 |

| Inventory Flows Statement Year Ended 2016-12-31 | |
|---|---|
| Computer4-C1-20161121-COM4-146 | $770.00 |
| Computer4-C1-20161121-COM4-147 | $770.00 |
| Computer4-C1-20161121-COM4-148 | $770.00 |
| Computer4-C1-20161121-COM4-149 | $770.00 |
| Computer4-C1-20161121-COM4-150 | $770.00 |
| Computer4-C1-20161121-COM4-151 | $770.00 |
| Computer4-C1-20161121-COM4-152 | $770.00 |
| Computer4-C1-20161121-COM4-153 | $770.00 |
| Computer4-C1-20161121-COM4-154 | $770.00 |
| Computer4-C1-20161121-COM4-155 | $770.00 |
| Net Inventory provided by Computer-inventory | $80,640.00 |
| | |
| Inven2 | |
| ASD parts | -$600.00 |
| Inven21 | -$750.00 |
| Inven21-C3-20150922-In21-1250T | $0.00 |
| Inven22 | -$800.00 |
| Net Inventory provided by Inven2 | -$2,150.00 |
| | |
| Net change in Inventory | $128,890.00 |
| Inventory, Begining | $357,130.00 |
| Inventory, Ending | $486,020.00 |
| | |
| Total Inventory, Ending | $374,638.00 |

Figure 4.1-1   Company1 Inventory Flows

From the Figure 4.1-1, the Company1's computer products have two class of the Computer server-inventory and the Computer-inventory, which are also the one-level subaccounts of the Inventory account. For these computer server products, they have still two-level and three-level subaccounts, so the Inventory flows only shows the balance of the two-level subaccounts. For these computer products of the Computer1 to the Computer4, they have only two-level subaccounts, so the Inventory flows shows the detail information of the Computer1 to the Computer4.

For getting the detail information of the computer server, the searching function of the "EachSubAccount" box in the MathAccounting software can be used. The Figure 4.1-2 shows the detail information of the two-level subaccount "Computer server-inventory".

Inventory: Computer server-inventory

| ID | Multi-Name | Amount | Unit | General ID | Transaction Date |
|---|---|---|---|---|---|
| 54 | Computer server1-C1-201501007-COMS1-039 < Computer server-inventory < Computer-inventory | $1,600.00 | 1 | 14 | 2015-12-31 |
| 55 | Computer server1-C1-201501007-COMS1-040 < Computer server-inventory < Computer-inventory | $1,600.00 | 1 | 14 | 2015-12-31 |
| 56 | Computer server1-C1-201501008-COMS1-041 < Computer server-inventory < Computer-inventory | $1,600.00 | 1 | 14 | 2015-12-31 |
| 57 | Computer server2-C1-201501008-COMS2-045 < Computer server-inventory < Computer-inventory | $1,500.00 | 1 | 15 | 2015-12-31 |
| 58 | Computer server2-C1-201501008-COMS2-046 < Computer server-inventory < Computer-inventory | $1,500.00 | 1 | 15 | 2015-12-31 |
| 136 | Computer server1-C1-20160430-COMS1-042 < Computer server-inventory < Computer-inventory | $1,600.00 | 1 | 64 | 2016-04-30 |
| 137 | Computer server1-C1-20160430-COMS1-043 < Computer server-inventory < Computer-inventory | $1,600.00 | 1 | 64 | 2016-04-30 |
| 138 | Computer server1-C1-20160430-COMS1-044 < Computer server-inventory < Computer-inventory | $1,600.00 | 1 | 64 | 2016-04-30 |
| 139 | Computer server1-C1-20160430-COMS1-045 < Computer server-inventory < Computer-inventory | $1,600.00 | 1 | 64 | 2016-04-30 |
| 140 | Computer server2-C1-20160430-COMS2-047 < Computer server-inventory < Computer-inventory | $1,500.00 | 1 | 64 | 2016-04-30 |
| 141 | Computer server2-C1-20160430-COMS2-048 < Computer server-inventory < Computer-inventory | $1,500.00 | 1 | 64 | 2016-04-30 |
| 142 | Computer server2-C1-20160430-COMS2-049 < Computer server-inventory < Computer-inventory | $1,500.00 | 1 | 64 | 2016-04-30 |
| 143 | Computer server2-C1-20160430-COMS2-050 < Computer server-inventory < Computer-inventory | $1,500.00 | 1 | 64 | 2016-04-30 |
| 191 | Computer server1-C1-201501007-COMS1-039 < Computer server-inventory < Computer-inventory | -$1,600.00 | -1 | 71 | 2016-05-01 |
| 344 | Computer server2-C1-201501008-COMS2-045 < Computer server-inventory < Computer-inventory | -$1,500.00 | -1 | 97 | 2016-06-01 |
| 347 | Computer server1-C1-20160430-COMS1-044 < Computer server-inventory < Computer-inventory | -$1,600.00 | -1 | 98 | 2016-06-01 |
| 351 | Computer server1-C1-201501008-COMS1-041 < Computer server-inventory < Computer-inventory | -$1,600.00 | -1 | 107 | 2016-08-01 |
| 355 | Computer server1-C1-20160430-COMS1-043 < Computer server-inventory < Computer-inventory | -$1,600.00 | -1 | 109 | 2016-08-01 |
| 361 | Computer server1-C1-201501007-COMS1-040 < Computer server-inventory < Computer-inventory | -$1,600.00 | -1 | 125 | 2016-10-01 |
| 364 | Computer server1-C1-20160430-COMS1-042 < Computer server-inventory < Computer-inventory | -$1,600.00 | -1 | 126 | 2016-10-01 |
| 367 | Computer server2-C1-20160430-COMS2-047 < Computer server-inventory < Computer-inventory | -$1,500.00 | -1 | 127 | 2016-10-01 |
| 371 | Computer server1-C1-20161121-COMS1-080 < Computer server-inventory < Computer-inventory | $1,600.00 | 1 | 138 | 2016-11-21 |
| 372 | Computer server1-C1-20161121-COMS1-081 < Computer server-inventory < Computer-inventory | $1,600.00 | 1 | 138 | 2016-11-21 |
| 373 | Computer server1-C1-20161121-COMS1-082 < Computer server-inventory < Computer-inventory | $1,600.00 | 1 | 138 | 2016-11-21 |
| 374 | Computer server1-C1-20161121-COMS1-083 < Computer server-inventory < Computer-inventory | $1,600.00 | 1 | 138 | 2016-11-21 |
| 375 | Computer server1-C1-20161121-COMS1-084 < Computer server-inventory < Computer-inventory | $1,600.00 | 1 | 138 | 2016-11-21 |
| 376 | Computer server2-C1-20161121-COMS2-091 < Computer server-inventory < Computer-inventory | $1,500.00 | 1 | 138 | 2016-11-21 |
| 377 | Computer server2-C1-20161121-COMS2-092 < Computer server-inventory < Computer-inventory | $1,500.00 | 1 | 138 | 2016-11-21 |
| 378 | Computer server2-C1-20161121-COMS2-093 < Computer server-inventory < Computer-inventory | $1,500.00 | 1 | 138 | 2016-11-21 |
| 379 | Computer server2-C1-20161121-COMS2-094 < Computer server-inventory < Computer-inventory | $1,500.00 | 1 | 138 | 2016-11-21 |
| 380 | Computer server2-C1-20161121-COMS2-095 < Computer server-inventory < Computer-inventory | $1,500.00 | 1 | 138 | 2016-11-21 |
| 444 | Computer server1-C1-20160430-COMS1-045 < Computer server-inventory < Computer-inventory | -$1,600.00 | -1 | 151 | 2016-12-01 |
| | | $21,500.00 | 14 | | |

Figure 4.1-2   Detail Information of Computer Server-inventory

## 4.2 Function of Internet of Things

The combination of internet and the digital inventory is the Internet of Things. The Internet of Things will realize the intelligent recognition, tracking, monitoring and management of all inventories.

## 4.2.1 Data Integrity

For ensuring data integrity of the public database dcj200, I can compare a sum (unit) of a three-level subaccount for all recorders to a sum (unit) of a three-level subaccount of a producer by using of SQL Server query. Due to possible different names of the two-level and the one-level subaccounts in the organizations (companies), searching standard is only the three-level subaccount plus general character "%". If the absolute values of the two sums are equal, then the data of this product is complete and correct. Repeating this process can ensure data integrity of the public database dcj200.

Please pay attention. As a producer, its products can also be used by itself except for sales. Therefore, only the products with the Symbol "c" can be included in the summing process. As a customer, the interior transactions cannot be included in the summing process, which means that only transaction with the Symbol "t' can be included in the summing process. In a word, the interior transactions are not considered in the summing process for any organizations (companies). By using of this method, the Government can monitor and manage all inventory at any time.

The Figure 4.2-1 respectively shows searching results of the three products for the Company1, the Proprietorship1, and the Proprietorship2. Their absolute values of the sums all are equal.

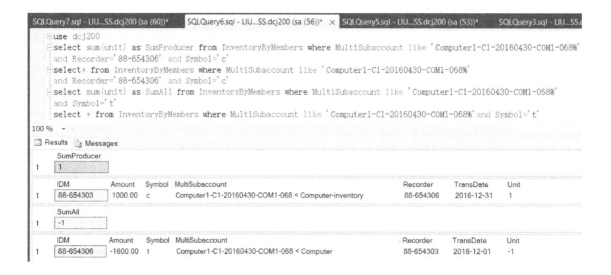

The Figure 4.2-1   Three Different Companies Products

## 4.2.2 Recognition of Product Producer

For a product on my hand, I want to know its producer. Then, I can also search it in the public database dcj200 by using of SQL Server query. The Figure 4.2-2 shows searching results. From the Figure 4.2-2, the three products' producers are the Company1 (Recorder: 88-654306), the Proprietorship1 (Recorder: 88-654309), and the Proprietorship2 (Recorder: 88-654310) respectively.

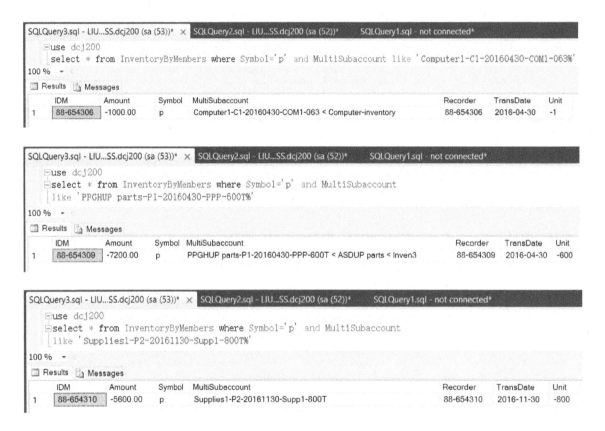

Figure 4.2-2   Recognition of Product Producer

## 4.2.3 Tracing Product

When I want to know a product distribution process, I can also search it in the public database dcj200 by using of SQL Server query. The results of searching the "Computer2-C1-201501008-COM2-066 < Computer-inventory" is in the Figure 4.2-3. From this figure, there are three recorders which are the Company1 (ID: 88-654306), the Tax Bureau (ID: 88-654303), and the Proprietorship2 (ID: 88-654310) in an order according to the time.

First, when the Company1 converted to the Mathaccounting software on December 31, 2015, this Computer2 was recorded by the Company1 itself with the Order 1.

Second, there are the three transactions on October, 1, 2016. The Company1 sold this Computer2 to the Tax Bureau and recorded this transaction with the Order 4. And the Tax Bureau purchased this Computer2 from the Company1 and recorded this transaction with the Order 2. Meanwhile, the Tax Bureau transferred this Coputer2 to the Equipment and recorded this interior transaction with the Order 3.

Last, there are the four transactions on December, 1, 2016. The Tax Bureau transferred the used Computer2 to the Inventory account for sales and recorded this interior transaction with the Order 6. Then the Tax Bureau sold this used Computer2 to the Proprietorship2 and recorded the transaction with the Order 7. On the other hand, the Proprietorship2 purchased the used Computer2 and recorded the transaction with the Order 8. Meanwhile, the Proprietorship2 transferred the used Computer2 to the Equipment and recorded the interior transaction with the Order 5.

Figure 4.2-3   Tracing Computer2 Distribution Process

The Figure 4.2-4 on the next page shows the distribution process of the "Supplies1-P2-20160430-Supp1-200T". There are four recorders which are the Company1 (ID: 88-654306), the Proprietorship2 (ID: 88-654310), the Proprietorship1 (ID: 88-654309), and the Company3 (ID: 88-654308) in an order according to the time.

First, when the Proprietorship2 produced the Supplies1 (200) on April 30, 2016 and recorded the interior transaction with the Order 3 and the Symbol "p". Then the Proprietorship2 sold the Supplies1 (110) to the Company1 and recorded the transaction with the Order 2. Meanwhile, the Company1 purchased the Supplies1 (110) and recorded the transaction with the Order 1.

Second, there are the three transactions on May 1, 2016. The Proprietorship2 sold the Supplies1 (50) to the Proprietorship1 and recorded this transaction with the Order 4. And the Proprietorship2 transferred Supplies1 (27) to the Cost of goods manufactured account and recorded this interior transaction with the Order 5. Meanwhile, the Proprietorship1 purchased the Supplies1 (50) from the Proprietorship2 and recorded this transaction with the Order 6.

Then, on May 2, 2016, the Proprietorship1 transferred Supplies1 (48) to the Cost of goods manufactured account and recorded this interior transaction with the Order 7.

Then, on May 20, 2016, the Company1 transferred Supplies1 (96) to the Cost of goods manufactured account and recorded this interior transaction with the Order 8.

Then, on June 15, 2016, The Proprietorship2 sold the Supplies1 (6) to the Company3 and recorded this transaction with the Order 10. Meanwhile, the Company3 purchased the Supplies1 (6) from the Proprietorship2 and recorded this transaction with the Order 9.

Then, on November 30, 2016, the Proprietorship1 transferred Supplies1 (2) to the Cost of goods manufactured account and recorded this interior transaction with the Order11.

Last, there are the four transactions on December, 31, 2016. The Proprietorship1 transferred the Supplies1 (4) to the XXX expenses account and recorded this interior transaction with the Order 12. And the Proprietorship2 transferred the Supplies1 (11) to the XXX expenses account and recorded this interior transaction with the Order 15. In addition, I made a mistake in entering a Proprietorship2's interior transaction, so I entered an interior transaction with the Order 13 and the Order 14 to correct this mistake.

```
use dcj200
select * from InventoryByMembers where MultiSubaccount like 'Supplies1-P2-20160430-Supp1-200T%'
order by TransDate
```

100 %  ▾

▦ Results  🗐 Messages

|    | IDM | Amount | Symbol | MultiSubaccount | Recorder | TransDate | Unit |
|----|-----|--------|--------|-----------------|----------|-----------|------|
| 1  | 88-654310 | -1540.00 | t | Supplies1-P2-20160430-Supp1-200T | 88-654306 | 2016-04-30 | -110 |
| 2  | 88-654306 | 770.00 | c | Supplies1-P2-20160430-Supp1-200T | 88-654310 | 2016-04-30 | 110 |
| 3  | 88-654310 | -1400.00 | p | Supplies1-P2-20160430-Supp1-200T | 88-654310 | 2016-04-30 | -200 |
| 4  | 88-654309 | 350.00 | c | Supplies1-P2-20160430-Supp1-200T | 88-654310 | 2016-05-01 | 50 |
| 5  | 88-654310 | 189.00 | f | Supplies1-P2-20160430-Supp1-200T | 88-654310 | 2016-05-01 | 27 |
| 6  | 88-654310 | -700.00 | t | Supplies1-P2-20160430-Supp1-200T | 88-654309 | 2016-05-01 | -50 |
| 7  | 88-654309 | 672.00 | f | Supplies1-P2-20160430-Supp1-200T | 88-654309 | 2016-05-02 | 48 |
| 8  | 88-654306 | 1344.00 | f | Supplies1-P2-20160430-Supp1-200T | 88-654306 | 2016-05-20 | 96 |
| 9  | 88-654310 | -84.00 | t | Supplies1-P2-20160430-Supp1-200T | 88-654308 | 2016-06-15 | -6 |
| 10 | 88-654308 | 42.00 | c | Supplies1-P2-20160430-Supp1-200T | 88-654310 | 2016-06-15 | 6 |
| 11 | 88-654309 | -28.00 | f | Supplies1-P2-20160430-Supp1-200T | 88-654309 | 2016-11-30 | -2 |
| 12 | 88-654309 | 56.00 | s | Supplies1-P2-20160430-Supp1-200T | 88-654309 | 2016-12-31 | 4 |
| 13 | 88-654310 | 91.00 | s | Supplies1-P2-20160430-Supp1-200T | 88-654310 | 2016-12-31 | 13 |
| 14 | 88-654310 | -91.00 | s | Supplies1-P2-20160430-Supp1-200T | 88-654310 | 2016-12-31 | -13 |
| 15 | 88-654306 | 154.00 | s | Supplies1-P2-20160430-Supp1-200T | 88-654306 | 2016-12-31 | 11 |

Figure 4.2-4   Tracing Supplies1 Distribution Process

# 4.3 Mixed Digital Inventory Model

The mixed digital inventory model is based on the mixed digital currency model. The mixed digital currency means that there is some paper money in the process of money circulation. In this situation, the MathAccounting software is also a good solution and the possibility of drawing up false accounts, tax evasion, and money laundering is very small. Moreover, taking some measures and doing analysis can prevent them to occur.

In the mixed digital currency model, there should be not any cash transaction between organizations (companies) because an organization (company) only pay cash to its employees. Therefore, cash transaction can only be occurred between an organization (company) and an individual or between an individual and another individual.

When an individual pays (or receives) some paper money to another individual (from another individual), this transaction does not have any issue of the taxation. In this situation, the accounting principle can discard this kind of transaction.

When an organization (company) received paper cash from an individual for sales, the organization (company) may record this transaction. Therefore, I define a public individual ID 999999999. When any organization (company) received paper cash from an individual, the multi-subaccount name of the Cash account is the "9999999999-c-paper < Cash receipts from customers < Operating activities".

Of course, for purpose of tax evasion, when an organization (company) received paper cash from an individual, it does not record this transaction. In addition, some transactions may use paper cash between the organizations (companies) and they are not recorded. In this situation, only method is to monitor these organizations' (companies') bank deposits.

# APPENDIXES

## Appendixes A    Deposit Transactions in the Business Bank1

**Cash Management Center**
- On January 2, 2016, the Cash Management Center's cash deposit decreases -$85,000. Please pay attention. The multi-subaccount name of the Cash account and transaction sub-equation respectively are:

    88-654300-d-deposits < Cash receipts from customers deposits < Operating activities

    Cash (1): -85000 = Deposits payable (2): -85000 = 0

- On January 2, 2016, the Cash Management Center's cash deposit decreases -$90,000.
- On January 2, 2016, the Cash Management Center's cash deposit decreases -$95,000.
- On June 1, 2016, the Cash Management Center's cash deposit decreases -$25,000.
- On December 31, 2016, the Cash Management Center's cash deposit decreases -$2,400.
- On December 31, 2016, individual A1's cash deposit increases $200.
- On December 31, 2016, individual A2's cash deposit increases $200.
- On December 31, 2016, individual A3's cash deposit increases $200.
- On December 31, 2016, individual A7's cash deposit increases $200.
- On December 31, 2016, individual A9's cash deposit increases $200
- On December 31, 2016, individual A15's cash deposit increases $200.
- On December 31, 2016, individual A16's cash deposit increases $200.
- On December 31, 2016, the Cash Management Center's cash deposit decreases -$2,500.
- On December 31, 2016, the Cash Management Center's cash deposit increases $656.25.
- On December 31, 2016, the Cash Management Center's cash deposit increases $xxx.

**Central Bank.**
- On January 18, 2016, the A1's cash deposit decreases -$39.
- On January 21, 2016, the A1's cash deposit increases $176.56.
- On January 31, 2016, the A1's cash deposit increases $2,800.
- On January 31, 2016, the A2's cash deposit increases $2,850.
- On February 28, 2016, the A1's cash deposit increases $2,800.
- On February 28, 2016, the A2's cash deposit increases $2,850.
- On March 26, 2016, the A2's cash deposit decreases -$72.
- On March 28, 2016, the A2's cash deposit increases $459.61.
- On March 31, 2016, the A1's cash deposit increases $2,800.
- On March 31, 2016, the A2's cash deposit increases $2,850.
- On April 15, 2016, the A2's cash deposit decreases -$50.
- On April 19, 2016, the A2's cash deposit increases $159.78.
- On April 30, 2016, the A1's cash deposit increases $2,800.
- On April 30, 2016, the A2's cash deposit increases $2,850.
- On May 31, 2016, the A1's cash deposit increases $2,800.
- On May 31, 2016, the A2's cash deposit increases $2,850.
- On June 18, 2016, the A2's cash deposit decreases -$136.
- On June 22, 2016, the A2's cash deposit increases $477.25.
- On June 30, 2016, the A1's cash deposit increases $2,800.
- On June 30, 2016, the A2's cash deposit increases $2,850.
- On July 31, 2016, the A1's cash deposit increases $2,800.
- On July 31, 2016, the A2's cash deposit increases $2,850.
- On August 31, 2016, the A1's cash deposit increases $2,800.
- On August 31, 2016, the A2's cash deposit increases $2,850.
- On September 5, 2016, the A2's cash deposit decreases -$59.
- On September 7, 2016, the A2's cash deposit increases $233.16.
- On September 30, 2016, the A1's cash deposit increases $2,800.
- On September 30, 2016, the A2's cash deposit increases $2,850.
- On October 31, 2016, the A1's cash deposit increases $2,800.
- On October 31, 2016, the A2's cash deposit increases $2,850.
- On November 30, 2016, the A1's cash deposit increases $2,800.
- On November 30, 2016, the A2's cash deposit increases $2,850.
- On December 8, 2016, the A1's cash deposit decreases -$120.

- On December 11, 2016, the A2's cash deposit increases $233.16.
- On December 31, 2016, the A1's cash deposit increases $2,800.
- On December 31, 2016, the A2's cash deposit increases $2,850.

**Government1**
- On January 2, 2016, the Government1's cash deposit increases $90,000.
- On January 6, 2016, the A3's cash deposit decreases -$108.
- On January 9, 2016, the Government1's cash deposit decreases -$307.23.
- On January 9, 2016, the A3's cash deposit increases $307.23.
- On January 15, 2016, the Government1's cash deposit increases $600.
- On January 31, 2016, the Government1's cash deposit decreases -$5,660.
- On January 31, 2016, the A3's cash deposit increases $2,810.
- On January 31, 2016, the A4's cash deposit increases $2,850.
- On February 21, 2016, the Government1's cash deposit decreases -$500.
- On February 25, 2016, the A3's cash deposit decreases -$99.
- On February 28, 2016, the Government1's cash deposit decreases -$5,660.
- On February 28, 2016, the A3's cash deposit increases $2,810.
- On February 28, 2016, the A4's cash deposit increases $2,850.
- On February 28, 2016, the Government1's cash deposit decreases -$295.17.
- On February 28, 2016, the A3's cash deposit increases $295.17.
- On March 19, 2016, the A4's cash deposit decreases -$172.
- On March 22, 2016, the Government1's cash deposit decreases -$558.34.
- On March 22, 2016, the A4's cash deposit increases $558.34.
- On March 31, 2016, the Government1's cash deposit decreases -$5,660.
- On March 31, 2016, the A3's cash deposit increases $2,810.
- On March 31, 2016, the A4's cash deposit increases $2,850.
- On April 20, 2016, the A4's cash deposit decreases -$100.
- On April 24, 2016, the Government1's cash deposit decreases -$283.53.
- On April 24, 2016, the A4's cash deposit increases $283.53.
- On April 30, 2016, the Government1's cash deposit decreases -$5,660.
- On April 30, 2016, the A3's cash deposit increases $2,810.
- On April 30, 2016, the A4's cash deposit increases $2,850.
- On April 30, 2016, the Government1's cash deposit decreases -$330.
- On April 30, 2016, the Government1's cash deposit decreases -$60.
- On May 1, 2016, the Government1's cash deposit decreases -$8,000.
- On May 14, 2016, the A3's cash deposit decreases -$105.
- On May 16, 2016, the Government1's cash deposit decreases -$415.97.
- On May 16, 2016, the A3's cash deposit increases $415.97.
- On May 31, 2016, the Government1's cash deposit decreases -$5,660.
- On May 31, 2016, the A3's cash deposit increases $2,810.
- On May 31, 2016, the A4's cash deposit increases $2,850.
- On June 1, 2016, the Government1's cash deposit decreases -$5,000.
- On June 15, 2016, the A3's cash deposit decreases -$93.
- On June 17, 2016, the Government1's cash deposit decreases -$272.59.
- On June 17, 2016, the A3's cash deposit increases $272.59.
- On June 30, 2016, the Government1's cash deposit decreases -$5,660.
- On June 30, 2016, the A3's cash deposit increases $2,810.
- On June 30, 2016, the A4's cash deposit increases $2,850.
- On July 16, 2016, the A4's cash deposit decreases -$112.
- On July 19, 2016, the Government1's cash deposit decreases -$336.87.
- On July 19, 2016, the A4's cash deposit increases $336.87.
- On July 31, the Government1's cash deposit decreases -$5,660.
- On July 31, 2016, the A3's cash deposit increases $2,810.
- On July 31, 2016, the A4's cash deposit increases $2,850.
- On August 10, 2016, the A3's cash deposit decreases -$150.
- On August 13, 2016, the Government1's cash deposit decreases -$481.11.
- On August 13, 2016, the A3's cash deposit increases $481.11.
- On August 31, the Government1's cash deposit decreases -$5,660.
- On August 31, 2016, the A3's cash deposit increases $2,810.
- On August 31, 2016, the A4's cash deposit increases $2,850.
- On September 5, 2016, the A4's cash deposit decreases -$86.
- On September 7, 2016, the Government1's cash deposit decreases -$384.46.

- On September 7, 2016, the A4's cash deposit increases $384.46.
- On September 25, 2016, the Government1's cash deposit decreases -$3,200.
- On September 30, the Government1's cash deposit decreases -$5,660.
- On September 30, 2016, the A3's cash deposit increases $2,810.
- On September 30, 2016, the A4's cash deposit increases $2,850.
- On October 3, the Government1's cash deposit decreases -$990.
- On October 21, 2016, the A3's cash deposit decreases -$121.
- On October 24, 2016, the Government1's cash deposit decreases -$377.77.
- On October 24, 2016, the A3's cash deposit increases $377.77.
- On October 31, the Government1's cash deposit decreases -$5,660.
- On October 31, 2016, the A3's cash deposit increases $2,810.
- On October 31, 2016, the A4's cash deposit increases $2,850.
- On November 11, 2016, the A4's cash deposit decreases -$85.
- On November 14, 2016, the Government1's cash deposit decreases -$375.39.
- On November 14, 2016, the A4's cash deposit increases $375.39.
- On November 30, the Government1's cash deposit decreases -$5,660.
- On November 30, 2016, the A3's cash deposit increases $2,810.
- On November 30, 2016, the A4's cash deposit increases $2,850.
- On December 20, 2016, the A3's cash deposit decreases -$129.
- On December 23, 2016, the Government1's cash deposit decreases -$514.62.
- On December 23, 2016, the A3's cash deposit increases $514.62.
- On December 30, the Government1's cash deposit decreases -$2,000.
- On December 31, the Government1's cash deposit decreases -$5,660.
- On December 31, 2016, the A3's cash deposit increases $2,810.
- On December 31, 2016, the A4's cash deposit increases $2,850.
- On December 31, 2016, the Government1's cash deposit increases $240.
- On December 31, 2016, the Government1's cash deposit increases $500.25.
- On December 31, 2016, the Government1's cash deposit increases $120.

**Tax Bureau**
- On January 2, 2016, the Tax Bureau's cash deposit increases $95,000.
- On January 10, 2016, the A5's cash deposit decreases -$98.
- On January 10, 2016, the A6's cash deposit decreases -$92.
- On January 12, 2016, the Tax Bureau's cash deposit decreases -$283.71.
- On January 12, 2016, the A5's cash deposit increases $283.71.
- On January 12, 2016, the Tax Bureau's cash deposit decreases -$277.71.
- On January 12, 2016, the A6's cash deposit increases $277.71.
- On January 13, 2016, the Tax Bureau's cash deposit decreases -$60.
- On January 31, 2016, the Tax Bureau's cash deposit decreases -$5,670.
- On January 31, 2016, the A5's cash deposit increases $2,810.
- On January 31, 2016, the A6's cash deposit increases $2,860.
- On February 2, 2016, the Tax Bureau's cash deposit decreases -$500.
- On February 11, 2016, the Tax Bureau's cash deposit decreases -$400.
- On February 23, 2016, the Tax Bureau's cash deposit decreases -$300.
- On February 24, 2016, the A5's cash deposit decreases -$110.
- On February 26, 2016, the Tax Bureau's cash deposit decreases -$335.63.
- On February 26, 2016, the A5's cash deposit increases $335.63.
- On February 28, 2016, the Tax Bureau's cash deposit decreases -$5,670.
- On February 28, 2016, the A5's cash deposit increases $2,810.
- On February 28, 2016, the A6's cash deposit increases $2,860.
- On March 10, 2016, the A6's cash deposit decreases -$123.
- On March 12, 2016, the Tax Bureau's cash deposit decreases -$419.99.
- On March 12, 2016, the A6's cash deposit increases $419.99.
- On March 31, 2016, the Tax Bureau's cash deposit decreases -$5,670.
- On March 31, 2016, the A5's cash deposit increases $2,810.
- On March 31, 2016, the A6's cash deposit increases $2,860.
- On April 13, 2016, the A5's cash deposit decreases -$112.
- On April 16, 2016, the Tax Bureau's cash deposit decreases -$358.13.
- On April 16, 2016, the A5's cash deposit increases $358.13.
- On April 30, 2016, the Tax Bureau's cash deposit decreases -$5,670.
- On April 30, 2016, the A5's cash deposit increases $2,810.
- On April 30, 2016, the A6's cash deposit increases $2,860.

- On May 8, 2016, the Tax Bureau's cash deposit decreases -$300.
- On May 13, 2016, the A6's cash deposit decreases -$112.
- On May 16, 2016, the Tax Bureau's cash deposit decreases -$443.18.
- On May 16, 2016, the A6's cash deposit increases $443.18.
- On May 31, 2016, the Tax Bureau's cash deposit decreases -$5,670.
- On May 31, 2016, the A5's cash deposit increases $2,810.
- On May 31, 2016, the A6's cash deposit increases $2,860.
- On June 1, 2016, the Tax Bureau's cash deposit decreases -$5,000.
- On June 17, 2016, the A5's cash deposit decreases -$93.
- On June 17, 2016, the A6's cash deposit decreases -$90.
- On June 20, 2016, the Tax Bureau's cash deposit decreases -$364.55.
- On June 20, 2016, the A5's cash deposit increases $364.55.
- On June 20, 2016, the Tax Bureau's cash deposit decreases -$361.55.
- On June 20, 2016, the A6's cash deposit increases $361.55.
- On June 29, 2016, the Tax Bureau's cash deposit decreases -$2,000.
- On June 30, 2016, the Tax Bureau's cash deposit decreases -$5,670.
- On June 30, 2016, the A5's cash deposit increases $2,810.
- On June 30, 2016, the A6's cash deposit increases $2,860.
- On July 22, 2016, the A5's cash deposit decreases -$105.
- On July 24, 2016, the Tax Bureau's cash deposit decreases -$317.22.
- On July 24, 2016, the A5's cash deposit increases $317.22.
- On July 31, 2016, the Tax Bureau's cash deposit decreases -$5,670.
- On July 31, 2016, the A5's cash deposit increases $2,810.
- On July 31, 2016, the A6's cash deposit increases $2,860.
- On August 9, 2016, the A6's cash deposit decreases -$114.
- On August 11, 2016, the Tax Bureau's cash deposit decreases -$395.47.
- On August 11, 2016, the A6's cash deposit increases $395.47.
- On August 31, 2016, the Tax Bureau's cash deposit decreases -$5,670.
- On August 31, 2016, the A5's cash deposit increases $2,810.
- On August 31, 2016, the A6's cash deposit increases $2,860.
- On September 15, 2016, the A6's cash deposit decreases -$105.
- On September 17, 2016, the Tax Bureau's cash deposit decreases -$399.36.
- On September 17, 2016, the A6's cash deposit increases $399.36.
- On September 30, 2016, the Tax Bureau's cash deposit decreases -$5,670.
- On September 30, 2016, the A5's cash deposit increases $2,810.
- On September 30, 2016, the A6's cash deposit increases $2,860.
- On October 1, 2016, the Tax Bureau's cash deposit decreases -$2,400.
- On October 3, 2016, the Tax Bureau's cash deposit decreases -$4,500.
- On October 22, 2016, the A5's cash deposit decreases -$116.
- On October 25, 2016, the Tax Bureau's cash deposit decreases -$369.53.
- On October 25, 2016, the A5's cash deposit increases $369.53.
- On October 31, 2016, the Tax Bureau's cash deposit decreases -$5,670.
- On October 31, 2016, the A5's cash deposit increases $2,810.
- On October 31, 2016, the A6's cash deposit increases $2,860.
- On November 15, 2016, the A6's cash deposit decreases -$93.
- On November 18, 2016, the Tax Bureau's cash deposit decreases -$388.19.
- On November 18, 2016, the A6's cash deposit increases $388.19.
- On November 19, 2016, the Tax Bureau's cash deposit decreases -$1,400.
- On November 30, 2016, the Tax Bureau's cash deposit decreases -$5,670.
- On November 30, 2016, the A5's cash deposit increases $2,810.
- On November 30, 2016, the A6's cash deposit increases $2,860.
- On December 26, 2016, the A5's cash deposit decreases -$192.
- On December 26, 2016, the A6's cash deposit decreases -$198.
- On December 28, 2016, the Tax Bureau's cash deposit decreases -$664.58.
- On December 28, 2016, the A5's cash deposit increases $664.58.
- On December 28, 2016, the Tax Bureau's cash deposit decreases -$670.58.
- On December 28, 2016, the A6's cash deposit increases $670.58.
- On December 28, 2016, the Tax Bureau's cash deposit decreases -$2500.
- On December 29, 2016, the Tax Bureau's cash deposit decreases -$2400.
- On December 31, 2016, the Tax Bureau's cash deposit decreases -$5,670.
- On December 31, 2016, the A5's cash deposit increases $2,810.
- On December 31, 2016, the A6's cash deposit increases $2,860.

- On December 31, 2016, the Tax Bureau's cash deposit increases $200.
- On December 31, 2016, the Tax Bureau's cash deposit increases $459.25.
- On December 31, 2016, the Tax Bureau's cash deposit increases $120.
- On December 31, 2016, the Tax Bureau's cash deposit increases $x1.
- On December 31, 2016, the Tax Bureau's cash deposit increases $x2.
- On December 31, 2016, the Tax Bureau's cash deposit increases $x3.
- On December 31, 2016, the Tax Bureau's cash deposit increases $x4.
- On December 31, 2016, the Tax Bureau's cash deposit increases $x5.
- On December 31, 2016, the Tax Bureau's cash deposit increases $x6.
- On December 31, 2016, the Tax Bureau's cash deposit increases $x7.
- On December 31, 2016, the Tax Bureau's cash deposit decreases -$XX.

**Company1**
- On January 2, 2016, the Company1's cash deposit decreases -$200.
- On January 13, 2016, the Company1's cash deposit increases $60.
- On January 14, 2016, the Company1's cash deposit decreases -$11,000.
- On January 14, 2016, the Company1's cash deposit decreases -$8,000.
- On January 15, 2016, the Company1's cash deposit decreases -$415.67.
- On January 15, 2016, the A13's cash deposit increases $415.67.
- On January 16, 2016, the Company1's cash deposit decreases -$42.12.
- On January 16, 2016, the A15's cash deposit increases $42.12.
- On January 31, 2016, the Company1's cash deposit decreases -$2,040.
- On January 31, 2016, the Company1's cash deposit decreases -$1,000.
- On January 31, 2016, the Company1's cash deposit decreases -$8,400.
- On January 31, 2016, the A14's cash deposit increases $2,900.
- On January 31, 2016, the A13's cash deposit increases $2,600.
- On January 31, 2016, the A15's cash deposit increases $2,900.
- On February 1, 2016, the Company1's cash deposit increases $19,000.
- On February 1, 2016, the Company1's cash deposit increases $28,000.
- On February 1, 2016, the Company1's cash deposit increases $30,000.
- On February 1, 2016, the Company1's cash deposit decreases -$49.68.
- On February 1, 2016, the A14's cash deposit increases $49.68.
- On February 2, 2016, the Company1's cash deposit increases $500.
- On February 13, 2016, the Company1's cash deposit increases $800.
- On February 20, 2016, the Company1's cash deposit decreases -$557.83.
- On February 20, 2016, the A13's cash deposit increases $557.83.
- On February 25, 2016, the Company1's cash deposit increases $600.
- On February 27, 2016, the Company1's cash deposit increases $900.
- On February 28, 2016, the Company1's cash deposit decreases -$8,400.
- On February 28, 2016, the A14's cash deposit increases $2,900.
- On February 28, 2016, the A13's cash deposit increases $2,600.
- On February 28, 2016, the A15's cash deposit increases $2,900.
- On March 1, 2016, the Company1's cash deposit increases $19,000.
- On March 4, 2016, the Company1's cash deposit decreases -$2,400.
- On March 4, 2016, the Company1's cash deposit decreases -$1,600.
- On March 6, 2016, the Company1's cash deposit increases $1,000.
- On March 9, 2016, the Company1's cash deposit increases $2,000.
- On March 23, 2016, the Company1's cash deposit decreases -$516.37.
- On March 23, 2016, the A13's cash deposit increases $516.37.
- On March 25, 2016, the Company1's cash deposit increases $600.
- On March 30, 2016, the Company1's cash deposit decreases -$239.73.
- On March 30, 2016, the A14's cash deposit increases $239.73.
- On March 31, 2016, the Company1's cash deposit decreases -$8,400.
- On March 31, 2016, the A14's cash deposit increases $2,900.
- On March 31, 2016, the A13's cash deposit increases $2,600.
- On March 31, 2016, the A15's cash deposit increases $2,900.
- On April 28, 2016, the Company1's cash deposit decreases -$717.38.
- On April 28, 2016, the A13's cash deposit increases $717.38.
- On April 29, 2016, the Company1's cash deposit decreases -$1,000.
- On April 30, 2016, the Company1's cash deposit increases $60.
- On April 12, 2016, the Company1's cash deposit decreases -$1,300.
- On April 30, 2016, the Company1's cash deposit decreases -$8,400.

- On April 30, 2016, the A14's cash deposit increases $2,900.
- On April 30, 2016, the A13's cash deposit increases $2,600.
- On April 30, 2016, the A15's cash deposit increases $2,900.
- On May 1, 2016, the Company1's cash deposit increases $1,900.
- On May 1, 2016, the Company1's cash deposit increases $8,000.
- On May 1, 2016, the Company1's cash deposit decreases -$15,000.
- On May 1, 2016, the Company1's cash deposit decreases -$3,250.
- On May 1, 2016, the Company1's cash deposit decreases -$2,300.
- On May 24, 2016, the Company1's cash deposit decreases -$623.75.
- On May 24, 2016, the A13's cash deposit increases $623.75.
- On May 31, 2016, the Company1's cash deposit decreases -$8,400.
- On May 31, 2016, the A14's cash deposit increases $2,900.
- On May 31, 2016, the A13's cash deposit increases $2,600.
- On May 31, 2016, the A15's cash deposit increases $2,900.
- On June 1, 2016, the Company1's cash deposit increases $3,000.
- On June 10, 2016, the Company1's cash deposit decreases -$15,000.
- On June 12, 2016, the Company1's cash deposit decreases -$64,000.
- On June 23, 2016, the Company1's cash deposit decreases -$580.91.
- On June 23, 2016, the A13's cash deposit increases $580.91.
- On June 30, 2016, the Company1's cash deposit decreases -$8,400.
- On June 30, 2016, the A14's cash deposit increases $2,900.
- On June 30, 2016, the A13's cash deposit increases $2,600.
- On June 30, 2016, the A15's cash deposit increases $2,900.
- On July 7, 2016, the Company1's cash deposit decreases -$442.56.
- On July 7, 2016, the A14's cash deposit increases $442.56.
- On July 19, 2016, the Company1's cash deposit increases $1,300.
- On July 19, 2016, the A8's cash deposit decreases -$1,300.
- On July 25, 2016, the Company1's cash deposit decreases -$487.84.
- On July 25, 2016, the A13's cash deposit increases $487.84.
- On July 31, 2016, the Company1's cash deposit decreases -$8,400.
- On July 31, 2016, the A14's cash deposit increases $2,900.
- On July 31, 2016, the A13's cash deposit increases $2,600.
- On July 31, 2016, the A15's cash deposit increases $2,900.
- On August 1, 2016, the Company1's cash deposit increases $5,000.
- On August 1, 2016, the Company1's cash deposit increases $38,000.
- On August 1, 2016, the A16's cash deposit decreases -$10,000.
- On August 1, 2016, the A23's cash deposit decreases -$11,500.
- On August 1, 2016, the Company1's cash deposit increases $3,000.
- On August 2, 2016, the Company1's cash deposit increases $1,600.
- On August 2, 2016, the A1's cash deposit decreases -$1,600.
- On August 3, 2016, the Company1's cash deposit decreases -$12,000.
- On August 10, 2016, the Company1's cash deposit increases $1,500.
- On August 14, 2016, the Company1's cash deposit increases $1,040.
- On August 17, 2016, the Company1's cash deposit decreases -$386.36.
- On August 17, 2016, the A15's cash deposit increases $386.36.
- On August 25, 2016, the Company1's cash deposit decreases -$501.22.
- On August 25, 2016, the A13's cash deposit increases $501.22.
- On August 31, 2016, the Company1's cash deposit decreases -$8,400.
- On August 31, 2016, the A14's cash deposit increases $2,900.
- On August 31, 2016, the A13's cash deposit increases $2,600.
- On August 31, 2016, the A15's cash deposit increases $2,900.
- On September 2, 2016, the Company1's cash deposit increases $18,000.
- On September 12, 2016, the Company1's cash deposit increases $18,000.
- On September 13, 2016, the Company1's cash deposit decreases -$25,000.
- On September 14, 2016, the Company1's cash deposit decreases -$10,000.
- On September 26, 2016, the Company1's cash deposit increases $17,000.
- On September 26, 2016, the Company1's cash deposit decreases -$8,000.
- On September 28, 2016, the Company1's cash deposit decreases -$658.33.
- On September 28, 2016, the A13's cash deposit increases $658.33.
- On September 30, 2016, the Company1's cash deposit decreases -$8,400.
- On September 30, 2016, the A14's cash deposit increases $2,900.
- On September 30, 2016, the A13's cash deposit increases $2,600.

- On September 30, 2016, the A15's cash deposit increases $2,900.
- On October 1, 2016, the Company1's cash deposit increases $2,400.
- On October 1, 2016, the Company1's cash deposit increases $5,000.
- On October 1, 2016, the Company1's cash deposit increases $5,500.
- On October 3, 2016, the Company1's cash deposit increases $990.
- On October 5, 2016, the Company1's cash deposit increases $39,000.
- On October 5, 2016, the A13's cash deposit decreases -$10,000.
- On October 5, 2016, the A25's cash deposit decreases -$10,500.
- On October 7, 2016, the Company1's cash deposit decreases -$392.36.
- On October 7, 2016, the A15's cash deposit increases $392.36.
- On October 27, 2016, the Company1's cash deposit decreases -$607.57.
- On October 27, 2016, the A13's cash deposit increases $607.57.
- On October 31, 2016, the Company1's cash deposit decreases -$8,400.
- On October 31, 2016, the A14's cash deposit increases $2,900.
- On October 31, 2016, the A13's cash deposit increases $2,600.
- On October 31, 2016, the A15's cash deposit increases $2,900.
- On November 5, 2016, the Company1's cash deposit increases $2,900.
- On November 19, 2016, the Company1's cash deposit decreases -$551.13.
- On November 19, 2016, the A13's cash deposit increases $551.13.
- On November 19, 2016, the Company1's cash deposit increases $1,400.
- On November 19, 2016, the Company1's cash deposit decreases -$401.13.
- On November 19, 2016, the A15's cash deposit increases $401.13.
- On November 29, 2016, the Company1's cash deposit decreases -$14,420.
- On November 29, 2016, the Company1's cash deposit decreases -$3,000.
- On November 29, 2016, the Company1's cash deposit increases $1,500.
- On November 29, 2016, the A4's cash deposit decreases -$1,500.
- On November 30, 2016, the Company1's cash deposit increases $1,500.
- On November 30, 2016, the A18's cash deposit decreases -$1,500.
- On November 30, 2016, the Company1's cash deposit increases $1,300.
- On November 30, 2016, the A6's cash deposit decreases -$1,300.
- On November 30, 2016, the Company1's cash deposit decreases -$8,400.
- On November 30, 2016, the A14's cash deposit increases $2,900.
- On November 30, 2016, the A13's cash deposit increases $2,600.
- On November 30, 2016, the A15's cash deposit increases $2,900.
- On December 1, 2016, the Company1's cash deposit increases $5.000.
- On December 10, 2016, the Company1's cash deposit increases $1,600.
- On December 10, 2016, the A24's cash deposit decreases -$1,600.
- On December 11, 2016, the Company1's cash deposit increases $1,500.
- On December 16, 2016, the Company1's cash deposit decreases -$638.34.
- On December 16, 2016, the A13's cash deposit increases $638.34.
- On December 19, 2016, the Company1's cash deposit increases $1,600.
- On December 19, 2016, the Company1's cash deposit increases $2,800.
- On December 22, 2016, the Company1's cash deposit increases $1,400.
- On December 22, 2016, the A2's cash deposit decreases -$1,400.
- On December 23, 2016, the Company1's cash deposit decreases -$444.45.
- On December 23, 2016, the A14's cash deposit increases $444.45.
- On December 23, 2016, the Company1's cash deposit decreases -$5,500.
- On December 23, 2016, the Company1's cash deposit decreases -$18,000.
- On December 29, 2016, the Company1's cash deposit increases $2,400.
- On December 29, 2016, the Company1's cash deposit increases $10,000.
- On December 29, 2016, the Company1's cash deposit increases $27,000.
- On December 29, 2016, the Company1's cash deposit decreases -$39,700.
- On December 30, 2016, the Company1's cash deposit increases $2,000.
- On December 30, 2016, the Company1's cash deposit increases $1,400.
- On December 31, 2016, the Company1's cash deposit increases $3,500.
- On December 31, 2016, the Company1's cash deposit increases $40,000.
- On December 31, 2016, the A7's cash deposit decreases -$40,000.
- On December 31, 2016, the Company1's cash deposit increases $40,000.
- On December 31, 2016, the Company1's cash deposit decreases -$8,400.
- On December 31, 2016, the A14's cash deposit increases $2,900.
- On December 31, 2016, the A13's cash deposit increases $2,600.
- On December 31, 2016, the A15's cash deposit increases $2,900.

- On December 31, 2016, the Company1's cash deposit increases $38,000.
- On December 31, 2016, the A24's cash deposit decreases -$38,000.
- On December 31, 2016, the Company1's cash deposit decreases -$55,000.
- On December 31, 2016, the Company1's cash deposit decreases -$22,500.
- On December 31, 2016, the Company1's cash deposit decreases -$16,150.
- On December 31, 2016, the Company1's cash deposit decreases -$19,800.
- On December 31, 2016, the Company1's cash deposit decreases -$230.
- On December 31, 2016, the Company1's cash deposit decreases -$138.
- On December 31, 2016, the A1's cash deposit increases $138.
- On December 31, 2016, the Company1's cash deposit decreases -$276.
- On December 31, 2016, the A2's cash deposit increases $276.
- On December 31, 2016, the Company1's cash deposit decreases -$230.
- On December 31, 2016, the A8's cash deposit increases $230.
- On December 31, 2016, the Company1's cash deposit decreases -$322.
- On December 31, 2016, the Company1's cash deposit decreases -$92.
- On December 31, 2016, the A14's cash deposit increases $92.
- On December 31, 2016, the Company1's cash deposit decreases -$184.
- On December 31, 2016, the A16's cash deposit increases $184.
- On December 31, 2016, the Company1's cash deposit decreases -$92.
- On December 31, 2016, the A18's cash deposit increases $92.
- On December 31, 2016, the Company1's cash deposit decreases -$138.
- On December 31, 2016, the Company1's cash deposit decreases -$230.
- On December 31, 2016, the Company1's cash deposit decreases -$138.
- On December 31, 2016, the A24's cash deposit increases $138.
- On December 31, 2016, the Company1's cash deposit decreases -$230.
- On December 31, 2016, the A25's cash deposit increases $230.
- On December 31, 2016, the Company1's cash deposit increases $400.
- On December 31, 2016, the Company1's cash deposit increases $135.
- On December 31, 2016, the Company1's cash deposit increases $369.
- On December 31, 2016, the Company1's cash deposit increases $120.

**Company2**
- On January 12, 2016, the A25's cash deposit decreases -$360.
- On January 15, 2016, the A16's cash deposit increases $411.32.
- On January 30, 2016, the A18's cash deposit increases $379.78.
- On January 31, 2016, the A16's cash deposit increases $2,610.
- On January 31, 2016, the A18's cash deposit increases $2,880.
- On February 20, 2016, the A16's cash deposit increases $557.83.
- On February 28, 2016, the A16's cash deposit increases $2,610.
- On February 28, 2016, the A18's cash deposit increases $2,880.
- On March 1, 2016, the A18's cash deposit increases $221.16.
- On March 23, 2016, the A16's cash deposit increases $347.65.
- On March 31, 2016, the A16's cash deposit increases $2,610.
- On March 31, 2016, the A18's cash deposit increases $2,880.
- On April 12, 2016, the A1's cash deposit decreases -$310.
- On April 26, 2016, the A16's cash deposit increases $369.88.
- On April 30, 2016, the A16's cash deposit increases $2,610.
- On April 30, 2016, the A18's cash deposit increases $2,880.
- On May 2, 2016, the A18's cash deposit increases $307.09.
- On May 3, 2016, the A13's cash deposit decreases -$290.
- On May 24, 2016, the A16's cash deposit increases $366.59.
- On May 31, 2016, the A16's cash deposit increases $2,610.
- On May 31, 2016, the A18's cash deposit increases $2,880.
- On June 23, 2016, the A16's cash deposit increases $362.81.
- On June 30, 2016, the A16's cash deposit increases $2,610.
- On June 30, 2016, the A18's cash deposit increases $2,880.
- On July 11, 2016, the A5's cash deposit decreases -$290.
- On July 13, 2016, the A7's cash deposit decreases -$320.
- On July 27, 2016, the A16's cash deposit increases $307.41.
- On July 31, 2016, the A16's cash deposit increases $2,610.
- On July 31, 2016, the A18's cash deposit increases $2,880.
- On August 23, 2016, the A16's cash deposit increases $392.33.

- On August 31, 2016, the A16's cash deposit increases $2,610.
- On August 31, 2016, the A18's cash deposit increases $2,880.
- On September 28, 2016, the A16's cash deposit increases $410.89.
- On September 30, 2016, the A16's cash deposit increases $2,610.
- On September 30, 2016, the A18's cash deposit increases $2,880.
- On October 6, 2016, the A18's cash deposit increases $377.63.
- On October 27, 2016, the A16's cash deposit increases $396.27.
- On October 31, 2016, the A16's cash deposit increases $2,610.
- On October 31, 2016, the A18's cash deposit increases $2,880.
- On November 19, 2016, the A16's cash deposit increases $399.28.
- On November 20, 2016, the A18's cash deposit decreases -$360.
- On November 30, 2016, the A16's cash deposit increases $2,610.
- On November 30, 2016, the A18's cash deposit increases $2,880.
- On December 17, 2016, the A16's cash deposit increases $395.88.
- On December 20, 2016, the A18's cash deposit increases $424.37.
- On December 31, 2016, the A16's cash deposit increases $2,610.
- On December 31, 2016, the A18's cash deposit increases $2,880.
- On December 31, 2016, the A4's cash deposit increases $188.
- On December 31, 2016, the A5's cash deposit increases $94.
- On December 31, 2016, the A6's cash deposit increases $47
- On December 31, 2016, the A13's cash deposit increases $235.
- On December 31, 2016, the A15's cash deposit increases $94.
- On December 31, 2016, the A24's cash deposit increases $235.
- On December 31, 2016, the A25's cash deposit increases $94.

**Company3**
- On January 31, 2016, the A6's cash deposit decreases -$350
- On February 1, 2016, the A24's cash deposit decreases -$10,010.
- On February 1, 2016, the A25's cash deposit decreases -$10,270.
- On March 24, 2016, the A2's cash deposit decreases -$3,500.
- On July 11, 2016, the A4's cash deposit decreases -$250.
- On August 13, 2016, the A13's cash deposit decreases -$700.
- On September 4, 2016, the A18's cash deposit decreases -$520.
- On October 3, 2016, the A15's cash deposit decreases -$550.
- On November 20, 2016, the A6's cash deposit decreases -$640.
- On December 31, 2016, the A1's cash deposit increases $288.
- On December 31, 2016, the A2's cash deposit increases $192.
- On December 31, 2016, the A3's cash deposit increases $336.
- On December 31, 2016, the A7's cash deposit increases $288.
- On December 31, 2016, the A8's cash deposit increases $192.
- On December 31, 2016, the A9's cash deposit increases $240.
- On December 31, 2016, the A14's cash deposit increases $240.
- On December 31, 2016, the A16's cash deposit increases $336.
- On December 31, 2016, the A18's cash deposit increases $288.

**Proprietorship1**
- On January 2, 2016, the Proprietorship1's cash deposit decreases -$450.
- On January 2, 2016, the Proprietorship1's cash deposit decreases -$10,000.
- On January 3, 2016, the Proprietorship1's cash deposit increases $9,300.
- On January 6, 2016, the Proprietorship1's cash deposit increases $108.
- On January 10, 2016, the Proprietorship1's cash deposit increases $98.
- On January 10, 2016, the Proprietorship1's cash deposit increases $92.
- On January 13, 2016, the Proprietorship1's cash deposit decreases -$150.
- On January 13, 2016, the Proprietorship1's cash deposit increases $20.
- On January 13, 2016, the A15's cash deposit decreases -$20.
- On January 13, 2016, the Proprietorship1's cash deposit increases $192.
- On January 13, 2016, the A16's cash deposit decreases -$192.
- On January 16, 2016, the Proprietorship1's cash deposit increases $57.
- On January 16, 2016, the A8's cash deposit decreases -$57.
- On January 16, 2016, the Proprietorship1's cash deposit increases $44.
- On January 18, 2016, the Proprietorship1's cash deposit increases $51.
- On January 18, 2016, the Proprietorship1's cash deposit decreases -$153.87.

- On January 19, 2016, the Proprietorship1's cash deposit increases $57.
- On January 19, 2016, the A25's cash deposit decreases -$57.
- On January 25, 2016, the Proprietorship1's cash deposit increases $100.
- On January 25, 2016, the A9's cash deposit decreases -$100.
- On January 26, 2016, the Proprietorship1's cash deposit increases $1,300.
- On January 27, 2016, the Proprietorship1's cash deposit decreases -$250.
- On January 27, 2016, the Proprietorship1's cash deposit increases $57.
- On January 28, 2016, the Proprietorship1's cash deposit increases $144.
- On January 28, 2016, the A18's cash deposit decreases -$144.
- On January 28, 2016, the Proprietorship1's cash deposit increases $42.
- On January 28, 2016, the Proprietorship1's cash deposit increases $44.
- On January 30, 2016, the Proprietorship1's cash deposit increases $500.
- On January 30, 2016, the Proprietorship1's cash deposit decreases -$145.54.
- On January 31, 2016, the Proprietorship1's cash deposit increases $2,040.
- On January 31, 2016, the Proprietorship1's cash deposit decreases -$5,670.
- On January 31, 2016, the Proprietorship1's cash deposit increases $10,400.
- On January 31, 2016, the A12 (secondary card)'s cash deposit decreases -$10,400.
- On January 31, 2016, the Proprietorship1's cash deposit increases $14,560.
- On January 31, 2016, the A1's cash deposit decreases -$14,560.
- On January 31, 2016, the Proprietorship1's cash deposit increases $13,000.
- On January 31, 2016, the A2's cash deposit decreases -$13,000.
- On January 31, 2016, the Proprietorship1's cash deposit increases $13,130.
- On January 31, 2016, the A3's cash deposit decreases -$13,130.
- On January 31, 2016, the Proprietorship1's cash deposit increases $14,430.
- On January 31, 2016, the A4's cash deposit decreases -$14,430.
- On January 31, 2016, the Proprietorship1's cash deposit increases $14,170.
- On January 31, 2016, the A5's cash deposit decreases -$14,170.
- On January 31, 2016, the Proprietorship1's cash deposit increases $12,610.
- On January 31, 2016, the A6's cash deposit decreases -$12,610.
- On January 31, 2016, the Proprietorship1's cash deposit increases $12,400.
- On January 31, 2016, the A7's cash deposit decreases -$12,400.
- On January 31, 2016, the Proprietorship1's cash deposit increases $13,000.
- On January 31, 2016, the A8's cash deposit decreases -$13,000.
- On January 31, 2016, the Proprietorship1's cash deposit increases $18,460.
- On January 31, 2016, the A9's cash deposit decreases -$18,460.
- On January 31, 2016, the Proprietorship1's cash deposit increases $13,900.
- On January 31, 2016, the Proprietorship1's cash deposit increases $14,430.
- On January 31, 2016, the Proprietorship1's cash deposit increases $14,560.
- On January 31, 2016, the Proprietorship1's cash deposit increases $18,460.
- On January 31, 2016, the A13's cash deposit decreases -$18,460.
- On February 1, 2016, the Proprietorship1's cash deposit decreases -$28,000.
- On February 17, 2016, the Proprietorship1's cash deposit increases $310.
- On February 17, 2016, the A13's cash deposit decreases -$310.
- On February 20, 2016, the Proprietorship1's cash deposit increases $400.
- On February 21, 2016, the Proprietorship1's cash deposit decreases -$300.
- On February 23, 2016, the Proprietorship1's cash deposit increases $124.
- On February 24, 2016, the Proprietorship1's cash deposit increases $110.
- On February 25, 2016, the Proprietorship1's cash deposit increases $99.
- On February 28, 2016, the Proprietorship1's cash deposit increases $102.
- On February 28, 2016, the A18's cash deposit decreases -$102.
- On February 28, 2016, the Proprietorship1's cash deposit increases $102.
- On February 28, 2016, the Proprietorship1's cash deposit decreases -$5,670.
- On March 6, 2016, the Proprietorship1's cash deposit decreases -$1,000.
- On March 7, 2016, the Proprietorship1's cash deposit increases $78.
- On March 7, 2016, the A25's cash deposit decreases -$78.
- On March 10, 2016, the Proprietorship1's cash deposit increases $123.
- On March 11, 2016, the Proprietorship1's cash deposit increases $50.
- On March 19, 2016, the Proprietorship1's cash deposit increases $172.
- On March 23, 2016, the Proprietorship1's cash deposit decreases -$159.45.
- On March 26, 2016, the Proprietorship1's cash deposit increases $72.
- On March 27, 2016, the Proprietorship1's cash deposit increases $51.
- On March 27, 2016, the A8's cash deposit decreases -$51.

- On March 31, 2016, the Proprietorship1's cash deposit decreases -$5,670.
- On April 13, 2016, the Proprietorship1's cash deposit increases $69.
- On April 22, 2016, the Proprietorship1's cash deposit increases $75.
- On April 22, 2016, the A24's cash deposit decreases -$75.
- On April 24, 2016, the Proprietorship1's cash deposit increases $156.
- On April 24, 2016, the A16's cash deposit decreases -$156.
- On April 24, 2016, the Proprietorship1's cash deposit increases $78.
- On April 27, 2016, the Proprietorship1's cash deposit increases $102.
- On April 27, 2016, the A7's cash deposit decreases -$102.
- On April 29, 2016, the Proprietorship1's cash deposit decreases -$5,000.
- On April 30, 2016, the Proprietorship1's cash deposit decreases -$5,670.
- On May 1, 2016, the Proprietorship1's cash deposit decreases -$800.
- On May 1, 2016, the Proprietorship1's cash deposit decreases -$5,000.
- On May 1, 2016, the Proprietorship1's cash deposit increases $3,250.
- On May 1, 2016, the Proprietorship1's cash deposit increases $9,000.
- On May 1, 2016, the Proprietorship1's cash deposit increases $90.
- On May 1, 2016, the A18's cash deposit decreases -$90.
- On May 1, 2016, the Proprietorship1's cash deposit increases $50.
- On May 12, 2016, the Proprietorship1's cash deposit increases $112.
- On May 12, 2016, the A9's cash deposit decreases -$112.
- On May 12, 2016, the Proprietorship1's cash deposit increases $50.
- On May 13, 2016, the Proprietorship1's cash deposit increases $112.
- On May 14, 2016, the Proprietorship1's cash deposit decreases -$166.23.
- On May 14, 2016, the Proprietorship1's cash deposit increases $105.
- On May 20, 2016, the Proprietorship1's cash deposit increases $56.
- On May 22, 2016, the Proprietorship1's cash deposit increases $403.
- On May 22, 2016, the A13's cash deposit decreases -$403.
- On May 22, 2016, the Proprietorship1's cash deposit increases $155.
- On May 22, 2016, the A16's cash deposit decreases -$155.
- On May 22, 2016, the Proprietorship1's cash deposit increases $138.
- On May 24, 2016, the Proprietorship1's cash deposit decreases -$176.95.
- On May 31, 2016, the Proprietorship1's cash deposit decreases -$5,670.
- On June 14, 2016, the Proprietorship1's cash deposit increases $96.
- On June 14, 2016, the A9's cash deposit decreases -$96.
- On June 16, 2016, the Proprietorship1's cash deposit increases $300.
- On June 18, 2016, the Proprietorship1's cash deposit increases $109.
- On June 20, 2016, the Proprietorship1's cash deposit increases $310.
- On June 20, 2016, the A13's cash deposit decreases -$310.
- On June 20, 2016, the Proprietorship1's cash deposit increases $163.
- On June 20, 2016, the A16's cash deposit decreases -$163.
- On June 21, 2016, the Proprietorship1's cash deposit increases $108
- On June 23, 2016, the Proprietorship1's cash deposit decreases -$157.37.
- On June 30, 2016, the Proprietorship1's cash deposit decreases -$5,670.
- On July 4, 2016, the Proprietorship1's cash deposit decreases -$55,000.
- On July 5, 2016, the Proprietorship1's cash deposit increases $180.
- On July 5, 2016, the A14's cash deposit decreases -$180.
- On July 16, 2016, the Proprietorship1's cash deposit increases $112.
- On July 21, 2016, the Proprietorship1's cash deposit increases $125.
- On July 22, 2016, the Proprietorship1's cash deposit increases $302.
- On July 22, 2016, the A13's cash deposit decreases -$302.
- On July 22, 2016, the Proprietorship1's cash deposit increases $105.
- On July 25, 2016, the Proprietorship1's cash deposit increases $118.
- On July 25, 2016, the A16's cash deposit decreases -$118.
- On July 25, 2016, the Proprietorship1's cash deposit increases $88.
- On July 25, 2016, the Proprietorship1's cash deposit increases $64.
- On July 27, 2016, the Proprietorship1's cash deposit decreases -$187.55.
- On July 31, 2016, the Proprietorship1's cash deposit decreases -$5,670.
- On July 31, 2016, the Proprietorship1's cash deposit increases $10,270.
- On July 31, 2016, the Proprietorship1's cash deposit increases $18,460.
- On July 31, 2016, the A14's cash deposit decreases -$18,460.
- On July 31, 2016, the Proprietorship1's cash deposit increases $18,200.
- On July 31, 2016, the A15's cash deposit decreases -$18,200.

- On July 31, 2016, the Proprietorship1's cash deposit increases $18,720.
- On July 31, 2016, the A16's cash deposit decreases -$18,720.
- On July 31, 2016, the Proprietorship1's cash deposit increases $17,940.
- On July 31, 2016, the Proprietorship1's cash deposit increases $18,460.
- On July 31, 2016, the A18's cash deposit decreases -$18,460.
- On July 31, 2016, the Proprietorship1's cash deposit increases $18,590.
- On July 31, 2016, the Proprietorship1's cash deposit increases $10,400.
- On July 31, 2016, the Proprietorship1's cash deposit increases $10,660.
- On July 31, 2016, the Proprietorship1's cash deposit increases $10,530.
- On July 31, 2016, the Proprietorship1's cash deposit increases $11,050.
- On July 31, 2016, the Proprietorship1's cash deposit increases $11,570.
- On July 31, 2016, the A24's cash deposit decreases -$11,570.
- On July 31, 2016, the Proprietorship1's cash deposit increases $12,090.
- On July 31, 2016, the A25's cash deposit decreases -$12,090.
- On August 10, 2016, the Proprietorship1's cash deposit increases $150.
- On August 14, 2016, the Proprietorship1's cash deposit increases $120.
- On August 17, 2016, the Proprietorship1's cash deposit decreases -$65,000.
- On August 17, 2016, the Proprietorship1's cash deposit increases $63.
- On August 20, 2016, the Proprietorship1's cash deposit increases $162.
- On August 20, 2016, the A16's cash deposit decreases -$162.
- On August 21, 2016, the Proprietorship1's cash deposit increases $78.
- On August 22, 2016, the Proprietorship1's cash deposit increases $112.
- On August 22, 2016, the Proprietorship1's cash deposit increases $312.
- On August 22, 2016, the A13's cash deposit decreases -$312.
- On August 23, 2016, the Proprietorship1's cash deposit decreases -$166.18.
- On August 31, 2016, the Proprietorship1's cash deposit decreases -$5,670.
- On September 15, 2016, the Proprietorship1's cash deposit increases $300.
- On September 17, 2016, the Proprietorship1's cash deposit increases $112.
- On September 17, 2016, the A9's cash deposit decreases -$112.
- On September 17, 2016, the Proprietorship1's cash deposit increases $104.
- On September 19, 2016, the Proprietorship1's cash deposit increases $99.
- On September 19, 2016, the A24's cash deposit decreases -$99.
- On September 26, 2016, the Proprietorship1's cash deposit increases $451.
- On September 26, 2016, the A13's cash deposit decreases -$451.
- On September 26, 2016, the Proprietorship1's cash deposit decreases -$1,800.
- On September 26, 2016, the Proprietorship1's cash deposit increases $183.
- On September 26, 2016, the A16's cash deposit decreases -$183.
- On September 26, 2016, the Proprietorship1's cash deposit increases $87.
- On September 30, 2016, the Proprietorship1's cash deposit decreases -$5,670.
- On October 1, 2016, the Proprietorship1's cash deposit decreases -$5,500.
- On October 8, 2016, the Proprietorship1's cash deposit decreases -$168.73.
- On October 12, 2016, the Proprietorship1's cash deposit decreases -$31,000.
- On October 16, 2016, the Proprietorship1's cash deposit increases $108.
- On October 21, 2016, the Proprietorship1's cash deposit increases $121.
- On October 22, 2016, the Proprietorship1's cash deposit increases $116.
- On October 22, 2016, the Proprietorship1's cash deposit increases $114.
- On October 22, 2016, the A9's cash deposit decreases -$114.
- On October 24, 2016, the Proprietorship1's cash deposit increases $383.
- On October 24, 2016, the A13's cash deposit decreases -$383.
- On October 25, 2016, the Proprietorship1's cash deposit increases $25,000.
- On October 25, 2016, the Proprietorship1's cash deposit increases $174.
- On October 25, 2016, the A16's cash deposit decreases -$174.
- On October 25, 2016, the Proprietorship1's cash deposit increases $90.
- On October 31, 2016, the Proprietorship1's cash deposit decreases -$5,670.
- On November 15, 2016, the Proprietorship1's cash deposit increases $93.
- On November 15, 2016, the Proprietorship1's cash deposit increases $361.
- On November 15, 2016, the A13's cash deposit decreases -$361.
- On November 17, 2016, the Proprietorship1's cash deposit increases $184.
- On November 17, 2016, the A16's cash deposit decreases -$184.
- On November 17, 2016, the Proprietorship1's cash deposit increases $87.
- On November 19, 2016, the Proprietorship1's cash deposit increases $100.
- On November 19, 2016, the Proprietorship1's cash deposit decreases -$177.16.

- On November 30, 2016, the Proprietorship1's cash deposit decreases -$5,670.
- On December 13, 2016, the Proprietorship1's cash deposit increases $413.
- On December 13, 2016, the A13's cash deposit decreases -$413.
- On December 15, 2016, the Proprietorship1's cash deposit increases $99.
- On December 15, 2016, the A9's cash deposit decreases -$99.
- On December 15, 2016, the Proprietorship1's cash deposit increases $104.
- On December 15, 2016, the Proprietorship1's cash deposit increases $74.
- On December 15, 2016, the Proprietorship1's cash deposit increases $174.
- On December 15, 2016, the A16's cash deposit decreases -$174.
- On December 17, 2016, the Proprietorship1's cash deposit decreases -$207.52.
- On December 19, 2016, the Proprietorship1's cash deposit decreases -$198.35.
- On December 20, 2016, the Proprietorship1's cash deposit increases $129.
- On December 23, 2016, the Proprietorship1's cash deposit increases $18,000.
- On December 26, 2016, the Proprietorship1's cash deposit increases $192.
- On December 26, 2016, the Proprietorship1's cash deposit increases $198.
- On December 27, 2016, the Proprietorship1's cash deposit increases $125.
- On December 29, 2016, the Proprietorship1's cash deposit decreases -$10,000.
- On December 31, 2016, the Proprietorship1's cash deposit decreases -$4,300.
- On December 31, 2016, the Proprietorship1's cash deposit decreases -$5,670.
- On December 31, 2016, the Proprietorship1's cash deposit decreases -$11,280.
- On December 31, 2016, the Proprietorship1's cash deposit decreases -$2,500.
- On December 31, 2016, the A4's cash deposit increases $150.
- On December 31, 2016, the A5's cash deposit increases $200.
- On December 31, 2016, the A6's cash deposit increases $250.
- On December 31, 2016, the A8's cash deposit increases $100.
- On December 31, 2016, the A13's cash deposit increases $250.
- On December 31, 2016, the A15's cash deposit increases $200.
- On December 31, 2016, the A16's cash deposit increases $100.
- On December 31, 2016, the A18's cash deposit increases $150.
- On December 31, 2016, the Proprietorship1's cash deposit increases $416.
- On December 31, 2016, the Proprietorship1's cash deposit increases $352.
- On December 31, 2016, the Proprietorship1's cash deposit increases $120.

**Proprietorship2**
- On January 12, 2016, the A24's cash deposit decreases -$118.
- On January 13, 2016, the A13's cash deposit decreases -$208.
- On January 14, 2016, the A24's cash deposit increases $255.37.
- On January 15, 2016, the A11's cash deposit decreases -$54.
- On January 20, 2016, the A7's cash deposit decreases -$82.
- On January 21, 2016, the A25's cash deposit increases $149.65.
- On January 31, 2016, the A14's cash deposit decreases -$24.
- On January 31, 2016, the A24's cash deposit increases $2,870.
- On January 31, 2016, the A25's cash deposit increases $2,790.
- On January 31, 2016, the A14's cash deposit decreases -$10,920.
- On January 31, 2016, the A15's cash deposit decreases -$11,050.
- On January 31, 2016, the A16's cash deposit decreases -$11,180.
- On January 31, 2016, the A18's cash deposit decreases -$11,830.
- On January 31, 2016, the A24's cash deposit decreases -$10,010.
- On January 31, 2016, the A25's cash deposit decreases -$10,270.
- On February 6, 2016, the A12's cash deposit decreases -$116 (second card).
- On February 17, 2016, the A16's cash deposit decreases -$310.
- On February 19, 2016, the A9's cash deposit decreases -$112.
- On February 22, 2016, the A8's cash deposit decreases -$96.
- On February 23, 2016, the A24's cash deposit decreases -$62.
- On February 25, 2016, the A24's cash deposit increases $187.84.
- On February 28, 2016, the A24's cash deposit increases $2,870.
- On February 28, 2016, the A25's cash deposit increases $2,790.
- On March 7, 2016, the A12's cash deposit decreases -$100.
- On March 7, 2016, the A25's cash deposit increases $201.66.
- On March 18, 2016, the A9's cash deposit decreases -$104.
- On March 20, 2016, the A13's cash deposit decreases -$290.
- On March 20, 2016, the A16's cash deposit decreases -$131.

- On March 22, 2016, the A7's cash deposit decreases -$96.
- On March 25, 2016, the A25's cash deposit decreases -$70.
- On March 27, 2016, the A25's cash deposit increases $191.43.
- On March 28, 2016, the A14's cash deposit decreases -$84.
- On March 31, 2016, the A24's cash deposit increases $2,870.
- On March 31, 2016, the A25's cash deposit increases $2,790.
- On April 6, 2016, the A9's cash deposit decreases -$108.
- On April 24, 2016, the A24's cash deposit increases $236.37.
- On April 26, 2016, the A13's cash deposit decreases -$470.
- On April 30, 2016, the A24's cash deposit increases $2,870.
- On April 30, 2016, the A25's cash deposit increases $2,790.
- On May 15, 2016, the A24's cash deposit decreases -$78.
- On May 17, 2016, the A24's cash deposit increases $210.77.
- On May 31, 2016, the A24's cash deposit increases $2,870.
- On May 31, 2016, the A25's cash deposit increases $2,790.
- On June 3, 2016, the A8's cash deposit decreases -$54.
- On June 17, 2016, the A24's cash deposit decreases -$74.
- On June 19, 2016, the A24's cash deposit increases $196.83.
- On June 30, 2016, the A24's cash deposit increases $2,870.
- On June 30, 2016, the A25's cash deposit increases $2,790.
- On July 2, 2016, the A9's cash deposit decreases -$117.
- On July 21, 2016, the A25's cash deposit decreases -$108.
- On July 23, 2016, the A25's cash deposit increases $251.19.
- On July 31, 2016, the A24's cash deposit increases $2,870.
- On July 31, 2016, the A25's cash deposit increases $2,790.
- On July 31, 2016, the A12's cash deposit decreases -$10,920.
- On July 31, 2016, the A1's cash deposit decreases -$11,050.
- On July 31, 2016, the A2's cash deposit decreases -$11,180.
- On July 31, 2016, the A3's cash deposit decreases -$11,310.
- On July 31, 2016, the A4's cash deposit decreases -$11,440.
- On July 31, 2016, the A5's cash deposit decreases -$11,830.
- On July 31, 2016, the A6's cash deposit decreases -$10,790.
- On July 31, 2016, the A7's cash deposit decreases -$11,310.
- On July 31, 2016, the A8's cash deposit decreases -$11,570.
- On July 31, 2016, the A9's cash deposit decreases -$12,090.
- On July 31, 2016, the A13's cash deposit decreases -$11,830.
- On August 12, 2016, the A9's cash deposit decreases -$118.
- On August 14, 2016, the A15's cash deposit decreases -$123.
- On August 15, 2016, the A8's cash deposit decreases -$52.
- On August 16, 2016, the A24's cash deposit decreases -$74.
- On August 18, 2016, the A24's cash deposit increases $203.47.
- On August 31, 2016, the A24's cash deposit increases $2,870.
- On August 31, 2016, the A25's cash deposit increases $2,790.
- On September 7, 2016, the A7's cash deposit decreases -$90.
- On September 21, 2016, the A24's cash deposit increases $256.18.
- On September 30, 2016, the A24's cash deposit increases $2,870.
- On September 30, 2016, the A25's cash deposit increases $2,790.
- On October 3, 2016, the A15's cash deposit decreases -$129.
- On October 4, 2016, the A18's cash deposit decreases -$117.
- On October 6, 2016, the A22's cash deposit decreases -$54 (second card).
- On October 8, 2016, the A8's cash deposit decreases -$56.
- On October 16, 2016, the A24's cash deposit decreases -$86.
- On October 18, 2016, the A24's cash deposit increases $228.66.
- On October 31, 2016, the A24's cash deposit increases $2,870.
- On October 31, 2016, the A25's cash deposit increases $2,790.
- On November 16, 2016, the A9's cash deposit decreases -$124.
- On November 16, 2016, the A15's cash deposit decreases -$132.
- On November 18, 2016, the A24's cash deposit decreases -$86.
- On November 20, 2016, the A24's cash deposit increases $204.61.
- On November 30, 2016, the A24's cash deposit increases $2,870.
- On November 30, 2016, the A25's cash deposit increases $2,790.
- On December 15, 2016, the A24's cash deposit decreases -$108.

- On December 17, 2016, the A24's cash deposit increases $277.93.
- On December 18, 2016, the A18's cash deposit decreases -$144.
- On December 18, 2016, the A25's cash deposit decreases -$98.
- On December 20, 2016, the A14's cash deposit decreases -$162.
- On December 20, 2016, the A25's cash deposit increases $249.51.
- On December 26, 2016, the A7's cash deposit decreases -$108.
- On December 31, 2016, the A24's cash deposit increases $2,870.
- On December 31, 2016, the A25's cash deposit increases $2,790.
- On December 31, 2016, the A1's cash deposit increases $364.
- On December 31, 2016, the A2's cash deposit increases $312.
- On December 31, 2016, the A4's cash deposit increases $260.
- On December 31, 2016, the A7's cash deposit increases $312.
- On December 31, 2016, the A9's cash deposit increases $312.
- On December 31, 2016, the A16's cash deposit increases $364.
- On December 31, 2016, the A18's cash deposit increases $312.
- On December 31, 2016, the A4's cash deposit increases $220.
- On December 31, 2016, the A5's cash deposit increases $275.
- On December 31, 2016, the A6's cash deposit increases $330.
- On December 31, 2016, the A8's cash deposit increases $275.
- On December 31, 2016, the A13's cash deposit increases $220.
- On December 31, 2016, the A15's cash deposit increases $275.
- On December 31, 2016, the A16's cash deposit increases $330.
- On December 31, 2016, the A18's cash deposit increases $220.

**Business Bank2**
- On December 31, 2016, the A7's cash deposit increases $164.
- On December 31, 2016, the A9's cash deposit increases $246.
- On December 31, 2016, the A13's cash deposit increases $123.
- On December 31, 2016, the A14's cash deposit increases $205.
- On December 31, 2016, the A18's cash deposit increases $123.
- On December 31, 2016, the A3's cash deposit increases $264.
- On December 31, 2016, the A4's cash deposit increases $308.
- On December 31, 2016, the A6's cash deposit increases $264.

# Appendixes B   Deposit Transactions in the Business Bank2

**Cash Management Center**
- On December 31, 2016, individual A10's cash deposit increases $200.
- On December 31, 2016, individual A11's cash deposit increases $200.
- On December 31, 2016, individual A12's cash deposit increases $200.
- On December 31, 2016, individual A21's cash deposit increases $200.
- On December 31, 2016, individual A22's cash deposit increases $200.

**Central Bank**
- On January 2, 2016, the Central Bank's cash deposit increases $85,000. The multi-subaccount name of the Cash account and transaction sub-equation  respectively are:

    88-654301-d-deposits < Cash receipts from customers deposits < Operating activities

    Cash (1): 85000 = Deposits payable (2): 85000 = 0

- On January 21, 2016, the Central Bank's cash deposit decreases -$176.56.
- On January 31, 2016, the Central Bank's cash deposit decreases -$5,650.
- On February 13, 2016, the Central Bank's cash deposit decreases -$800.
- On February 13, 2016, the Central Bank's cash deposit decreases -$200.
- On February 22, 2016, the Central Bank's cash deposit decreases -$3,600.
- On February 28, 2016, the Central Bank's cash deposit decreases -$5,650.
- On March 25, 2016, the Central Bank's cash deposit decreases -$600.
- On March 28, 2016, the Central Bank's cash deposit decreases -$459.61.
- On March 31, 2016, the Central Bank's cash deposit decreases -$5,650.
- On April 19, 2016, the Central Bank's cash deposit decreases -$159.78.
- On April 30, 2016, the Central Bank's cash deposit decreases -$5,650.
- On May 1, 2016, the Central Bank's cash deposit decreases -$1,900.
- On May 16, 2016, the Central Bank's cash deposit decreases -$316.
- On May 31, 2016, the Central Bank's cash deposit decreases -$5,650.
- On June 1, 2016, the Central Bank's cash deposit decreases -$5,000.
- On June 22, 2016, the Central Bank's cash deposit decreases -$477.25.
- On June 30, 2016, the Central Bank's cash deposit decreases -$5,650.
- On July 31, 2016, the Central Bank's cash deposit decreases -$5,650.
- On August 14, 2016, the Central Bank's cash deposit decreases -$1,040.
- On August 31, 2016, the Central Bank's cash deposit decreases -$5,650.
- On September 7, 2016, the Central Bank's cash deposit decreases -$233.16.
- On September 30, 2016, the Central Bank's cash deposit decreases -$5,650.
- On October 31, 2016, the Central Bank's cash deposit decreases -$5,650.
- On November 30, 2016, the Central Bank's cash deposit decreases -$5,650.
- On December 11, 2016, the Central Bank's cash deposit decreases -$552.37.
- On December 31, 2016, the Central Bank's cash deposit decreases -$5,650.
- On December 31, 2016, the Central Bank's cash deposit increases $131.25.
- On December 31, 2016, the Central Bank's cash deposit increases $120.
- On December 31, 2016, the Central Bank's cash deposit decreases -$3,500.

**Company1**
- On August 1, 2016, individual A16's cash deposit decreases -$11,000.
- On August 1, 2016, the A23's cash deposit decreases -$5,500.
- On August 10, 2016, the A11's cash deposit decreases -$1,500.
- On October 5, 2016, the A13's cash deposit decreases -$11,500.
- On October 5, 2016, the A25's cash deposit decreases -$7,000.
- On December 19, 2016, the A22's cash deposit decreases -$1,600.
- On December 31, 2016, the A10's cash deposit decreases -$40,000.
- On December 31, 2016, the A11's cash deposit increases $322.
- On December 31, 2016, the A21's cash deposit increases $138.
- On December 31, 2016, the A22's cash deposit increases $230.

**Company2**
- On January 2, 2016, the Company2's cash deposit decreases -$500.
- On January 12, 2016, the Company2's cash deposit increases $360.
- On January 14, 2016, the Company2's cash deposit increases $11,000.

- On January 15, 2016, the Company2's cash deposit decreases -$5000.
- On January 15, 2016, the Company2's cash deposit decreases -$411.32.
- On January 18, 2016, the Company2's cash deposit decreases -$112.57.
- On January 18, 2016, the A17's cash deposit increases $112.57.
- On January 24, 2016, the Company2's cash deposit increases $600.
- On January 27, 2016, the Company2's cash deposit increases $250.
- On January 28, 2016, the Company2's cash deposit increases $7000.
- On January 30, 2016, the Company2's cash deposit decreases -$379.78.
- On January 30, 2016, the Company2's cash deposit decreases -$500.
- On January 30, 2016, the Company2's cash deposit decreases -$300.
- On January 31, 2016, the Company2's cash deposit decreases -$8,380.
- On January 31, 2016, the A17's cash deposit increases $2,890.
- On February 11, 2016, the Company2's cash deposit increases $400.
- On February 20, 2016, the Company2's cash deposit decreases -$557.83.
- On February 21, 2016, the Company2's cash deposit increases $500.
- On February 25, 2016, the Company2's cash deposit decreases -$600.
- On February 26, 2016, the Company2's cash deposit increases $5200.
- On February 28, 2016, the Company2's cash deposit decreases -$8,380.
- On February 28, 2016, the A17's cash deposit increases $2,890.
- On March 1, 2016, the Company2's cash deposit decreases -$221.16.
- On March 4, 2016, the Company2's cash deposit increases $2,400.
- On March 23, 2016, the Company2's cash deposit decreases -$347.65.
- On March 26, 2016, the Company2's cash deposit decreases -$253.93.
- On March 26, 2016, the A17's cash deposit increases $253.93.
- On March 30, 2016, the Company2's cash deposit decreases -$700.
- On March 31, 2016, the Company2's cash deposit decreases -$8,380.
- On March 31, 2016, the A17's cash deposit increases $2,890.
- On April 12, 2016, the Company2's cash deposit increases $310.
- On April 26, 2016, the Company2's cash deposit decreases -$369.88.
- On April 29, 2016, the Company2's cash deposit increases $5,000.
- On April 30, 2016, the Company2's cash deposit decreases -$8,380.
- On April 30, 2016, the A17's cash deposit increases $2,890.
- On May 1, 2016, the Company2's cash deposit increases $15,000.
- On May 2, 2016, the Company2's cash deposit decreases -$307.09.
- On May 3, 2016, the Company2's cash deposit increases $290.
- On May 24, 2016, the Company2's cash deposit decreases -$366.59.
- On May 31, 2016, the Company2's cash deposit decreases -$8,380.
- On May 31, 2016, the A17's cash deposit increases $2,890.
- On June 12, 2016, the Company2's cash deposit increases $64,000.
- On June 14, 2016, the Company2's cash deposit decreases -$255.54.
- On June 14, 2016, the A17's cash deposit increases $255.54.
- On June 23, 2016, the Company2's cash deposit decreases -$362.81.
- On June 30, 2016, the Company2's cash deposit decreases -$8,380.
- On June 30, 2016, the A17's cash deposit increases $2,890.
- On July 11, 2016, the Company2's cash deposit increases $290.
- On July 13, 2016, the Company2's cash deposit increases $320.
- On July 27, 2016, the Company2's cash deposit decreases -$307.41.
- On July 31, 2016, the Company2's cash deposit decreases -$8,380.
- On July 31, 2016, the A17's cash deposit increases $2,890.
- On August 1, 2016, the Company2's cash deposit decreases -$3,000.
- On August 3, 2016, the Company2's cash deposit increases $12,000.
- On August 13, 2016, the Company2's cash deposit increases $360.
- On August 13, 2016, the A11's cash deposit decreases -$360.
- On August 16, 2016, the Company2's cash deposit decreases -$373.77.
- On August 16, 2016, the A17's cash deposit increases $373.77.
- On August 23, 2016, the Company2's cash deposit decreases -$392.33.
- On August 31, 2016, the Company2's cash deposit decreases -$8,380.
- On August 31, 2016, the A17's cash deposit increases $2,890.
- On September 3, 2016, the Company2's cash deposit increases $310.
- On September 3, 2016, the A19's cash deposit decreases -$310.
- On September 10, 2016, the Company2's cash deposit increases $320.
- On September 10, 2016, the A22's cash deposit decreases -$320.

- On September 12, 2016, the Company2's cash deposit increases $4,000.
- On September 14, 2016, the Company2's cash deposit decreases -$380.
- On September 14, 2016, the Company2's cash deposit increases $10,000.
- On September 26, 2016, the Company2's cash deposit increases $1,800.
- On September 28, 2016, the Company2's cash deposit decreases -$410.89.
- On September 30, 2016, the Company2's cash deposit decreases -$8,380.
- On September 30, 2016, the A17's cash deposit increases $2,890.
- On October 3, 2016, the Company2's cash deposit increases $4,500.
- On October 6, 2016, the Company2's cash deposit decreases -$377.63.
- On October 27, 2016, the Company2's cash deposit decreases -$396.27.
- On October 31, 2016, the Company2's cash deposit decreases -$8,380.
- On October 31, 2016, the A17's cash deposit increases $2,890.
- On November 19, 2016, the Company2's cash deposit decreases -$399.28.
- On November 20, 2016, the Company2's cash deposit increases $360.
- On November 29, 2016, the Company2's cash deposit increases $14,420.
- On November 30, 2016, the Company2's cash deposit decreases -$8,380.
- On November 30, 2016, the A17's cash deposit increases $2,890.
- On December 17, 2016, the Company2's cash deposit decreases -$395.88.
- On December 20, 2016, the Company2's cash deposit decreases -$424.37.
- On December 29, 2016, the Company2's cash deposit increases $39,700.
- On December 30, 2016, the Company2's cash deposit decreases -$600.
- On December 31, 2016, the Company2's cash deposit increases $55,000.
- On December 31, 2016, the Company2's cash deposit decreases -$8,380.
- On December 31, 2016, the A17's cash deposit increases $2,890.
- On December 31, 2016, the Company2's cash deposit decreases -$35,600.
- On December 31, 2016, the Company2's cash deposit decreases -$21,600.
- On December 31, 2016, the Company2's cash deposit decreases -$1,880 (total amount of Bond41).
- On December 31, 2016, the A10's cash deposit increases $141.
- On December 31, 2016, the A19's cash deposit increases $141.
- On December 31, 2016, the A20's cash deposit increases $94.
- On December 31, 2016, the A23's cash deposit increases $141.
- On December 31, 2016, the Company2's cash deposit increases $336.
- On December 31, 2016, the Company2's cash deposit increases $264.
- On December 31, 2016, the Company2's cash deposit increases $120.

**Company3**

- On January 2, 2016, the Company3's cash deposit decreases -$316.
- On January 2, 2016, the Company3's cash deposit increases $10,000.
- On January 2, 2016, the Company3's cash deposit increases $8,000.
- On January 3, 2016, the Company3's cash deposit decreases -$9,300.
- On January 3, 2016, the Company3's cash deposit decreases -$6,000.
- On January 13, 2016, the Company3's cash deposit increases $150.
- On January 13, 2016, the Company3's cash deposit increases $2,000.
- On January 14, 2016, the Company3's cash deposit increases $8,000.
- On January 15, 2016, the Company3's cash deposit increases $5,000.
- On January 18, 2016, the Company3's cash deposit decreases -$261.26.
- On January 18, 2016, the A19's cash deposit increases $261.26.
- On January 19, 2016, the Company3's cash deposit decreases -$143.68.
- On January 19, 2016, the A20's cash deposit increases $143.68.
- On January 23, 2016, the Company3's cash deposit increases $230.
- On January 23, 2016, the A22's cash deposit decreases -$230.
- On January 24, 2016, the Company3's cash deposit decreases -$600.
- On January 26, 2016, the Company3's cash deposit decreases -$1,300.
- On January 26, 2016, the Company3's cash deposit decreases -$800.
- On January 28, 2016, the Company3's cash deposit increases $200.
- On January 28, 2016, the Company3's cash deposit decreases -$7,000.
- On January 30, 2016, the Company3's cash deposit decreases -$143.33.
- On January 30, 2016, the A21's cash deposit increases $143.33.
- On January 31, 2016, the Company3's cash deposit increases $350.
- On January 31, 2016, the Company3's cash deposit decreases -$8,370.
- On January 31, 2016, the A20's cash deposit increases $2,880.
- On January 31, 2016, the A19's cash deposit increases $2,700.

- On January 31, 2016, the A21's cash deposit increases $2,790.
- On February 13, 2016, the Company3's cash deposit increases $200.
- On February 22, 2016, the Company3's cash deposit increases $1,500.
- On February 23, 2016, the Company3's cash deposit increases $300.
- On February 25, 2016, the Company3's cash deposit decreases -$339.49.
- On February 25, 2016, the A19's cash deposit increases $339.49.
- On February 27, 2016, the Company3's cash deposit decreases -$900.
- On February 27, 2016, the Company3's cash deposit increases $1,050.
- On February 27, 2016, the A23's cash deposit decreases -$1,050.
- On February 28, 2016, the Company3's cash deposit decreases -$8,370.
- On February 28, 2016, the A20's cash deposit increases $2,880.
- On February 28, 2016, the A19's cash deposit increases $2,700.
- On February 28, 2016, the A21's cash deposit increases $2,790.
- On March 1, 2016, the Company3's cash deposit decreases -$225.64.
- On March 1, 2016, the A21's cash deposit increases $225.64.
- On March 4, 2016, the Company3's cash deposit increases $1,600.
- On March 23, 2016, the Company3's cash deposit decreases -$198.56.
- On March 23, 2016, the A19's cash deposit increases $198.56.
- On March 24, 2016, the Company3's cash deposit increases $3,500.
- On March 30, 2016, the Company3's cash deposit increases $700.
- On March 31, 2016, the Company3's cash deposit decreases -$8,370.
- On March 31, 2016, the A20's cash deposit increases $2,880.
- On March 31, 2016, the A19's cash deposit increases $2,700.
- On March 31, 2016, the A21's cash deposit increases $2,790.
- On April 6, 2016, the Company3's cash deposit increases $1,500.
- On April 14, 2016, the Company3's cash deposit increases $4,160.
- On April 14, 2016, the A10's cash deposit decreases -$4,160.
- On April 26, 2016, the Company3's cash deposit decreases -$236.37.
- On April 26, 2016, the A19's cash deposit increases $236.37.
- On April 30, 2016, the Company3's cash deposit decreases -$8,370.
- On April 30, 2016, the A20's cash deposit increases $2,880.
- On April 30, 2016, the A19's cash deposit increases $2,700.
- On April 30, 2016, the A21's cash deposit increases $2,790.
- On May 2, 2016, the Company3's cash deposit decreases -$167.19.
- On May 2, 2016, the A21's cash deposit increases $167.19.
- On May 3, 2016, the Company3's cash deposit increases $880.
- On May 24, 2016, the Company3's cash deposit decreases -$339.55.
- On May 24, 2016, the A19's cash deposit increases $339.55.
- On May 31, 2016, the Company3's cash deposit decreases -$8,370.
- On May 31, 2016, the A20's cash deposit increases $2,880.
- On May 31, 2016, the A19's cash deposit increases $2,700.
- On May 31, 2016, the A21's cash deposit increases $2,790.
- On June 1, 2016, the Company3's cash deposit decreases -$3000.
- On June 10, 2016, the Company3's cash deposit increases $15,000.
- On June 14, 2016, the Company3's cash deposit decreases -$193.49.
- On June 14, 2016, the A20's cash deposit increases $193.49.
- On June 15, 2016, the Company3's cash deposit increases $84.
- On June 16, 2016, the Company3's cash deposit decreases -$300.
- On June 23, 2016, the Company3's cash deposit decreases -$254.33.
- On June 23, 2016, the A19's cash deposit increases $254.33.
- On June 29, 2016, the Company3's cash deposit increases $2,000.
- On June 30, 2016, the Company3's cash deposit decreases -$8,370.
- On June 30, 2016, the A20's cash deposit increases $2,880.
- On June 30, 2016, the A19's cash deposit increases $2,700.
- On June 30, 2016, the A21's cash deposit increases $2,790.
- On July 3, 2016, the Company3's cash deposit increases $53,000.
- On July 4, 2016, the Company3's cash deposit increases $55,000.
- On July 11, 2016, the Company3's cash deposit increases $250.
- On July 13, 2016, the Company3's cash deposit increases $780.
- On July 13, 2016, the A21's cash deposit decreases -$780.
- On July16, 2016, the Company3's cash deposit decreases -$13,000.
- On July 27, 2016, the Company3's cash deposit decreases -$221.14.

- On July 27, 2016, the A19's cash deposit increases $221.14.
- On July 31, 2016, the Company3's cash deposit decreases -$8,370.
- On July 31, 2016, the A20's cash deposit increases $2,880.
- On July 31, 2016, the A19's cash deposit increases $2,700.
- On July 31, 2016, the A21's cash deposit increases $2,790.
- On August 3, 2016, the Company3's cash deposit increases $550.
- On August 3, 2016, the A17's cash deposit decreases -$550.
- On August 13, 2016, the Company3's cash deposit increases $700.
- On August 15, 2016, the Company3's cash deposit increases $66,000.
- On August 17, 2016, the Company3's cash deposit increases $65,000.
- On August 23, 2016, the Company3's cash deposit decreases -$208.31.
- On August 23, 2016, the A19's cash deposit increases $208.31.
- On August 31, 2016, the Company3's cash deposit decreases -$8,370.
- On August 31, 2016, the A20's cash deposit increases $2,880.
- On August 31, 2016, the A19's cash deposit increases $2,700.
- On August 31, 2016, the A21's cash deposit increases $2,790.
- On September 4, 2016, the Company3's cash deposit increases $520.
- On September 10, 2016, the Company3's cash deposit increases $550.
- On September 10, 2016, the A23's cash deposit decreases -$550.
- On September 12, 2016, the Company3's cash deposit decreases -$4,000.
- On September 13, 2016, the Company3's cash deposit increases $25,000.
- On September 15, 2016, the Company3's cash deposit decreases -$300.
- On September 25, 2016, the Company3's cash deposit increases $3,200.
- On September 26, 2016, the Company3's cash deposit increases $8,000.
- On September 28, 2016, the Company3's cash deposit decreases -$214.84.
- On September 28, 2016, the A19's cash deposit increases $214.84.
- On September 30, 2016, the Company3's cash deposit decreases -$8,370.
- On September 30, 2016, the A20's cash deposit increases $2,880.
- On September 30, 2016, the A19's cash deposit increases $2,700.
- On September 30, 2016, the A21's cash deposit increases $2,790.
- On October 3, 2016, the Company3's cash deposit increases $550.
- On October 8, 2016, the Company3's cash deposit decreases -$218.66.
- On October 8, 2016, the A21's cash deposit increases $218.66.
- On October 11, 2016, the Company3's cash deposit increases $41,000.
- On October 12, 2016, the Company3's cash deposit increases $31,000.
- On October 18, 2016, the Company3's cash deposit increases $2,660.
- On October 25, 2016, the Company3's cash deposit decreases -$25,000.
- On October 27, 2016, the Company3's cash deposit decreases -$242.23.
- On October 27, 2016, the A19's cash deposit increases $242.23.
- On October 31, 2016, the Company3's cash deposit decreases -$8,370.
- On October 31, 2016, the A20's cash deposit increases $2,880.
- On October 31, 2016, the A19's cash deposit increases $2,700.
- On October 31, 2016, the A21's cash deposit increases $2,790.
- On November 5, 2016, the Company3's cash deposit decreases -$2,900.
- On November 17, 2016, the A19's cash deposit decreases -$87.
- On November 19, 2016, the Company3's cash deposit decreases -$223.61.
- On November 19, 2016, the A19's cash deposit increases $223.61.
- On November 20, 2016, the Company3's cash deposit increases $640.
- On November 29, 2016, the Company3's cash deposit increases $3,000.
- On November 30, 2016, the Company3's cash deposit decreases -$8,370.
- On November 30, 2016, the A20's cash deposit increases $2,880.
- On November 30, 2016, the A19's cash deposit increases $2,700.
- On November 30, 2016, the A21's cash deposit increases $2,790.
- On December 17, 2016, the Company3's cash deposit decreases -$272.78.
- On December 17, 2016, the A19's cash deposit increases $272.78.
- On December 20, 2016, the Company3's cash deposit decreases -$248.53.
- On December 20, 2016, the A21's cash deposit increases $248.53.
- On December 28, 2016, the Company3's cash deposit increases $2,500.
- On December 30, 2016, the Company3's cash deposit increases $600.
- On December 31, 2016, the Company3's cash deposit decreases -$8,370.
- On December 31, 2016, the A20's cash deposit increases $2,880.
- On December 31, 2016, the A19's cash deposit increases $2,700.

- On December 31, 2016, the A21's cash deposit increases $2,790.
- On December 31, 2016, the Company3's cash deposit decreases -$18,000.
- On December 31, 2016, the Company3's cash deposit decreases -$16,200.
- On December 31, 2016, the Company3's cash deposit decreases -$18,200.
- On December 31, 2016, the Company3's cash deposit decreases -$288 (actually enter total $3,840).
- On December 31, 2016, the Company3's cash deposit decreases -$192.
- On December 31, 2016, the Company3's cash deposit decreases -$336.
- On December 31, 2016, the Company3's cash deposit decreases -$88.
- On December 31, 2016, the Company3's cash deposit decreases -$192.
- On December 31, 2016, the Company3's cash deposit decreases -$240.
- On December 31, 2016, the Company3's cash deposit decreases -$192.
- On December 31, 2016, the A11's cash deposit increases $192.
- On December 31, 2016, the Company3's cash deposit decreases -$384.
- On December 31, 2016, the A12's cash deposit increases $384.
- On December 31, 2016, the Company3's cash deposit decreases -$240.
- On December 31, 2016, the Company3's cash deposit decreases -$336.
- On December 31, 2016, the Company3's cash deposit decreases -$240.
- On December 31, 2016, the A17's cash deposit increases $240.
- On December 31, 2016, the Company3's cash deposit decreases -$288.
- On December 31, 2016, the Company3's cash deposit decreases -$192.
- On December 31, 2016, the A21's cash deposit increases $192.
- On December 31, 2016, the Company3's cash deposit decreases -$288.
- On December 31, 2016, the A22's cash deposit increases $288.
- On December 31, 2016, the Company3's cash deposit increases $320.
- On December 31, 2016, the Company3's cash deposit increases $492.
- On December 31, 2016, the Company3's cash deposit increases $120.

**Proprietorship1**
- On January 16, 2016, individual A17's cash deposit decreases -$44.
- On January 18, 2016, the A20's cash deposit decreases -$51.
- On January 18, 2016, the A22's cash deposit increases $153.87.
- On January 27, 2016, the A10's cash deposit decreases -$57.
- On January 28, 2016, the A21's cash deposit decreases -$42.
- On January 28, 2016, the A23's cash deposit decreases -$44.
- On January 30, 2016, the A23's cash deposit increases $145.54.
- On January 31, 2016, the A22's cash deposit increases $2,870.
- On January 31, 2016, the A23's cash deposit increases $2,800.
- On January 31, 2016, the A10's cash deposit decreases -$13,900.
- On January 31, 2016, the A11's cash deposit decreases -$14,430.
- On January 31, 2016, the A12's cash deposit decreases -$14,560.
- On February 23, 2016, the A19's cash deposit decreases -$124.
- On February 28, 2016, the A21's cash deposit decreases -$102.
- On February 28, 2016, the A22's cash deposit increases $2,870.
- On February 28, 2016, the A23's cash deposit increases $2,800.
- On March 11 2016, the A11's cash deposit decreases -$50.
- On March 23, 2016, the A22's cash deposit increases $159.45.
- On March 31, 2016, the A22's cash deposit increases $2,870.
- On March 31, 2016, the A23's cash deposit increases $2,800.
- On April 13, 2016, the A11's cash deposit decreases -$69.
- On April 24, 2016, the A19's cash deposit decreases -$78.
- On April 30, 2016, the A22's cash deposit increases $2,870.
- On April 30, 2016, the A23's cash deposit increases $2,800.
- On May 1, 2016, the A21's cash deposit decreases -$50.
- On May 12, 2016, the A23's cash deposit decreases -$50.
- On May 14, 2016, the A23's cash deposit increases $166.23.
- On May 20, 2016, the A11's cash deposit decreases -$56.
- On May 22, 2016, the A19's cash deposit decreases -$138.
- On May 24, 2016, the A22's cash deposit increases $176.95.
- On May 31, 2016, the A22's cash deposit increases $2,870.
- On May 31, 2016, the A23's cash deposit increases $2,800.
- On June 18, 2016, the A12's cash deposit decreases -$109.
- On June 21, 2016, the A19's cash deposit decreases -$108.

- On June 23, 2016, the A22's cash deposit increases $157.37.
- On June 30, 2016, the A22's cash deposit increases $2,870.
- On June 30, 2016, the A23's cash deposit increases $2,800.
- On July 21, 2016, the A12's cash deposit decreases -$125.
- On July 25, 2016, the A19's cash deposit decreases -$88.
- On July 25, 2016, the A23's cash deposit decreases -$64.
- On July 27, 2016, the A23's cash deposit increases $187.55.
- On July 31, 2016, the A22's cash deposit increases $2,870.
- On July 31, 2016, the A23's cash deposit increases $2,800.
- On July 31, 2016, the A1 (secondary card)'s cash deposit decreases -$10,270.
- On July 31, 2016, the A17's cash deposit decreases -$17,940.
- On July 31, 2016, the A19's cash deposit decreases -$18,590.
- On July 31, 2016, the A20's cash deposit decreases -$10,400.
- On July 31, 2016, the A21's cash deposit decreases -$10,660.
- On July 31, 2016, the A22's cash deposit decreases -$10,530.
- On July 31, 2016, the A23's cash deposit decreases -$11,050.
- On August 14, 2016, the A17's cash deposit decreases -$120.
- On August 17, 2016, the A10's cash deposit decreases -$63.
- On August 21, 2016, the A19's cash deposit decreases -$78.
- On August 22, 2016, the A12's cash deposit decreases -$112.
- On August 23, 2016, the A22's cash deposit increases $166.18.
- On August 31, 2016, the A22's cash deposit increases $2,870.
- On August 31, 2016, the A23's cash deposit increases $2,800.
- On September 17, 2016, the A12's cash deposit decreases -$104.
- On September 26, 2016, the A19's cash deposit decreases -$87.
- On September 30, 2016, the A22's cash deposit increases $2,870.
- On September 30, 2016, the A23's cash deposit increases $2,800.
- On October 8, 2016, the A22's cash deposit increases $168.73.
- On October 16, 2016, the A12's cash deposit decreases -$108.
- On October 25, 2016, the A19's cash deposit decreases -$90.
- On October 31, 2016, the A22's cash deposit increases $2,870.
- On October 31, 2016, the A23's cash deposit increases $2,800.
- On November 17, 2016, the A19's cash deposit decreases -$87.
- On November 19, 2016, the A12's cash deposit decreases -$100.
- On November 19, 2016, the A22's cash deposit increases $177.16.
- On November 30, 2016, the A22's cash deposit increases $2,870.
- On November 30, 2016, the A23's cash deposit increases $2,800.
- On December 15, 2016, the A19's cash deposit decreases -$104.
- On December 15, 2016, the A23's cash deposit decreases -$74.
- On December 17, 2016, the A23's cash deposit increases $207.52.
- On December 19, 2016, the A22's cash deposit increases $198.35.
- On December 27, 2016, the A12's cash deposit decreases -$125.
- On December 31, 2016, the A22's cash deposit increases $2,870.
- On December 31, 2016, the A23's cash deposit increases $2,800.
- On December 31, 2016, the A10's cash deposit increases $150.
- On December 31, 2016, the A17's cash deposit increases $250.
- On December 31, 2016, the A19's cash deposit increases $250.
- On December 31, 2016, the A20's cash deposit increases $150.
- On December 31, 2016, the A21's cash deposit increases $200.
- On December 31, 2016, the A22's cash deposit increases $100.

**Proprietorship2**
- On January 2, 2016, the Proprietorship2's cash deposit increases $316.
- On January 2, 2016, the Proprietorship2's cash deposit increases $200.
- On January 2, 2016, the Proprietorship2's cash deposit increases $450.
- On January 2, 2016, the Proprietorship2's cash deposit decreases -$8,000.
- On January 2, 2016, the Proprietorship2's cash deposit increases $500.
- On January 3, 2016, the Proprietorship2's cash deposit increases $6,000.
- On January 12, 2016, the Proprietorship2's cash deposit increases $118.
- On January 13, 2016, the Proprietorship2's cash deposit increases $208.
- On January 14, 2016, the Proprietorship2's cash deposit decreases -$255.37.
- On January 15, 2016, the Proprietorship2's cash deposit increases $54.

- On January 16, 2016, the Proprietorship2's cash deposit increases $122.
- On January 16, 2016, the A19's cash deposit decreases -$122.
- On January 16, 2016, the Proprietorship2's cash deposit increases $48.
- On January 16, 2016, the A22's cash deposit decreases -$48.
- On January 18, 2016, the Proprietorship2's cash deposit increases $39.
- On January 20, 2016, the Proprietorship2's cash deposit increases $82.
- On January 21, 2016, the Proprietorship2's cash deposit decreases -$149.65.
- On January 22, 2016, the Proprietorship2's cash deposit increases $120.
- On January 22, 2016, the A12's cash deposit decreases -$120.
- On January 26, 2016, the Proprietorship2's cash deposit increases $800.
- On January 28, 2016, the Proprietorship2's cash deposit decreases -$200.
- On January 30, 2016, the Proprietorship2's cash deposit increases $300.
- On January 31, 2016, the Proprietorship2's cash deposit increases $1,000.
- On January 31, 2016, the Proprietorship2's cash deposit increases $24.
- On January 31, 2016, the Proprietorship2's cash deposit decreases -$5,660.
- On January 31, 2016, the Proprietorship2's cash deposit increases $10,790.
- On January 31, 2016, the A1's cash deposit decreases -$10,790.
- On January 31, 2016, the Proprietorship2's cash deposit increases $10,920.
- On January 31, 2016, the Proprietorship2's cash deposit increases $11,050.
- On January 31, 2016, the Proprietorship2's cash deposit increases $11,180.
- On January 31, 2016, the Proprietorship2's cash deposit increases $10,270.
- On January 31, 2016, the A17's cash deposit decreases -$10,270.
- On January 31, 2016, the Proprietorship2's cash deposit increases $11,830.
- On January 31, 2016, the Proprietorship2's cash deposit increases $11,570.
- On January 31, 2016, the A19's cash deposit decreases -$11,570.
- On January 31, 2016, the Proprietorship2's cash deposit increases $12,090.
- On January 31, 2016, the A20's cash deposit decreases -$12,090.
- On January 31, 2016, the Proprietorship2's cash deposit increases $12,870.
- On January 31, 2016, the A21's cash deposit decreases -$12,870.
- On January 31, 2016, the Proprietorship2's cash deposit increases $10,790.
- On January 31, 2016, the A22's cash deposit decreases -$10,790.
- On January 31, 2016, the Proprietorship2's cash deposit increases $12,350.
- On January 31, 2016, the A23's cash deposit decreases -$12,350.
- On January 31, 2016, the Proprietorship2's cash deposit increases $10,010.
- On January 31, 2016, the Proprietorship2's cash deposit increases $10,270.
- On February 1, 2016, the Proprietorship2's cash deposit decreases -$30,000.
- On February 6, 2016, the Proprietorship2's cash deposit increases $116.
- On February 17, 2016, the Proprietorship2's cash deposit increases $310.
- On February 19, 2016, the Proprietorship2's cash deposit increases $112.
- On February 20, 2016, the Proprietorship2's cash deposit decreases -$400.
- On February 21, 2016, the Proprietorship2's cash deposit increases $300.
- On February 22, 2016, the Proprietorship2's cash deposit increases $96.
- On February 23, 2016, the Proprietorship2's cash deposit increases $62.
- On February 25, 2016, the Proprietorship2's cash deposit decreases -$187.84.
- On February 28, 2016, the Proprietorship2's cash deposit decreases -$5,660.
- On March 7, 2016, the Proprietorship2's cash deposit increases $100.
- On March 7, 2016, the Proprietorship2's cash deposit decreases -$201.66.
- On March 9, 2016, the Proprietorship2's cash deposit decreases -$2,000.
- On March 18, 2016, the Proprietorship2's cash deposit increases $104.
- On March 20, 2016, the Proprietorship2's cash deposit increases $290.
- On March 20, 2016, the Proprietorship2's cash deposit increases $131.
- On March 21, 2016, the Proprietorship2's cash deposit increases $73.
- On March 21, 2016, the A19's cash deposit decreases -$73.
- On March 21, 2016, the Proprietorship2's cash deposit increases $58.
- On March 21, 2016, the A22's cash deposit decreases -$58.
- On March 22, 2016, the Proprietorship2's cash deposit increases $96.
- On March 24, 2016, the Proprietorship2's cash deposit increases $87.
- On March 24, 2016, the A17's cash deposit decreases -$87.
- On March 25, 2016, the Proprietorship2's cash deposit increases $70.
- On March 27, 2016, the Proprietorship2's cash deposit decreases -$191.43.
- On March 28, 2016, the Proprietorship2's cash deposit increases $84.
- On March 31, 2016, the Proprietorship2's cash deposit decreases -$5,660.

- On April 6, 2016, the Proprietorship2's cash deposit increases $108.
- On April 13, 2016, the Proprietorship2's cash deposit increases $112.
- On April 15, 2016, the Proprietorship2's cash deposit increases $50.
- On April 17, 2016, the Proprietorship2's cash deposit increases $120.
- On April 17, 2016, the A12's cash deposit decreases -$120.
- On April 20, 2016, the Proprietorship2's cash deposit increases $100.
- On April 24, 2016, the Proprietorship2's cash deposit decreases -$236.37.
- On April 26, 2016, the Proprietorship2's cash deposit increases $470.
- On April 29, 2016, the Proprietorship2's cash deposit increases $1,000.
- On April 30, 2016, the Proprietorship2's cash deposit increases $330.
- On April 30, 2016, the Proprietorship2's cash deposit increases $1,300.
- On April 30, 2016, the Proprietorship2's cash deposit decreases -$5,660.
- On May 1, 2016, the Proprietorship2's cash deposit decreases -$9,000.
- On May 1, 2016, the Proprietorship2's cash deposit increases $2,300.
- On May 1, 2016, the Proprietorship2's cash deposit increases $5,000.
- On May 1, 2016, the Proprietorship2's cash deposit increases $800.
- On May 8, 2016, the Proprietorship2's cash deposit increases $300.
- On May 15, 2016, the Proprietorship2's cash deposit increases $78.
- On May 16, 2016, the Proprietorship2's cash deposit increases $316.
- On May 17, 2016, the Proprietorship2's cash deposit decreases -$210.77.
- On May 22, 2016, the Proprietorship2's cash deposit increases $56.
- On May 22, 2016, the A22's cash deposit decreases -$56.
- On May 24, 2016, the Proprietorship2's cash deposit increases $108.
- On May 24, 2016, the A12's cash deposit decreases -$108.
- On May 31, 2016, the Proprietorship2's cash deposit decreases -$5,660.
- On June 3, 2016, the Proprietorship2's cash deposit increases $54.
- On June 12, 2016, the Proprietorship2's cash deposit increases $68.
- On June 12, 2016, the A17's cash deposit decreases -$68.
- On June 12, 2016, the Proprietorship2's cash deposit increases $68.
- On June 12, 2016, the A20's cash deposit decreases -$68.
- On June 15, 2016, the Proprietorship2's cash deposit increases $84.
- On June 15, 2016, the Proprietorship2's cash deposit increases $93.
- On June 17, 2016, the Proprietorship2's cash deposit increases $93.
- On June 17, 2016, the Proprietorship2's cash deposit increases $90.
- On June 17, 2016, the Proprietorship2's cash deposit increases $74.
- On June 18, 2016, the Proprietorship2's cash deposit increases $136.
- On June 19, 2016, the Proprietorship2's cash deposit decreases -$196.83.
- On June 21, 2016, the Proprietorship2's cash deposit increases $48.
- On June 21, 2016, the A22's cash deposit decreases -$48.
- On June 30, 2016, the Proprietorship2's cash deposit decreases -$5,660.
- On July 2, 2016, the Proprietorship2's cash deposit increases $117.
- On July 3, 2016, the Proprietorship2's cash deposit decreases -$53,000.
- On July 9, 2016, the Proprietorship2's cash deposit increases $74.
- On July 9, 2016, the A11's cash deposit decreases -$74.
- On July 16, 2016, the Proprietorship2's cash deposit increases $13,000.
- On July 21, 2016, the Proprietorship2's cash deposit increases $108.
- On July 23, 2016, the Proprietorship2's cash deposit decreases -$251.19.
- On July 31, 2016, the Proprietorship2's cash deposit decreases -$5,660.
- On July 31, 2016, the Proprietorship2's cash deposit increases $10,920.
- On July 31, 2016, the Proprietorship2's cash deposit increases $11,050.
- On July 31, 2016, the Proprietorship2's cash deposit increases $11,180.
- On July 31, 2016, the Proprietorship2's cash deposit increases $11,310.
- On July 31, 2016, the Proprietorship2's cash deposit increases $11,440.
- On July 31, 2016, the Proprietorship2's cash deposit increases $11,830.
- On July 31, 2016, the Proprietorship2's cash deposit increases $10,790.
- On July 31, 2016, the Proprietorship2's cash deposit increases $11,310.
- On July 31, 2016, the Proprietorship2's cash deposit increases $11,570.
- On July 31, 2016, the Proprietorship2's cash deposit increases $12,090.
- On July 31, 2016, the Proprietorship2's cash deposit increases $11,570.
- On July 31, 2016, the A10's cash deposit decreases -$11,570.
- On July 31, 2016, the Proprietorship2's cash deposit increases $10,270.
- On July 31, 2016, the A11's cash deposit decreases -$10,270.

- On July 31, 2016, the Proprietorship2's cash deposit increases $11,830.
- On July 31, 2016, the A12's cash deposit decreases -$11,830.
- On July 31, 2016, the Proprietorship2's cash deposit increases $11,830.
- On August 9, 2016, the Proprietorship2's cash deposit increases $114.
- On August 12, 2016, the Proprietorship2's cash deposit increases $118.
- On August 14, 2016, the Proprietorship2's cash deposit increases $123.
- On August 15, 2016, the Proprietorship2's cash deposit decreases -$66,000.
- On August 15, 2016, the Proprietorship2's cash deposit increases $52.
- On August 16, 2016, the Proprietorship2's cash deposit increases $74.
- On August 18, 2016, the Proprietorship2's cash deposit decreases -$203.47.
- On August 21, 2016, the Proprietorship2's cash deposit increases $56.
- On August 21, 2016, the A22's cash deposit decreases -$56.
- On August 31, 2016, the Proprietorship2's cash deposit decreases -$5,660.
- On September 2, 2016, the Proprietorship2's cash deposit decreases -$18,000.
- On September 5, 2016, the Proprietorship2's cash deposit increases $59.
- On September 5, 2016, the Proprietorship2's cash deposit increases $86.
- On September 7, 2016, the Proprietorship2's cash deposit increases $90.
- On September 14, 2016, the Proprietorship2's cash deposit increases $380.
- On September 15, 2016, the Proprietorship2's cash deposit increases $105.
- On September 21, 2016, the Proprietorship2's cash deposit decreases -$256.18.
- On September 30, 2016, the Proprietorship2's cash deposit decreases -$5,660.
- On October 3, 2016, the Proprietorship2's cash deposit increases $129.
- On October 4, 2016, the Proprietorship2's cash deposit increases $117.
- On October 6, 2016, the Proprietorship2's cash deposit increases $78.
- On October 6, 2016, the A21's cash deposit decreases -$78.
- On October 6, 2016, the Proprietorship2's cash deposit increases $54.
- On October 8, 2016, the Proprietorship2's cash deposit increases $56.
- On October 11, 2016, the Proprietorship2's cash deposit decreases -$41,000.
- On October 16, 2016, the Proprietorship2's cash deposit increases $86.
- On October 18, 2016, the Proprietorship2's cash deposit decreases -$228.66.
- On October 31, 2016, the Proprietorship2's cash deposit decreases -$5,660.
- On November 1, 2016, the Proprietorship2's cash deposit increases $61.
- On November 1, 2016, the A11's cash deposit decreases -$61.
- On November 11, 2016, the Proprietorship2's cash deposit increases $85.
- On November 16, 2016, the Proprietorship2's cash deposit increases $124.
- On November 16, 2016, the Proprietorship2's cash deposit increases $132.
- On November 18, 2016, the Proprietorship2's cash deposit increases $86.
- On October 20, 2016, the Proprietorship2's cash deposit decreases -$204.61.
- On November 30, 2016, the Proprietorship2's cash deposit decreases -$5,660.
- On December 1, 2016, the Proprietorship2's cash deposit decreases -$5,000.
- On December 2, 2016, the Proprietorship2's cash deposit increases $76.
- On December 2, 2016, the A10's cash deposit decreases -$76.
- On December 8, 2016, the Proprietorship2's cash deposit increases $120.
- On December 15, 2016, the Proprietorship2's cash deposit increases $108.
- On December 17, 2016, the Proprietorship2's cash deposit decreases -$277.93.
- On December 17, 2016, the Proprietorship2's cash deposit increases $68.
- On December 17, 2016, the A22's cash deposit decreases -$68.
- On December 18, 2016, the Proprietorship2's cash deposit increases $144.
- On December 18, 2016, the Proprietorship2's cash deposit increases $88.
- On December 18, 2016, the A21's cash deposit decreases -$88.
- On December 18, 2016, the Proprietorship2's cash deposit increases $98.
- On December 20, 2016, the Proprietorship2's cash deposit increases $162.
- On December 20, 2016, the Proprietorship2's cash deposit decreases -$249.51.
- On December 23, 2016, the Proprietorship2's cash deposit increases $5,500.
- On December 26, 2016, the Proprietorship2's cash deposit increases $108.
- On December 29, 2016, the Proprietorship2's cash deposit decreases -$27,000.
- On December 31, 2016, the Proprietorship2's cash deposit increases $4,300.
- On December 31, 2016, the Proprietorship2's cash deposit decreases -$5,660.
- On December 31, 2016, the Proprietorship2's cash deposit decreases -$3,640 (total amount).
- On December 31, 2016, the A11's cash deposit increases $260.
- On December 31, 2016, the A12's cash deposit increases $208.
- On December 31, 2016, the A17's cash deposit increases $260.

- On December 31, 2016, the A19's cash deposit increases $260.
- On December 31, 2016, the A20's cash deposit increases $416.
- On December 31, 2016, the Proprietorship2's cash deposit decreases -$2,750 (total amount).
- On December 31, 2016, the A10's cash deposit increases $330.
- On December 31, 2016, the A17's cash deposit increases $275.
- On December 31, 2016, the Proprietorship2's cash deposit increases $252.
- On December 31, 2016, the Proprietorship2's cash deposit increases $463.
- On December 31, 2016, the Proprietorship2's cash deposit increases $120.

**Business Bank1**
- On December 31, 2016, the A21's cash deposit increases $252.
- On December 31, 2016, the A17's cash deposit increases $225.
- On December 31, 2016, the A19's cash deposit increases $270.
- On December 31, 2016, the A21's cash deposit increases $180.

# REFERENCES

[JIE] Guoping Jie, *A Mathematical Accounting Model and its MathAccounting Software*
First Edition. Guoping Jie Press. Ontario, 2016.

[JIE] Guoping Jie, *A Mathematical Accounting Model and its MathAccounting Software*
Second Edition. Guoping Jie Press. Ontario, 2017.

[JIE] Guoping Jie, *Digital Currency Embedded In Identities of All Society Members I*
First Edition. Guoping Jie Press. Ontario, 2017.

[JIE] Guoping Jie, *Digital Currency Embedded In Identities of All Society Members II*
First Edition. Guoping Jie Press. Ontario, 2017.

www.ingramcontent.com/pod-product-compliance
Lightning Source LLC
Chambersburg PA
CBHW080143060326
40689CB00018B/3833